.NET E-Commerce Programming

Mike Gunderloy
Noel Jerke

SYBEX

San Francisco · London

Associate Publisher: Richard Mills
Acquisitions Editor: Denise Santoro Lincoln
Developmental Editor: Jim Gabbert
Editors: Jim Gabbert, Susan Berge
Production Editor: Kelly Winquist
Technical Editor: Acey J. Bunch
Graphic Illustrator: Tony Jonick
Electronic Publishing Specialist: Nila Nichols
Proofreaders: Laurie O'Connell, Yariv Rabinovitch, Dave Nash, Abigail Sawyer, Emily Hsuan, Nancy Riddiough
Indexer: Lynzee Elze
CD Coordinator: Dan Mummert
CD Technician: Kevin Ly
Cover Designer: Caryl Gorska, Gorska Design
Cover Photographer: PhotoDisc: D. Normark/PhotoLink

An earlier version of this book was published under the title *Visual Basic Developer's Guide to E-Commerce with ASP and SQL Server*, ISBN 0-7821-2621-9 © 2000 SYBEX Inc.

Library of Congress Card Number: 2002103167

ISBN: 0-7821-4056-4

For Ken Getz, for bringing a rare combination of inspiration, support, and friendship to my life.
—MG

I would like to dedicate this book to my children, Gabrielle, Grayson, and Gianna. I love each of you dearly and thank God for each of you.
—NJ

Foreword

As I write this in May 2002, the dot-com world is still in a state of shock. Young millionaires are frantically selling their expensive toys at garage sales, behemoths like Amazon .com are still promising profitability any day now, and former Top-100 IT executives are standing in bread lines. Well, maybe the last one is a stretch, but times really are tough all over.

Does this mean that e-commerce is dead? Of course not. Now that many websites are maturing and the borderline sites are history, the Web and the commerce on it are poised to become better than ever. The Web is becoming even more pervasive, reaching into more and more homes and businesses in most countries—developed or developing. The Web is here to stay, and it continues to spawn more and better ways to conduct commerce. You shouldn't shy away from e-commerce just because the market is correcting. If anything, there are more real opportunities now than ever before.

This state of turmoil, however, does mean that you have to be smarter about investing in e-commerce technology. An e-commerce investment should become more like any other business investment: It should meet projected return-on-income targets, integrate sensibly into the organization's overall line of business, use the right technologies for the job, and not overtax resources. Certainly, gone are the days when a single Super Bowl ad represented the entire marketing strategy of a dot-com. Pure dot-com companies are still possible—witness Amazon.com's continuing flirtation with profitability—but we're going to see more brick-and-mortar companies expand to clicks and mortar. And they'll be much stronger for it. Many people won't consider doing business with organizations that don't have at least a minimal Web presence, even the mom-and-pop shop around the corner.

Success in e-commerce is still quite possible, but now, more than ever, you have to carefully plan and think through your strategy. I can't think of anyone better than Mike Gunderloy and Noel Jerke to provide wise strategic and technical e-commerce guidance. Between them, they have the street smarts, experience, and insight to help you make the right decisions for expanding your environment into e-commerce. Far too many books cover the cool technology, but far too few provide the perspective of how to put technology to effective use. New stuff is always cool—well, most of the time—until you have to use it to get the job done.

Scan the table of contents to see what I mean. When you read *.NET E-Commerce Programming*, you're going to get information about the tools and technologies, of course, but you're also going to learn how to put them to use to manage your website once it's built. For example, you'll learn to implement product promotions, conduct online sales, manage security, localize your e-commerce application for use in other countries, and on and on.

One of the many things I like about this book is that it will be useful to different kinds of readers. If you already know a lot about e-commerce applications, you can learn how to build them using Microsoft technologies that are new to you. Or, if you're already a whiz with Microsoft tools, you can learn the right ways to build e-commerce sites. This book won't give you detailed, in-depth knowledge of the technologies; 12 books of this size couldn't do that. But you'll gain a solid understanding of what you need to do to design and build an app, a clear understanding of what knowledge areas you need to explore further to make it successful, and plenty of useful code and data structures for a solid start. And you'll know the kind of experts you need to bring to the team that's building the app.

Okay, that's enough gushing. Reading this book isn't going to make building your next e-commerce application easy. It won't guarantee the app's success. It isn't going to protect you from making some of the lamebrain decisions that went to waste with so many dot-coms that existed only to suck down rivers of venture capital money. But it *will* give you a solid foundation for success.

I close with my highest compliment: Guys, I wish *I* had written this book!

Don Kiely
Third Sector Technologies
Fairbanks, Alaska

Acknowledgments

Thanks to Denise Santoro Lincoln and my coauthor, Noel Jerke, for bringing me on board for the second edition of this book. Noel was the sole author of the first edition (titled *Visual Basic Developer's Guide to E-Commerce with ASP and SQL Server*) and continued to be the lead architect of the e-commerce application, even as I translated the code to work with the latest .NET platform.

Ken Getz, Mary Chipman, Andy Baron, and Brian Randell all helped with software questions at one point or another. There is far too much software in the world for any person to know it all, so I'm happy to have such a great network of contacts to consult on knotty problems.

Special thanks to Ulrika Korkala for providing Swedish translation services.

As always, I couldn't have written a single word without the eternal support of Dana Jones, who helps raise kids, feed horses, can tomatoes, and otherwise make this house in the country a home. Adam did his best to add his own twist to the manuscript, but fortunately, Word's revision marks made that easy to deal with. The cuddles make it worth dealing with, in any case.

—Mike Gunderloy

I would like to thank all the folks at Sybex who have supported this book continuously from its first edition to this new version. I'm especially grateful to Acquisitions Editor Denise Santoro Lincoln for supporting the idea from the start. I would also thank all the readers of the first edition for your kind comments, many questions, support, and enthusiasm.

I want to thank my wife, Maria, for supporting me through all of my writing. I love you! Finally, I thank God for his many blessings.

—Noel Jerke

Of course, no book could ever happen without an editorial team. We were blessed this time with an exceptionally good one, including Editors Jim Gabbert and Susan Berge and Production Editor Kelly Winquist. Technical Editor Acey Bunch was always willing to go a few extra rounds in e-mail to help locate intractable bugs, and he put up with far too many formatting nuisances without complaining. Thanks also to the production team—Nila Nichols, Tony Jonick, Dan Mummert, and Kevin Ly—who worked hard to turn a set of Word documents and sketches into an actual printed book and a CD.

Contents at a Glance

Contents

Introduction

Electronic commerce is a hot topic in just about every industry today. Whether trying to reach consumers directly, working with trading partners, or making online purchases, almost everyone seems to be involved with e-commerce these days. It's a rare business that doesn't have plans to hawk its goods online.

This book doesn't pretend to be the ultimate book on the technical topic of e-commerce. That would require many volumes. What it *does* do is demonstrate to the programming community how e-commerce storefronts can be built on the latest Microsoft technology platform, the .NET Framework.

Noel brings to this book nearly eight years' experience on the front lines of the e-commerce battleground, having worked on websites such as Martha Stewart (www.marthastewart.com), Electronics Boutique (www.ebworld.com), and Ulla Popken (www.ullapopken.com). Noel is now focusing on helping companies ensure that they are organizationally ready for the use of new technology. Mike has been writing code with Microsoft tools since well before the advent of Windows and has worked on several successful websites, including QuiltIndex (www.quiltindex.com). Together, we've tried to distill the core development requirements of e-commerce software into an easy-to-follow case study example of a CD and T-shirt store. All of the key processes and tools are covered in this store, from the retail storefront to back-end management.

Throughout the book, you'll find numerous notes, tips, and warnings, as well as sidebars that present additional information on specific topics. These should all be helpful guides to any particular issues surrounding the topic at hand.

Microsoft Tools and Other Technologies

Recently, Microsoft made it easier to choose the proper set of tools for a web application. That's because just about everything you need, including the desktop version of SQL Server, is found in the new Visual Studio .NET. This platform forms the core of our e-commerce solution. Of course, the parts that we develop in our solution depend on other Microsoft software, including Internet Information Services and Internet Explorer. We'll discuss some of these choices in Chapter 2.

Finally, just a brief note on technology alternatives. You have the options of using Sun technology, the up-and-coming Linux operating system, and many other platforms. There are valid arguments that these solutions may be able to scale faster or better in superscaled websites such as eBay. But we can say from experience that Windows and SQL Server can scale to handle substantial site traffic if the site's architecture is designed properly.

Who Should Read This Book

This book is intended for anyone who is ready to implement an e-commerce website. Although the implementation here is in ASP.NET, the principles that we discuss are appropriate for any e-commerce application. Of course, we hope you'll agree with our choice of tools, because we find Visual Studio .NET to be a powerful and easy-to-use development environment. But we don't assume that you have any previous .NET experience. As we design our e-commerce site, we'll also show you how to use the Visual Studio .NET integrated development environment (IDE) and demonstrate how the various pieces fit together.

Structure of This Book

This book is divided into five parts. These parts take you through the entire process of building an e-commerce store, from initial planning to ongoing management operations.

Part I: Designing an E-Commerce Solution

Part I of this book walks you through the planning process and introduces the tools that we'll be using in the rest of the book.

The first two chapters introduce all the key concepts of e-commerce. These chapters define much of the terminology and review the processes involved. Chapter 2 also reviews the tools that we'll be using, particularly Visual Studio .NET, and shows how they fit into the overall development process.

The last three chapters in Part I begin the design process for building a business-to-consumer storefront. We start by designing the database for the store, using the new Visio for Enterprise Architects to help us translate requirements into SQL code. We also look at the issues involved in choosing and managing servers for an e-commerce site.

The final chapter of Part I kicks off the programming phase by building a simple subscription request form. Although this isn't a full-fledged e-commerce solution in the shopping-basket sense, it does provide some of the basics of utilizing the Microsoft tool set for web development.

Part II: Building the Shopping Experience

In Part II, we build the parts of our store that the shopper will see. These include all the web pages through which shoppers can navigate while browsing the catalog, purchasing goods, and reviewing their orders.

Chapter 6 begins Part II by implementing department and product browsing. Chapter 7 adds the function of putting items into the shopper's basket, and Chapter 8 works through the checkout process. Finally, Chapter 9 shows how we can add order history and profile management to the store.

Part III: Managing the Solution

In Part III, we tackle the side of the store that the shopper doesn't see—the store manager application. Certainly, there are many ways to approach store management, which may contain a mix of traditional LAN-based client-server tools as well as browser-based tools. In our own case study, we've chosen to implement all the management tools in a browser interface. Chapter 10 discusses this choice and shows the product management functions that we've implemented.

Chapter 11 adds tax and shipping management to the mix, and Chapter 12 covers the all-important subject of managing orders. We've tried to provide a flexible set of tools for customer service in this chapter so that we can keep our shoppers happy with a minimum of effort.

Part IV: Promotions

We can't leave marketing out of the building of our e-commerce shopping and management processes. The Web offers unique opportunities to leverage the medium to promote products and generate sales. Part IV shows how we can integrate some marketing features directly into our website.

Chapter 13 shows how to implement "up-sell" and "cross-sell" functionality to tempt the shopper to buy more products. Chapter 14 brings the idea of featured products into the mix, and Chapter 15 helps us offer sale prices and free shipping. Throughout this part, we show how to upgrade the behind-the-scenes store manager application as well as the public e-commerce store so that they can support the new features.

Part V: Advanced Topics

Finally, Part V of the book deals with some advanced topics that don't fit neatly into the earlier chapters. Chapter 16 discusses the tools that .NET offers for localizing applications, and Chapter 17 introduces some of the administrative tasks involved in keeping an e-commerce store running smoothly.

Appendix A: Database Tables and Stored Procedures

We've added an appendix that contains the SQL statements required to build all the tables and stored procedures that are used by our e-commerce application. These are listed in alphabetical order for easy reference as you're reading through the book. If you should ever need a reminder as to the data types or columns in a particular table, or the code in a particular stored procedure, you'll find it in Appendix A.

About the CD

The companion CD contains the entire code for the e-commerce storefront and store manager applications that are developed throughout this book. It also contains supporting code, such as the Visio model for the database and the Cultures sample, to help you understand how the .NET globalization classes work. The following table shows the folders that you'll find on the CD.

Folder Name	Contents
Database	The Visio model for the database, build scripts for the database itself, and individual SQL files for the parts of the database
Utility	Code to help you successfully install the .NET applications from the companion CD
Subscriptions	The subscription application developed in Chapter 5
ManageSubscriptions	The subscription manager application developed in Chapter 5
CDStore	The first version of the e-commerce store itself, as developed in Part II
CDStoreTaxShipping	The tax and shipping Web Service developed in Chapter 8
StoreManager	The first version of the store manager application, as developed in Part III
CDStore2	The advanced version of the e-commerce application, as developed in Part IV
StoreManager2	The advanced version of the store manager application, as developed in Part IV
Culture	The globalization sample from Chapter 16
StoreManagerLocalize	Sample localized pages from the store manager application, as developed in Chapter 16

> **NOTE** Before installing any of this software, you should refer to the `readme.txt` file, located in the root folder of the CD. It contains important information on installing the sample projects successfully.

Keeping Up-to-Date

This book was written in early 2002 using the then-current versions of the software it discusses:

- SQL Server 2000 with Service Pack 2
- Visual Studio .NET
- Windows 2000 with Service Pack 2

We started this project working with a late beta version of Visual Studio .NET and finished it with the release version. All the code on the companion CD has been updated to use the final release version of Visual Studio .NET and the .NET Framework. We've also tested with .NET Framework Service Pack 1 without problems.

Inevitably, the software we've written about will be updated. Sharp-eyed readers will let Sybex and us know when they find bugs. If we have any major changes to the sample projects, we'll make copies available on the Sybex website, `www.sybex.com`. On the Sybex home page, enter this book's ISBN code, **4056**, in the Search box to locate the web page for the book.

If you do find any problems with the sample projects or have any questions or suggestions, we'll be happy to hear from you via e-mail. You can reach us at `MikeG1@larkfarm.com`. or `noeljerke@att.net`. Of course, we can't guarantee an answer to every question, but we'll do our best.

PART I

Designing an E-Commerce Solution

CHAPTER 1

Defining E-Commerce

- Electronic Commerce Phases

- Managing the Storefront

Everywhere you look, electronic commerce, or *e-commerce*, is one of the buzzwords of the day. Ten years ago, mail-order catalogs were all the rage. Now we have this new medium in the Internet for transacting business. And that word *business* may be the most critical aspect of what e-commerce is all about.

Most people think of e-commerce as online shopping. That is typically called business-to-consumer (B-to-C or B2C) e-commerce and is the traditional retail, or storefront, type of business. On the Web today, examples of such businesses are Martha Stewart (www.marthastewart.com) and Amazon.com (www.amazon.com). Companies such as Dell Computer (www.dell.com) are finding that sales on their websites are beginning to equal or surpass those made through the companies' more traditional retail channels. There is no doubt that sites like these are gaining critical market space and will continue to grow. In addition, traditional "bricks and mortar" stores such as Wal-Mart (www.walmart.com) and Target (www.target.com) are slowly easing into the e-commerce space with great success.

E-commerce also includes the business-to-business (B-to-B or B2B) market space, which accounts for a significant amount of activity on the Internet. Just think of all the supply-chain purchasing that takes place to manufacture and support many of the products and services we use every day! Examples of B-to-B e-commerce include wholesale companies selling to end retailers—for instance, a PC manufacturer selling to distributors and large retailers. Although many B-to-B vendors were launched unsuccessfully during the first rush to exploit this technology, some (for example, Covisint, www.covisint.com) have quietly continued brokering large deals. As we write this book, General Motors has announced that their purchases through Covisint are nearing $100 billion!

As B-to-B e-commerce grows, businesses will come to rely on this type of e-commerce as an everyday business solution. Your favorite restaurant down the street will probably purchase from different suppliers using this technology, as will your local grocery store, bookshop, and other traditional businesses. The day will come when the Internet will be a standard place for businesses to communicate with other businesses, and that day is just around the corner.

The last few years have seen spectacular successes and notable failures in e-commerce. Some websites have gained a large and devoted customer following, while others have spent amazing amounts of money on marketing, only to go bankrupt. We remain convinced that e-commerce has staying power as one of the backbone applications that will continue to drive the Internet. Our goal in this book is to show you how you can get your own e-commerce site up and running quickly, so that you can test your own ideas for doing business via the Net.

Electronic Commerce Phases

In this book, we are going to focus on the core concepts of purchasing, which are typically related to retail shopping but are also relevant to business-to-business purchasing. Before we start, though, it's important for you to grasp the complete e-commerce food chain in order to understand where the Internet storefront begins and ends and where more traditional back-office technology comes into play.

Figure 1.1 diagrams the phases of the purchasing process. The flat boxes show the customer's activities, and the three-dimensional boxes show business processes not performed by the customer. Note that not all of these steps are necessarily required in every e-commerce transaction.

FIGURE 1.1:

E-commerce phases

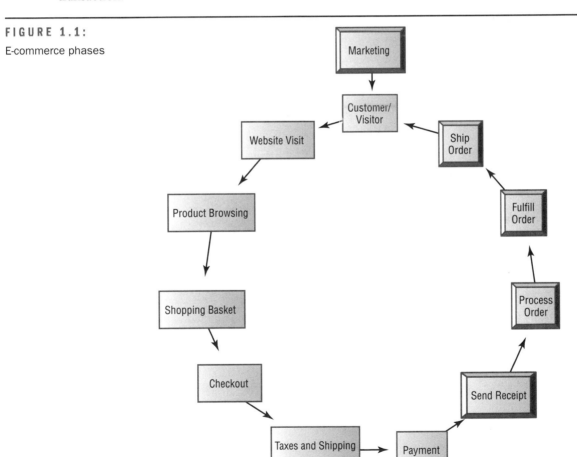

Let's take a look at each of these phases and see how their roles fit into the overall e-commerce process.

Marketing

There is nothing new about the need to market your products and to target consumers. The general goal is to target potential buyers and entice them to give your website a whirl. What's new is the ability to use the medium of the Internet to target consumers in different ways. Although we might not think of banner advertising, targeted e-mails, sweepstakes, and so on, as e-commerce, they can be a critical part of the process in the e-commerce cycle.

Another hot topic on the Internet today is building communities and creating "sticky" applications. The goal is to provide an environment that will entice the website visitor to come back repeatedly. Examples of techniques to bring people back to your site include discussion forums, chat rooms, polls, and surveys. Frequently updated content such as how-to articles and news sections will also entice people to return.

TIP	To learn more about building Internet communities, see Noel Jerke's *E-Commerce Developer's Guide to Building Community and Using Promotional Tools* (Sybex, 2001).

In this book, we won't cover the technology behind using the Internet as a marketing and community-building tool; rather, we'll focus on how to use technology to market to the consumer who has found your website (see Part IV, "Promotions").

Customer/Visitor

Of course, there is no e-commerce without the customer! In this case, your customer is the web surfer who has decided to type in your URL or click a link to visit your website. The biggest distinction we need to make here is the difference between the business-to-business customer and the business-to-consumer customer. Typically when we talk about business to business, the customer is another business entity who will need to have various purchasing options, including credit card, purchase order, and/or credit account (with terms such as net 30 days for payment). The seller may need to provide a purchase order number to the customer. There may be additional requirements for large-dollar and mission-critical purchases, including authenticated receipt of order, electronic transfer of funds, and so on. Many of these issues have been addressed traditionally through the Electronic Data Interchange (EDI), which provides agreed-upon data interchange standards for businesses.

In the traditional B-to-C model, the customer is typically an individual who is going to pay with a credit card and have the item shipped to their home. In this book, we're going to look at the technology behind the core shopping process, with a specific focus on B-to-C purchasing; but many of the core processes are equally applicable to B-to-B transactions.

Website Visit

Once the potential customer visits the website, the fun begins. When a page from a business site is downloaded, a number of things can happen to begin building the e-commerce experience for the customer. You can immediately begin tracking and profiling this customer. And, based on that information, you can start to target products that the customer may be most interested in. This step begins the e-commerce shopping process. As you can see, while the shopper is interacting with the site, some of the back-end business processes will intermingle with the front-end shopper experience.

Product Browsing

If the shopper likes what they see after entering your website, they will hopefully begin to browse through the site's product pages. Typically, a shopper will browse through departments and then products within those departments. As a shopper goes through this experience, they may be enticed with products on sale, promotions, related or upgraded products, and so on.

When you're building an e-commerce site, you need to give some consideration to organizing your products for easy browsing. The most critical decisions are how many products to group on a page and how many levels of classification shoppers have to browse through before they get to a product. You need to balance the speed at which the pages load against the amount of time it takes to find a particular product. Remember, if your site is too slow to load or too hard to use, shoppers will just go to the mall instead. Many e-commerce sites feature a few of their most popular products (or products that they would *like* to be popular) on their opening page to increase the odds that shoppers will immediately see something that interests them.

Shopping Basket

The next step is for the shopper to add products to their *shopping basket*. The shopping basket is simply a list of products the shopper has selected, the quantities, prices, attributes (color, size, and so on), and anything else related to the potential order. Shopping baskets often offer options to clear the basket, remove items, and update quantities. In Part II, "Building the Shopping Experience," we'll explore the basics of the shopping process, including product browsing and the shopping basket.

Checkout

Once the shopper has all of their items ready for purchase, they will begin the checkout process. In the B-to-C model, the shopper will typically enter their shipping and billing address information. The shopper might also input additional information for a gift greeting, gift wrapping, and other ancillary services.

Taxes and Shipping

Once the business site knows where the items are going to be shipped and billed, the site can execute two important business-rule calculations for taxes and shipping. Computing the taxes can be as easy as simply charging for a state tax if the shopper lives in a nexus (physical location) for the business. Or, in rare cases, your site may need to provide local tax-rate support, usually only when you have local representation such as storefronts in multiple states. If so, you may also need to consider support for local county or city taxes based on the shopper's zip code. Likewise, computing the shipping charge can be as simple as charging a flat fee or as complex as calculating charges specific to each product purchased and correlated with the shipping distance or the carrier that will deliver the product.

Both of these issues can be even more challenging when it comes to handling international purchases. But, make no mistake about it, after your site launches, people from other countries will find it, one way or another.

TIP   We'll cover the mechanics of implementing and maintaining processes for taxes and shipping in Chapter 8, "Checking Out," and Chapter 11, "Managing Taxes and Shipping."

Payment

Once the website calculates the subtotal, taxes, and shipping for the product purchase, it's time for the shopper to present payment. As mentioned earlier, the options will be quite different for business-to-business and business-to-consumer transactions. In B-to-C e-commerce, the typical purchase is through a credit card; or, depending on the situation, COD or invoice options may be available. In B-to-B e-commerce, *all* options may need to be available, including purchase orders. Also, for large-ticket purchases, where inventory, advanced availability, and other issues may come up, a quote or follow-up with final pricing, ship time, and so on, may be required.

With credit cards, there are options to either clear/transact the credit cards offline or transact them online. Online processing is over the Internet via a service such as CyberCash or VeriFone; the credit card data is securely transmitted over the Internet, and a response is sent back, indicating whether or not the charge was approved.

Send Receipt

Once the purchaser has placed the order, you might want to send a receipt to the purchaser. For B-to-B e-commerce, the receipt might be a listing that's attached to a purchase order. For the consumer, it might be a recap of the order on the screen in a format optimized for printing or a listing that's e-mailed to the consumer. In both cases, this process can be automated easily (as we'll demonstrate in Chapter 8).

Process Order

At this stage, the customer leaves the picture, and we reach the back end of the e-commerce process. If your site didn't handle the credit card automatically, the next task is to process the financial transaction. In general, standard business rules take over in this phase, just as though the order came in via the phone or mail. As with traditional purchases, the Internet provides the option to keep the customer informed about the order status; for example, you may want to show that the order has been processed, that all items are in stock, and so on. To do this, you'll need to set up a method on the website for the customer to check the status of their order. We will explore this further in Chapter 8.

NOTE   If you are shipping digital goods, such as music or movie files, over the Internet, you may need to provide fulfillment of the goods to the customer immediately after the credit card has been verified. In that case, you'll need to provide a link and some kind of access to the digital files. Everything will take place in one action.

Fulfill Order

Once you have a valid order, it needs to be fulfilled. This can actually be the most challenging business process to work on. Many different scenarios come into play, depending on your type of business.

If you are a traditional retailer with storefronts, there may be an issue of having central inventory to fulfill from. And, even if more than 90% of the transactions are electronic, there will be customers who need to make a phone call or send an e-mail to the business.

If you provide fulfillment via a fulfillment house or service, there might be integration issues with the fulfillment house's system. Even if you do your own fulfillment, there may be integration issues between the web server and your back-end fulfillment system.

Ship Order

The last step in the process is to get the product to the customer. As in the Process Order stage, you can provide the order status to the customer. In this case, it may include the UPS or FedEx shipping number so that the customer can track the shipment.

Managing the Storefront

There is more to an e-commerce website than just the user side of things. There are also all the aspects of managing the store. The right tools for managing the e-commerce site are as critical as the right tools for engaging the site visitor.

The management tools needed can range from those used for simple order reporting and tracking to tools for full-fledged database management. Table 1.1 shows some of the sample functionality that a solid management interface may need. Keep in mind that all these tools can be built on the same technology as the storefront. It's entirely possible to do all of your store management via applications hosted in your web browser. Or, in some cases, you may want to build more traditional client-server applications to handle some of the management tasks.

TABLE 1.1: Storefront Management Tools

Function	Description
Security	High levels of security will be critical for ensuring that the right people have the right access to the appropriate functions. Customers, too, need to have confidence that their credit cards and order details won't be compromised en route to the supplier.
Product management	The products in the storefront can be managed directly on the web servers if desired. You can add, update, or delete products directly in a web page environment. An automated process might be necessary to reconcile the online store with a traditional product management system.
Order tracking and reporting	There are many opportunities to perform order tracking and general order management. You can download order data into a local database format such as a Microsoft Access or comma-delimited ASCII file, perhaps for integration with separate data analysis tools. This data can help you analyze order history, product-buying patterns, and so on.
Department/category management	Along with managing products, you can build in functionality to manage product categorization into departments.
Promotion management	A critical aspect of managing the site might include administering product promotions, sales, message text, cross-sells, up-sells, and anything else your marketers can come up with.
Shopper management	If your e-commerce site has profiling of shoppers and shopper recognition, you may need features to manage those profiles.
Business rule management	Virtually any aspect of the site should be customizable from a solid management tool. Taxes, shipping, and other critical business rules of the website can be managed easily from a web interface.

The technology behind the management interface doesn't have to be in a web page. Traditional graphical user interface (GUI) client-server development can also provide all the tools needed to manage the online store. By using the .NET Framework to build your e-commerce site, you'll find that managing your servers from a remote location becomes almost as easy as working with them directly.

Summary

E-commerce can be as simple as creating a single online form that accepts a credit card or as complex as integrating disparate vendor systems to support supply-chain purchasing.

In this book, we are going to focus on the technology behind the business-to-consumer e-commerce process. It's important to point out that underlying e-commerce are the basics of any business—customer service, fulfillment, marketing, inventory management, and much more. We won't try to teach you all of these business basics. Just keep in mind that e-commerce isn't magic; you still need to have a viable business model behind your e-commerce site.

A lot of planning needs to go into a successful e-commerce business. This book will show you how to utilize the products you already know—Visual Basic .NET, SQL Server, the Windows 2000 family of servers, and others—to build a successful, feature-rich, online presence for your business.

The Microsoft Tool Set

- The Microsoft Tool Set

- Building the Functionality

Although Visual Basic .NET will be the key tool in our plans for e-commerce development, many other tools are used in a successful e-commerce deployment. In this chapter, we'll look at the contents of our e-commerce toolbox and explore how all the pieces will fit together as we set out to construct our e-commerce website.

Introducing the Microsoft Tool Set

We'll be using tools from Microsoft almost exclusively for our solution. These tools range from server software to programming languages to encryption technology. Each has its place in building the complete solution. In this chapter, we'll give you an overview of each of the tools we're going to use in the rest of the book, along with the features that they bring to the e-commerce world. Our tool set includes these Microsoft software packages:

- Windows 2000
- Internet Information Server
- Microsoft .NET, including ASP.NET, ADO.NET, and Web Services, as well as the underlying .NET Framework
- SQL Server 2000
- Visual Basic .NET
- Secure Sockets Layer (SSL)
- Other tools, including Microsoft Exchange, FrontPage 2002, Office XP, Visual Source-Safe, and Internet Explorer

Microsoft Windows 2000 and Beyond

Windows 2000 is the foundation for building a .NET solution. It provides the core security, TCP/IP functionality, and other fundamental requirements for a web server operating system. Table 2.1 discusses the key features that this operating system supplies for e-commerce.

NOTE   As we write this book, Microsoft Windows .NET Server is in serious beta testing. We expect it to provide an even more attractive platform for e-commerce than Windows 2000, thanks to increased "out of the box" support for the .NET Framework and other improvements. The code in this book, though, should work unchanged across the entire range of Windows 2000 and Windows .NET servers.

TABLE 2.1: Windows 2000 E-Commerce/Web Features

Feature	Description
Security	As with any web server, it's critical to provide solid security to protect the network and operating system from the rest of the world.
TCP/IP networking	TCP/IP is, of course, the standard networking protocol used across the Internet that allows computers to communicate with each other.
Component Object Model (COM) support	When .NET code needs to interoperate with business components built using older languages, COM is a key tool.
Common Language Runtime (CLR) support	Although the CLR doesn't ship with Windows 2000, it is tightly integrated with the Windows 2000 operating system.
Web server	Internet Information Server (IIS) is the server that supports the core web server functionality (see the next section). Our code will target IIS for maximum performance and flexibility.

There are many excellent references available for setting up and administering Windows 2000 as a web server. It is important that Windows be set up properly to ensure security integrity, scalability, and other key requirements. Security, in particular, is a very real issue that any system administrator must consider carefully these days. We recommend that, at the very least, you keep up with the Microsoft security bulletins that you'll find online at www.microsoft.com/technet/itsolutions/security/current.asp.

Internet Information Server 5

IIS 5 is the web server that's provided as a part of Windows 2000. A new version of IIS will be released with Windows .NET, but that's not a matter of great concern for developers; Microsoft has a very good track record of preserving backward compatibility for IIS applications. Table 2.2 gives an overview of some of the key features of IIS.

TABLE 2.2: IIS Web Server Features

Feature	Description
Index Server	Index Server supports website content indexing, including HTML pages and Word documents. This enables your website to have site search functionality.
FTP service	IIS provides the basic functionality to support the File Transfer Protocol (FTP).
HTTP service	IIS provides the basic Hypertext Transfer Protocol (HTTP) service.
SMTP service	IIS also provides the support for the Simple Mail Transfer Protocol (SMTP) for sending e-mail from the web server.

Continued on next page

TABLE 2.2 CONTINUED: IIS Web Server Features

Feature	Description
NNTP service	IIS supports the Network News Transport Protocol (NNTP), with which you can set up Internet newsgroups.
Certificate Server	Certificate Server allows you to manage your own set of certificates to enable authentication between the server and the client.
MMC integration	The web server can be managed entirely from Microsoft Management Console (MMC).
Active Server Pages	Active Server Pages (ASP) represent the foundation for web server development. The ASP engine provides a hosting environment for several scripting languages, with integrated support for VBScript and JavaScript (JScript). Note that this is the original scripting technology provided by Microsoft in earlier versions of IIS.
FrontPage extensions	The FrontPage extensions are a key tool for supporting website development in Microsoft FrontPage. These extensions allow FrontPage to manage the site over a standard TCP/IP connection.
ASP.NET support	The IIS architecture supports additional languages, such as ASP.NET, even when they're not included as part of the base product.
Application protection	IIS allows you to isolate applications from one another even when they're running on the same physical server. If one application crashes, other applications on the same web server will continue to function.

Microsoft .NET

The core of our e-commerce development efforts is the Microsoft .NET Framework. This is a major upgrade to Microsoft's development languages that was first rolled out in beta form in mid-2001. Microsoft describes the .NET Framework variously as "a new computing platform designed to simplify application development in the highly distributed environment of the Internet" and as "an XML Web Services platform that will enable developers to create programs that transcend device boundaries and fully harness the connectivity of the Internet."

.NET Overview

.NET has an impressive array of features designed to make application development faster and the resulting applications more robust. Table 2.3 summarizes some of the features that we'll be using as we build our e-commerce solution.

TABLE 2.3: Microsoft .NET Features

Feature	Description
Common Language Runtime	The CLR executes all .NET code and provides common services, including memory management, security, and interoperability services to all .NET applications.
Managed execution	All .NET languages compile to a common Microsoft Intermediate Language (MSIL) format that includes metadata for the CLR to use.
Common Type System	The Common Type System (CTS) is an extensible library of data types available to all .NET languages.
Cross-language interoperability	.NET languages can call code or subclass types from other .NET languages.
.NET Framework class library	The class library contains hundreds of classes for working with system resources, data structures, XML (Extensible Markup Language), and other common application features.
Security	.NET includes pervasive code-access and role-based security features.
Simple deployment	.NET applications can be deployed in a variety of ways, including simply copying the files involved to the target computer.
Versioning	.NET has a complete set of versioning rules designed to eliminate component incompatibilities.

ASP.NET

ASP.NET is the web development platform for Active Server Pages applications. You may be familiar with ASP, the web development platform that ships as part of IIS 5. ASP supports a variety of scripting languages via an interpreter on the IIS computer. Code written in VBScript, JScript, or other scripting languages is saved on the server in files with an .asp extension. When an HTTP client requests an ASP page, the IIS server loads it into the ASP interpreter, which executes the code to produce a standard HTML (Hypertext Markup Language) page. It's this interpreted HTML page that is actually returned to the client. The code stays entirely on the server (which leads to ASP being referred to as a server-side scripting solution).

ASP.NET is conceptually similar to ASP in that the code is executed entirely on the server. However, ASP.NET is vastly more powerful than ASP and offers advanced features that aren't available in ASP. With ASP.NET, the .NET CLR is completely integrated into the web server. This means that ASP.NET pages take advantage of all the CLR features that we've mentioned previously. Table 2.4 shows some additional ASP.NET features that we'll take advantage of as we develop our e-commerce solution.

TABLE 2.4: Features of ASP.NET

Feature	Description
Compiled page support	ASP.NET pages are compiled rather than interpreted, offering significant speed increases over ASP pages.
Support for all .NET languages	You can write ASP.NET code in any .NET language, including Visual Basic .NET, C#, and many others. You no longer need to use a separate scripting language for authoring web pages.
Web Forms	These forms provide a set of controls and themes used for rapid web-page GUI development.
XML configuration files	All configuration settings are human-readable and may be changed with any text editor.
Authorization	Default authorization and authentication schemes are built into ASP.NET.

ADO.NET

ADO.NET is the data access portion of the .NET Framework. As the name indicates, it's an upgrade path from ADO (ActiveX Data Objects), Microsoft's premier COM-based data access library. ADO.NET is optimized for access to the types of data that you're most likely to need in a web-based application, including SQL Server data and data stored as XML files.

ADO.NET is explicitly designed to support disconnected scenarios. That is, you can load data into a DataSet (an ADO.NET object that can hold a set of tables, their data, and the relations between them) and then move that DataSet to another tier of your application for display and editing without maintaining a connection to the original data source. Later on, you can move the data back and reconnect to the original data source to perform any updates.

We'll be using ADO.NET consistently as the data access layer in our e-commerce solution.

Web Services

You're going to hear a lot (if you haven't heard enough already!) about *Web Services* as .NET catches on. You may also read a lot of complex and confusing explanations of the architecture of these Web Services. But at their most basic, Web Services are simple: They are a means for interacting with objects over the Internet.

The key to Web Services is that they are built with common, pervasive Internet protocols: All communication between Web Services clients and servers is over HTTP and XML by default (although developers may use other protocols if they wish). For this to work, there has to be a way to translate objects (as well as their methods and properties) into XML. This way is called SOAP, the Simple Object Access Protocol. SOAP is a way to encapsulate object calls as XML sent via HTTP.

There are two major advantages to using SOAP to communicate with Web Services. First, because HTTP is so pervasive, it can travel to any point on the Internet, regardless of intervening hardware or firewalls. Second, because it is XML-based, SOAP can be interpreted by a wide variety of software on many operating systems.

There are two other important acronyms you'll run into when learning about Web Services in .NET. UDDI, which stands for Universal Description, Discovery, and Integration, is a method for finding new Web Services by referring to a central directory. WSDL stands for Web Services Description Language, a standard by which a Web Service can tell clients what messages it accepts and which results it will return.

Using the .NET tools, you can take any data and define it as a Web Service. For example, you could develop a Customer object that retrieves address information from a database via ADO.NET, and wrap it as a Web Service. Once you've done that, client programs would be able to create new Customer objects and retrieve addresses from anywhere on the Internet.

SQL Server 2000

As critical to e-commerce as programming is, even more critical is the database. Without a database to store products, baskets, orders, and much more, there would be no e-commerce at all. Microsoft SQL Server 2000 provides a robust development platform for building multi-tiered web applications. You can place as much or as little logic in the database tier (using stored procedures) as needed. If you are running a multi-server web farm, partitioning the client, web server, and database tiers becomes critical to ensuring solid performance and balancing server load.

SQL Server 2000 supports advanced database features, including a high level of security, replication, clustering, XML input and output, and more. In conjunction with ADO.NET, data stored in SQL Server 2000 is available to any portion of a solution written in any .NET language.

NOTE   The next version of SQL Server (which will probably be called SQL Server .NET), due out in 2003, is expected to contain support for writing stored procedures directly in .NET languages.

Visual Basic .NET

We'll be using Visual Basic .NET, or VB .NET, as the programming language for the entire e-commerce application (with the exception of SQL Server stored procedures, which must be written in the Transact-SQL language). One of the nicest things about working in Visual Basic .NET is that the same language can be used for a variety of purposes. Table 2.5 shows the types of applications that we can create using Visual Basic .NET. Although we won't use all of these types in building the e-commerce solution, we'll take advantage of Visual Basic .NET's flexibility to locate code in stand-alone applications, class libraries, or ASP.NET pages, as appropriate to the situation.

TABLE 2.5: Visual Basic .NET Application Types

Type	Description
Windows application	A desktop application with a graphical user interface
Class library	A set of components designed to be shared by multiple applications
Windows control library	A set of controls that can be used in Windows application projects
ASP.NET web application	A web application that will run using ASP.NET on a computer with IIS 5 or later
ASP.NET Web Service	A Web Service that can be consumed by other Web Services or web applications
Web control library	A set of controls that can be used in ASP.NET web application projects
Console application	A stand-alone application designed to be run from the Windows command line, with no graphical user interface
Windows service	An application that runs as a service under Windows NT or Windows 2000

In this book, we are going to focus on using Visual Basic .NET code directly in ASP.NET pages. We'll also have the opportunity to construct some useful class libraries and stand-alone components.

Secure Sockets Layer and Certificates

Security on an e-commerce website is crucial for securing private data, especially credit card data. On the management side of things, passwords and other business-critical data should be encrypted between the browser and the server.

IIS 5 supports Secure Sockets Layer (SSL) 3. There is a simple process for requesting a certificate on the server and then submitting the certificate request to an authority, such as VeriSign (www.verisign.com). Once the certificate request is made, the keys will be sent back and installed on the server. We'll discuss the process of obtaining a server certificate in detail in Chapter 4, "System Configuration."

Miscellaneous Tools

Many other tools are available for Internet development. Certainly, many non-Microsoft tools are available for website development on Windows and other operating systems. Table 2.6 reviews some of the other Microsoft tools that can be used for e-commerce site development.

TABLE 2.6: Microsoft's Web-Enabled Tools

Tool	Description
Microsoft Exchange Server 2000	If you want to build extended capabilities for targeting via e-mail, provide e-mail boxes for customer support, and other related functions, Exchange Server provides a robust e-mail platform.
Microsoft FrontPage 2002	FrontPage 2002 is an excellent WYSIWYG HTML editing tool for creating static content on the website. FrontPage also includes some database features that are suitable for very simple sites.
Microsoft Office XP	Microsoft Office provides extended tools for working with the Web. Microsoft Word can be utilized for creating and editing web-page documents. Microsoft Access Data Projects (ADPs) can be an excellent tool to use in conjunction with Microsoft SQL Server. Office also includes the Office Web Components (a set of controls designed for use on web pages) and SharePoint Team Services (a product for managing collaboration via an intranet site).
Internet Explorer	Internet Explorer (IE) provides much more than standard web-page display; besides the browser, it includes a number of tools. Remote Data Service (RDS) objects are provided for interfacing with data on the web server via HTTP; ActiveX controls can run in the browser interface; and IE can execute client-side scripting in VBScript and JScript.
Visual SourceSafe	Visual SourceSafe provides a source-code-control tool set for storing source code and related files in a source database. It includes source-code version management as well as an infrastructure for checking code in and out; this is particularly useful for avoiding version conflicts in team-based environments.
Remote Data Service	RDS contains a tool set for querying databases across the Internet via HTTP. It provides a direct link between the browser and the database without having to go to the server to work through ASP or some other server-side development tool. RDS is included with MDAC, the Microsoft Data Access Components. For new websites, you should use the ability of ADO.NET to send disconnected DataSet objects as XML instead of RDS.
Microsoft Visual Studio .NET	We have already mentioned Visual Basic .NET, but there are many other tools within the Visual Studio .NET package. These include the C++ and C# programming languages, the Visual Studio Analyzer, templates for distributed applications, and more. All of these may be useful at various points in the development process.
Commerce Server 2000	Commerce Server 2000 is Microsoft's own prepackaged e-commerce software, designed for both B-to-B and B-to-C sites. It offers extensive customization, work flow, and analysis features. The main drawback to Commerce Server for many small sites is its $13,000 price tag.

Browser Issues

Two browsers primarily are used on the Internet: Internet Explorer 6 and Netscape Navigator (or Communicator) 6.1; Figures 2.1 and 2.2 show these two browsers. Even though Internet Explorer has seen strong growth in utilization, Netscape is still a significant player in the marketplace. Other browsers with significant usage in some sectors are Opera, Mozilla, and the Konqueror web browser on Linux.

FIGURE 2.1:

Internet Explorer 6

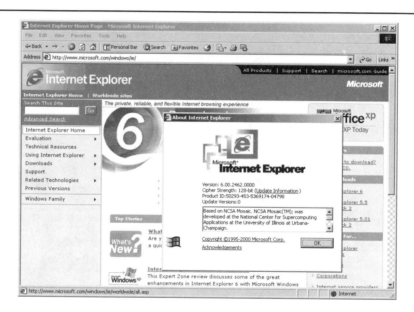

All of these browsers support standard HTML and some extended features such as cascading style sheets (CSS), dynamic HTML, and JavaScript. However, the level of support and the completeness of implementation of these features vary from browser to browser. The only thing you can be sure will work in all browsers is standard HTML, and even then the visual rendering might be a little different in each. One of the advantages of using ASP.NET as our main development interface is that all of the code runs on the server, and only standard HTML is sent back to the client.

Trying to design a truly unique, advanced interface on the client side can be very tricky when you're trying to ensure support in multiple browsers. Even if you decide to build different interfaces for the different browsers, you will still have issues of supporting browsers having a smaller market share, such as earlier versions and specialized browsers. In most cases, you're much better off using standard HTML than targeting a specific browser.

FIGURE 2.2:

Netscape
Navigator 6.1

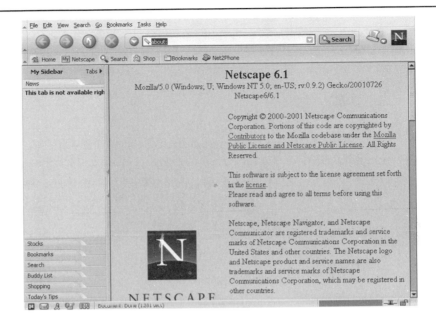

Building the Functionality

So, how will all these tools be utilized to build the e-commerce functionality laid out in this book? Table 2.7 breaks down the process as outlined in Chapter 1.

TABLE 2.7: Using Microsoft Tools to Build an E-Commerce Solution

Phase of the Process	Tools Used
Marketing	ASP.NET, SQL
Customer/Visitor	ASP.NET, SQL
Website Visit	ASP.NET, SQL
Product Browsing	ASP.NET, SQL
Shopping Basket	ASP.NET, SQL
Checkout	ASP.NET, SQL
Taxes and Shipping	ASP.NET, VB .NET, SQL
Payment	ASP.NET, VB .NET, SQL
Send Receipt	ASP.NET, SQL
Process Order	ASP.NET, SQL (order status)
Fulfill Order	ASP.NET, SQL (order status)
Ship Order	ASP.NET, SQL (order status)
Manage the Storefront	ASP.NET, VB .NET, SQL, IE

In the last part of the book, we'll explore some advanced topics, including localization and internationalization, system architecture design, and best practices. These topics cut across the entire Microsoft tool set.

Summary

In this book, we are going to focus on the technology behind the e-commerce process. It's important to point out that e-commerce is built on the basics of any business—customer service, fulfillment, marketing, inventory management, and much more. To a large degree, these basics will dictate the design of our application. In the next chapter, we'll begin exploring the database requirements that underlie an e-commerce solution.

CHAPTER 3

E-Commerce Database Design

- Microsoft SQL Server

- Data Modeling with Visio

- The Store Database

- The Final SQL Scripts

A t the core of almost any interactive website is a well-designed database. Before we jump into programming the website, we need to know the core design for all the key components of the site. This is just good development practice: You'll get the job done faster if you plan before you code.

The database system we'll use for this book is Microsoft SQL Server. SQL Server is a good choice for .NET development because of the tight integration of the System.Data.SqlClient namespace with SQL Server. But we could also implement that database using the Microsoft Jet or Oracle database engine, or nearly any database for which we have an ODBC driver. Throughout this book, the SQL code and related development will be as server-agnostic as possible so that the code can be utilized on different database platforms.

Microsoft SQL Server

SQL Server is Microsoft's enterprise-level database offering, designed for use on servers accessed by multiple users. (Microsoft Access is the company's entry-level offering for basic application development as a desktop database.) The current version of SQL Server is SQL Server 2000, and there are six editions of it, as shown in Table 3.1. We'll be using SQL Server 2000 Enterprise Edition with Service Pack 2 as our test database.

TABLE 3.1: SQL Server 2000 Editions

Edition	Features
SQL Server Enterprise Edition	Failover clustering, support for 32 processors and 64GB RAM, federated servers, Storage Area Network (SAN) support, increased parallelism.
SQL Server Standard Edition	Support for 4 processors; includes Analysis Services and English Query.
SQL Server Personal Edition	Support for 2 processors; runs on Windows 98 with some tools unavailable. Performance degrades with more than 5 simultaneous connections.
SQL Server Developer Edition	Includes all features of SQL Server Enterprise Edition but is licensed only for use on development and test systems.
SQL Server Evaluation Edition	Includes all features of SQL Server Enterprise Edition but expires after 120 days.
SQL Server Desktop Engine	Zero-management version with no graphical management tools. Performance degrades with more than 5 simultaneous connections.

NOTE   SQL Server provides a robust relational database architecture for building high-transaction e-commerce websites. It's the server technology behind many high-profile e-commerce sites. The databases created in this book, although developed on Microsoft SQL Server, could be ported to Oracle or even Microsoft Access. To use those platforms, some of the SQL queries, stored procedures, and other database components would have to be redesigned.

SQL Development

The primary tool that we'll use for writing application code to work with SQL Server will be Visual Studio .NET. Specifically, we'll use the Visual Basic .NET and ASP.NET development tools, all of which are hosted in the Visual Studio .NET environment. Visual Studio .NET also provides query development tools, server management tools, and other development tools.

For direct development, we'll work with SQL Server Enterprise Manager and Query Analyzer. SQL Server Enterprise Manager provides powerful administration tools that you can use to manage multiple servers. With Enterprise Manager, you can configure, start, pause, and stop SQL Servers, monitor current server activity, and view the SQL Server error log. You can create and manage databases, tables, stored procedures, views, and other objects. You can manage security, including logins, database users, and permissions. SQL Server Enterprise Manager and the SQL Server Agent service provide a way to set alerts for various server events and to schedule server tasks. Enterprise Manager also provides a graphical way to set up and manage replication, and it enables you to execute and analyze queries, back up and restore databases, and generate SQL scripts.

Query Analyzer provides a development environment for SQL queries that includes an object browser, color-coded syntax, and the ability to manage multiple simultaneous queries. It's an ideal tool for ad hoc queries of SQL Server data.

Transact-SQL Language

Microsoft SQL Server supports the Transact-SQL (T-SQL) language, which is a dialect of Structured Query Language (SQL, often pronounced "sequel"), the leading standard for querying relational databases. T-SQL has been certified as compliant with the ANSI SQL-92 standard, but any code taking advantage of proprietary extensions will not, of course, be easily portable. As much as possible, SQL code written in this book will be ANSI compliant.

Database Administration

Although our focus in this book is on creating a database and the code that will use it, in a real-world installation, you also need to worry about database administration. Most SQL Server installations will have a dedicated database administrator, whose duties include the following:

- Configuring the SQL Server
- Backing up and restoring data
- Managing database users and permissions
- Monitoring server performance and identifying bottlenecks
- Updating indexes
- Removing unneeded transaction logs
- Shrinking databases where rows have been removed
- Configuring replication between multiple servers

If you're approaching e-commerce as a developer, you ignore these tasks at your peril. When you're implementing a new website, take the time to identify the person responsible for database administration and to develop emergency plans. The Maintenance Plan Wizard, built into SQL Server Enterprise Manager, can help you schedule some of the necessary tasks.

NOTE   We'll discuss some SQL Server configuration issues in Chapter 4, "System Configuration." Detailed instructions for using the SQL Server tools and administering databases are beyond the scope of this book. A good reference is *Mastering SQL Server 2000* by Mike Gunderloy and Joseph L. Jorden (Sybex, 2000).

Data Modeling with Visio

Before we begin developing the actual database structure, we'll look at the data modeling tools that are available with Visual Studio .NET. Many developers are accustomed to developing a database design on paper and then creating the database directly (or even creating the database without any preliminary design at all). But there are more structured ways to proceed, and it's worth knowing about these ways when you're building a complex solution. In particular, Visual Studio .NET supports Object Role Modeling (ORM) through the included Visio for Enterprise Architects (VEA). With ORM, you enter facts about objects and relationships, and the tool figures out how to represent those facts in a database. Using ORM allows you to concentrate on the logical design of your database rather than the physical design. In this section, we'll show how you can use ORM to build up a database from a logical model to the final product.

NOTE   VEA is included in the Enterprise Edition of Visual Studio .NET. If you're using one of the other editions, you won't be able to follow the steps in this section. But you can still use the SQL scripts generated by VEA (which are included on the companion CD) to build your database.

NOTE   Our treatment of ORM only scratches the surface of this powerful tool. For more information, a good place to start is www.orm.net.

Entering Facts

To get started, launch Visio for Enterprise Architects by selecting Start ➤ Programs ➤ Microsoft Visio. Visio will open to the Choose Drawing Type interface. Select the Database category, then click the ORM Source Model template. Visio will open with its interface split into three main sections, as shown in Figure 3.1:

• To the left, the ORM Source template has objects that you can drag to your Visio drawing.

• At the top, the ORM Source Model drawing will be your documentation of the model.

• At the bottom, the Business Rules editor allows you to enter the facts that will describe your data.

FIGURE 3.1:

New ORM Source
Model project

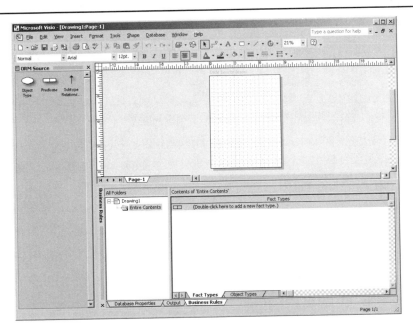

To get started building a model, double-click in the Fact Types area or click in Fact Types and press F2. This will open the Fact Editor. You can start with anything that you know about your data; part of the job of VEA is to organize your collection of facts into a sensible database.

We'll start with some facts about departments. To enter the first fact into the model, follow these steps:

1. Type **Department** in the first Object Name combo box, **has** in the Relationship text box, and **DepartmentName** in the second Object Name combo box. Leave the Inverse Relationship text box blank. Figure 3.2 shows the new fact in the Fact Editor.

TIP   If you don't want spaces in the column names in the physical database, you can't include spaces in the names in the model.

FIGURE 3.2:

Creating a new fact

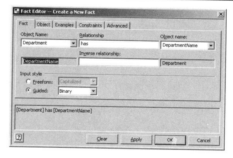

2. Click the Object tab in the Fact Editor. Select the Department object in the Select Object list. Because you just added this name to the model, the Object Kind will be set to Entity, which is correct; a Department is an entity, or "thing," in the model.

3. Enter **ID** in the Reference/Identifier text box, and select Identification as the Ref Type. VEA will use this information when building the physical database.

4. In the Notes text box, type **Department is a grouping for products.** This information is strictly for your own reference; notes are not used in the construction of the database. Figure 3.3 shows the Object tab of the Fact Editor.

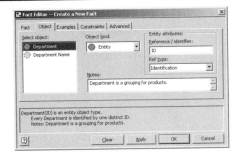

5. Select the DepartmentName object in the Select Object list. Change the Object Kind to Value. Department Name is something that describes the Department; it isn't a thing in its own right.

6. Click the Examples tab in the Fact Editor. Here you can enter sample data. VEA will use this data to help determine the constraints that apply to data entry. Enter these pairs of Department and Department Name:

   - Music—Music
   - Books—Books
   - Clothing—Clothing

NOTE   The sample data doesn't have to be actual data from your application; it just has to have the same structure as the actual data.

7. As you enter each example, the Fact Editor will convert it into a natural-language sentence at the bottom of the Examples tab. These particular examples get converted into sentences such as "Department Music has Department Name Music." This makes sense, because the name of the department is the same as the department's name. When you've finished entering the examples, click the Analyze button. This will open the Example Analysis Results dialog box, as shown in Figure 3.4.

FIGURE 3.4:

Analyzing
example data

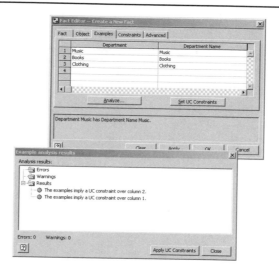

8. VEA will use the sample data to determine uniqueness constraints (UCs) for your data. Click the Apply UC Constraints button to include as part of the database model the uniqueness constraints that VEA deduced from your examples.

9. Select the Constraints tab of the Fact Editor. You'll see that VEA has deduced a pair of constraints from the data:

   • For each Department Name y, at most one Department has Department Name y.

   • Each Department has at most one Department Name.

10. In fact, we know that there is an even stronger constraint that can be applied to naming: Each Department has exactly one Department Name. In the combo box for Constraint Question #1, select Exactly One. Figure 3.5 shows the Constraints tab after this change. On the other hand, you know it's possible that there are names that don't actually get used for any Department. In the combo box for Constraint Question #2, select Zero or One.

FIGURE 3.5:

Defining uniqueness
constraints

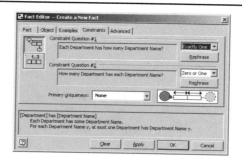

11. Click OK to add the fact to the model.

12. Click the Object Types tab at the bottom of the Business Rules window. You'll see that both the Department and DepartmentName objects default to being represented by char(10) columns. You can click in the Physical Data Type column to change these selections. Change Department to use int for its physical data type, and DepartmentName to use varchar(255).

13. Repeat the process to enter two more facts about Departments:

    • Department has Department Description, stored as text. A Department can have zero or one Department Descriptions.

    • Department has Department Image, stored as varchar(255). A Department can have zero or one Department Images.

TIP   You can use the Apply button to simultaneously enter a new fact and clear the Fact Editor for further data entry.

Building the Database

Of course, we'll have many more than three facts in the model for our online store database. But before we enter more facts, let's take a look at the process of turning an ORM model into a physical database. To do so, follow these steps:

1. Save the model as `store.vsd`.

2. Select File ➢ New ➢ Database ➢ Database Model Diagram.

3. Select Database ➢ Project ➢ Add Existing Document. In the Add Document to Project dialog box, select the `store.vsd` document and click Open.

4. Select Database ➢ Options ➢ Drivers. Select Microsoft SQL Server on the Drivers tab of the Database Drivers dialog box. Click the Setup button in this dialog box.

5. Select 2000 as the Preferred Version on the Preferred Settings tab of the Microsoft SQL Server Setup dialog box. Click OK to return to the Database Drivers dialog box. Click OK to return to the drawing.

6. Select Database ➢ Project ➢ Build. This will prompt you to save the current drawing. Save it as `StoreLogical.vsd`.

7. VEA will print some status messages to the Output window, which should end with "0 error(s), and (1) warning(s)." It will also create the Department table in the Tables and Views window. You can drag this table to the Visio drawing area to see the structure that VEA has developed for the table, based on the facts that you entered into the ORM Source Model.

8. Select Database ➤ Generate to launch the Generate Wizard.

9. On the first panel of the Generate Wizard, check the box to generate a text file of the DDL script. Name the script `Store.ddl`. Check the box for Generate New Database. Check the box to store the current database image. Click Next.

10. On the second panel of the Generate Wizard, select the Microsoft SQL Server driver. Select the Create Database radio button. Click the New button.

11. In the Create New Data Source dialog box, select System Data Source and click Next.

12. Select the SQL Server driver and click Next.

13. Click Finish to create the data source.

14. In the Create a New Data Source to SQL Server dialog box, name the data source **Store**. Choose the database server where you wish to create the database and click Next.

15. Choose the appropriate authentication method for your SQL Server and click Next three times to create the data source.

16. Now you'll be back in the Generate Wizard. Enter **Store** as the Database name and click Next.

17. Fill in the appropriate authentication information in the Connect Data Source dialog box and click OK.

18. Review the tables that will be created (in this case, only the Department table, because that's the only one that you've modeled so far) and click Next.

19. Visio will prompt for filenames, but you don't need to supply them. Click Close.

VEA will generate a build script and create the database for you. Alternatively, you can have it generate the script but not build the database. This allows you to execute the script manually through SQL Server Query Analyzer. If you like, you can view the generated script. Listing 3.1 shows a sample script derived from the model that we've created to this point.

Listing 3.1   Initial Build Script

```
/*    This SQL DDL script was generated by Microsoft Visual Studio
➡ (Release Date    LOCAL BUILD). */

/*    Driver Used : Microsoft Visual Studio -
   Microsoft SQL Server Driver. */
/*    Document    : C:\DOCUMENTS AND SETTINGS\MIKE.LARKGROUP.000\
➡ MY DOCUMENTS\STORE\STORELOGICAL.VSD. */
/*    Time Created: December 08, 2001 9:04 PM. */
/*    Operation   : From Visio Generate Wizard.  */
```

```
/*      Connected data source : Store */
/*      Connected server      : SKYROCKET */
/*      Connected database    : master */

/* Create Store database. */
use master

go

create database "Store"

go

use "Store"

go

/* Create new table "Department". */
/* "Department" : Department is a grouping for products. */
/*      "Department ID" : Department is a grouping for products. */
/*      "DepartmentName" : Department has DepartmentName */
/*      "DepartmentDescription" : Department has DepartmentDescription */
/*      "DepartmentImage" : Department has DepartmentImage */
create table "Department" (
    "Department ID" int not null,
    "DepartmentName" varchar(255) not null,
    "DepartmentDescription" text null,
    "DepartmentImage" varchar(255) null)

go

alter table "Department"
    add constraint "Department_PK" primary key ("Department ID")

go

/* This is the end of the Microsoft Visual Studio generated
   SQL DDL script. */
```

NOTE   We've removed some white space from the comments in the generated script to make it fit better on the printed page.

Adding a Related Object

The real power of ORM comes into play when you're modeling more than one object. To see how this works, you'll first need to enter some additional facts, this time about Product.

Here are the relevant facts about the Product object:

- Product has exactly one ProductName.
- Product has zero or one ProductDescription.
- Product has zero or one ProductImage.
- Product has zero or one ProductPrice.
- Product has zero or one ProductSaleStart.
- Product has zero or one ProductSaleEnd.
- Product has zero or one ProductSalePrice.
- Product has zero or one ProductActive.
- Product has zero or one ProductFeatured.
- Product has zero or one ProductFeaturedStart.
- Product has zero or one ProductFeaturedEnd.

We'll discuss the actual meaning of these various characteristics later in the chapter.

Figure 3.6 shows the Object Types tab of the Business Rules designer, which displays the physical data types for these objects.

There's one more fact that needs to be entered, and in some ways, it's the most important. So far, all the facts we've entered have had to do with one object and the values that characterize it. However, we know something about Departments and Products: Departments contain Products. Figure 3.7 shows this fact open in the Fact Editor.

FIGURE 3.7:

A fact that relates two objects

On the Constraints tab of the Fact Editor, we entered some additional information:

- Each Department contains zero or more Products.
- Each Product belongs to one or more Departments.

That is, we can have a department with no products, but every product belongs to at least one department, and some products are sold through multiple departments.

After adding these facts, it's time to rebuild the database:

1. Save the ORM model.

2. Switch back to the Database Model Diagram (or open it if you closed it).

3. Select Database ➢ Project ➢ Build; this will prompt you to save the current drawing. Save it as StoreLogical.vsd.

4. VEA now builds three tables: Department, Department Product, and Product. If you drag these three tables to the drawing surface, you'll get the view shown in Figure 3.8. VEA automatically draws the join lines between the tables. As you can see, it has figured out that it needs to create a linking table to implement the many-to-many relationship between the Department and Product tables that the constraints imply.

FIGURE 3.8:

Automatic creation of a linking table

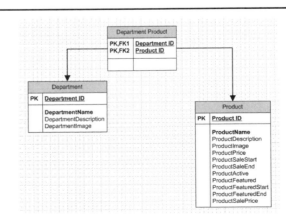

5. Select Database ➤ Generate to launch the Generate Wizard.

6. On the first panel of the Generate Wizard, check the box to generate a text file of the DDL script. Name the script `Store.ddl`. Enter **Store** as the Database Name. Click Next.

7. On the second panel of the Generate Wizard, select the Microsoft SQL Server driver. Click Next.

8. Fill in the appropriate authentication information in the Connect Data Source dialog box and click OK.

9. Review the tables that will be created and click Finish.

10. Visio will prompt for filenames, but you don't need to supply them. Click Close.

This procedure will produce a new version of the `Store.ddl` script, but it won't execute the script on your database server. You can use the SQL Server tools to drop the existing version of the database and then run the new script to recreate it.

Tweaking the Results

Although ORM will produce a database for you, it may not, in all cases, make exactly the choices that you might have preferred. Two areas in particular will probably require attention: names and additional properties.

VEA will automatically derive names for tables and columns based on the information that you enter through the Fact Editor. For example, if you tell it that the entity named Tax is identified by an ID, it will generate the name *Tax ID* for the corresponding column in the Tax table. Depending on your own preferences, you may not want the embedded space in the name. You can change names in the logical model by following these steps:

1. Open the logical model in VEA.

2. Select the Database Properties tab in the Output window.

3. In the Tables and Views window, select the table containing the column of interest.

4. To change the name of the table, select the Definition category in the Database Properties window and enter a new physical name.

5. To change the name of a column, select the Columns category in the Database Properties window and enter a new physical name.

6. Save the logical model. VEA will ask you whether you'd like to save the changes back to the Source Model as well. Generally, you'll want to choose Yes here. If you choose No, your changes will be overwritten the next time you rebuild the logical model.

When you use the ORM tools, VEA builds these items into the DDL script:

- Table names
- Column names
- Data types and sizes
- Primary keys
- Foreign keys

Of course, there is other information that you need in order to define the tables in a database. Notably absent from this list are identity column properties and default values. You have two choices for handling these items. The first is to modify the DDL script before you run it. This option requires experience with SQL Server's CREATE TABLE and ALTER TABLE statements, but it has the advantage of allowing you to recreate the database with those items by re-running the DDL script. The second choice is to add default values, identity properties, and any other additional information by using SQL Server Enterprise Manager (or other tools) after the database has been created.

By now, you should have some idea how Object Role Modeling can help you design a database. Rather than spend several pages here entering every fact about our data, we've included the full ORM Source Model and Database Model Diagram on the companion CD. In the next section, we'll describe all the tables that we produced in our database.

The Store Database

Our online store is going to sell CDs and a few T-shirts. We are going to need an appropriate database that will define music departments/genres, products, basket storage, and order data. Now that we've developed the model for this database and generated the actual physical database, we'll take a column-by-column look at the information that we've chosen to store.

Departments

The top-level categorization of products will be departments. If we were selling sporting goods, for example, we might have rackets and tennis balls in the Tennis department, whereas the hoop, backboard, and net would be in the Basketball department. In the case of our CD store, CDs will be classified according to music categories, or departments, such as Jazz and Country.

Conceivably, a store could also have multilevel departments. For example, a top-level department, such as Sporting Goods, could have several departments below it, such as Tennis and Basketball. Our database won't implement multilevel departments.

TIP   The simplest way to handle multilevel departments is to implement a self-join on the Department table so that each department can also have a ParentDepartment column.

Table 3.2 lists the columns in the Department table in the Store database.

TABLE 3.2: Department Table Columns

Column	Description
DepartmentID	The ID will be auto-incremented to give a unique identifier to the Department table.
DepartmentName	The name will be the displayed name in the store.
DepartmentDescription	The department description can be used for internal business use or external display.
DepartmentImage	Included in our database might be a pointer to an image that's representative of the department. We'll store a filename here, rather than the actual image, because that's easier to handle when we're generating HTML pages from the database.

Next, we'll define the products that will be categorized into the departments.

NOTE   As you can see, we've chosen a naming scheme that includes the table name in each column name. We've found that this makes the SQL statements involved in the application easier to write and understand, but this is certainly not a requirement. Other developers prefer names that don't include the table name (ID, Name) or names that include a tag for the data type (intID, chrName). It's important that you choose and stick to a standard, but it's not important which standard you choose.

Products

Offering products in a store would seem pretty simple. But when you begin to think about defining a generic product, things can get rather complicated. For example, a computer will have many attributes, including processor speed, drive size, and RAM, whereas a simple paper clip may not have any specific attributes.

Sample Database Tables

In our sample store for the website, we'll assume that our products (such as T-shirts) can have only two specific attributes: size and color. This will help us keep the code simple while still demonstrating how you can handle attributes. But our relational table structure will allow for more attribute types. In fact, we'll allow each product to have an arbitrary number of attributes. Figure 3.9 shows the product-related tables for our database.

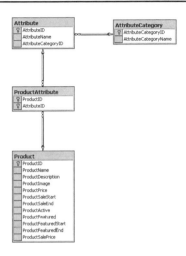

There are four tables in this diagram:

Product table   This table stores the primary product data.

Attribute table   This table stores all the attributes (for example, red, green, X, and XL).

ProductAttribute table   This table is the link between the attributes a product has and the product itself.

AttributeCategory table   This table categorizes each attribute (for example, size, color, and weight).

Two other key relationships to note are that our products are categorized into departments and we need to be able to depict a relationship between products. For example, a basketball may be related to a basketball backboard. That would be a *cross-sell*. Another type of relationship would be the *up-sell*. In that case, we might want to tempt the customer to switch from a lower-cost product to a more expensive one. Figure 3.10 shows the core products table as it relates to departments and other products. Each product can be in multiple departments and can have multiple related products.

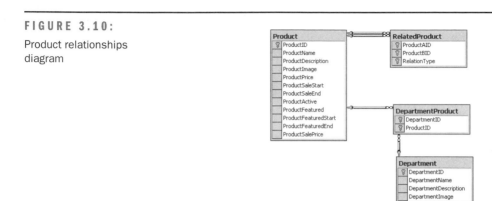

The Product Table

Each product must be categorized into at least one department. In our case, we are allowing a product to be categorized into multiple departments. And, of course, one department must be able to hold multiple products. These requirements are handled by a "linking table" named DepartmentProduct. Also, we have a relationship table of products related to other products in RelatedProduct. Later in the book, we'll show you the SQL statements that create products and departments and that build the relationships among them. Table 3.3 details the columns for the main Product table.

TABLE 3.3: Product Table Columns

Column	Description
ProductID	The ID will be auto-incremented to give a unique identifier to the product.
ProductName	Name of the product as displayed to the shopper.
ProductDescription	A description of the product. The information will be stored as text, but HTML tagging can be placed in the text for display purposes.
ProductImage	Name of the image to be displayed. We'll store a filename or hyperlink here for easier processing; the actual images will be saved in separate files.
ProductPrice	Price of the product. To avoid rounding issues with decimal numbers, the price will be stored using the SQL Server money data type, which stores exact amounts.
ProductSaleStart	Date the sale price of the product is available.
ProductSaleEnd	Date the sale price of the product ends.
ProductActive	Flag to indicate whether or not the product is active.
ProductFeatured	Flag to indicate whether or not the product is featured.
ProductFeaturedStart	First date that the product is featured.
ProductFeaturedEnd	Last date that the product is featured.
ProductSalePrice	Sale price of the product.

The Attribute Table

Now that we have the Product table columns defined, we can take a look at the columns in the Attribute table. Table 3.4 shows these columns.

TABLE 3.4: Attribute Table Columns

Column	Description
AttributeID	The ID will be auto-incremented to give a unique identifier to each attribute.
AttributeName	Name of the attribute as displayed to the shopper.
AttributeCategoryID	Link to the category to which this attribute is assigned.

This simple table will assign an ID to the attribute and will store a description. Example data would include an AttributeID of *1* and an AttributeName of *red*.

The ProductAttribute Table

The ProductAttribute table is what ties the particular product's attributes to the list in the Attribute table. Table 3.5 shows the columns in this table.

TABLE 3.5: ProductAttribute Table Columns

Column	Description
AttributeID	The ID of the attribute.
ProductID	The ID of the product to which the attribute is related.

As you can see, this table is a simple cross-reference listing of the attributes of a product. Note that at this level, we're not assigning any type of categorization to the attributes. There's no need for a separate ID column in this table, because the combination of Product-ID and AttributeID is unique for each row.

The AttributeCategory Table

Finally, we can assign a categorization to the attributes in the attribute list. Table 3.6 shows the columns.

TABLE 3.6: AttributeCategory Table Columns

Column	Description
AttributeCategoryID	The ID will be auto-incremented to give a unique identifier to each category.
AttributeCategoryName	Name of the category.

This table is a simple lookup table of attribute categories.

NOTE   If we want to list the attributes of a product by category, we'll need to build a query that returns a unique list of categories based on the set of attributes assigned to a product.

Categorizing Products into Multiple Departments

As we mentioned earlier, each product will be assigned to at least one department, although we want our database to be flexible enough to support categorizing products into multiple departments. For example, although a blouse may be categorized in the Blouses department, it can also be part of the Spring Collection department. A CD might fall into a Jazz category as well as a Blues category. Table 3.7 shows the columns for the DepartmentProduct table.

TABLE 3.7: DepartmentProduct Table Columns

Column	Description
DepartmentID	The ID of the department.
ProductID	The ID of the product categorized into the department.

As with the ProductAttribute table, this table simply contains a listing of relationships between products and departments.

Linking Two Products Together

Finally, with regard to products, we need a way to link two products together. To the shopper, this may show up as a listing of *related* products, or it may appear as a suggestion to *upgrade* to a better product. These will be items that the shopper will be interested in or need to know about when purchasing another product. Table 3.8 shows the columns for the table that accomplishes this task.

TABLE 3.8: RelatedProduct Table Columns

Column	Description
ProductAID	The ID of the product.
ProductBID	The ID of the related product.
RelationType	A numeric code that indicates whether the product relation is an up-sell or a cross-sell. We'll use the value *1* for an up-sell and *2* for a cross-sell.

Again, this table is simply a listing of relationships between products.

TIP Reporting inventory availability to the user can be critical if the shopping site will have a high level of order volume or limited inventory at any time. If this is the case for your store, product definitions may require an inventory column or a link to an inventory database to keep track of availability. And, in the ordering process, you'll need to decrement the inventory availability to maintain an accurate count. In our store, we're assuming that this isn't an issue.

Defining the proper product definitions and relationships is critical to properly presenting your product line to the shopper. The structure outlined here for products will most likely work for simple products with minimal attribute requirements. In more complex stores, the data diagram for products can become much more intricate.

Most established companies will already have a product database. Although that database may not be in the right form for use in the online store, a close link between the two databases will be necessary to ensure that the two are reconciled.

Shoppers

Next, we need to think about shoppers. Obviously, we are going to have to store some information about them, especially when they order products from our store. The options in this area range widely from the storing of minimal shopper data to a complete shopper profile. A complete profile would include the ability to do one-click shopping (as at Amazon.com) and to record a lot of information about the shopper. In the simplest of cases, only the shipping, billing, and payment information would be stored for each order, with no persistent customer information at all.

NOTE It's important to remember that stores can be as different and as complex as people. We all share the same elements (head, heart, body), but the character and nature of each person are quite different. Thus, it will be important to thoroughly understand what your store's requirements are and how the template provided in this book will be best applied, as well as which pieces you might need to customize.

If you store shopper information on an ongoing basis, you'll have many options for customizing your website. If you have a bit of profile data on the shoppers, you can begin to target product offerings and other types of promotions at them when they log on to the site. Also, you can provide extended customer service information, such as the order status and the shipping tracking number.

For the purposes of this book, we will store shopper information and allow the shopper to retrieve it at a later date by setting a cookie or by entering a username and password.

Our shopper data is going to be fairly straightforward. It will primarily store the contact information for the shopper. Because each order will have the shopper's ID stored in it for the long term, we could do some correlation between what the shopper has been ordering and how we might present the site to the shopper in the future (this is known as *personalization*). Table 3.9 shows the columns for the Shopper table.

WARNING   Because of the increased threat of theft, you need to be aware of the security concerns surrounding long-term storage of credit card data. Storage of credit card data can be an issue for your shoppers, and forcing that option on shoppers might turn them away. The Shopper table in this scenario doesn't enable long-term storage of payment information in shoppers' records. Instead, we'll store payment information separately in its own table, which can be purged periodically.

TABLE 3.9: Shopper Table Columns

Column	Description
ShopperID	The ID will be auto-incremented to give a unique identifier to each shopper.
ShopperFirstName	Shopper's first name.
ShopperLastName	Shopper's last name.
ShopperAddress	Address of the shopper.
ShopperCity	City of the shopper.
ShopperState	State of the shopper.
ShopperProvince	International province location of the shopper.
ShopperCountry	Country of the shopper.
ShopperZipCode	Zip code of the shopper.
ShopperPhone	Phone number of the shopper.
ShopperFax	Fax number of the shopper.
ShopperEmail	E-mail address of the shopper.
ShopperDateEntered	Date on which the shopper information was first entered.
ShopperPassword	Password used by the shopper to access their profile and order status.
ShopperCookie	Flag indicating whether the shopper wishes to have no username/password requirement for accessing their profile. This will allow the shopper to be recognized immediately when they log on from their own computer.

In this table, we've chosen to include only one address: the billing address for the shopper. Of course, not everyone wants goods shipped to the same address as the bill. It's not unusual for a company to have different shipping and billing addresses, and even individuals may prefer to receive goods at their home but bills at a Post Office box. When we define our Order table, we'll include places to store both billing and shipping information.

NOTE   In our example, we aren't storing any payment information with the shopper profile. Instead, we store this information on a per-order basis in a separate table. We could have a secondary table of credit card types, expiration dates, and so on. In the business-to-business environment, payment methods such as COD, invoice, and purchase order may need to be stored in the profile.

Keep in mind that in many cases, a shopper profile will be created with each order, even though the shopper may order more than once. The shopper may simply choose not to participate in using their profile. There is no real way to keep the shopper from doing this without severely locking down the website, which will make things harder for your customers—and tend to drive them away.

Shopping Basket

While the shopper is maneuvering through the website, we'll need to store their selected products in their shopping basket. Ultimately, this task serves as a way to store data about the selected products. Thus, we'll need to keep in mind a few pieces of information about the *state* of these products.

For example, if the shopper selects a product to be added to the basket and it's on sale, we don't want them to be shocked if the sale ends while they are shopping and the price suddenly jumps up. Or, for that matter, if the store manager initiates a pricing update, we don't want the prices changing on the fly for the shopper.

Figure 3.11 shows the Basket tables in relation to the Shopper table.

FIGURE 3.11:

Basket tables diagram

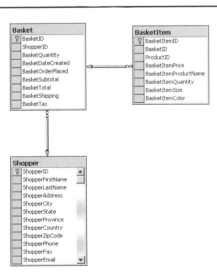

In the diagram, each shopper has a basket. In fact, if the shopper is returning and pulling up their profile, they may have several baskets. Each basket will then have one or more items in it. Table 3.10 defines the Basket table columns.

TABLE 3.10: Basket Table Columns

Column	Description
BasketID	The ID will be auto-incremented to give a unique identifier to each basket.
ShopperID	ID of the shopper for whom the basket was created.
BasketQuantity	Total number of items in the basket.
BasketDateCreated	Date on which the basket was created.
BasketOrderPlaced	Flag that will indicate whether the basket was ordered by the shopper.
BasketSubtotal	Subtotal cost of the basket without any shipping, tax, handling, or other charges.
BasketTotal	Total cost of the order with all charges included.
BasketShipping	Shipping charge for the order. The calculation will be based on the appropriate business logic.
BasketTax	Tax charge for the order. The calculation will be based on the appropriate business logic.

Note that the basket totals store the actual costs and totals of the order. These will be stored at the time of the order in case the business logic behind any of the costs changes or there are any promotions that happen based on the type of order. If you don't store this information, you run the risk of not being able to accurately calculate in the future what the shopper was charged.

With each basket, there will be a listing of items that have been added. This table will store the basic information about each product and will be used to create a receipt for the order. Table 3.11 defines the items placed in the basket.

TABLE 3.11: BasketItem Table Columns

Column	Description
BasketItemID	The ID will be auto-incremented to give a unique identifier to each basket.
BasketID	ID of the basket to which these items belong.
ProductID	ID of the product added to the basket.
BasketItemPrice	Price of the product at the time it is added to the basket. Note that this price may be a sale price.

Continued on next page

TABLE 3.11 CONTINUED: BasketItem Table Columns

Column	Description
BasketItemProductName	Name of the product.
BasketItemQuantity	Number of units of the product ordered.
BasketItemSize	Size value of the product.
BasketItemColor	Color value of the product.

TIP   A key issue related to database management is managing the basket and basket item tables. On high-volume websites, the number of baskets generated can be far more than just the number of orders placed. It can be important to put in place a process to clear out abandoned baskets that are older than a specified amount of time (for example, 24 or 48 hours).

While the shopper browses through the website and chooses products to buy, we'll run application code to add, update, or delete items in the basket. You'll see all of this code later in the book. Next, we'll look at storing orders placed on the site.

Orders

This is the part of the process that every businessperson likes to deal with—the collection of money. When the shopper checks out from the store, we'll need to store the basic order information, including shipping and billing addresses, payment data, and items ordered.

The order data relates to the shopping basket—specifically, the items in the basket. Figure 3.12 shows the relationship between the Order table, the Basket tables, and the shopper data (if present).

In this case, the order will be related to the shopping basket and the shopper. Each basket, and each order, must have a shopper assigned to it.

The payment data will be stored in a separate table in case we wish to easily delete this data on a frequent basis (for security reasons) and yet keep the primary contact information on the order for later reference. Table 3.12 defines the columns for the Order table.

FIGURE 3.12:

Order tables diagram

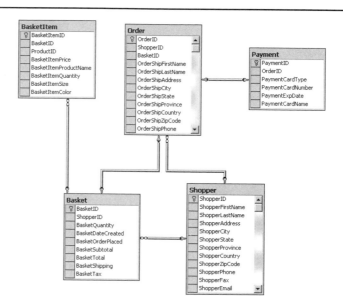

TABLE 3.12: Order Table Columns

Column	Description
OrderID	The ID will be auto-incremented to give a unique identifier to each order.
ShopperID	ID of the shopper placing the order.
BasketID	ID of the basket that this order fulfills.
OrderShipFirstName	First name of the person to whom the product will be shipped.
OrderShipLastName	Last name of the person to whom the product will be shipped.
OrderShipAddress	Address where the product will be shipped.
OrderShipCity	City where the product will be shipped.
OrderShipState	State where the product will be shipped. This will also potentially have a bearing on tax and shipping calculations.
OrderShipProvince	Province where the product will be shipped, for an international order.
OrderShipCountry	Country where the product will be shipped.
OrderShipZipCode	Zip code to which the product will be shipped. In complex tax situations, taxes may be calculated down to the zip code level.
OrderShipPhone	Phone number at the "ship to" location.
OrderShipFax	Fax number at the "ship to" location.
OrderShipEmail	E-mail address for the person to whom the product will be shipped.

Continued on next page

TABLE 3.12 CONTINUED: Order Table Columns

Column	Description
OrderBillFirstName	First name of the billing contact.
OrderBillLastName	Last name of the billing contact.
OrderBillAddress	Address of the billing contact.
OrderBillCity	City of the billing contact.
OrderBillState	State of the billing contact.
OrderBillProvince	Province of the billing contact.
OrderBillCountry	Country of the billing contact.
OrderBillZipCode	Zip code of the billing contact.
OrderBillPhone	Phone number of the billing contact.
OrderBillFax	Fax number of the billing contact.
OrderBillEmail	E-mail address of the billing contact.
OrderDateOrdered	Date on which the order was placed.

NOTE   For many orders, the shipping and billing address information will be the same. But we'll store it twice in case there's a need to update one or the other because of a change. In the interface, an option should be provided to enter the address information only once if the billing and shipping address are identical.

Next, we need to define the table to store the payment data for the shopper. We'll need to store the three key items of credit card data to facilitate payment authorization: the type of credit card used, the credit card number, and the expiration date. Table 3.13 reviews the columns for the payment data.

TABLE 3.13: Payment Table Columns

Column	Description
PaymentID	The ID will be auto-incremented to give a unique identifier to each payment.
OrderID	ID of the order to which the payment is related.
PaymentCardType	Type of credit card (Visa, American Express, and so on).
PaymentCardNumber	Credit card number.
PaymentExpDate	Expiration date of the credit card.
PaymentCardName	Name of the card owner.

TIP   If you do your own credit card processing, you may need to store additional information, such as the authorization code and authorization time, in the Payment table.

Again, it's critical to manage this data securely and to ensure that it is deleted after it has been processed.

Now that we've captured the order data, it will be used in the order processing stage. To provide good customer service, we will want to provide a way for the customers to see their order status.

Order Status

Every order has a status that indicates what actions have been taken. We'll store status information at three different stages in our application so that the shopper will be able to return to the site and view the current status of their order. In low-volume stores, this data can be entered automatically. In high-volume stores, this data may be updated automatically from an internal order-management system.

The order status will be updated at these stages:

1. The order has been received and is ready to be fulfilled.

2. The order has been fulfilled.

3. The order has been shipped. The shipping tracking number is provided in this status update.

As a result, each order will have three entries in the OrderStatus table as it proceeds through the system. Table 3.14 shows the definitions for the OrderStatus table.

TABLE 3.14: OrderStatus Table Columns

Column	Description
OrderStatusID	The ID will be auto-incremented to give a unique identifier to each payment.
OrderID	ID of the order to which the payment is related.
OrderStatusStage	Code indicating the current stage of the order. We'll use 1, 2, or 3, corresponding to the stage number.
OrderStatusDateShipped	Date on which the order was shipped (stage 3).
OrderStatusDateFulfilled	Date on which the order was fulfilled from inventory (stage 2).
OrderStatusDateProcessed	Date on which the order was processed from the Web (stage 1).

Continued on next page

TABLE 3.14 CONTINUED: OrderStatus Table Columns

Column	Description
OrderStatusNotes	Any notes related to the order status—for example, notes about any problems with the order.
OrderStatusShippingNumber	Shipping number for the shipment of the order to the customer.
OrderStatusProcessed	Flag that indicates whether or not the order has been processed for fulfillment.

The OrderStatus table could be much more complex than what is represented here. We could have more than three stages, and ideally this status data would be plugged directly into a back-end order processing system.

Shipping Tables

Shipping can be calculated in a number of ways, including these methods:

Item Quantity   The total shipping charge is based on the number of items in the order. Variations can include a per-item fee or a fee based on ranges. An example of range-based fees would $3 for 1 to 5 items, $6 for 6 to 10 items, and so on.

Order Total   Instead of the number of items, the shipping charge is based on the total amount of the order. For example, if the order total is $5 or less, the shipping cost is $1; if the total is between $5.01 and $10, the shipping cost is $3.

Weight   Weight can also be a factor in situations where the products are unusually large or vary in size. Weight calculations need to be related to the Product table, where, presumably, the weight of the product is stored.

Shipping Distance   Perhaps the most complicated of the shipping models is the one based on shipping distance. If you use zip codes to determine distance, the calculations can become complex. A simpler model specifies costs for shipping within a region and costs for shipping between regions.

These are just four examples of how shipping can be calculated, but many combinations and variations are possible, depending on the business requirements. For example, you might want to combine shipping distance with the weights of the products to come up with the final charges.

For the example in this book, we'll use a simple table of shipping fees based on item quantities. The table will list quantity ranges and the fee for each range. Table 3.15 defines the Shipping table columns.

TABLE 3.15: Shipping Table Columns

Column	Description
ShippingID	The ID will be auto-incremented to give a unique identifier to each fee range.
ShippingLowQuantity	The low-end number of items for this range.
ShippingHighQuantity	The high-end number of items for this range.
ShippingFee	Shipping fee for this range.

When the shopper checks out, the number of items ordered will be checked against the data in the table to find the appropriate shipping fee. Table 3.16 shows example data for the sample code in this book.

TABLE 3.16: Shipping Fees

Low Quantity	High Quantity	Fee
0	5	$5.00
6	10	$7.50
11	20	$10.00
21	99,999	$15.00

In most cases, there will be a maximum shipping fee for any order over a certain size. In this case, our highest fee will apply to quantities in the range of 21 to 99,999 (a number that's safely higher than the maximum number of items that anyone will ever order). Another variation on this shipping option would be to use a dynamic formula that calculates the shipping fee if the shopper orders more than 20 items.

NOTE   Options for next-day and two-day shipping, resulting in higher fees, are often available. For example, if the customer wants the product shipped within two days, $5 might be added to the order. For next-day shipping, $10 might be added.

We may also want to offer free shipping on certain days as a promotional device. We'll implement this, of course, by adding one more table to our database. The FreeShip table, shown in Table 3.17, tracks the dates on which shipping charges are waived.

TABLE 3.17: FreeShip Table Columns

Column	Description
FreeShipID	The ID will be auto-incremented to give a unique identifier to each free shipping period.
FreeShipStartDate	Date that free shipping begins.
FreeShipEndDate	Date that free shipping ends.

Tax Tables

Similar to shipping, we also need to be able to calculate the tax. Figuring the tax can be fairly complicated or quite simple—it all depends on the state tax requirements and the location of nexus points for shipping the product. In this book, we are going to calculate the tax based on simple state tax requirements. We'll assume that we have shipping nexus locations in only two or three states, so that the tax rate for all other states is zero.

Based on these requirements, Table 3.18 simply defines the storing of tax rates by state.

TABLE 3.18: Tax Table Columns

Column	Description
TaxID	The ID will be auto-incremented to give a unique identifier to each state.
TaxState	State abbreviation.
TaxRate	Tax rate for the state.

Table 3.19 shows some sample data as it might be entered into the Tax table.

TABLE 3.19: Tax Rate Sample Data

State	Tax Rate
TX	5% (0.05)
VA	10% (0.10)
DC	25% (0.25)

In the order process, we will simply check the state entered as the shipping address against the Tax table to compute the tax for the store.

Final Database Design

Now that we've defined our database tables, we can produce a final relationship diagram. Figure 3.13 shows the complete set of tables and their relationships.

FIGURE 3.13:

The Store database

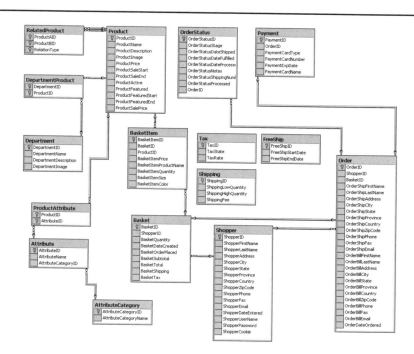

TIP The database diagram shown in Figure 3.13 is saved in the sample database with the name *dgmMain*.

Putting it all together provides the complete data picture needed for our e-commerce store. Next, we'll take a look at the script programming needed to create our tables.

The Final SQL Scripts

Now that we have our database columns designed, let's review the SQL scripts behind all the tables. These scripts were created by using the scripting facility built into SQL Server Enterprise Manager, which provides a convenient way to document the final design.

NOTE All the code presented in this chapter was tested on SQL Server 2000 with Service Pack 2 installed.

These tables are only part of what's in the database, of course. We'll also need stored procedures and other objects that interact with the tables. We'll present scripts for these other objects as we introduce them in later chapters.

NOTE   The readme.txt file on the companion CD has full instructions for installing the Store database on your own server.

The first script, shown in Listing 3.2, is for the Attribute table. The AttributeID column is the primary key.

Listing 3.2   Attribute Table

```
CREATE TABLE [dbo].[Attribute] (
    [AttributeID] [int] IDENTITY (1, 1) NOT NULL ,
    [AttributeName] [varchar] (255) NOT NULL ,
    [AttributeCategoryID] [int] NOT NULL
) ON [PRIMARY]
GO

ALTER TABLE [dbo].[Attribute] WITH NOCHECK ADD
    CONSTRAINT [Attribute_PK] PRIMARY KEY  CLUSTERED
    (
        [AttributeID]
    ) ON [PRIMARY]
GO

ALTER TABLE [dbo].[Attribute] ADD
    CONSTRAINT [AttributeCategory_Attribute_FK1] FOREIGN KEY
    (
        [AttributeCategoryID]
    ) REFERENCES [dbo].[AttributeCategory] (
        [AttributeCategoryID]
    )
GO
```

TIP   There are dependencies among the scripts that create the various tables. For example, the AttrributeCategory table must be created before the Attribute table. The build script on the companion CD organizes everything in the correct order.

Next is the AttributeCategory table, shown in Listing 3.3. Note that the primary key for the table is the AttributeCategoryID column.

Listing 3.3   **AttributeCategory Table**

```
CREATE TABLE [dbo].[AttributeCategory] (
    [AttributeCategoryID] [int] IDENTITY (1, 1) NOT NULL ,
    [AttributeCategoryName] [varchar] (255) NOT NULL
) ON [PRIMARY]
GO

ALTER TABLE [dbo].[AttributeCategory] WITH NOCHECK ADD
    CONSTRAINT [AttributeCategory_PK] PRIMARY KEY  CLUSTERED
    (
        [AttributeCategoryID]
    ) ON [PRIMARY]
GO
```

In the Basket table, the BasketID column is the primary key. The BasketDateCreated column will be defaulted with the getdate() statement call. All of the monetary columns will also be defaulted to a value of 0. Listing 3.4 shows the script for this table.

Listing 3.4   **Basket Table**

```
CREATE TABLE [dbo].[Basket] (
    [BasketID] [int] IDENTITY (1, 1) NOT NULL ,
    [ShopperID] [int] NOT NULL ,
    [BasketQuantity] [int] NOT NULL ,
    [BasketDateCreated] [datetime] NOT NULL ,
    [BasketOrderPlaced] [int] NOT NULL ,
    [BasketSubtotal] [money] NOT NULL ,
    [BasketTotal] [money] NOT NULL ,
    [BasketShipping] [money] NOT NULL ,
    [BasketTax] [money] NOT NULL
) ON [PRIMARY]
GO

ALTER TABLE [dbo].[Basket] WITH NOCHECK ADD
    CONSTRAINT [DF_Basket_BasketQuantity] DEFAULT (0)
     FOR [BasketQuantity],
    CONSTRAINT [DF_Basket_BasketDateCreated] DEFAULT (getdate())
     FOR [BasketDateCreated],
    CONSTRAINT [DF_Basket_BasketOrderPlaced] DEFAULT (0)
     FOR [BasketOrderPlaced],
    CONSTRAINT [DF_Basket_BasketSubtotal] DEFAULT (0)
     FOR [BasketSubtotal],
    CONSTRAINT [DF_Basket_BasketTotal] DEFAULT (0)
     FOR [BasketTotal],
    CONSTRAINT [DF_Basket_BasketShipping]
     DEFAULT (0) FOR [BasketShipping],
    CONSTRAINT [DF_Basket_BasketTax] DEFAULT (0)
```

```
    FOR [BasketTax],
    CONSTRAINT [Basket_PK] PRIMARY KEY  CLUSTERED
    (
        [BasketID]
    )  ON [PRIMARY]
GO

ALTER TABLE [dbo].[Basket] ADD
    CONSTRAINT [Shopper_Basket_FK1] FOREIGN KEY
    (
        [ShopperID]
    ) REFERENCES [dbo].[Shopper] (
        [ShopperID]
    )
GO
```

In the BasketItem table, the BasketItemID column is the primary key. The BasketItem-Price and BasketItemQuantity columns will both default to 0. This table is shown in Listing 3.5.

Listing 3.5   BasketItem Table

```
CREATE TABLE [dbo].[BasketItem] (
    [BasketItemID] [int] IDENTITY (1, 1) NOT NULL ,
    [BasketID] [int] NOT NULL ,
    [ProductID] [int] NOT NULL ,
    [BasketItemPrice] [money] NOT NULL ,
    [BasketItemProductName] [varchar] (255) NOT NULL ,
    [BasketItemQuantity] [int] NOT NULL ,
    [BasketItemSize] [varchar] (50) NULL ,
    [BasketItemColor] [varchar] (50) NULL
) ON [PRIMARY]
GO

ALTER TABLE [dbo].[BasketItem] WITH NOCHECK ADD
    CONSTRAINT [DF_BasketItem_BasketItemPrice] DEFAULT (0)
     FOR [BasketItemPrice],
    CONSTRAINT [DF_BasketItem_BasketItemQuantity] DEFAULT (0)
     FOR [BasketItemQuantity],
    CONSTRAINT [BasketItem_PK] PRIMARY KEY  CLUSTERED
    (
        [BasketItemID]
    )  ON [PRIMARY]
GO

ALTER TABLE [dbo].[BasketItem] ADD
    CONSTRAINT [Basket_BasketItem_FK1] FOREIGN KEY
    (
        [BasketID]
```

```
    ) REFERENCES [dbo].[Basket] (
        [BasketID]
    ),
    CONSTRAINT [Product_BasketItem_FK1] FOREIGN KEY
    (
        [ProductID]
    ) REFERENCES [dbo].[Product] (
        [ProductID]
    )
GO
```

Our next two tables are the Department and DepartmentProduct tables, which define how the department products are assigned. In the case of the Department table, the primary key is defined as an Identity column. Listing 3.6 defines the Department table, and Listing 3.7 defines the DepartmentProduct table.

Listing 3.6   **Department Table**

```
CREATE TABLE [dbo].[Department] (
    [DepartmentID] [int] IDENTITY (1, 1) NOT NULL ,
    [DepartmentName] [varchar] (255) NOT NULL ,
    [DepartmentDescription] [text] NULL ,
    [DepartmentImage] [varchar] (255) NULL
) ON [PRIMARY] TEXTIMAGE_ON [PRIMARY]
GO

ALTER TABLE [dbo].[Department] WITH NOCHECK ADD
    CONSTRAINT [Department_PK] PRIMARY KEY  CLUSTERED
    (
        [DepartmentID]
    ) ON [PRIMARY]
GO
```

Listing 3.7   **DepartmentProduct Table**

```
CREATE TABLE [dbo].[DepartmentProduct] (
    [DepartmentID] [int] NOT NULL ,
    [ProductID] [int] NOT NULL
) ON [PRIMARY]
GO

ALTER TABLE [dbo].[DepartmentProduct] WITH NOCHECK ADD
    CONSTRAINT [Department Product_PK] PRIMARY KEY  CLUSTERED
    (
        [DepartmentID],
        [ProductID]
    ) ON [PRIMARY]
```

```
GO

ALTER TABLE [dbo].[DepartmentProduct] ADD
    CONSTRAINT [Department_Department Product_FK1] FOREIGN KEY
    (
        [DepartmentID]
    ) REFERENCES [dbo].[Department] (
        [DepartmentID]
    ),
    CONSTRAINT [Product_Department Product_FK1] FOREIGN KEY
    (
        [ProductID]
    ) REFERENCES [dbo].[Product] (
        [ProductID]
    )
GO
```

The FreeShip table, shown in Listing 3.8, defines the dates on which we offer promotional free shipping.

Listing 3.8   FreeShip table

```
CREATE TABLE [dbo].[FreeShip] (
    [FreeShipID] [int] IDENTITY (1, 1) NOT NULL ,
    [FreeShipStartDate] [datetime] NOT NULL ,
    [FreeShipEndDate] [datetime] NOT NULL
) ON [PRIMARY]
GO

ALTER TABLE [dbo].[FreeShip] WITH NOCHECK ADD
    CONSTRAINT [FreeShip_PK] PRIMARY KEY  CLUSTERED
    (
        [FreeShipID]
    )  ON [PRIMARY]
GO
```

The Order table, shown in Listing 3.9, defines OrderID as its primary key column. The OrderDateOrdered column is defaulted with the getdate() function call. Thus, the order insertion date will be set to the server time when the customer placed the order.

Listing 3.9   Order Table

```
CREATE TABLE [dbo].[Order] (
    [OrderID] [int] IDENTITY (1, 1) NOT NULL ,
    [ShopperID] [int] NOT NULL ,
    [BasketID] [int] NOT NULL ,
    [OrderShipFirstName] [varchar] (50) NULL ,
    [OrderShipLastName] [varchar] (50) NULL ,
```

```
        [OrderShipAddress] [varchar] (150) NULL ,
        [OrderShipCity] [varchar] (150) NULL ,
        [OrderShipState] [varchar] (50) NULL ,
        [OrderShipProvince] [varchar] (150) NULL ,
        [OrderShipCountry] [varchar] (100) NULL ,
        [OrderShipZipCode] [varchar] (15) NULL ,
        [OrderShipPhone] [varchar] (25) NULL ,
        [OrderShipFax] [varchar] (25) NULL ,
        [OrderShipEmail] [varchar] (100) NULL ,
        [OrderBillFirstName] [varchar] (50) NULL ,
        [OrderBillLastName] [varchar] (50) NOT NULL ,
        [OrderBillAddress] [varchar] (150) NULL ,
        [OrderBillCity] [varchar] (150) NULL ,
        [OrderBillState] [varchar] (50) NULL ,
        [OrderBillProvince] [varchar] (150) NULL ,
        [OrderBillCountry] [varchar] (100) NULL ,
        [OrderBillZipCode] [varchar] (15) NULL ,
        [OrderBillPhone] [varchar] (25) NULL ,
        [OrderBillFax] [varchar] (25) NULL ,
        [OrderBillEmail] [varchar] (100) NULL ,
        [OrderDateOrdered] [datetime] NOT NULL
) ON [PRIMARY]
GO

ALTER TABLE [dbo].[Order] WITH NOCHECK ADD
    CONSTRAINT [DF_Order_OrderDateOrdered] DEFAULT (getdate())
     FOR [OrderDateOrdered],
    CONSTRAINT [Order_PK] PRIMARY KEY  CLUSTERED
    (
        [OrderID]
    )  ON [PRIMARY] ,
    CONSTRAINT [Order_AK1_UC1] UNIQUE  NONCLUSTERED
    (
        [BasketID]
    )  ON [PRIMARY]
GO

ALTER TABLE [dbo].[Order] ADD
    CONSTRAINT [Basket_Order_FK1] FOREIGN KEY
    (
        [BasketID]
    ) REFERENCES [dbo].[Basket] (
        [BasketID]
    ),
    CONSTRAINT [Shopper_Order_FK1] FOREIGN KEY
    (
        [ShopperID]
    ) REFERENCES [dbo].[Shopper] (
        [ShopperID]
    )
GO
```

In the OrderStatus table, shown in Listing 3.10, we default the OrderStatusStage value to 0. This will indicate that the order has not yet been processed. The OrderStatusID column is the primary key.

Listing 3.10   **OrderStatus Table**

```
CREATE TABLE [dbo].[OrderStatus] (
    [OrderStatusID] [int] IDENTITY (1, 1) NOT NULL ,
    [OrderStatusStage] [int] NOT NULL ,
    [OrderStatusDateShipped] [datetime] NULL ,
    [OrderStatusDateFulfilled] [datetime] NULL ,
    [OrderStatusDateProcessed] [datetime] NULL ,
    [OrderStatusNotes] [text] COLLATE SQL_Latin1_General_CP1_CI_AS NULL ,
    [OrderStatusShippingNumber] [varchar] (30) COLLATE
SQL_Latin1_General_CP1_CI_AS NULL ,
    [OrderStatusProcessed] [int] NOT NULL ,
    [OrderID] [int] NOT NULL
) ON [PRIMARY] TEXTIMAGE_ON [PRIMARY]
GO

ALTER TABLE [dbo].[OrderStatus] WITH NOCHECK ADD
    CONSTRAINT [DF_OrderStatus_OrderStatusStage]
        DEFAULT (0) FOR [OrderStatusStage],
    CONSTRAINT [OrderStatus_PK] PRIMARY KEY  CLUSTERED
    (
        [OrderStatusID]
    )  ON [PRIMARY]
GO

ALTER TABLE [dbo].[OrderStatus] ADD
    CONSTRAINT [Order_OrderStatus_FK1] FOREIGN KEY
    (
        [OrderID]
    ) REFERENCES [dbo].[Order] (
        [OrderID]
    )
GO
```

Listing 3.11 shows the Payment table. The PaymentID column is the primary key.

Listing 3.11   **Payment Table**

```
CREATE TABLE [dbo].[Payment] (
    [PaymentID] [int] IDENTITY (1, 1) NOT NULL ,
    [OrderID] [int] NOT NULL ,
    [PaymentCardType] [varchar] (50) NOT NULL ,
    [PaymentCardNumber] [varchar] (30) NOT NULL ,
    [PaymentExpDate] [varchar] (25) NOT NULL ,
    [PaymentCardName] [varchar] (150) NOT NULL
```

```
) ON [PRIMARY]
GO

ALTER TABLE [dbo].[Payment] WITH NOCHECK ADD
    CONSTRAINT [Payment_PK] PRIMARY KEY  CLUSTERED
    (
        [PaymentID]
    ) ON [PRIMARY] ,
    CONSTRAINT [Payment_AK1_UC1] UNIQUE  NONCLUSTERED
    (
        [OrderID]
    ) ON [PRIMARY]
GO

ALTER TABLE [dbo].[Payment] ADD
    CONSTRAINT [Order_Payment_FK1] FOREIGN KEY
    (
        [OrderID]
    ) REFERENCES [dbo].[Order] (
        [OrderID]
    )
GO
```

The Product table, shown in Listing 3.12, defines the product data for the store, with the ProductID column as the primary key.

Listing 3.12   Product Table

```
CREATE TABLE [dbo].[Product] (
    [ProductID] [int] IDENTITY (1, 1) NOT NULL ,
    [ProductName] [varchar] (255) NOT NULL ,
    [ProductDescription] [text] NULL ,
    [ProductImage] [varchar] (255) NULL ,
    [ProductPrice] [money] NULL ,
    [ProductSaleStart] [datetime] NULL ,
    [ProductSaleEnd] [datetime] NULL ,
    [ProductActive] [bit] NULL ,
    [ProductFeatured] [bit] NULL ,
    [ProductFeaturedStart] [datetime] NULL ,
    [ProductFeaturedEnd] [datetime] NULL ,
    [ProductSalePrice] [money] NULL
) ON [PRIMARY] TEXTIMAGE_ON [PRIMARY]
GO

ALTER TABLE [dbo].[Product] WITH NOCHECK ADD
    CONSTRAINT [DF_Product_ProductActive] DEFAULT (1)
     FOR [ProductActive],
    CONSTRAINT [DF_Product_ProductFeatured] DEFAULT (0)
     FOR [ProductFeatured],
    CONSTRAINT [Product_PK] PRIMARY KEY  CLUSTERED
```

```
    (
        [ProductID]
    ) ON [PRIMARY]
GO
```

The ProductAttribute table links the products with their assigned attributes. This table uses a composite primary key made up of the ProductID and AttributeID columns. Listing 3.13 shows this table.

Listing 3.13   ProductAttribute Table

```
CREATE TABLE [dbo].[ProductAttribute] (
    [ProductID] [int] NOT NULL ,
    [AttributeID] [int] NOT NULL
) ON [PRIMARY]
GO

ALTER TABLE [dbo].[ProductAttribute] WITH NOCHECK ADD
    CONSTRAINT [ProductAttribute_PK] PRIMARY KEY  CLUSTERED
    (
        [ProductID],
        [AttributeID]
    ) ON [PRIMARY]
GO

ALTER TABLE [dbo].[ProductAttribute] ADD
    CONSTRAINT [Attribute_ProductAttribute_FK1] FOREIGN KEY
    (
        [AttributeID]
    ) REFERENCES [dbo].[Attribute] (
        [AttributeID]
    ),
    CONSTRAINT [Product_ProductAttribute_FK1] FOREIGN KEY
    (
        [ProductID]
    ) REFERENCES [dbo].[Product] (
        [ProductID]
    )
GO
```

The RelatedProduct table defines the relationships between products. The primary key defines a composite key that encompasses all the columns in the table. Listing 3.14 shows the SQL script for this table.

Listing 3.14   RelatedProduct Table

```
CREATE TABLE [dbo].[RelatedProduct] (
    [ProductAID] [int] NOT NULL ,
```

```
        [ProductBID] [int] NOT NULL ,
        [RelationType] [int] NOT NULL
) ON [PRIMARY]
GO

ALTER TABLE [dbo].[RelatedProduct] WITH NOCHECK ADD
    CONSTRAINT [RelatedProduct_PK] PRIMARY KEY  CLUSTERED
    (
        [ProductAID],
        [ProductBID],
        [RelationType]
    ) ON [PRIMARY]
GO

ALTER TABLE [dbo].[RelatedProduct] ADD
    CONSTRAINT [Product_RelatedProduct_FK1] FOREIGN KEY
    (
        [ProductAID]
    ) REFERENCES [dbo].[Product] (
        [ProductID]
    ),
    CONSTRAINT [Product_RelatedProduct_FK2] FOREIGN KEY
    (
        [ProductBID]
    ) REFERENCES [dbo].[Product] (
        [ProductID]
    )
GO
```

The Shipping table defines the shipping rates for the store. The `ShippingID` column is the primary key. Listing 3.15 shows this table.

Listing 3.15   Shipping Table

```
CREATE TABLE [dbo].[Shipping] (
    [ShippingID] [int] IDENTITY (1, 1) NOT NULL ,
    [ShippingLowQuantity] [int] NOT NULL ,
    [ShippingHighQuantity] [int] NOT NULL ,
    [ShippingFee] [money] NOT NULL
) ON [PRIMARY]
GO

ALTER TABLE [dbo].[Shipping] WITH NOCHECK ADD
    CONSTRAINT [Shipping_PK] PRIMARY KEY  CLUSTERED
    (
        [ShippingID]
    ) ON [PRIMARY]
GO
```

The Shopper table, shown in Listing 3.16, defines the shopper data for the store. The ShopperDateEntered column is defaulted to the current date with the getdate() function to indicate when the shopper record was created. Also, the ShopperCookie column is defaulted to 0 to indicate that a cookie should *not* be set to store the shopper's ID unless the shopper specifically requests this. The ShopperID column is the primary key.

Listing 3.16   Shopper Table

```
CREATE TABLE [dbo].[Shopper] (
    [ShopperID] [int] IDENTITY (1, 1) NOT NULL ,
    [ShopperFirstName] [varchar] (50) NULL ,
    [ShopperLastName] [varchar] (50) NOT NULL ,
    [ShopperAddress] [varchar] (150) NULL ,
    [ShopperCity] [varchar] (100) COLLATE NULL ,
    [ShopperState] [varchar] (2) NULL ,
    [ShopperProvince] [varchar] (150) NULL ,
    [ShopperCountry] [varchar] (100) NULL ,
    [ShopperZipCode] [varchar] (15) NULL ,
    [ShopperPhone] [varchar] (30) NULL ,
    [ShopperFax] [varchar] (30) NULL ,
    [ShopperEmail] [varchar] (150) NULL ,
    [ShopperDateEntered] [datetime] NOT NULL ,
    [ShopperUserName] [varchar] (25) NOT NULL ,
    [ShopperPassword] [varchar] (25) NOT NULL ,
    [ShopperCookie] [tinyint] NOT NULL
) ON [PRIMARY]
GO

ALTER TABLE [dbo].[Shopper] WITH NOCHECK ADD
    CONSTRAINT [DF_Shopper_ShopperDateEntered] DEFAULT (getdate())
     FOR [ShopperDateEntered],
    CONSTRAINT [DF_Shopper_ShopperCookie] DEFAULT (0)
     FOR [ShopperCookie],
    CONSTRAINT [Shopper_PK] PRIMARY KEY  CLUSTERED
    (
        [ShopperID]
    ) ON [PRIMARY]
GO
```

Finally, the Tax table defines our tax rates by state. The primary key is the TaxID column. Listing 3.17 shows this table.

Listing 3.17   Tax Table

```
CREATE TABLE [dbo].[Tax] (
    [TaxID] [int] IDENTITY (1, 1) NOT NULL ,
    [TaxState] [varchar] (50) NOT NULL ,
    [TaxRate] [float] NOT NULL
```

```
) ON [PRIMARY]
GO

ALTER TABLE [dbo].[Tax] WITH NOCHECK ADD
    CONSTRAINT [Tax_PK] PRIMARY KEY  CLUSTERED
    (
        [TaxID]
    ) ON [PRIMARY]
GO
```

With that, our core tables are created, with all the appropriate primary keys set and with default values set for specific columns. You're now ready to create the tables in your database.

Summary

A solid, fundamental database design is the key to any successful e-commerce website. In this chapter, you've seen the design for our Store database pass through stages of Object Role Modeling, logical design, and physical design. At this point, we've defined the core tables that will be used in building our e-commerce solution.

In the next chapter, we'll look at the issues of designing and managing the actual servers that will hold this database as well as the rest of our e-commerce application.

CHAPTER 4

System Configuration

- Designing the Server Farm

- Managing the Server Farm

Configuring the systems appropriately for running an e-commerce website is critical to the site's success. Setting up the server farm properly is crucial whether the e-commerce store is simple and meant to sell just a few products or it's complex and intended for prime-time e-commerce retailing.

Also, issues such as backups, the development environment, product staging, and source code control become critical in a 24×7×365, real-time, production environment, where any downtime may mean a substantial loss of revenue.

NOTE   For the purposes of this book, we presume that from a business perspective, your organization is ready to begin selling its products and/or services online.

Designing the Server Farm

The *server farm* will consist of all the servers required to run the website. It may contain only one server or many servers with different roles such as database management, website serving, and so on. When you're developing an e-commerce system, you need to consider many aspects of setting up the server farm, including the number of servers needed. Although it's possible to run all the functions on one server, doing this could compromise security and reliability. Indeed, you may find that you want to run some functions (such as delivering web pages) on multiple servers simultaneously to spread the load and provide redundancy. Let's explore the options for building a server farm.

Web Servers

WARNING   The e-commerce store will need to run on a Windows 2000 or later web server. For our example, which is based on ASP.NET and Visual Basic .NET, you will also need Internet Information Server 5 or later. The website should also run fine on Windows .NET Server, once that version of Windows is released. An advantage of Windows .NET Server is that the .NET Framework is already installed, making it easier to deploy ASP.NET websites. ASP.NET requires a Windows 2000, Windows XP, or Windows .NET server. You cannot use Windows NT 4 or any member of the Windows 9x family as your web server.

TIP   Typically, a website will encompass more than just an e-commerce store. Other features might be more content focused and not necessarily commerce related.

Usually, the e-commerce web server will be set up separately from the database server and the main corporate web server. Only in cases of very simple sites with minimal traffic should all three be combined. Table 4.1 describes some key requirements for you to consider.

TABLE 4.1: E-Commerce Configuration Requirements

Requirement	Description
E-commerce management interface	A management interface will be built during the store's design process. Security is essential, so the management interface URL should be distinct (for example, `https://admin.ecstore.schmoop.com`) from that of the user shopping site (for example, `http://www.ecstore.schmoop.com`). Security can be implemented in a number of ways. NT Challenge and Response authentication can be required with directory-level security, or, as will be explored later in the book, a code-based security system can be implemented.
SSL security	Secure Sockets Layer security will be required for encrypting private data between the browser and the server.
Database connection	Presuming the database server isn't on the same machine, we'll need an OLE DB link to the database on the e-commerce web server. That also presumes that the database server is easily accessible on the network.

The e-commerce web server is like any other web server. But, unlike a server that primarily serves static pages, this web server will primarily deliver template- and data-driven web pages.

If a web server that's separate from the e-commerce server is required, it will be configured in much the same way as the e-commerce web server. The primary requirement will be an appropriate link to the web store. An excellent example of how this type of server configuration can be accomplished is the American Diabetes Association's websites. The primary website is at `www.diabetes.org`, and the e-commerce store is hosted at `store.diabetes.org`.

Database Server

Typically, you don't want the database server to be accessible to the outside world. It should sit behind a firewall and not be directly accessible to the Internet. In that case, it will be accessible via the LAN environment behind the firewall. If the web server and the database server are on the same machine, the database is directly exposed to outside access. This has the potential of permitting access to private data such as credit cards. Although SQL Server certainly provides login access security and other means of locking down the database, making the database publicly inaccessible helps to ensure security.

Multiple Servers

As mentioned, the simplest of websites can be run from a single web server, with all functionality on that server, as shown in Figure 4.1. The next level of division, as shown in Figure 4.2, is the separation of any web server support from database support. This configuration requires two servers in the data farm. More challenging are situations where multiple web servers and database servers are needed to support a high volume of transactions, as shown in Figure 4.3. Although the fundamental coding and database functionality are the same, new issues of data synchronization, content synchronization, load balancing, and so on, will need to be addressed. Tackling those issues specifically is beyond the scope of this book, but you should consider these issues carefully before launching a website that will potentially attract a high transaction volume.

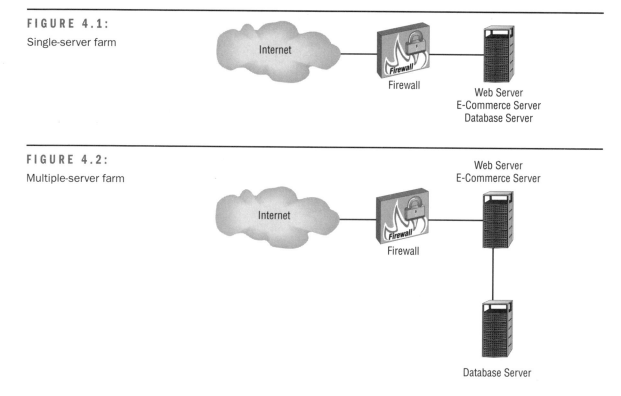

FIGURE 4.1:

Single-server farm

Internet — Firewall — Web Server / E-Commerce Server / Database Server

FIGURE 4.2:

Multiple-server farm

Web Server / E-Commerce Server

Internet — Firewall — Database Server

FIGURE 4.3:

Server farm with a high transaction volume

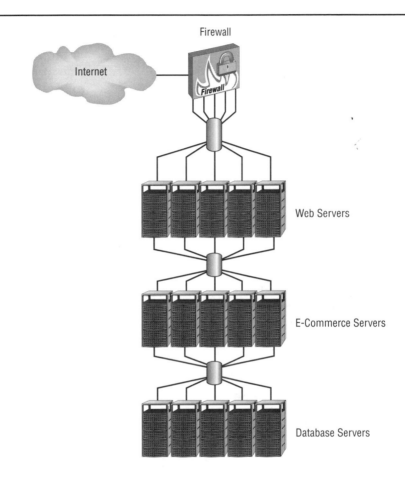

TIP   For development purposes, there is no problem in having all of the functionality on a single server. But it's important to test the solution on the full server farm to ensure that all items are linking up properly.

WARNING   When the requirement for load balancing comes into play in a multiple-server environment, additional functionality will be needed to serve the web requests to the different servers. Load balancing can be implemented in software, such as the Windows Load Balancing Service, or in dedicated hardware that handles switching sessions among different servers.

It's also important to point out that as a website grows and different levels of traffic spiking occur, the server farm configuration may need to change. You should plan for a flexible system right from the start of your e-commerce project. This means that, to the extent possible, you should isolate specific server names in small portions of the code so that the names can be changed quickly to redirect components to new servers.

Development and Staging Servers

Although you'll devote much of your attention to the production web server farm, you should also spend some time planning the related roles of the *development server* and the *staging server*. The development server is where ongoing development will take place for new functionality on the e-commerce web server. Typically, the development server can be a computer without the full resources needed by the production servers, because it will be used only for preliminary testing under low loads.

The staging server will be utilized for migrating website updates from the development server to the production web server farm, to ensure that everything is working. The staging server is used primarily by the quality assurance team to confirm that any updates work as specified and that they don't break existing functionality. This phase is particularly critical if updates will be ongoing and frequent, especially in a multi-server production environment. If the updates to the website are significant, it may be vital to do proper load testing to ensure that the changes will not fail under a full production load.

Application Deployment

The backbone of our store's code will use the ASP.NET components of Microsoft's .NET Framework. ASP.NET was designed for ease of deployment to staging and production servers after the development cycle is finished. You can FTP, XCOPY, or otherwise copy all the files in the application to the production server and set up a virtual root pointing to the files, and everything will just work.

ASP.NET functionality is grouped into programming units called *assemblies*. ASP.NET allows you to designate an assembly cache directory on your production server. When you copy an assembly into this directory, ASP.NET automatically registers it. There's no need to log on to the server or register the assembly. This makes it possible to add new functionality via new objects without stopping the server or interrupting existing sessions.

When users interact with an application, ASP.NET makes shadow copies of the files in the application and runs from the shadow copies. At any time, you can upgrade an application by copying new files into the application's directory. ASP.NET monitors the files in an application for changes and loads newer versions as they are detected. The end result is that you should never have to shut down a web server to upgrade an ASP.NET application.

Scaling

As your store's business increases, you'll find that you need to add additional hardware capacity to handle the server load. Four key terms you need to understand in this connection are *scale up*, *scale out*, *clustering*, and *failover*.

Scale up   To "scale up" a server, you simply add more hardware resources—more RAM, bigger hard drives, more CPUs. The Enterprise Edition of SQL Server 2000 running on Windows 2000 Datacenter Server can make use of 64GB of RAM and 32 CPUs and will support databases up to a million terabytes in size.

Scale out   As your database needs grow, scaling up may become prohibitively expensive. SQL Server also supports "scaling out," which refers to distributing a database across multiple servers. SQL Server 2000 supports distributed partitioned views, which allow you to store portions of a table on many different servers and yet treat it as one large table when you're writing queries. Replication and log shipping (the ability to take transaction logs from a production server and apply them to a backup server) also help you scale out a SQL Server solution by maintaining copies of your data on multiple servers.

Clustering   Clustering is designed to increase the reliability of a server by running one logical server on multiple physical computers. In a typical clustering installation, all data is kept on an external disk array that is available through two or more SCSI controller cards. This disk array is storage space that is shared by every server in the cluster.

Failover   If a server in a cluster fails, failover takes place. With failover, running services are transparently moved from one physical server to another. For example, if you have a cluster composed of two servers, and the SQL Server service on the first server fails, the second server will immediately take over running queries and storing data.

Managing the Server Farm

Many of the challenges of managing a server farm for a web application are like the challenges of managing a traditional client-server application. Key aspects of any good development and production management process include source code control, backups, and so on. In this section, we'll review some of those requirements. Also, we'll discuss the basics of setting up the website so that we can kick off our development in the next chapter.

Development Environment

Building an e-commerce store isn't significantly different in scope or complexity from building an internal client-server application. Good development techniques and tools are critical.

Visual SourceSafe is an excellent tool for managing source code for a project, and it does a very good job of managing code check-in and checkout in a group-project development environment. The SourceSafe database can reside on the development server or preferably on a separate server on the network. With all files from all developers checked in to SourceSafe, you have several options for managing the development environment. If server hardware is scarce, you may opt to have all developers actively working on their pieces of the project on one, central development server. With more resources, you may find it makes more sense to give each developer their own development server, where they can maintain a full copy of the project. This insulates developers from crashes caused by others on the team, but it increases the difficulty of making sure all of the development servers have identical configurations and requires increased attention to keeping all of the source-code files up to date.

Web Server Setup

To create our development environment, we'll go through the steps to configure Internet Information Server (IIS) and FrontPage Server Extensions, and then install the .NET Framework.

NOTE   Our instructions use the Windows 2000 user interface. You'll find some differences in the location of menu items and the appearance of the user interface on the other supported operating systems—Windows XP and Windows .NET Server. For the latest information on each of these operating systems, refer to the WebServer.htm file in the Setup folder on Disk 1 of Visual Studio .NET.

Before you begin, you need to make sure that you have the proper security updates available. To install a web server safely, you must first download the current security updates to the computer and then physically disconnect the computer from the Internet. If you neglect this step, you run a high risk of having the computer rendered worthless by a malicious attack between the time that you install the web server and the time that you install the security updates. You can find a listing of the latest required security updates at http://msdn .microsoft.com/vstudio/security/. At a minimum, a Windows 2000 computer should be updated with Windows 2000 Service Pack 2 and the latest IIS security update.

Now you can install IIS on the computer. To do so, follow these steps:

1. Select Start ➤ Settings ➤ Control Panel.
2. In Control Panel, double-click the Add/Remove Programs applet.
3. Select the Add/Remove Windows Components icon at the left side of the Add/Remove Programs dialog box.

4. Select Internet Information Services (IIS) in the Windows Component Wizard.

5. Click the Details button and select the IIS components that you wish to install on the server. At the minimum, you'll need the Common Files, FrontPage 2000 Server Extensions, Internet Information Services Snap-In, SMTP Service, and World Wide Web Service. Don't install components that you don't need (this would present an unnecessary security risk).

TIP   You can use the FrontPage 2002 Server Extensions from the Office XP package instead of the FrontPage 2000 Server Extensions.

6. Click OK and then Next to install the IIS components. You may need your Windows 2000 CD-ROM to complete this step.

7. Click Finish and then Close to close the Add/Remove Programs dialog box.

The next task is to make sure that FrontPage Server Extensions are properly configured. This step needs to be performed only if the server uses the FAT file system; the step will already have been done by the installation program if the server uses the NTFS file system. But it doesn't hurt to check. To do so, follow these steps:

1. Select Start ➤ Settings ➤ Control Panel.

2. In Control Panel, double-click the Administrative Tools applet.

3. Select Computer Management. This will launch an instance of Microsoft Management Console with the Computer Management snap-in loaded, as shown in Figure 4.4.

FIGURE 4.4:

The Microsoft Management Console with IIS snap-ins loaded

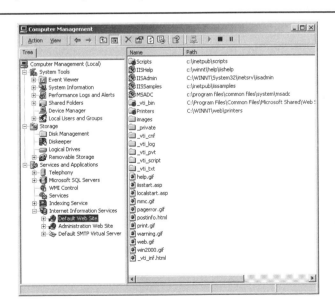

4. Expand the Services and Applications node and then the Internet Information Services node.

5. Right-click Default Web Site and select All Tasks ➤ Configure Server Extensions. (If this menu item is missing, it means that the extensions were automatically configured and you can skip the rest of these steps.)

6. Click Next.

7. Respond Yes to the Warning dialog box.

8. Respond No when asked about configuring mail server settings.

9. Click Next and then Finish to configure the FrontPage Server Extensions.

At this point, you should install the security updates that you downloaded before you began the installation process. After doing this, reboot the machine. It's then safe to reconnect it to the Internet.

Now you can install the .NET Framework on the web server. Follow these steps:

1. Insert Disk 1 of Visual Studio .NET in the web server. If Visual Studio .NET Setup doesn't launch automatically, run the setup.exe program from the root of the CD or DVD.

2. Click step 1 in the Visual Studio .NET Setup dialog box, as shown in Figure 4.5, and follow the instructions to install the Windows Component Update.

FIGURE 4.5:

Visual Studio .NET
Setup

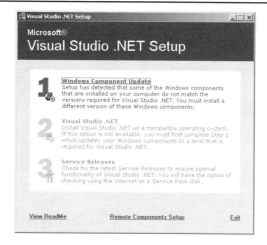

3. When the Windows Component Update has finished installing updates, it will display the Visual Studio .NET Setup dialog box again. Click step 2 to install Visual Studio .NET.

4. Accept the license agreement, enter your product key, and click Next.

5. On the Options page of Visual Studio .NET Setup, deselect all the options except Server Components. Expand the Server Components node and select the Full Remote Debugging and Web Development options. These are the components that are necessary to allow us to develop ASP.NET pages on this server. Figure 4.6 shows the selected options. Click Install Now to install the components.

FIGURE 4.6:

Installing the necessary server components

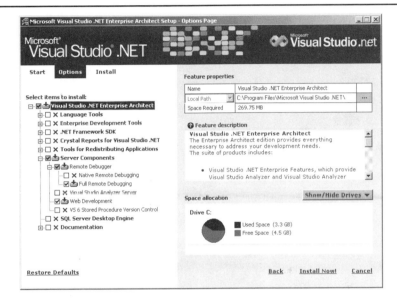

6. After Visual Studio .NET has installed the server components, it will display the Visual Studio .NET Setup dialog box again. Click step 3 and follow the on-screen instructions to download any available service releases.

7. Select Start ➢ Settings ➢ Control Panel.

8. In Control Panel, double-click the Administrative Tools applet.

9. Select Computer Management.

10. Expand the System Tools node, then the Local Users and Groups node.

11. Click Groups.

12. Double-click the VS Developers group.

13. In the VS Developers Properties dialog box, click the Add button. Select the users on your network who will need to be able to develop pages for this server. Click OK twice to add these users to the VS Developers group.

That's it! Now your server is ready to start delivering ASP.NET pages, and you're ready to have your developers start producing them. We'll test these capabilities in the next chapter, but first, there are some other configuration tasks to think about.

Server Backups

Backing up server data is critical, of course. Backing up an e-commerce website can be even more critical, for two reasons: The site will be recording new transactions constantly as shoppers select products and place orders, and the site needs to be available 24 hours a day, 7 days a week, 365 days a year.

Table 4.2 provides an overview of the key items to back up.

TABLE 4.2: Server Backup Considerations

Requirement	Description
ASP.NET and other key web files	Of course, the code, images, HTML pages, and other files on the website should be backed up frequently. Keeping backups over time may also be important in case past content needs to be resurrected.
.NET objects	Business objects that we will create in Visual Basic .NET will also need to be backed up when they're updated. The source code for these objects (stored in Visual SourceSafe) should be backed up as well.
SSL certificates	Often missed in the backup process is the requirement to store the SSL certificates in a backed-up location. If the certificates are lost, the only option is to request a new set of certificates.
IIS configuration settings	If you are making changes to the default IIS configuration settings, they should also be noted and saved in case the web server needs to be rebuilt.
SQL Server configuration settings	As with the IIS configuration settings, any changes to the default SQL Server configuration settings should be noted and saved.
Operating system and other server files	As with any good, standard backup and for a quick recovery, the full system should be backed up frequently.

Security

As mentioned earlier in the chapter, security is a key issue for configuring the website. We can secure our site directly at the web level in IIS. This is opposed to implementing database security and not allowing access to content via ASP coding.

Figure 4.7 shows the Authentication Methods dialog box for an IIS 5 website. You can get to this dialog box by right-clicking the website in Internet Services Manager and selecting Properties. Then click the Edit button in the Anonymous Access section of the Directory Security tab. In general, Anonymous Access is the appropriate setting for providing public access to a website. If a particular virtual root or directory needs to be locked down further, you can implement Basic Authentication and Windows NT Challenge/Response. Basic Authentication sends passwords across the Internet in clear text. In Windows NT Challenge/Response, you have to use Internet Explorer to gain access to the website. In either case, the user is prompted with a dialog box requesting the username and password.

FIGURE 4.7:

Security settings for the website

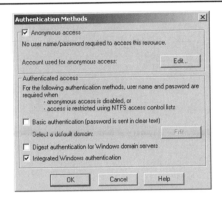

Also on the security front, management of SSL certificates is critical. SSL certificates allow users to connect to your website by using the secure HTTPS protocol in addition to the standard HTTP protocol. To install a certificate, click the Server Certificate button in the Secure Communications section of the Directory Security tab of the website's Properties dialog box.

For a public website (such as an e-commerce site), you'll need to obtain a certificate from a certificate authority such as VeriSign. Certificate authorities provide a guarantee of identity to concerned web surfers. For a good list of certificate authorities and other information on public-key infrastructure (PKI), try the PKI Page at www.pki-page.org.

Database Setup

Configuring the database is as important as setting up the web server. Although going through all the ins and outs of database configuration is beyond the scope of this book, Table 4.3 shows a few items for you to consider.

TABLE 4.3: Database Configuration Considerations

Configuration	Description
Peak loading	Unlike the traditional business environment, where the peak spike load may be a moderate blip on the radar, websites often have peaks at unusual times, requiring far more resources than the average load on the server might lead you to expect. Holidays, sales promotions, and other events may entail significant loading requirements. You should ensure that the web server can support extended connections and data objects. Each of these will affect the server configuration requirements.
Drive space	Transaction logs and web activity logs, as well as the information stored in the database itself, can quickly add up to a lot of data. This can affect drive storage requirements. Continuing to monitor the drive utilization is critical. If backups are temporarily stored on the hard drive, they must be removed to tape on a regular basis to ensure that the hard drive doesn't run out of space.
Multiple server support	If multiple database servers are in place, you should ensure the synchronization of product data, orders, customer profiles, and other issues as part of the basic system design.

Database backup and replication are also critical issues. You should consider several scenarios when building in redundancy and backup for the database server. Table 4.4 suggests some options.

TABLE 4.4: Database Backup and Replication Scenarios

Configuration	Description
Device backup	Simple device backup with nightly backup to tape can provide basic backup capabilities. The only downside is that there is no real-time backup to ensure that the website will stay up without significant downtime.
Warm backup	There are possible *warm* backup scenarios in which the database data is transferred or replicated infrequently (perhaps hourly or even less often). If the database server should go down, a simple reconfiguration of ASP.NET settings to point at the warm backup will keep the website up and functioning.
Real-time replication	The best of all worlds is real-time replication between database servers. Putting this kind of requirement on the database server calls for significant planning for resource loading, depending on the different transaction levels.

You also need to carefully plan your process for applying any database updates to the production server. Any time updates are made to the production database server from the development server, issues such as ensuring that peak loading will not be affected and providing security become critical to the website's success. Database updates, like website updates, should be tested on a staging server before being rolled out to the live server.

Load Planning

As illustrated several times in this chapter on system design, load planning is critical. Coding of the e-commerce platform for core functionality may have a minimal impact, but if you're planning for substantial load, it's important to ensure that the code is solid and capable of handling multiple server requirements.

You can find some excellent load-planning tools on the Web. If you are working with an ISP to run and manage the server farm, the ISP will likely have load-testing capabilities to assist you in planning for different traffic loads. It's particularly important to test the key code-heavy sections of the website.

TIP   The Windows 2000 Server Resource Kit contains a tool, WCAT (Web Capacity Analysis Test), that can help you perform automated load testing on a web server.

Browser Considerations

Finally, a key part of system planning is understanding the browser requirements that the system will need to support. Although much of this relates to design, the type of browser may be dictated if certain parts of the website are coded to use extended browser features (such as ActiveX or DHTML). An example of this is a store manager that is developed to use a specific browser for extended functionality. In some situations, Internet Explorer may be required for Windows NT Challenge/Response.

In general, of course, you want to avoid limiting your potential customer base. This means that you must support the widest possible browser selection. ASP.NET is designed to produce standard HTML 3.2 output without any vendor-specific extensions, which means that Version 4.x or later of any major browser should have no trouble with the store that we're going to build.

Summary

System design for a website is critical to ensuring the success of all that hard work that goes into the code development of the site. In some respects, the issues aren't all that different from designing a traditional client-server application or n-tier server farm. The primary differences are in planning for different server loads, a somewhat different set of tools, different clients, and the potential for the environment to change rapidly.

In this chapter, we've shown you how to set up your server for ASP.NET development and suggested areas that you'll need to investigate further with your IT department to ensure a successful rollout. Now we'll turn to the development process itself, starting with a test project to check that everything is properly configured.

CHAPTER 5

Building a Sample Application

- Building the Data Table

- Building the Subscription Form

- Managing ASP.NET Web Pages

- Programming the Subscription Process

- Managing the Application

- Thinking about Potential Enhancements

Before we go full bore into the development process based on the database design in Chapter 3, we are going to build a very simple e-commerce application based on ASP.NET and SQL Server. This will help you get your feet wet with the Visual Studio .NET development environment and the other tools that we'll be using in building the full store application.

Our sample application will be a simple form for purchasing a subscription to a publication. This form will receive the subscriber's name, address, and credit card data.

Building the Data Table

The first thing we'll need is a simple database table where we can insert our subscriptions. Obviously, the table must contain columns for the subscriber's name, address, and credit card information. Because this application is so simple, we won't need to use Visio to design the database. Instead, we can just build the database directly using SQL Server's Query Analyzer tool. Listing 5.1 shows the SQL script that we'll use to create the database and build the Subscriptions table in it.

Listing 5.1   Subscriptions Database Table

```
USE master
GO
CREATE DATABASE Subscriptions
GO
USE subscriptions
GO
CREATE TABLE dbo.Subscriptions (
    SubscriptionID int IDENTITY (1, 1) NOT NULL,
    FirstName varchar (100) NULL ,
    LastName varchar (100) NULL ,
    Address varchar (150) NULL ,
    City varchar (100) NULL ,
    State varchar (10) NULL ,
    ZipCode varchar (15) NULL ,
    Phone varchar (25) NULL ,
    Email varchar (100) NULL ,
    CardName varchar (150) NULL ,
    CardType varchar (50) NULL ,
    CardNumber varchar (25) NULL ,
    ExpirationDate varchar (50) NULL ,
    Processed bit NULL DEFAULT 0,
       /* Default to 0 */
    DateEntered datetime NULL
      DEFAULT GETDATE(),
       /* Default to current date */
    Length tinyint NULL
)
```

```
GO
ALTER TABLE dbo.Subscriptions ADD
    CONSTRAINT PK_Subscriptions PRIMARY KEY CLUSTERED
      (
        SubscriptionID
      )
  GO
```

A couple of status columns are included in the table. The Processed column will be used to flag the order as processed so that fulfillment information can be easily tracked. This column is defaulted to 0, to indicate "unprocessed." The other status column is the DateEntered field. This defines the date when the subscription was entered into the database. This automatically defaults to the current date.

To create this table by using SQL Query Analyzer, follow these steps:

1. Select Start ➤ Programs ➤ Microsoft SQL Server ➤ Query Analyzer.

2. In the Connect to SQL Server dialog box, enter the name of the SQL Server where you would like to create the Subscriptions database. If you're working on the same computer where the database will be created, you can use the special name *(local)* in place of the server name. Select the Windows Authentication option and then click OK.

3. In SQL Query Analyzer, select File ➤ Open. Browse to the Subscription.sql file on the companion CD and then click Open.

4. Press F5 or click the Execute button on the toolbar. This will run the SQL statements to create the database and the table.

Figure 5.1 shows SQL Query Analyzer after running the query. In this case, we used a SQL Server named HOURGLASS to hold the database.

FIGURE 5.1:

Using SQL Query Analyzer to create a table

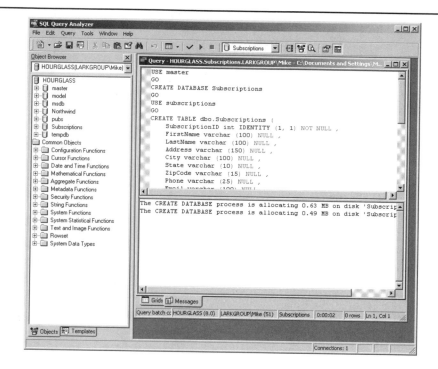

Building the Subscription Form

We'll use Visual Studio .NET to build our web application, including the subscription form and the other pages that we'll need to manage subscriptions. To get started, you'll need to create a new web application by following these steps:

1. Select Start ➤ Programs ➤ Microsoft Visual Studio .NET ➤ Microsoft Visual Studio .NET.

2. On the Start Page, click the New Project button.

3. Select the Visual Basic Projects project type and the ASP.NET Web Application template. Specify a location for your project on the server where you'll be running the ASP.NET pages. For example, Figure 5.2 shows the New Project dialog box preparing to create a project named Subscriptions on a server named HOURGLASS.

FIGURE 5.2:

Creating a new web application

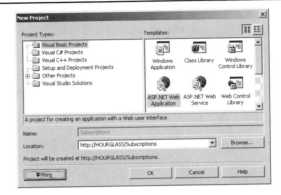

4. Click OK to create the new application on your web server.

5. Visual Studio .NET will open the new web application in its IDE (integrated development environment), as shown in Figure 5.3. Right-click the WebForm1.aspx item in the Solution Explorer and select Rename. Rename the Web Form subscription.aspx.

FIGURE 5.3:

A new web application

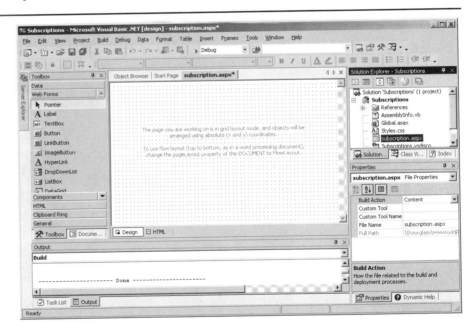

NOTE   Because we chose to create a Visual Basic .NET project, the IDE is labeled "Visual Basic .NET" in its title bar. You'll find, though, that the tools and process of web application design are much the same, whether you use Visual Basic or C# as your programming language.

The Visual Basic .NET Design Environment

When you first open a Visual Basic .NET project, you may be overwhelmed by the sheer number of windows and buttons available. Here's what you'll find in the default set of Visual Basic .NET windows.

In the center of the work area is the *designer*. This is the portion of Visual Basic .NET where you can design forms (both Windows Forms and Web Forms) and write code, as well as design other specialized objects.

In the upper-right corner of the work area, the *Solution Explorer* and *Class View* share a window. Tabs at the bottom of the window let you move back and forth between these two tools. The Solution Explorer provides a file-based view of the components within your Visual Basic .NET project. You can double-click a file here to open it in the designer. The Solution Explorer also shows you the .NET namespaces and other components that you have referenced from the current project. The Class View provides a logical view of the classes within your project. It presents a treeview that lets you drill down to individual classes, methods, and properties.

In the lower-right corner of the work area, the *Properties window* and the *Dynamic Help* share a window. Tabs at the bottom of the window let you move back and forth between these two tools. The Properties window shows you the properties of the object currently selected in the Solution Explorer or the designer. Buttons on this window's toolbar let you choose whether to view the properties alphabetically or by category. The Dynamic Help window provides hyperlinks to the Visual Studio .NET help files that match what you're doing in the design interface. For example, if you select the Calendar in the Toolbox, the Dynamic Help window will show you topic titles related to the Calendar. If you click one of these titles, the corresponding help topic will open in the main designer window.

At the bottom of the work area, you'll see the *Output window*. Visual Basic .NET uses this window to send you informational messages. For example, when you run a Visual Basic .NET project, this window will tell you exactly which .NET assemblies are loaded to provide functionality for the project.

The *Toolbox* is to the left of the design surface. The Toolbox contains controls and other components that you can add to your project. In a web application, some of these are Web Form controls, while others (for example, those on the Data tab) are nongraphical controls. The tabs on the Toolbox (Data, Web Forms, Components, Clipboard Ring, and General, by default) allow you to keep components sorted into various categories. You can right-click the Toolbox and select Add Tab to add your own custom categories to the list.

At the far left of the work area, you'll see a tab for the *Server Explorer*. If you hover over this tab, the Server Explorer window will slide out and cover the Toolbox. You can control this sliding behavior by clicking the tiny pushpin icon in the Server Explorer's title bar. The Server Explorer lets you explore databases, message queues, and other system services that are available to your application.

Of course, the entire Visual Basic .NET interface is customizable. You can drag windows around, leave them free-floating or dock them, and hide or display them. The View menu offers options to display the default windows as well as some other useful windows like the Object Browser and the Command window.

Creating the Subscription Form

We're going to build the subscription form as a Web Form. Web Forms are ASPX files that are stored on the computer where IIS is running. When the user requests a Web Form, the ASP.NET runtime compiles the ASPX file into a .NET class. The class then processes requests for that Web Form. Although the contents of the Web Form can include code in any .NET language, that code is never sent to the client browser. Instead, the ASP.NET runtime executes the compiled form to return HTML to the browser. You can think of a Web Form as a self-contained program whose output is pure HTML.

The HTML that ASP.NET sends depends on the browser making the request for the page. ASP.NET classifies browsers as *uplevel* and *downlevel* browsers. Uplevel browsers support ECMAScript (JScript or JavaScript) version 1.2, HTML version 4, and Cascading Style Sheets. When ASP.NET detects one of these browsers, it may make use of those capabilities to create a richer user experience. For downlevel browsers, ASP.NET sends only HTML version 3.2 tags and doesn't use any client-side scripting. The net result is that ASP.NET pages should display properly in nearly any browser, although some capabilities may not work as well in downlevel browsers. For example, most controls don't support a BackColor property in HTML 3.2.

Because of this runtime translation to pure HTML, you don't have to worry about browser capabilities when you're designing Web Forms. You can use all of the Visual Studio .NET design tools and let ASP.NET worry about how to render the results.

The ASP.NET page designer lets you develop the graphical interface of your pages in three different modes:

- In *HTML mode*, selected by choosing the HTML tab at the bottom of the designer window, you can work with the raw HTML code for the page.

- In *grid layout mode*, selected by choosing the Design tab at the bottom of the designer page and setting the pageLayout property of the document to GridLayout, you can place controls anywhere on the page and size them precisely.

- In *flow layout mode*, selected by choosing the Design tab at the bottom of the designer page and setting the pageLayout property of the document to FlowLayout, controls are laid out from top to bottom as you add them to the page.

For this sample layout, we'll use grid layout mode to design the pages. If you've worked with any modern forms-based layout tool (such as Visual Basic 6), page layout using grid layout mode should seem natural. For example, we'll start by putting a title containing the company name at the top of the page. To do so, follow these steps:

1. Select the Label control on the Web Forms tab of the Toolbox.

2. Click on the design surface of the Web Form, hold down the mouse button, and drag to create a rectangular area. The default text *Label* will appear in this area.

3. Click the Text property in the Properties window and type **XYZ Publications**.

4. Click the plus sign next to the Font property in the Properties window. Click the Size property underneath Font, then click the drop-down arrow that appears. Select X-Large as the font size.

5. You can click the label and drag to reposition it, or click one of the grab handles at the side or corner of the label and then drag to resize it.

You can use the other controls in the Toolbox in much the same way as the Label control. Use these controls to create the user interface for the subscription form, as shown in Figure 5.4. Table 5.1 lists the non-label controls on this Web Form as well as the properties that you'll need to set.

FIGURE 5.4:

Designing the subscription form

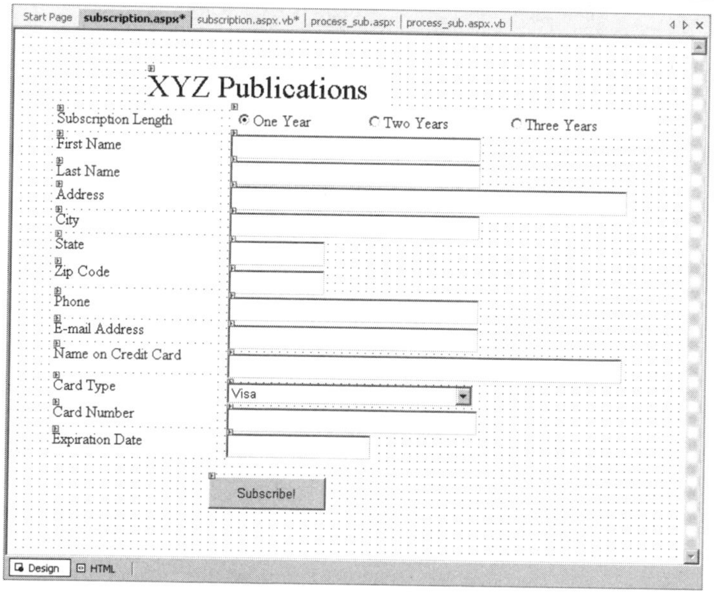

TIP   On the Format menu, you'll find commands to help you manage the alignment, size, and spacing of controls.

TABLE 5.1: Controls for the Subscription Form

Control Type	ID	Other Properties
RadioButtonList	rbLength	RepeatColumns=3; Items=One Year, Two Years, Three Years
TextBox	txtFirstName	
TextBox	txtLastName	
TextBox	txtAddress	
TextBox	txtCity	
TextBox	txtState	
TextBox	txtZip	
TextBox	txtPhone	
TextBox	txtEmail	
TextBox	txtCardName	
DropDownList	ddlCardType	Items=Visa, MasterCard, Discover, American Express
TextBox	txtCardNumber	
TextBox	txtExpirationDate	
Button	btnSubscribe	Text=Subscribe!

Both the RadioButtonList control and the DropDownList control allow the user to choose one from a set of items. To add choices to these controls, you use their Items property. Visual Basic .NET provides a special dialog box for adding items. For example, to add items to the DropDownList, follow these steps:

1. Select the DropDownList control in the designer window.

2. Click the Items property in the Properties window. This will cause a build button to display in the property.

3. Click the build button to open the ListItem Collection Editor.

4. Click the Add button to add a new item.

5. Set the Text property of the new item to Visa and the Value property of the new item to Visa.

6. Repeat steps 4 and 5 to add items for MasterCard, American Express, and Discover. Figure 5.5 shows the ListItem Collection Editor with all four items.

7. Click OK to save the changes to the Items property.

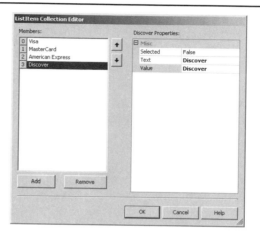

For the RadioButtonList Items property, the Text and Value properties of the items will be different. Table 5.2 shows the values to use in this list. You should also set the Selected property of the first item to True, to ensure that there's a reasonable default when the user first loads the form.

TABLE 5.2: RadioButtonList Items

Text	Value
One Year	1
Two Years	2
Three Years	3

Validating the Data

One of the common tasks for data-entry web pages is validating the data that the user has entered. That is, all data should be checked to make sure that it's reasonable before you try to save it to the database. If any data is obviously wrong, you should prompt the user to fix it before proceeding. For example, you might want to check that a phone number includes an area code, or that a United States zip code has either five or nine digits. ASP.NET supplies a group of six controls that are designed to help you validate data. These controls are listed in Table 5.3.

TABLE 5.3: ASP.NET Validation Server Controls

Control	Purpose
RequiredFieldValidator	Validate that a control's value has been changed.
CompareValidator	Validate that two controls have the same value.
RangeValidator	Validate that a control's value falls within a specified range.
RegularExpressionValidator	Validate that a control's value matches a specified regular expression.
CustomValidator	Validate a control using custom code.
ValidationSummary	Display a list of all validation errors on a page.

The validation controls work by being bound to another control through their ControlTo-Validate property. This property holds the ID of another control on which the validation control should act. As an example, here's how to add a validation control to make sure that the user enters some text in the txtFirstName control:

1. Place a RequiredFieldValidator control on the form to the right of the txtFirstName text box.

2. Set the ErrorMessage property of the RequiredFieldValidator control to **You must enter a first name.**

3. Set the ControlToValidate property of the RequiredFieldValidator control to **txtFirst-Name**.

4. Place a ValidationSummary control on the form beneath the Subscribe button.

At this point, you can test the project to see how the validation controls work. Besides, you're probably about ready to see it work in any case. To do so, follow these steps:

1. Right-click subscription.aspx in the Solution Explorer window and select Set as Start Page.

2. Select Debug ➢ Start without Debugging or press Ctrl+F5. This will launch your default web browser and contact the server to get a copy of the web application's start page.

TIP   Visual Studio .NET can debug both local (running on the client) and remote (running on the server) code. In this case, we launched the project without debugging so that it would run faster, and because we didn't have any code that we wanted to debug.

3. Without entering a first name, click the Submit button.

4. This will cause both the RequiredFieldValidator control and the ValidationSummary control to become visible, as shown in Figure 5.6.

5. Close your web browser to stop the application.

Validation controls

By default, validation is performed twice—once by client-side JavaScript code and once by ASP.NET on the server. These two validations have different purposes. The client-side validation can catch errors without needing a round-trip to the server, thereby keeping processing time and server load at a minimum. But a malicious user could craft an HTTP request that appeared to come from this form and so bypassed client-side validation. In that case, the server-side validation would catch the problem. If you don't want client-side validation (for example, you might be targeting a population of largely downlevel browsers), you can set the EnableClientScript property of each validation control to False.

TIP   In most cases, you'll want to leave client-side validation active in order to catch as many errors as possible without a round-trip to the server.

Validation on the server takes place after the Page Load event but before any control events. You can check whether any particular validation control is reporting a problem by retrieving the Page.IsValid property. However, you should be aware that this property will always return True in the Page Load event, unless you first explicitly call the Page Validate method from within the Page Load event.

Custom Validation

In some cases, you'll want to use your own custom logic to validate the contents of a control. You can use the CustomValidator control for this purpose. As an example, let's add a control to check that the user entered precisely two characters in the txtState text box:

1. Place a RequiredFieldValidator control on the form to the right of the txtState text box.

2. Set the ErrorMessage property of the RequiredFieldValidator control to **You must enter a state.**

3. Set the ControlToValidate property of the RequiredFieldValidator control to **txtState**.

4. Place a CustomValidator control on the form to the right of the txtState text box.

5. Set the ErrorMessage property of the CustomValidator control to **You must enter a 2-character state abbreviation.**

6. Set the ControlToValidate property of the CustomValidator control to **txtState**.

7. Double-click the CustomValidator control. This will open the code module for the ASP.NET page to the ServerValidate procedure for the control. Enter the following code into this procedure:

```
Private Sub CustomValidator1_ServerValidate( _
ByVal source As System.Object, _
ByVal args As System.Web.UI.WebControls.ServerValidateEventArgs) _
Handles CustomValidator1.ServerValidate
    ' Check for a 2-character entry in the State TextBox
    Try
        args.IsValid = (args.Value.Length = 2)
    Catch ex As Exception
        Args.IsValid = False
    End Try
End Sub
```

8. Switch back to the design surface for the `subscription.aspx` page. Click the HTML tab below the design surface. Enter this HTML for client-side validation just before the `</HEAD>` tag of the page:

```
<SCRIPT language="VBScript">
    Sub validateState(source, arguments)
        arguments.IsValid = Len(arguments.Value = 2)
    End Sub
</SCRIPT>
```

9. Set the ClientValidationFunction property of the CustomValidator control to **validateState**.

Inline Code and Code-Behind

ASP.NET supports two ways to add Visual Basic (or other) code to Web Forms. In the *inline code* model, source code for processing at the server is interspersed with the HTML code that defines the look of the final web page. This is the model that's used by regular ASP code in pre-.NET applications. In the *code-behind* model—new with .NET—source code for processing at the server is stored in a separate module. This is similar to the way that Visual Basic .NET Windows Forms work, with separate files for the controls and the code.

In this book, we've chosen to design our Web Forms using the code-behind model. Although this may seem confusing at first, we think the separation of business logic from the user interface code makes sense as a way to organize your applications.

Why use two different validations for one control? Because, counterintuitive as it may seem, all the validation controls except the RequiredFieldValidator control consider an empty control to be valid, no matter what properties you set for the validation control. So you need to use a RequiredFieldValidator to catch blank controls, and then add other controls as necessary to perform more detailed validation. Try out the application again to see how this works:

1. Select Debug ➢ Start without Debugging or press Ctrl+F5.

2. Enter a first name and then click the Submit button.

3. You'll see the RequiredFieldValidator control for the txtState text box, but not the CustomValidator control.

4. Now enter data for a new subscription, but use a three-character state such as **CAL**; then click the Submit button again.

5. At this point, the CustomValidator will appear, as shown in Figure 5.7.

6. Close your web browser to stop the application.

FIGURE 5.7:

A CustomValidator
control in action

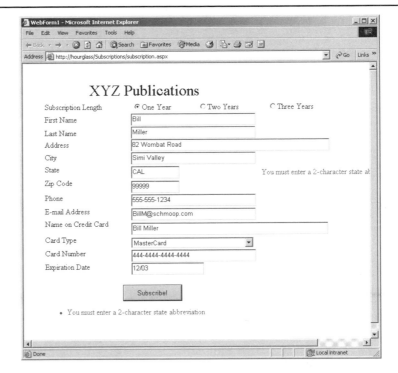

Validating with Regular Expressions

Figure 5.8 shows the subscription Web Form in design view, with all of the validation controls added. Most of these are RequiredFieldValidator controls. The exceptions are the custom validation control for the txtState text box (which we examined in the previous section) and the control that checks that the expiration date is entered in the format MM/YY.

To validate the expiration date, we used a RegularExpressionValidator control. This control checks the contents of the validated control to see whether those contents match a particular pattern. The pattern is specified with a *regular expression*—a specially formatted character string. There are two ways to specify the regular expression to be used with a RegularExpressionValidator control. First, you can click the control's ValidationExpression property and then click the build button that appears. This will open the Regular Expression Editor dialog box, as shown in Figure 5.9. The Regular Expression Editor contains entries for some common regular expressions.

FIGURE 5.8:

Subscription form with validation controls

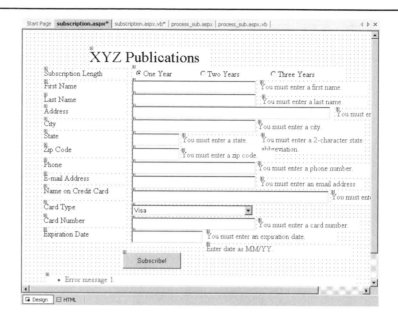

FIGURE 5.9:

Specifying a regular expression

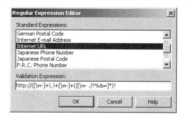

The other way to specify a regular expression is by simply typing it into the Validation-Expression property. The .NET Framework supports a rich set of patterns in regular expressions. Some of these are listed in Table 5.4.

TABLE 5.4: Regular Expression Patterns

Pattern	Matches
.	Any single character
[abc]	A single a, b, or c character
[^abc]	Any character except a, b, or c
\w	Any single word
\s	Any white space character

Continued on next page

TABLE 5.4 CONTINUED: Regular Expression Patterns

Pattern	Matches
\d	Any decimal digit
\D	Any non-digit
/	A single / character
{n}	Exactly n matches
{n.m}	At least n, but no more than m, matches

Managing ASP.NET Web Pages

Now that we've designed the data entry page, the next step is to write the code that will actually process subscriptions. Before doing that, though, we'll review some of the details of how ASP.NET processes web pages. Understanding these concepts will help you manage your web applications more productively. In particular, we'll look at the life cycle of Web Forms and at the issues around maintaining state within a web application.

The Life Cycle of Web Forms

Although a Web Form using code-behind resembles a Windows Form, there are some major distinctions between the two. The first thing to understand is that processing code behind a Web Form requires a round-trip for the form. That is, although the Web Form is displayed in the user's browser, the actual code runs at the IIS computer. When the user clicks a button, their browser packages the entire page and submits it to the server. The server then executes the code, rebuilds the web page, and returns the page to the browser. This means that you need to be somewhat careful about which events you choose to react to on a Web Form. Indiscriminately writing code for many events can lead to severe performance problems.

TIP   You can run code in the user's browser by embedding VBScript or JavaScript in the web page. This is the approach taken by the validation controls for client-side validation. In general, though, the complexity of the code that you can execute in this fashion is limited, and the technique won't work in downlevel browsers.

It's convenient to break up ASP.NET's page processing into a series of stages, each of which is useful for particular purposes. The first of these stages is the page initialization. During this stage, ASP.NET creates the controls for the page and restores any ViewState data (you'll learn about ViewState data when we discuss maintaining state, in the next section). The Page_Init event is raised during this stage, although this is not usually an event that you'll want to react to, because the web page hasn't been fully created at that point.

The next stage occurs when the page is fully created, the Page_Load event is raised, and it's time to initialize things. This is a good time to execute your own initialization code. You can check the Page.IsPostBack property to determine whether this is the first time that this page has been created; the property returns False if the page is being shown for the first time. This event is the appropriate place to perform initial data binding, for example.

The third stage of page processing is the validation stage. This is the point at which any server-side validation control code is executed.

The next stage is event handling. This is the point at which the event that actually triggered rebuilding the page gets raised. For example, if you clicked a button, this is where the button's click procedure is executed. This is the point at which you'll typically execute your own code to handle whatever action the user has performed.

Finally, there's a cleanup stage, in which the Page_Unload event is raised. This doesn't mean that the page is actually being closed in the user's browser—in fact, it's just being sent to the browser! This event means that ASP.NET has finished rendering the page and that, as far as it's concerned, the page is history. You should use this event to close any database connections, files, or other server-side resources that you opened in the Page_Load event. Now that the page is on its way to the browser, it's time to give those resources back to the system.

Maintaining State in a Web Application

Another consequence of the round-trip processing model for web pages in general is that web pages are *stateless*. That is, by default, a web page knows nothing about what was on the page before the previous round-trip. This contrasts with the functioning of other event-driven programs that you may be familiar with. For example, in Visual Basic, you can assume that the contents of the FirstName control will remain unchanged while your code processes a button-click event elsewhere on the form. In HTML pages, that's not true; the web page is completely rebuilt, and the contents of the FirstName control are no longer available.

This stateless aspect of HTML processing can quickly become a problem in a complex application. Fortunately, there are ways to maintain the state of a page from one invocation to the next. ASP.NET provides both client-side and server-side ways to maintain state.

Client-Side Methods

Client-side methods of storing state save the information in the web page somehow. These methods still send the information to the server, of course, but it isn't stored permanently on the server. Client-side methods include the ViewState property, hidden form fields, cookies, and query strings.

Controls have a ViewState property that can be used to store their state. When the page is sent to the server, the contents of this property are hashed into a string, which is then stored in a hidden field on the page. When the page is initialized, the contents of this field are used to rebuild the controls. You can also store your own string values in ViewState if you like. For example, you could save a custom property named Receipt to the ViewState this way:

```
ViewState("Receipt") = "Yes"
```

To retrieve this property, you could use code like this:

```
Dim strReceipt As String
strReceipt = CStr(ViewState("Receipt"))
```

You can also skip the ViewState property entirely and just use hidden HTML fields to store information. You can drag a Hidden control from the HTML tab of the Toolbox to your Web Form and use the Value property of the control to hold whatever information you like.

Another means of storing information on the client side is to use an HTML cookie. ASP.NET provides the HttpResponse.Cookie property, which allows you to set and retrieve the value of cookies. Although cookies provide a relatively simple and secure method of storing information, you need to be aware that some users will have disabled cookies in their browser. If you depend on cookies, you should have an alternative method of data storage available for these users.

Finally, you can use a query string to hold information. A query string appends information to the end of a URL, separated from the main URL by a question mark. For example, if the subscription.aspx page were stored on a server named HOURGLASS, a request with a query string might look like this:

```
http://HOURGLASS/subscriptions/subscription.aspx?subscriptionterm=1year
```

Many browsers limit URLs to 255 characters, which means that you can't pass much information in a query string.

Server-Side Methods

You can also save state information on the server. The advantage is that the information doesn't have to make extra round-trips to the client. The disadvantage is that you will have to dedicate server resources to each client session, which can be quite expensive. Options for storing state on the server include application state, session state, and custom code.

Each active web application has an instance of the HttpApplicationState class available for storing application-related state information. This information is shared by all sessions using the application, so it's not suitable for storing state that relates to an individual browser session.

For individual information, each session has an instance of the HttpSessionState class available. You can treat this instance as a simple collection named Session. For example, you can store a property in session state this way:

```
Session("Receipt") = "Yes"
```

To retrieve this property, you could use code like this:

```
Dim strReceipt As String
strReceipt = CStr(Session("Receipt"))
```

Finally, you can make use of any other code running on the server to store state information. Typically, this will involve opening a connection to a database and storing values in a table, but you could also use an XML file, a text file, or even registry entries to store server-side state information.

Given all these choices, how do you decide which method to use in a particular application? Here are some things to consider when choosing a state-management option:

- ViewState and hidden fields are good when you have a limited amount of information to store and high security isn't necessary. For large amounts of information, ViewState or hidden fields can severely diminish the application's speed.

- Cookies are simple to use but may not be available with all users.

- Query strings are also simple, but they're severely limited in the amount of information that they can contain.

- Application state is best suited for information that must be stored by multiple sessions. An example would be some sort of counter that needs to assign a sequential number to each session.

- Session state is easy to use and doesn't require sending excess information back and forth from client to server, but it does require server resources.

WARNING   One caution applies when using session state to store information: While there's an open session, that session won't use any new code that's inserted into the application. You'll need to watch out for this when you're debugging an application that uses session state. Close all browser windows that you're using to test the application, and open new browser windows after you've saved your changes.

In our sample application, we'll use session state to store the information that the user entered when clicking the Subscribe button. After all the information is stored, our code will open a new Web Form named process_sub.aspx. Here's the code for the Subscribe button to handle these tasks:

```
Private Sub btnSubscribe_Click(ByVal sender As System.Object, _
    ByVal e As System.EventArgs) Handles btnSubscribe.Click
```

```
        Session("Length") = rbLength.SelectedItem.Value
        Session("FirstName") = txtFirstName.Text
        Session("LastName") = txtLastName.Text
        Session("Address") = txtAddress.Text
        Session("City") = txtCity.Text
        Session("State") = txtState.Text
        Session("Zip") = txtZip.Text
        Session("Phone") = txtPhone.Text
        Session("Email") = txtEmail.Text
        Session("CardName") = txtCardName.TemplateSourceDirectory
        Session("CardType") = ddlCardType.SelectedItem.Value
        Session("ExpirationDate") = txtExpirationDate.Text
        Server.Transfer("process_sub.aspx")
    End Sub
```

TIP The Server.Transfer method performs a server-side redirect, delivering the specified page, instead of the original page, to the user's browser.

NOTE Because we're using validation controls to check the data, we're sure that only valid data will be placed in the session-state variables. As you saw in the discussion of the web page's life cycle, if validation fails, the event code for the button will never actually be executed.

Programming the Subscription Process

Now we can begin programming the processing of the subscription request. Our goal in this page is twofold. First, we want to thank the user; as part of this feedback, we'll redisplay the input data so that the user can check it for accuracy. Second, of course, we need to insert the subscription data into the database for later retrieval.

As with the subscription.aspx page, we've used the grid layout capabilities of ASP.NET to position the controls on the process_sub.aspx page. Figure 5.10 shows this page in the designer.

FIGURE 5.10:

The process_sub
.aspx page

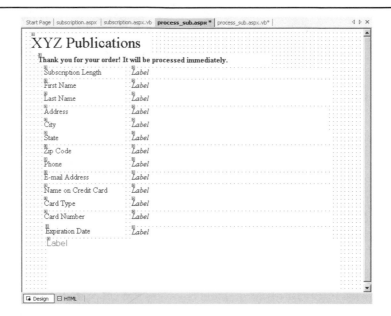

Saving the Subscription Information

All of the processing takes place in the Page_Load event. Listing 5.2 shows the start of the
event procedure for this event.

Listing 5.2   **Saving Information to the Database**

```
Private Sub Page_Load(ByVal sender As System.Object, _
  ByVal e As System.EventArgs) Handles MyBase.Load
    Try
        ' Drop the data into the database
        Dim cnn As SqlConnection = _
        New SqlClient.SqlConnection("Data Source=(local);" & _
        "Initial Catalog=Subscriptions;Integrated Security=SSPI")
        Dim strQuery As String = "INSERT INTO Subscriptions " & _
        "(FirstName, LastName, Address, City, State, ZipCode, Phone, " & _
        "Email, CardName, CardType, CardNumber, ExpirationDate, " & _
        "Length) " & _
        "VALUES ('" & CStr(Session("FirstName")).Replace("'", "''") & _
        "', '" & CStr(Session("LastName")).Replace("'", "''") & _
        "', '" & CStr(Session("Address")).Replace("'", "''") & _
        "', '" & CStr(Session("City")).Replace("'", "''") & _
        "', '" & CStr(Session("State")).Replace("'", "''") & _
        "', '" & CStr(Session("Zip")).Replace("'", "''") & _
        "', '" & CStr(Session("Phone")).Replace("'", "''") & _
        "', '" & CStr(Session("Email")).Replace("'", "''") & _
```

```
    "', '" & CStr(Session("CardName")).Replace("'", "''") & _
    "', '" & CStr(Session("CardType")).Replace("'", "''") & _
    "', '" & CStr(Session("CardNumber")).Replace("'", "''") & _
    "', '" & CStr(Session("ExpirationDate")).Replace("'", "''") & _
    "', " & CInt(Session("Length")) & ")"
Dim cmd As New SqlCommand(strQuery, cnn)
cmd.Connection.Open()
cmd.ExecuteNonQuery()
cnn.Close()
```

This first portion of the code uses two of the ADO.NET objects to insert data into the SQL Server database:

- The SqlConnection object represents a connection to a SQL Server database.

- The SqlCommand object represents a SQL string that can be used to retrieve data or to make changes in the database.

The code takes these steps to insert the data:

1. Prepare to connect to the database by creating a SqlConnection object and initializing it with a connection string. The connection string specifies the server, the database, and the security credentials to use when accessing the data.

NOTE   In the examples in this book, we're assuming that the web server and the SQL Server are running on the same computer. This allows us to use the special name *(local)* instead of an actual computer name when supplying connection information. If your SQL Server and web server are on different computers, you'll need to change the connection string accordingly.

2. Create a SQL string that performs an INSERT operation to place a new row of data into the database. This SQL string uses the information that was stored in the session state by the subscription.aspx page.

3. Create a SqlCommand object that uses the SqlConnection and the SQL string.

4. Open the connection that the SqlCommand object will use.

5. Call the ExecuteNonQuery method of the SqlCommand object to actually execute the SQL string. This is the step that puts the data into the database.

6. Close the connection. It's important to do this so that server resources can be freed as quickly as possible.

NOTE   There's much more to ADO.NET than the two objects that we used in this simple example. We'll be introducing other ADO.NET objects as we use them in this book. For a more systematic introduction to ADO.NET, see Mike Gunderloy's *ADO and ADO.NET Programming* (Sybex, 2002).

As you can see, we had to clean up the data a bit for insertion into the database. We need to ensure that any single quotes that the user enters will be doubled so that they can be inserted and not interpreted by SQL Server as delimiters. Examples of this problem would include some last names (O'Brien, for instance), cities, and addresses. Using the Replace method of the String class makes it easy to replace these single quotes with doubles. We've called the Replace method on every piece of text information entered by the user.

TIP   In a literal string (such as data to be inserted), SQL Server will interpret two single quotes together ('') as only one single quote. We need to double all single quotes that are part of the data to be stored in a field. After we've doubled the single quotes in the values to be inserted, we surround them with single quotes to indicate that they're literal strings.

Displaying the Thank-You Message

The next chunk of code in the Page_Load event procedure, shown in Listing 5.3, handles displaying the information entered by the user on the previous page.

Listing 5.3   **Displaying Information on the User Interface**

```
' And put the information on the form
lblFirstName.Text = CStr(Session("FirstName"))
lblLastName.Text = CStr(Session("LastName"))
lblAddress.Text = CStr(Session("Address"))
lblCity.Text = CStr(Session("City"))
lblState.Text = CStr(Session("State"))
lblZip.Text = CStr(Session("Zip"))
lblPhone.Text = CStr(Session("Phone"))
lblEmail.Text = CStr(Session("Email"))
lblCardName.Text = CStr(Session("CardName"))
lblCardType.Text = CStr(Session("CardType"))
lblCardNumber.Text = CStr(Session("CardNumber"))
lblExpirationDate.Text = CStr(Session("ExpirationDate"))
Select Case CInt(Session("Length"))
    Case 1
        lblLength.Text = "1 year"
    Case 2
        lblLength.Text = "2 years"
    Case 3
        lblLength.Text = "3 years"
End Select
```

As you can see, ASP.NET lets us treat all of the displayed information on the HTML page as properties of objects. When this code is actually executed by ASP.NET, the results will be HTML. But we don't have to think about it at that level. Instead of intermingling markup and code, as was necessary in ASP, we can simply set object properties and let the ASP.NET processor take care of the rest.

Figure 5.11 shows the confirmation page in the user's browser.

FIGURE 5.11:

Displaying a confirmation message

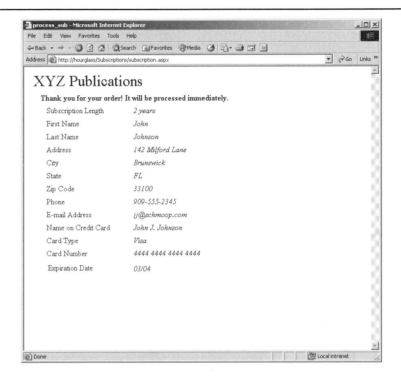

Two Kinds of Error Handling

The process_sub.aspx page also includes two different kinds of error handling. First, the Page_Load event procedure includes a Try/Catch error trap:

```
Catch ex As Exception
    lblError.Text = ex.ToString
    lblError.Visible = True
End Try
```

If any error occurs in the Page_Load event procedure, execution will jump to this code. The code converts the error into a string, displays it in a Label control on the Web Form, and then makes the normally invisible control visible.

TIP   In a production application, we'd probably choose to e-mail such error information to the developer or save it in a server-side log rather than expose it to the end user.

Although this error trap will handle any coding errors, it won't do anything about HTML errors. For example, the user might click a bad hyperlink on the page. To trap HTML errors, you can use the Page_Error event. The process_sub.aspx page includes this Page_Error event procedure:

```
Private Sub Page_Error(ByVal sender As Object, _
  ByVal e As System.EventArgs) Handles MyBase.Error
    Dim strMessage As String = "<font face=verdana color=red>" & _
      "<h4>" & Request.Url.ToString() & "</h4>" & _
      "<pre><font color='red'>" & Server.GetLastError().ToString() & _
      "</pre></font>"
    Response.Write(strMessage)
End Sub
```

This procedure uses the Response.Write method to simply write text out to the HTML page. There's no need to use the lblError label, because in the case of an HTML error, the page will never be constructed.

Managing the Application

Now that we've completed the user experience, we need to focus on the back-end management of the subscription data. We will need a way to retrieve the subscriptions.

The last piece of our e-commerce sample application is the reporting form. The purpose of the form is to report the subscription data that has been entered since the last subscriptions were processed. It will also provide an option for the user to mark the current listing of subscriptions as processed. We'll use some of the rapid application development (RAD) tools built into Visual Studio .NET to quickly build this form, and then fine-tune the results.

Building the Management Application

We'll build a separate web application to manage the subscriptions, rather than add more pages to the application that enters the subscriptions. This way, we can limit access to the management application by allowing only users from certain domains or IP addresses to view the management information.

Follow these steps to build a new application that will display the current crop of subscription requests on a grid on a Web Form:

1. Select Start ➢ Programs ➢ Microsoft Visual Studio .NET ➢ Microsoft Visual Studio .NET.

2. On the Start Page, click the New Project button.

3. Select the Visual Basic Projects project type and the ASP.NET Web Application template. Name the new project **ManageSubscriptions** and place it on the same web server that hosts the Subscriptions application.

4. Click OK to create the new application on your web server.

5. Visual Studio .NET will open the new web application. Right-click the `WebForm1.aspx` item in the Solution Explorer and select Rename. Rename the Web Form `main_report.aspx`.

6. Click the Server Explorer tab at the left of the Visual Studio .NET workspace to display the Server Explorer window. You can use the pushpin control in this window's title bar if you'd like to keep it on-screen while you work with it.

7. Right-click the Data Connections node in Server Explorer and select Add Connection. This will open the Data Link Properties dialog box.

8. Select the Microsoft OLE DB Provider for SQL Server on the Provider tab of the Data Link Properties dialog box.

9. On the Connection tab of the Data Link Properties dialog box, select or enter the name of your database server, enter your login credentials, and select the Subscriptions database. Click OK to add the new connection to Server Explorer.

10. Expand the new data connection so that you can see its subsidiary nodes. Right-click the Views node and select New View.

11. Select the Subscriptions table in the Add Table dialog box and then click Add; then click Close.

12. Check the check box to add all columns to the view.

13. On the second row of the view designer, select the Processed column. Uncheck the Output column for this column. Type **=0** in the Criteria column for this row. Figure 5.12 shows the completed view in the designer.

14. Save the view as **vwUnprocessedSubscriptions** and then close the view designer.

15. Now, drag vwUnprocessedSubscriptions from Server Explorer and drop it on the design surface of the `sub_report.aspx` page. You'll get a Data Adapter Configuration Error dialog box, warning you that UPDATE and DELETE statements could not be generated. This isn't a problem, because we're going to use this view only to retrieve data, not to change data. When you click OK to dismiss the dialog box, Visual Studio .NET will create a SqlConnection object named SqlConnection1 and a SqlDataAdapter object named SqlDataAdapter1 at the bottom of the design surface.

Designing a view in
Visual Studio .NET

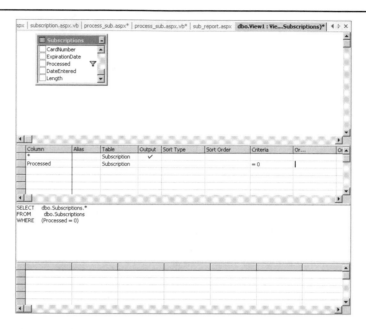

16. Select the SqlDataAdapter1 object and then click the Generate DataSet hyperlink in the
Properties window. This will open the Generate DataSet dialog box, shown in Figure 5.13. Create a new DataSet named dsSubscriptions and add it to the designer by
clicking OK.

The Generate DataSet
dialog box

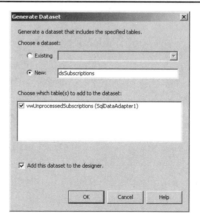

17. Select the DataGrid control on the Web Forms tab in the Toolbox and draw a DataGrid
control on the Web Form design surface.

18. Set the DataSource property of the DataGrid control to **DsSubscriptions1**.

19. Set the DataMember property of the DataGrid control to **vwUnprocessedSubscriptions**.

20. Click the Auto Format hyperlink in the Properties window and select the Classic 2 format. Click OK.

21. Double-click the design surface of the Web Form to open the code-behind module; then enter this code for the Page Load procedure:

```
Private Sub Page_Load(ByVal sender As System.Object, _
  ByVal e As System.EventArgs) Handles MyBase.Load
    SqlDataAdapter1.Fill(DsSubscriptions1, "vwUnprocessedSubscriptions")
    DataBind()
End Sub
```

22. Save the project and start it without debugging. You should see the subscriptions that you've entered, as shown in Figure 5.14.

FIGURE 5.14:

Viewing unprocessed subscriptions

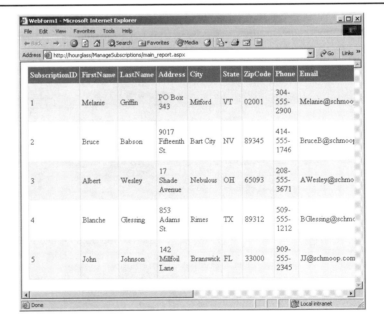

Reviewing the Data Access Code

Although you needed to write only two lines of code to enable the grid functionality, there's actually a lot more code involved in this particular Web Form. That's because the drag-and-drop operations in Visual Studio .NET generate their own code. Listing 5.4 shows the code behind this Web Form at this point.

Listing 5.4   Data Access Code for Managing Subscriptions

```
Public Class WebForm1
    Inherits System.Web.UI.Page
    Protected WithEvents SqlSelectCommand1 As
System.Data.SqlClient.SqlCommand
    Protected WithEvents SqlInsertCommand1 As
System.Data.SqlClient.SqlCommand
    Protected WithEvents SqlConnection1 As
System.Data.SqlClient.SqlConnection
    Protected WithEvents SqlDataAdapter1 As
System.Data.SqlClient.SqlDataAdapter
    Protected WithEvents DsSubscriptions1 As
ManageSubscriptions.dsSubscriptions
    Protected WithEvents DataGrid1 As
System.Web.UI.WebControls.DataGrid

#Region " Web Form Designer Generated Code "

    'This call is required by the Web Form Designer.
    <System.Diagnostics.DebuggerStepThrough()>
Private Sub InitializeComponent()
        Me.SqlSelectCommand1 = New System.Data.SqlClient.SqlCommand()
        Me.SqlInsertCommand1 = New System.Data.SqlClient.SqlCommand()
        Me.SqlConnection1 = New System.Data.SqlClient.SqlConnection()
        Me.SqlDataAdapter1 = New System.Data.SqlClient.SqlDataAdapter()
        Me.DsSubscriptions1 = New ManageSubscriptions.dsSubscriptions()
        CType(Me.DsSubscriptions1,
System.ComponentModel.ISupportInitialize).BeginInit()
        '
        'SqlSelectCommand1
        '
        Me.SqlSelectCommand1.CommandText = "SELECT SubscriptionID,
FirstName, LastName, Address, City, State, ZipCode, Phone," & _
" Email, CardName, CardType, CardNumber, ExpirationDate,
Processed, DateEntered, " & _
        "Length FROM vwUnprocessedSubscriptions"
        Me.SqlSelectCommand1.Connection = Me.SqlConnection1
        '
        'SqlInsertCommand1
        '
        Me.SqlInsertCommand1.CommandText = "INSERT INTO
vwUnprocessedSubscriptions(FirstName, LastName, Address, City,
State," & _
        " ZipCode, Phone, Email, CardName, CardType, CardNumber,
ExpirationDate, Processe" & _
        "d, DateEntered, Length) VALUES (@FirstName, @LastName,
```

```
➡ @Address, @City, @State, " & _
        "@ZipCode, @Phone, @Email, @CardName, @CardType, @CardNumber,
➡ @ExpirationDate, @P" & _
        "rocessed, @DateEntered, @Length); SELECT SubscriptionID,
➡ FirstName, LastName, Ad" & _
        "dress, City, State, ZipCode, Phone, Email, CardName, CardType,
➡ CardNumber, Expir" & _
        "ationDate, Processed, DateEntered, Length FROM
➡ vwUnprocessedSubscriptions"
        Me.SqlInsertCommand1.Connection = Me.SqlConnection1
        Me.SqlInsertCommand1.Parameters.Add(New
➡ System.Data.SqlClient.SqlParameter("@FirstName",
➡ System.Data.SqlDbType.VarChar, 100, "FirstName"))
        Me.SqlInsertCommand1.Parameters.Add(New
➡ System.Data.SqlClient.SqlParameter("@LastName",
➡ System.Data.SqlDbType.VarChar, 100, "LastName"))
        Me.SqlInsertCommand1.Parameters.Add(New
➡ System.Data.SqlClient.SqlParameter("@Address",
➡ System.Data.SqlDbType.VarChar, 150, "Address"))
        Me.SqlInsertCommand1.Parameters.Add(New
➡ System.Data.SqlClient.SqlParameter("@City",
➡ System.Data.SqlDbType.VarChar, 100, "City"))
        Me.SqlInsertCommand1.Parameters.Add(New
➡ System.Data.SqlClient.SqlParameter("@State",
➡ System.Data.SqlDbType.VarChar, 10, "State"))
        Me.SqlInsertCommand1.Parameters.Add(New
➡ System.Data.SqlClient.SqlParameter("@ZipCode",
➡ System.Data.SqlDbType.VarChar, 15, "ZipCode"))
        Me.SqlInsertCommand1.Parameters.Add(New
➡ System.Data.SqlClient.SqlParameter("@Phone",
➡ System.Data.SqlDbType.VarChar, 25, "Phone"))
        Me.SqlInsertCommand1.Parameters.Add(New
➡ System.Data.SqlClient.SqlParameter("@Email",
➡ System.Data.SqlDbType.VarChar, 100, "Email"))
        Me.SqlInsertCommand1.Parameters.Add(New
➡ System.Data.SqlClient.SqlParameter("@CardName",
➡ System.Data.SqlDbType.VarChar, 150, "CardName"))
        Me.SqlInsertCommand1.Parameters.Add(New
➡ System.Data.SqlClient.SqlParameter("@CardType",
➡ System.Data.SqlDbType.VarChar, 50, "CardType"))
        Me.SqlInsertCommand1.Parameters.Add(New
➡ System.Data.SqlClient.SqlParameter("@CardNumber",
➡ System.Data.SqlDbType.VarChar, 25, "CardNumber"))
        Me.SqlInsertCommand1.Parameters.Add(New
➡ System.Data.SqlClient.SqlParameter("@ExpirationDate",
➡ System.Data.SqlDbType.VarChar, 50, "ExpirationDate"))
        Me.SqlInsertCommand1.Parameters.Add(New
➡ System.Data.SqlClient.SqlParameter("@Processed",
➡ System.Data.SqlDbType.Bit, 1, "Processed"))
        Me.SqlInsertCommand1.Parameters.Add(New
➡ System.Data.SqlClient.SqlParameter("@DateEntered",
```

```
➦ System.Data.SqlDbType.DateTime, 8, "DateEntered"))
        Me.SqlInsertCommand1.Parameters.Add(New
➦ System.Data.SqlClient.SqlParameter("@Length",
➦ System.Data.SqlDbType.TinyInt, 1, "Length"))
        '
        'SqlConnection1
        '
        Me.SqlConnection1.ConnectionString = "data
➦ source=HOURGLASS;initial catalog=Subscriptions;integrated
➦ security=SSPI;pers" & _
        "ist security info=False;workstation id=SEESAW;packet
➦ size=4096"
        '
        'SqlDataAdapter1
        '
        Me.SqlDataAdapter1.InsertCommand = Me.SqlInsertCommand1
        Me.SqlDataAdapter1.SelectCommand = Me.SqlSelectCommand1
        Me.SqlDataAdapter1.TableMappings.AddRange(
➦ New System.Data.Common.DataTableMapping() {New
➦ System.Data.Common.DataTableMapping("Table",
➦ "vwUnprocessedSubscriptions", New
➦ System.Data.Common.DataColumnMapping() {New
➦ System.Data.Common.DataColumnMapping("SubscriptionID",
➦ "SubscriptionID"), New
➦ System.Data.Common.DataColumnMapping("FirstName", "FirstName"), New
➦ System.Data.Common.DataColumnMapping("LastName", "LastName"), New
➦ System.Data.Common.DataColumnMapping("Address", "Address"), New
➦ System.Data.Common.DataColumnMapping("City", "City"), New
➦ System.Data.Common.DataColumnMapping("State", "State"), New
➦ System.Data.Common.DataColumnMapping("ZipCode", "ZipCode"), New
➦ System.Data.Common.DataColumnMapping("Phone", "Phone"), New
➦ System.Data.Common.DataColumnMapping("Email", "Email"), New
➦ System.Data.Common.DataColumnMapping("CardName", "CardName"), New
➦ System.Data.Common.DataColumnMapping("CardType", "CardType"), New
➦ System.Data.Common.DataColumnMapping("CardNumber", "CardNumber"),
➦ New System.Data.Common.DataColumnMapping("ExpirationDate",
➦ "ExpirationDate"), New
➦ System.Data.Common.DataColumnMapping("Processed", "Processed"), New
➦ System.Data.Common.DataColumnMapping("DateEntered", "DateEntered"),
➦ New System.Data.Common.DataColumnMapping("Length", "Length")}})
        '
        'DsSubscriptions1
        '
        Me.DsSubscriptions1.DataSetName = "dsSubscriptions"
        Me.DsSubscriptions1.Locale = New
➦ System.Globalization.CultureInfo("en-US")
        Me.DsSubscriptions1.Namespace =
➦ "http://www.tempuri.org/dsSubscriptions.xsd"
        CType(Me.DsSubscriptions1,
➦ System.ComponentModel.ISupportInitialize).EndInit()
```

```
    End Sub

    Private Sub Page_Init(ByVal sender As System.Object, ByVal e As
➡ System.EventArgs) Handles MyBase.Init
        'CODEGEN: This method call is required by the Web Form Designer
        'Do not modify it using the code editor.
        InitializeComponent()
    End Sub

#End Region

    Private Sub Page_Load(ByVal sender As System.Object, _
     ByVal e As System.EventArgs) Handles MyBase.Load
        SqlDataAdapter1.Fill(DsSubscriptions1, _
        "vwUnprocessedSubscriptions")
        DataBind()
    End Sub

End Class
```

NOTE   In the copy of the project on the companion CD, we've modified the connection string to use *(local)* rather than a server name to connect to the SQL Server.

This code introduces several new ADO.NET objects and demonstrates some of the key concepts of ADO.NET. It starts by declaring the objects that will be used to retrieve data. Table 5.5 lists these objects.

TABLE 5.5: Data Retrieval Objects for the Management Form

Object Name	Object Class	Comments
SqlSelectCommand1	SqlCommand	Provides the SQL statement used for selecting data.
SqlInsertCommand1	SqlCommand	Provides the SQL statement used for inserting data. Our code doesn't use this object.
SqlConnection1	SqlConnection	Provides a connection to the SQL Server database.
SqlDataAdapter1	SqlDataAdapter	Provides a connection between the SQL Server–specific objects and the more general DataSet object. You can think of this as a pipeline between your database and the actual data-containing objects within ASP.NET.
DsSubscriptions1	dsSubscriptions	This is actually a subclassed DataSet object. Generally, the DataSet is a container for data that can hold any number of tables as well as the relations between them. We'll discuss the subclassing later in this section.
DataGrid1	DataGrid	This is the visual grid of data on the Web Form.

The code then initializes the various objects. The SQL statements for the SqlSelectCommand1 and SqlInsertCommand1 objects are automatically generated by Visual Studio .NET as a result of the drag-and-drop operations that were used to construct this form. These two objects are assigned to the SelectCommand and InsertCommand properties of the SqlDataAdapter1 object. The DataAdapter will choose the appropriate command to execute, depending on what you're trying to do with the data.

In the code that we actually wrote, the call to the Fill method of the DataAdaper pulls the data from the SQL Server database to the DataSet. The Fill method takes as parameters the name of the target DataSet and the name of the table to be created within the DataSet. These, in turn, must match the DataSource and DataMember properties that we set for the DataGrid control on the user interface.

Although the DataGrid is a bound control, ASP.NET doesn't actually bind any data without an explicit call to the DataBind method. This allows you to manage the performance impact of loading data more carefully. In the case of this particular Web Form, we're assuming that there isn't a vast amount of data to display, and we simply bind the data whenever the page is loaded.

The DataSet used in this particular example is a *strongly typed* DataSet. With such a DataSet, you can treat the names of objects within the DataSet as properties of their parent objects. This leads to your code being easier to understand and allows the compiler to perform some design-time error checking. We aren't actually using this capability in this example, but the DataSets that Visual Studio .NET generates for you are always strongly typed. If you inspect the Solution Explorer for the project, you'll discover an object named dsSubscriptions.xsd. This is an XML Schema file that describes the particular DataSet that you told Visual Studio .NET to create. You can double-click this object to open it in the designer, where you'll discover that it has both a visual and an XML representation. Listing 5.5 shows the XML that describes the DataSet, while Figure 5.15 shows the XSD file open in the designer.

Listing 5.5   dsSubscriptions.xsd

```
<?xml version="1.0" standalone="yes" ?>
<xs:schema id="dsSubscriptions"
➥ targetNamespace="http://www.tempuri.org/dsSubscriptions.xsd"
➥ xmlns:mstns="http://www.tempuri.org/dsSubscriptions.xsd"
➥ xmlns="http://www.tempuri.org/dsSubscriptions.xsd"
➥ xmlns:xs="http://www.w3.org/2001/XMLSchema"
➥ xmlns:msdata="urn:schemas-microsoft-com:xml-msdata"
➥ attributeFormDefault="qualified" elementFormDefault="qualified">
    <xs:element name="dsSubscriptions" msdata:IsDataSet="true">
        <xs:complexType>
            <xs:choice maxOccurs="unbounded">
```

```
                    <xs:element name="vwUnprocessedSubscriptions">
                        <xs:complexType>
                            <xs:sequence>
                                <xs:element name="SubscriptionID"
➤   msdata:ReadOnly="true" msdata:AutoIncrement="true" type="xs:int" />
                                <xs:element name="FirstName"
➤ type="xs:string" minOccurs="0" />
                                <xs:element name="LastName"
➤ type="xs:string" minOccurs="0" />
                                <xs:element name="Address"
➤ type="xs:string" minOccurs="0" />
                                <xs:element name="City"
➤ type="xs:string" minOccurs="0" />
                                <xs:element name="State"
➤ type="xs:string" minOccurs="0" />
                                <xs:element name="ZipCode"
➤ type="xs:string" minOccurs="0" />
                                <xs:element name="Phone"
➤ type="xs:string" minOccurs="0" />
                                <xs:element name="Email"
➤ type="xs:string" minOccurs="0" />
                                <xs:element name="CardName"
➤ type="xs:string" minOccurs="0" />
                                <xs:element name="CardType"
➤ type="xs:string" minOccurs="0" />
                                <xs:element name="CardNumber"
➤ type="xs:string" minOccurs="0" />
                                <xs:element name="ExpirationDate"
➤ type="xs:string" minOccurs="0" />
                                <xs:element name="Processed"
➤ type="xs:boolean" minOccurs="0" />
                                <xs:element name="DateEntered"
➤ type="xs:dateTime" minOccurs="0" />
                                <xs:element name="Length"
➤ type="xs:unsignedByte" minOccurs="0" />
                            </xs:sequence>
                        </xs:complexType>
                    </xs:element>
                </xs:choice>
            </xs:complexType>
            <xs:unique name="Constraint1" msdata:PrimaryKey="true">
                <xs:selector xpath=".//mstns:vwUnprocessedSubscriptions" />
                <xs:field xpath="mstns:SubscriptionID" />
            </xs:unique>
        </xs:element>
    </xs:schema>
```

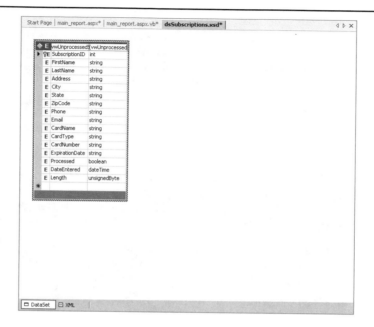

Managing the Subscriptions

To wrap up the functionality in our sample application, we'll add a button to mark the displayed subscriptions as having been processed. The plan is that users will view the pending subscriptions on this report, process them through some other interface, and then mark them as processed. Here's how to add the button:

1. Select the Button control from the Web Forms tab in the Toolbox and then draw a button on the Web Form.

2. Set the Text property of the button to **Mark as Processed**.

3. Set the ID property of the button to **btnProcess**.

4. Double-click the button to open the code for its Click event. Enter this code:

```
Private Sub btnProcess_Click(ByVal sender As System.Object, _
ByVal e As System.EventArgs) Handles btnProcess.Click
    Dim cnn As System.Data.SqlClient.SqlConnection = _
    New SqlClient.SqlConnection("Data Source=(local);" & _
    "Initial Catalog=Subscriptions;Integrated Security=SSPI")
    Dim r As dsSubscriptions.vwUnprocessedSubscriptionsRow
    Dim cmd As System.Data.SqlClient.SqlCommand = _
    cnn.CreateCommand()
    cmd.Connection.Open()
```

```
        For Each r In DsSubscriptions1.vwUnprocessedSubscriptions
            cmd.CommandText = "UPDATE Subscriptions " & _
              "SET Processed = 1 WHERE SubscriptionID = " & _
              r.SubscriptionID
            cmd.ExecuteNonQuery()
        Next
        cnn.Close()
        DsSubscriptions1.Clear()
        SqlDataAdapter1.Fill(DsSubscriptions1, "vwUnprocessedSubscriptions")
        DataBind()
    End Sub
```

This code first uses some of the features of the strongly typed DataSet to move through the data that the Web Form is displaying. The object named "r" represents a single row in the DataSet. This object has a SubscriptionID property that holds the value that the original view retrieved from the SubscriptionID column in the database. The code builds and executes a separate SQL statement for each row. By taking this approach, it will mark as processed only those rows that are actually displayed on the Web Form.

After all the rows have been processed, the code uses the Clear method of the DsSubscriptions1 object to clear the DataSet. This illustrates an important aspect of ADO.NET data processing: Changes to a database don't automatically show up in a DataSet based on that database, or vice versa. To copy information from the database to the DataSet, you must explicitly call the Fill method of the DataAdapter. To post changes from the DataSet back to the database, you must explicitly call the Update method of the DataAdapter. By taking this "always disconnected" approach, ADO.NET offers superior performance for distributed applications.

In this particular case, we refill the DataSet and bind it to the DataGrid control again when we're done processing subscriptions. This way, the Web Form will show any new subscriptions that have come in when the form is reloaded.

Of course, this example is incomplete in a business sense. We might want to provide a richer interface for searching for subscriptions, both processed and unprocessed. We could also offer search options such as date entered, length of subscription, and so on. As we continue to build the full e-commerce application, you'll see many more examples of interactivity between the user and the database.

Thinking about Potential Enhancements

There are a few implementation details to consider, which we skipped earlier in this chapter. The first of these is security. Certainly the subscription form should be encrypted with Secure Sockets Layer (SSL) to ensure that the data cannot be easily *sniffed* (retrieved by another user) on the Internet. Also, the manager page should not be readily accessible to just anybody. You'll want to secure it with a method such as IP authentication, a password-protected form, or Windows NT Authentication and an Access Control List (ACL) on the directory where the management application exists.

Second, you may want to provide an order number to the purchaser so that they can reference that number when making queries. The best way to implement that would be to build a stored procedure that inserts the subscription data into the database and then returns a parameter that holds the new value from the identity column in the table. That data could then be displayed in the thank-you message to the purchaser. We'll demonstrate this technique in Chapter 8, "Checking Out."

Finally, if you want to provide immediate processing of the credit card data, you might consider using a service such as CyberCash (`www.cybercash.com`) or VeriFone (`www.verifone.com`). Then, if the purchaser's order is approved, you could immediately give them online access to content, without needing to wait for a human being to verify the order.

Summary

Our sample application uses the key tools that we'll be utilizing for development: ASP.NET, ADO.NET, Visual Basic .NET, SQL Server, HTML, XML, and a browser. For a website that needs a simple way to process subscriptions, memberships, or other data, this type of form is more than adequate.

This example concludes the first part of the book. We're now well positioned to move to the next phase: beginning the development of our full-blown e-commerce application.

PART II

Building the Shopping Experience

CHAPTER 6

Building the User Interface

- Designing the Store Foundation

- Building the Page Structure

- Browsing Departments and Products

- Searching

So far, we've only built the database for our online store. The database is a necessity for taking orders, but it's not all that we need to build before we can do business. We need to provide a user interface that shoppers can visit so that they can place orders with our store. These orders, of course, will end up being stored in the database.

The user interface of an e-commerce store is a fundamental part of the shopper's experience. You can offer the best merchandise in the world, but if users get frustrated while trying to order things, you won't make any sales. In this chapter, we'll build the core pieces of the store, including navigation, website structure, and product data.

Designing the Store Foundation

Our store will be composed of multiple ASP.NET pages combined with a Visual Basic .NET application for business-rule management and some web services for essential infrastructure. The ASP.NET pages will draw their data from the database design that we developed in Chapter 3, "E-Commerce Database Design." Table 6.1 lists the pages in our store, the function of each, and the chapter where you'll find more discussion of each page.

TABLE 6.1: Web Pages in the E-Commerce Store

Page	Description	Chapter
Footer.inc	Included at the bottom of every display page on the site. It provides the closing structure for the navigation and primary content area.	Chapter 6
Header.inc	Included at the top of every display page on the site. It provides the navigation structure.	Chapter 6
AddItem.aspx	Adds items to the shopping basket when the shopper selects a product.	Chapter 7
Basket.aspx	Displays all the items in the shopper's basket.	Chapter 7
Confirmed.aspx	Provides a confirmation message and thank-you when the shopper has completed an order.	Chapter 8
Default.aspx	Home page for the store.	Chapter 6
Dept.aspx	Lists all the departments in the store.	Chapter 6
EmailPassword.aspx	Provides a way for shoppers to get an e-mail containing their profile password.	Chapter 9
EmailPasswordPrompt.aspx	Prompts shoppers for their e-mail address so that they can be sent their password.	Chapter 9

Continued on next page

TABLE 6.1 CONTINUED: Web Pages in the E-Commerce Store

Page	Description	Chapter
Global.asax	Application-level file that is executed each time a new application or session is started.	Chapter 6
GlobalProcedures.vb	Code called from more than one web page	Chapter 6
OrderHistoryDisplay.aspx	Displays the order history of the shopper.	Chapter 9
OrderReceipt.aspx	Displays an on-screen order receipt.	Chapter 8
OrderStatus.aspx	Login page for the shopper's order history.	Chapter 9
Payment.aspx	Provides data input for the shopper's billing information.	Chapter 8
Product.aspx	Displays information on the specified product.	Chapter 6
Products.aspx	Displays all the products in the specified department.	Chapter 6
Profile.aspx	Login page for the shopper to retrieve and edit their profile.	Chapter 9
ProfileDisplay.aspx	Displays the profile data for the specified shopper.	Chapter 9
Search.aspx	Provides search capabilities for finding products in the database.	Chapter 6
Shipping.aspx	Provides data input for the shipping information for the order.	Chapter 8

These core pages will provide an environment for easy shopping and ordering. The site architecture is designed to help users move through the shopping process in an organized way.

NOTE   This part of the book covers building the portion of the application that shoppers use to place orders. In Part III, "Managing the Solution," we'll build tools for managing the data in the store. In Part IV, "Promotions," we'll add support for promotional functions such as up-sells and cross-sells.

Site Architecture

When the shopper enters the store, they'll typically follow one of two steps for beginning their shopping process. Either they'll look at department and product data through browsing the store, or they'll search for something specific.

We hope that this browsing phase will culminate in items added to the shopping basket and ready for purchase. We'll offer the shopper the opportunity to manage their shopping basket (for example, by changing quantities or deleting items) and then check out. The checkout process will collect all of their key data (such as shipping and billing information). Once processed, they can then check their order history through a profile they set up online. Figure 6.1 diagrams the shopping process.

FIGURE 6.1:

The shopping process

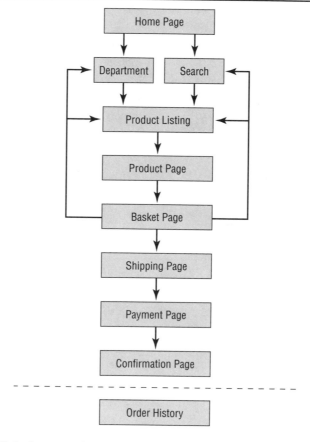

The navigation that we'll design into the system certainly needs to provide ways to move between the various states of the shopping process. But, for example, we should not allow the shopper to go to the payment page if there are no items in their shopping basket. Likewise, if the shopper goes to the basket before adding any items to it, we need to provide appropriate feedback.

Finally, it will be critical that we maintain *state* throughout the entire process. We'll need to be able to track the current shopper's ID so we can maintain their basket. Also, we'll need to be able to maintain state on data entered into the various forms. For example, if the shopper gets to the payment page and decides that they want one more item, we don't want them to have to enter their shipping information all over again. Asking the shopper to do additional work for no apparent reason is sure to cost you sales.

To track the data for these tasks, we'll use application state, session state, cookies, and ViewState at various points throughout the site.

TIP   For a discussion of the options for maintaining state in ASP.NET applications, see Chapter 5, "Building a Sample Application."

Project Setup

As you learned in Chapter 5, we'll need to set up a new development project on our web server. Our sample store for this demonstration is called Wild Willie's CD Store. The store is going to sell some very unusual CD titles and T-shirts—some that even the biggest Internet retailers probably don't carry (or don't *want* to carry). To create the ASP.NET project for the store, follow these steps:

1. Select Start ➢ Programs ➢ Microsoft Visual Studio .NET ➢ Microsoft Visual Studio .NET.

2. On the Start Page, click the New Project button.

3. Select the Visual Basic Projects project type and the ASP.NET Web Application template. Name the project **CDStore**. Specify a location for your project on the server where you'll be running the ASP.NET pages. In our case, that's a server named HOURGLASS.

4. Click OK to create the new application on your web server.

The database for the store will be the one that we designed in Chapter 3. If you haven't yet installed the SQL scripts from that chapter, you'll need to do so now before proceeding with the ASP.NET project. We've tried to keep the ASP.NET code simple and easy to understand, while allowing room for future growth.

TIP   For full instructions on installing the sample code, see the `readme.txt` file on the companion CD.

The first file that we'll customize is the `Global.asax` file, as shown in Listing 6.1. This file, also known as the ASP.NET application file, contains code that responds to application-level events. Procedures from this file are called every time a new application is started (when the website is started or restarted) or a new user session is started, among other times. It contains specific procedures that are fired off depending on the request. For example, the Application_Start procedure will be executed when the website application is started. This is useful for initializing any parameters or settings upon startup. There is also a corresponding Application_End procedure. Although we don't use these two in our sample store, they might be useful for storing global data such as statistical counts across the store or variable data related to the specific server. When you create a new ASP.NET project, Visual Studio .NET automatically creates a Global.asax file and populates it with empty procedures for the events that it can handle. You can view these empty procedures by right-clicking the file in the Solution Explorer and selecting View Code.

We do use the Session_Start procedure. One thing that we'll need to do is track shoppers as they proceed through the store. When the shopper first visits, we don't know what their shopper ID is, or even whether they already have a shopper ID. We'll eventually need to see if they have their profile set as a cookie on their computer. But to ensure that the key variable *idShopper* is initialized properly, the code sets it to 0 at the start of every session. This variable will later get set to either a new shopper ID or an existing one from a stored profile on the user's computer. There's also a corresponding Session_End procedure, which is not utilized.

NOTE   In Listing 6.1 and in other listings throughout the book, we've added additional line continuations to automatically generated code to make it fit more easily on the book page.

Listing 6.1   Global.asax

```
Imports System.Web
Imports System.Web.SessionState

Public Class Global
    Inherits System.Web.HttpApplication

#Region " Component Designer Generated Code "

    Public Sub New()
        MyBase.New()

        'This call is required by the Component Designer.
        InitializeComponent()

        'Add any initialization after the InitializeComponent() call

    End Sub

    'Required by the Component Designer
    Private components As System.ComponentModel.IContainer
```

```
'NOTE: The following procedure is required by the Component Designer
'It can be modified using the Component Designer.
'Do not modify it using the code editor.
<System.Diagnostics.DebuggerStepThrough()> _
 Private Sub InitializeComponent()
     components = New System.ComponentModel.Container()
 End Sub

#End Region

    Sub Application_Start(ByVal sender As Object, ByVal e As EventArgs)
        ' Fires when the application is started
    End Sub

    Sub Session_Start(ByVal sender As Object, ByVal e As EventArgs)
        ' Fires when the session is started
        Session("idShopper") = 0
    End Sub

    Sub Application_BeginRequest(ByVal sender As Object, ByVal e As EventArgs)
        ' Fires at the beginning of each request
    End Sub

    Sub Application_AuthenticateRequest(ByVal sender As Object, _
    ByVal e As EventArgs)
        ' Fires upon attempting to authenticate the use
    End Sub

    Sub Application_Error(ByVal sender As Object, ByVal e As EventArgs)
        ' Fires when an error occurs
    End Sub

    Sub Session_End(ByVal sender As Object, ByVal e As EventArgs)
        ' Fires when the session ends
    End Sub

    Sub Application_End(ByVal sender As Object, ByVal e As EventArgs)
        ' Fires when the application ends
    End Sub

End Class
```

NOTE   As you can see from Listing 6.1, much of the code in our application will be automatically generated by Visual Studio .NET. For example, the code that initializes the Global.asax file, as well as the empty procedure stubs, is generated automatically. We'll include it in our listings to show you the complete application code, but you should almost never need to alter this code.

We also need to prepare a database connection for the ASP.NET project to use. We can use Visual Studio .NET's Server Explorer to create this connection, which can later be placed on any ASP.NET page via drag-and-drop. To create the new connection, follow these steps:

1. Click the Server Explorer tab at the left side of Visual Studio .NET to open the Server Explorer window.

2. Right-click the Data Connections node and select Add Connection.

3. Click the Provider tab of the Data Link Properties dialog box and select the Microsoft OLE DB Provider for SQL Server.

4. Click the Connection tab and enter the name of your database server. In our samples, this is HOURGLASS.

5. Enter authentication information and select the Store database on the server.

6. Click the Test Connection button to ensure that you've entered all the necessary information.

7. Click OK to create the new data connection.

Loading Data

Since we haven't built the management side of the store yet, we'll populate the store with some sample data "by hand" by running SQL scripts in SQL Server Query Analyzer. The companion CD includes SQL scripts for inserting the data. In this section, we'll review the data inserts to ensure that it's clear how the tables are being populated.

First, we'll need to load the Department table with department data. This will include the department ID, department name, description, and name of the corresponding image file. Listing 6.2 shows the SQL statements that load the Department table.

TIP   All of the INSERT statements in this section are contained in a single file, SampleData.sql.

Listing 6.2   **Loading Departments**

```
SET IDENTITY_INSERT Department ON
INSERT INTO Department(DepartmentID, DepartmentName,
 DepartmentDescription
 DepartmentImage)
 VALUES(1, 'Funky Wacky Music',
   'The craziest music you have ever seen. Is it even music?', 'funk.gif')
INSERT INTO Department(DepartmentID, DepartmentName,
```

```
DepartmentDescription,
DepartmentImage)
VALUES(2, 'Cool Backstreet Jazz', 'Jazz that will make you dance.',
  'dance.gif')
INSERT INTO Department(DepartmentID, DepartmentName,
DepartmentDescription,
DepartmentImage)
VALUES(3, 'Crying Westerns',
  'The stories are so sad and the twangs so deep, you will cry.', 'Western.gif')
INSERT INTO Department(DepartmentID, DepartmentName,
DepartmentDescription,
DepartmentImage)
VALUES(4, 'Punked Out',
  'All of these titles are just on the edge of being punk (but worse).',
  'punk.gif')
INSERT INTO Department(DepartmentID, DepartmentName,
DepartmentDescription,
DepartmentImage)
VALUES(5, 'Wild T-Shirts',
  'The coolest ... everyone will be wearing them!',
  'tshirts.gif')
SET IDENTITY_INSERT Department OFF
```

TIP The SET IDENTITY_INSERT statement allows you to insert values into an identity column, which is otherwise read-only. If you turn this option on for a table, you must remember to turn it off when you're done, because it can only be set on for one table at a time.

Next, we'll load product data and then designate which department the products are assigned to. Listing 6.3 shows the SQL statements that insert the product information.

TIP Remember to check for single quotes in the data and double them for proper insertion into the database.

Listing 6.3   Loading Products

```
SET IDENTITY_INSERT Product ON
INSERT INTO Product(ProductID, ProductName, ProductDescription,
 ProductImage,
 ProductPrice, ProductActive)
 VALUES(1, 'Joe Bob''s Thimble Sounds',
  'Great thimble music that you will love!', 'thimble.gif', 10.00, 1)
INSERT INTO Product(ProductID, ProductName, ProductDescription,
 ProductImage,
 ProductPrice, ProductActive)
VALUES(2, 'The sounds of silence (for real).',
  '120 minutes of blank static.
```

```
➡ Nothing like it to drive your neighbors nuts!',
   'static.gif', 8.75, 1)
INSERT INTO Product(ProductID, ProductName, ProductDescription,
 ProductImage,
 ProductPrice, ProductActive)
 VALUES(3, 'Alley Jazz.',
   'Recorded in an alley in New Orleans during Mardi Gras',
   'jazz.gif', 18.75, 1)
INSERT INTO Product(ProductID, ProductName, ProductDescription,
 ProductImage,
 ProductPrice, ProductActive)
 VALUES(4, 'Circle Sax', 'The circle ensemble plays sax while spinning.',
   'circle.gif', 8.25, 1)
INSERT INTO Product(ProductID, ProductName, ProductDescription,
 ProductImage,
 ProductPrice, ProductActive)
 VALUES(5, 'Hats Off',
   'Sad songs of cowboy''s hats falling off on the trail.', 'hatsoff.gif',
   9.00, 1)
INSERT INTO Product(ProductID, ProductName, ProductDescription,
 ProductImage,
 ProductPrice, ProductActive)
 VALUES(6, 'Lassos of Love',
   'Heartwarming a capella country love songs.
   ➡ Includes the soothing sounds ' +
   'of the swirling lasso in the background.', 'lassos.gif', 89.00, 1)
INSERT INTO Product(ProductID, ProductName, ProductDescription,
 ProductImage,
 ProductPrice, ProductActive)
 VALUES(7, 'My Dog is a Cat',
   'Bizarre songs about animals being other animals.',
   'DogCat.gif', 5.00, 1)
INSERT INTO Product(ProductID, ProductName, ProductDescription,
 ProductImage,
 ProductPrice, ProductActive)
 VALUES(8, 'Candle Sticks are Falling',
   'Poems about candles read with smash punk in the background.',
   'candles.gif', 9.99, 1)
INSERT INTO Product(ProductID, ProductName, ProductDescription,
 ProductImage,
 ProductPrice, ProductActive)
 VALUES(9, 'T-Shirt Rip', 'Full of holes and totally cool!', 'hole.gif',
   80.00, 1)
INSERT INTO Product(ProductID, ProductName, ProductDescription,
 ProductImage,
 ProductPrice, ProductActive)
 VALUES(10, 'Undershirt', 'It looks like an undershirt, but it is better!',
   'under.gif', 20.00, 1)
SET IDENTITY_INSERT Product OFF
```

TIP You can use the + operator to concatenate two string constants into a longer string, as we did in the description for the "Lassos of Love" album.

The set of INSERT statements, shown in Listing 6.4, tie each of the new products to one of the departments.

Listing 6.4   **Loading the DepartmentProduct Table**

```
INSERT INTO DepartmentProduct(DepartmentID, ProductID)
  VALUES (1, 1)
INSERT INTO DepartmentProduct(DepartmentID, ProductID)
  VALUES(1 ,2)
INSERT INTO DepartmentProduct(DepartmentID, ProductID)
  VALUES(2 ,3)
INSERT INTO DepartmentProduct(DepartmentID, ProductID)
  VALUES(2 ,4)
INSERT INTO DepartmentProduct(DepartmentID, ProductID)
  VALUES(3 ,5)
INSERT INTO DepartmentProduct(DepartmentID, ProductID)
  VALUES(3 ,6)
INSERT INTO DepartmentProduct(DepartmentID, ProductID)
  VALUES(4 ,7)
INSERT INTO DepartmentProduct(DepartmentID, ProductID)
  VALUES(4 ,8)
INSERT INTO DepartmentProduct(DepartmentID, ProductID)
  VALUES(5 ,9)
INSERT INTO DepartmentProduct(DepartmentID, ProductID)
  VALUES(5 ,10)
```

WARNING Because we have chosen to enforce referential integrity in the database, we must load both the Product table and the Department table before the DepartmentProduct table.

Some of our products will have attributes that we need to load. For example, the T-shirts will be available in different colors and sizes. Listing 6.5 shows the SQL statements that insert two attribute categories, Size and Color, for our sample store.

Listing 6.5   **Loading Attribute Categories**

```
SET IDENTITY_INSERT AttributeCategory ON
INSERT INTO AttributeCategory(AttributeCategoryID, AttributeCategoryName)
  VALUES(1, 'Size')
INSERT INTO AttributeCategory(AttributeCategoryID, AttributeCategoryName)
  VALUES(2, 'Color')
SET IDENTITY_INSERT AttributeCategory OFF
```

Next, we need to load the names of the attributes in these categories. For example, in the Size category, we will have Small, Medium, Large, and X-Large. The SQL INSERT statements in Listing 6.6 create the attributes for the different categories.

Listing 6.6 **Loading Attributes**

```
SET IDENTITY_INSERT Attribute ON
INSERT INTO Attribute(AttributeID, AttributeName, AttributeCategoryID)
 VALUES(1, 'Small', 1)
INSERT INTO Attribute(AttributeID, AttributeName, AttributeCategoryID)
 VALUES(2, 'Medium', 1)
INSERT INTO Attribute(AttributeID, AttributeName, AttributeCategoryID)
 VALUES(3, 'Large', 1)
INSERT INTO Attribute(AttributeID, AttributeName, AttributeCategoryID)
 VALUES(4, 'X-Large', 1)
INSERT INTO Attribute(AttributeID, AttributeName, AttributeCategoryID)
 VALUES(5, 'Red', 2)
INSERT INTO Attribute(AttributeID, AttributeName, AttributeCategoryID)
 VALUES(6, 'Blue', 2)
INSERT INTO Attribute(AttributeID, AttributeName, AttributeCategoryID)
 VALUES(7, 'Green', 2)
INSERT INTO Attribute(AttributeID, AttributeName, AttributeCategoryID)
 VALUES(8, 'White', 2)
SET IDENTITY_INSERT Attribute OFF
```

Finally, we need to hook up our products to the different attributes. In this case, the products will be the two T-shirts in Wild Willie's store. The SQL statements in Listing 6.7 build the table that links products and attributes.

Listing 6.7 **Assigning Attributes to Products**

```
INSERT INTO ProductAttribute(AttributeID, ProductID)
 VALUES(1, 9)
INSERT INTO ProductAttribute(AttributeID, ProductID)
 VALUES(2, 9)
INSERT INTO ProductAttribute(AttributeID, ProductID)
 VALUES(3, 9)
INSERT INTO ProductAttribute(AttributeID, ProductID)
 VALUES(4, 9)
INSERT INTO ProductAttribute(AttributeID, ProductID)
 VALUES(5, 9)
INSERT INTO ProductAttribute(AttributeID, ProductID)
 VALUES(6, 9)
INSERT INTO ProductAttribute(AttributeID, ProductID)
 VALUES(7, 9)
INSERT INTO ProductAttribute(AttributeID, ProductID)
 VALUES(8, 9)
INSERT INTO ProductAttribute(AttributeID, ProductID)
```

```
  VALUES(1, 10)
INSERT INTO ProductAttribute(AttributeID, ProductID)
  VALUES(2, 10)
INSERT INTO ProductAttribute(AttributeID, ProductID)
  VALUES(3, 10)
INSERT INTO ProductAttribute(AttributeID, ProductID)
  VALUES(4, 10)
INSERT INTO ProductAttribute(AttributeID, ProductID)
  VALUES(5, 10)
INSERT INTO ProductAttribute(AttributeID, ProductID)
  VALUES(6, 10)
INSERT INTO ProductAttribute(AttributeID, ProductID)
  VALUES(7, 10)
INSERT INTO ProductAttribute(AttributeID, ProductID)
  VALUES(8, 10)
```

This initial load of data will take care of the data requirements in this chapter. We'll load additional data in later chapters.

Building the Page Structure

A good store design should provide consistent navigation throughout the shopping experience. Key navigational elements include links to the department page, the shopping basket, the checkout process, and the search page. We'll also provide a link to retrieve order status and one to manage the shopper's profile, which the shopper can update even when they're not shopping. Figure 6.2 shows the page layout. Note the additional elements at the bottom of the page.

We'll want to wrap our pages in a navigational structure that will be easy to manage. For example, perhaps down the road, we may wish to add a link to specials on the site, and we'll want to avoid revising all the pages in the store in order to accommodate this new link. Instead, we should encapsulate the header and footer into include files that will build the page structure.

The store's navigation interface

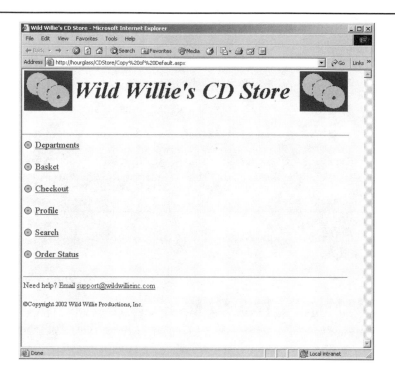

Header and Footer Files

The Header.inc page, shown in Listing 6.8, builds the main navigational structure of the site.

Listing 6.8   Header.inc

```
<!-- Header.inc - This page should be included at the
top of all pages in the store to define the navigation
and layout of the pages. -->

<!-- Set the default body tag for all of the pages -->
<body bgcolor="lightgoldenrodyellow" topmargin="0" leftmargin="0">

<!-- This table defines the header for the page -->
<table width="680" border="0">
<tr>
    <td align="right" valign="center"><img src="images/cdlogo.gif"></td>
    <td><font size="7" color="blue">
        <b><i>Wild Willie's CD Store</i></b></font></td>
    <td align="right" valign="center"><img src="images/cdlogo.gif"></td>
</tr>
</table>
```

```
<br><br>
<!-- Dividing line -->
<hr width="680" align="left">

<!-- This table defines the navigation for the page
and the structure for placing the page content. -->
<table width="680" border="0">
<tr>
    <!-- Navigation column -->
    <td width="130" valign="top">
        <img src="images/cdbullet.gif" border="0" align="center">
        <font color="blue" size="4">
        <a href="dept.aspx">Departments</a></font>
        <br><br>

        <img src="images/cdbullet.gif" border="0" align="center">
        <font color="blue" size="4">
        <a href="basket.aspx">Basket</a></font>
        <br><br>

        <img src="images/cdbullet.gif" border="0" align="center">
        <font color="blue" size="4">
        <a href="shipping.aspx">Checkout</a></font>
        <br><br>

        <img src="images/cdbullet.gif" border="0" align="center">
        <font color="blue" size="4">
        <a href="profile.aspx">Profile</a></font>
        <br><br>

        <img src="images/cdbullet.gif" border="0" align="center">
        <font color="blue" size="4">
        <a href="search.aspx">Search</a></font>
        <br><br>

        <img src="images/cdbullet.gif" border="0" align="center">
        <font color="blue" size="4">
        <a href="OrderStatus.aspx">Order Status</a></font>
        <br><br>

    </td>

    <!-- Spacing column between navigation and core content area -->
    <td width="10"> <td>

    <!-- Start the column for the main page content -->
    <td valign="top" width="540">

    <!--  Note that the Footer.inc include must close out any page
    that has the header include. The table will be closed out by
    the footer include-->
```

The point of the `Header.inc` file is to set up a standard structure for each page on our website. We do this by creating a structure of tables to define the physical layout of the pages. The first section of the page is the top row, where the CD logo and the title of the page appear. Following that table is the table that structures the navigation section of the page. The first column in the first row builds out the navigation links for each of the key sections. The second column is where the core content of the page will be displayed.

To match the header, we'll need to include the `Footer.inc` file at the bottom of any page that uses the header. This file closes out the tags started in the header. It also gives us an opportunity to show on each page a copyright notice, an e-mail address for support, or other standard information. Listing 6.9 shows the `Footer.inc` file.

Listing 6.9   **Footer.inc**

```
<!-- Footer.inc - This page should be included at the
bottom of all pages in the store to close out the
structure of the page. -->
    <!--  Close out the content column
          started in the header -->
    </td>

<!-- Close out the row -->
</tr>

<!-- Start a new row to display the footer information -->
<tr>
    <!--  Start a column, note the display across the four columns -->
    <td colspan="4" width="680">
    <HR>
    <!-- Display the help email -->
    Need help?  Email
    <a href="mailto:support@wildwillieinc.com">
    support@wildwillieinc.com</a>
    <BR><BR>
    <!-- Show the copyright -->
    <font size="2">&copy;Copyright 2002 Wild Willie
    Productions, Inc.</font>
    </td>
</tr>
</table>
</body>
```

It's important to include the `Header.inc` and `Footer.inc` files at the top and bottom of all pages that display content to the user. If only one or the other is included, the page will not build properly because the files contain opening and closing tags that relate to one another.

The SessionCheck Procedure

In addition to the standard layout for each page on our website, we want to execute some standard code. No matter where the user enters the site, whether through the home page or through a bookmark or link to some other page, we'll need to check their identity and see whether they have an open shopping basket. We'll do this by calling the SessionCheck procedure, which is a part of the GlobalProcedures.vb file, from the Page_Load event procedure of each Web Form. Listing 6.10 shows this procedure.

Listing 6.10   The SessionCheck Procedure

```
Friend Sub SessionCheck(ByVal Session As HttpSessionState, _
  ByVal objCookie As HttpCookie, ByVal strError As String)
    Try
        ' Check to see if the shopper session is 0. If so
        ' then we will need to create a shopper ID for tracking
        ' the shopper.
        If (Session("idShopper") = "0") Or _
            (Session ("idShopper") Is  Nothing) Then
            ' Next we look to see if a Wild Willie cookie
            ' has been set with the shopper ID.
            If objCookie Is Nothing Then
                ' Connect to the database and set up to
                ' insert a new shopper
                Dim cnn As SqlConnection = _
                 New SqlClient.SqlConnection("Data Source=(local);" & _
                 "Initial Catalog=Subscriptions;Integrated Security=SSPI")
                Dim cmd As New SqlCommand()
                With cmd
                    .Connection = cnn
                    .CommandText = "procInsertShopper"
                    .CommandType = CommandType.StoredProcedure
                End With
                cnn.Open()
                ' Execute the stored procedure, placing the results
                ' in the session state
                Session("idShopper") = CType(cmd.ExecuteScalar, String)
                cnn.Close()
                ' Indicate that a profile has NOT been retrieved.
                Session("ProfileRetrieve") = "0"
            Else ' There is a shopper ID in the cookie
                ' Retrieve the shopper ID from the cookie
                Session("idShopper") = objCookie.Value
                ' Now use the shopper ID to retrieve the
                ' ID of the last basket this shopper used
                Dim cnn As SqlConnection = _
                 New SqlClient.SqlConnection("Data Source=(local);" & _
                 "Initial Catalog=Subscriptions;Integrated Security=SSPI")
                Dim cmd As New SqlCommand()
                With cmd
```

```
                    .Connection = cnn
                    .CommandText = "procRetrieveLastBasket"
                    .CommandType = CommandType.StoredProcedure
                End With
                Dim prm As New SqlParameter("@ShopperID", SqlDbType.Int)
                prm.Direction = ParameterDirection.Input
                prm.Value = CType(objCookie.Value, Integer)
                cmd.Parameters.Add(prm)
                cnn.Open()
                ' Execute the stored procedure, placing the results
                ' in the session state
                Session("idBasket") = CType(cmd.ExecuteScalar, String)
            End If
        End If
    Catch ex As Exception
        strError = ex.ToString
    End Try

End Sub
```

The SessionCheck procedure takes three arguments. The Session argument is a copy of the ASP.NET Session object from the calling page. The objCookie argument is a copy of the shopper's cookie, also passed in. The third argument, strError, is used to pass any error message back to the calling page.

This procedure starts by checking to see whether there's a nonzero *idShopper* value assigned to this session. You'll recall that we initialize *idShopper* to zero in the Global.asax file. This means that the first time this procedure is executed, no matter where it's called from, the first If statement will be true.

If there is no shopper ID yet, we need to see whether the user has a stored shopper ID on their own computer. We can do this by checking a cookie that's passed into this procedure in the *objCookie* variable. If there's nothing in the variable, we were unable to retrieve a cookie from the user. In this case, we need to assign a shopper ID for this session. We do that by executing the procInsertShopper stored procedure, which you'll see a bit later in this section. This stored procedure returns a single value: the new ShopperID value from the Shopper table. The ADO.NET Command object allows us to easily retrieve a single value from a stored procedure by calling the ExecuteScalar method.

When we create a new shopper ID, we also set a session variable to indicate that we haven't loaded a profile for this shopper.

NOTE　　We'll discuss profiles in Chapter 9, "Order Status and Profile Management."

If we were able to retrieve our cookie from the user's computer, we can use the Value property of the HttpCookie object to retrieve the actual shopper ID and store it in the *idShopper* session variable. In this case, we also want to retrieve any shopping basket that the user was filling the last time they visited the site. That's the job of the procRetrieveLastBasket stored procedure, which takes the shopper ID as a parameter. It returns the BasketID column of the shopper's most recent open basket, or zero if they don't have an open basket. We store this value in another session variable.

If there are any errors in this procedure, we just pass them up to the calling procedure, which can decide whether and how to display the error text on the web page.

Now, let's look at the two stored procedures that are called from the SessionCheck procedure. The first, procInsertShopper, creates a new row in the Shopper table. Adding a new row to this table automatically assigns a value to the ShopperID column, which is an identity column. We return that by referencing the @@*identity* system variable, which contains the last value. Listing 6.11 shows the text of the procInsertShopper stored procedure.

Listing 6.11   procInsertShopper Stored Procedure

```
/* Insert a new shopper into the database, setting
   the required fields to empty strings

From .NET E-Commerce Programming
by Mike Gunderloy and Noel Jerke
Copyright 2002, Sybex Inc. All Rights Reserved. */
CREATE PROC procInsertShopper
AS
  INSERT INTO Shopper(ShopperLastName, ShopperUserName, ShopperPassword)
  VALUES('', '', '')
  SELECT @@IDENTITY
```

The second stored procedure, procRetrieveLastBasket, will return the last active basket the shopper was utilizing. It checks to ensure that only baskets that are not part of a completed order are returned. It ensures that only the last basket is returned by ordering the results in descending order by date created and then returning only the most recent one by invoking the TOP operator. Listing 6.12 shows the text of this stored procedure.

Listing 6.12   procRetrieveLastBasket Stored Procedure

```
/* Retrieve the last basket ID for the shopper,
   or 0 if there is no saved basket.

From .NET E-Commerce Programming
by Mike Gunderloy and Noel Jerke
Copyright 2002, Sybex Inc. All Rights Reserved. */
```

```
CREATE PROCEDURE procRetrieveLastBasket
    @ShopperID int
AS
 DECLARE @BasketID int
 SET @BasketID = (SELECT TOP 1 BasketID FROM Basket
  WHERE ShopperID = @ShopperID AND BasketOrderPlaced =0 AND BasketTotal = 0
  ORDER BY BasketDateCreated DESC)
 IF @BasketID IS NULL
  SELECT 0
 ELSE
  SELECT @BasketID
```

The Home Page

Now we're ready to put all these pieces together into a Web Form. The home page for the store, Default.aspx, puts our header and footer into place and gives an entry point for the shopper. Right after the opening tags for the page, we include the Header.inc file by using the ASP.NET include syntax. Then we put in the core information for the page, which, in this case, is just a welcome message. Following that, we close out the page with the Footer.inc file.

The home page code is shown in Listing 6.13. As with other ASP.NET pages, this page contains much code that's auto-generated by Visual Studio .NET when you create a new page. For example, the opening comments that define the page language and event hookup, as well as the meta tags that are used by Visual Studio .NET, are all automatically generated. You must not alter these tags; they are essential to the functioning of ASP.NET.

Listing 6.13   **Default.aspx**

```
<%@ Page Language="vb" AutoEventWireup="false"
  Codebehind="Default.aspx.vb" Inherits="CDStore._Default"%>
<!DOCTYPE HTML PUBLIC "-//W3C//DTD HTML 4.0 Transitional//EN">
<HTML>
    <HEAD>
        <TITLE>Default</TITLE>
    </HEAD>
    <!--Default.aspx - Home page and welcome message for the store -->
    <meta name="GENERATOR" content="Microsoft Visual Studio.NET 7.0">
    <meta name="CODE_LANGUAGE" content="Visual Basic 7.0">
    <meta name="vs_defaultClientScript" content="JavaScript">
    <meta name="vs_targetSchema"
    content="http://schemas.microsoft.com/intellisense/ie5">
    <!-- #Include File="Header.inc" -->
    <form id="Form1" method="post" runat="server">
```

```
    </form>
    <!-- Opening screen text -->
    Welcome to <font color="blue"><b>Wild Willie's CRAZY CD
    </b></font> store!
    We have some of the wildest CDs that not even the biggest of the CD
    stores have.
    <br>
    <br>
    Select "Departments" on the left to start your shopping experience!
    <!-- #Include File="Footer.inc" -->
    </HTML>
```

In addition to the HTML code, we need to insert a call to the SessionCheck procedure in the code-behind file for this Web Form. Listing 6.14 shows the procedures on this page.

Listing 6.14   Event Procedures from Default.aspx.vb

```
Private Sub Page_Load(ByVal sender As System.Object, _
 ByVal e As System.EventArgs) Handles MyBase.Load
    'Put user code to initialize the page here
    Dim strError As String
    SessionCheck(Session, Request.Cookies("WWCD"), strError)
End Sub

Private Sub Page_Error(ByVal sender As Object, _
 ByVal e As System.EventArgs) Handles MyBase.Error
    Dim strMessage As String = "<font face=verdana color=red>" & _
     "<h4>" & Request.Url.ToString() & "</h4>" & _
     "<pre><font color='red'>" & Server.GetLastError().ToString() & _
     "</pre></font>"
    Response.Write(strMessage)
End Sub
```

Figure 6.3 shows the store's home page in all its glory. Now we'll move on to exploring some of the functionality of the store.

FIGURE 6.3:

Default page for the
store

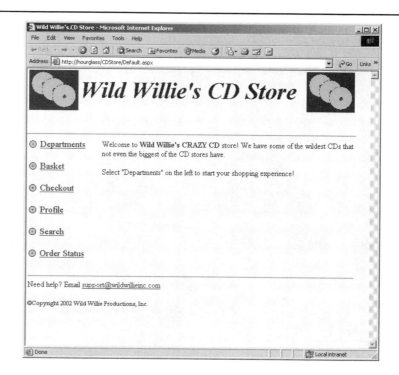

Browsing Departments and Products

In the rest of this chapter, we'll concentrate on implementing browsing of departments and products. Now that we've defined the core page structure and loaded the database, we're ready to get started.

From a marketing standpoint, the browsing experience can be the most critical aspect of enticing the consumer to do some window shopping and maybe coming in to buy. Browsing is part of the core functionality that must be present regardless of the visual design of the store. Whether your store is as simple as Wild Willie's or loaded with extra features, shoppers should be able to browse easily through the products that you offer.

Departments

The department page is built to display a list of departments in the store. For our sample store, we are going to show the department name and a corresponding image that represents the department. Listing 6.15 shows the HTML code for our department page, Dept.aspx.

Listing 6.15   **Dept.aspx**

```
<%@ Page Language="vb" AutoEventWireup="false"
  Codebehind="Dept.aspx.vb" Inherits="CDStore.Dept"%>
<!DOCTYPE HTML PUBLIC "-//W3C//DTD HTML 4.0 Transitional//EN">
<HTML>
    <HEAD>
        <TITLE>Departments</TITLE>
    </HEAD>
    <!--Dept.aspx - Department listing -->
    <meta content="Microsoft Visual Studio.NET 7.0" name="GENERATOR">
    <meta content="Visual Basic 7.0" name="CODE_LANGUAGE">
    <meta content="JavaScript" name="vs_defaultClientScript">
    <meta content="http://schemas.microsoft.com/intellisense/ie5"
     name="vs_targetSchema">
    <!-- #Include File="Header.inc" -->
    <form id="Form1" method="post" runat="server">
        <asp:datalist id="dlDepts" runat="server" BorderColor="Tan"
          ForeColor="Black" BackColor="LightGoldenrodYellow" CellPadding="2"
          BorderWidth="1px">
            <SelectedItemStyle ForeColor="GhostWhite"
            BackColor="DarkSlateBlue"></SelectedItemStyle>
            <AlternatingItemStyle BackColor="PaleGoldenrod">
            </AlternatingItemStyle>
            <ItemTemplate>
                <TABLE style="FONT: 10pt verdana" cellPadding="10">
                    <TR>
                        <TD vAlign="top">
                          <A href='<%# DataBinder.Eval(Container.DataItem,
                            "DepartmentID",
                            "Products.aspx?idDept={0}") %>'>
                          <IMG src='<%# DataBinder.Eval(Container.DataItem,
                            "DepartmentImage", "images/{0}") %>' align=top>
                          </A>
                        </TD>
                        <TD vAlign="top">
                          <B><A href='<%# DataBinder.Eval(Container.DataItem,
                            "DepartmentID",
                            "Products.aspx?idDept={0}") %>'>
                          <%# DataBinder.Eval(Container.DataItem,
                            "DepartmentName") %></A></B><BR>
                          <%# DataBinder.Eval(Container.DataItem,
                            "DepartmentDescription") %>
                          <BR>
                        </TD>
                    </TR>
                </TABLE>
            </ItemTemplate>
            <FooterStyle BackColor="Tan"></FooterStyle>
            <HeaderStyle Font-Bold="True" BackColor="Tan"></HeaderStyle>
            <AlternatingItemTemplate>
                <TABLE id="Table1" style="FONT: 10pt verdana"
                  cellPadding="10">
                    <TR>
```

```
            <TD vAlign="top">·
              <B><A href='<%# DataBinder.Eval(Container.DataItem,
                "DepartmentID",
                "Products.aspx?idDept={0}") %>'>
                <%# DataBinder.Eval(Container.DataItem,
                "DepartmentName") %></A></B><BR>
                <%# DataBinder.Eval(Container.DataItem,
                "DepartmentDescription") %>
                <BR>
            </TD>
            <TD vAlign="top">
              <A href='<%# DataBinder.Eval(Container.DataItem,
                "DepartmentID",
                "Products.aspx?idDept={0}") %>'>
                <IMG src='<%# DataBinder.Eval(Container.DataItem,
                "DepartmentImage", "images/{0}") %>' align=top>
                </A>
            </TD>
          </TR>
        </TABLE>
      </AlternatingItemTemplate>
    </asp:datalist></form>
  <!-- #Include File="Footer.inc" -->
</HTML>
```

Figure 6.4 shows this page open in the Visual Studio .NET designer. The bulk of the code in Listing 6.15 exists to define the DataList control, which presents the entire visual interface of the page. We'll discuss the DataList in more detail shortly, but first, let's look at the code-behind file for this Web Form.

FIGURE 6.4:

The Dept.aspx Web Form in the designer

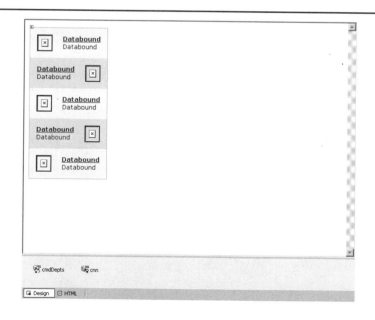

Retrieving Departments

Listing 6.16 shows the event procedures from Dept.aspx.vb, the code-behind file for the Dept.aspx Web Form.

Listing 6.16   Code for Retrieving Departments

```
Private Sub Page_Load(ByVal sender As System.Object, _
 ByVal e As System.EventArgs) Handles MyBase.Load
    'Put user code to initialize the page here
    Dim strError As String
    SessionCheck(Session, Request.Cookies("WWCD"), strError)
    Dim dsDepts As New DataSet()
    Dim daDepts As New SqlDataAdapter()
    daDepts.SelectCommand = cmdDepts
    daDepts.Fill(dsDepts, "Departments")
    dlDepts.DataSource = dsDepts
    dlDepts.DataMember = "Departments"
    DataBind()

End Sub

Private Sub Page_Error(ByVal sender As Object, _
 ByVal e As System.EventArgs) Handles MyBase.Error
    Dim strMessage As String = "<font face=verdana color=red>" & _
     "<h4>" & Request.Url.ToString() & "</h4>" & _
     "<pre><font color='red'>" & Server.GetLastError().ToString() & _
     "</pre></font>"
    Response.Write(strMessage)
End Sub
```

The Page_Load procedure takes care of retrieving data and displaying it on the Web Form. It uses the same ADO.NET objects that you've already seen: a SqlCommand object to retrieve data from the SQL Server database, a DataSet to hold the retrieved data, and a DataAdapter to make the connection between the two. Because we're only retrieving data, not editing it, the DataAdapter only needs its SelectCommand property initialized. The Sql-Connection and SqlCommand objects were created by drag-and-drop from Server Explorer; you can see them at the bottom of Figure 6.4.

The SqlCommand object is based on the procRetrieveDepts stored procedure, which is shown in Listing 6.17.

Listing 6.17   procRetrieveDepts Stored Procedure

```
/* Retrieve departments from the store.
```

From .NET E-Commerce Programming

```
by Mike Gunderloy and Noel Jerke
Copyright 2002, Sybex Inc. All Rights Reserved. */
CREATE PROCEDURE procRetrieveDepts
AS
  SELECT * FROM Department
```

Calling the Fill method of the DataAdaptor object uses this stored procedure to retrieve all the rows from the Department table into the DataSet. Then this data is assigned to the DataList control through its DataSource and DataMember properties.

Using the DataList Control

In Chapter 5, you saw the DataGrid Web Forms control, which provides an easy data-bound interface for displaying data from a DataSet. But the DataGrid, while convenient, is somewhat inflexible. We've chosen to use a different data-bound control, the DataList, on the Dept.aspx Web Form.

Like the DataGrid, the DataList is bound by setting its DataSource and DataMember properties and then calling the DataBind method. But unlike the DataGrid, the DataList has no built-in formatting. Rather, you need to supply formatting in a series of templates. Table 6.2 lists the templates that you can create for a DataList control.

TABLE 6.2: DataList Templates

Template	Used for
Header template	Formatting a single header row at the top of the DataList
Footer template	Formatting a single footer row at the bottom of the DataList
Item template	Formatting each row of data
Alternating Item template	Formatting alternating rows of data
Selected Item template	Formatting the currently selected row of data
Edit Item template	Formatting the row of data that's currently being edited
Separator template	Formatting separators between items

At a minimum, you need to supply an Item template. We've chosen to supply both the Item template and the Alternating Item template for the Depts.aspx Web Form. ASP.NET will use the Item template for the first row of data and the Alternating Item template for the second row of data and will continue alternating the two as long as there is data to display.

What can go in a template? Any valid HTML, as well as data binding commands, can be placed in a template. Data binding commands are sections of ASP.NET code set off by <%#

and %> markers. These commands are executed only when you call the DataBind method of the page or control.

For example, consider this snippet of code from within the ItemTemplate tag:

```
<A href='<%# DataBinder.Eval(Container.DataItem,
"DepartmentID", "Products.aspx?idDept={0}") %>'>
```

When you invoke the DataBind method, this bit of code builds a hyperlink tag. The Data-Binder.Eval method specifies the code to be evaluated at runtime. The first argument to this method (in this case, Container.DataItem) specifies the object reference to be evaluated. Container in this case refers to the ASP.NET page, and the DataItem property returns the current row of data. The second argument is the name of the column to be evaluated, and the third argument is a format string. The {0} token in the format string is replaced with the results of the evaluation.

With that, we have our first interactive display page built for the store—the department page. Figure 6.5 shows the page with the sample data populated. Note that the images rotate from left to right around the product name, thanks to the two Item templates in the Data-List. And each department is linked to display the products in the department.

FIGURE 6.5:

Department page

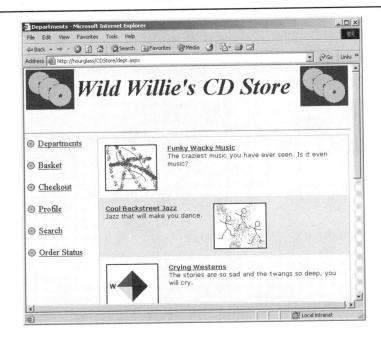

TIP
A tip on designing the department page: If you have a large number of departments, you may want to list them in multiple columns rather than in a direct top-to-bottom list. You can manage this easily by setting the RepeatColumns property of the DataList control to the number of columns that you'd like to display.

Listing Products

Next, we move to the page that will display the products in the department that was selected from the Dept.aspx page. The ID of the department is passed as part of the URL to the Products.aspx page, which is shown in Listing 6.18.

Listing 6.18   Products.aspx

```
<%@ Page Language="vb" AutoEventWireup="false" Codebehind="Products.aspx.vb"
  Inherits="CDStore.Products"%>
<!DOCTYPE HTML PUBLIC "-//W3C//DTD HTML 4.0 Transitional//EN">
<HTML>
    <HEAD>
        <TITLE>Products</TITLE>
    </HEAD>
    <!--Products.aspx - Products in a particular department -->
    <meta content="Microsoft Visual Studio.NET 7.0" name="GENERATOR">
    <meta content="Visual Basic 7.0" name="CODE_LANGUAGE">
    <meta content="JavaScript" name="vs_defaultClientScript">
    <meta content="http://schemas.microsoft.com/intellisense/ie5"
      name="vs_targetSchema">
    <!-- #Include File="Header.inc" -->
    <form id="Form1" method="post" runat="server">
        <!--  Display the department information -->
        <asp:datalist id="dlDept" runat="server" BorderColor="Tan"
         ForeColor="Black" BackColor="LightGoldenrodYellow" CellPadding="2"
         BorderWidth="0px">
            <SelectedItemStyle ForeColor="GhostWhite"
             BackColor="DarkSlateBlue"></SelectedItemStyle>
            <AlternatingItemStyle BackColor="PaleGoldenrod">
            </AlternatingItemStyle>
            <ItemTemplate>
              <CENTER>
                <IMG src='<%# DataBinder.Eval(Container.DataItem,
                  "DepartmentImage", "images/{0}") %>' align=middle>
                    <FONT size="4"><B>
                      <%# DataBinder.Eval(Container.DataItem,
                        "DepartmentName") %>
                    </B></FONT>
                    <BR>
                    <BR>
              </CENTER>
              <%# DataBinder.Eval(Container.DataItem,
```

```
                "DepartmentDescription") %>  <br>
              Select a product:<BR><BR>
            </ItemTemplate>
            <FooterStyle BackColor="Tan"></FooterStyle>
            <HeaderStyle Font-Bold="True" BackColor="Tan"></HeaderStyle>
        </asp:datalist>
        <asp:datalist id="dlProducts" runat="server" BorderColor="Tan"
         ForeColor="Black" BackColor="LightGoldenrodYellow" CellPadding="2"
         BorderWidth="1px" Width="100%">
            <SelectedItemStyle ForeColor="GhostWhite"
             BackColor="DarkSlateBlue"></SelectedItemStyle>
            <AlternatingItemStyle BackColor="PaleGoldenrod">
            </AlternatingItemStyle>
            <ItemTemplate>
              <a href='Product.aspx?idProduct=
              <%# DataBinder.Eval(Container.DataItem, "ProductID") %>'>
              <img src='images/products/sm_
              <%# DataBinder.Eval(Container.DataItem, "ProductImage") %>'
              align="middle" border="0">
              <%# DataBinder.Eval(Container.DataItem, "ProductName") %>
              </a>
              <BR>
              <BR>
            </ItemTemplate>
            <FooterStyle BackColor="Tan"></FooterStyle>
            <HeaderStyle Font-Bold="True" BackColor="Tan"></HeaderStyle>
            <AlternatingItemTemplate>
              <a href='Product.aspx?idProduct=
              <%# DataBinder.Eval(Container.DataItem, "ProductID") %>'>
              <%# DataBinder.Eval(Container.DataItem, "ProductName") %>
              <img src='images/products/sm_
              <%# DataBinder.Eval(Container.DataItem, "ProductImage") %>'
              align="middle" border="0">
              </a><BR>
              <BR>
            </AlternatingItemTemplate>
        </asp:datalist></form>
      <!-- #Include File="Footer.inc" -->
    </HTML>
```

The code for this page consists primarily of two DataList controls. The first one repeats the data for the selected department. Because this data will always be a single row, we don't need to define an Alternating Item template for this DataList. We will show the department image, name, and description. This will help to serve as a visual placeholder to indicate where the shopper has navigated to.

The second DataList control on the page displays the information on the products within the selected department. It uses two templates to alternate the image's placement to the left and the right of the product name. As we did on the department page, we link the image and name to a page containing more information. In this case, we're linking to the `Product.aspx` page and passing the product ID as part of the URL.

Listing 6.19 shows the event procedures from the code-behind file for this Web Form.

Listing 6.19   **Event Procedures from Products.aspx.vb**

```
Private Sub Page_Load(ByVal sender As System.Object, _
  ByVal e As System.EventArgs) Handles MyBase.Load
    Dim strError As String
    SessionCheck(Session, Request.Cookies("WWCD"), strError)
    ' Set up the department data
    cmdRetrieveDept.Parameters("@idDepartment").Value = _
      Request("idDept")
    Dim dsDept As New DataSet()
    Dim daDept As New SqlDataAdapter()
    daDept.SelectCommand = cmdRetrieveDept
    daDept.Fill(dsDept, "Department")
    dlDept.DataSource = dsDept
    dlDept.DataMember = "Department"
    ' Set up the product data
    cmdRetrieveDeptProducts.Parameters("@idDept").Value = _
      Request("idDept")
    Dim dsProducts As New DataSet()
    Dim daProducts As New SqlDataAdapter()
    daProducts.SelectCommand = cmdRetrieveDeptProducts
    daProducts.Fill(dsProducts, "Products")
    dlProducts.DataSource = dsProducts
    dlProducts.DataMember = "Products"
    ' And bind it all to the user interface
    DataBind()
    ' Store the department ID for later use in building links
    Session("LastIDDept") = Request("idDept")
End Sub

Private Sub Page_Error(ByVal sender As Object, _
  ByVal e As System.EventArgs) Handles MyBase.Error
    Dim strMessage As String = "<font face=verdana color=red>" & _
      "<h4>" & Request.Url.ToString() & "</h4>" & _
      "<pre><font color='red'>" & Server.GetLastError().ToString() & _
      "</pre></font>"
    Response.Write(strMessage)
End Sub
```

This code uses two stored procedures to retrieve data. Each of these takes a single parameter, the department ID. Because we created the SqlCommand objects by drag-and-drop, the SqlParameter objects are waiting for us when we start to run code. All we need to do is fill in their values from the department ID that's passed as part of the URL to this page, which we can retrieve through the Request() collection. The first stored procedure, shown in Listing 6.20, retrieves the information on a single department.

Listing 6.20   **procRetrieveDept Stored Procedure**

```
/*  Retrieve the information about a specified department

From .NET E-Commerce Programming
by Mike Gunderloy and Noel Jerke
Copyright 2002, Sybex Inc. All Rights Reserved. */
CREATE PROCEDURE procRetrieveDept
  @idDepartment int
AS
  SELECT * FROM Department
  WHERE DepartmentID = @idDepartment
```

The second stored procedure returns the products assigned to a particular department. To find the proper products, we need to join together the Product table and the Department-Products table. The stored procedure, shown in Listing 6.21, returns all the products that have an entry for the selected department in the DepartmentProducts table.

Listing 6.21   **procRetrieveDeptProducts Stored Procedure**

```
/*  Retrieve the products for a specified department

From .NET E-Commerce Programming
by Mike Gunderloy and Noel Jerke
Copyright 2002, Sybex Inc. All Rights Reserved. */
CREATE PROCEDURE procRetrieveDeptProducts
  @idDept int
AS
  SELECT Product.ProductID, ProductName, ProductImage
  FROM Product INNER JOIN DepartmentProduct
  ON Product.ProductID = DepartmentProduct.ProductID
  WHERE DepartmentProduct.DepartmentID = @idDept
```

The code also stores the ID of the department requested in a session variable, *LastIDDept*. That way, when the shopper goes to the basket page, we can build a link back to the department where the shopper was. This allows the shopper to continue selecting items from a department where they've already shown interest.

Now we can click any department listed on the Dept.aspx page and bring up a listing of the products on the Products.aspx page. The shopper can surf through each of the departments quickly by clicking the Departments link on the navigation bar. Figure 6.6 shows the Funky Wacky music department in our store.

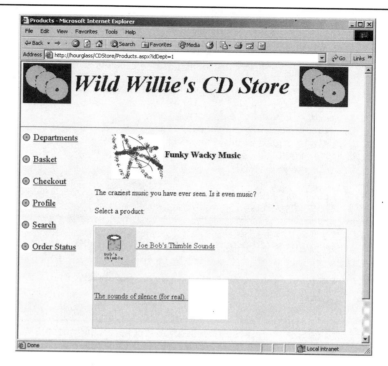

In this case, we have two products tied to that department, "Joe Bob's Thimble Sounds"
and "The Sounds of Silence (for Real)." Note the display of department information right
below the page's header. As you can see, the DataList controls have provided us with very
flexible formatting for this page.

If you click back to the Departments listing, you can select a new department such as Cry-
ing Westerns, and the data for the new department will display in the browser.

Now we're ready to look at some actual product data. This is the next step toward reaching
our ultimate goal of selling things to the shopper.

Displaying Individual Products

The Product.aspx page, shown in Listing 6.22, displays the data on the product that the
shopper selected on the Products.aspx page. This is where the shopper will be able to view
the product data in more detail and make a purchasing decision.

Listing 6.22   Product.aspx

```
<%@ Page Language="vb" AutoEventWireup="false" Codebehind="Product.aspx.vb"
Inherits="CDStore.Product"%>
<!DOCTYPE HTML PUBLIC "-//W3C//DTD HTML 4.0 Transitional//EN">
```

```html
<HTML>
    <HEAD>
        <TITLE>Product Detail</TITLE>
    </HEAD>
    <!-- Product.aspx - Details and order form for a particular product -->
    <meta name="GENERATOR" content="Microsoft Visual Studio.NET 7.0">
    <meta name="CODE_LANGUAGE" content="Visual Basic 7.0">
    <meta name="vs_defaultClientScript" content="JavaScript">
    <meta name="vs_targetSchema"
     content="http://schemas.microsoft.com/intellisense/ie5">
    <!-- #Include File="Header.inc" -->
    <form id="Form1" method="post" runat="server">
        <P>
            <asp:datalist id="dlProduct" runat="server" BorderColor="Tan"
             ForeColor="Black" BackColor="LightGoldenrodYellow"
             CellPadding="2" BorderWidth="1px">
                <SelectedItemStyle ForeColor="GhostWhite"
                 BackColor="DarkSlateBlue"></SelectedItemStyle>
                <AlternatingItemStyle BackColor="PaleGoldenrod">
                </AlternatingItemStyle>
                <ItemTemplate>
                    <table>
                        <tr>
                            <td><img src='images/products/
                             <%# DataBinder.Eval(Container.DataItem,
                             "ProductImage") %>'></td>
                            <td valign="top">
                                <center><b><font size="5">
                                 <%# DataBinder.Eval(Container.DataItem,
                                 "ProductName") %></font></b></center>
                                <br>
                                <br>
                                <%# DataBinder.Eval(Container.DataItem,
                                 "ProductDescription") %>
                                <br>
                                <br>
                            </td>
                        </tr>
                        <tr>
                            <td align="center"><b>Price:
                                    <%# DataBinder.Eval(Container.DataItem,
                                     "ProductPrice", "{0:c}") %>
                                </b>
                            </td>
                            <td align="center">
                                <b>Quantity: <input type="text" value="1"
                                 name="quantity" size="2"></b>
                                <input type="hidden" value='
                                 <%# DataBinder.Eval(Container.DataItem,
                                 "ProductID") %>' name="ProductID">
                                <input type="hidden" value='
```

```
                              <%# DataBinder.Eval(Container.DataItem,
                                "ProductName") %>' name="ProductName">
                              <input type="hidden" value='
                                <%# DataBinder.Eval(Container.DataItem,
                                "ProductPrice") %>' name="ProductPrice">
                          </td>
                        </tr>
                      </table>
                    </ItemTemplate>
                    <FooterStyle BackColor="Tan"></FooterStyle>
                    <HeaderStyle Font-Bold="True"
                      BackColor="Tan"></HeaderStyle>
                </asp:datalist></P>
            <P>
                <asp:Label id="lblColor" runat="server">Color: </asp:Label>
                <asp:DropDownList id="ddlColor"
                  runat="server"></asp:DropDownList>
                <asp:Label id="lblSize" runat="server">Size: </asp:Label>
                <asp:DropDownList id="ddlSize"
                  runat="server"></asp:DropDownList>
            </P>
            <P></P>
            <P></P>
            <P>
                <INPUT type="submit" value="Order" name="Submit">
            </P>
        </form>
            </form>
        <!-- #Include File="Footer.inc" -->
    </HTML>
```

Like the other Web Forms we've seen, this one uses a DataList control to handle the formatting of the product information. The page also contains two other types of controls. First, there are some standard HTML input controls. One of these is visible, and holds the quantity; the other two are hidden, and hold the product name and product price. As you can see, you can easily mix traditional HTML controls with the newer ASP.NET controls on the same page.

The second group of controls are from the Web Forms tab of the Toolbox: two Label controls and two DropDownList controls. These controls are used to choose the product size and product color if a product has those attributes. You'll see in Listing 6.23 how these controls can be manipulated from the VB .NET code behind the Web Form.

Listing 6.23   **Product.aspx.vb Event Procedures**

```
Private Sub Page_Load(ByVal sender As System.Object, _
  ByVal e As System.EventArgs) Handles MyBase.Load
    Dim strError As String
    SessionCheck(Session, Request.Cookies("WWCD"), strError)
```

```
                ' Set up the department data
                cmdRetrieveDept.Parameters("@idDepartment").Value = _
                 Request("idDept")
                Dim dsDept As New DataSet()
                Dim daDept As New SqlDataAdapter()
                daDept.SelectCommand = cmdRetrieveDept
                daDept.Fill(dsDept, "Department")
                dlDept.DataSource = dsDept
                dlDept.DataMember = "Department"
                ' Set up the product data
                cmdRetrieveDeptProducts.Parameters("@idDept").Value = _
                 Request("idDept")
                Dim dsProducts As New DataSet()
                Dim daProducts As New SqlDataAdapter()
                daProducts.SelectCommand = cmdRetrieveDeptProducts
                daProducts.Fill(dsProducts, "Products")
                dlProducts.DataSource = dsProducts
                dlProducts.DataMember = "Products"
                ' And bind it all to the user interface
                DataBind()
                ' Store the department ID for later use in building links
                Session("LastIDDept") = Request("idDept")
        End Sub

        Private Sub Page_Frror(ByVal sender As Object, _
         ByVal e As System.EventArgs) Handles MyBase.Error
                Dim strMessage As String = "<font face=verdana color=red>" & _
                 "<h4>" & Request.Url.ToString() & "</h4>" & _
                 "<pre><font color='red'>" & Server.GetLastError().ToString() & _
                 "</pre></font>"
                Response.Write(strMessage)
        End Sub
```

The Page_Load procedure in this page is the most complex one we've seen so far. It starts by checking the value of the *IsPostBack* system variable. Remember, Web Forms are reloaded every time the user submits them to the server. *IsPostBack* is false the very first time the page is loaded, and false thereafter. By checking this variable, we know whether we're just building the page or responding to user input.

If the value of *IsPostBack* is false, we need to retrieve the data from the database to build the page. This uses three SqlCommand objects but only two stored procedures. The cmdRetrieve-Product command is based on the procRetrieveProduct stored procedure, which is shown in Listing 6.24. Both the cmdColor and the cmdSize commands are based on the procProduct-Attributes stored procedure, which is shown in Listing 6.25.

The procRetrieveProduct stored procedure takes a product ID as a parameter and returns selected fields from the Product table for that product. There are many other fields in the

Product table, which is why we didn't use a SELECT * statement here. By retrieving only the necessary data, we can keep things moving more quickly.

Listing 6.24   **procRetrieveProduct Stored Procedure**

```
/*  Retrieve the product data

From .NET E-Commerce Programming
by Mike Gunderloy and Noel Jerke
Copyright 2002, Sybex Inc. All Rights Reserved. */
CREATE PROCEDURE procRetrieveProduct
  @idProduct int
AS
  SELECT ProductID, ProductName, ProductImage, ProductPrice,
  ProductDescription
  FROM Product
  WHERE ProductID = @idProduct
```

The procProductAttributes stored procedure returns all the attributes for the specified product in a specified category. To do this, it has to join four tables: Product, ProductAttribute, Attribute, and AttributeCategory.

Listing 6.25   **procProductAttributes Stored Procedure**

```
/*  Returns the attributes of a specified type
for a specified product

From .NET E-Commerce Programming
by Mike Gunderloy and Noel Jerke
Copyright 2002, Sybex Inc. All Rights Reserved. */
CREATE PROCEDURE procProductAttributes
  @idProduct int, @AttributeCategoryName varchar(255)
AS
  SELECT Attribute.AttributeName
  FROM ((Product INNER JOIN ProductAttribute
  ON Product.ProductID = ProductAttribute.ProductID)
  INNER JOIN Attribute
  ON ProductAttribute.AttributeID = Attribute.AttributeID)
  INNER JOIN AttributeCategory
  ON Attribute.AttributeCategoryID =
  AttributeCategory.AttributeCategoryID
  WHERE Product.ProductID = @idProduct
  AND AttributeCategory.AttributeCategoryName =
  @AttributeCategoryNameHandling
```

Product SKUs

Different businesses handle product SKUs (stock-keeping units) differently. Some use the ID of the core product as the primary SKU, with the attributes recorded as just part of the order data. That's how we're handling attributes in our sample store. But many store SKUs are combinations of the product ID, any attributes, and other data.

When storing attribute and product data, you need to keep in mind that what you're storing is information about the product at the time that it was ordered by the shopper. You wouldn't want a price change, for example, to occur right after a shopper orders and then have the shopper charged the new price. In our store, we take a "snapshot" of the product information at the time of purchase, storing all the necessary information with the order itself rather than referring back to the Product and Attribute tables.

The procProductAttributes stored procedure accepts two parameters, the product ID and the attribute category name. To create the SqlCommand objects that the `Product.aspx` page uses, we dragged this stored procedure from Server Explorer to the Web Form design surface twice. Then we customized the individual instances. For example, here are the steps that we followed to create the cmdSize object:

1. Drag an instance of the procProductAttribute stored procedure from Server Explorer to the Web Form's design surface.

2. Use the Properties window to change the Name property of the new object to cmdSize.

3. Click the Parameters property to reveal the build button, then click the build button. This opens the SqlParameter Collection Editor dialog box, shown in Figure 6.7.

FIGURE 6.7:

The SqlParameter Collection Editor

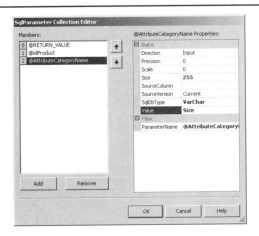

4. Select the @AttributeCategoryName member in the Members listbox.

5. Enter **Size** on the Value line in the Properties list for this member.

6. Click OK.

We followed a similar procedure to create the cmdSize object.

Returning to Listing 6.23, you can see that if *IsPostBack* is false, we retrieve data from the database into three different DataSet objects. The code binds the dsProduct DataSet to the DataList on the Web Form to supply the visual representation of the product. With the other two DataSets, the situation is a bit more complex. We don't want to show controls for selecting the size or color of an item if it doesn't have any size or color attributes. So the code checks the row count within the DataSets. If there are rows, it sets the properties of the DropDownList controls to display the possible values for the attribute. If there are no rows, it hides the DropDownList and Label controls so that they won't distract the user.

Finally, after setting all the data properties, the code calls the DataBind method to build the page for the user's browser.

On the other hand, if *IsPostBack* is true, the user has clicked the Order button to order the current product. In this case, we use the Request.Form method to retrieve data from the visible and hidden controls on the form. The code places this data into session variables and then calls the Server.Transfer method to load the `AddItem.aspx` Web Form. Server.Transfer performs the redirection entirely on the web server, unlike the Response.Redirect method, which requires a round-trip to the client.

NOTE   We'll dig into the `AddItem.aspx` Web Form in Chapter 7, "Making a Basket Case."

Figure 6.8 shows one of our sample product pages. The product image is placed on the left, with the product data on the right. The price appears directly below the image. To order the product, the shopper can click the Order button. That loads the data into the session variables and then returns the `AddItem.aspx` page to the user's browser.

Figure 6.9 shows a product that has attributes. It's the lovely and unique "Undershirt" that costs $20. And, much to every shopper's delight, it comes in four different colors and four different sizes. The shopper can select a size-and-color combination and then add the shirt to the basket.

FIGURE 6.8:

Product page—
"Alley Jazz"

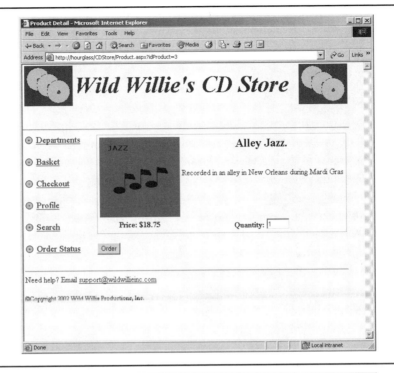

FIGURE 6.9:

Product page—
"Undershirt"

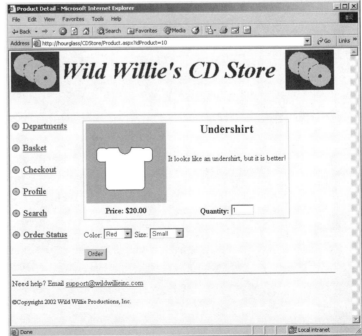

The shopper can now accomplish basic navigation through departments and products. To conclude this chapter, we'll take a look at how the shopper can find products through the search feature.

Searching

The search feature on the website is critical for enabling users to find products that meet their specific needs. In our store, we're going to provide two basic kinds of searches. The first is the standard keyword search; it will be executed against the Name and Description columns using SQL syntax.

The second option is a search for products that fall into a certain price range. The shopper will be able to combine the two options in a single search. For example, the shopper could search for products in the $10-to-$20 price range that also have "jazz" in their title or description.

Listing 6.26 shows the user interface code for the search page.

Listing 6.26   Search.aspx

```
<%@ Page Language="vb" AutoEventWireup="false" Codebehind="Search.aspx.vb"
 Inherits="CDStore.Search"%>
<!DOCTYPE HTML PUBLIC "-//W3C//DTD HTML 4.0 Transitional//EN">
<HTML>
    <HEAD>
        <TITLE>Search</TITLE>
    </HEAD>
    <!-- Search.aspx - Search for products by text or price -->
    <meta name="GENERATOR" content="Microsoft Visual Studio.NET 7.0">
    <meta name="CODE_LANGUAGE" content="Visual Basic 7.0">
    <meta name="vs_defaultClientScript" content="JavaScript">
    <meta name="vs_targetSchema"
     content="http://schemas.microsoft.com/intellisense/ie5">
    <!-- #Include File="Header.inc" -->
    <form id="Form1" method="post" runat="server">
        <TABLE id="Table1" cellSpacing="1" cellPadding="1" border="0"
        borderColor="white">
            <TR>
                <TD><STRONG>Enter your search text:</STRONG></TD>
                <TD></TD>
                <TD>
                    <asp:TextBox id="txtSearchText" runat="server">
                    </asp:TextBox></TD>
            </TR>
            <TR>
                <TD><STRONG>Price Range:</STRONG></TD>
                <TD>Low</TD>
                <TD>
```

```
                              <asp:TextBox id="txtLow" runat="server">
                              </asp:TextBox></TD>
              </TR>
              <TR>
                  <TD></TD>
                  <TD>High</TD>
                  <TD>
                      <asp:TextBox id="txtHigh" runat="server">
                      </asp:TextBox></TD>
              </TR>
              <TR>
                  <TD></TD>
                  <TD>
                      <asp:Button id="Button1" runat="server" Text="Search">
                      </asp:Button></TD>
                  <TD></TD>
              </TR>
          </TABLE>
      </form>
      <asp:DataList id="dlResults" runat="server" BorderColor="Tan"
       ForeColor="Black" BackColor="LightGoldenrodYellow" CellPadding="2"
       BorderWidth="1px">
          <SelectedItemStyle ForeColor="GhostWhite"
           BackColor="DarkSlateBlue">
          </SelectedItemStyle>
          <AlternatingItemStyle BackColor="PaleGoldenrod">
          </AlternatingItemStyle>
          <FooterStyle BackColor="Tan"></FooterStyle>
          <HeaderStyle Font-Bold="True" BackColor="Tan"></HeaderStyle>
          <ItemTemplate>
              <a href='Product.aspx?idProduct=
                <%# DataBinder.Eval(Container.DataItem, "ProductID") %>'>
                  <%# DataBinder.Eval(Container.DataItem, "ProductName") %>
              </a>
              <BR>
              <BR>
          </ItemTemplate>
      </asp:DataList>
      <!-- #Include File="Footer.inc" -->
</HTML>
```

This HTML defines a page that has some data entry controls, a command button, and a DataList. We'll use the same page both to prompt for search parameters and to display the search results. That way, the shopper can easily begin a new search or refine their existing search after receiving the results. Because we're using Web Forms controls, the data that the user enters into the controls is automatically preserved when the page is posted to the server and rebuilt.

Listing 6.27 shows the code-behind event procedures for the search page.

Listing 6.27   **Search.aspx.vb Event Procedures**

```vb
Private Sub Page_Load(ByVal sender As System.Object, _
  ByVal e As System.EventArgs) Handles MyBase.Load
    'Put user code to initialize the page here
    Dim strError As String
    SessionCheck(Session, Request.Cookies("WWCD"), strError)
    If IsPostBack Then
        Dim dsSearch As New DataSet()
        Dim daSearch As New SqlDataAdapter()
        cmdSearch.Parameters("@SearchText").Value = txtSearchText.Text
        If txtLow.Text = "" Then
            cmdSearch.Parameters("@Low").Value = 0
        Else
            cmdSearch.Parameters("@Low").Value = _
            CType(txtLow.Text, Integer)
        End If
        If txtHigh.Text = "" Then
            cmdSearch.Parameters("@High").Value = 99999999
        Else
            cmdSearch.Parameters("@High").Value = _
            CType(txtHigh.Text, Integer)
        End If
        daSearch.SelectCommand = cmdSearch
        daSearch.Fill(dsSearch, "Search")
        dlResults.DataSource = dsSearch
        dlResults.DataMember = "Search"
        DataBind()
        dlResults.Visible = True
    Else
        dlResults.Visible = False
    End If

End Sub

Private Sub Page_Error(ByVal sender As Object, _
  ByVal e As System.EventArgs) Handles MyBase.Error
    Dim strMessage As String = "<font face=verdana color=red>" & _
    "<h4>" & Request.Url.ToString() & "</h4>" & _
    "<pre><font color='red'>" & Server.GetLastError().ToString() & _
    "</pre></font>"
    Response.Write(strMessage)
End Sub
```

Once again, we're using the *IsPostBack* variable to determine whether this is the first time the page has been displayed. If it's being displayed for the first time, the code simply makes the DataList control (which won't contain any results yet) invisible. Otherwise, it fills in the parameters on a SqlCommand object based on the information that the user has entered, and binds the results to the DataList, which it then makes visible. The actual searching is done by the procSearchProducts stored procedure, shown in Listing 6.28.

The procSearchProducts stored procedure takes in three parameters: the search text, the low price, and the high price. The SQL query uses the LIKE capability to check the product names and the descriptions to see if they contain the search text. Then the prices are checked against the low and high prices.

Listing 6.28   **procSearchProducts Stored Procedure**

```
/*  Stored procedure to search for products based
    on passed in parameters.

From .NET E-Commerce Programming
by Mike Gunderloy and Noel Jerke
Copyright 2002, Sybex Inc. All Rights Reserved. */
CREATE PROCEDURE procSearchProducts
  @SearchText varchar(255),
  @Low int,
  @High int
AS
  SELECT ProductID, ProductName from Product
   WHERE (ProductName LIKE '%' + @SearchText+ '%' OR
    ProductDescription LIKE '%' + @SearchText + '%') AND
    (ProductPrice >= @low and ProductPrice <= @High)
   ORDER BY ProductName
```

Site Searching

Searching is an interesting topic when it comes to websites. Two types of searches are typically found on websites. The first is the unstructured type of search that a typical site search accomplishes. Tools such as Microsoft Index Server "crawl" content files and then index key words in the content into a specialized database. Then a special query language is used to query the database. The second type is the database search, which is normally accomplished through languages such as SQL. Product searches in e-commerce stores are an example of a database search.

In an e-commerce site, especially one with lots of products, the search page may be one of the most popular pages. The designer can develop spiffy features such as tracking the key words on which shoppers search and building special key word fields into the database to increase the possibility of search hits. You can get even more sophisticated and use software that automatically recommends products based on what the shopper has been searching for. Amazon.com, for example, does this.

Continued on next page

You should give special focus to the search features of your e-commerce store. Although the traditional practice of browsing through departments, department products, and so on, is critical, don't overlook the important nature of the search. A good product database search can help shoppers find exactly what they are looking for—while the urge to buy is hot.

Figure 6.10 shows the site's search page. Note the three input fields. To build a sample search, type **jazz** in the search text box, **10** in the low price box, and **20** in the high price box.

FIGURE 6.10:

Search page

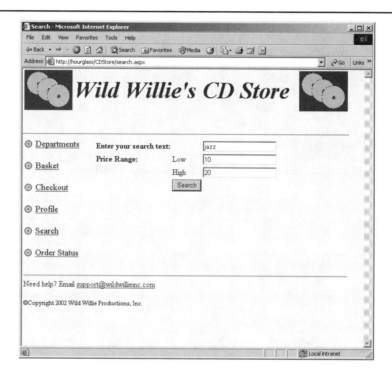

Figure 6.11 shows the results of the sample search. One product, "Alley Jazz," has been returned. Now the shopper can simply click the link and then be ready to buy.

FIGURE 6.11:

Search results

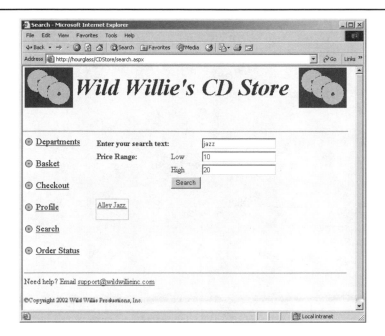

Summary

With the default, department, product, and search pages, we have built the core infrastructure for presenting the e-store to the shopper. This infrastructure is also where much of the marketing focus of a website is typically targeted, although we haven't done any promotional programming yet. In Part IV, "Promotions," you'll learn how to build promotions into your website.

There are two key concepts to note about the build of these pages. The first is the use of the include files to provide the overall framework of the pages. Using these files enables us to build a very encapsulated approach to the user interface that will be easy to change down the road.

The second concept is the implementation of the database structure. Using only stored procedures for data access insulates us from any possible changes to the database schema, without needing to do any Web Form reprogramming.

Now we're ready to build the other half of the store—the portion that supports the basket and checkout processes. In the next chapter, we'll tackle the basket management phase of the shopping process.

CHAPTER 7

Making a Basket Case

- Designing the Basket

- Adding Items

- Displaying the Basket

- Testing the Basket

N ow that we've built the functionality for finding products by either browsing or searching, it's time to turn our attention to the purchasing process. We'll start with the shopping basket. This is where we want the shopper to park products that they are interested in, allowing them to decide later which products they will ultimately purchase.

Designing the Basket

The shopping basket allows several key functions that make it a very dynamic aspect of the website. Table 7.1 shows the core functions that we'll be adding to the shopping basket section of the site.

TABLE 7.1: Basket Functionality

Core Function	Description
Add item to basket	When the shopper is on a product page and clicks the Order button, some magic needs to happen to add the product to the shopping basket. We need to keep track of key business rules as we add the product.
Display basket	When the shopper visits the basket page, we need to be able to list all the items the shopper has added to the basket and to display the quantities.
Update quantity of basket item	We need to allow the shopper to change the quantity of any item in their basket.
Remove item	If the shopper decides they don't want a certain item that's in their basket, we need to provide a method for removing the item.
Empty basket	If, for some reason, the shopper decides they just want to dump the whole thing, we can provide a function to empty the basket completely.

Figure 7.1 shows how the functions of the basket interact dynamically. At the top of the diagram, the shopper adds items to the basket. After that, the shopper can empty the basket, adjust quantities, or remove items. Let's dig into the programming that makes all of this work.

NOTE   We'll cover the final stages of placing an order in Chapter 8, "Checking Out.".

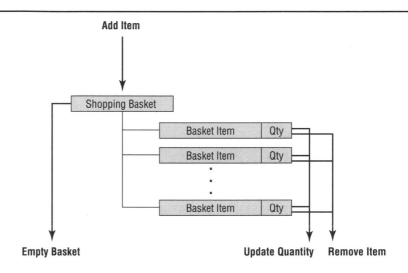

FIGURE 7.1:
Basket functions inter-
act dynamically.

Adding Items

The first step in the process is adding items to the basket. This page is called when the shopper clicks the Order button on the product page, as you saw in the preceding chapter. Note
that this page, AddItem.aspx, performs processing only—that is, it doesn't display any information directly to the shopper. When the page finishes adding the item, it redirects the
shopper's browser to the Basket.aspx page to display their basket. Listing 7.1 shows the code
for the event processing in AddItem.aspx.

Listing 7.1   AddItem.aspx.vb

```
Private Sub Page_Load(ByVal sender As System.Object, _
ByVal e As System.EventArgs) Handles MyBase.Load
    ' Check for a valid session ID
    Dim strError As String
    SessionCheck(Session, Request.Cookies("WWCD"), strError)

    ' Check to make sure the user supplied a quantity
    If Session("Quantity") = 0 Then
        ' No quantity? Go back where we came from
        Server.Transfer("Product.aspx?idProduct=" & Session("ProductID"))
    Else
        ' Ready to order this product, check to see if there
        ' is a basket for this session yet
        If CType(Session("idBasket"), String) = "" Then
            ' No basket yet, need to create one
```

```
                    cmdCreateBasket.Parameters("@ShopperID").Value = _
                     Session("idShopper")
                    cnn.Open()
                    cmdCreateBasket.ExecuteNonQuery()
                    Session("idBasket") = _
                     cmdCreateBasket.Parameters("@BasketID").Value
                    cnn.Close()
                End If
                ' When we get here, we will have a basket, either existing or new
                ' So insert or update the basket item
                cmdInsertBasketItem.Parameters("@BasketID").Value = _
                 Session("idBasket")
                cmdInsertBasketItem.Parameters("@Quantity").Value = _
                 Session("Quantity")
                cmdInsertBasketItem.Parameters("@Price").Value = _
                 Session("ProductPrice")
                cmdInsertBasketItem.Parameters("@ProductName").Value = _
                 Session("ProductName")
                cmdInsertBasketItem.Parameters("@ProductID").Value = _
                 Session("ProductID")
                cmdInsertBasketItem.Parameters("@Size").Value = _
                 Session("Size")
                cmdInsertBasketItem.Parameters("@Color").Value = _
                 Session("Color")
                cnn.Open()
                cmdInsertBasketItem.ExecuteNonQuery()
                cnn.Close()
                ' And take the user to their basket
                Server.Transfer("Basket.aspx")
            End If
    End Sub

    Private Sub Page_Error(ByVal sender As Object, _
      ByVal e As System.EventArgs) Handles MyBase.Error
        Dim strMessage As String = "<font face=verdana color=red>" & _
         "<h4>" & Request.Url.ToString() & "</h4>" & _
         "<pre><font color='red'>" & Server.GetLastError().ToString() & _
         "</pre></font>"
        Response.Write(strMessage)
    End Sub
```

As with the other ASP.NET pages in the CD store application, this one starts by calling the SessionCheck procedure to make sure that a session ID has been assigned to this session. It then checks to see if the quantity of product ordered was 0. We don't want to add the product to the basket if that is the case. If the quantity is 0, we send the shopper back to the product page, using the *ProductID* session variable to make sure that the correct product is loaded.

Two Ways to Transfer Control

The AddItem.aspx page uses the Server.Transfer method to transfer control to a different ASP.NET page. An alternative to this is the Response.Redirect method, which has the identical syntax. That is, the following two lines of code produce the same effect:

```
Server.Transfer("Basket.aspx")
Response.Redirect("Basket.aspx")
```

Although the two methods have the same ultimate effect, they are implemented differently. When the ASP.NET processor executes the Server.Transfer method, control is immediately transferred on the server to the specified page. The execution of the current page is terminated as soon as the Server.Transfer method is encountered. Response.Redirect, on the other hand, is a directive to the client web browser. ASP.NET continues to execute the code on the current page, but it sends the client a message telling it to load the new page.

In most cases, you'll want to use Server.Transfer to switch pages in an ASP.NET application. This is generally faster than performing a client-side redirect with Response.Redirect.

Next, we have to ensure that there is a basket for this order session. We can't insert a basket item without a basket. The code checks the *idBasket* session variable to see whether it has been initialized.

If it hasn't, we execute the procCreateBasket stored procedure. In order to create a new basket, we have to assign a shopper ID, so that it is passed into the stored procedure. Note that we need to explicitly open and close the connection that's used to execute the stored procedure.

TIP All the stored procedures used in this chapter were added to the appropriate ASP.NET pages with drag-and-drop from Server Explorer, and then renamed with the "cmd" prefix. For example, the procCreateBasket stored procedure is represented in code by a SqlCommand variable named *cmdCreateBasket*.

The procCreateBasket stored procedure, shown in Listing 7.2, has an output parameter that is set from the SQL Server *@@IDENTITY* system variable. This makes the new value of the BasketID column available in the output parameter. The code stores the value of this parameter in a session variable for future use.

Listing 7.2   **procCreateBasket Procedure**

```
/*  Creates a new basket and returns the ID
```

```
by Mike Gunderloy and Noel Jerke
Copyright 2002, Sybex Inc. All Rights Reserved. */
CREATE PROCEDURE procCreateBasket
/*  Pass in the ID of the shopper that
    the basket will belong to, and return
    the ID of the newly created basket
*/
  @ShopperID int,
  @BasketID int OUTPUT
AS
  INSERT INTO Basket(ShopperID)
    VALUES (@ShopperID)
  SELECT @BasketID = @@IDENTITY
```

After creating the basket (if necessary), we're ready to insert the item into the basket. There are two possibilities:

- The item isn't already in the basket. In that case, we need to add a new row to the BasketItem table to hold the new item.

- The item is already in the basket. In that case, we need to locate the current row in the BasketItem table and increase the quantity by the amount that the shopper is now ordering.

We could write code to check these situations and handle them separately, but that would require multiple trips to the database server. Instead, we use a single stored procedure, procInsertBasketItem, which can handle both situations. The code sets the parameters of this stored procedure from the session variables (which, in turn, were set by the Product.aspx page when the shopper clicked Order) and then calls the ExecuteNonQuery method of the SqlCommand object to execute the stored procedure. Listing 7.3 shows the procInsertBasketItem stored procedure.

TIP   In general, your code will run more quickly if you minimize the number of times that you switch control from one component to another. If, for example, you have multiple SQL Server operations to perform, you should write a single stored procedure to handle them all, rather than call multiple stored procedures (which would involve switching between .NET code and SQL Server code multiple times).

Listing 7.3   procInsertBasketItem Procedure

```
/* Insert an item into the shopper's basket.
   If they already have this item in their basket,
   increase the quantity for the item instead of
   adding a second instance

From .NET E-Commerce Programming
by Mike Gunderloy and Noel Jerke
```

```
Copyright 2002, Sybex Inc. All Rights Reserved. */
CREATE PROCEDURE procInsertBasketItem
/* Pass in the ID of the basket, quantity, price,
   product name, ID of the product,
   size of the product, and color
*/
  @BasketID int,
  @Quantity int,
  @Price money,
  @ProductName varchar(255),
  @ProductID int,
  @Size varchar(50) = NULL,
  @Color varchar(50) = NULL
AS
  DECLARE @Current int
  /* First, see if it's already in the basket */
  SELECT @Current = COUNT(*)
    FROM BasketItem
    WHERE BasketID = @BasketID AND ProductID = @ProductID
  IF @Current = 0
  /* Not already there, so insert it */
    INSERT INTO BasketItem(BasketID, BasketItemQuantity,
      BasketItemPrice, BasketItemProductName, ProductID,
      BasketItemSize, BasketItemColor)
    VALUES(@BasketID, @Quantity, @Price, @ProductName,
      @ProductID, @Size, @Color)
  ELSE
  /* Already there, update quantity */
    UPDATE BasketItem
      SET BasketItemQuantity = @Quantity + BasketItemQuantity
      WHERE BasketID = @BasketID AND ProductID = @ProductID
```

NOTE Many of the sample products in our database don't include the size or color attributes. If these attributes don't exist, nothing is returned from the corresponding session variables, and the fields will default to Null in the database.

Finally, after the item has been added or updated, the code transfers control to the Basket.aspx page, which you'll see in the next section.

Figure 7.2 shows a product page featuring "Joe Bob's Thimble Sounds." When the shopper clicks the Order button, the item will be added to the basket, which will then be displayed.

FIGURE 7.2:

Preparing to add a
product to the basket

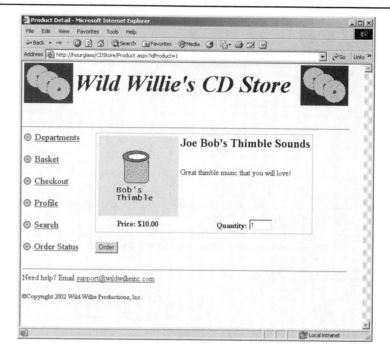

Figure 7.3 shows the basket after the item was added (we'll review the basket code in the next section). Note that the quantity shown is 1, since the shopper selected that quantity prior to adding the item.

Figure 7.4 shows the effect when the same item is added again. This time, the shopper has set the quantity to 3. Because that item is already in the basket, the code doesn't add it again; instead, the quantity of the existing item is simply updated to reflect the total quantity of 4.

Now that you've seen the basket, we'll take a look at the code that makes it work.

FIGURE 7.3:

Basket containing the product

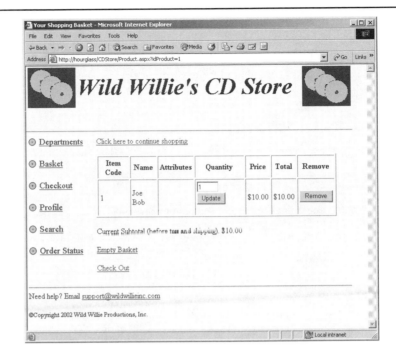

FIGURE 7.4:

The basket page with the quantity updated

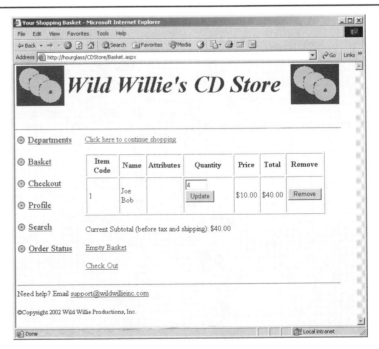

Displaying the Basket

The shopping basket displays a tabular list of all the items the shopper has selected. As you can see in Figure 7.4, the Basket.aspx page also includes some additional links and information, as well as controls to let the shopper update the quantity of an item or remove an item from the basket.

The Basket Web Form

Listing 7.4 shows the HTML code for the Basket.aspx page.

Listing 7.4   Basket.aspx

```
<%@ Page Language="vb" AutoEventWireup="false" Codebehind="Basket.aspx.vb"
  Inherits="CDStore.Basket"%>
<!DOCTYPE HTML PUBLIC "-//W3C//DTD HTML 4.0 Transitional//EN">
<HTML>
    <HEAD>
        <TITLE>Your Shopping Basket</TITLE>
    </HEAD>
    <!-- Basket.aspx - Display the contents of the shopper's basket -->
    <meta content="Microsoft Visual Studio.NET 7.0" name="GENERATOR">
    <meta content="Visual Basic 7.0" name="CODE_LANGUAGE">
    <meta content="JavaScript" name="vs_defaultClientScript">
    <meta content="http://schemas.microsoft.com/intellisense/ie5"
      name="vs_targetSchema">
    <!-- #Include File="Header.inc" -->
    <form id="Form1" method="post" runat="server">
        <font size="4">
            <P><asp:label id="lblEmpty" runat="server" Visible="False">
              Your basket is empty</asp:label></P>
            <P>
        </font>
        <asp:hyperlink id="hlDepartment" runat="server">
          Click here to continue shopping</asp:hyperlink>
        <P><asp:repeater id="rptBasket" runat="server">
              <HeaderTemplate>
                  <table border="1" cellpadding="3"
                    cellspacing="2" width="500">
                    <tr>
                        <th>
                            Item Code</th>
                        <th>
                            Name</th>
                        <th>
                            Attributes</th>
                        <th>
                            Quantity</th>
                        <th>
                            Price</th>
```

```
                    <th>
                        Total</th>
                    <th>
                        Remove</th>
                </tr>
            </HeaderTemplate>
            <ItemTemplate>
                <tr>
                    <td><%# DataBinder.Eval(Container.DataItem,
                        "ProductID") %></td>
                    <td><%# DataBinder.Eval(Container.DataItem,
                        "BasketItemProductName") %></td>
                    <!-- Show the product attributes -->
                    <td>
                        <%# DataBinder.Eval(Container.DataItem,
                            "BasketItemColor") %>
                         
                        <%# DataBinder.Eval(Container.DataItem,
                            "BasketItemSize") %>
                    </td>
                    <td>
                      <input type="text"
                        value='<%# DataBinder.Eval(Container.DataItem,
                        "BasketItemQuantity") %>'
                        name="quantity" size="2">
                      <input type="hidden"
                        value='<%# DataBinder.Eval(Container.DataItem,
                            "ProductID") %>' name="ProductID">
                      <asp:Button id="btnUpdate" runat="server"
                        Text="Update" CommandName="update">
                      </asp:Button></P>
                    </td>
                    <td><%# DataBinder.Eval(Container.DataItem,
                        "BasketItemPrice", "{0:c}") %></td>
                    <!-- Show the product total cost -->
                    <td><%# DataBinder.Eval(Container.DataItem,
                        "BasketItemTotal", "{0:c}") %>
                    </td>
                    <!-- Show the remove option --><td>
                    <input type="hidden"
                        value='<%# DataBinder.Eval(Container.DataItem,
                            "BasketItemID") %>' name="BasketItemID">
                    <asp:Button id="btnRemove"
                        runat="server" Text="Remove"
                        CommandName="remove"></asp:Button>
                    </td>
                </tr>
            </ItemTemplate>
            <FooterTemplate>
              </table>
            </FooterTemplate>
```

```
        </asp:repeater>
        <P></P>
        <P></P>
        <P>
            <asp:Label id="lblSubtotal" runat="server">
              Current Subtotal (before tax and shipping):</asp:Label></P>
        <P>
            <asp:LinkButton id="lbEmptyBasket" runat="server">
              Empty Basket</asp:LinkButton></P>
        <P>
            <asp:HyperLink id="hlCheckout" runat="server"
              NavigateUrl="Shipping.aspx">Check Out</asp:HyperLink></P>
    </form>
    <!-- #Include File="Footer.inc" -->
</HTML>
```

This page has the same general structure as the pages you saw in Chapter 6, "Building the User Interface": It includes the standard header and footer files that all the pages on the site use. The first thing that gets displayed on the page is a label control, with the ID value of lblEmpty, that informs the user when their shopping basket is empty. A bit later, you'll see that we can toggle the Visible property of this control from code so that it displays when we need it.

The next control on the page is a hyperlink control named hlDepartment. This control, too, will be customized in code.

E-Commerce Store Navigation

We have built into our store's core a navigation structure that allows the shopper to move back and forth between the shopping, basket, and checkout pages.

The link back to the department on the basket page helps to facilitate the shopping process that the shopper was following. In a bricks-and-mortar store, of course, we wouldn't make the shopper go to a basket somewhere else and then walk all the way back to the department they were in. This link makes it easy for the shopper to continue where they left off.

There are some other elements of the navigation process that we might want to consider. For example, many online stores implement a forward/back feature on the product page to allow the shopper to move back and forth between products without navigating back to the department page.

Other possibilities would involve selling products in groups. For example, if we were selling a selection of bedding, many shoppers would buy a complete set (for example, pillowcases, sheets, and a blanket). In that case, we might have other product templates that would allow multiple products to be displayed on one page and purchased in one group.

Continued on next page

Considering these navigational issues is one of the keys to ensuring that your shoppers have the best experience while navigating your store. The navigational requirements are somewhat dependent on the types of products being sold, but many of the principles outlined here can be applied widely.

The main section of the page, dealing with the table of items in the basket, is implemented as a Repeater control. You can think of the Repeater as a sort of lightweight DataList control. It's not as flexible as the DataList, but it does a fine job of displaying tabular information. Like the DataList, the Repeater control includes multiple templates that are filled in with data at runtime. Table 7.2 lists the templates that are available in a Repeater control.

TABLE 7.2: Repeater Control Templates

Template	Use
HeaderTemplate	Output once at the start of the control. You can't use data-bound elements in the HeaderTemplate.
ItemTemplate	Output once for each row in the data source that's attached to the control.
AlternatingItemTemplate	Output once for each alternate row in the data source that's attached to the control.
SeparatorTemplate	Output once between each row of data. You can't use data-bound elements in the SeparatorTemplate.
FooterTemplate	Output once at the end of the control. You can't use data-bound elements in the FooterTemplate.

The Repeater control on the `Basket.aspx` page is fairly typical. It uses the HeaderTemplate to render an opening `<table>` tag and a table header, the ItemTemplate to render rows of the table, and the FooterTemplate to render the closing `</table>` tag.

Within the ItemTemplate, the Repeater control uses the same data-binding syntax that you're already familiar with from the DataList controls that you've seen. Later in the chapter, we'll take a look at the SQL query that supplies data for these items.

In addition to the bound data, the ItemTemplate contains several other objects. There are three standard HTML input controls. One of these, the quantity control, displays the quantity being ordered in a text box. The other two controls are hidden and are used to store the product ID and basket item ID for the current row. There are also two ASP.NET button controls, which the shopper can use to update quantities or delete items entirely.

TIP   You can use an HTML input control to display bound data within a template-based control (such as a DataList or Repeater), as demonstrated in this example. You can't use an ASP.NET text box control for this purpose; you'll get an error message if you try.

There are three other controls on the page after the Repeater control:

- The lblSubtotal label control displays the total cost of the items in the shopper's basket. We'll set the amount in this control at runtime.

- The lbEmptyBasket control is used to empty the shopper's basket.

- The hlCheckout control is a standard hyperlink control that will take the shopper to the Shipping.aspx page to begin the checkout process.

Three Kinds of Buttons

The ASP.NET Web Forms Toolbox provides three different button controls:

- The *Button* control is displayed as a standard push button.

- The *LinkButton* control is displayed as a hyperlink.

- The *ImageButton* control is displayed as an image.

Although these three controls look different, they have exactly the same functionality. A LinkButton control triggers a click event; it doesn't act as a hyperlink. Because users are accustomed to clicking hyperlinks to carry out actions in a web application, the LinkButton can be used (as it is here) as a way to attach functionality without displaying a standard button.

Code behind the Basket

As you've probably guessed, there's a fair amount of code behind the Basket.aspx page. Listing 7.5 shows the Page_Load procedure, which is called every time the page is loaded.

Listing 7.5   **Basket.aspx.vb Page_Load Procedure**

```
Private Sub Page_Load(ByVal sender As System.Object, _
   ByVal e As System.EventArgs) Handles MyBase.Load
      If Not IsPostBack Then
         ' Check for a valid session ID
         Dim strError As String
         SessionCheck(Session, Request.Cookies("WWCD"), strError)
         ' Make sure there IS a basket by checking basket ID, and
         ' creating one if necessary
```

```
        If CType(Session("idBasket"), String) = "" Then
            ' No basket yet, need to create one
            cmdCreateBasket.Parameters("@ShopperID").Value = _
             Session("idShopper")
            cnn.Open()
            cmdCreateBasket.ExecuteNonQuery()
            Session("idBasket") = _
             cmdCreateBasket.Parameters("@BasketID").Value
            cnn.Close()
        End If
        UpdatePage()
    End If
End Sub
```

This procedure starts by checking the *IsPostBack* variable to make sure that it's executed only the first time the page is loaded. It then carries out the standard check for a session ID and creates a basket ID if necessary. Finally, it calls a procedure named UpdatePage, shown in Listing 7.6.

Listing 7.6   **Basket.aspx.vb UpdatePage Procedure**

```
Private Sub UpdatePage()
    ' Update the various bits of the user interface
    ' Get the current basket contents
    cmdRetrieveBasket.Parameters("@BasketID").Value = _
     Session("idBasket")
    Dim dsBasket As New DataSet()
    Dim daBasket As New SqlDataAdapter()
    daBasket.SelectCommand = cmdRetrieveBasket
    daBasket.Fill(dsBasket, "BasketItems")
    rptBasket.DataSource = dsBasket
    rptBasket.DataMember = "BasketItems"
    ' And bind it all to the user interface
    DataBind()
    ' Check to see whether the basket is empty
    If dsBasket.Tables("BasketItems").Rows.Count = 0 Then
        lblEmpty.Visible = True
        rptBasket.Visible = False
    Else
        lblEmpty.Visible = False
        rptBasket.Visible = True
    End If
    ' Set up the department hyperlink
    If Session("LastIDDept") <> "" Then
        hlDepartment.NavigateUrl = "Products.aspx?idDept=" & _
         Session("LastIDDept")
    Else
        hlDepartment.Visible = False
    End If
```

```
' Fill in the subtotal
cmdBasketSubtotal.Parameters("@BasketID").Value = _
 Session("idBasket")
cnn.Open()
lblSubtotal.Text = "Current Subtotal (before tax and shipping): " & _
 Format(cmdBasketSubtotal.ExecuteScalar, "Currency")
cnn.Close()
End Sub
```

The UpdatePage procedure handles all of the user interface updates for the page. The reason that we've split this off into a separate procedure is to avoid duplicating code; this procedure is called from several other events, as you'll see later in this section. The first thing that the UpdatePage procedure does is call the procRetrieveBasket procedure, shown in Listing 7.7, to get the contents of the current shopping basket.

Listing 7.7   **procRetrieveBasket Procedure**

```
/*  Retrieve the contents of a specified basket by BasketID

From .NET E-Commerce Programming
by Mike Gunderloy and Noel Jerke
Copyright 2002, Sybex Inc. All Rights Reserved. */
CREATE PROCEDURE procRetrieveBasket
  @BasketID int
AS
 SELECT ProductID, BasketItemProductName, BasketItemColor, BasketItemSize,
   BasketItemPrice, BasketItemQuantity, BasketItemID,
   BasketItemPrice * BasketItemQuantity AS BasketItemTotal
   FROM BasketItem
   WHERE BasketID = @BasketID
```

As you can see, the procRetrieveBasket procedure performs the necessary calculation to get the total for the item (by multiplying the price by the quantity). By returning this as a single column, the stored procedure makes it easy to bind this calculated total to a field inside the Repeater control.

After creating a DataSet from this stored procedure and binding it to the Repeater control, the UpdatePage procedure calls the DataBind method to display the table of data on the page. But that's not the end of the user interface update process. This procedure performs several other tasks:

- If there aren't any items in the basket, it sets the Visible properties of the controls to display the empty basket message and hide the Repeater control.

- If there are items in the basket, it sets the Visible properties of the controls to hide the empty basket message and display the Repeater control.

- If there is a value in the *LastIDDept* session variable, it uses this value to build the hyperlink to the department by setting the NavigateUrl property of the hlDepartment control.

- It calls the procBasketSubtotal stored procedure to calculate the subtotal for the items in the basket and uses this to build the Text property for the lblSubtotal control. Listing 7.8 shows this stored procedure.

Listing 7.8   **procBasketSubtotal Procedure**

```
/*  Get the subtotal for a basket

From .NET E-Commerce Programming
by Mike Gunderloy and Noel Jerke
Copyright 2002, Sybex Inc. All Rights Reserved. */
CREATE PROCEDURE procBasketSubtotal
  @BasketID money
AS
  DECLARE @Subtotal money
  SELECT @Subtotal = SUM(BasketItemQuantity * BasketItemPrice)
    FROM BasketItem
    WHERE BasketID = @BasketID
  IF @Subtotal IS NULL
    SELECT 0
  ELSE
    SELECT @Subtotal
```

Note that the procBasketSubtotal stored procedure includes code to return zero rather than Null for the subtotal of an empty basket. That makes it possible to format the returned value as currency, for display on the user interface, no matter what the value is. You can't format a Null value as currency directly.

Handling Item Commands

If you look again at Figure 7.4, you'll see that each row of the Repeater control contains two buttons. These are referred to as *item commands*. The Repeater control provides a single event procedure to handle all of the item commands. Listing 7.9 shows this event procedure.

TIP   You can also use item commands in a DataList control.

Listing 7.9   **Basket.aspx.vb rptBasket_ItemCommand Procedure**

```
Private Sub rptBasket_ItemCommand(ByVal source As System.Object, _
  ByVal e As System.Web.UI.WebControls.RepeaterCommandEventArgs) _
  Handles rptBasket.ItemCommand
    ' Handle button clicks within the Repeater control
```

```
    If (e.CommandName = "update") Then
        ' To update quantity, call the procBasketItemQuantity
        ' stored procedure
        cmdUpdateBasketItemQuantity.Parameters("@BasketID").Value = _
          CType(Session("idBasket"), Integer)
        cmdUpdateBasketItemQuantity.Parameters("@ProductID").Value = _
          CType(Split(Request("ProductID"), ",")(e.Item.ItemIndex), Integer)
        cmdUpdateBasketItemQuantity.Parameters("@Quantity").Value = _
          CType(Split(Request("Quantity"), ",")(e.Item.ItemIndex), Integer)
        cnn.Open()
        cmdUpdateBasketItemQuantity.ExecuteNonQuery()
        cnn.Close()
    ElseIf (e.CommandName = "remove") Then
        ' To remove an item, call the procRemoveBasketItem
        ' stored procedure
        cmdRemoveBasketItem.Parameters("@BasketID").Value = _
          Session("idBasket")
        cmdRemoveBasketItem.Parameters("@BasketItemID").Value = _
          CType(Split(Request("BasketItemID"), ",")(e.Item.ItemIndex), _
          Integer)
        cnn.Open()
        cmdRemoveBasketItem.ExecuteNonQuery()
        cnn.Close()
    End If
    ' Update the user interface to show the changes
    UpdatePage()
End Sub
```

The ItemCommand event procedure can determine which button was clicked within the Repeater control by examining the value of the e.CommandName property. If you refer to the HTML code in Listing 7.4, you'll see those CommandName properties assigned as part of the tags that define the button controls. If the shopper clicks the Update button, the code calls the procUpdateBasketItemQuantity stored procedure, shown in Listing 7.10, to update the quantity of the chosen item in the basket. This stored procedure uses a SQL UPDATE statement to locate and change the correct row of data.

Listing 7.10   **procUpdateBasketItemQuantity Procedure**

```
From .NET E-Commerce Programming
by Mike Gunderloy and Noel Jerke
Copyright 2002, Sybex Inc. All Rights Reserved. */
CREATE PROCEDURE procUpdateBasketItemQuantity
  @BasketID int,
  @ProductID int,
  @Quantity int
AS
```

```
UPDATE BasketItem
SET BasketItemQuantity = @Quantity
WHERE BasketID = @BasketID AND ProductID = @ProductID
```

You'll notice some peculiar expressions involved in retrieving values for the parameters of the stored procedures. For instance, the `@Quantity` parameter of the procUpdateBasketItemQuantity stored procedure is set using this expression:

```
CType(Split(Request("Quantity"), ",")(e.Item.ItemIndex), Integer)
```

This expression is necessary because ASP.NET does not automatically return the values of other controls in the selected row as part of the Request object. Instead, the Request object returns a comma-separated list of values. For instance, if there are two items in the basket, with quantities of 3 and 4, `Request("Quantity")` will return the string "3,4".

One of the event procedure's arguments, named *e*, has some information about the Repeater control. The e.Item property returns a RepeaterItem object representing the row of data in which the shopper clicked. You can't get at the particular element you need from the Request item directly through this object, but you can retrieve its index in the control. So, for example, if the shopper clicks the Update button in the second row of the control, `e.Item.ItemIndex` returns 1 (the index is zero-based).

The Split function takes a string and a separator and returns an array of elements from the original string, broken at instances of the separator. If the original string is "3,4" and the separator character is ",", the array returned has two elements, the first being "3" and the second being "4". This array also has a zero-based index.

Finally, the CType() function is used to convert a string value to an integer value. This is necessary because the stored procedure expects integer parameters, not string parameters.

So, to sum things up, you could read the original expression as follows:

1. Use the Request object to get the value of the Quantity control from the Repeater.

2. Use the Split function to split this value into an array of individual values.

3. Use the e.Item.ItemIndex property to locate the desired member of this array.

4. Use the CType() function to convert the located member to an integer.

If the shopper clicks the Remove button, the code calls the procRemoveBasketItem stored procedure, which uses a SQL DELETE statement to delete the entire row of data from the underlying table. Listing 7.11 shows this stored procedure.

Listing 7.11   **procRemoveBasketItem Procedure**

```
/*  Remove a particular item from the basket

From .NET E-Commerce Programming
by Mike Gunderloy and Noel Jerke
Copyright 2002, Sybex Inc. All Rights Reserved. */
CREATE PROCEDURE procRemoveBasketItem
   @BasketID int,
   @BasketItemID int
AS
   DELETE BasketItem
   WHERE BasketID = @BasketID AND BasketItemID = @BasketItemID
```

The final bit of code in the Basket.aspx.vb code-behind file handles clicks on the Empty Basket LinkButton control. Remember that although this control is displayed as a hyperlink, it actually functions as a button. The code triggered by clicking this control is shown in Listing 7.12.

Listing 7.12   **Basket.aspx.vb lbEmptyBasket_Click Procedure**

```
Private Sub lbEmptyBasket_Click(ByVal sender As Object, _
  ByVal e As System.EventArgs) Handles lbEmptyBasket.Click
     ' Call the procClearBasketItems stored procedure to
     ' clear the current shopping basket
     cmdClearBasketItems.Parameters("@BasketID").Value = _
       Session("idBasket")
     cnn.Open()
     cmdClearBasketItems.ExecuteNonQuery()
     cnn.Close()
     ' And update the user interface
     UpdatePage()
End Sub
```

This event procedure calls the procClearBasketItems stored procedure, which uses a SQL DELETE statement to remove all matching rows from the BasketItem table. Listing 7.13 shows this stored procedure.

Listing 7.13   **procClearBasketItems Procedure**

```
/*  Clear all items from a basket

From .NET E-Commerce Programming
by Mike Gunderloy and Noel Jerke
Copyright 2002, Sybex Inc. All Rights Reserved. */
CREATE PROCEDURE procClearBasketItems
```

```
    @BasketID int
AS
    DELETE FROM BasketItem
    WHERE BasketID = @BasketID
```

Now you've seen the code that makes the basket functional. Figure 7.5 shows the basket with several items already chosen by the shopper. Note the different quantities for the items and the Total column, which shows the multiplied price. A subtotal for the entire basket appears below the table. Also note the link *Click here to continue shopping*; that will take the shopper back to the department in which they were shopping.

NOTE   We're showing only the subtotal, exclusive of tax and shipping charges, in the basket. The shipping and tax will be added during the checkout process. If your store has large shipping costs or unusual tax requirements, it may be prudent to show these charges at the basket level; but in many cases, this will require the shopper to enter at least a shipping and/or billing zip code.

FIGURE 7.5:

Basket page

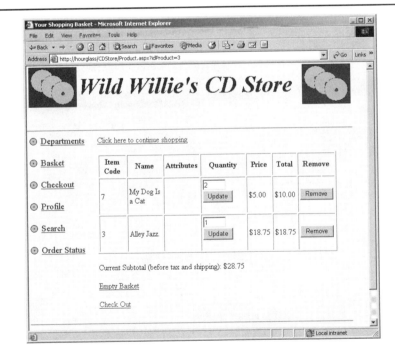

Testing the Basket

Now that we've built the shopping basket, it's a good idea to test all of its functionality. This includes updating the quantity of an item, removing an item entirely, and emptying the basket.

Updating the Basket

The first function to check is updating the quantity of an item. We can start with the basket shown in Figure 7.5, which contains two copies of "My Dog Is a Cat" and one copy of "Alley Jazz." (To create this basket, of course, you need to navigate to the appropriate departments, enter quantities for the desired items, and click Order each time.) Change the quantity of "Alley Jazz" to 3 and click the Update button. Figure 7.6 shows the result. Note that both the total for the item and the subtotal for the overall basket are updated.

FIGURE 7.6:

Updated basket

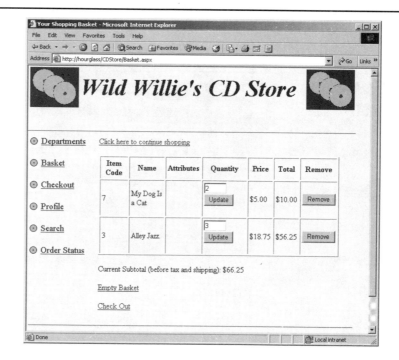

Deleting from the Basket

The next thing to check is that the shopper can properly remove items from the basket. Starting with the basket shown in Figure 7.6, click the Remove button in the row for "My Dog Is a Cat." The result is shown in Figure 7.7.

FIGURE 7.7:

An item has been
removed from the
basket.

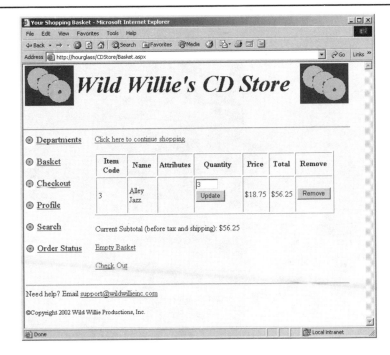

Note that the subtotal is once again updated and the remaining item, "Alley Jazz," is unchanged.

Emptying the Basket

The last function that we need to check is the ability of the shopper to empty the shopping basket completely. Click the Empty Basket hyperlink. Figure 7.8 shows that all the items have been removed from the basket. In this case, the shopper sees the default message indicating that the basket is empty.

The basket has been cleared of all items.

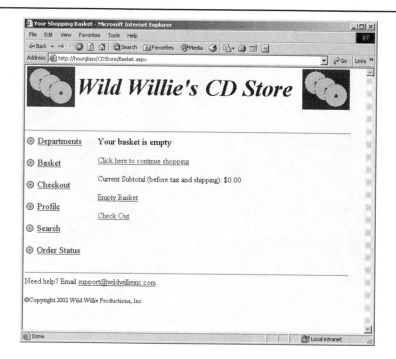

Summary

In the last chapter, we explored the basic functions of browsing through departments and products and executing searches. These functions are the key focus of the shopper's initial activities in the online store.

This chapter dealt with the shopping basket and its role in the e-commerce process. The shopping basket is a key tool in the online shopping experience; it's the tool that the shopper uses to keep track of their interests and to manage the items that they will ultimately purchase. It's also the stepping-off point for making the purchase.

In the next chapter, we'll explore the next phase of the process: checking out. We'll deal with validation issues, calculate shipping and taxes, and generally ensure that the order is executed properly.

CHAPTER 8

Checking Out

- Defining the Checkout Process

- Defining the Shopper Profile Process

- Loading Tax and Shipping Data

- The Shipping Page

- Calculating Shipping and Taxes

- The Payment Page

- Processing the Order

- The Confirmation Page

We've finally come to the stage where the shopper is ready to check out and place their order. It's important at this stage to make the process as smooth and seamless as possible and to ensure that all data is captured correctly. In this chapter, we'll look at the pages that manage the actual purchase process. Chapter 9, "Order Status and Profile Management," will cover the pages that let the customer follow up on their shopping experience.

Defining the Checkout Process

Although the user interface for the checkout process is easy for the shopper to understand, there is a lot going on behind the scenes. Table 8.1 lists and describes the pages involved in this process.

TABLE 8.1: Checkout Process

Page	Description
Shipping.aspx	The first step is for the shopper to enter the shipping information for the order. Taxes and shipping fees can't be calculated until we've collected this information. As soon as the shopper submits their data, we will need to validate it. We need to ensure that all of the appropriate data has been entered to make the order complete.
Payment.aspx	The payment page is where the shopper enters their billing information as well as their credit card data. This page also displays the shipping and taxes for the order. As with the shipping data, we will need to validate the billing data.
Confirmation.aspx	Once the shopper has successfully completed the order, the confirmation page will return the shopper's order number and invite them to continue shopping.

Figure 8.1 shows a diagram of the checkout process. Although the process is fairly straightforward, it also contains the core of the business-rule logic behind the e-commerce store.

The checkout process starts with the shopping basket. As shown in the figure, the shipping is the next step, and then the validation is done on the shipping data. If there is an error in the shipping information, the shopper is sent back to the shipping page, where the error is stated.

When the shopper jumps to the payment process, we'll calculate the tax and shipping fee. We'll do this by calling a Web Service that will provide the necessary data, given the details about the shopper's order.

The payment phase follows in the same fashion as the shipping phase. The shopper will enter their payment data, which will then be validated. If the validation is successful, an e-mail receipt will be sent to the shopper, and the confirmation page will appear.

FIGURE 8.1:

Checkout process

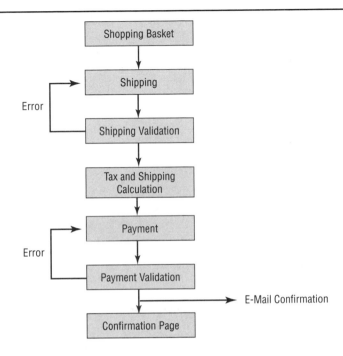

Checkout Page Approaches

Although the processes modeled in our sample store are pretty standard, there are many variations on the theme. In our example, we'll allow shipping to Canada or Mexico, but the checkout process will be the same for all addresses. Many stores provide different checkout processes based on whether they are serving an international shopper or a domestic one.

Another approach is to combine the shipping and payment pages into one page. In that case, it's important to give the shopper the option of making the billing data the same as the shipping data so the shopper doesn't have to rekey data. If this approach is taken, the shipping and tax calculations should still be shown at some point in the checkout process.

Some online stores, such as Amazon.com, provide sophisticated checkout processes in which multiple addresses and payment options are remembered to facilitate easy purchasing. Also, Amazon.com and other stores provide features such as one-click shopping to make buying as simple as possible.

Defining the Shopper Profile Process

Another key part of the shopping process is storing the shopper information in a profile. The basic idea behind the profile is to remember the shopper's data down the road in order to minimize rekeying in the checkout process and to facilitate the shopper's retrieval of an order status once their order is placed. Also, if the shopper wishes to keep a cookie on their system, the shopper's previous basket will be retrieved (if that basket wasn't converted to a completed order).

You may remember that the navigation bar contains a hyperlink labeled *Profile*. That link allows the shopper to edit an existing profile. The profile is created when the shopper first enters the checkout process. At that time, the shopper has the option of saving their profile. Table 8.2 shows the key profile functions.

TABLE 8.2: Profile Functions

Core Function	Description
Create Profile	A shopper profile is created when the shopper enters the checkout process. On the payment page, they will have the option of creating a new profile or updating an existing one.
Retrieve Profile	If the shopper has a cookie, their profile will be retrieved automatically upon return to the store. It will also be retrieved when the shopper enters their username and password.
Edit Profile	When a profile exists for the shopper, they can edit it by selecting the option on the navigation bar. They also will edit their profile every time they place an order.
E-Mail Password	If the shopper wishes to retrieve the profile (or order history), they will need to enter their username and password. If they have forgotten their password, they can have it e-mailed to them.

Figure 8.2 shows the points where the profile is used in the shopping process.

As the figure shows, the profile data interacts with the shopping process in a number of ways. We have direct pages for editing the profile data. The basket page will retrieve a previous in-process basket if the shopper has one. The checkout pages will provide a vehicle for retrieving and updating the data. And, finally, the shopper will be able to retrieve their order history through their profile as well.

NOTE   We'll discuss some of these processes in more detail in Chapter 9.

FIGURE 8.2:

Profile data interaction

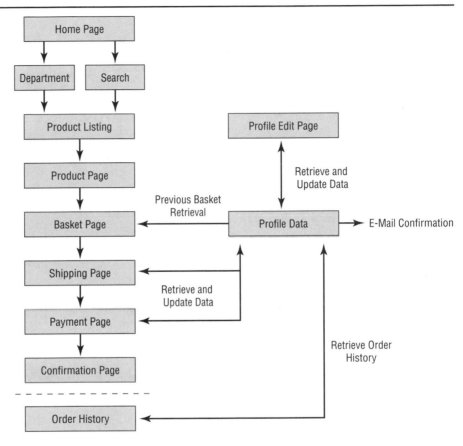

Profile-related code turns up on a number of pages in our application. The Header.inc page (as noted in earlier chapters) will look for a shopper cookie to retrieve shopper data. There are also other ways to retrieve a profile; these are summarized in Table 8.3.

TABLE 8.3: Profile Retrieval Scenarios

Scenario	Description
No cookie	If there is no cookie, the shopper can supply a username and password to retrieve an existing profile. If they choose not to do so, the system will create a new profile for them.
Cookie	The Header.inc page will retrieve the ID of the shopper from the cookie. Then a check is done to see if an existing unfinished basket is available.

Continued on next page

TABLE 8.3 CONTINUED: Profile Retrieval Scenarios

Scenario	Description
No cookie—username and password are entered	If the shopper has no cookie but retrieves a previous profile, only the billing and shipping information will be retrieved. We don't want to overwrite any basket the shopper may have in progress by retrieving a previous basket that was unfinished.
No previous profile	If there was no previous profile, a profile will be created when the shopper checks out, regardless of whether they enter a password for later retrieval. They will be able to retrieve the profile only if they enter a password.

The profiling done in our sample store is really just the beginning of what is possible. By tracking order history, shopping history, and so on, we have many options available for targeting the shopper with additional data down the road and for analyzing shopping patterns.

TIP   If you wish to test different scenarios for how shopper profile data is retrieved, be sure to look in the local cookies folder for the Wild Willie cookie. That can be deleted to clear any automatic retrieval. The way cookies are stored varies by browser and browser version; for specific instructions, refer to the documentation or help files that came with your browser.

Loading Tax and Shipping Data

For the checkout process, we need to set up our data for tax and shipping calculations. Recall that we have two tables in the database for storing this data.

The Shipping table stores the shipping data. The calculation of the shipping fee is based on a low item quantity and a high item quantity, and each quantity range has a specific price.

Listing 8.1 shows the SQL statements that we used to set up the initial shipping data. In the sample shipping data, we have four levels of shipping costs. Note that the last level is essentially a set price for all orders containing 31 items or more.

Listing 8.1   **Loading the Shipping Table**

```
INSERT INTO Shipping (ShippingLowQuantity,
 ShippingHighQuantity, ShippingFee)
 VALUES (1, 10, 2)
INSERT INTO Shipping (ShippingLowQuantity,
 ShippingHighQuantity, ShippingFee)
 VALUES (11, 20, 4)
INSERT INTO Shipping (ShippingLowQuantity,
```

```
ShippingHighQuantity, ShippingFee)
VALUES (21, 30, 6)
INSERT INTO Shipping (ShippingLowQuantity,
ShippingHighQuantity, ShippingFee)
VALUES (31, 999999, 8)
```

TIP   The ShippingRates.sql file on the companion CD contains these SQL statements.

For the tax data, the database contains a table named *Tax*, which stores a value for each state. To start, we'll set specific tax rates for only two states, Virginia and Texas; we'll set all the other states to a default tax rate of zero. This setup is done by the SQL statements shown in Listing 8.2.

Listing 8.2   Loading the Tax Table

```
INSERT INTO Tax (TaxState, TaxRate)
VALUES ('AL', 0)
INSERT INTO Tax (TaxState, TaxRate)
VALUES ('AK', 0)
INSERT INTO Tax (TaxState, TaxRate)
VALUES ('AZ', 0)
INSERT INTO Tax (TaxState, TaxRate)
VALUES ('AR', 0)
INSERT INTO Tax (TaxState, TaxRate)
VALUES ('CA', 0)
INSERT INTO Tax (TaxState, TaxRate)
VALUES ('CO', 0)
INSERT INTO Tax (TaxState, TaxRate)
VALUES ('CT', 0)
INSERT INTO Tax (TaxState, TaxRate)
VALUES ('DE', 0)
INSERT INTO Tax (TaxState, TaxRate)
VALUES ('DC', 0)
INSERT INTO Tax (TaxState, TaxRate)
VALUES ('FL', 0)
INSERT INTO Tax (TaxState, TaxRate)
VALUES ('GA', 0)
INSERT INTO Tax (TaxState, TaxRate)
VALUES ('HI', 0)
INSERT INTO Tax (TaxState, TaxRate)
VALUES ('ID', 0)
INSERT INTO Tax (TaxState, TaxRate)
VALUES ('IL', 0)
INSERT INTO Tax (TaxState, TaxRate)
VALUES ('IN', 0)
INSERT INTO Tax (TaxState, TaxRate)
VALUES ('IA', 0)
INSERT INTO Tax (TaxState, TaxRate)
```

```
 VALUES ('KS', 0)
INSERT INTO Tax (TaxState, TaxRate)
 VALUES ('KY', 0)
INSERT INTO Tax (TaxState, TaxRate)
 VALUES ('LA', 0)
INSERT INTO Tax (TaxState, TaxRate)
 VALUES ('ME', 0)
INSERT INTO Tax (TaxState, TaxRate)
 VALUES ('MD', 0)
INSERT INTO Tax (TaxState, TaxRate)
 VALUES ('MA', 0)
INSERT INTO Tax (TaxState, TaxRate)
 VALUES ('MI', 0)
INSERT INTO Tax (TaxState, TaxRate)
 VALUES ('MN', 0)
INSERT INTO Tax (TaxState, TaxRate)
 VALUES ('MS', 0)
INSERT INTO Tax (TaxState, TaxRate)
 VALUES ('MO', 0)
INSERT INTO Tax (TaxState, TaxRate)
 VALUES ('MT', 0)
INSERT INTO Tax (TaxState, TaxRate)
 VALUES ('NE', 0)
INSERT INTO Tax (TaxState, TaxRate)
 VALUES ('NV', 0)
INSERT INTO Tax (TaxState, TaxRate)
 VALUES ('NH', 0)
INSERT INTO Tax (TaxState, TaxRate)
 VALUES ('NJ', 0)
INSERT INTO Tax (TaxState, TaxRate)
 VALUES ('NM', 0)
INSERT INTO Tax (TaxState, TaxRate)
 VALUES ('NY', 0)
INSERT INTO Tax (TaxState, TaxRate)
 VALUES ('NC', 0)
INSERT INTO Tax (TaxState, TaxRate)
 VALUES ('ND', 0)
INSERT INTO Tax (TaxState, TaxRate)
 VALUES ('OH', 0)
INSERT INTO Tax (TaxState, TaxRate)
 VALUES ('OK', 0)
INSERT INTO Tax (TaxState, TaxRate)
 VALUES ('OR', 0)
INSERT INTO Tax (TaxState, TaxRate)
 VALUES ('PA', 0)
INSERT INTO Tax (TaxState, TaxRate)
 VALUES ('RI', 0)
INSERT INTO Tax (TaxState, TaxRate)
 VALUES ('SC', 0)
INSERT INTO Tax (TaxState, TaxRate)
 VALUES ('SD', 0)
```

```
INSERT INTO Tax (TaxState, TaxRate)
 VALUES ('TN', 0)
INSERT INTO Tax (TaxState, TaxRate)
 VALUES ('TX', .08)
INSERT INTO Tax (TaxState, TaxRate)
 VALUES ('UT', 0)
INSERT INTO Tax (TaxState, TaxRate)
 VALUES ('VT', 0)
INSERT INTO Tax (TaxState, TaxRate)
 VALUES ('VA', .045)
INSERT INTO Tax (TaxState, TaxRate)
 VALUES ('WA', 0)
INSERT INTO Tax (TaxState, TaxRate)
 VALUES ('WV', 0)
INSERT INTO Tax (TaxState, TaxRate)
 VALUES ('WI', 0)
INSERT INTO Tax (TaxState, TaxRate)
 VALUES ('WY', 0)
```

TIP The TaxRates.sql file on the companion CD contains these SQL statements.

As we noted in Chapter 3, "E-Commerce Database Design," there are many options for calculating the tax and shipping fee. For example, if there are more than 31 items in the shopping basket, we may wish to instead calculate the shipping fee based on a percentage of the order total or some other method.

Later in this chapter, we'll build an ASP.NET Web Service for tax and shipping calculations. This Web Service will encapsulate the rules for calculating tax and shipping. The idea is that down the road, we may need to change how our tax and shipping business rules work. If that happens, we'll be able to change our underlying database structure and the code in the Web Service to handle the new rules, without having to worry about changing our front-end shopper code.

Now that you have an overview of all the facets of the checkout process, shopper profiling, and the tax and shipping business rules, we're ready to dive into the code to see how all of this will work.

The Shipping Page

The first step in our checkout process is collecting the shipping information from the shopper. Figure 8.3 shows the Shipping.aspx page open in the designer.

Designing the shipping page

The HTML code for this page, shown in Listing 8.3, is straightforward. For the most part, it's composed of a set of Web Form controls in a table structure, along with associated validation controls.

Listing 8.3   Shipping.aspx

```
<%@ Page Language="vb" AutoEventWireup="false"
 Codebehind="Shipping.aspx.vb"
 Inherits="CDStore.Shipping"%>
<!DOCTYPE HTML PUBLIC "-//W3C//DTD HTML 4.0 Transitional//EN">
<HTML>
    <HEAD>
        <TITLE>Shipping</TITLE>
    </HEAD>
    <meta content="Microsoft Visual Studio.NET 7.0" name="GENERATOR">
    <meta content="Visual Basic 7.0" name="CODE_LANGUAGE">
    <meta content="JavaScript" name="vs_defaultClientScript">
    <meta content="http://schemas.microsoft.com/intellisense/ie5"
     name="vs_targetSchema">
    <!-- Shipping.aspx - Retrieve or enter shipping data for the user -->
    <!-- #Include File="Header.inc" -->
    <form id="Form1" method="post" runat="server">
        <P align="center"><font size="5"><b>Shipping Information</b></font>
```

```
        </P>
        <P><asp:hyperlink id="hlProfile" runat="server" Visible="False"
            NavigateUrl="Profile.aspx">
            Click here to retrieve an existing profile</asp:hyperlink></P>
<P><asp:label id="lblInstructions" runat="server">
            Enter your shipping address
            </asp:label></P>
        <P><asp:validationsummary id="ValidationSummary1" runat="server">
            </asp:validationsummary></P>
        <P>
            <TABLE id="Table1" cellSpacing="2" cellPadding="2" width="100%"
            border="0">
                <TR>
                    <TD>
                        <P align="right"><asp:requiredfieldvalidator
                        id="RequiredFieldValidator1" runat="server"
                        ErrorMessage="You must enter a first name."
                        ControlToValidate="txtFirstName">*
                        </asp:requiredfieldvalidator>First Name</P>
                    </TD>
                    <TD><asp:textbox id="txtFirstName" runat="server"
                     Width="394px"></asp:textbox></TD>
                </TR>
                <TR>
                    <TD>
                        <P align="right"><asp:requiredfieldvalidator
                        id="RequiredFieldValidator2" runat="server"
                        ErrorMessage="You must enter a last name."
                        ControlToValidate="txtLastName">*
                        </asp:requiredfieldvalidator>Last Name</P>
                    </TD>
                    <TD><asp:textbox id="txtLastName" runat="server"
                     Width="395px"></asp:textbox></TD>
                </TR>
                <TR>
                    <TD>
                        <P align="right"><asp:requiredfieldvalidator
                        id="RequiredFieldValidator3" runat="server"
                        ErrorMessage="You must enter an address."
                        ControlToValidate="txtAddress">*
                        </asp:requiredfieldvalidator>Address</P>
                    </TD>
                    <TD><asp:textbox id="txtAddress" runat="server"
                     Width="396px"></asp:textbox></TD>
                </TR>
                <TR>
                    <TD>
                        <P align="right"><asp:requiredfieldvalidator
                        id="RequiredFieldValidator4" runat="server"
                        ErrorMessage="You must enter a city."
                        ControlToValidate="txtCity">*
```

```
                    </asp:requiredfieldvalidator>City</P>
        </TD>
        <TD><asp:textbox id="txtCity" runat="server"
         Width="395px"></asp:textbox></TD>
    </TR>
    <TR>
        <TD>State
        </TD>
        <TD><asp:dropdownlist id="ddlState" runat="server"
        Width="154px">
                <asp:ListItem Value="">Select a state
                </asp:ListItem>
                <asp:ListItem value="AL">Alabama
                </asp:ListItem>
                <asp:ListItem value="AK">Alaska
                </asp:ListItem>
                <asp:ListItem value="AZ">Arizona
                </asp:ListItem>
                <asp:ListItem value="AR">Arkansas
                </asp:ListItem>
                <asp:ListItem value="CA">California
                </asp:ListItem>
                <asp:ListItem value="CT">Connecticut
                </asp:ListItem>
                <asp:ListItem value="CO">Colorado
                </asp:ListItem>
                <asp:ListItem value="DC">D.C.
                </asp:ListItem>
                <asp:ListItem value="DE">Delaware
                </asp:ListItem>
                <asp:ListItem value="FL">Florida
                </asp:ListItem>
                <asp:ListItem value="GA">Georgia
                </asp:ListItem>
                <asp:ListItem value="HI">Hawaii
                </asp:ListItem>
                <asp:ListItem value="ID">Idaho
                </asp:ListItem>
                <asp:ListItem value="IL">Illinois
                </asp:ListItem>
                <asp:ListItem value="IN">Indiana
                </asp:ListItem>
                <asp:ListItem value="IA">Iowa
                </asp:ListItem>
                <asp:ListItem value="KS">Kansas
                </asp:ListItem>
                <asp:ListItem value="KY">Kentucky
                </asp:ListItem>
                <asp:ListItem value="LA">Louisiana
                </asp:ListItem>
                <asp:ListItem value="ME">Maine
```

```
</asp:ListItem>
<asp:ListItem value="MA">Massachusetts
</asp:ListItem>
<asp:ListItem value="MD">Maryland
</asp:ListItem>
<asp:ListItem value="MI">Michigan
</asp:ListItem>
<asp:ListItem value="MN">Minnesota
</asp:ListItem>
<asp:ListItem value="MS">Mississippi
</asp:ListItem>
<asp:ListItem value="MO">Missouri
</asp:ListItem>
<asp:ListItem value="MT">Montana
</asp:ListItem>
<asp:ListItem value="NE">Nebraska
</asp:ListItem>
<asp:ListItem value="NV">Nevada
</asp:ListItem>
<asp:ListItem value="NH">New Hampshire
</asp:ListItem>
<asp:ListItem value="NJ">New Jersey
</asp:ListItem>
<asp:ListItem value="NM">New Mexico
</asp:ListItem>
<asp:ListItem value="NY">New York
</asp:ListItem>
<asp:ListItem value="NC">North Carolina
</asp:ListItem>
<asp:ListItem value="ND">North Dakota
</asp:ListItem>
<asp:ListItem value="OH">Ohio
</asp:ListItem>
<asp:ListItem value="OK">Oklahoma
</asp:ListItem>
<asp:ListItem value="OR">Oregon
</asp:ListItem>
<asp:ListItem value="PA">Pennsylvania
</asp:ListItem>
<asp:ListItem value="RI">Rhode Island
</asp:ListItem>
<asp:ListItem value="SC">South Carolina
</asp:ListItem>
<asp:ListItem value="SD">South Dakota
</asp:ListItem>
<asp:ListItem value="TN">Tennessee
</asp:ListItem>
<asp:ListItem value="TX">Texas
</asp:ListItem>
<asp:ListItem value="UT">Utah
</asp:ListItem>
```

```
                <asp:ListItem value="VT">Vermont
                </asp:ListItem>
                <asp:ListItem value="VA">Virginia
                </asp:ListItem>
                <asp:ListItem value="WA">Washington
                </asp:ListItem>
                <asp:ListItem value="WY">Wyoming
                </asp:ListItem>
                <asp:ListItem value="WI">Wisconsin
                </asp:ListItem>
                <asp:ListItem value="WV">West Virginia
                </asp:ListItem>
            </asp:dropdownlist> or
            Province
            <asp:textbox id="txtProvince" runat="server">
            </asp:textbox></TD>
    </TR>
    <TR>
        <TD>
            <P align="right">
                <asp:RequiredFieldValidator
                 id="RequiredFieldValidator5" runat="server"
                 ErrorMessage="You must select a country."
                 ControlToValidate="ddlCountry">*
                 </asp:RequiredFieldValidator>Country</P>
        </TD>
        <TD><asp:dropdownlist id="ddlCountry" runat="server"
            Width="154px">
                <asp:ListItem>Select a country</asp:ListItem>
                <asp:ListItem Value="US">United States
                 </asp:ListItem>
                <asp:ListItem Value="CA">Canada</asp:ListItem>
                <asp:ListItem Value="MX">Mexico</asp:ListItem>
            </asp:dropdownlist></TD>
    </TR>
    <TR>
        <TD>
            <P align="right">
                <asp:RequiredFieldValidator
                 id="RequiredFieldValidator6" runat="server"
                 ErrorMessage=
                 "You must enter a zip or postal code."
                 ControlToValidate="txtZipcode">*
                 </asp:RequiredFieldValidator>Zip/
                 Postal Code</P>
        </TD>
        <TD><asp:textbox id="txtZipcode" runat="server"
        Width="152px"></asp:textbox></TD>
    </TR>
    <TR>
        <TD>
```

```
                    <P align="right">
                        <asp:RequiredFieldValidator
                         id="RequiredFieldValidator7" runat="server"
                         ErrorMessage="You must enter a phone number."
                         ControlToValidate="txtPhone">*
                         </asp:RequiredFieldValidator>Phone</P>
                </TD>
                <TD><asp:textbox id="txtPhone" runat="server"
                 Width="397px">
                        </asp:textbox></TD>
            </TR>
            <TR>
                <TD>
                    <P align="right">
                        <asp:RegularExpressionValidator
                         id="RegularExpressionValidator1"
                         runat="server"
                         ErrorMessage=
                         "You must enter an e-mail address."
                         ControlToValidate="txtEmail"
                         ValidationExpression=
                         "\w+([-+.]\w+)*@\w+([-.]\w+)*\.\w+([-.]\w+)*">*
                         </asp:RegularExpressionValidator>E-mail</P>
                </TD>
                <TD>
                    <asp:TextBox id="txtEmail" runat="server"
                     Width="397px"></asp:TextBox></TD>
            </TR>
            <TR>
                <TD>
                    <P align="center"> </P>
                </TD>
                <TD>
                    <P align="center">
                        <asp:Button id="Button1" runat="server"
                         Text="Submit"></asp:Button></P>
                </TD>
            </TR>
        </TABLE>
    </P>
  </form>
  <!-- #Include File="Footer.inc" -->
</HTML>
```

The meat of this page, of course, is in the code-behind file. The first section of this file handles the checking that must be done the first time the page is loaded by the shopper. The first check, shown in Listing 8.4, ensures that a basket has already been created in this session. If there isn't a basket, obviously we can't allow the shopper to check out, and instead must direct them to the Basket.aspx page. On that page, the shopper will get the message that their basket is empty. If they do have a basket, the next check is to see whether there's already a session ID in place for this session.

Listing 8.4   **Shipping.aspx.vb Page_Load Procedure**

```
Private Sub Page_Load(ByVal sender As System.Object, _
  ByVal e As System.EventArgs) Handles MyBase.Load
    ' Checks to make only on first load
  If Not IsPostBack Then
      ' Check to make sure they have a basket when they
      ' get to this page. If not, send them to a page to get one
      If Session("idBasket").ToString = "" Then
          Server.Transfer("Basket.aspx")
      End If

      ' Check for a valid session ID
      Dim strError As String
      SessionCheck(Session, Request.Cookies("WWCD"), strError)
```

The next check we perform is to see whether a profile has been retrieved. The *ProfileRetrieve* session variable is set to 1 if a profile has already been retrieved in this session. Note that we want to retrieve a shopper's profile only once each session (unless the shopper retrieves it themselves through the Profile link in the main navigation area). The reason for this is that the shopper may be updating their shipping and billing information, and we don't want to overwrite their changes should they reload this page. This will happen, for example, if some piece of information fails a validation check.

If no profile has been retrieved, we'll provide a link to the Profile.aspx page so that the shopper can retrieve a past profile. This link will typically show up only if there is no cookie for a past profile or the shopper simply has no previous profile. The link is hard-coded as a Hyperlink control named hlProfile, whose Visible property is normally set to False. To show the link, the code simply sets this property to True, as shown in Listing 8.5.

Listing 8.5   **Shipping.aspx.vb Page_Load Procedure (continued)**

```
    ' If no profile has been retrieved, show the
    ' link to retrieve one. The ProfileRetrieve variable
    ' is set to zero in the SessionCheck procedure
  If Session("ProfileRetrieve") = "0" Then
      hlProfile.Visible = True
```

Next, the code uses the shopper ID stored for the current session to try to retrieve a stored profile. This shopper ID might have come from a cookie on the shopper's computer (in which case we'll already have a profile in the system), or it might have been arbitrarily assigned by the system when the shopper started interacting with the site. In the latter case, the procRetrieveProfileByID stored procedure simply won't return any data.

Once the profile is retrieved, the code reads the values from the profile into the session variables that will track the shipping data for the shopper. Then it sets the *ProfileRetrieve* session variable to 1, which indicates that the address information has been retrieved once and should not be retrieved again. This block of code is shown in Listing 8.6.

Listing 8.6   **Shipping.aspx.vb Page_Load Procedure (continued)**

```
' And while we're here, see whether there is
' profile information to retrieve based on a
' Shopper ID from a cookie
With cmdRetrieveProfileByID
    .Parameters("@ShopperID").Value = _
     Session("idShopper")
    cnn.Open()
    .ExecuteNonQuery()
    cnn.Close()
    ' Store the values if we got anything back
    If Not IsDBNull(.Parameters("@ShopperFirstName").Value) Then
        Session("ShopperFirstName") = _
         .Parameters("@ShopperFirstName").Value
        Session("ShopperLastName") = _
         .Parameters("@ShopperLastName").Value
        Session("ShopperAddress") = _
         .Parameters("@ShopperAddress").Value
        Session("ShopperCity") = _
         .Parameters("@ShopperCity").Value
        Session("ShopperState") = _
         .Parameters("@ShopperState").Value
        Session("ShopperProvince") = _
         .Parameters("@ShopperProvince").Value
        Session("ShopperCountry") = _
         .Parameters("@ShopperCountry").Value
        Session("ShopperZipCode") = _
         .Parameters("@ShopperZipCode").Value
        Session("ShopperPhone") = _
         .Parameters("@ShopperPhone").Value
        Session("ShopperEmail") = _
         .Parameters("@ShopperEmail").Value
        Session("ShopperPassword") = _
         .Parameters("@ShopperPassword").Value
        Session("ShopperCookie") = _
         .Parameters("@ShopperCookie").Value
    End If
End With
' Either way, there's no point in trying to retrieve
' this info again, so make note that we tried
Session("ProfileRetrieve") = 1
End If
```

Listing 8.7 shows the procRetrieveProfileByID stored procedure, which returns profile information when supplied with a Shopper ID. If there's no profile for the supplied Shopper ID, the stored procedure returns Null for each column requested.

Listing 8.7   **procRetrieveProfileByID**

```
/*  Retrieve the shopper profile */
/* Given a shopper's ID, retrieve their other
   information. All information is put into
   output parameters to avoid the overhead of
   building a DataSet to hold one row of data

From .NET E-Commerce Programming
by Mike Gunderloy and Noel Jerke
Copyright 2002, Sybex Inc. All Rights Reserved. */
CREATE PROCEDURE procRetrieveProfileByID
  @ShopperID int,
  @ShopperFirstName varchar(50) OUTPUT,
  @ShopperLastName varchar(50) OUTPUT,
  @ShopperAddress varchar(50) OUTPUT,
  @ShopperCity varchar(100) OUTPUT,
  @ShopperState varchar(2) OUTPUT,
  @ShopperProvince varchar(150) OUTPUT,
  @ShopperCountry varchar(100) OUTPUT,
  @ShopperZipCode varchar(15) OUTPUT,
  @ShopperPhone varchar(30) OUTPUT,
  @ShopperEmail varchar(150) OUTPUT,
  @ShopperPassword varchar(25) OUTPUT,
  @ShopperCookie tinyint OUTPUT
AS
  SELECT @ShopperFirstName = ShopperFirstName,
    @ShopperLastName = ShopperLastName,
    @ShopperAddress = ShopperAddress,
    @ShopperCity = ShopperCity,
    @ShopperState = ShopperState,
    @ShopperProvince = ShopperProvince,
    @ShopperCountry = ShopperCountry,
    @ShopperZipCode = ShopperZipCode,
    @ShopperPhone = ShopperPhone,
    @ShopperEmail = ShopperEmail,
    @ShopperPassword = ShopperPassword,
    @ShopperCookie = ShopperCookie
  FROM Shopper
  WHERE ShopperID = @ShopperID
```

Any profile information that we're able to retrieve should be displayed on the form for the shopper to verify. This simplifies the shopping process if the shopper is shipping to the same address as in a previous order. In ASP.NET, we can do this by setting the Text properties of

TextBox controls and by finding the matching items in DropDownList controls. Listing 8.8 shows the code that handles these tasks.

Listing 8.8   *Shipping.aspx.vb Page_Load Procedure (continued)*

```
' Move any info that we have to the User Interface
txtFirstName.Text = Session("ShopperFirstName")
txtLastName.Text = Session("ShopperLastName")
txtAddress.Text = Session("ShopperAddress")
txtCity.Text = Session("ShopperCity")
Dim li As ListItem
For Each li In ddlState.Items
        li.Selected = True
        Exit For
    End If
Next
txtProvince.Text - Session("ShopperProvince")
For Each li In ddlCountry.Items
    If li.Value = Session("ShopperCountry") Then
        li.Selected = True
        Exit For
    End If
Next
txtZipcode.Text = Session("ShopperZipCode")
txtPhone.Text = Session("ShopperPhone")
txtEmail.Text = Session("ShopperEmail")
```

That's all of the code that runs when the page is first loaded. At this point, the shopper is free to interact with the page, filling in their shipping information, until they click the Submit button (or, of course, until they navigate away from the page by some means). At that point, the validation controls on the page take over. Most of these controls are simple required-field validators that ensure that the shopper has actually entered data. There's also a regular-expression validation control that checks the formatting of the e-mail address, using a regular expression that .NET supplies.

However, the state and province controls have more complex validation rules:

- If the United States is selected as the shipping country, the shopper must select a state.
- If any other country is selected as the shipping country, the shopper must supply a province.
- The shopper cannot both select a state and supply a province.

After the data that's entered by the shopper passes all the client-side validations, the page will reload and the Page_Load procedure will run again. This time, though, the *IsPostBack* variable will be set to True by ASP.NET. These validation rules are then handled by more code in the Page_Load procedure that is invoked only on postback. Listing 8.9 shows the code that performs these validations.

WARNING   You can't use a CustomValidator control to validate these conditions, because the custom validation code won't be executed if the control is left empty.

NOTE   For more information on ASP.NET validation controls, refer to Chapter 5, "Building a Sample Application."

Listing 8.9   Shipping.aspx.vb Page_Load Procedure (continued)

```
Else ' IsPostBack
    ' Perform validations that are too complex for
    ' the validation controls
    ' First check: make sure a state is selected
    ' if this is a US address, or a province if
    ' this is a non-US address
    lblError.Visible = False
    If ddlCountry.SelectedItem.Value = "US" Then
        If ddlState.SelectedItem.Value = "" Then
            lblError.Text = "You must select a state."
            lblError.Visible = True
        End If
    Else ' Country other than US
        If txtProvince.Text = "" Then
            lblError.Text = "You must specify a province."
            lblError.Visible = True
        End If
    End If
    ' Second check: make sure they haven't selected
    ' both a state and a province. In this case, need
    ' to change the error message
    If (ddlState.SelectedItem.Value <> "") And _
      (txtProvince.Text <> "") Then
        lblError.Text = _
          "You cannot specify both a state and a province."
        lblError.Visible = True
    End If
```

After the final round of validations, the code checks to see whether the lblError control was made visible. If it wasn't, it's safe to proceed. In this case, the remaining Page_Load code will run, saving the shopper's shipping data to a set of session variables. Finally, the page uses the Server.Transfer method to move from this page to the Payment.aspx page, which we'll look at next. Listing 8.10 shows this code.

Note that the shopper's shipping address is saved as the default billing address for the transaction as well. That way, the shopper won't have to enter the information twice if the billing and shipping addresses are the same.

Listing 8.10   Shipping.aspx.vb Page_Load Procedure (continued)

```
If Not lblError.Visible Then
   ' If we get this far, and it's a postback, then
   ' all of the validation passed. In this case,
   ' save the information for shipping and as the default
   ' for billing, and redirect to the payment page
   Session("ShipFirstName") = txtFirstName.Text
   Session("ShipLastName") = txtLastName.Text
   Session("ShipAddress") = txtAddress.Text
   Session("ShipCity") = txtCity.Text
   Session("ShipState") = ddlState.SelectedItem.Value
   Session("ShipProvince") = txtProvince.Text
   Session("ShipCountry") = ddlCountry.SelectedItem.Value
   Session("ShipZipcode") = txtZipcode.Text
   Session("ShipPhone") = txtPhone.Text
   Session("ShipEmail") = txtEmail.Text
   Session("BillFirstName") = txtFirstName.Text
   Session("BillLastName") = txtLastName.Text
   Session("BillAddress") = txtAddress.Text
   Session("BillCity") = txtCity.Text
   Session("BillState") = ddlState.SelectedItem.Value
   Session("BillProvince") = txtProvince.Text
   Session("BillCountry") = ddlCountry.SelectedItem.Value
   Session("BillZipcode") = txtZipcode.Text
   Session("BillPhone") = txtPhone.Text
   Session("BillEmail") = txtEmail.Text
   Server.Transfer("Payment.aspx")
End If

End Sub
```

To test the page, let's begin without a saved profile. To do this, be sure to delete any profile cookies you may have already set by working with the sample code. Then, after adding several items to the shopping basket, navigate to the shipping page by clicking one of the Checkout links. Figure 8.4 shows the blank shipping page. Note the text indicating where to click to retrieve a previous profile.

FIGURE 8.4:

Blank shipping page

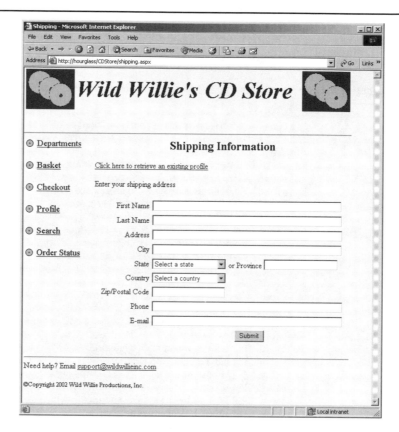

Now let's enter some data into the page. Fill in all the items except the state and the province. Figure 8.5 shows a page containing the sample data entry.

FIGURE 8.5:

Shipping page filled
out with an error

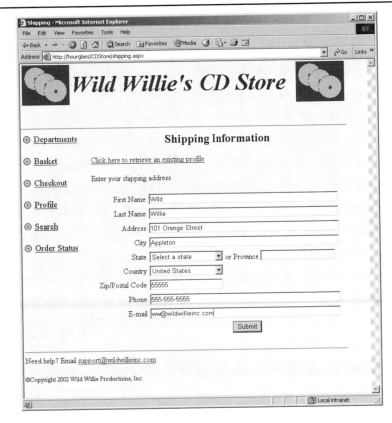

Next, click the Submit button. The server-side validation functions will be invoked. Validation will show that there is an error in your page because you didn't select a state (see Figure 8.6).

FIGURE 8.6:

Shipping page with an
error message

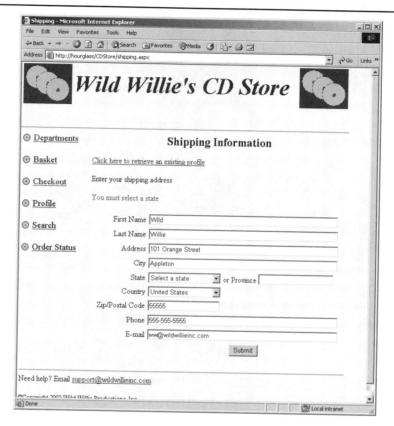

Now, fill in a state as appropriate, click Submit, and continue to shop.

Data Validation

In our sample application, we simply check to ensure that a province or state is entered in conjunction with a proper country. We also ensure that a zip code of some kind has been entered. But if we are dealing in volume orders to many international locations, the potential costs of receiving bad data could be quite high.

There are more options. For example, zip code lookup data is available for validating zip codes against the selected states. Also, data is available for providing province selection options based on the selected country. If needed, this level of validation could be performed, by adding additional tests in the code at the point where the page has been posted back.

Calculating Shipping and Taxes

Now that we have valid shipping data, the shopper moves to the next step: entering their billing information. Before we look at the payment page, though, we're going to take a side trip to the world of Web Services. As mentioned earlier, we want to build our "line of business" logic (such as tax and shipping calculations) into a Web Service that will be accessible from our ASP.NET pages.

You've undoubtedly heard the term *Web Service* by now, but you may still be a bit hazy on what it means. Part of the problem is that there are many definitions of Web Services, depending on which vendor you're listening to.

If you've studied software development at all, you understand the importance of separating interface and implementation. That's one of the basic ways that we make large amounts of source code comprehensible to our limited brains. For example, if you understand that the interface of a Customer object includes a CollectOverdueInvoices method, you can call Customer.CollectOverdueInvoices from your Visual Basic .NET code without knowing the details of the code inside the object that actually performs the operation. And indeed, the developer of the Customer object can change those details without affecting your code at all.

That sets the stage for a simple definition of a Web Service: an object whose interface can be invoked via common Internet protocols without knowing about the object's implementation. (You can read a more detailed definition that boils down to the same thing at `http://msdn.microsoft.com/library/default.asp?url=/library/en-us/dnWebsrv/html/Websvcs_platform.asp`.) So what's the big deal? Well, the key is those common protocols. Web Services use XML protocols, which travel via HTTP. This means that Web Services can be used through firewalls and across platforms. In particular, there are three protocols you should know about:

Simple Object Access Protocol (SOAP)   Defines a standard for passing data and messages (such as remote procedure calls) via XML. SOAP is also extensible, so other bits of information can be tucked into a SOAP message as necessary.

Web Services Description Language (WSDL)   A specialized type of XML that describes a Web Service's interface. Put another way, WSDL tells you what methods and properties a Web Service makes available, and then SOAP gives you the way to use them.

Universal Description, Discovery, and Integration specification (UDDI)   Essentially a language for advertising Web Services. UDDI is understood by UDDI registries; by sending SOAP messages to such a registry, you can find out about available Web Services. `http://uddi.microsoft.com/default.aspx`, for example, is Microsoft's own UDDI registry.

So, to sum up: You use UDDI to find Web Services, WSDL to find out their interfaces, and then SOAP to interact with them. Except, of course, in most cases, you're better off using tools that hide all of that low-level stuff from you. That's one of the best things about developing with .NET: It lets you write Web Services, or interact with existing Web Services, without writing code to handle the XML directly.

One more point: You shouldn't think of Web Services only as something you use over the Internet; they're equally useful on an intranet, or potentially even on a single computer. In fact, for our example, we'll deploy a Web Service on the same computer that's serving our ASP.NET pages and handling the SQL Server duties. Web Services are easily redeployed, though. If our store grows large enough that having everything on the same server presents performance problems, we could easily move the Web Service to another computer and call it from there.

Web Services can be created in the Visual Studio .NET interface, just like any other ASP.NET application. To create a new Web Service, follow these steps:

1. Launch Visual Studio .NET.

2. On the Start Page, click the New Project button.

3. Select Visual Basic Projects in the Project Types list, and ASP.NET Web Service in the Templates list. Assign a location to the project using your web server name and CDStore-TaxShipping as the base name. For example, Figure 8.7 shows the creation of this service on a server named HOURGLASS.

FIGURE 8.7:

Creating a new Web Service

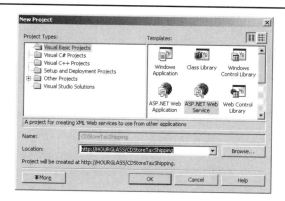

4. Click OK to create the Web Service.

5. Highlight the Service1.asmx class in the Solution Explorer window and rename it **CDStoreServices.asmx**.

6. Drag the procGetShippingFee stored procedure from Server Explorer to the design surface for the Web Service. Rename the SqlConnection object that this creates as **cnn**, and rename the SqlCommand object **cmdGetShippingFee**.

7. Drag the procGetTaxRate stored procedure from Server Explorer to the Web Service. Rename the SqlCommand object that this generates as **cmdGetTaxRate**.

8 Right-click on the design surface and select View Code. This will open the code-behind-page window for CDStoreServices.asmx.vb.

9. Change the name of the class in the code to **CDStoreServices**. Change the namespace for the Web Service to **http://CDStore.WildWillys.com**.

TIP   Namespaces for Web Services should be unique, but they need not be actual URLs that you could follow in a browser.

---

10. Enter this code to create two new WebMethods as a part of the CDStoreServices class:

```
<WebMethod()> Public Function GetShippingFee(_
ByVal intQuantity As Integer) As Double
    ' Invoke the stored procedure to retrieve the
    ' shipping fee for the specified quantity
    cmdGetShippingFee.Parameters("@Quantity").Value = intQuantity
    cnn.Open()
    GetShippingFee = CType(cmdGetShippingFee.ExecuteScalar, Double)
    cnn.Close()
End Function

<WebMethod()> Public Function GetTaxRate(ByVal strState As String) _
  As Double
    ' Invoke the stored procedure to retrieve the
    ' tax rate for the specified state
    cmdGetTaxRate.Parameters("@State").Value = strState
    cnn.Open()
    GetTaxRate = CType(cmdGetTaxRate.ExecuteScalar, Double)
    cnn.Close()
End Function
```

Except for the <WebMethod()> tags, this is exactly the code that you could use to create these methods in a regular Windows application.

At this point, you're ready to test the Web Service. To do so, follow these steps:

1. Save the project and select Debug ➤ Start to run it. This will open a page with general information on the Web Service, including hyperlinks to the GetShippingFee and Get-TaxRate methods.

2. Click the GetShippingFee link. This will open a page of information about the GetShippingFee method, as shown in Figure 8.8. This page gives the details of the SOAP messages that can be used to invoke the GetCustomers method.

FIGURE 8.8:

Information on Get-
ShippingFee

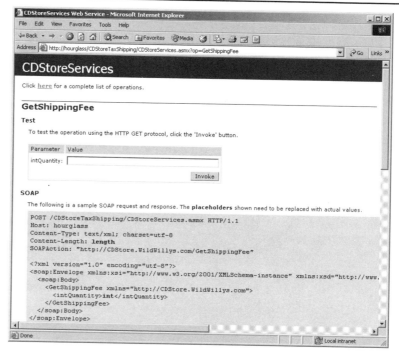

3. Enter a value for the intQuantity parameter on the GetShippingFee page; then click the Invoke button. This will open a second browser window with the results of the GetShippingFee call. The results will automatically be formatted as XML, which is the language that Web Services use to return information.

4. Close the browser windows to stop the debugging session.

Finally, with the Web Service running properly, it can be deployed to the production server. In this case, we developed the Web Service directly on the production server, so deployment is simple. Choose Build ➤ Build Solution to deploy the Web Service on your IIS server.

NOTE To deploy a Web Service to a server other than the one where it was developed, you need to copy the .asmx, .disco, and any private assemblies to a folder on the deployment server. This folder should normally be an IIS application folder. For more information, search the .NET Framework documentation for "Deploying Web Services."

The Web Service depends on two stored procedures—one for calculating shipping and one for calculating tax. Listing 8.11 shows the details of the procGetShippingFee stored procedure that is used to calculate shipping fees.

Listing 8.11   **procGetShippingFee Stored Procedure**

```
/*  Retrieve the shipping fee for
    a particular quantity

From .NET E-Commerce Programming
by Mike Gunderloy and Noel Jerke
Copyright 2002, Sybex Inc. All Rights Reserved. */
CREATE PROCEDURE procGetShippingFee
   @Quantity int
AS
   SELECT ShippingFee FROM Shipping
      WHERE ShippingLowQuantity <= @Quantity
      AND ShippingHighQuantity >= @Quantity
```

Listing 8.12 shows the procGetTaxRate stored procedure. This stored procedure looks up the tax rate for the state passed in by the calling procedure.

Listing 8.12   **procGetTaxRate Stored Procedure**

```
/*  Return the tax rate for
    a particular state

From .NET E-Commerce Programming
by Mike Gunderloy and Noel Jerke
Copyright 2002, Sybex Inc. All Rights Reserved. */
CREATE PROCEDURE procGetTaxRate
   @State varchar(2)
AS
   SELECT TaxRate FROM Tax
      WHERE TaxState = @State
```

To use the Web Service in the CDStore project, we need to add a web reference to the project. This is similar to a regular reference, in that it tells the project where to find a particular object. To add a web reference to the Web Service, open the CDStore project and follow these steps:

1. Select Project ➢ Add Web Reference.

2. In the Add Web Reference dialog box, enter **http://*ServerName*/CDStoreTaxShipping/ CDStoreServices.asmx**; then press Enter. This should open the descriptive page for the Web Service, as shown in Figure 8.9.

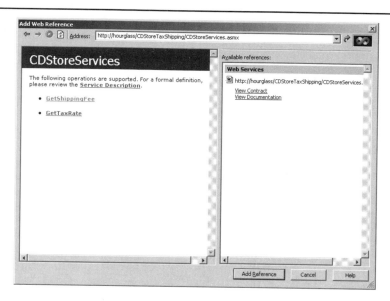

3. Click Add Reference to make this Web Service available to the project.

The Payment Page

Now that the Web Service for calculating tax rates and shipping fees is in place, we can
return to the main CDStore project and continue to develop the website. The next page the
shopper will see is the Payment.aspx page. This is where the shopper will enter their credit
card data and their billing address information. The HTML code for this page, shown in
Listing 8.13, is relatively extensive.

Listing 8.13   **Payment.aspx**

```
<%@ Page Language="vb" AutoEventWireup="false" Codebehind="Payment.aspx.vb"
 Inherits="CDStore.Payment"%>
<!DOCTYPE HTML PUBLIC "-//W3C//DTD HTML 4.0 Transitional//EN">
<HTML>
    <HEAD>
        <TITLE>Payment</TITLE>
    </HEAD>
    <meta content="Microsoft Visual Studio.NET 7.0" name="GENERATOR">
    <meta content="Visual Basic 7.0" name="CODE_LANGUAGE">
    <meta content="JavaScript" name="vs_defaultClientScript">
    <meta content="http://schemas.microsoft.com/intellisense/ie5"
     name="vs_targetSchema">
    <!-- Payment.aspx - Enter payment information -->
    <!-- #Include File="Header.inc" -->
```

```
<form id="Form1" method="post" runat="server">
    <H2>Order Recap:
    </H2>
    <TABLE id="Table1" cellSpacing="1" cellPadding="1" width="100%"
     border="0">
        <TR>
            <TD>
                <P align="right">Subtotal:  </P>
            </TD>
            <TD><asp:label id="lblSubtotal" runat="server"
             Width="51px">
             Label</asp:label></TD>
        </TR>
        <TR>
            <TD>
                <P align="right">Shipping:  </P>
            </TD>
            <TD><asp:label id="lblShipping" runat="server">Label
             </asp:label></TD>
        </TR>
        <TR>
            <TD>
                <P align="right">Tax:  </P>
            </TD>
            <TD><asp:label id="lblTax" runat="server"
             Visible="False">Label</asp:label>
            </TD>
        </TR>
        <TR>
            <TD>
                <P align="right"><STRONG>Total:  </STRONG></P>
            </TD>
            <TD><asp:label id="lblTotal" runat="server">
             Label</asp:label>
            </TD>
        </TR>
    </TABLE>
    <H2>Payment Information:
    </H2>
    <P><asp:validationsummary id="ValidationSummary1" runat="server">
    </asp:validationsummary></P>
    <P>
        <asp:Label id="lblError" runat="server" ForeColor="Red">Label
        </asp:Label></P>
    <P>
        <TABLE id="Table2" cellSpacing="1" cellPadding="1" width="100%"
         border="0">
            <TR>
                <TD>
                    <P align="right"><asp:requiredfieldvalidator
                     id="RequiredFieldValidator8" runat="server"
```

```
            ErrorMessage="You must enter a name."
            ControlToValidate="txtCCName">*
            </asp:requiredfieldvalidator>Name
                on credit card:   </P>
        </TD>
        <TD><asp:textbox id="txtCCName" runat="server">
        </asp:textbox></TD>
    </TR>
    <TR>
        <TD>
            <P align="right"><asp:regularexpressionvalidator
            id="RegularExpressionValidator4" runat="server"
            ErrorMessage="Invalid credit card number"
            ControlToValidate="txtCCNumber"
            ValidationExpression="[-0-9]+">*
            </asp:regularexpressionvalidator>Credit
                card number:  </P>
        </TD>
        <TD><asp:textbox id="txtCCNumber" runat="server">
         </asp:textbox></TD>
    </TR>
    <TR>
        <TD>
            <P align="right">Card type:  </P>
        </TD>
        <TD><asp:dropdownlist id="ddlCardType" runat="server"
         Width="154px">
                <asp:ListItem Value="Visa">Visa</asp:ListItem>
                <asp:ListItem Value="MasterCard">MasterCard
                 </asp:ListItem>
                <asp:ListItem Value="Amex">American Express
                 </asp:ListItem>
            </asp:dropdownlist></TD>
    </TR>
    <TR>
        <TD>
            <P align="right">Expiration month:  </P>
        </TD>
        <TD><asp:dropdownlist id="ddlMonth" runat="server"
         Width="155px">
                <asp:ListItem Value="1">January</asp:ListItem>
                <asp:ListItem Value="2">February</asp:ListItem>
                <asp:ListItem Value="3">March</asp:ListItem>
                <asp:ListItem Value="4">April</asp:ListItem>
                <asp:ListItem Value="5">May</asp:ListItem>
                <asp:ListItem Value="6">June</asp:ListItem>
                <asp:ListItem Value="7">July</asp:ListItem>
                <asp:ListItem Value="8">August</asp:ListItem>
                <asp:ListItem Value="9">September
                </asp:ListItem>
                <asp:ListItem Value="10">October</asp:ListItem>
```

```
                          <asp:ListItem Value="11">November
                          </asp:ListItem>
                          <asp:ListItem Value="12">December
                          </asp:ListItem>
                    </asp:dropdownlist></TD>
            </TR>
            <TR>
                <TD>
                    <P align="right">Expiration year:  </P>
                </TD>
                <TD><asp:dropdownlist id="ddlYear" runat="server"
                 Width="155px">
                          <asp:ListItem Value="2002">2002</asp:ListItem>
                          <asp:ListItem Value="2003">2003</asp:ListItem>
                          <asp:ListItem Value="2004">2004</asp:ListItem>
                          <asp:ListItem Value="2005">2005</asp:ListItem>
                          <asp:ListItem Value="2006">2006</asp:ListItem>
                          <asp:ListItem Value="2007">2007</asp:ListItem>
                          <asp:ListItem Value="2008">2008</asp:ListItem>
                          <asp:ListItem Value="2009">2009</asp:ListItem>
                    </asp:dropdownlist></TD>
            </TR>
        </TABLE>
</P>
<H2>Billing Address:</H2>
<P>
        <TABLE id="Table1" cellSpacing="2" cellPadding="2"
        width="100%" border="0">
            <TR>
                <TD>
                    <P align="right"><asp:requiredfieldvalidator
                     id="RequiredFieldValidator1" runat="server"
                     ErrorMessage="You must enter a first name."
                     ControlToValidate="txtFirstName">*
                     </asp:requiredfieldvalidator>First Name</P>
                </TD>
                <TD><asp:textbox id="txtFirstName" runat="server"
                 Width="394px"></asp:textbox></TD>
            </TR>
            <TR>
                <TD>
                    <P align="right"><asp:requiredfieldvalidator
                     id="RequiredFieldValidator2" runat="server"
                     ErrorMessage="You must enter a last name."
                     ControlToValidate="txtLastName">*
                     </asp:requiredfieldvalidator>Last Name</P>
                </TD>
                <TD><asp:textbox id="txtLastName" runat="server"
                Width="395px"></asp:textbox></TD>
            </TR>
            <TR>
```

```
<TD>
    <P align="right"><asp:requiredfieldvalidator
     id="RequiredFieldValidator3" runat="server"
     ErrorMessage="You must enter an address."
     ControlToValidate="txtAddress">*
     </asp:requiredfieldvalidator>Address</P>
</TD>
<TD><asp:textbox id="txtAddress" runat="server"
 Width="396px"></asp:textbox></TD>
</TR>
<TR>
    <TD>
        <P align="right"><asp:requiredfieldvalidator
         id="RequiredFieldValidator4" runat="server"
         ErrorMessage="You must enter a city."
         ControlToValidate="txtCity">*
         </asp:requiredfieldvalidator>City</P>
    </TD>
    <TD><asp:textbox id="txtCity" runat="server"
     Width="395px">
     </asp:textbox></TD>
</TR>
<TR>
    <TD>
        <P align="right">State</P>
    </TD>
    <TD><asp:dropdownlist id="ddlState" runat="server"
     Width="154px">
            <asp:ListItem Value="">Select a state
            </asp:ListItem>
            <asp:ListItem value="AL">Alabama
            </asp:ListItem>
            <asp:ListItem value="AK">Alaska
            </asp:ListItem>
            <asp:ListItem value="AZ">Arizona
            </asp:ListItem>
            <asp:ListItem value="AR">Arkansas
            </asp:ListItem>
            <asp:ListItem value="CA">California
            </asp:ListItem>
            <asp:ListItem value="CT">Connecticut
            </asp:ListItem>
            <asp:ListItem value="CO">Colorado
            </asp:ListItem>
            <asp:ListItem value="DC">D.C.
            </asp:ListItem>
            <asp:ListItem value="DE">Delaware
            </asp:ListItem>
            <asp:ListItem value="FL">Florida
            </asp:ListItem>
            <asp:ListItem value="GA">Georgia
```

```
      </asp:ListItem>
      <asp:ListItem value="HI">Hawaii
      </asp:ListItem>
      <asp:ListItem value="ID">Idaho
      </asp:ListItem>
      <asp:ListItem value="IL">Illinois
      </asp:ListItem>
      <asp:ListItem value="IN">Indiana
      </asp:ListItem>
      <asp:ListItem value="IA">Iowa
      </asp:ListItem>
      <asp:ListItem value="KS">Kansas
      </asp:ListItem>
      <asp:ListItem value="KY">Kentucky
      </asp:ListItem>
      <asp:ListItem value="LA">Louisiana
      </asp:ListItem>
      <asp:ListItem value="ME">Maine
      </asp:ListItem>
      <asp:ListItem value="MA">Massachusetts
      </asp:ListItem>
      <asp:ListItem value="MD">Maryland
      </asp:ListItem>
      <asp:ListItem value="MI">Michigan
      </asp:ListItem>
      <asp:ListItem value="MN">Minnesota
      </asp:ListItem>
      <asp:ListItem value="MS">Mississippi
      </asp:ListItem>
      <asp:ListItem value="MO">Missouri
      </asp:ListItem>
      <asp:ListItem value="MT">Montana
      </asp:ListItem>
      <asp:ListItem value="NE">Nebraska
      </asp:ListItem>
      <asp:ListItem value="NV">Nevada
      </asp:ListItem>
      <asp:ListItem value="NH">New Hampshire
      </asp:ListItem>
      <asp:ListItem value="NJ">New Jersey
      </asp:ListItem>
      <asp:ListItem value="NM">New Mexico
      </asp:ListItem>
      <asp:ListItem value="NY">New York
      </asp:ListItem>
      <asp:ListItem value="NC">North Carolina
      </asp:ListItem>
      <asp:ListItem value="ND">North Dakota
      </asp:ListItem>
      <asp:ListItem value="OH">Ohio
      </asp:ListItem>
```

```
                        <asp:ListItem value="OK">Oklahoma
                        </asp:ListItem>
                        <asp:ListItem value="OR">Oregon
                        </asp:ListItem>
                        <asp:ListItem value="PA">Pennsylvania
                        </asp:ListItem>
                        <asp:ListItem value="RI">Rhode Island
                        </asp:ListItem>
                        <asp:ListItem value="SC">South Carolina
                        </asp:ListItem>
                        <asp:ListItem value="SD">South Dakota
                        </asp:ListItem>
                        <asp:ListItem value="TN">Tennessee
                        </asp:ListItem>
                        <asp:ListItem value="TX">Texas
                        </asp:ListItem>
                        <asp:ListItem value="UT">Utah
                        </asp:ListItem>
                        <asp:ListItem value="VT">Vermont
                        </asp:ListItem>
                        <asp:ListItem value="VA">Virginia
                        </asp:ListItem>
                        <asp:ListItem value="WA">Washington
                        </asp:ListItem>
                        <asp:ListItem value="WY">Wyoming
                        </asp:ListItem>
                        <asp:ListItem value="WI">Wisconsin
                        </asp:ListItem>
                        <asp:ListItem value="WV">West Virginia
                        </asp:ListItem>
                    </asp:dropdownlist> or Province
                    <asp:textbox id="txtProvince" runat="server">
                    </asp:textbox></TD>
            </TR>
            <TR>
                <TD>
                    <P align="right"><asp:requiredfieldvalidator
                     id="RequiredFieldValidator5" runat="server"
                    ErrorMessage="You must select a country."
                    ControlToValidate="ddlCountry">*
                    </asp:requiredfieldvalidator>Country</P>
                </TD>
                <TD><asp:dropdownlist id="ddlCountry" runat="server"
                 Width="154px">
                        <asp:ListItem>Select a country</asp:ListItem>
                        <asp:ListItem Value="US">United States
                         </asp:ListItem>
                        <asp:ListItem Value="CA">Canada</asp:ListItem>
                        <asp:ListItem Value="MX">Mexico</asp:ListItem>
                    </asp:dropdownlist></TD>
            </TR>
```

```
<TR>
    <TD>
        <P align="right"><asp:requiredfieldvalidator
        id="RequiredFieldValidator6" runat="server"
        ErrorMessage=
        "You must enter a zip or postal code."
        ControlToValidate="txtZipcode">*
        </asp:requiredfieldvalidator>Zip/Postal Code</P>
    </TD>
    <TD><asp:textbox id="txtZipcode" runat="server"
    Width="152px"></asp:textbox></TD>
</TR>
<TR>
    <TD>
        <P align="right"><asp:requiredfieldvalidator
        id="RequiredFieldValidator7" runat="server"
        ErrorMessage="You must enter a phone number."
        ControlToValidate="txtPhone">*
        </asp:requiredfieldvalidator>Phone</P>
    </TD>
    <TD><asp:textbox id="txtPhone" runat="server"
    Width="397px"></asp:textbox></TD>
</TR>
<TR>
    <TD>
        <P align="right"><asp:regularexpressionvalidator
        id="RegularExpressionValidator1" runat="server"
        ErrorMessage="You must enter an e-mail address."
        ControlToValidate="txtEmail" ValidationExpression=
        "\w+([-+.]\w+)*@\w+([-.]\w+)*\.\w+([-.]\w+)*">*
        </asp:regularexpressionvalidator>Email</P>
    </TD>
    <TD><asp:textbox id="txtEmail" runat="server"
    Width="397px"></asp:textbox></TD>
</TR>
<TR>
    <TD>
        <P align="right">Save Profile Cookie? </P>
    </TD>
    <TD><asp:radiobuttonlist id="rblProfile" runat="server"
    RepeatColumns="2">
        <asp:ListItem Value="1" Selected="True">Yes
        </asp:ListItem>
        <asp:ListItem Value="0">No</asp:ListItem>
    </asp:radiobuttonlist></TD>
</TR>
<TR>
    <TD>
        <P align="right">Password for Profile</P>
    </TD>
    <TD><asp:textbox id="txtPassword" runat="server"
```

```
            Width="397px" TextMode="Password"></asp:textbox></TD>
        </TR>
        <TR>
            <TD>
                <P align="center"> </P>
            </TD>
            <TD>
                <P align="center"><asp:button id="Button1"
                    runat="server" Text="Submit"></asp:button></P>
            </TD>
        </TR>
    </TABLE>
</P>
</form>
<!-- #Include File="Footer.inc" -->
</HTML>
```

Although there is a lot of HTML to this page, it's all HTML that you've seen before. As usual, we've used server-side Web Form controls to build the user interface. This gives us easy access to properties of the controls from the code behind the Web Form.

NOTE   Note that we've hard-coded expiration years from 2002 to 2009 into the code. That means that when it's no longer 2002, we'll need to remove that option and probably tack a new option year onto the end. Alternatively, client-side code could be written to automate building the list of years for x years, starting from the current year, if this becomes a maintenance problem.

This page is the critical last step in the ordering process. The first thing we do is check to see whether the shopper has come to this page via an appropriate route. This page should only be loaded from the shipping page, or as a postback from itself. We can check the Request.UrlReferrer.AbsolutePath property of the page to determine the shopper's origin. If it was neither Shipping.aspx nor Payment.aspx, we send the shopper back to the shopping basket, as shown in Listing 8.14.

Listing 8.14   **Payment.aspx.vb Page_Load Procedure**

```
Private Sub Page_Load(ByVal sender As System.Object, _
ByVal e As System.EventArgs) Handles MyBase.Load
    If Not IsPostBack Then
        'One-time page initialization tasks

        ' Check that the user came from the shipping page
        ' or from a refresh of this page
        If (LCase(Request.UrlReferrer.AbsolutePath) <> _
        "/cdstore/payment.aspx") And _
        (LCase(Request.UrlReferrer.AbsolutePath) <> _
```

```
        "/cdstore/shipping.aspx") Then
            ' Send them back to the basket
            Server.Transfer("Basket.aspx")
        End If
```

Next, we move on to the display of the shopper's final charges for the order. The code uses the procBasketDetails stored procedure to retrieve the current subtotal for the shopping basket and the number of items in the basket. Both of these pieces of information get stored in session variables, as shown in Listing 8.15. The VB .NET code uses the data returned from the stored procedure to see whether there are any items in the basket. If not, it's back to the Basket.aspx page again.

Listing 8.15   **Payment.aspx.vb Page_Load Procedure (continued)**

```
' Retrieve details of the current basket
With cmdBasketDetails
    .Parameters("@BasketID").Value = _
     Session("idBasket")
    cnn.Open()
    .ExecuteNonQuery()
    Session("Subtotal") = .Parameters("@Subtotal").Value
    Session("Quantity") = .Parameters("@Quantity").Value
    cnn.Close()
End With

' If there's nothing IN the basket, might as well
' skip this page and send 'em back to the basket
If Session("Quantity") = 0 Then
    Server.Transfer("Basket.aspx")
End If
```

Now we are ready to work with our Web Services object to calculate the tax and shipping fee for this order. The code uses the As New syntax to create this object, just like any other object. Listing 8.16 shows the code that uses this object to calculate the tax and shipping for the order. After retrieving the tax and shipping amounts, the code can calculate the total for the order.

WARNING   As you can see, the server name is hard-coded. Before testing this code, you'll need to change the web reference and the line of code that invokes the Web Service to point to your own server.

Listing 8.16   **Payment.aspx.vb Page_Load Procedure (continued)**

```
' Use the Web Services to get the tax and shipping charges
Dim TaxShip As New hourglass.CDStoreServices()
```

```
Session("Tax") = TaxShip.GetTaxRate(Session("ShipState")) * _
  Session("Subtotal")
Session("Shipping") = TaxShip.GetShippingFee(Session("Quantity"))

' Calculate and store the total for this basket
Session("Total") = Session("Subtotal") + Session("Tax") + _
  Session("Shipping")
```

Once we have all the checking and calculations out of the way, we are ready to begin filling in the payment page. The first step is to fill in the order recap section based on the calculations that the code has just performed. Using Web Form controls makes this easy, as shown in Listing 8.17.

Listing 8.17   Payment.aspx.vb Page_Load Procedure (continued)

```
' Fill in the table on screen
lblSubtotal.Text = Format(Session("Subtotal"), "Currency")
lblTax.Text = Format(Session("Tax"), "Currency")
lblShipping.Text = Format(Session("Shipping"), "Currency")
lblTotal.Text = Format(Session("Total"), "Currency")
```

The next section of the code fills in any credit card information that the shopper has already entered. This will be available if, for example, the shopper partially filled in the page and clicked the Submit button. In that case, we can use the session variables to retain the information already entered. Listing 8.18 shows this block of code.

TIP The first time the payment page is accessed, you might consider setting the name on the credit card to the name in the profile. The only danger here is that if the name in the profile is something like John Doe and the name on the card is John E. Doe, the shopper may not think to enter the middle initial. This could cause a problem when validating the credit card.

Listing 8.18   Payment.aspx.vb Page_Load Procedure (continued)

```
' Show any credit card info entered earlier in this session
txtCCName.Text = Session("CCName")
txtCCNumber.Text = Session("CCNumber")
Dim li As ListItem
For Each li In ddlCardType.Items
    If li.Value = Session("CCType") Then
        li.Selected = True
        Exit For
    End If
Next
For Each li In ddlMonth.Items
```

```
        If li.Value = Session("CCExpMonth") Then
            li.Selected = True
            Exit For
        End If
    Next
    For Each li In ddlYear.Items
        If li.Value = Session("CCExpYear") Then
            li.Selected = True
            Exit For
        End If
    Next
```

The last task on the initial load of the page is to move the billing information to the user interface. This will be the default information from the shipping page. Listing 8.19 shows the code that fills out the billing form with the default address.

TIP　　It may be wise, depending on the types of shoppers visiting the store, to give them the option on the shipping page of having that data automatically copied to the billing page. If you have a lot of business purchasers, the shipping and billing addresses will usually be different. In these cases, it could get tedious for the shoppers to always have to overwrite the defaulted data.

Listing 8.19　　**Payment.aspx.vb Page_Load Procedure (continued)**

```
    ' Move any billing info that we have to the User Interface
    txtFirstName.Text = Session("BillFirstName")
    txtLastName.Text = Session("BillLastName")
    txtAddress.Text = Session("BillAddress")
    txtCity.Text = Session("BillCity")
    For Each li In ddlState.Items
        If li.Value = Session("BillState") Then
            li.Selected = True
            Exit For
        End If
    Next
    txtProvince.Text = Session("BillProvince")
    For Each li In ddlCountry.Items
        If li.Value = Session("BillCountry") Then
            li.Selected = True
            Exit For
        End If
    Next
    txtZipcode.Text = Session("BillZipCode")
    txtPhone.Text = Session("BillPhone")
    txtEmail.Text = Session("BillEmail")
    For Each li In rblProfile.Items
        If li.Value = Session("Cookie") Then
            li.Selected = True
```

```
        Exit For
    End If
Next
```

After the billing information has been added to the page, it will be displayed for the shopper to confirm or modify. Here, they can also make some choices about their profile. We want to provide two options for the shopper. The first is to have their profile saved as a cookie on their machine; that way, it will be automatically accessed the next time they return. The second option is to have a password saved with the profile so the shopper can retrieve their order status, or retrieve their profile from another machine where the cookie is not set.

NOTE   The shopper could have the cookie set and have their profile retrieved on the next visit. But, if they don't have a password set, they won't be able to access the order status portion of the site. Even if a cookie is set, we will still require that the shopper enter their e-mail address and password to retrieve their order status, as you'll see in Chapter 9.

When the shopper finishes entering information and clicks the Submit button, the data that they've entered is validated by the validation controls. As with the shipping page, most of these are RequiredFieldValidator controls. However, for the credit card number field, we've used a RegularExpressionValidator with this expression:

```
[-0-9]+
```

The square brackets define a set of characters that are acceptable within this field: a hyphen or any numeric character from zero through nine. The plus sign at the end specifies that the regular expression matches one or more such characters. Another option (which we didn't use) is to specify exactly how many characters can be entered. For example, we could validate for 16 to 20 characters consisting of hyphens and numerals with this regular expression:

```
[-0-9]{16,20}
```

There is additional code that gets invoked on postback to finish the validation. Similar to the code that you've already seen for the Shipping.aspx page, this code verifies that either a state or a province, but not both, was filled in as appropriate. Listing 8.20 shows this code.

Listing 8.20   **Payment.aspx.vb Form_Load Procedure (continued)**

```
Else ' IsPostBack
    ' Perform validations that are too complex for
    ' the validation controls
    ' First check: make sure a state is selected
    ' if this is a US address, or a province if
    ' this is a non-US address
    lblError.Visible = False
```

```
If ddlCountry.SelectedItem.Value = "US" Then
    If ddlState.SelectedItem.Value = "" Then
        lblError.Text = "You must select a state."
        lblError.Visible = True
    End If
Else ' Country other than US
    If txtProvince.Text = "" Then
        lblError.Text = "You must specify a province."
        lblError.Visible = True
    End If
End If
' Second check: make sure they haven't selected
' both a state and a province. In this case, need
' to change the error message
If (ddlState.SelectedItem.Value <> "") And _
(txtProvince.Text <> "") Then
    lblError.Text = _
      "You cannot specify both a state and a province."
    lblError.Visible = True
End If
```

Assuming the data passes all the validation steps, we can finally insert the order into the database. We'll do that in the next section. But first, let's look at the stored procedure that we called when filling in this page. The procBasketDetails stored procedure is used to retrieve the total number of basket items in the shopper's order and the subtotal for those items. Listing 8.21 shows the SQL code that performs these functions.

Listing 8.21   procBasketDetails Stored Procedure

```
/* Return the number of items in a shopping
   basket and their current subtotal, given
   the basket ID.

From .NET E-Commerce Programming
by Mike Gunderloy and Noel Jerke
Copyright 2002, Sybex Inc. All Rights Reserved. */
CREATE PROCEDURE procBasketDetails
  @BasketID int,
  @Quantity int OUTPUT,
  @Subtotal money OUTPUT
AS
  SELECT @Quantity = SUM(BasketItemQuantity)
    FROM BasketItem
    WHERE BasketID = @BasketID
  SELECT @Subtotal = SUM(BasketItemQuantity *
    BasketItemPrice)
    FROM BasketItem
    WHERE BasketID = @BasketID
```

Figure 8.10 shows the payment page as it initially loads, containing the data entered from the shopper's last interaction with the basket on the shipping page. Note that the payment data is blank, since this is the first visit to the page. The billing address is automatically filled in with the shipping information, but the shopper can change that here if they like.

The order recap is displayed at the top of the page. In this case, there's a tax amount because the shipping address is Virginia, where we charge a tax of 4.5%. The shipping fee is $2.00 because there were between 1 and 10 items in the shopping basket.

FIGURE 8.10:

Payment page

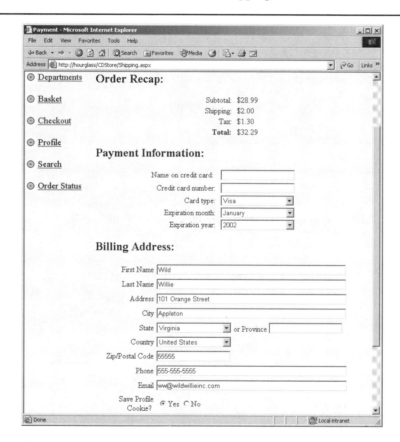

Figure 8.11 shows the payment page after some payment data has been filled in.

FIGURE 8.11:

Payment page ready to submit

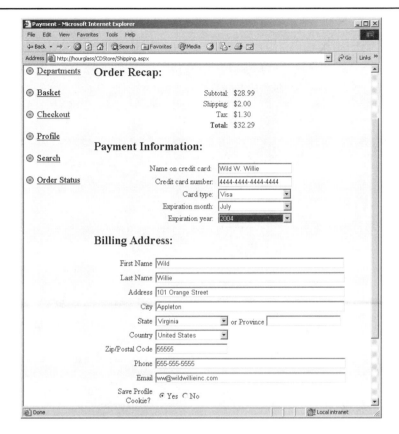

Now that the shopper can enter their payment data and we have seen it validated, let's explore the payment validation phase of the checkout process.

Credit Card Validation

Making certain that proper credit card data has been retrieved is critical to ensuring that we receive the payment properly. There are a number of additional validation steps we can take to ensure that the data is correct, beyond those that we've taken in our sample. The first is to utilize checksum calculations to confirm that the credit card number meets the proper validation set forth by the credit card companies. For each type of credit card (MasterCard, Visa, and so on), there are mathematical calculations that can tell you whether a card number is valid or is just a string of numbers that someone made up. Another possible step is to check the expiration date to confirm that it's in or after the current month.

Continued on next page

> We can also use tools such as VeriSign's PayFlow to do live validation and clearing at the point the data is entered. There are even tools on the market that maintain lists of fraudulent cards that can be checked against your customers' cards to ensure that a valid payment is being received. Delving into these tools is beyond the scope of this book. One useful reference is a Microsoft white paper titled "Collecting Payment with an Online Business," which is available at `http://msdn.microsoft.com/library/default.asp?url=/library/en-us/dnduwam/html/d4paymnt.asp`.

Processing the Order

If all of the billing information is valid, we start the process of completing the order. This happens in several steps:

1. Clean the shipping data, to ensure that it's ready for insertion into the SQL database.

2. Clean the billing data so that it's ready for insertion.

3. Insert the order data into the database.

4. Insert the payment data into the database.

5. Initialize the order status tracking to indicate that the order is received.

6. Update the basket with the final order data.

7. Update the shopper's profile based on the new billing data.

8. Send an e-mail receipt to the shopper.

9. Set a cookie containing the profile ID.

Now, let's take a look at the code behind each of these steps. First, we'll clean the shipping data. We need to ensure that any single quotes (or apostrophes) that may be entered in the shipping data (like O'Malley) are doubled for our insert into the database. Remember, single quotes need to be doubled in a string so that they will insert properly via SQL. Listing 8.22 shows this step.

Listing 8.22   Payment.aspx.vb Page_Load Procedure (continued)

```
If Not lblError.Visible Then
    ' User has submitted data. We won't actually get
    ' here unless the data is passed by all of the
    ' validation controls

    ' Store all of the data
```

```
Session("CCName") = txtCCName.Text
Session("CCNumber") = txtCCNumber.Text
Session("CCType") = ddlCardType.SelectedItem.Value
Session("CCExpMonth") = ddlMonth.SelectedItem.Value
Session("CCExpYear") = ddlYear.SelectedItem.Value
Session("BillFirstName") = txtFirstName.Text
Session("BillLastName") = txtLastName.Text
Session("BillAddress") = txtAddress.Text
Session("BillCity") = txtCity.Text
Session("BillState") = ddlState.SelectedItem.Value
Session("BillProvince") = txtProvince.Text
Session("BillCountry") = ddlCountry.SelectedItem.Value
Session("BillZipcode") = txtZipcode.Text
Session("BillEmail") = txtEmail.Text
Session("Password") = txtPassword.TemplateSourceDirectory
Session("Cookie") = rblProfile.SelectedItem.Value

'  We are ready to store and finish the order.  This happens
'  in many steps.

'***************************************************
'**** 1.  Clean the shipping data.
'***************************************************

'  Ensure that the shipping data is validated for SQL inserts.
'  We will check for single quotes and double them up
Session("ShipFirstName") = _
 Replace(Session("ShipFirstName"), "'", "''")
Session("ShipLastName") = _
 Replace(Session("ShipLastName"), "'", "''")
Session("ShipAddress") = _
 Replace(Session("ShipAddress"), "'", "''")
Session("ShipCity") = _
 Replace(Session("ShipCity"), "'", "''")
Session("ShipProvince") = _
 Replace(Session("ShipProvince"), "'", "''")
```

The next step is to similarly clean the billing data, as shown in Listing 8.23. Note that here, we remove any hyphens that were entered as part of the credit card number.

Listing 8.23   **Payment.aspx.vb Page_Load Procedure (continued)**

```
'***************************************************
'**** 2.  Clean the billing data.
'***************************************************

'  Prepare the billing data for inserts
Session("CCName") = _
 Replace(Session("ShipFirstName"), "'", "''")
'  For the credit card number, strip out hyphens
```

```
Session("CCNumber") = _
 Replace(Session("CCNumber"), "-", "")
Session("BillFirstName") = _
 Replace(Session("BillFirstName"), "'", "''")
Session("BillLastName") = _
 Replace(Session("BillLastName"), "'", "''")
Session("BillAddress") = _
 Replace(Session("BillAddress"), "'", "''")
Session("BillCity") = _
 Replace(Session("BillCity"), "'", "''")
Session("BillProvince") = _
 Replace(Session("BillProvince"), "'", "''")
```

Next, we insert the actual order into the database, using the procInsertOrderData stored procedure. Pay particular attention to the code that sets the @State and @Province parameters. If the shopper hasn't entered anything into one of these fields, their value will be Nothing, which is different from the DBNull that a database expects for indicating an empty field. Listing 8.24 shows this code.

Listing 8.24   Payment.aspx.vb Page_Load Procedure (continued)

```
'***************************************************
'**** 3.  Insert the order information into
'****     the database.
'***************************************************

With cmdInsertOrderData
    .Parameters("@ShopperID").Value = _
     Session("idShopper")
    .Parameters("@ShipFirstName").Value = _
     Session("ShipFirstName")
    .Parameters("@ShipLastName").Value = _
     Session("ShipLastName")
    .Parameters("@ShipAddress").Value = _
     Session("ShipAddress")
    .Parameters("@ShipCity").Value = _
     Session("ShipCity")
    If Session("ShipState") Is Nothing Then
        .Parameters("@ShipState").Value = DBNull.Value
    Else
        .Parameters("@ShipState").Value = _
         Session("ShipState")
    End If
    If Session("ShipProvince") Is Nothing Then
        .Parameters("@ShipProvince").Value = DBNull.Value
    Else
        .Parameters("@ShipProvince").Value = _
         Session("ShipProvince")
    End If
    .Parameters("@ShipCountry").Value = _
```

```
        Session("ShipCountry")
        .Parameters("@ShipZipCode").Value = _
        Session("ShipZipCode")
        .Parameters("@ShipPhone").Value = _
        Session("ShipPhone")
        .Parameters("@ShipEmail").Value = _
        Session("ShipEmail")
        .Parameters("@BillFirstName").Value = _
        Session("BillFirstName")
        .Parameters("@BillLastName").Value = _
        Session("BillLastName")
        .Parameters("@BillAddress").Value = _
        Session("BillAddress")
        .Parameters("@BillCity").Value = _
        Session("BillCity")
        If Session("BillState") Is Nothing Then
            .Parameters("@BillState").Value = DBNull.Value
        Else
            .Parameters("@BillState").Value = _
            Session("BillState")
        End If
        If Session("BillProvince") Is Nothing Then
            .Parameters("@BillProvince").Value = DBNull.Value
        Else
            .Parameters("@BillProvince").Value = _
            Session("BillProvince")
        End If
        .Parameters("@BillCountry").Value = _
        Session("BillCountry")
        .Parameters("@BillZipCode").Value = _
        Session("BillZipCode")
        .Parameters("@BillPhone").Value = _
        Session("BillPhone")
        .Parameters("@BillEmail").Value = _
        Session("BillEmail")
        .Parameters("@BasketID").Value = _
        Session("idBasket")
        cnn.Open()
        Session("idOrder") = .ExecuteScalar
        cnn.Close()
    End With
```

Remember that we are storing the payment data separately from the order data. This is to allow easy management of credit card data, which we probably won't store for the long term (due to privacy concerns). The code calls the procInsertPaymentData stored procedure, passing the order ID along with the payment data, as shown in Listing 8.25.

Listing 8.25   **Payment.aspx.vb Page_Load Procedure (continued)**

```
'*************************************************
'**** 4.  Insert the payment information into
'****      the database.
'*************************************************

'   Insert the payment data into the Payment table
With cmdInsertPaymentData
    .Parameters("@OrderID").Value = _
     Session("idOrder")
    .Parameters("@CardType").Value() = _
     Session("CCType")
    .Parameters("@CardNumber").Value() = _
     Session("CCNumber")
    .Parameters("@ExpDate").Value() = _
     Session("CCExpMonth") & " " & Session("CCExpYear")
    .Parameters("@CardName").Value() = _
     Session("CCName")
    cnn.Open()
    .ExecuteNonQuery()
    cnn.Close()
End With
```

Next, we need to initialize the order history for the order. The first status is that of the order being received. The procInitializeOrderStatus stored procedure will do this. Note that using the stored procedure encapsulates the business rules behind order tracking. That way, if the codes for initial status change, the programming in this page won't have to be changed. Listing 8.26 shows this section of the code.

Listing 8.26   **Payment.aspx.vb Page_Load Procedure (continued)**

```
'*************************************************
'**** 5.  Initialize the order status tracking
'****      to indicate the order is received.
'*************************************************

cmdInitializeOrderStatus.Parameters("@OrderID").Value = _
  Session("idOrder")
cnn.Open()
cmdInitializeOrderStatus.ExecuteNonQuery()
cnn.Close()
```

The next step is to ensure that the shopping basket has the final data. Remember that the basket stores the total quantity, subtotal, shipping fee, tax fee, and final total. We're storing this information with the basket because business rules such as shipping and tax calculations can change over time. We want the basket to hold a snapshot of what the charges are at this point in time. The code uses the procUpdateBasket stored procedure for this purpose, as shown in Listing 8.27.

Listing 8.27 **Payment.aspx.vb Page_Load Procedure (continued)**

```
'****************************************************
'**** 6.  Update the basket with the final
'****     order data.
'****************************************************

With cmdUpdateBasket
    .Parameters("@BasketID").Value = _
    Session("idBasket")
    .Parameters("@Quantity").Value = _
    Session("Quantity")
    .Parameters("@Subtotal").Value = _
    Session("Subtotal")
    .Parameters("@Tax").Value = _
    Session("Tax")
    .Parameters("@Shipping").Value = _
    Session("Shipping")
    .Parameters("@Total").Value = _
    Session("Total")
    cnn.Open()
    .ExecuteNonQuery()
    cnn.Close()
End With
```

Next, we need to update the profile of the shopper. Remember that if no previous profile can be retrieved, a new profile is created when the shopper begins browsing through the store; thus, we can be sure that the shopper has a profile record before this code is executed.

The procUpdateShopper stored procedure handles updating the profile data, as shown in Listing 8.28. We are using the billing information as the long-term profile data. It's conceivable that we could also store the shipping data and have that retrieved at a later date.

Note that both the cookie and the password are set as well. If the shopper doesn't enter a password, there is no way they can retrieve the profile for accessing the order history status. If they have the cookie set, the profile will be retrieved automatically at the next visit.

Listing 8.28 **Payment.aspx.vb Page_Load Procedure (continued)**

```
'****************************************************
'**** 7.  Update the profile based on the new
'****     billing information.
'****************************************************
```

```
With cmdUpdateShopper
    .Parameters("@ShopperID").Value = _
    Session("idShopper")
    .Parameters("@FirstName").Value = _
    Session("BillFirstName")
    .Parameters("@LastName").Value = _
    Session("BillLastName")
    .Parameters("@Address").Value = _
    Session("BillAddress")
    .Parameters("@City").Value = _
    Session("BillCity")
    If Session("BillState") Is Nothing Then
        .Parameters("@State").Value = DBNull.Value
    Else
        .Parameters("@State").Value = _
        Session("BillState")
    End If
    If Session("BillProvince") Is Nothing Then
        .Parameters("@Province").Value = DBNull.Value
    Else
        .Parameters("@Province").Value = _
        Session("BillProvince")
    End If
    .Parameters("@Country").Value = _
    Session("BillCountry")
    .Parameters("@ZipCode").Value = _
    Session("BillZipcode")
    .Parameters("@Phone").Value = _
    Session("BillPhone")
    .Parameters("@Email").Value = _
    Session("BillEmail")
    .Parameters("@Password").Value = _
    Session("Password")
    .Parameters("@Cookie").Value = _
    Session("Cookie")
    cnn.Open()
    .ExecuteNonQuery()
    cnn.Close()
End With
```

It has become almost mandatory to send an e-mail confirmation receipt when an order is completed. The .NET Framework makes this task easier by supplying the MailMessage and SmtpMail classes. These classes provide a wrapper around the native Windows SMTP mailing service. Table 8.4 outlines the key properties and methods of the MailMessage object.

TABLE 8.4: Key Properties and Methods of the MailMessage Object

Property/Method	Description
Attachments	List of attachments to send with the message.
Bcc	E-mail addresses of recipients of a blind copy.

Continued on next page

TABLE 8.4 CONTINUED: Key Properties and Methods of the MailMessage Object

Property/Method	Description
Body	Text of the e-mail message.
BodyFormat	Sets the text format of the message. Options include HTML or Text.
Cc	E-mail addresses of recipients of a copy.
From	E-mail address of the message's sender.
Priority	Sets the importance associated with the e-mail address.
Subject	Sets the subject of the message.

The code creates an instance of the MailMessage object using the As New syntax. It then sets the appropriate properties of the object. For example, the To property is the e-mail address of the billing recipient. The Subject is set to indicate that this is a receipt.

The code then builds the body of the e-mail. In this case, we are going to send an order ID and the final totals on the basket. If we wanted, we could also loop through the basket items and provide complete details of the order—but the shopper can always retrieve that information by visiting the site.

Finally, the code sends the e-mail message by calling the Send method of the SmtpMail object. Note that this object is automatically instantiated for you by the .NET Framework; you don't have to create it yourself. Listing 8.29 shows the e-mailing code.

Listing 8.29   Payment.aspx.vb Page_Load Procedure (continued)

```
'*******************************************************
'**** 8.  Send an e-mail receipt to the shopper.
'*******************************************************
Dim msg As New MailMessage()
msg.From = "support@wildwillieinc.com"
msg.To = Session("BillEmail")
msg.Subject = "Wild Willie CD Receipt"
msg.Body = "Thank You for your Order!" & vbCrLf & vbCrLf & _
  "Order Id = " & Session("idOrder") & vbCrLf & _
  "Subtotal = " & Format(Session("Subtotal"), "Currency") & _
  vbCrLf & _
  "Subtotal = " & Format(Session("Shipping"), "Currency") & _
  vbCrLf & _
  "Subtotal = " & Format(Session("Tax"), "Currency") & _
  vbCrLf & _
  "Subtotal = " & Format(Session("Total"), "Currency") & _
  vbCrLf & vbCrLf & _
  "Please call 1-800-555-Wild with any questions.  " & _
  "Be sure to check back to retrieve your order status."
SmtpMail.Send(msg)
```

The last step in the process is to see whether the shopper wants a cookie to be set, to simplify the retrieval of their profile. To do this, we will use the Cookies collection of the Response object. The name of our cookie is WWCD (for Wild Willie's CDs). All we need to store in the cookie is the ID of the shopper, which we can use to retrieve all of the other shopper information if the shopper returns to the store.

We also need to set an expiration date to make the cookie stay "permanently" on the machine. That's done with the Expires property of the cookie item, as shown in Listing 8.30. Once this step is completed, we are ready to send the shopper on to the confirmation page.

Listing 8.30   **Payment.aspx.vb Page_Load Procedure (continued)**

```
'*************************************************
'**** 9.  Write out a cookie if the user
'****       requested it to be written.
'*************************************************

If Session("Cookie") = 1 Then
    Response.Cookies("WWCD").Value = Session("idShopper")
    Response.Cookies("WWCD").Expires = _
    DateTime.Today.AddDays(365).ToShortDateString
End If

' Processing is finished!
' Send the user to the confirmation page
    Server.Transfer("Confirmed.aspx")
        End If
    End If
End Sub
```

Now we'll look at the stored procedures that are used on this page to handle the checkout process. The first is procInsertOrderData. This stored procedure takes all the information about the order and adds a row to the Order table, as shown in Listing 8.31. Note the use of the @@IDENTITY variable from SQL Server to return the order ID of the new order.

Listing 8.31   **procInsertOrderData Stored Procedure**

```
/*  Insert the basic order information
by Mike Gunderloy and Noel Jerke

From .NET E-Commerce Programming
by Mike Gunderloy and Noel Jerke
Copyright 2002, Sybex Inc. All Rights Reserved. */
CREATE PROCEDURE procInsertOrderData
    @ShopperID int,
    @ShipFirstName varchar(50),
    @ShipLastName varchar(50),
```

```
     @ShipAddress varchar(150),
     @ShipCity varchar(150),
     @ShipState varchar(50),
     @ShipProvince varchar(150),
     @ShipCountry varchar(100),
     @ShipZipCode varchar(15),
     @ShipPhone varchar(25),
     @ShipEmail varchar(100),
     @BillFirstName varchar(50),
     @BillLastName varchar(150),
     @BillAddress varchar(150),
     @BillCity varchar(150),
     @BillState varchar(50),
     @BillProvince varchar(150),
     @BillCountry varchar(100),
     @BillZipCode varchar(15),
     @BillPhone varchar(25),
     @BillEmail varchar(100),
     @BasketID int
AS
  INSERT INTO [Order](ShopperID, OrderShipFirstName,
     OrderShipLastName, OrderShipAddress,
     OrderShipCity, OrderShipState,
     OrderShipProvince, OrderShipCountry,
     OrderShipZipCode, OrderShipPhone,
     OrderShipEmail, OrderBillFirstName,
     OrderBillLastName, OrderBillAddress,
     OrderBillCity, OrderBillState,
     OrderBillProvince, OrderBillCountry,
     OrderBillZipCode, OrderBillPhone,
     OrderBillEmail, BasketID)
  VALUES(@ShopperID, @ShipFirstName,
     @ShipLastName, @ShipAddress,
     @ShipCity, @ShipState,
     @ShipProvince, @ShipCountry,
     @ShipZipCode, @ShipPhone,
     @ShipEmail, @BillFirstName,
     @BillLastName, @BillAddress,
     @BillCity, @BillState,
     @BillProvince, @BillCountry,
     @BillZipCode, @BillPhone,
     @BillEmail, @BasketID)
  /* Return the autogenerated ID as the value
     of this stored procedure */
  SELECT @@IDENTITY
```

The next stored procedure, shown in Listing 8.32, inserts the payment data into the database. The stored procedure, procInertPaymentData, takes in the ID of the order, the card type, the card number, the expiration date, and the cardholder's name. Note that the expiration date is the combination of the expiration month and expiration year from the Web Form. The stored procedure then inserts the data into the Payment table.

Listing 8.32   **procInsertPaymentData Stored Procedure**

```
CREATE PROCEDURE procInsertPaymentData
  @OrderID int,
  @CardType varchar(50),
  @CardNumber varchar(30),
  @ExpDate varchar(25),
  @CardName varchar(150)
AS
  INSERT INTO Payment (OrderID, PaymentCardType,
    PaymentCardNumber, PaymentExpDate,
    PaymentCardName)
  VALUES (@OrderID, @CardType,
    @CardNumber, @ExpDate,
    @CardName)
```

The procInitializeOrderStatus stored procedure adds a row to the OrderStatus table to indicate that we've taken, but not yet processed, the order. Listing 8.33 shows this stored procedure.

Listing 8.33   **procInitializeOrderStatus Stored Procedure**

```
/*  Initialize the order status table for
    a new order

From .NET E-Commerce Programming
by Mike Gunderloy and Noel Jerke
Copyright 2002, Sybex Inc. All Rights Reserved. */
CREATE PROCEDURE procInitializeOrderStatus
  @OrderID int
AS
  INSERT INTO OrderStatus(OrderID, OrderStatusProcessed)
  VALUES(@OrderID, 0)
```

The procUpdateBasket stored procedure, shown in Listing 8.34, takes the information that we calculated for the overall order and inserts it into the Basket table.

Listing 8.34   **procUpdateBasket Stored Procedure**

```
/*  Update the basket with final order totals

From .NET E-Commerce Programming
by Mike Gunderloy and Noel Jerke
Copyright 2002, Sybex Inc. All Rights Reserved. */
```

```
CREATE PROCEDURE procUpdateBasket
  @BasketID int,
  @Quantity int,
  @Subtotal money,
  @Shipping money,
  @Tax money,
  @Total money
AS
  UPDATE Basket
    SET BasketQuantity = @Quantity,
    BasketSubtotal = @Subtotal,
    BasketShipping = @Shipping,
    BasketTax = @Tax,
    BasketTotal = @Total
  WHERE
    BasketID = @BasketID
```

Finally, the procUpdateShopper stored procedure updates the shopper's profile. This stored procedure, shown in Listing 8.35, saves the billing information for the shopper so that it will be available when they revisit the store.

Listing 8.35   **procUpdateShopper Stored Procedure**

```
/*  Update the shopper with final billing information

From .NET E-Commerce Programming
by Mike Gunderloy and Noel Jerke
Copyright 2002, Sybex Inc. All Rights Reserved. */
CREATE PROCEDURE procUpdateShopper
  @ShopperID int,
  @FirstName varchar(50),
  @LastName varchar(50),
  @Address varchar(150),
  @City varchar(100),
  @State varchar(2),
  @Province varchar(150),
  @Country varchar(100),
  @ZipCode varchar(15),
  @Phone varchar(30),
  @Email varchar(150),
  @Password varchar(25),
  @Cookie tinyint
AS
  UPDATE Shopper
    SET ShopperFirstName = @FirstName,
    ShopperLastName = @LastName,
    ShopperAddress = @Address,
    ShopperCity = @City,
    ShopperState = @State,
```

```
ShopperProvince = @Province,
ShopperCountry = @Country,
ShopperZipCode = @ZipCode,
ShopperPhone = @Phone,
ShopperEmail = @Email,
ShopperPassword = @Password,
ShopperCookie = @Cookie
```

That does it for validating and storing payment data. At the end of this code, the shopper has successfully completed an order and updated their profile. Now they are ready to get their order number and move on to other activities—in our store or elsewhere.

The Confirmation Page

The confirmation page is fairly straightforward. Its primary purpose is to provide an initial indicator that the order is completed. The shopper is thanked for their order and receives their order number for tracking. The HTML code for the page simply contains a thank-you message and a label control that the code can fill in with the order number. Listing 8.36 shows the HTML for this page.

Listing 8.36   Confirmed.aspx

```
<%@ Page Language="vb" AutoEventWireup="false"
 Inherits="CDStore.Confirmed"%>
<!DOCTYPE HTML PUBLIC "-//W3C//DTD HTML 4.0 Transitional//EN">
<HTML>
    <HEAD>
        <TITLE>Order Confirmation</TITLE>
    </HEAD>
    <meta content="Microsoft Visual Studio.NET 7.0" name="GENERATOR">
    <meta content="Visual Basic 7.0" name="CODE_LANGUAGE">
    <meta content="JavaScript" name="vs_defaultClientScript">
    <meta content="http://schemas.microsoft.com/intellisense/ie5"
     name="vs_targetSchema">
    <!-- Confirmed.aspx: confirm that the order was processed -->
    <!-- #Include File="Header.inc" -->
    <form id="Form1" method="post" runat="server">
        <P>
            <asp:Label id="Label1" runat="server" Height="21px">
            Thank you for your order! Have fun grooving to the cool
            music that you ordered! </asp:Label></P>
        <P>
            <asp:Label id="lblOrderID" runat="server">Label</asp:Label></P>
    </form>
    <!-- #Include File="Footer.inc" -->
</HTML>
```

The first thing we do in the code-behind file for this page is check to ensure that an order ID is set for the session. If not, the shopper should not be accessing this page; in this case, the shopper is sent back to the basket page, where they can continue shopping. Listing 8.37 shows the code.

Listing 8.37   **Confirmed.aspx.vb Page_Load Procedure**

```
Private Sub Page_Load(ByVal sender As System.Object, _
  ByVal e As System.EventArgs) Handles MyBase.Load
    ' If for some reason they're on this page
    ' without an Order ID, just go back to the basket
    If CType(Session("idOrder"), String) = "" Then
        Server.Transfer("Basket.aspx")
    End If
```

The code then fills in the Text property for the lblOrderID control with a message that includes the actual order ID for this order.

The last thing we want to do is ensure that all session data is cleared in case the shopper decides to continue shopping. This is done using the Abandon method of the session object. If we didn't do this, we'd risk alienating customers by accidentally shipping them the same merchandise twice. Listing 8.38 shows the code that concludes this page.

Listing 8.38   **Confirmed.aspx.vb Page_Load Procedure (continued)**

```
    ' Otherwise, show the Order ID
    lblOrderID.Text = "Your Order ID is " & _
    CType(Session("idOrder"), String) & _
    ". You should receive a confirmation " & _
    "e-mail shortly."

    ' And clear out this session
    Session.Abandon()

End Sub
```

Figure 8.12 shows the confirmation page after the shopper completes an order. If the shopper clicks the shopping basket at this point, the contents will be cleared and a new shopping session will be started.

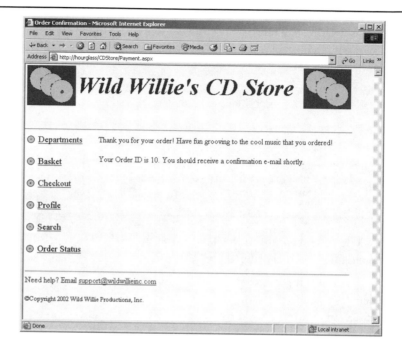

Summary

The shopper has finally completed an order! Our sample shopping system provides all the key processes for browsing, managing a basket, and checking out. As noted throughout this chapter, there are many different options for managing the checkout process. But the ultimate goal is to allow the shopper to check out quickly and ensure that the data we collect is as valid as possible.

The goal in the next chapter will be to manage the shopper's interaction the next time they visit the store. This includes both profile management and order history retrieval.

CHAPTER 9

Order Status and Profile Management

- Profile Interface

- Order History Interface

W e're on the last leg of building the shopper experience. In this chapter, we'll look at the various web pages that allow a shopper to manage their profile or review their order history. These are the post-purchasing functions that help to minimize the need for a shopper to contact a customer service representative.

Profile Interface

On the navigation menu for the shopper, we've included an option to work with the profile, but we haven't explored it yet. When the shopper clicks the Profile link, they're given an option to log in with an e-mail address and password.

TIP   Why not just use the shopper ID if we've already retrieved it from a cookie? The answer is that requiring the shopper to know a piece of information that's stored only on the server helps ensure the privacy of the shopper's sensitive information.

The Profile.aspx page provides the login form for the profile process. Figure 9.1 shows this form in action, and Listing 9.1 shows its HTML code.

FIGURE 9.1:

Retrieving a profile

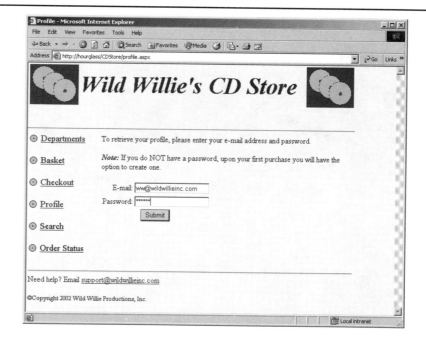

Listing 9.1   **Profile.aspx**

```
<%@ Page Language="vb" AutoEventWireup="false" Codebehind="Profile.aspx.vb"
 Inherits="CDStore.Profile"%>
<!DOCTYPE HTML PUBLIC "-//W3C//DTD HTML 4.0 Transitional//EN">
<HTML>
    <HEAD>
        <TITLE>Profile</TITLE>
    </HEAD>
    <meta name="GENERATOR" content="Microsoft Visual Studio.NET 7.0">
    <meta name="CODE_LANGUAGE" content="Visual Basic 7.0">
    <meta name="vs_defaultClientScript" content="JavaScript">
    <meta name="vs_targetSchema" content=
     "http://schemas.microsoft.com/intellisense/ie5">
    <!-- Profile.asp - Display a login in to the profile. -->
    <!-- #include file="Header.inc" -->
    To retrieve your profile, please enter your e-mail address and password.
    <BR>
    <BR>
    <b><i>Note:</b></I> If you do NOT have a password, upon your first
    purchase you will have the option to create one.
<BR>
    <BR>
    <!--  Form to post the request -->
    <form method="post" action="ProfileDisplay.aspx">
        <!--  Table that allows the user to enter an e-mail address
      and password. -->
        <table>
            <tr>
                <td align="right">
                    E-mail:
                </td>
                <td>
                    <input type="text" name="email">
                </td>
            </tr>
            <tr>
                <td align="right">
                    Password:
                </td>
                <td>
                    <input type="password" name="password">
                </td>
            </tr>
            <tr>
                <td colspan="2" align="middle">
                    <input type="submit" value="Submit" name="submit">
                </td>
            </tr>
        </table>
    </form>
    <!-- #include file="Footer.inc" -->
</HTML>
```

If you inspect Listing 9.1, you'll see that the `Profile.aspx` page is just a standard HTML input form. There's nothing .NET-specific about this page at all. This points out something that we haven't emphasized in this book—namely, that there's no need for every part of a .NET web application to use the new .NET features. In this case, all that the form needs to do is collect two pieces of information and forward them to another page. HTML works perfectly well for this, so why not use it?

Suppose the shopper enters an invalid e-mail address or password in the profile form? Figure 9.2 shows the resulting page.

FIGURE 9.2:

Error page when logging in

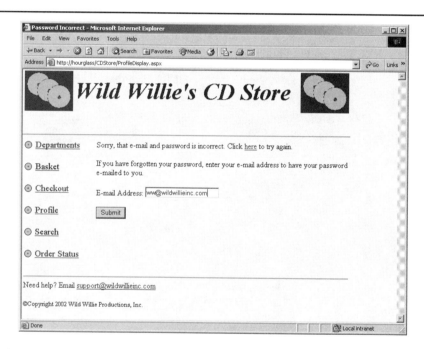

The point of this page is to allow the shopper to retrieve their password if they've forgotten it. The e-mail password page will use the .NET Web.Mail classes to e-mail the password to the shopper. For security purposes, we will e-mail a password only to a corresponding e-mail address. That way, only the e-mail address owner can receive their own password. So, if someone is trying to breach security and get into a shopper's profile or order history, they would first have to get into the e-mail of the targeted shopper.

Let's take a look at this page, `EmailPasswordPrompt.aspx`. Once again, this page is an HTML Web Form that simply posts its data to another page. Listing 9.2 shows the HTML code for `EmailPasswordPrompt.aspx`.

⤳ Listing 9.2   **EmailPasswordPrompt.aspx**

```
<%@ Page Language="vb" AutoEventWireup="false"
 Codebehind="EmailPasswordPrompt.aspx.vb"
 Inherits="CDStore.EmailPasswordPrompt"%>
<!DOCTYPE HTML PUBLIC "-//W3C//DTD HTML 4.0 Transitional//EN">
<HTML>
     <HEAD>
         <TITLE>Password Incorrect</TITLE>
     </HEAD>
     <meta name="GENERATOR" content="Microsoft Visual Studio.NET 7.0">
     <meta name="CODE_LANGUAGE" content="Visual Basic 7.0">
     <meta name="vs_defaultClientScript" content="JavaScript">
     <meta name="vs_targetSchema" content=
      "http://schemas.microsoft.com/intellisense/ie5">
     <!-- EmailPasswordPrompt.aspx: Prompt for the shopper's password -->
     <!-- #Include File="Header.inc" -->
     Sorry, that e-mail and password is incorrect. Click
     <a href="profile.aspx">here</a> to try again.<BR>
     <BR>
     If you have forgotten your password,
     enter your e-mail address to have
     your password e-mailed to you.<BR>
     <BR>
     <!--  Display a form that will e-mail the password
       to the user if it has been forgotten -->
     <form method="post" action="EmailPassword.aspx">
         E-mail Address: <input type="text" name="email"><BR>
         <BR>
         <input type="submit" value="Submit" name="submit">
     </form>
     <!-- #Include File="Footer.inc" -->
 </HTML>
```

This form posts to another Web Form, EmailPassword.aspx. The HTML code for this form is absurdly simple, as shown in Listing 9.3.

⤳ Listing 9.3   **EmailPassword.aspx**

```
<%@ Page Language="vb" AutoEventWireup="false"
 Codebehind="EmailPassword.aspx.vb" Inherits="CDStore.EmailPassword"%>
<!DOCTYPE HTML PUBLIC "-//W3C//DTD HTML 4.0 Transitional//EN">
<HTML>
     <HEAD>
         <TITLE>EmailPassword</TITLE>
     </HEAD>
     <meta name="GENERATOR" content="Microsoft Visual Studio.NET 7.0">
     <meta name="CODE_LANGUAGE" content="Visual Basic 7.0">
     <meta name="vs_defaultClientScript" content="JavaScript">
     <meta name="vs_targetSchema"
```

```
      content="http://schemas.microsoft.com/intellisense/ie5">
      <!-- EmailPassword.aspx: Send the user their password -->
      <!-- #Include File="Header.inc" -->
      <b>Your password has been sent to your e-mail address.</b>
      <!-- #Include File="Footer.inc" -->
</HTML>
```

As you can see, the user interface of this confirmation page consists of a single piece of text. Obviously, there must be more going on somewhere. As you'd expect, the real action for this page is in the code-behind file. Listing 9.4 shows this code, which works in two steps:

1. Execute a stored procedure to retrieve the shopper's password.

2. E-mail the password to the shopper.

Listing 9.4   EmailPassword.aspx.vb Page_Load Procedure

```vb
Private Sub Page_Load(ByVal sender As System.Object, _
  ByVal e As System.EventArgs) Handles MyBase.Load
    Dim strPassword As SqlTypes.SqlString
    ' Make sure they entered an e-mail address
    If Len(Request("Email")) = 0 Then
        Server.Transfer("EmailPasswordPrompt.aspx")
    End If
    ' Retrieve the shopper's password
    With cmdGetShopperPassword
        .Parameters("@Email").Value = Request("Email")
        strPassword = .ExecuteScalar
    End With
    ' If we found a password, send it to the shopper
    If Not strPassword.Value Is DBNull.Value Then
        Dim msg As New MailMessage()
        msg.From = "support@wildwillieinc.com"
        msg.To = Request("Email")
        msg.Subject = "Wild Willie Password"
        msg.Body = "Here is your password: " & _
        CType(strPassword.Value, String)
        SmtpMail.Send(msg)
    End If
End Sub
```

If the shopper enters a valid e-mail address in the request form, the password will be sent to that e-mail address. Note that, either way, we indicate that it was sent; for security purposes, we don't want to give any clues about whether a password does or does not exist.

This code uses a stored procedure to retrieve the password, based on the supplied e-mail, as shown in Listing 9.5.

Listing 9.5   **procGetShopperPassword Procedure**

```
/* Given a shopper's e-mail, retrieve their password

From .NET E-Commerce Programming
by Mike Gunderloy and Noel Jerke
Copyright 2002, Sybex Inc. All Rights Reserved. */
CREATE PROCEDURE procGetShopperPassword
  @Email varchar(150)
AS
  SELECT ShopperPassword
    FROM Shopper
    WHERE ShopperEmail = @Email
```

What happens if the supplied e-mail address doesn't correspond to a row in the Shopper table? This stored procedure will return a Null in place of the password. That's why the code shown in Listing 9.4 uses the SqlString data type to hold the returned password. The .NET Framework includes a System.SqlTypes namespace that contains classes to represent each of the SQL Server data types. For example, the SqlString data type can hold a string value (SQL Server data types varchar, char, nvarchar, nchar, and so on) or a Null. This prevents the code from raising an error if a Null is returned.

To test whether the value returned was Null, we compare the Value property of the str-Password object to the Value property of the built-in DBNull class. This special class exists only to perform Null comparisons. If the value isn't Null, that means that the stored procedure returned an actual password. In this case, the code uses the MailMessage and SmtpMail classes (which you first saw in Chapter 8, "Checking Out") to send the password back to the shopper.

Once the shopper supplies a working e-mail and password pair, we're ready to handle the display of the profile. This is the task of the ProfileDisplay.aspx page. If you recall that we store the shopper's shipping information in their profile, you won't be surprised that this page is very similar to the Shipping.aspx page that you saw in Chapter 8. The major difference is that, in this case, we're retrieving the information from the database to allow the shopper to view or edit it without necessarily having an order in progress. Listing 9.6 shows the HTML for this page. It consists primarily of a series of Web Form controls and the validation controls necessary to ensure that the shopper enters acceptable data.

Listing 9.6   **ProfileDisplay.aspx**

```
<%@ Page Language="vb" AutoEventWireup="false"
  Codebehind="ProfileDisplay.aspx.vb" Inherits="CDStore.ProfileDisplay"%>
<!DOCTYPE HTML PUBLIC "-//W3C//DTD HTML 4.0 Transitional//EN">
<HTML>
```

```
<HEAD>
    <TITLE>ProfileDisplay</TITLE>
</HEAD>
<meta content="Microsoft Visual Studio.NET 7.0" name="GENERATOR">
<meta content="Visual Basic 7.0" name="CODE_LANGUAGE">
<meta content="JavaScript" name="vs_defaultClientScript">
<meta content="http://schemas.microsoft.com/intellisense/ie5"
 name="vs_targetSchema">
<!-- ProfileDisplay.aspx: Display the shopper's profile -->
<!-- #Include File="Header.inc" -->
<form id="Form1" method="post" runat="server">
    <H2>Edit your profile:
    </H2>
    <P><asp:validationsummary id="ValidationSummary1" runat="server">
        </asp:validationsummary></P>
    <P><asp:label id="lblError" runat="server" Visible="False"
     ForeColor="Red">Label</asp:label></P>
    <P><asp:label id="lblUpdated" runat="server" Visible="False">
     Your profile has been updated!</asp:label></P>
    <P>
        <TABLE id="Table1" cellSpacing="2" cellPadding="2" width="100%"
        border="0">
            <TR>
                <TD>
                    <P align="right"><asp:requiredfieldvalidator
                     id="RequiredFieldValidator1" runat="server"
                     ControlToValidate="txtFirstName"
                     ErrorMessage="You must enter a first name.">*
                     </asp:requiredfieldvalidator>First Name</P>
                </TD>
                <TD><asp:textbox id="txtFirstName" runat="server"
                 Width="394px"></asp:textbox></TD>
            </TR>
            <TR>
                <TD>
                    <P align="right"><asp:requiredfieldvalidator
                     id="RequiredFieldValidator2" runat="server"
                     ControlToValidate="txtLastName"
                     ErrorMessage="You must enter a last name.">*
                     </asp:requiredfieldvalidator>Last Name</P>
                </TD>
                <TD><asp:textbox id="txtLastName" runat="server"
                 Width="395px"></asp:textbox></TD>
            </TR>
            <TR>
                <TD>
                    <P align="right"><asp:requiredfieldvalidator
                     id="RequiredFieldValidator3" runat="server"
                     ControlToValidate="txtAddress"
                     ErrorMessage="You must enter an address.">*
                     </asp:requiredfieldvalidator>Address</P>
```

```
        </TD>
        <TD><asp:textbox id="txtAddress" runat="server"
        Width="396px"></asp:textbox></TD>
    </TR>
    <TR>
        <TD>
            <P align="right"><asp:requiredfieldvalidator
             id="RequiredFieldValidator4" runat="server"
             ControlToValidate="txtCity"
             ErrorMessage="You must enter a city.">*
             </asp:requiredfieldvalidator>City</P>
        </TD>
        <TD><asp:textbox id="txtCity" runat="server"
        Width="395px"></asp:textbox></TD>
    </TR>
    <TR>
        <TD>
            <P align="right">State</P>
        </TD>
        <TD><asp:dropdownlist id="ddlState" runat="server"
        Width="154px">
                <asp:ListItem Value="">Select a state
                </asp:ListItem>
                <asp:ListItem value="AL">Alabama
                </asp:ListItem>
                <asp:ListItem value="AK">Alaska
                </asp:ListItem>
                <asp:ListItem value="AZ">Arizona
                </asp:ListItem>
                <asp:ListItem value="AR">Arkansas
                </asp:ListItem>
                <asp:ListItem value="CA">California
                </asp:ListItem>
                <asp:ListItem value="CT">Connecticut
                </asp:ListItem>
                <asp:ListItem value="CO">Colorado
                </asp:ListItem>
                <asp:ListItem value="DC">D.C.
                </asp:ListItem>
                <asp:ListItem value="DE">Delaware
                </asp:ListItem>
                <asp:ListItem value="FL">Florida
                </asp:ListItem>
                <asp:ListItem value="GA">Georgia
                </asp:ListItem>
                <asp:ListItem value="HI">Hawaii
                </asp:ListItem>
                <asp:ListItem value="ID">Idaho
                </asp:ListItem>
                <asp:ListItem value="IL">Illinois
                </asp:ListItem>
```

```
<asp:ListItem value="IN">Indiana
</asp:ListItem>
<asp:ListItem value="IA">Iowa
</asp:ListItem>
<asp:ListItem value="KS">Kansas
</asp:ListItem>
<asp:ListItem value="KY">Kentucky
</asp:ListItem>
<asp:ListItem value="LA">Louisiana
</asp:ListItem>
<asp:ListItem value="ME">Maine
</asp:ListItem>
<asp:ListItem value="MA">Massachusetts
</asp:ListItem>
<asp:ListItem value="MD">Maryland
</asp:ListItem>
<asp:ListItem value="MI">Michigan
</asp:ListItem>
<asp:ListItem value="MN">Minnesota
</asp:ListItem>
<asp:ListItem value="MS">Mississippi
</asp:ListItem>
<asp:ListItem value="MO">Missouri
</asp:ListItem>
<asp:ListItem value="MT">Montana
</asp:ListItem>
<asp:ListItem value="NE">Nebraska
</asp:ListItem>
<asp:ListItem value="NV">Nevada
</asp:ListItem>
<asp:ListItem value="NH">New Hampshire
</asp:ListItem>
<asp:ListItem value="NJ">New Jersey
</asp:ListItem>
<asp:ListItem value="NM">New Mexico
</asp:ListItem>
<asp:ListItem value="NY">New York
</asp:ListItem>
<asp:ListItem value="NC">North Carolina
</asp:ListItem>
<asp:ListItem value="ND">North Dakota
</asp:ListItem>
<asp:ListItem value="OH">Ohio
</asp:ListItem>
<asp:ListItem value="OK">Oklahoma
</asp:ListItem>
<asp:ListItem value="OR">Oregon
</asp:ListItem>
<asp:ListItem value="PA">Pennsylvania
</asp:ListItem>
<asp:ListItem value="RI">Rhode Island
```

```
                        </asp:ListItem>
                        <asp:ListItem value="SC">South Carolina
                        </asp:ListItem>
                        <asp:ListItem value="SD">South Dakota
                        </asp:ListItem>
                        <asp:ListItem value="TN">Tennessee
                        </asp:ListItem>
                        <asp:ListItem value="TX">Texas
                        </asp:ListItem>
                        <asp:ListItem value="UT">Utah
                        </asp:ListItem>
                        <asp:ListItem value="VT">Vermont
                        </asp:ListItem>
                        <asp:ListItem value="VA">Virginia
                        </asp:ListItem>
                        <asp:ListItem value="WA">Washington
                        </asp:ListItem>
                        <asp:ListItem value="WY">Wyoming
                        </asp:ListItem>
                        <asp:ListItem value="WI">Wisconsin
                        </asp:ListItem>
                        <asp:ListItem value="WV">West Virginia
                        </asp:ListItem>
                </asp:dropdownlist> or Province
                <asp:textbox id="txtProvince" runat="server">
                </asp:textbox></TD>
        </TR>
        <TR>
            <TD>
                <P align="right"><asp:requiredfieldvalidator
                 id="RequiredFieldValidator5" runat="server"
                 ControlToValidate="ddlCountry"
                 ErrorMessage="You must select a country.">*
                 </asp:requiredfieldvalidator>Country</P>
            </TD>
            <TD><asp:dropdownlist id="ddlCountry" runat="server"
             Width="154px">
                    <asp:ListItem>Select a country</asp:ListItem>
                    <asp:ListItem Value="US">United States
                     </asp:ListItem>
                    <asp:ListItem Value="CA">Canada</asp:ListItem>
                    <asp:ListItem Value="MX">Mexico</asp:ListItem>
                </asp:dropdownlist></TD>
        </TR>
        <TR>
            <TD>
                <P align="right"><asp:requiredfieldvalidator
                 id="RequiredFieldValidator6" runat="server"
                 ControlToValidate="txtZipcode"
                 ErrorMessage=
                 "You must enter a zip or postal code.">*
```

```
                    </asp:requiredfieldvalidator>Zip/Postal Code</P>
                </TD>
                <TD><asp:textbox id="txtZipcode" runat="server"
                Width="152px"></asp:textbox></TD>
            </TR>
            <TR>
                <TD>
                    <P align="right"><asp:requiredfieldvalidator
                    id="RequiredFieldValidator7" runat="server"
                    ControlToValidate="txtPhone"
                    ErrorMessage="You must enter a phone number.">*
                    </asp:requiredfieldvalidator>Phone</P>
                </TD>
                <TD><asp:textbox id="txtPhone" runat="server"
                Width="397px"></asp:textbox></TD>
            </TR>
            <TR>
                <TD>
                    <P align="right"><asp:regularexpressionvalidator
                    id="RegularExpressionValidator1" runat="server"
                    ControlToValidate="txtEmail"
                    ErrorMessage="You must enter an e-mail address."
                    ValidationExpression=
                    "\w+([-+.]\w+)*@\w+([-.]\w+)*\.\w+([-.]\w+)*">*
                    </asp:regularexpressionvalidator>Email</P>
                </TD>
                <TD><asp:textbox id="txtEmail" runat="server"
                Width="397px"></asp:textbox></TD>
            </TR>
            <TR>
                <TD>
                    <P align="right">Save Profile Cookie? </P>
                </TD>
                <TD><asp:radiobuttonlist id="rblProfile" runat="server"
                RepeatColumns="2">
                        <asp:ListItem Value="1" Selected="True">Yes
                        </asp:ListItem>
                        <asp:ListItem Value="0">No</asp:ListItem>
                    </asp:radiobuttonlist></TD>
            </TR>
            <TR>
                <TD>
                    <P align="right">Password for Profile</P>
                </TD>
                <TD><asp:textbox id="txtPassword" runat="server"
                Width="397px" TextMode="Password"></asp:textbox></TD>
            </TR>
            <TR>
                <TD>
                    <P align="center"> </P>
                </TD>
```

```
                              <TD>
                                  <P align="center"><asp:button id="Button1"
                                     runat="server" Text="Submit"></asp:button></P>
                              </TD>
                          </TR>
                      </TABLE>
                  </P>
              </form>
              <!-- #Include File="Footer.inc" -->
          </HTML>
```

As with many other web pages in the CDStore application, this one loads differently depending on whether it's the initial load of the page or the loading is in response to a post-back action. Listing 9.7 shows the code that runs when the page is first loaded.

Listing 9.7   ProfileDisplay.aspx.vb Form_Load Procedure

```vb
Private Sub Page_Load(ByVal sender As System.Object, _
  ByVal e As System.EventArgs) Handles MyBase.Load
    Dim dr As SqlDataReader
    If Not IsPostBack Then
        If Request("email") <> "" Then
            Session("email") = Request("email")
        End If
        If Request("password") <> "" Then
            Session("password") = Request("password")
        End If
        ' If no e-mail, prompt for it
        If Len(Request("email")) = 0 Then
            Server.Transfer("EmailPasswordPrompt.aspx")
        End If        cnn.Open()
        With cmdRetrieveProfile
            .Parameters("@Email").Value = Session("email")
            .Parameters("@Password").Value = Session("password")
            dr = .ExecuteReader()
        End With

        If dr.Read() Then
            ' Save the shopper ID for later. Note that the Get methods
            ' take zero-based ordinals to identify columns
            Session("idShopper") = dr.GetInt32(0)
            ' Mark this profile as not current, because they can
            ' now edit it
            Session("ProfileRetrieve") = "0"
            ' And fill in the information on the UI
            txtFirstName.Text = dr.GetString(1)
            txtLastName.Text = dr.GetString(2)
            txtAddress.Text = dr.GetString(3)
            txtCity.Text = dr.GetString(4)
```

```
        Dim li As ListItem
        If Not dr.IsDBNull(5) Then
            For Each li In ddlState.Items
                If li.Value = dr.GetString(5) Then
                    li.Selected = True
                    Exit For
                End If
            Next
        End If
        If Not dr.IsDBNull(6) Then
            txtProvince.Text = dr.GetString(6)
        End If
        For Each li In ddlCountry.Items
            If li.Value = dr.GetString(7) Then
                li.Selected = True
                Exit For
            End If
        Next
        txtZipcode.Text = dr.GetString(8)
        txtPhone.Text = dr.GetString(9)
        txtEmail.Text = dr.GetString(11)
        txtPassword.Text = dr.GetString(14)
        For Each li In rblProfile.Items
            If li.Value = dr.GetByte(15) Then
                li.Selected = True
                Exit For
            End If
        Next

    Else
        ' Read returns False if no data is available.
        ' In this case, send them to a form to
        ' try again
        Server.Transfer("EmailPasswordPrompt.aspx")
    End If
    dr.Close()
    cnn.Close()
```

This code begins by making sure that the desired e-mail address and password are available in session variables. Depending on the path that the shopper took to get to this page, these values may have been passed in a request from the Profile.aspx page. If the request variables aren't empty, the code copies their values to the session variables.

The next step is to set the parameters of the stored procedure that will be used to retrieve information from the database. In this case, rather than pass everything back in parameters or open a DataSet, the code uses a SqlDataReader to retrieve the results of the stored procedure. The SqlDataReader class provides fast access to data with a minimum of overhead, but there are a few catches. First, you can only move forward, never backward, in the data returned by the SqlDataReader. Second, as you can see in the calls to the GetString and GetInt32 methods of this class, you must refer to columns by number rather than by name. This tends to make the code somewhat more confusing.

If you're going to be working extensively with SqlDataReader objects, you may want to define constants to represent the columns in your data. That will allow you to use friendly names rather than numbers when retrieving the data.

When it's initially opened, the SqlDataReader object contains no data. Each call to its Read method loads one row of data. When there is no more data, the Read method returns False. We know that we'll get back one row at most from the SqlDataReader in this case (because we don't save duplicate customer records in the database), so we can test the initial call to Read to know whether we got any data at all.

Assuming that there is data, the code uses calls to the Get methods of the SqlDataReader object to return the data to the user interface. Note also the use of the IsDBNull method of the SqlDataReader. This method tests a specified column to see whether the value contained in that column is a Null. In this particular code, the IsDBNull method is used to determine whether the data contains a state or province value.

On the other hand, it's possible that the SqlDataReader will return no data. This could happen, for example, if the shopper deliberately passed bad data to this page as part of the URL. In that case, the code uses the Server.Transfer method to redirect execution to the EmailPasswordPrompt.aspx page.

Listing 9.8 shows the procRetrieveProfile stored procedure that this page uses to get its data.

Listing 9.8   **procRetrieveProfile Procedure**

```
/*  Retrieve a profile based on e-mail and password

From .NET E-Commerce Programming
by Mike Gunderloy and Noel Jerke
Copyright 2002, Sybex Inc. All Rights Reserved. */
CREATE PROCEDURE procRetrieveProfile
  @Email varchar(150),
  @Password varchar(25)
AS
  SELECT * FROM Shopper
    WHERE ShopperEmail = @Email
    AND ShopperPassword = @Password
```

After the data is loaded, it's displayed on the user interface in a series of TextBox, Drop-DownList, and other controls. The page also displays a Submit button. If the shopper clicks this button, the form will post its data back to the server. In that case, the postback code executes. The start of this code validates user input, as shown in Listing 9.9. This is identical to the validation that we reviewed in the last chapter when we discussed the Shipping.aspx page.

Listing 9.9   **ProfileDisplay.aspx.vb Form_Load Procedure (continued)**

```
Else
    ' This is a postback, so we need to save changes to
    ' the profile
    ' Perform validations that are too complex for
    ' the validation controls
    ' First check: make sure a state is selected
    ' if this is a US address, or a province if
    ' this is a non-US address
    lblError.Visible = False
    If ddlCountry.SelectedItem.Value = "US" Then
        If ddlState.SelectedItem.Value = "" Then
            lblError.Text = "You must select a state."
            lblError.Visible = True
        End If
    Else ' Country other than US
        If txtProvince.Text = "" Then
            lblError.Text = "You must specify a province."
            lblError.Visible = True
        End If
    End If
    ' Second check: make sure they haven't selected
    ' both a state and a province. In this case, need
    ' to change the error message
    If (ddlState.SelectedItem.Value <> "") And _
      (txtProvince.Text <> "") Then
        lblError.Text = _
          "You cannot specify both a state and a province."
        lblError.Visible = True
    End Ifelse
```

Finally, if the new data passes all the validation checks (both those in the code and those performed by the validator controls on the web page), the code uses the cmdUpdateShopper SqlCommand object to write the new data to the database, as shown in Listing 9.10.

Listing 9.10   **ProfileDisplay.aspx.vb Page_Load Procedure (continued)**

```
If Not lblError.Visible Then
    ' If we get here, all data is valid and can be saved
```

```
        With cmdUpdateShopper
            .Parameters("@ShopperID").Value = _
            Session("idShopper")
            .Parameters("@FirstName").Value = _
            txtFirstName.Text
            .Parameters("@LastName").Value = _
            txtLastName.Text
            .Parameters("@Address").Value = _
            txtAddress.Text
            .Parameters("@City").Value = _
            txtCity.Text
            If ddlState.SelectedItem.Value Is Nothing Then
                .Parameters("@State").Value = DBNull.Value
            Else
                .Parameters("@State").Value = _
                ddlState.SelectedItem.Value
            End If
            If txtProvince.Text Is Nothing Then
                .Parameters("@Province").Value = DBNull.Value
            Else
                .Parameters("@Province").Value = _
                txtProvince.Text
            End If
            .Parameters("@Country").Value = _
            ddlCountry.SelectedItem.Value
            .Parameters("@ZipCode").Value = _
            txtZipcode.Text
            .Parameters("@Phone").Value = _
            txtPhone.Text
            .Parameters("@Email").Value = _
            txtEmail.Text
            .Parameters("@Password").Value = _
            txtPassword.Text
            .Parameters("@Cookie").Value = _
            rblProfile.SelectedItem.Value
            cnn.Open()
            .ExecuteNonQuery()
            cnn.Close()
        End With
        ' Save the cookie if desired
        If Session("Cookie") = 1 Then
            Response.Cookies("WWCD").Value = Session("idShopper")
            Response.Cookies("WWCD").Expires = _
            DateTime.Today.AddDays(365).ToShortDateString
        End If
        ' And note the update on the UI
        lblUpdated.Visible = True
        End If
    End If
End Sub
```

As you can see, this block of code closes by making a label on the form visible. This provides the shopper with a visual cue that their profile information has been updated in the database. After the update, the new data is displayed on the form, and the shopper can either make further edits or proceed to other parts of the store.

Listing 9.11 shows the stored procedure that this form uses to update the shopper information.

Listing 9.11   procUpdateShopper Procedure

```
/*  Update the shopper with final billing information

From .NET E-Commerce Programming
by Mike Gunderloy and Noel Jerke
Copyright 2002, Sybex Inc. All Rights Reserved. */
CREATE   PROCEDURE procUpdateShopper
  @ShopperID int,
  @FirstName varchar(50),
  @LastName varchar(50),
  @Address varchar(150),
  @City varchar(100),
  @State varchar(2),
  @Province varchar(150),
  @Country varchar(100),
  @ZipCode varchar(15),
  @Phone varchar(30),
  @Email varchar(150),
  @Password varchar(25),
  @Cookie tinyint
AS
  UPDATE Shopper
    SET ShopperFirstName = @FirstName,
    ShopperLastName = @LastName,
    ShopperAddress = @Address,
    ShopperCity = @City,
    ShopperState = @State,
    ShopperProvince = @Province,
    ShopperCountry = @Country,
    ShopperZipCode = @ZipCode,
    ShopperPhone = @Phone,
    ShopperEmail = @Email,
    ShopperPassword = @Password,
    ShopperCookie = @Cookie
    WHERE ShopperID = @ShopperID
```

Figure 9.3 shows the displayed profile. Note that the form displays the data that's already in the shopper's profile. At this point, the shopper can make any changes they would like and then click Submit to perform the update.

WARNING There's a problem with the Password text box on this form. If you set the TextBox control to the Password TextMode, so that it doesn't display the data typed in, it's impossible to set a value for the TextBox programmatically. This means that we have the choice of requiring the shopper to retype their password, or displaying it in plain text. We've chosen the former resolution in this case.

FIGURE 9.3:

Profile display

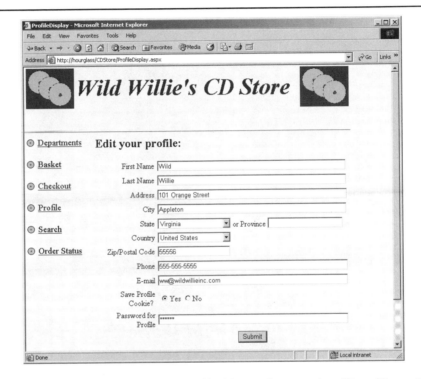

Now let's make some updates to the shopper profile. To test the error handling, Figure 9.4 shows the error message when an invalid country is entered into the profile.

When a correct profile is entered, the profile is updated. The appropriate message is shown in Figure 9.5.

That's it for our profile management. Don't forget about the various interactions with the profile throughout the shopping process, as outlined in Chapter 8.

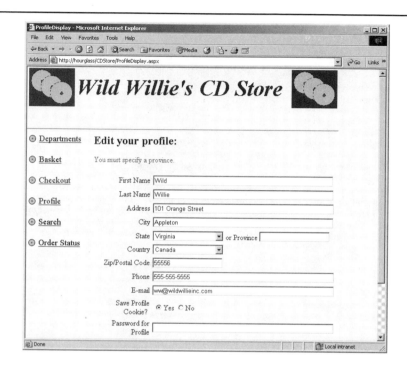

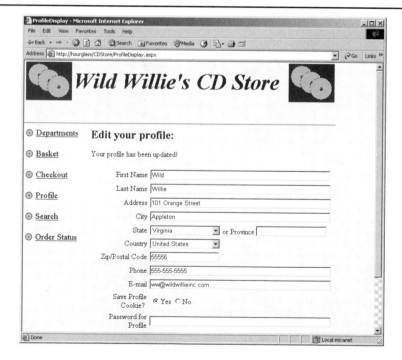

Order History Interface

The final basic feature of our store is the order status section. This is the feature that allows the shopper to return to the website and see what the status of their order is.

We hope we have built a store that will entice shoppers to purchase many times, again and again. We want to make it possible for the shopper to retrieve their order history right up to the status of the last order. Table 9.1 outlines the order status options that we'll track on each order.

TABLE 9.1: Order Status Settings

Order Status Setting	Description
0	The order has been retrieved from the system.
1	The order has been fulfilled and is ready for shipment.
2	The order has been shipped. A corresponding shipping number can be provided.

At the time an order is placed, the initial order status is set to 0. In Chapter 12, "Managing Orders," we'll build management tools for updating the order status.

The process for retrieving the order history is fairly straightforward. When the shopper clicks Order Status, they will be presented with a simple login page, where they will be required to enter their username and password. If the shopper cannot remember their username and password, they will have the option of having the password e-mailed to the profile's e-mail address. If they do remember their username and password, they're granted access to a listing of their orders and the status of each. They can then select an order and get a complete order recap.

The first task is to have the shopper log in to retrieve their list of orders. The OrderStatus.aspx page that handles this task is similar to the Profile.aspx page that you saw earlier in the chapter. Listing 9.12 shows the HTML code for this page.

Listing 9.12   **OrderStatus.aspx**

```
<%@ Page Language="vb" AutoEventWireup="false" Codebehind="OrderStatus.aspx.vb"
 Inherits="CDStore.OrderStatus"%>
<!DOCTYPE HTML PUBLIC "-//W3C//DTD HTML 4.0 Transitional//EN">
<HTML>
    <HEAD>
        <TITLE>Retrieve Order Status</TITLE>
    </HEAD>
    <meta name="GENERATOR" content="Microsoft Visual Studio.NET 7.0">
    <meta name="CODE_LANGUAGE" content="Visual Basic 7.0">
```

```
<meta name="vs_defaultClientScript" content="JavaScript">
<meta name="vs_targetSchema" content=
 "http://schemas.microsoft.com/intellisense/ie5">
<!-- OrderStatus.aspx - Login page to retrieve order status -->
<!-- #Include File="Header.inc" -->
To retrieve your order history, please enter your e-mail address and
password.
<BR>
<BR>
<!-- Display a form that allows data entry -->
<form method="post" action="OrderHistoryDisplay.aspx">
    <table>
        <tr>
            <td align="right">
                E-mail:
            </td>
            <td>
                <input type="text" name="email">
            </td>
        </tr>
        <tr>
            <td align="right">
                Password:
            </td>
            <td>
                <input type="password" name="password">
            </td>
        </tr>
        <tr>
            <td colspan="2" align="middle">
                <input type="submit" value="Submit" name="submit">
            </td>
        </tr>
    </table>
</form>
<!-- #Include File="Footer.inc" -->
</HTML>
```

As with the Profile.aspx page, this page is a standard HTML form. Once again, the Password field uses the HTML password element type. That way, the actual password isn't displayed on-screen.

Figure 9.6 shows an order status login page. As mentioned, it's a simple page where shoppers can identify themselves.

FIGURE 9.6:

Order status
login page

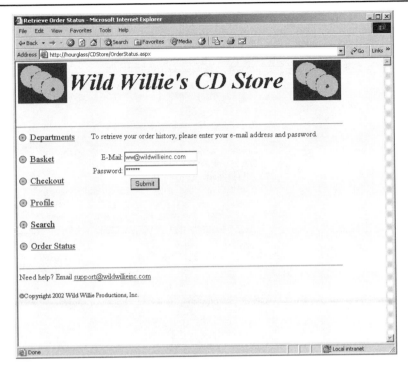

When the shopper submits the information on this page, the application loads the Order-HistoryDisplay.aspx page. The purpose of this page is to provide a list of all orders placed by the shopper and to show the status of each. This page uses a DataList control for the bulk of its user interface, as shown in Listing 9.13.

Listing 9.13   **OrderHistoryDisplay.aspx**

```
<%@ Page Language="vb" AutoEventWireup="false"
 Codebehind="OrderHistoryDisplay.aspx.vb"
 Inherits="CDStore.OrderHistoryDisplay"%>
<!DOCTYPE HTML PUBLIC "-//W3C//DTD HTML 4.0 Transitional//EN">
<HTML>
    <HEAD>
        <title>Order History Display</title>
        <meta name="GENERATOR" content="Microsoft Visual Studio.NET 7.0">
        <meta name="CODE_LANGUAGE" content="Visual Basic 7.0">
        <meta name="vs_defaultClientScript" content="JavaScript">
        <meta name="vs_targetSchema" content=
          "http://schemas.microsoft.com/intellisense/ie5">
    </HEAD>
    <!-- OrderHistoryDisplay.aspx - Show all orders for this shopper -->
    <!-- #Include File="Header.inc" -->
```

```
<form id="Form1" method="post" runat="server">
    <P>
        <asp:Label id="lblInfo" runat="server">Label</asp:Label></P>
    <P>
         
        <asp:datalist id="dlOrders" runat="server" BorderColor="Tan"
         ForeColor="Black" BackColor="LightGoldenrodYellow"
          CellPadding="2"
         BorderWidth="0px">
            <SelectedItemStyle ForeColor="GhostWhite"
             BackColor="DarkSlateBlue"></SelectedItemStyle>
            <AlternatingItemStyle BackColor="PaleGoldenrod">
            </AlternatingItemStyle>
            <ItemTemplate>
                    Order #<a href='OrderReceipt.aspx?
                     idOrder=<%# DataBinder.Eval(Container.DataItem,
                     "OrderID") %>&idShopper=
                    <%# DataBinder.Eval(Container.DataItem,
                     "ShopperID") %>'>
                    <%# DataBinder.Eval(Container.DataItem,
                     "OrderID") %>
                </a>: Placed
                    <%# DataBinder.Eval(Container.DataItem,
                     "OrderDateOrdered") %>
                    <br>
                    Order Total:
                    <%# DataBinder.Eval(Container.DataItem,
                     "BasketTotal", "{0:c}") %>
                    <br>
                    Order Status:
                    <%# DataBinder.Eval(Container.DataItem,
                     "OrderStatus") %><br><br>
            </ItemTemplate>
            <FooterStyle BackColor="Tan"></FooterStyle>
            <HeaderStyle Font-Bold="True" BackColor="Tan">
            </HeaderStyle>
        </asp:datalist></P>
    </form>
    <!-- #Include File="Footer.inc" -->
</HTML>
```

The HTML code uses the OrderID and ShopperID values for each order to build a hyperlink to the OrderReceipt.aspx page, which you'll see later in the chapter.

The code for the OrderHistoryDisplay.aspx page begins by using the *email* and *password* session variables to retrieve the ShopperID, as shown in Listing 9.14.

Listing 9.14 **OrderHistoryDisplay.aspx Page_Load Procedure**

```
Private Sub Page_Load(ByVal sender As System.Object, _
    ByVal e As System.EventArgs) Handles MyBase.Load
```

```
Dim dr As SqlDataReader
If Not IsPostBack Then
    If Request("email") <> "" Then
        Session("email") = Request("email")
    End If
    If Request("password") <> "" Then
        Session("password") = Request("password")
    End If
    cnn.Open()
    With cmdRetrieveProfile
        .Parameters("@Email").Value = Session("email")
        .Parameters("@Password").Value = Session("password")
        dr = .ExecuteReader()
    End With

    If dr.Read() Then
        ' Save the shopper ID for later. Note that the Get methods
        ' take zero-based ordinals to identify columns
        Session("idShopper") = dr.GetInt32(0)
        dr.Close()
        cnn.Close()
```

The return value from the Read method of the SqlDataReader object tells us again whether we were successful in retrieving a profile. If a profile is returned, we are ready to list the orders. To do so, we base a DataSet on the procRetrieveOrders stored procedure. This stored procedure will retrieve all orders that the shopper has placed. Listing 9.15 shows the code that retrieves the DataSet and binds it to the user interface of the Web Form.

Listing 9.15   OrderHistoryDisplay.aspx Page_Load Procedure (continued)

```
' Now that we have the Shopper ID, retrieve their orders
cmdRetrieveOrders.Parameters("@ShopperID").Value = _
 Session("idShopper")
Dim dsOrders As New DataSet()
Dim daOrders As New SqlDataAdapter()
daOrders.SelectCommand = cmdRetrieveOrders
daOrders.Fill(dsOrders, "Orders")

' If there are any orders, show them
If dsOrders.Tables("Orders").Rows.Count > 0 Then
    lblInfo.Text = "Here are your orders:"
    dlOrders.DataSource = dsOrders
    dlOrders.DataMember = "Orders"
    DataBind()
Else
    ' No orders, let the shopper know that
    lblInfo.Text = "You have not placed any orders"
    dlOrders.Visible = False
End Ifset rsOrders = dbOrders.Execute(sql)
```

If there are no rows in the DataSet, it means that we don't have any record of orders from this shopper. In this case, a label control on the form is set to some informational text, and the code hides the DataList control. The last possibility is that we can't find the shopper ID. The code that handles this possibility also uses the informational label, as shown in Listing 9.16.

Listing 9.16   OrderHistoryDisplay.aspx Page_Load Procedure (continued)

```
        Else
            ' No records returned when trying to get Profile
            ' Probably wrong email/password
            lblInfo.Text = "Sorry, we could not retrieve your order " & _
                "status. Please call 1-800-555-wild for help."
            dlOrders.Visible = False
            dr.Close()
            cnn.Close()

        End If

    Else
        ' Is Postback
    End If
End Sub
```

We have some options on how we handle this case. We could tell the shopper that they can have their password e-mailed to them. We could also give the shopper the option of trying again. But it seems most likely that they were really trying to get their order history and need assistance (or that they simply haven't placed any orders).

This page uses a couple of stored procedures for handling the order data. The first of these, procRetrieveOrders, uses the ShopperID to get data from the OrderData, OrderStatus, and Basket tables, as shown in Listing 9.17.

Listing 9.17   procRetrieveOrders Procedure

```
/*  Retrieve basic order information for a shopper

From .NET E-Commerce Programming
by Mike Gunderloy and Noel Jerke
Copyright 2002, Sybex Inc. All Rights Reserved. */
CREATE PROCEDURE procRetrieveOrders
  @ShopperID int
AS
  SELECT
    OrderStatus = CASE OrderStatus.OrderStatusStage
      WHEN 0 THEN 'Order received and to be processed'
      WHEN 1 THEN 'Order ready to ship'
```

```
WHEN 2 THEN 'Order Shipped, Confirmation #' +
    OrderStatus.OrderStatusShippingNumber
END,
[Order].OrderID, [Order].ShopperID,
[Order].OrderDateOrdered, Basket.BasketTotal
FROM ([Order] INNER JOIN OrderStatus
  ON [Order].OrderID = OrderStatus.OrderID)
INNER JOIN Basket
  ON [Order].BasketID = Basket.BasketID
WHERE [Order].ShopperID = @ShopperID
ORDER BY [Order].OrderDateOrdered
```

Note the use of the Transact-SQL CASE statement to translate the numeric status values in the table to text strings for the benefit of the shopper. This is one more way to do some of the processing on the SQL Server rather than on the shopper's computer. This stored procedure returns only selected columns, rather than use the * selector to return every column in the tables. This helps it to execute more quickly. Note also that we've used square brackets around the name of the Order table to distinguish it from the ORDER keyword.

The other stored procedure used by this page is procRetrieveProfile, which is shown in Listing 9.18.

Listing 9.18   procRetrieveProfile Procedure

```
/* Retrieve a profile based on e-mail and password

From .NET E-Commerce Programming
by Mike Gunderloy and Noel Jerke
Copyright 2002, Sybex Inc. All Rights Reserved. */
CREATE PROCEDURE procRetrieveProfile
  @Email varchar(150),
  @Password varchar(25)
AS
  SELECT * FROM Shopper
    WHERE ShopperEmail = @Email
    AND ShopperPassword = @Password        (chrPassword = @Password)
```

Figure 9.7 shows a sample order history display. Note that the order ID is linked so that the shopper can access the full receipt. The status of each order is also indicated. (A reminder that we'll build a tool to update the order status settings in Chapter 12.)

FIGURE 9.7:

Order status history

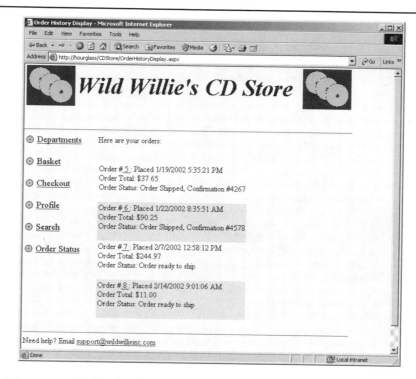

The last step of the process is for the shopper to print out a complete receipt. There are links to this page, OrderReceipt.aspx, from each Order ID on the order history display. The page uses a Repeater control to display the line items in the order, and a series of labels for other information. Listing 9.19 shows the start of the HTML code for this page.

Listing 9.19   **OrderReceipt.aspx**

```
<%@ Page Language="vb" AutoEventWireup="false"
 Codebehind="OrderReceipt.aspx.vb" Inherits="CDStore.OrderReceipt"%>
<!DOCTYPE HTML PUBLIC "-//W3C//DTD HTML 4.0 Transitional//EN">
<HTML>
    <HEAD>
        <TITLE>Order Receipt</TITLE>
    </HEAD>
    <meta name="GENERATOR" content="Microsoft Visual Studio.NET 7.0">
    <meta name="CODE_LANGUAGE" content="Visual Basic 7.0">
    <meta name="vs_defaultClientScript" content="JavaScript">
    <meta name="vs_targetSchema" content=
     "http://schemas.microsoft.com/intellisense/ie5">
    <!-- OrderReceipt.asp - Displays the items in the shoppers receipt. -->
    <!-- #Include File="Header.inc" -->
    <form id="Form1" method="post" runat="server">
```

```
<P>
    <TABLE id="Table1" cellSpacing="1" cellPadding="1"
    width="100%" border="0">
        <TR>
            <TD>
                <asp:Label id="lblOrderID" runat="server">Label
                </asp:Label></TD>
            <TD>
                <asp:Label id="lblOrderDate" runat="server">Label
                </asp:Label></TD>
        </TR>
        <TR>
            <TD><STRONG>Bill To:</STRONG></TD>
            <TD><STRONG>Ship To:</STRONG></TD>
        </TR>
        <TR>
            <TD>
                <asp:Label id="lblBillName" runat="server">Label
                </asp:Label></TD>
            <TD>
                <asp:Label id="lblShipName" runat="server">Label
                </asp:Label></TD>
        </TR>
        <TR>
            <TD>
                <asp:Label id="lblBillAddress" runat="server">Label
                </asp:Label></TD>
            <TD>
                <asp:Label id="lblShipAddress" runat="server">Label
                </asp:Label></TD>
        </TR>
        <TR>
            <TD>
                <asp:Label id="lblBillCity" runat="server">Label
                </asp:Label></TD>
            <TD>
                <asp:Label id="lblShipCity" runat="server">Label
                </asp:Label></TD>
        </TR>
        <TR>
            <TD>
                <asp:Label id="lblBillPhone" runat="server">Label
                </asp:Label></TD>
            <TD>
                <asp:Label id="lblShipPhone" runat="server">Label
                </asp:Label></TD>
        </TR>
        <TR>
            <TD>
                <asp:Label id="lblBillEmail" runat="server">Label
                </asp:Label></TD>
```

```
            <TD>
                <asp:Label id="lblShipEmail" runat="server">Label
                </asp:Label></TD>
        </TR>
    </TABLE>
</P>
```

This first part of the page uses a table with a series of Label controls to lay out a header section for the receipt. The text in the labels is just placeholder text; as you'll see a bit later in this chapter, the real text is filled in at runtime. The next section of HTML defines the Repeater control that will show the item detail for the receipt. This section is shown in Listing 9.20.

Listing 9.20   **OrderReceipt.aspx (continued)**

```
<P>
     
    <asp:repeater id="rptItems" runat="server">
        <ItemTemplate>
            <tr>
                <td><%# DataBinder.Eval(Container.DataItem,
                    "ProductID") %></td>
                <td><%# DataBinder.Eval(Container.DataItem,
                    "BasketItemProductName") %></td>
                <!-- Show the product attributes -->
                <td>
                    <%# DataBinder.Eval(Container.DataItem,
                        "BasketItemColor") %>
                     
                    <%# DataBinder.Eval(Container.DataItem,
                        "BasketItemSize") %>
                </td>
                <td>
                    <%# DataBinder.Eval(Container.DataItem,
                        "BasketItemQuantity") %>
                </td>
                <td><%# DataBinder.Eval(Container.DataItem,
                    "BasketItemPrice", "{0:c}") %></td>
                <!-- Show the product total cost -->
                <td><%# DataBinder.Eval(Container.DataItem,
                    "BasketItemTotal", "{0:c}") %>
                </td>
            </tr>
        </ItemTemplate>
        <HeaderTemplate>
            <table border="1" cellpadding="3" cellspacing="2"
            width="500">
                <tr>
                    <th>
```

```
                    Item Code</th>
                <th>
                    Name</th>
                <th>
                    Attributes</th>
                <th>
                    Quantity</th>
                <th>
                    Price</th>
                <th>
                    Total</th>
            </tr>
        </HeaderTemplate>
        <FooterTemplate>
            </table>
        </FooterTemplate>
    </asp:repeater></P>
<P>
```

The final section of the page, shown in Listing 9.21, defines another small table. This one will hold the total charges for the order.

Listing 9.21   **OrderReceipt.aspx (continued)**

```
<TABLE id="Table2" cellSpacing="1" cellPadding="1" width="100%"
border="0">
    <TR>
        <TD align="right">
            <asp:Label id="lblSubtotal" runat="server">Label
            </asp:Label></TD>
    </TR>
    <TR>
        <TD align="right">
            <asp:Label id="lblShipping" runat="server">Label
            </asp:Label></TD>
    </TR>
    <TR>
        <TD align="right">
            <asp:Label id="lblTax" runat="server">Label
            </asp:Label></TD>
    </TR>
    <TR>
        <TD align="right">
            <asp:Label id="lblTotal" runat="server">Label
            </asp:Label></TD>
    </TR>
</TABLE>
</P>
</form>
<!-- #Include File="Footer.inc" -->
</HTML>
```

Of course, all those placeholders wouldn't do any good without code to fill them in. The code behind this form starts by using a SqlDataReader to retrieve and fill in all of the header and footer information for the order. This portion of the code is shown in Listing 9.22.

TIP You'll see that we close the SqlDataReader as soon as we've finished retrieving information from it. That's because ADO.NET can maintain only a single open SqlDataReader on a single connection at one time. The SqlDataAdapter class uses a hidden SqlDataReader of its own when you call its Fill method, which means that we have to close our own SqlDataReader before we call that method. The alternative would be to open a second connection for the second SqlDataReader to use.

Listing 9.22   OrderReceipt.aspx.vb Page_Load Procedure

```
Private Sub Page_Load(ByVal sender As System.Object, _
  ByVal e As System.EventArgs) Handles MyBase.Load
    ' Get the header information
    Dim dr As SqlDataReader
    With cmdRetrieveReceiptHeader
        .Parameters("@ShopperID").Value = _
        Request("idShopper")
        .Parameters("@OrderID").Value = _
        Request("idOrder")
        cnn.Open()
        dr = .ExecuteReader
    End With

    ' Get the first (only) row of information
    dr.Read()
    ' Add header information to the page
    lblOrderID.Text = "Order Number " & dr.GetInt32(0).ToString
    lblOrderDate.Text = dr.GetDateTime(25)
    lblShipName.Text = dr.GetString(3) & " " & dr.GetString(4)
    lblShipAddress.Text = dr.GetString(5)
    ' Choose either state or province, whichever is not null
    If Not dr.IsDBNull(7) Then
        lblShipCity.Text = dr.GetString(6) & ", " & _
        dr.GetString(7) & dr.GetString(10)
    Else
        lblShipCity.Text = dr.GetString(6) & ", " & _
        dr.GetString(8) & dr.GetString(10)
    End If
    lblShipEmail.Text = dr.GetString(13)
    lblShipPhone.Text = dr.GetString(11)
    lblBillName.Text = dr.GetString(14) & " " & dr.GetString(15)
    lblBillAddress.Text = dr.GetString(16)
    ' Choose either state or province, whichever is not null
    If Not dr.IsDBNull(18) Then
```

```
        lblBillCity.Text = dr.GetString(17) & ", " & _
            dr.GetString(18) & dr.GetString(21)
Else
        lblBillCity.Text = dr.GetString(17) & ", " & _
            dr.GetString(19) & dr.GetString(21)
End If
lblBillEmail.Text = dr.GetString(24)
lblBillPhone.Text = dr.GetString(22)
lblSubtotal.Text = "Subtotal: " & _
 Format(dr.GetSqlMoney(31).Value, "C")
lblTotal.Text = "Total: " & _
 Format(dr.GetSqlMoney(32).Value, "C")
lblShipping.Text = "Shipping: " & _
 Format(dr.GetSqlMoney(33).Value, "C")
lblTax.Text = "Tax: " & _
 Format(dr.GetSqlMoney(34).Value, "C")

dr.Close()
cnn.Close()
```

You'll see that we need to go through a bit of extra effort to format the currency values (such as Subtotal) for display. The GetSqlMoney method returns a SqlMoney object. This object implements a Value method to return the actual value from the column, which can be formatted by the Format function.

The rest of the code behind this Web Form, shown in Listing 9.23, uses another stored procedure to fill a DataSet with item information, and then binds the DataSet to the Repeater control.

Listing 9.23   **OrderReceipt.aspx.vb Page_Load Procedure (continued)**

```
' Get the item information
With cmdRetrieveReceiptItems
    .Parameters("@ShopperID").Value = _
     Request("idShopper")
    .Parameters("@OrderID").Value = _
     Request("idOrder")
End With
Dim dsItems As New DataSet()
Dim daItems As New SqlDataAdapter()
daItems.SelectCommand = cmdRetrieveReceiptItems
daItems.Fill(dsItems, "Items")
' And bind the items to the user interface
rptItems.DataSource = dsItems
rptItems.DataMember = "Items"
DataBind()

End Sub
```

We use a couple of stored procedures to retrieve the order data. The procRetrieveReceipt-Header stored procedure will get the basic customer order data that we use for header and footer information on the receipt. This stored procedure returns fields from the Order and Basket tables, as shown in Listing 9.24.

Listing 9.24   **procRetrieveReceiptHeader Procedure**

```
/* Retrieve the header information for a receipt,
   given the Order ID and the Shopper ID

From .NET E-Commerce Programming
by Mike Gunderloy and Noel Jerke
Copyright 2002, Sybex Inc. All Rights Reserved. */
CREATE PROCEDURE procRetrieveReceiptHeader
  @ShopperID int,
  @OrderID int
AS
  SELECT * FROM [ORDER] INNER JOIN Basket
    ON [Order].BasketID = Basket.BasketID
    WHERE [Order].OrderID = @OrderID
      AND [Order].ShopperID = @ShopperID
```

The procRetrieveReceiptItems stored procedure gets the items in the basket for the completed order. In order to get all of the right data, it needs to join the BasketItem, Basket, and Order tables. It uses the ID of the order and the shopper ID to locate the correct data, as shown in Listing 9.25.

Listing 9.25   **procRetrieveReceiptItems Procedure**

```
/* Retrieve the item information for a receipt,
   given the Order ID and the Shopper ID

From .NET E-Commerce Programming
by Mike Gunderloy and Noel Jerke
Copyright 2002, Sybex Inc. All Rights Reserved. */
CREATE PROCEDURE procRetrieveReceiptItems
  @ShopperID int,
  @OrderID int
AS
  SELECT BasketItem.*, BasketItemTotal =
  BasketItemQuantity * BasketItemPrice
  FROM (BasketItem INNER JOIN Basket
    ON BasketItem.BasketID = Basket.BasketID)
  INNER JOIN [Order]
    ON [Order].BasketID = Basket.BasketID
    WHERE [Order].OrderID = @OrderID
      AND [Order].ShopperID = @ShopperID
```

Figure 9.8 shows the completed order receipt. Such a receipt should be printable, be easily readable by the shopper, and contain all of the appropriate data to answer most questions about the order.

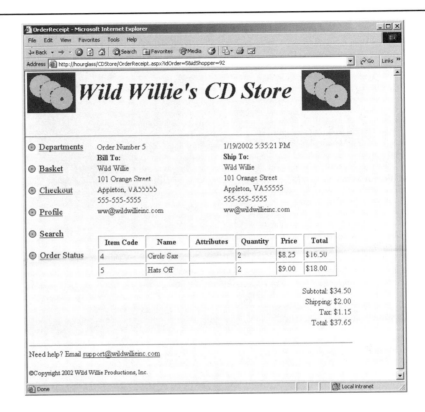

Summary

That does it for Part II of the book. By now, you should have a good understanding of the ins and outs of building a functioning e-commerce store from the shopper's perspective.

But that's only half the picture. In Parts III and IV, we'll cover the management tools that you'll need to run a store efficiently. We'll also look at the marketing tools that will hopefully entice shoppers to explore the store and spend more money.

PART III

Managing the Solution

CHAPTER 10

Product Management

- Designing the Store Manager

- Managing Security

- Managing Products

- Managing Departments

n the last several chapters, we designed the part of our e-commerce site that the shopper will see. In those chapters, we presumed that all the data was already loaded and ready to go. Now we need to work on the other half of the job: store management. This can be a vast topic and has the potential to be exceedingly complex, depending on your business needs.

In this and the next two chapters, we'll tackle the basics of product, department, tax, shipping, and order management. These are key tools that will be useful in any online store. Even if most of the data is being imported automatically from some other system, on-the-fly changes to the data in the live store will most likely be necessary.

We're going to start our store management interface by designing functionality to manage products and departments. We want to provide the ability to add, update, and delete products and departments. This will include managing department assignments, attributes, images, and the other data associated with departments and products.

We also need to define the interface for our store manager, in much the same way we did for the shopping side of the store.

Designing the Store Manager

The store manager is a fairly complex application for working with the database behind our online store. The interface that we'll build in this chapter will provide the fundamental tools for product and department management. The chart in Figure 10.1 shows the key functional items that we'll create.

FIGURE 10.1:
Store manager
functionality

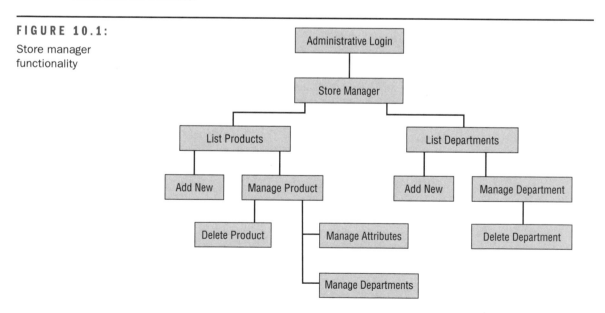

At the top level, the user must log in to the store manager. Then the user will have initial options: product listing, department listing, tax, shipping, and order reporting. From there, the functional tree expands into management actions for each area. Table 10.1 outlines the core functionality that we'll develop in this chapter.

TABLE 10.1: Store Manager Core Functionality for Products and Departments

Functionality	Description
Administrative login	Provides login security for the store manager.
Product listing	Lists products in the database.
Product search	Searches for products in the database.
Add new product	Adds a new product to the store.
Delete product	Deletes a product from the database.
Product update	Updates the product data.
Product attribute management	Adds, updates, and deletes product attributes.
Department listing	Lists departments in the database.
Add new department	Adds a new department to the database.
Delete department	Deletes a department from the database.
Department update	Updates the department data.

Before we can start implementing the store manager interface, we need to choose the platform and language that we'll use to write the code. Because the store manager will be used only by our own staff, we have more flexibility than we did with the store itself. We could choose to build a stand-alone Visual Basic .NET application, a Microsoft Access project, or an ASP.NET Web Application to manage the store. We've chosen an ASP.NET application, for these reasons:

- By using ASP.NET, we can leverage the skills that we've built in designing and developing the store interface.

- Although this application is only for our own staff, we may want to update the store from remote locations. Using an ASP.NET Web Application allows our staff to manage the store from anywhere with an Internet connection.

- Using ASP.NET means that we don't have to add the overhead of managing more servers or development tools than we're already using for the store itself.

- Using ASP.NET allows the store to be hosted on any server and administered from anywhere. For instance, we might want to have the store at a collocated server at our ISP to handle an anticipated heavy traffic load. ASP.NET lets us manage that server without a direct LAN connection.

Our store manager, then, will be a new ASP.NET Web Application. We've named this application StoreManager, and you'll find it on the companion CD. The rest of this chapter will explore and explain the code that's used in StoreManager to manage products and departments.

NOTE   See the `readme.txt` file on the companion CD for full instructions on installing the Store-Manager application.

One key element we'll need in the website for store management is straightforward navigation to the different product management features. Figure 10.2 shows the navigation style that we've chosen: a simple navigation bar at the top of each page within the store manager.

FIGURE 10.2:

Manager navigation

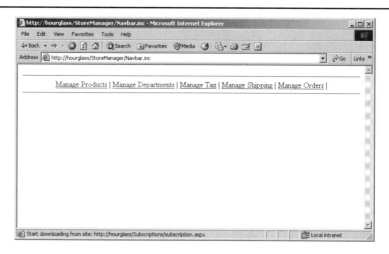

We'll use the same method that we used on the shopper side of the store for making sure that the navigation bar is consistent across all the pages in the site: We'll include a single file in every page. Listing 10.1 shows the navigation bar's include code.

Listing 10.1   Navbar.inc

```
<!-- Navbar.inc - Top navigation include for the store manager -->
<hr>
<center>

<!-- Link to the listing of products  -->
<a href="ListProducts.aspx">
Manage Products<a> |

<!-- Link to the listing of departments  -->
<a href="ListDepts.aspx">
```

```
Manage Departments</a> |

<!-- Link to the management page for tax settings  -->
<a href="ManageTax.aspx">
Manage Tax</a> |

<!-- Link to the management page for shipping settings  -->
<a href="ManageShipping.aspx">
Manage Shipping</a> |

<!-- Link to the management page for orders  -->
<a href="ManageOrders.aspx">
Manage Orders</a> |

</center>
<hr>
```

The navigation bar is basically a series of links to the core pages for the management features of the store. This navigation bar will appear at the top of each page as an ASP.NET include file so that we will be able to update the navigation easily when new features are added.

Managing Security

We'll need to have security for our store manager—we don't want just anybody getting into the management functions. But because we're assuming that all the users will be internal to our company, we're not going to implement particularly heavy-duty security.

The first item we'll need is the login page. Figure 10.3 shows the login page from the StoreManager application.

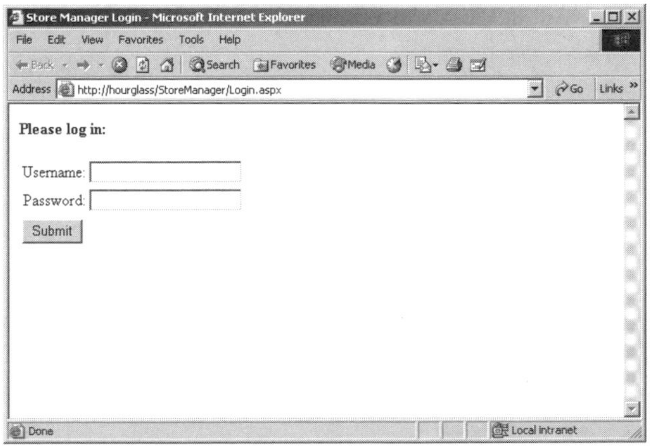

FIGURE 10.3:

Login page

The login page is a simple form with fields for inputting the username and password. As with some of the pages in the CDStore application, this one uses a traditional HTML form for data input. Listing 10.2 shows the HTML code for the Login.aspx page.

Listing 10.2   **Login.aspx**

```
<%@ Page Language="vb" AutoEventWireup="false" Codebehind="Login.aspx.vb"
 Inherits="StoreManager.Login"%>
<!DOCTYPE HTML PUBLIC "-//W3C//DTD HTML 4.0 Transitional//EN">
<HTML>
    <HEAD>
        <title>Store Manager Login</title>
        <meta name="GENERATOR" content="Microsoft Visual Studio.NET 7.0">
        <meta name="CODE_LANGUAGE" content="Visual Basic 7.0">
        <meta name="vs_defaultClientScript" content="JavaScript">
        <meta name="vs_targetSchema" content=
         "http://schemas.microsoft.com/intellisense/ie5">
        <!-- Login.aspx - Login page for the site administrator. -->
    </HEAD>
    <BODY>
        <B>Please log in:</B><BR>
        <BR>
        <!--  Start the form for the user to enter
    their username and password.  -->
        <form method="post" action="ManagerMenu.aspx">
            <table>
                <tr>
                    <td align="right">Username:</td>
                    <td>
                        <!--  The input text box for the username.  -->
                        <input type="text" name="username">
                    </td>
                </tr>
                <tr>
                    <td align="right">Password:</td>
                    <td>
                        <!--  The input text box for the password.  -->
                        <input type="password" name="password">
                    </td>
                <tr>
                <tr>
                    <td colspan="2">
                        <!--  The submit button for the form.  -->
                        <input type="submit" value="Submit" name="Submit">
                    </td>
                </tr>
            </table>
        </form>
    </BODY>
</HTML>
```

Note that this page doesn't include the menu bar; we don't want to give the user a way to go elsewhere before they've even logged in! When the user fills out the form, the login name and password are passed to the ManagerMenu.aspx page. The Page_Load procedure of this page makes a very simple check to determine whether the user should be allowed to proceed, as shown in Listing 10.3.

Listing 10.3   ManagerMenu.aspx.vb Page_Load Procedure

```
Private Sub Page_Load(ByVal sender As System.Object, _
ByVal e As System.EventArgs) Handles MyBase.Load
    ' Validate the user's login before proceeding.
    ' We use a very simple model, with a hard-coded
    ' username and password
    If Request("username") <> "Admin" Or _
    Request("password") <> "Password" Then
        ' Login failed. Back to the login page
        Server.Transfer("Login.aspx")
    Else
        ' Login succeeded, set a session variable to indicate this
        Session("Validated") = True
    End If
End Sub
```

If the login and password entered by the user match those that are hard-coded on this page, the code continues loading the page. If not, the user is sent back to the login page. If the login information is correct, the code sets a session variable to indicate that the user has successfully logged in. That variable will be checked throughout the rest of the site to ensure validation.

Listing 10.4 shows the HTML code for this page, which mainly consists of another rendition of the application's menu choices. Because we don't know which task a user will have in mind when they log in to the application, we need to present them with the menu rather than jump directly to one of the functional pages.

Listing 10.4   ManagerMenu.aspx

```
<%@ Page Language="vb" AutoEventWireup="false"
 Codebehind="ManagerMenu.aspx.vb"
 Inherits="StoreManager.ManagerMenu"%>
<!DOCTYPE HTML PUBLIC "-//W3C//DTD HTML 4.0 Transitional//EN">
<HTML>
    <HEAD>
        <title>Manager Menu</title>
        <meta name="GENERATOR" content="Microsoft Visual Studio.NET 7.0">
        <meta name="CODE_LANGUAGE" content="Visual Basic 7.0">
        <meta name="vs_defaultClientScript" content="JavaScript">
```

```
        <meta name="vs_targetSchema" content=
         "http://schemas.microsoft.com/intellisense/ie5">
    </HEAD>
    <body>
        <!-- ManagerMenu.aspx: Welcome the manager
             and show the main menu -->
        <center>
            <BR>
            <BR>
            <b>Welcome to Wild Willie's CD Store Manager. Select a function
             below: </b>
            <br>
            <br>
            <table border="1" cellpadding="3" cellspacing="3">
                <tr>
                    <th>
                        <B>Functions</B></th>
                </tr>
                <tr>
                    <td><a href="ListProducts.aspx"> Manage Products<a></a>
                    </td>
                </tr>
                <tr>
                    <td><a href="ListDepts.aspx">
                     Manage Departments</a></td>
                </tr>
                <tr>
                    <td><a href="ManageTax.aspx"> Manage Tax</a></td>
                </tr>
                <tr>
                    <td><a href="ManageShipping.aspx">
                     Manage Shipping</a></td>
                </tr>
                <tr>
                    <td><a href="ManageOrders.aspx"> Manage Orders</a></td>
                </tr>
            </table>
        </center>
    </body>
</HTML>
```

Figure 10.4 shows the page. Of course, it's not necessary to have two copies of the menu on the same page, so this page doesn't feature the navigation bar.

FIGURE 10.4:

Manager menu page

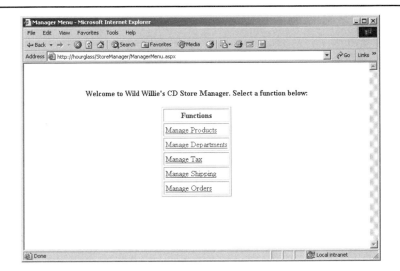

We'll also include a simple security check at the top of each page. Listing 10.5 shows this code, which is saved as a separate include file.

Listing 10.5   ValidateCheck.inc

```
<%
'   ValidateCheck.inc - Ensures that the manager has
'   been validated.
'   Check our session variable to see if the user has
'   been validated. This will help to ensure that
'   none of the admin pages are accessed without
'   authorization
If Not Session("Validated") Then
    ' Redirect back to the login page
    Server.Transfer("Login.aspx")
End If
%>
```

This page checks to see whether the session variable *Validated* has the value that was set during the login process. If not, the user is sent back to the login page. This prevents users from jumping into the application without going through the login page first.

NOTE   If the default timeout period of the user's session elapses, the session variable will be cleared and the user will have to log in again. The default session timeout is 20 minutes of inactivity, but this can be adjusted from within the IIS management tools or by setting the HttpSessionState.Timeout property in ASP.NET code.

Login Security

In this example, we're using a very simple security model for validating the user and protecting the pages. But there are many more options for implementing security. For example, we may want only certain users to manage products and departments, while other users may only need to access order management. Thus, we would need different levels of access. This could be implemented with a database of usernames and references.

We also might want to go to extended lengths to tighten the security. For example, we could place the store manager pages on a different server under a different domain name. We could also place directory-level security on the store manager directory. In that case, the user would log in with Windows NT Authentication.

In general, security for .NET applications is a complex topic and is thus beyond the scope of this book. If you'd like to dig deeper into .NET security, see John Paul Mueller's *Visual C# .NET Developer's Handbook* (Sybex, 2002).

Managing Products

Now we are ready to begin working on the product management. The first two capabilities we need to provide are a way to list all the products and a way to search for products. Because we potentially may have many products in the database, we'll want to enable the user to browse through the products easily, with only a subset of the products appearing on each page.

Listing Products

Listing 10.6 shows the start of the HTML for the ListProducts.aspx page. This page controls the display of a set number of products on the page. The code begins with the usual Visual Studio .NET meta tags and page properties; then it continues with our two standard files for handling login validation and the navigation bar.

Listing 10.6   **ListProducts.aspx**

```
<%@ Page Language="vb" AutoEventWireup="false"
 Codebehind="ListProducts.aspx.vb" Inherits="StoreManager.ListProducts"%>
<!DOCTYPE HTML PUBLIC "-//W3C//DTD HTML 4.0 Transitional//EN">
<HTML>
    <HEAD>
        <title>Product Listing</title>
        <meta content="Microsoft Visual Studio.NET 7.0" name="GENERATOR">
        <meta content="Visual Basic 7.0" name="CODE_LANGUAGE">
```

```
<meta content="JavaScript" name="vs_defaultClientScript">
<meta content=
  "http://schemas.microsoft.com/intellisense/ie5"
  name="vs_targetSchema">
<!-- ListProducts.aspx - Page through products in the store -->
</HEAD>
<body>
    <!-- #Include File="ValidateCheck.inc" -->
    <!-- #Include File="Navbar.inc" -->
```

The rest of this page is a server-side ASP.NET form. It starts with a Hyperlink control that the user can click when they're ready to add a new product to the database, as shown in Listing 10.7. This hyperlink leads to the NewProduct.aspx page, which you'll see later in the chapter.

Listing 10.7   ListProducts.aspx (continued)

```
<form id="Form1" method="post" runat="server">
    <P>
        <asp:HyperLink id="HyperLink1" runat="server"
         NavigateUrl="NewProduct.aspx">Click here to add a new product
        </asp:HyperLink></P>
```

Next comes a DataGrid control that will display the actual products. Listing 10.8 shows this portion of the HTML code. Most of this HTML is concerned with formatting the DataGrid properly. We'll discuss it in detail after we've finished showing you the code for this page.

NOTE We've chosen to use the DataGrid control in the StoreManager application rather than the DataList control that we used in the CDStore application. We did this for two reasons. First, the store manager doesn't need the fancy display that we created for the store itself. Second, we want you to get some experience with the different controls so that you'll know how they all work.

Listing 10.8   ListProducts.aspx (continued)

```
<P>To edit a product, select from the list below</P>
<P>
    <asp:DataGrid id="dgProducts" runat="server" PageSize="4"
     AllowPaging="True" BorderColor="#DEDFDE" BorderStyle="None"
     BorderWidth="1px" BackColor="White" CellPadding="4"
     GridLines="Vertical" ForeColor="Black"
     AllowCustomPaging="True" AutoGenerateColumns="False">
        <SelectedItemStyle Font-Bold="True" ForeColor="White"
```

```
        BackColor="#CE5D5A"></SelectedItemStyle>
        <AlternatingItemStyle BackColor="White">
        </AlternatingItemStyle>
        <ItemStyle BackColor="#F7F7DE"></ItemStyle>
        <HeaderStyle Font-Bold="True" ForeColor="White"
         BackColor="#6B696B"></HeaderStyle>
        <FooterStyle BackColor="#CCCC99"></FooterStyle>
        <Columns>
            <asp:BoundColumn DataField="ProductID"
             HeaderText="Product ID"></asp:BoundColumn>
            <asp:BoundColumn DataField="ProductName"
             HeaderText="Product Name"></asp:BoundColumn>
            <asp:BoundColumn DataField="ProductPrice"
             HeaderText="Price"
             DataFormatString="{0:C}"></asp:BoundColumn>
            <asp:ButtonColumn Text="Select"
             CommandName="Select"></asp:ButtonColumn>
        </Columns>
        <PagerStyle Visible="False" HorizontalAlign="Right"
         ForeColor="Black" BackColor="#F7F7DE"
         PageButtonCount="5" Mode="NumericPages"></PagerStyle>
    </asp:DataGrid></P>
   <P>
```

The page concludes with three navigation controls for the DataGrid, plus the search controls, as shown in Listing 10.9.

Listing 10.9   **ListProducts.aspx (continued)**

```
            <asp:LinkButton id="btnFirstProduct" runat="server">
             First Product</asp:LinkButton> 
            <asp:LinkButton id="btnPrevious" runat="server">
             Previous</asp:LinkButton> 
            <asp:LinkButton id="btnNext" runat="server">
             Next</asp:LinkButton></P>
        <P>
            <asp:Label id="Label1" runat="server">
             Search text: </asp:Label> 
            <asp:TextBox id="txtSearch" runat="server" Width="331px">
            </asp:TextBox></P>
        <P>
            <asp:Button id="btnSearch" runat="server" Text="Search">
            </asp:Button></P>
        <P> </P>
    </form>
   </body>
  </HTML>
```

All in all, that's quite a chunk of HTML to try to understand—and, in fact, if we had tried to write it in a text editor, it would have been difficult. But, of course, that's not how we created this page. Instead, the entire page was created from within the Visual Studio .NET IDE. Figure 10.5 shows this page open in Visual Studio .NET.

FIGURE 10.5:

Designing the
`ListProducts`
`.aspx` page

The HyperLink, DataGrid, LinkButton, Label, TextBox, and Button controls were all added to this page simply by dragging and dropping them from the Toolbox. Similarly, the SqlCommand and SqlConnection objects shown at the bottom of the page were added by drag-and-drop from the Server Explorer window.

Of course, even though controls could be added and sized through drag-and-drop, there was still cleanup work to do. Here's a summary of the steps that you would need to follow to create this page in the IDE after adding the controls and setting their sizes and text properties:

1. Rename all the controls using a sensible naming convention. Visual Studio .NET doesn't even try to assign good names to controls.

2. Edit the ConnectionString property of the Connection object to use the special (`local`) name to refer to the SQL Server. (If your SQL Server is on a computer other than the computer with your web server, you'll need to supply the appropriate server name here instead.)

3. Select the DataGrid control and click the AutoFormat link at the bottom of the Properties window. Choose the Classic 2 color scheme and then click OK.

4. Select the DataGrid control and then click the Property Builder link at the bottom of the Properties window. Select the Columns section within the Properties dialog box. Uncheck the Create Columns Automatically at Run Time check box. Create three bound columns (for the ProductID, ProductName, and Price columns) and one Select button column. Figure 10.6 shows this section of the Properties dialog box.

FIGURE 10.6:

Creating columns for the DataGrid control

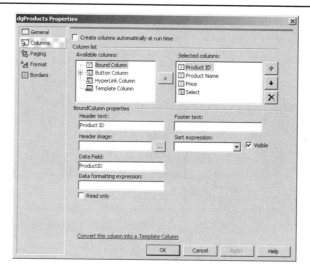

5. Select the Paging section in the left-hand column of the Properties dialog box. Check the Allow Paging and Allow Custom Paging check boxes and set the Page Size to four rows. Figure 10.7 shows this section of the Properties dialog box. Click OK to set the properties and dismiss the dialog box.

FIGURE 10.7:

Setting paging properties for the DataGrid control

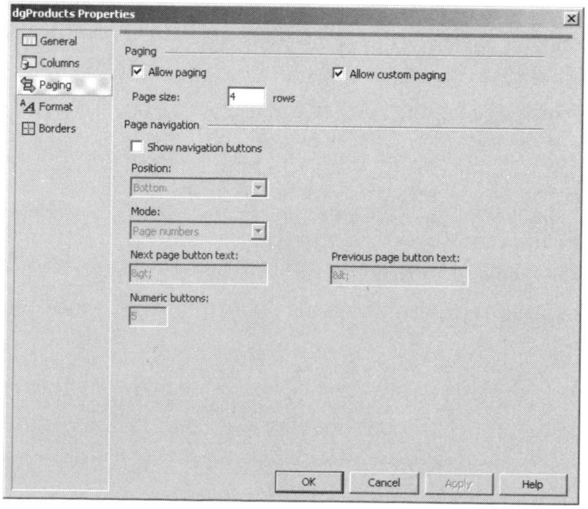

6. Set the NavigateURL property of the Hyperlink control at the top of the page to **New-Product.aspx**.

7. Add the include files and comments to the code by editing the page in HTML view.

This page also includes quite a bit of Visual Basic .NET code to handle its behavior. The Page_Load procedure, shown in Listing 10.10, uses the IsPostBack property to determine whether this is the first time the page has been loaded. If it is, the procedure executes a command to retrieve and store the highest ProductID in the database (this is used later in the paging code). It then sets parameters on a SqlCommand object to fetch the first four products from the database, and it passes this object to a subroutine named FillGrid. Finally, it stores the minimum ProductID that was retrieved and disables the Previous button (because it doesn't make any sense to try to retrieve previous products when the page is already displaying the first product in the database).

Listing 10.10   **ListProducts.aspx.vb Page_Load Procedure**

```
Private Sub Page_Load(ByVal sender As System.Object, _
  ByVal e As System.EventArgs) Handles MyBase.Load
    If Not IsPostBack Then
        ' Retrieve and store the highest product ID
        cnn.Open()
        ViewState("Max") = cmdManagerMaxProductID.ExecuteScalar
        cnn.Close()
        ' And load the initial data
        With cmdManagerRetrieveNextProducts
            .Parameters("@ProductID").Value = 0
            .Parameters("@Count").Value = 4
        End With
        FillGrid(cmdManagerRetrieveNextProducts)
        ' Store the lowest product ID
        ViewState("Min") = dgProducts.Items(0).Cells(0).Text
        ' Can't go backwards from the start
        btnPrevious.Enabled = False
    End If
End Sub
```

TIP   This page uses the ViewState collection to store pieces of information, including the highest and lowest ProductID values in the database. The difference between the ViewState and Session collections is that the former is valid only within the page, while the latter is valid throughout the browser session.

The FillGrid procedure, shown in Listing 10.11, handles the details of fetching a set of rows and displaying them on the DataGrid. It accepts as input a SqlCommand object that can be executed to return rows, and uses this object to create a DataReader object whose results can be bound to the DataGrid. It then uses the properties of the DataGrid to store the ProductID values from the first and last displayed rows into ViewState variables, and selectively disables the Previous and Next buttons by comparing those values to the minimum and maximum values that were determined by the Page_Load procedure.

Listing 10.11   **ListProducts.aspx.vb FillGrid Procedure**

```
Private Sub FillGrid(ByVal cmdCurrent As SqlCommand)
    Dim dr As SqlDataReader
    cnn.Open()
    dr = cmdCurrent.ExecuteReader()
    dgProducts.DataSource = dr
    dgProducts.DataBind()
    dr.Close()
    cnn.Close()
    ' Store the first and last rows retrieved
    ViewState("First") = dgProducts.Items(0).Cells(0).Text
    ViewState("Last") = dgProducts.Items(dgProducts.Items.Count - 1). _
     Cells(0).Text
    ' Disable the Next button if we're out of data
    If CType(ViewState("Last"), Integer) >= _
     CType(ViewState("Max"), Integer) Then
        btnNext.Enabled = False
    Else
        btnNext.Enabled = True
    End If
    ' Disable the Previous button if we're at the start
    If CType(ViewState("First"), Integer) <= _
     CType(ViewState("Min"), Integer) Then
        btnPrevious.Enabled = False
    Else
        btnPrevious.Enabled = True
    End If
End Sub
```

Each of the LinkButton controls, when clicked, calls a Click event on the server. Listing 10.12 shows the code that runs in response to these events. Each of these procedures constructs an appropriate SqlCommand object and passes it to the FillGrid procedure.

Listing 10.12   **ListProducts.aspx.vb LinkButton Click Procedures**

```
Private Sub btnFirstProduct_Click(ByVal sender As System.Object, _
  ByVal e As System.EventArgs) Handles btnFirstProduct.Click
    ' Fill the DataGrid with the first four rows of data
    With cmdManagerRetrieveNextProducts
        .Parameters("@ProductID").Value = 0
```

```
            .Parameters("@Count").Value = 4
        End With
        FillGrid(cmdManagerRetrieveNextProducts)
    End Sub

    Private Sub btnNext_Click(ByVal sender As System.Object, _
     ByVal e As System.EventArgs) Handles btnNext.Click
        ' Fill the DataGrid with the next four rows of data
        With cmdManagerRetrieveNextProducts
            .Parameters("@ProductID").Value = _
            CType(ViewState("Last"), Integer)
            .Parameters("@Count").Value = 4
        End With
        FillGrid(cmdManagerRetrieveNextProducts)
    End Sub

    Private Sub btnPrevious_Click(ByVal sender As System.Object, _
     ByVal e As System.EventArgs) Handles btnPrevious.Click
        ' Fill the DataGrid with the previous four rows of data
        With cmdManagerRetrievePreviousProducts
            .Parameters("@ProductID").Value = _
            CType(ViewState("First"), Integer)
            .Parameters("@Count").Value = 4
        End With
        FillGrid(cmdManagerRetrievePreviousProducts)
    End Sub
```

When the user clicks the Select link within the DataGrid, the DataGrid's ItemCommand property will be called. Listing 10.13 shows the code that's run in this case. This code sets a session variable to the ProductID from the specified product and redirects the browser to the ManageProduct.aspx page.

Listing 10.13   **ListProducts.aspx.vb dgProducts_ItemCommand Procedure**

```
    Private Sub dgProducts_ItemCommand(ByVal source As Object, _
     ByVal e As System.Web.UI.WebControls.DataGridCommandEventArgs) _
     Handles dgProducts.ItemCommand
        ' e.Item is the row of the DataGrid where the link was
        ' clicked.
        ' Store the ProductID
        Session("ProductID") = e.Item.Cells(0).Text
        ' And redirect to the management page
        Server.Transfer("ManageProduct.aspx")
    End Sub
```

The last piece of code behind this page is called when the user clicks the Search button. Listing 10.14 shows this procedure, which sets a session variable to the search text and then redirects the browser to the SearchProducts.aspx page.

Listing 10.14   **ListProducts.aspx.vb btnSearch_Click Procedure**

```
Private Sub btnSearch_Click(ByVal sender As System.Object, _
  ByVal e As System.EventArgs) Handles btnSearch.Click
    ' Store the search text
    Session("Search") = txtSearch.Text
    ' And redirect to the search page
    Server.Transfer("SearchProducts.aspx")
End Sub
```

This page uses three stored procedures from the database. The first, procManagerMax-ProductID, is shown in Listing 10.15. This stored procedure returns the highest ProductID currently in the database.

Listing 10.15   **procManagerMaxProductID Stored Procedure**

```
/* Get the highest product ID

From .NET E-Commerce Programming
by Mike Gunderloy and Noel Jerke
Copyright 2002, Sybex Inc. All Rights Reserved. */
CREATE PROCEDURE procManagerMaxProductID
AS
SELECT Max(ProductID) FROM Product
```

The procManagerRetrieveNextProducts stored procedure retrieves a set of products from the Product table. The parameters to the stored procedure specify how many products to retrieve and where to start the retrieval. The SQL for this stored procedure, shown in Listing 10.16, is a bit tricky. It actually builds a SQL statement by using the plus sign as a string concatenation operator and then calls the EXEC function to execute this statement. That's necessary because you can't use a SQL Server variable to directly specify the number of products to retrieve when using a TOP n SQL statement.

Listing 10.16   **procManagerRetrieveNextProducts Stored Procedure**

```
/* Retrieve basic product information

From .NET E-Commerce Programming
by Mike Gunderloy and Noel Jerke
Copyright 2002, Sybex Inc. All Rights Reserved. */
CREATE PROCEDURE procManagerRetrieveNextProducts
  @ProductID int,
  @Count int
```

```
AS
  EXEC('SELECT TOP ' + @Count + 'ProductID, ProductName, ProductPrice
    FROM Product
    WHERE ProductID > ' + @ProductID +
    ' ORDER BY ProductID')
```

The final stored procedure for this page, procManagerRetrievePreviousProducts, is even more complex, as shown in Listing 10.17. The added complexity comes from the fact that the TOP n SQL statement returns rows in reverse order when the table is sorted in descending order; this is necessary to have the statement return rows that start before a specified position. So the code retrieves the desired rows into a temporary table and then uses a second SELECT statement to reverse the order of the rows before returning them.

Listing 10.17   procManagerRetrievePreviousProducts Stored Procedure

```
CREATE PROCEDURE procManagerRetrievePreviousProducts
  @ProductID int,
  @Count int
AS
  CREATE TABLE #ProductTemp
    (ProductID int, ProductName varchar(255), ProductPrice money)
  INSERT #ProductTemp
    EXEC('SELECT TOP ' + @Count + 'ProductID, ProductName, ProductPrice
      FROM Product
      WHERE ProductID < ' + @ProductID +
      ' ORDER BY ProductID DESC')
  SELECT * FROM #ProductTemp ORDER BY ProductID
```

NOTE Note that both of the row retrieval stored procedures accept a parameter that specifies how many rows to retrieve. In the ListProducts.aspx page, we've hard-coded this variable to always return four rows. For additional flexibility, you could add a text box to the form to allow the user to specify the number of rows to return.

That does it for providing the key features of the product listing, which serves as the gateway to product management. Figure 10.8 shows the product listing page as it starts out, listing the first four products from the database.

FIGURE 10.8:

Product listing

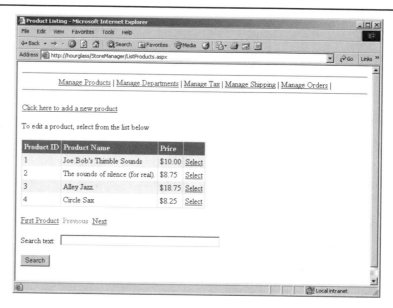

The user can click the Next link to move the listing to the next set of four products. Figure 10.9 shows the results. At this point, both the Previous link and the Next link are active.

FIGURE 10.9:

Second page in
product listing

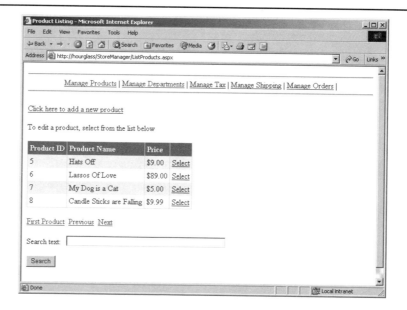

Searching for Products

The search page works in much the same way as the product listing page, but in this case, we are narrowing down the list to show only those products that contain the searched-for text. In fact, we could have used the same page for both regular listings and search listings, but the code is easier to understand when it's split between two pages.

Listing 10.18 shows the HTML code for the SearchProducts.aspx page.

Listing 10.18   SearchProducts.aspx

```
<%@ Page Language="vb" AutoEventWireup="false"
 Codebehind="SearchProducts.aspx.vb"
 Inherits="StoreManager.SearchProducts"%>
<!DOCTYPE HTML PUBLIC "-//W3C//DTD HTML 4.0 Transitional//EN">
<HTML>
    <HEAD>
        <title>Search Products</title>
        <meta name="GENERATOR" content="Microsoft Visual Studio.NET 7.0">
        <meta name="CODE_LANGUAGE" content="Visual Basic 7.0">
        <meta name="vs_defaultClientScript" content="JavaScript">
        <meta name="vs_targetSchema"
         content="http://schemas.microsoft.com/intellisense/ie5">
        <!-- SearchProducts.aspx -
            Page through products in search results -->
    </HEAD>
    <body>
        <!-- #Include File="ValidateCheck.inc" -->
        <!-- #Include File="Navbar.inc" -->
        <FORM id="Form1" method="post" runat="server">
            <P>
                <asp:Label id="lblInfo" runat="server">
                 Label</asp:Label></P>
            <P>
                <asp:HyperLink id="HyperLink1" runat="server"
                 NavigateUrl="NewProduct.aspx">
                  Click here to add a new product
                </asp:HyperLink></P>
            <P>
                <asp:Label id="lblEdit" runat="server">To edit a product,
                 select from the list below</asp:Label></P>
            <P>
                <asp:DataGrid id="dgProducts" runat="server"
                 AutoGenerateColumns="False" PageSize="4"
                 AllowPaging="True"
                 BorderColor="#DEDFDE" BorderStyle="None"
                 BorderWidth="1px"
                 BackColor="White" CellPadding="4" GridLines="Vertical"
                 ForeColor="Black" AllowCustomPaging="True">
                    <SelectedItemStyle Font-Bold="True" ForeColor="White"
```

```
                              BackColor="#CE5D5A"></SelectedItemStyle>
                              <AlternatingItemStyle BackColor="White">
                              </AlternatingItemStyle>
                              <ItemStyle BackColor="#F7F7DE"></ItemStyle>
                              <HeaderStyle Font-Bold="True" ForeColor="White"
                               BackColor="#6B696B"></HeaderStyle>
                              <FooterStyle BackColor="#CCCC99"></FooterStyle>
                              <Columns>
                                    <asp:BoundColumn DataField="ProductID"
                                      HeaderText="Product ID"></asp:BoundColumn>
                                    <asp:BoundColumn DataField="ProductName"
                                      HeaderText="Product Name"></asp:BoundColumn>
                                    <asp:BoundColumn DataField="ProductPrice"
                                      HeaderText="Price" DataFormatString="{0:C}">
                                    </asp:BoundColumn>
                                    <asp:ButtonColumn Text="Select"
                                     CommandName="Select">
                                    </asp:ButtonColumn>
                              </Columns>
                              <PagerStyle Visible="False" HorizontalAlign="Right"
                               ForeColor="Black" BackColor="#F7F7DE"
                               PageButtonCount="5"
                               Mode="NumericPages"></PagerStyle>
                        </asp:DataGrid></P>
                  <P>
                        <asp:LinkButton id="btnFirstProduct" runat="server">
                         First Product</asp:LinkButton> 
                        <asp:LinkButton id="btnPrevious" runat="server">Previous
                        </asp:LinkButton> 
                        <asp:LinkButton id="btnNext" runat="server">Next
                        </asp:LinkButton></P>
                  <P>
                        <asp:Label id="Label1" runat="server">Search text:
                        </asp:Label> 
                        <asp:TextBox id="txtSearch" runat="server" Width="331px">
                        </asp:TextBox></P>
                  <P>
                        <asp:Button id="btnSearch" runat="server" Text="Search">
                        </asp:Button></P>
                  <P> </P>
            </FORM>
      </body>
</HTML>
```

If you compare the HTML for the search page with the HTML for the listing page, you'll see that the major difference is that there's an additional label at the top of the search page. We'll use that label to convey information about the search back to the user, by setting its Text property at runtime.

The Page_Load procedure for this page, shown in Listing 10.19, first retrieves the highest ProductID for any product that meets the search criterion. If the stored procedure used for this purpose returns a Null instead of a value, that means that there are no matching products in the database. In that case, the lblInfo label is used to display a warning message to the user, and the actual data controls are made invisible. Otherwise, the lblInfo label displays the text that the user searched for, and the code calls the FillGrid procedure to load the actual data.

Listing 10.19   **SearchProducts.aspx.vb Page_Load Procedure**

```
Private Sub Page_Load(ByVal sender As System.Object, _
 ByVal e As System.EventArgs) Handles MyBase.Load
    If Not IsPostBack Then
        ' Retrieve and store the highest product ID
        cnn.Open()
        cmdManagerMaxSearchProductID.Parameters("@SearchText").Value = _
        Session("Search")
        Dim MaxID As Object = _
         cmdManagerMaxSearchProductID.ExecuteScalar
        cnn.Close()
        ' Check to make sure we got results, or put up
        ' a warning if we didn't
        If MaxID Is DBNull.Value Then
            lblInfo.Text = "Your search for '" & Session("Search") & _
            "' did not return any data."
            lblEdit.Visible = False
            dgProducts.Visible = False
            btnFirstProduct.Visible = False
            btnPrevious.Visible = False
            btnNext.Visible = False
        Else
            ViewState("Max") = MaxID
            lblInfo.Text = "Search results for '" & Session("Search") & _
            "'"
            lblEdit.Visible = True
            dgProducts.Visible = True
            btnFirstProduct.Visible = True
            btnPrevious.Visible = True
            btnNext.Visible = True
            ' And load the initial data
            With cmdManagerRetrieveSearchNextProducts
                .Parameters("@ProductID").Value = 0
                .Parameters("@Count").Value = 4
                .Parameters("@SearchText").Value = Session("Search")
            End With
            FillGrid(cmdManagerRetrieveSearchNextProducts)
            ' Store the lowest product ID
            ViewState("Min") = dgProducts.Items(0).Cells(0).Text
            ' Can't go backwards from the start
            btnPrevious.Enabled = False
```

```
                End If
            End If
        End Sub
```

The remaining code behind this page, shown in Listing 10.20, is very similar to the code for ListProducts.aspx. The major difference is that a different set of stored procedures are used to actually retrieve rows from the database.

Listing 10.20   **SearchProducts.aspx.vb Event Procedures**

```
    Private Sub FillGrid(ByVal cmdCurrent As SqlCommand)
        Dim dr As SqlDataReader
        cnn.Open()
        dr = cmdCurrent.ExecuteReader()
        dgProducts.DataSource = dr
        dgProducts.DataBind()
        dr.Close()
        cnn.Close()
        ' Store the first and last rows retrieved
        ViewState("First") = dgProducts.Items(0).Cells(0).Text
        ViewState("Last") = dgProducts.Items(dgProducts.Items.Count - 1). _
        Cells(0).Text
        ' Disable the Next button if we're out of data
        If CType(ViewState("Last"), Integer) >= _
        CType(ViewState("Max"), Integer) Then
            btnNext.Enabled = False
        Else
            btnNext.Enabled = True
        End If
        ' Disable the Previous button if we're at the start
        If CType(ViewState("First"), Integer) <= _
        CType(ViewState("Min"), Integer) Then
            btnPrevious.Enabled = False
        Else
            btnPrevious.Enabled = True
        End If
    End Sub

    Private Sub btnFirstProduct_Click(ByVal sender As System.Object, _
    ByVal e As System.EventArgs) Handles btnFirstProduct.Click
        ' Fill the DataGrid with the first four rows of data
        With cmdManagerRetrieveSearchNextProducts
            .Parameters("@ProductID").Value = 0
            .Parameters("@Count").Value = 4
            .Parameters("@SearchText").Value = Session("Search")
        End With
        FillGrid(cmdManagerRetrieveSearchNextProducts)
    End Sub
```

```
Private Sub btnNext_Click(ByVal sender As System.Object, _
 ByVal e As System.EventArgs) Handles btnNext.Click
     ' Fill the DataGrid with the next four rows of data
    With cmdManagerRetrieveSearchNextProducts
        .Parameters("@ProductID").Value = _
        CType(ViewState("Last"), Integer)
        .Parameters("@Count").Value = 4
        .Parameters("@SearchText").Value = Session("Search")
    End With
    FillGrid(cmdManagerRetrieveSearchNextProducts)
End Sub

Private Sub btnPrevious_Click(ByVal sender As System.Object, _
 ByVal e As System.EventArgs) Handles btnPrevious.Click
     ' Fill the DataGrid with the previous four rows of data
    With cmdManagerRetrieveSearchPreviousProducts
        .Parameters("@ProductID").Value = _
        CType(ViewState("First"), Integer)
        .Parameters("@Count").Value = 4
        .Parameters("@SearchText").Value = Session("Search")
    End With
    FillGrid(cmdManagerRetrieveSearchPreviousProducts)
End Sub

Private Sub dgProducts_ItemCommand(ByVal source As Object, _
 ByVal e As System.Web.UI.WebControls.DataGridCommandEventArgs) _
 Handles dgProducts.ItemCommand
     ' e.Item is the row of the DataGrid where the button was
     ' clicked.
     ' Store the ProductID
    Session("ProductID") = e.Item.Cells(0).Text
     ' And redirect to the management page
    Server.Transfer("ManageProduct.aspx")
End Sub

Private Sub btnSearch_Click(ByVal sender As System.Object, _
 ByVal e As System.EventArgs) Handles btnSearch.Click
     ' Store the search text
    Session("Search") = txtSearch.Text
     ' And redirect to the search page
    Server.Transfer("SearchProducts.aspx")
End Sub
```

Listing 10.21 shows the procManagerMaxSearchProductID stored procedure, which is used to determine the largest ProductID in the search results (and also to tell whether there are, in fact, any search results).

Listing 10.21   **procManagerMaxSearchProductID Stored Procedure**

```
/*  Get the highest product ID
    for a product search

From .NET E-Commerce Programming
by Mike Gunderloy and Noel Jerke
Copyright 2002, Sybex Inc. All Rights Reserved. */
CREATE PROCEDURE procManagerMaxSearchProductID
    @SearchText varchar(255)
AS
  SELECT Max(ProductID) FROM Product
    WHERE ProductName LIKE '%' + @SearchText + '%'
```

As you can see in the SQL, we're searching only the ProductName column of the database. In a more complex management application, you'd probably want to offer the option of searching other information as well. This stored procedure (as well as the ones that actually retrieve data) takes a parameter that holds the search string. Listing 10.22 shows the procManagerRetrieveSearchNextProducts stored procedure, which is used to return a batch of search results moving forward in the table.

Listing 10.22   **procManagerRetrieveSearchNextProducts Stored Procedure**

```
/*  Retrieve basic product information

From .NET E-Commerce Programming
by Mike Gunderloy and Noel Jerke
Copyright 2002, Sybex Inc. All Rights Reserved. */
CREATE PROCEDURE procManagerRetrieveSearchNextProducts
  @ProductID int,
  @Count int,
  @SearchText varchar(255)
AS
  EXEC('SELECT TOP ' + @Count + 'ProductID, ProductName, ProductPrice
    FROM Product
    WHERE ProductID > ' + @ProductID +
    ' AND ProductName LIKE ''%'' + ''' +
    @SearchText + ''' + ''%'' ORDER BY ProductID')
```

This stored procedure uses the same EXEC method as the procManagerRetrieveNextProducts stored procedure that you saw earlier. Note the use of two quotes within quoted text to represent a single quote in the final SQL statement.

Finally, the procManagerRetrieveSearchPreviousProducts stored procedure, shown in Listing 10.23, is used to move backward in the search results.

Listing 10.23 procManagerRetrieveSearchPreviousProducts Stored Procedure

```
/*  Retrieve basic product information

From .NET E-Commerce Programming
by Mike Gunderloy and Noel Jerke
Copyright 2002, Sybex Inc. All Rights Reserved. */
CREATE PROCEDURE procManagerRetrieveSearchPreviousProducts
  @ProductID int,
  @Count int,
  @SearchText varchar(255)
AS
  CREATE TABLE #ProductTemp
    (ProductID int, ProductName varchar(255), ProductPrice money)
  INSERT #ProductTemp
    EXEC('SELECT TOP ' + @Count + 'ProductID, ProductName, ProductPrice
      FROM Product
      WHERE ProductID < ' + @ProductID +
      ' AND ProductName LIKE ''%'' + ''' +
    @SearchText + ''' + ''%'' ORDER BY ProductID DESC')
  SELECT * FROM #ProductTemp ORDER BY ProductID
```

With this code in place, you can execute a product search from the product listing page. For example, if you type in the keyword **Dog** and click Search, you'll get the results shown in Figure 10.10.

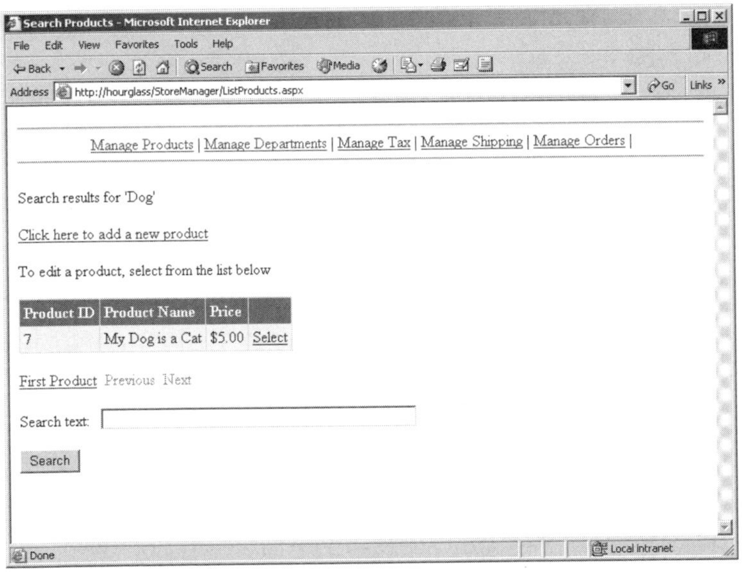

FIGURE 10.10:

Product search on "Dog"

Adding New Products

To begin the process of adding a new product to the database, the user can click the Add a New Product link on either the product listing page or the listing search page. Figure 10.11 shows the NewProduct.aspx page in the Visual Studio .NET IDE. As you can see, the page consists of a table containing data entry controls, together with a submit button and associated validation controls. Listing 10.24 contains the HTML code for this page.

FIGURE 10.11:

Design of the new product page

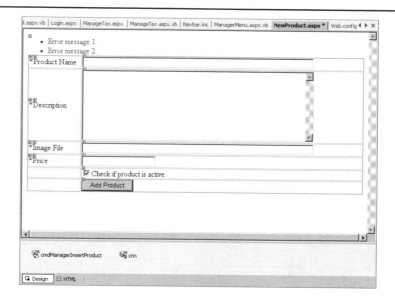

Listing 10.24   NewProduct.aspx

```
<%@ Page Language="vb" AutoEventWireup="false"
 Codebehind="NewProduct.aspx.vb"
 Inherits="StoreManager.NewProduct"%>
<!DOCTYPE HTML PUBLIC "-//W3C//DTD HTML 4.0 Transitional//EN">
<HTML>
    <HEAD>
        <title>New Product</title>
        <meta name="GENERATOR" content="Microsoft Visual Studio.NET 7.0">
        <meta name="CODE_LANGUAGE" content="Visual Basic 7.0">
        <meta name="vs_defaultClientScript" content="JavaScript">
        <meta name="vs_targetSchema" content=
         "http://schemas.microsoft.com/intellisense/ie5">
        <!-- NewProduct.aspx - Add a new product to the store -->
    </HEAD>
    <body>
        <!-- #Include File="ValidateCheck.inc" -->
        <!-- #Include File="Navbar.inc" -->
        <form id="Form1" method="post" runat="server">
```

```
<asp:ValidationSummary id="ValidationSummary1" runat="server">
</asp:ValidationSummary>
<TABLE id="Table1" cellSpacing="1" cellPadding="1" width="100%"
 border="0">
    <TR>
        <TD style="WIDTH: 97px">
            <asp:RequiredFieldValidator
             id="RequiredFieldValidator1" runat="server"
             ErrorMessage="You must enter a product name."
             ControlToValidate="txtProductName">*
            </asp:RequiredFieldValidator>
            <asp:Label id="Label1" runat="server">Product Name
            </asp:Label></TD>
        <TD>
            <asp:TextBox id="txtProductName" runat="server"
             Width="480px"></asp:TextBox></TD>
    </TR>
    <TR>
        <TD style="WIDTH: 97px">
            <asp:RequiredFieldValidator
             id="RequiredFieldValidator2" runat="server"
             ErrorMessage=
             "You must enter a product description."
             ControlToValidate="txtProductDescription">*
            </asp:RequiredFieldValidator>
            <asp:Label id="Label2" runat="server">Description
            </asp:Label></TD>
        <TD>
            <asp:TextBox id="txtProductDescription"
             runat="server"
             Width="482px" Height="145px" Rows="6"
             TextMode="MultiLine"></asp:TextBox></TD>
    </TR>
    <TR>
        <TD style="WIDTH: 97px">
            <asp:RequiredFieldValidator
             id="RequiredFieldValidator3" runat="server"
             ErrorMessage="You must enter an image file name."
             ControlToValidate="txtProductImage">*
            </asp:RequiredFieldValidator>
            <asp:Label id="Label3" runat="server">Image File
            </asp:Label></TD>
        <TD>
            <asp:TextBox id="txtProductImage" runat="server"
             Width="482px"></asp:TextBox></TD>
    </TR>
    <TR>
        <TD style="WIDTH: 97px">
            <asp:RequiredFieldValidator
             id="RequiredFieldValidator4" runat="server"
             ErrorMessage="You must enter a price."
```

```
                          ControlToValidate="txtProductPrice">*
                        </asp:RequiredFieldValidator>
                        <asp:Label id="Label4" runat="server">Price
                        </asp:Label></TD>
                    <TD>
                        <asp:TextBox id="txtProductPrice" runat="server">
                        </asp:TextBox></TD>
                </TR>
                <TR>
                    <TD style="WIDTH: 97px"></TD>
                    <TD>
                        <asp:CheckBox id="chkActive" runat="server"
                        Text="Check if product is active." Checked="True">
                        </asp:CheckBox></TD>
                </TR>
                <TR>
                    <TD style="WIDTH: 97px"></TD>
                    <TD>
                        <asp:Button id="btnAddProduct" runat="server"
                        Text="Add Product"></asp:Button></TD>
                </TR>
            </TABLE>
        </form>
    </body>
</HTML>
```

Listing 10.25 shows the Page_Load procedure for this page. Remember, when the user clicks the Add Product button, the validation controls will process the page contents first. Only if all the validations are satisfied will the Page_Load procedure be executed with the IsPostBack property set to True. So, if the code is in the Page_Load procedure and if IsPost-Back is true, we know that all the data has passed validation. In this case, the code uses a stored procedure to insert the new product into the database. It then sets a session variable to the ProductID of the new product and redirects the browser to a new page, Manage-Product.aspx, where the user can fill in further product details.

Listing 10.25   NewProduct.aspx.vb Page_Load Procedure

```
Private Sub Page_Load(ByVal sender As System.Object, _
ByVal e As System.EventArgs) Handles MyBase.Load
    ' If we're in a postback, data has passed validation
    If IsPostBack Then
        ' Save the new product to the database
        With cmdManagerInsertProduct
            .Parameters("@ProductName").Value = _
            txtProductName.Text()
            .Parameters("@ProductDescription").Value = _
            txtProductDescription.Text
            .Parameters("@ProductImage").Value = _
```

```
                    txtProductImage.Text
                    .Parameters("@ProductPrice").Value = _
                    txtProductPrice.Text
                    If chkActive.Checked Then
                        .Parameters("@ProductActive").Value = True
                    Else
                        .Parameters("@ProductActive").Value = False
                    End If
                    cnn.Open()
                    Session("ProductID") = .ExecuteScalar
                    cnn.Close()
                    ' And redirect to the management page
                    Server.Transfer("ManageProduct.aspx")
                End With
            End If
        End Sub
```

Listing 10.26 shows the procManagerInsertProduct stored procedure, which does the actual work of inserting the product data into the database. Note the use of the SELECT @@IDENTITY function to set the new ProductID as the return value of the stored procedure.

Listing 10.26   **procManagerInsertProduct Stored Procedure**

```
/*  Add a new product to the store

From .NET E-Commerce Programming
by Mike Gunderloy and Noel Jerke
Copyright 2002, Sybex Inc. All Rights Reserved. */
CREATE PROCEDURE procManagerInsertProduct
  @ProductName varchar(255),
  @ProductDescription text,
  @ProductImage varchar(255),
  @ProductPrice money,
  @ProductActive bit
AS
  INSERT INTO Product(ProductName, ProductDescription,
    ProductImage, ProductPrice, ProductActive)
  VALUES(@ProductName, @ProductDescription,
    @ProductImage, @ProductPrice, @ProductActive)
  /* Return the ID of the new product */
  SELECT @@IDENTITY
```

Figure 10.12 shows the add new product page in action. After the user fills in the form and the data is entered into the database, the application displays the new product on the product management page, which is the subject of the next section of this chapter.

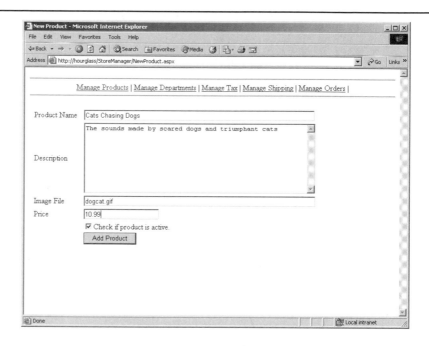

Managing a Product

The product management page provides, in a single view, all the settings for a particular product. The page starts out in the usual format with the page headers, security validation, and navigation bar. As shown in Listing 10.27, it continues with a Hyperlink control to preview the product, and a LinkButton control to delete the product. Note that we'll deal with the actions of these controls in code behind the page rather than in HTML.

Listing 10.27   **ManageProduct.aspx**

```
<%@ Page Language="vb" AutoEventWireup="false"
 Codebehind="ManageProduct.aspx.vb" Inherits="StoreManager.ManageProduct"%>
<!DOCTYPE HTML PUBLIC "-//W3C//DTD HTML 4.0 Transitional//EN">
<HTML>
    <HEAD>
        <title>Manage Product</title>
        <meta content="Microsoft Visual Studio.NET 7.0" name="GENERATOR">
        <meta content="Visual Basic 7.0" name="CODE_LANGUAGE">
        <meta content="JavaScript" name="vs_defaultClientScript">
        <meta content="http://schemas.microsoft.com/intellisense/ie5"
         name="vs_targetSchema">
        <!-- ManageProduct.aspx - Page to manage product data -->
    </HEAD>
    <body>
```

```
<!-- #Include File="ValidateCheck.inc" -->
<!-- #Include File="Navbar.inc" -->
<form id="Form1" method="post" runat="server">
    <P><asp:hyperlink id="hlPreview" runat="server">
    Preview in store</asp:hyperlink></P>
    <P><asp:linkbutton id="lbDelete" runat="server">
    Delete Product</asp:linkbutton></P>
```

The next part of the page contains data entry controls for the product data, along with validation controls for this data. This section, as shown in Listing 10.28, uses a table for layout and ends with a button to submit any changes.

Listing 10.28   ManageProduct.aspx (continued)

```
<P>
    <asp:ValidationSummary id="ValidationSummary1" runat="server">
    </asp:ValidationSummary></P>
<P>
    <TABLE id="Table1" cellSpacing="1" cellPadding="1" width="100%"
     border="0">
        <TR>
            <TD><asp:label id="Label1" runat="server">Product ID:
            </asp:label></TD>
            <TD><asp:textbox id="txtProductID"
             runat="server" Width="106px">
            </asp:textbox></TD>
        </TR>
        <TR>
            <TD>
                <asp:RequiredFieldValidator id="RequiredFieldValidator1"
                 runat="server"
                 ErrorMessage="You must enter a product name."
                 ControlToValidate="txtProductName">*
                </asp:RequiredFieldValidator>Product
                Name:</TD>
            <TD><asp:textbox id="txtProductName"
             runat="server" Width="343px">
            </asp:textbox></TD>
        </TR>
        <TR>
            <TD>
                <asp:RequiredFieldValidator id="RequiredFieldValidator2"
                 runat="server"
                 ErrorMessage="You must enter a product description."
                 ControlToValidate="txtProductDescription">*
                </asp:RequiredFieldValidator>Description:</TD>
            <TD><asp:textbox id="txtProductDescription" runat="server"
             Width="342px" Height="213px" Rows="10" TextMode="MultiLine">
            </asp:textbox></TD>
```

```
        </TR>
        <TR>
            <TD>
                <asp:RequiredFieldValidator id="RequiredFieldValidator3"
                 runat="server"
                 ErrorMessage="You must select a product image."
                 ControlToValidate="txtProductImage">*
                </asp:RequiredFieldValidator>Image
                 file:</TD>
            <TD><asp:textbox id="txtProductImage" runat="server"
             Width="342px"></asp:textbox><asp:image id="imgProduct"
             runat="server"></asp:image></TD>
        </TR>
        <TR>
            <TD>
                <asp:RequiredFieldValidator id="RequiredFieldValidator4"
                 runat="server"
                 ErrorMessage="You must enter a product price."
                 ControlToValidate="txtProductPrice">*
                </asp:RequiredFieldValidator>Price:</TD>
            <TD><asp:textbox id="txtProductPrice" runat="server"
             Width="108px"></asp:textbox></TD>
        </TR>
        <TR>
            <TD></TD>
            <TD><asp:checkbox id="chkActive" runat="server"
             Text="Check if product is active."></asp:checkbox></TD>
        </TR>
    </TABLE>
</P>
<P><asp:button id="btnUpdate" runat="server" Text="Update Product">
</asp:button></P>
```

The next section of the page displays all the departments that contain this product. The page uses a DataGrid to manage this display. There's also a DropDownList containing departments so that the user can add a new department for this product. Listing 10.29 shows this section of the page.

Listing 10.29   ManageProduct.aspx (continued)

```
<H3>Departments for this product:</H3>
<P><asp:datagrid id="dgDepartments" runat="server" ForeColor="Black"
 GridLines="Vertical" CellPadding="4" BackColor="White" BorderWidth="1px"
 BorderStyle="None" BorderColor="#DEDFDE" AutoGenerateColumns="False">
        <SelectedItemStyle Font-Bold="True" ForeColor="White"
         BackColor="#CE5D5A"></SelectedItemStyle>
        <AlternatingItemStyle BackColor="White"></AlternatingItemStyle>
        <ItemStyle BackColor="#F7F7DE"></ItemStyle>
        <HeaderStyle Font-Bold="True" ForeColor="White"
         BackColor="#6B696B">
```

```
        </HeaderStyle>
        <FooterStyle BackColor="#CCCC99"></FooterStyle>
        <Columns>
            <asp:BoundColumn Visible="False" DataField="DepartmentID"
             HeaderText="DepartmentID"></asp:BoundColumn>
            <asp:BoundColumn DataField="DepartmentName"
             HeaderText="Department"></asp:BoundColumn>
            <asp:ButtonColumn Text="Delete" CommandName="Delete">
            </asp:ButtonColumn>
        </Columns>
        <PagerStyle HorizontalAlign="Right" ForeColor="Black"
         BackColor="#F7F7DE" Mode="NumericPages"></PagerStyle>
    </asp:datagrid></P>
 <P>Select a Department to add:</P>
 <P><asp:dropdownlist id="ddlAddDept" runat="server" AutoPostBack="True">
    </asp:dropdownlist></P>
```

Note that the Visible property of the BoundColumn element that holds the DepartmentID field is set to False. This means that the user won't actually see this column, but that its contents will still be available in the ItemCommand procedure for this control.

The page closes with a similar DataGrid and DropDownList combination to manage the attributes for the product, as shown in Listing 10.30.

Listing 10.30   ManageProduct.aspx (continued)

```
        <H3>Attributes for this product:</H3>
        <P><asp:datagrid id="dgAttributes" runat="server"
         ForeColor="Black" GridLines="Vertical" CellPadding="4"
         BackColor="White" BorderWidth="1px" BorderStyle="None"
         BorderColor="#DEDFDE" AutoGenerateColumns="False">
                <SelectedItemStyle Font-Bold="True" ForeColor="White"
                 BackColor="#CE5D5A"></SelectedItemStyle>
                <AlternatingItemStyle BackColor="White">
                </AlternatingItemStyle>
                <ItemStyle BackColor="#F7F7DE"></ItemStyle>
                <HeaderStyle Font-Bold="True" ForeColor="White"
                 BackColor="#6B696B"></HeaderStyle>
                <FooterStyle BackColor="#CCCC99"></FooterStyle>
                <Columns>
                    <asp:BoundColumn Visible="False"
                     DataField="AttributeID" HeaderText="AttributeID">
                    </asp:BoundColumn>
                    <asp:BoundColumn DataField="AttributeCategoryName"
                     HeaderText="Category"></asp:BoundColumn>
                    <asp:BoundColumn DataField="AttributeName"
                     HeaderText="Attribute"></asp:BoundColumn>
                    <asp:ButtonColumn Text="Delete"
                     CommandName="Delete">
```

```
                    </asp:ButtonColumn>
                  </Columns>
                  <PagerStyle HorizontalAlign="Right" ForeColor="Black"
                    BackColor="#F7F7DE" Mode="NumericPages"></PagerStyle>
                </asp:datagrid></P>
            <P>Select an Attribute to add:</P>
            <P><asp:dropdownlist id="ddlAddAttribute" runat="server"
                AutoPostBack="True">
                </asp:dropdownlist></P>
        </form>
    </body>
</HTML>
```

Now let's look at the code that drives this page. The Page_Load procedure starts by setting the NavigateURL of the Hyperlink control that's used to preview the product. It builds a link including the ProductID of the selected product to point to the Product.aspx page in the main store. This allows the user to see how a product will appear in the store, even before they mark it as active.

As shown in Listing 10.31, the code then goes on to use a SqlCommand object to retrieve the basic information about the product and display it on the form, together with the appropriate image file. The control that displays the ProductID column is disabled. This prevents the user from changing the ProductID accidentally (or deliberately), which would overwrite information for another product.

WARNING This code assumes that both the CDStore application and the StoreManager application are running on the same web server. If they were on different servers, we would need to alter the URLs that point from one to the other.

Listing 10.31   ManageProduct.aspx.vb Page_Load Procedure

```
Private Sub Page_Load(ByVal sender As System.Object, _
  ByVal e As System.EventArgs) Handles MyBase.Load
    Dim dr As SqlClient.SqlDataReader
    ' Populate the UI with current information
    ' First, set the hyperlink jump into the store
    hlPreview.NavigateUrl = "../CDStore/Product.aspx?idProduct=" & _
    Session("ProductID")
    cnn.Open()
    If Not IsPostBack Then
        ' Get the product info from the database
        With cmdManagerRetrieveProduct
            .Parameters("@ProductID").Value = _
            Session("ProductID")
            dr = .ExecuteReader()
        End With
```

```
      dr.Read()
      txtProductID.Enabled = True
      txtProductID.Text = dr.GetInt32(0)
      ' Lock the Product ID so they can't change it
      txtProductID.Enabled = False
      txtProductName.Text = dr.GetString(1)
      txtProductDescription.Text = dr.GetString(2)
      txtProductImage.Text = dr.GetString(3)
      imgProduct.ImageUrl = "../CDStore/Images/Products/sm_" & _
       dr.GetString(3)
      txtProductPrice.Text = Format( _
       dr.GetSqlMoney(4).ToSqlString.Value, "currency")
      If dr.GetBoolean(7) Then
          chkActive.Checked = True
      Else
          chkActive.Checked = False
      End If
      dr.Close()
  End If
```

Note the code that's used to format the Price column for display. Because the price is stored using the money data type in SQL Server, the code uses the GetSqlMoney method of the DataReader object to retrieve the value. But that value can't be automatically converted to a string for display on the user interface. Instead, the code uses the ToSqlString method of the returned value to convert it to a SqlString object, then uses the Value property of that object to convert it to a regular string. Finally, the code uses the Format function to display the returned value with the proper currency symbol.

Listing 10.32 shows the procManagerRetrieveProduct stored procedure, which is used to get the product information out of the database. This stored procedure simply takes a ProductID and returns the corresponding row from the Product table.

Listing 10.32   procManagerRetrieveProduct Stored Procedure

```
/*  Retrieve all info on a product

From .NET E-Commerce Programming
by Mike Gunderloy and Noel Jerke
Copyright 2002, Sybex Inc. All Rights Reserved. */
CREATE PROCEDURE procManagerRetrieveProduct
  @ProductID int
AS
  SELECT * FROM Product
  WHERE ProductID = @ProductID
```

Next, the code retrieves the current departments and the current attributes for the product, and binds these to their respective DataGrid controls, as shown in Listing 10.33. Note that we use the DataBind method of the control to initialize a single control, rather than call the DataBind method of the entire page to bind all the controls at once. Remember, because we're using a DataReader to retrieve this data, we must finish with each batch of data and close the DataReader before trying to load the next batch.

Listing 10.33   ManageProduct.aspx.vb Page_Load Procedure (continued)

```
' Get the list of departments for this product
cmdManagerRetrieveDeptByProd.Parameters("@ProductID").Value = _
  Session("ProductID")
dr = cmdManagerRetrieveDeptByProd.ExecuteReader
dgDepartments.DataSource = dr
dgDepartments.DataBind()
dr.Close()

' Get the list of attributes for this product
cmdManagerRetrieveAttributeByProd.Parameters("@ProductID").Value = _
  Session("ProductID")
dr = cmdManagerRetrieveAttributeByProd.ExecuteReader
dgAttributes.DataSource = dr
dgAttributes.DataBind()
dr.Close()
cnn.Close()
```

This code uses another pair of stored procedures. First, Listing 10.34 shows the procManagerRetrieveDeptByProd stored procedure, which returns all the departments that contain the specified product. Because of the many-to-many relationship between products and departments, this stored procedure must join two tables to get the necessary information.

Listing 10.34   procManagerRetrieveDeptByProd Stored Procedure

```
/*  Retrieve all departments for a product

From .NET E-Commerce Programming
by Mike Gunderloy and Noel Jerke
Copyright 2002, Sybex Inc. All Rights Reserved. */
CREATE PROCEDURE procManagerRetrieveDeptByProd
  @ProductID int
AS
  SELECT Department.DepartmentID, DepartmentName
    FROM Department INNER JOIN DepartmentProduct
    ON Department.DepartmentID = DepartmentProduct.DepartmentID
    WHERE ProductID = @ProductID
```

Listing 10.35 shows the procManagerRetrieveAttributeByProd stored procedure, which performs the same job for attributes. In this case, the code joins three tables, because we want to display the attribute category as well as the attribute.

Listing 10.35   **procManagerRetrieveAttributeByProd Stored Procedure**

```
/*  Retrieve all attributes for a product

From .NET E-Commerce Programming
by Mike Gunderloy and Noel Jerke
Copyright 2002, Sybex Inc. All Rights Reserved. */
CREATE PROCEDURE procManagerRetrieveAttributeByProd
  @ProductID int
AS
  SELECT AttributeCategoryName, Attribute.AttributeID, AttributeName
    FROM (Attribute INNER JOIN AttributeCategory
    ON Attribute.AttributeCategoryID =
      AttributeCategory.AttributeCategoryID)
    INNER JOIN ProductAttribute
    ON Attribute.AttributeID = ProductAttribute.AttributeID
    WHERE ProductID = @ProductID
```

After loading the DataGrid controls, the Page_Load procedure goes on to load the rows into the DropDownList controls, as shown in Listing 10.36. This code is run only the first time the page is loaded; we assume that the Department and Attribute lists themselves are unlikely to change. Initializing a DropDownList requires retrieving data (in this case, into a DataSet object) and then performing five steps:

1. Set the DataSource property of the DropDownList control to the DataSet.

2. Set the DataMember property of the DropDownList control to the appropriate DataTable name within the DataSet.

3. Set the DataTextField property of the DropDownList control to the name of the column that contains the data that should be displayed in the list.

4. Set the DataValueField property of the DropDownList control to the name of the column that contains the data that should be returned when the user makes a selection in the list.

5. Call the DataBind method of the DropDownList control.

NOTE   Note that we're simply listing all departments and all attributes. But it may make more sense to list only the departments and attributes that are currently not assigned to this product. That's worth considering if you have a long list of departments or attributes to choose from.

Listing 10.36   **ManageProduct.aspx.vb Page_Load Procedure (continued)**

```
        If Not IsPostBack Then
            ' One-time initializations
            ' Stock the Departments dropdownlist
            Dim dsDepts As New DataSet()
            Dim daDepts As New SqlDataAdapter()
            daDepts.SelectCommand = cmdManagerRetrieveDepts
            daDepts.Fill(dsDepts, "Depts")
            ddlAddDept.DataSource = dsDepts
            ddlAddDept.DataMember = "Depts"
            ddlAddDept.DataTextField = "DepartmentName"
            ddlAddDept.DataValueField = "DepartmentID"
            ddlAddDept.DataBind()

            ' Stock the Attributes dropdownlist
            Dim dsAttributes As New DataSet()
            Dim daAttributes As New SqlDataAdapter()
            daAttributes.SelectCommand = cmdManagerRetrieveAttributes
            daAttributes.Fill(dsAttributes, "Attributes")
            ddlAddAttribute.DataSource = dsAttributes
            ddlAddAttribute.DataMember = "Attributes"
            ddlAddAttribute.DataTextField = "Attr"
            ddlAddAttribute.DataValueField = "AttributeID"
            ddlAddAttribute.DataBind()

        End If
End Sub
```

Listing 10.37 shows the procManagerRetrieveDepts stored procedure, which is used to provide data for the list of departments. As you can see, this procedure runs a UNION query to place a "dummy" row having a value of zero and a hyphen as its text at the top of the list. That way, there's a default value for the DropDownList control that we know doesn't belong to any actual department.

Listing 10.37   **procManagerRetrieveDepts Stored Procedure**

```
/*  Retrieve all departments in the store

From .NET E-Commerce Programming
by Mike Gunderloy and Noel Jerke
Copyright 2002, Sybex Inc. All Rights Reserved. */
CREATE PROCEDURE procManagerRetrieveDepts
AS
  SELECT 0 AS DepartmentID, '-' AS DepartmentName
    UNION
  SELECT DepartmentID, DepartmentName
    FROM Department
```

The procManagerRetrieveAttributes stored procedure similarly retrieves all the attributes from the database, along with a single dummy row. This stored procedure, shown in Listing 10.38, also concatenates the attribute category name and the attribute name into a single string so that both will be displayed in the list.

Listing 10.38   procManagerRetrieveAttributes Stored Procedure

```
/*  Retrieve all attributes in the database

From .NET E-Commerce Programming
by Mike Gunderloy and Noel Jerke
Copyright 2002, Sybex Inc. All Rights Reserved. */
CREATE PROCEDURE procManagerRetrieveAttributes
AS
  SELECT '-' AS Attr, 0 AS AttributeID
  UNION
  SELECT AttributeCategoryName + ': ' + AttributeName AS Attr,
  Attribute.AttributeID
    FROM Attribute INNER JOIN AttributeCategory
    ON Attribute.AttributeCategoryID =
    AttributeCategory.AttributeCategoryID
```

The rest of the code behind this page handles the various actions that the user can take with the data. The Update Product button is used to execute a stored procedure to return information from the user interface of the form to the database. This stored procedure uses the ProductID to locate the appropriate row and then writes the new values to it. Listing 10.39 shows the code for the Update Product button.

Listing 10.39   ManageProduct.aspx.vb btnUpdate_Click Procedure

```
Private Sub btnUpdate_Click(ByVal sender As System.Object, _
  ByVal e As System.EventArgs) Handles btnUpdate.Click
    ' Save the information from this page back
    ' to the database
    With cmdManagerUpdateProduct
        .Parameters("@ProductID").Value = _
        Session("ProductID")
        .Parameters("@ProductName").Value = _
        txtProductName.Text
        .Parameters("@ProductDescription").Value = _
        txtProductDescription.Text
        .Parameters("@ProductImage").Value = _
        txtProductImage.Text
        .Parameters("@ProductPrice").Value = _
        CType(txtProductPrice.Text, Decimal)
        If chkActive.Checked Then
            .Parameters("@ProductActive").Value = 1
```

```
        Else
            .Parameters("@ProductActive").Value = 0
        End If
        cnn.Open()
        .ExecuteNonQuery()
        cnn.Close()
    End With
End Sub
```

Listing 10.40 shows the stored procedure that this code calls to actually perform the updates.

Listing 10.40   procManagerUpdateProduct Stored Procedure

```
/*  Update information on a product

From .NET E-Commerce Programming
by Mike Gunderloy and Noel Jerke
Copyright 2002, Sybex Inc. All Rights Reserved. */
CREATE PROCEDURE procManagerUpdateProduct
  @ProductID int,
  @ProductName varchar(255),
  @ProductDescription text,
  @ProductImage varchar(255),
  @ProductPrice money,
  @ProductActive bit
AS
  UPDATE Product
    SET ProductName = @ProductName,
      ProductDescription = @ProductDescription,
      ProductImage = @ProductImage,
      ProductPrice = @ProductPrice,
      ProductActive = @ProductActive
    WHERE ProductID = @ProductID
```

When the user clicks the Delete Product link, the server responds by running the code shown in Listing 10.41. Remember, this control is a LinkButton, which looks like a hyperlink but behaves like any other command button. After deleting the product, of course, there's nothing left to display on this page, so the procedure redirects the browser back to the product list.

Listing 10.41   ManageProduct.asxp.vb lbDelete_Click Procedure

```
Private Sub lbDelete_Click(ByVal sender As System.Object, _
  ByVal e As System.EventArgs) Handles lbDelete.Click
    ' Delete this product
    With cmdManagerDeleteProduct
```

```
        .Parameters("@ProductID").Value = _
         Session("ProductID")
        cnn.Open()
        .ExecuteScalar()
        cnn.Close()
    End With
    ' And redirect back to the (remaining) product list
    Server.Transfer("ListProducts.aspx")
End Sub
```

The procManagerDeleteProduct stored procedure, shown in Listing 10.42, does the actual work of deleting the product. In addition to deleting the row from the Product table, this stored procedure also deletes the linking rows in other tables that associate this product with departments and attributes.

Listing 10.42   procManagerDeleteProduct Stored Procedure

```
/*  Delete a product from the database

From .NET E-Commerce Programming
by Mike Gunderloy and Noel Jerke
Copyright 2002, Sybex Inc. All Rights Reserved. */
CREATE PROCEDURE procManagerDeleteProduct
  @ProductID int
AS
  /* Delete department associations */
  DELETE FROM DepartmentProduct
    WHERE ProductID = @ProductID
  /* Delete attribute associations */
  DELETE FROM ProductAttribute
    WHERE ProductID = @ProductID
  /* Delete the product itself */
  DELETE FROM Product
    WHERE ProductID = @ProductID
```

There are two operations that the user can perform with a department or an attribute. First, they can click a link within the corresponding DataGrid control to delete the association between this particular product and the selected department or attribute. Second, they can make a selection from the DropDownList controls to add a new department or attribute association.

Listing 10.43 shows the code that runs when the user clicks the Delete link inside the department DataGrid control. This code first runs a stored procedure to delete the row from the linking table; then the code refreshes the list of departments for the product and rebinds the DataGrid control, to bring it up to date.

Listing 10.43   **ManageProduct.aspx.vb dgDepartments_ItemCommand Procedure**

```
Private Sub dgDepartments_ItemCommand(ByVal source As Object, _
  ByVal e As System.Web.UI.WebControls.DataGridCommandEventArgs) _
  Handles dgDepartments.ItemCommand
    ' Called when the Delete link is clicked for a Department.
    ' e.Item is the row of the table where the button was
    ' clicked
    Dim dr As SqlDataReader
    With cmdManagerRemoveProductDept
        .Parameters("@ProductID").Value = _
        Session("ProductID")
        .Parameters("@DepartmentID").Value = _
        e.Item.Cells(0).Text
        cnn.Open()
        .ExecuteNonQuery()
    End With
    ' Refresh the list of departments for this product
    cmdManagerRetrieveDeptByProd.Parameters("@ProductID").Value = _
      Session("ProductID")
    dr = cmdManagerRetrieveDeptByProd.ExecuteReader
    dgDepartments.DataSource = dr
    dgDepartments.DataBind()
    dr.Close()
    cnn.Close()
End Sub
```

Listing 10.44 shows the procManagerRemoveProductDept stored procedure, which deletes the association. As you can see, this stored procedure needs both the ProductID and the DepartmentID to locate the correct row to delete.

Listing 10.44   **procManagerRemoveProductDept Stored Procedure**

```
/*  Delete a department for a product

From .NET E-Commerce Programming
by Mike Gunderloy and Noel Jerke
Copyright 2002, Sybex Inc. All Rights Reserved. */
CREATE PROCEDURE procManagerRemoveProductDept
  @ProductID int,
  @DepartmentID int
AS
  DELETE FROM DepartmentProduct
    WHERE ProductID = @ProductID AND DepartmentID = @DepartmentID
```

When the user makes a selection from the DropDownList control that displays the departments, the SelectedIndexChanged event for the control fires. In response, the server runs the code shown in Listing 10.45. This code, as you'd expect, uses a stored procedure to add the new row to the DepartmentProduct table. What you might not expect is the use of the Try/Catch/Finally construction to handle errors in this case. The reason this is necessary is that the DropDownList control displays all the departments in the database. If the user attempts to add an association with a department that already contains this product, the stored procedure will raise an error. In response to this error, the code will simply close the connection and return control to the user. Otherwise (if there's no error), it refreshes the list of departments that is displayed in the DataGrid control.

Listing 10.45   ManageProduct.aspx.vb ddlAddDept_SelectedIndexChanged Procedure

```
Private Sub ddlAddDept_SelectedIndexChanged( _
 ByVal sender As System.Object, ByVal e As System.EventArgs) _
 Handles ddlAddDept.SelectedIndexChanged
    Dim dr As SqlDataReader
    ' Add a new department for this product
    Try
        If ddlAddDept.SelectedItem.Value <> 0 Then
            With cmdManagerAddProductDept
                .Parameters("@ProductID").Value = _
                Session("ProductID")
                .Parameters("@DepartmentID").Value = _
                ddlAddDept.SelectedItem.Value
                cnn.Open()
                .ExecuteNonQuery()
            End With
            ' Refresh the list of departments for this product
            cmdManagerRetrieveDeptByProd.Parameters("@ProductID").Value = _
             Session("ProductID")
            dr = cmdManagerRetrieveDeptByProd.ExecuteReader
            dgDepartments.DataSource = dr
            dgDepartments.DataBind()
            dr.Close()
        End If
    Catch ex As Exception
        ' Code will end up here on attempt to add a
        ' duplicate department. OK to just fall through
        ' in that case
    Finally
        cnn.Close()
    End Try
End Sub
```

Listing 10.46 shows the procManagerAddProductDept stored procedure that this code calls.

Listing 10.46   **procManagerAddProductDept Stored Procedure**

```
/*  Add a new department for a product

From .NET E-Commerce Programming
by Mike Gunderloy and Noel Jerke
Copyright 2002, Sybex Inc. All Rights Reserved. */
CREATE PROCEDURE procManagerAddProductDept
  @ProductID int,
  @DepartmentID int
AS
  INSERT INTO DepartmentProduct(ProductID, DepartmentID)
    VALUES(@ProductID, @DepartmentID)
```

The code and stored procedures that handle attributes are very similar to those for departments. First, Listing 10.47 shows the code that runs when a user clicks the link to delete an attribute from a product.

Listing 10.47   **ManageProduct.aspx.vb dgAttributes_ItemCommand Procedure**

```
Private Sub dgAttributes_ItemCommand(ByVal source As Object, _
  ByVal e As System.Web.UI.WebControls.DataGridCommandEventArgs) _
  Handles dgAttributes.ItemCommand
    ' Called when the Delete link is clicked for an attribute.
    ' e.Item is the row of the table where the button was
    ' clicked
    Dim dr As SqlDataReader
    With cmdManagerRemoveProductAttribute
        .Parameters("@ProductID").Value = _
         Session("ProductID")
        .Parameters("@AttributeID").Value = _
         e.Item.Cells(0).Text
        cnn.Open()
        .ExecuteNonQuery()
    End With
    ' Refresh the list of attributes for this product
    cmdManagerRetrieveAttributeByProd.Parameters("@ProductID").Value = _
      Session("ProductID")
    dr = cmdManagerRetrieveAttributeByProd.ExecuteReader
    dgAttributes.DataSource = dr
    dgAttributes.DataBind()
    dr.Close()
    cnn.Close()
End Sub
```

The corresponding stored procedure, procManagerRemoveProductAttribute, is shown in Listing 10.48.

Listing 10.48   procManagerRemoveProductAttribute Stored Procedure

```
/*  Remove an attribute for a product

From .NET E-Commerce Programming
by Mike Gunderloy and Noel Jerke
Copyright 2002, Sybex Inc. All Rights Reserved. */
CREATE PROCEDURE procManagerRemoveProductAttribute
   @ProductID int,
   @AttributeID int
AS
   DELETE FROM ProductAttribute
      WHERE ProductID = @ProductID AND AttributeID = @AttributeID
```

Listing 10.49 shows the code for adding an attribute to a product. Once again, this code requires error trapping to handle the case where the user tries to add a duplicate attribute.

Listing 10.49   ManageProduct.aspx.vb ddlAddAttribute_SelectedIndexChanged Procedure

```
Private Sub ddlAddAttribute_SelectedIndexChanged( _
 ByVal sender As Object, ByVal e As System.EventArgs) _
 Handles ddlAddAttribute.SelectedIndexChanged
    Dim dr As SqlDataReader
    ' Add a new attribute for this product
    Try
        If ddlAddAttribute.SelectedItem.Value <> 0 Then
            With cmdManagerAddProductAttribute
                .Parameters("@ProductID").Value = _
                 Session("ProductID")
                .Parameters("@AttributeID").Value = _
                 ddlAddAttribute.SelectedItem.Value
                cnn.Open()
                .ExecuteNonQuery()
            End With
            ' Refresh the list of attributes for this product
            cmdManagerRetrieveAttributeByProd.Parameters("@ProductID").Value = _
             Session("ProductID")
            dr = cmdManagerRetrieveAttributeByProd.ExecuteReader
            dgAttributes.DataSource = dr
            dgAttributes.DataBind()
            dr.Close()
        End If
    Catch ex As Exception
        ' Code will end up here on attempt to add a
        ' duplicate attribute. OK to just fall through
        ' in that case
    Finally
        cnn.Close()
    End Try
End Sub
```

To round out the code for this Web Form, Listing 10.50 shows the stored procedure that's used to add an attribute to a product.

Listing 10.50   procManagerAddProductAttribute Stored Procedure

```
/*  Add a new attribute for a product

From .NET E-Commerce Programming
by Mike Gunderloy and Noel Jerke
Copyright 2002, Sybex Inc. All Rights Reserved. */
CREATE PROCEDURE procManagerAddProductAttribute
  @ProductID int,
  @AttributeID int
AS
  INSERT INTO ProductAttribute(ProductID, AttributeID)
    VALUES(@ProductID, @AttributeID)
```

Figure 10.13 shows a product being edited. All of the current data is retrieved from the database and displayed on the form. Because this product was just added to the database, it has no department or attribute assignments yet.

FIGURE 10.13:

Editing a product

Now let's add a new department for the product. Select the Cool Backstreet Jazz department and wait for the page to refresh. Figure 10.14 shows the new department assignment for the product.

FIGURE 10.14:

Adding a new department

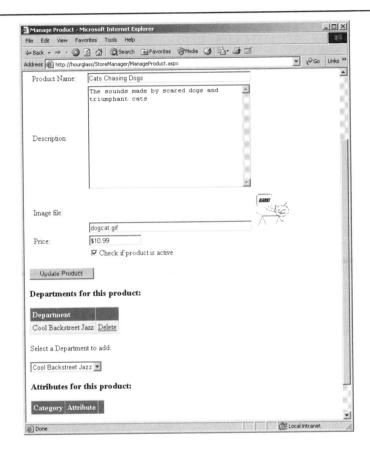

Next, let's add a second department for the product. Select the Punked Out department and add it to the list. Figure 10.15 shows the added department.

FIGURE 10.15:

Adding a second
department

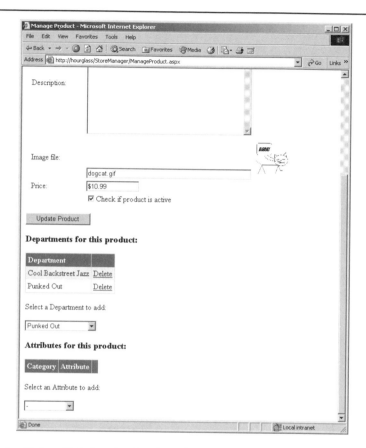

Now you can click the Delete link for the Cool Backstreet Jazz department to remove the product from that department. You can also experiment with the links to add and remove attributes. Figure 10.16 shows the product with two attributes added.

Finally, you can preview the product in the store by clicking the Preview link.

That does it for product management. The code that we created covers the tasks from listing and searching of products to adding and editing products. There are a few additional issues that we might want to address in implementing a store.

Many stores use preassigned SKUs (stock-keeping units) for tracking their products. Typically, a product's SKU is built from both an internal system's product ID and the product's attributes. For example, if product 1234 is purchased in yellow and size Large, the SKU might be 1234YL. In our sample application, we are allowing the product database to generate the SKU. We haven't provided any way for the user to edit the SKU. In your application, you may need to provide an additional functionality for SKU management and generation.

FIGURE 10.16:

Adding color and size
attributes

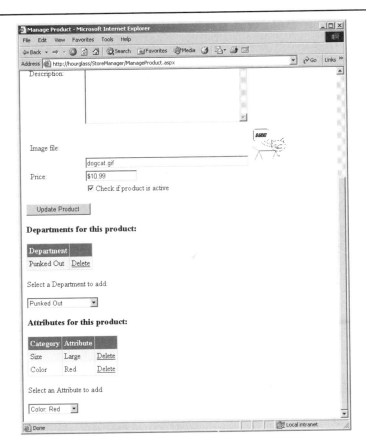

You might also consider the relationship of SKUs and prices. Some retailers, for example, charge more for XXL sizes or special versions of products. Our sample store assumes that there is only one price per product, no matter how many SKUs that product covers. If prices in your store will change by product attribute, you'll need to restructure the database to store prices by attribute.

With regard to images, we are assuming that the user will have direct network access to the location where the product images will be placed. If, however, the user is managing the products over the Internet, we may need to provide additional methods for accessing the location of the images. We could provide FTP access to the images directory, or we could provide an HTML file upload feature.

With product management covered, we can move on to the management of the departments.

Managing Departments

We want to be able to add, update, and delete departments in our store. Of course, the department data is much simpler than the product data.

Listing Departments

Listing 10.51 shows the HTML code for the ListDepts.aspx page. The departments list is created in a similar fashion to the list of the products, but we assume that the departments can easily be listed on one page and that the previous/next functionality isn't needed. With all the departments displayed at once, we've also omitted the search feature.

This page consists of a DataGrid control that displays the current departments and lets the user select one to edit, as well as a link for adding a new department.

Listing 10.51   ListDepts.aspx

```
<%@ Page Language="vb" AutoEventWireup="false"
 Codebehind="ListDepts.aspx.vb"
 Inherits="StoreManager.ListDepts"%>
<!DOCTYPE HTML PUBLIC "-//W3C//DTD HTML 4.0 Transitional//EN">
<HTML>
    <HEAD>
        <title>List Departments</title>
        <meta name="GENERATOR" content="Microsoft Visual Studio.NET 7.0">
        <meta name="CODE_LANGUAGE" content="Visual Basic 7.0">
        <meta name="vs_defaultClientScript" content="JavaScript">
        <meta name="vs_targetSchema"
         content="http://schemas.microsoft.com/intellisense/ie5">
        <!-- ListDepts.aspx - List all Departments in the store -->
    </HEAD>
    <body>
        <!-- #Include File="ValidateCheck.inc" -->
        <!-- #Include File="Navbar.inc" -->
        <form id="Form1" method="post" runat="server">
            <P>
                <asp:HyperLink id="HyperLink1" runat="server"
                 NavigateUrl="NewDept.aspx">
                 Click here to add a new department.
                </asp:HyperLink></P>
            <P>To edit a department, select from the list below.</P>
            <P>
                <asp:DataGrid id="dgDepartments" runat="server"
                 BorderColor="#DEDFDE" BorderStyle="None" BorderWidth="1px"
                 BackColor="White" CellPadding="4" GridLines="Vertical"
                 ForeColor="Black" AutoGenerateColumns="False">
                    <SelectedItemStyle Font-Bold="True" ForeColor="White"
                     BackColor="#CE5D5A"></SelectedItemStyle>
                    <AlternatingItemStyle BackColor="White">
                    </AlternatingItemStyle>
```

```
                        <ItemStyle BackColor="#F7F7DE"></ItemStyle>
                        <HeaderStyle Font-Bold="True" ForeColor="White"
                         BackColor="#6B696B"></HeaderStyle>
                        <FooterStyle BackColor="#CCCC99"></FooterStyle>
                        <Columns>
                            <asp:BoundColumn DataField="DepartmentID"
                             HeaderText="Department ID"></asp:BoundColumn>
                            <asp:BoundColumn DataField="DepartmentName"
                             HeaderText="Department Name"></asp:BoundColumn>
                            <asp:ButtonColumn Text="Select"
                             CommandName="Select"></asp:ButtonColumn>
                        </Columns>
                        <PagerStyle HorizontalAlign="Right" ForeColor="Black"
                         BackColor="#F7F7DE" Mode="NumericPages"></PagerStyle>
                    </asp:DataGrid></P>
                </form>
            </body>
        </HTML>%>
```

The code behind this page is fairly simple. The Page_Load procedure, shown in Listing 10.52, uses a stored procedure to get all the departments from the database and binds the list to the DataGrid control.

Listing 10.52   ListDepts.asxp.vb Page_Load Procedure

```
Private Sub Page_Load(ByVal sender As System.Object, _
 ByVal e As System.EventArgs) Handles MyBase.Load
    Dim dr As SqlDataReader
    If Not IsPostBack Then
        cnn.Open()
        dr = cmdManagerRetrieveDeptListing.ExecuteReader()
        dgDepartments.DataSource = dr
        dgDepartments.DataBind()
        dr.Close()
        cnn.Close()
    End If
End Sub
```

Listing 10.53 shows the procManagerRetrieveDeptListing stored procedure that this code uses to get the department information. Note that this stored procedure brings back only enough information to identify the departments. There's no need for the detailed department information on this page, and retrieving it would only slow things down.

Listing 10.53   procManagerRetrieveDeptListing Stored Procedure

```
/*  Retrieve all departments in the store
```

```
by Mike Gunderloy and Noel Jerke
Copyright 2002, Sybex Inc. All Rights Reserved. */
CREATE PROCEDURE procManagerRetrieveDeptListing
AS
   SELECT DepartmentID, DepartmentName
     FROM Department
```

Linking to the detailed page for a department is handled in the ItemCommand event procedure for the DataGrid control. Listing 10.54 shows this code, which places the DepartmentID into a session variable and then transfers control to the ManageDept.aspx page.

Listing 10.54   **ListDepts.aspx.vb dgDepartments_ItemCommand Procedure**

```
Private Sub dgDepartments_ItemCommand(ByVal source As Object, _
  ByVal e As System.Web.UI.WebControls.DataGridCommandEventArgs) _
  Handles dgDepartments.ItemCommand
      ' e.Item is the row of the table where the button was
      ' clicked.
      ' Store the DepartmentID
      Session("DepartmentID") = e.Item.Cells(0).Text
      ' And redirect to the management page
      Server.Transfer("ManageDept.aspx")
End Sub
```

Adding a Department

The link for adding a new department takes the user to the NewDept.aspx page. This page contains controls to allow the user to input the data about the new department, along with validation controls. Listing 10.55 shows the HTML code for this page, which uses a table for layout.

Listing 10.55   **NewDept.aspx**

```
<%@ Page Language="vb" AutoEventWireup="false" Codebehind="NewDept.aspx.vb"
 Inherits="StoreManager.NewDept"%>
<!DOCTYPE HTML PUBLIC "-//W3C//DTD HTML 4.0 Transitional//EN">
<HTML>
    <HEAD>
        <title>New Department</title>
        <meta name="GENERATOR" content="Microsoft Visual Studio.NET 7.0">
        <meta name="CODE_LANGUAGE" content="Visual Basic 7.0">
        <meta name="vs_defaultClientScript" content="JavaScript">
        <meta name="vs_targetSchema"
         content="http://schemas.microsoft.com/intellisense/ie5">
        <!-- NewDept.aspx - Add a new department to the store -->
    </HEAD>
```

```
<body>
    <!-- #Include File="ValidateCheck.inc" -->
    <!-- #Include File="Navbar.inc" -->
    <form id="Form1" method="post" runat="server">
        <asp:ValidationSummary id="ValidationSummary1" runat="server">
        </asp:ValidationSummary>
        <TABLE id="Table1" cellSpacing="1" cellPadding="1" width="100%"
         border="0">
            <TR>
                <TD style="WIDTH: 97px">
                    <asp:RequiredFieldValidator
                     id="RequiredFieldValidator1" runat="server"
                     ErrorMessage="You must enter a department name."
                     ControlToValidate="txtDepartmentName">*
                    </asp:RequiredFieldValidator>
                    <asp:Label id="Label1" runat="server">
                    Department Name
                    </asp:Label></TD>
                <TD>
                    <asp:TextBox id="txtDepartmentName" runat="server"
                     Width="480px"></asp:TextBox></TD>
            </TR>
            <TR>
                <TD style="WIDTH: 97px">
                    <asp:RequiredFieldValidator
                     id="RequiredFieldValidator2"
                     runat="server"
                     ErrorMessage="You must enter a department.
                     Description."
                     ControlToValidate="txtDepartmentDescription">*
                    </asp:RequiredFieldValidator>
                    <asp:Label id="Label2" runat="server">Description
                    </asp:Label></TD>
                <TD>
                    <asp:TextBox id="txtDepartmentDescription"
                     runat="server" Width="482px"
                     Height="145px" Rows="6"
                     TextMode="MultiLine"></asp:TextBox></TD>
            </TR>
            <TR>
                <TD style="WIDTH: 97px">
                    <asp:RequiredFieldValidator
                     id="RequiredFieldValidator3" runat="server"
                     ErrorMessage="You must enter an image file name."
                     ControlToValidate="txtDepartmentImage">*
                    </asp:RequiredFieldValidator>
                    <asp:Label id="Label3" runat="server">Image file
                    </asp:Label></TD>
                <TD>
                    <asp:TextBox id="txtDepartmentImage" runat="server"
                     Width="482px"></asp:TextBox></TD>
```

```
            </TR>
            <TR>
                <TD style="WIDTH: 97px"></TD>
                <TD>
                    <asp:Button id="btnAddDepartment" runat="server"
                    Text="Add Department"></asp:Button></TD>
            </TR>
        </TABLE>
    </form>
</body>
</HTML>
```

The Add Product button simply reloads this page if all the data passes validation. In that case, the Page_Load procedure, shown in Listing 10.56, adds the data to the database. This code retrieves the DepartmentID for the new department from the database, stores it in a session variable, and then transfers control to the ManageDept.aspx page so that the user can continue editing the new department.

Listing 10.56   **NewDept.aspx.vb Page_Load Procedure**

```
Private Sub Page_Load(ByVal sender As System.Object, _
  ByVal e As System.EventArgs) Handles MyBase.Load
    ' If we're in a postback, data has passed validation
    If IsPostBack Then
        ' Save the new department to the database
        With cmdManagerInsertDepartment
            .Parameters("@DepartmentName").Value = _
            txtDepartmentName.Text()
            .Parameters("@DepartmentDescription").Value = _
            txtDepartmentDescription.Text
            .Parameters("@DepartmentImage").Value = _
            txtDepartmentImage.Text
            cnn.Open()
            Session("DepartmentID") = .ExecuteScalar
            cnn.Close()
            ' And redirect to the management page
            Server.Transfer("ManageDept.aspx")
        End With
    End If
End Sub
```

Listing 10.57 shows the procManagerInsertDepartment stored procedure, which actually writes the new department to the database. This stored procedure uses the SELECT @@IDENTITY command to return the DepartmentID of the new department to the calling code.

Listing 10.57   **procManagerInsertDepartment Stored Procedure**

```
/*  Add a new department to the store

From .NET E-Commerce Programming
by Mike Gunderloy and Noel Jerke
Copyright 2002, Sybex Inc. All Rights Reserved. */
CREATE PROCEDURE procManagerInsertDepartment
  @DepartmentName varchar(255),
  @DepartmentDescription text,
  @DepartmentImage varchar(255)
AS
  INSERT INTO Department(DepartmentName,
    DepartmentDescription, DepartmentImage)
  VALUES(@DepartmentName,
    @DepartmentDescription, @DepartmentImage)
  /* Return the ID of the new department */
  SELECT @@IDENTITY
```

Editing and Deleting Departments

In our sample application, the ManageDept.aspx page will enable the user to edit the data for a department or to delete an entire department. The HTML code for this page, shown in Listing 10.58, starts with the standard page headers and include files and then presents links to preview or delete the department.

Listing 10.58   **ManageDept.aspx**

```
<%@ Page Language="vb" AutoEventWireup="false"
 Codebehind="ManageDept.aspx.vb"
 Inherits="StoreManager.ManageDept"%>
<!DOCTYPE HTML PUBLIC "-//W3C//DTD HTML 4.0 Transitional//EN">
<HTML>
    <HEAD>
        <title>Manage Department</title>
        <meta content="Microsoft Visual Studio.NET 7.0" name="GENERATOR">
        <meta content="Visual Basic 7.0" name="CODE_LANGUAGE">
        <meta content="JavaScript" name="vs_defaultClientScript">
        <meta content="http://schemas.microsoft.com/intellisense/ie5"
         name="vs_targetSchema">
        <!-- ManageDept.aspx - Page to manage department data -->
    </HEAD>
    <body>
        <!-- #Include File="ValidateCheck.inc" -->
        <!-- #Include File="Navbar.inc" -->
        <form id="Form1" method="post" runat="server">
            <P>
                <asp:HyperLink id="hlPreview" runat="server">
```

```
        Preview in store</asp:HyperLink></P>
    <P>
        <asp:LinkButton id="lbDelete" runat="server">
        Delete Department</asp:LinkButton></P>
    <P>
```

The remainder of the HTML code, shown in Listing 10.59, builds a data entry form with validation controls.

Listing 10.59   ManageDept.aspx (continued)

```
        <asp:ValidationSummary id="ValidationSummary1"
        runat="server">
        </asp:ValidationSummary></P>
    <P>
        <TABLE id="Table1" cellSpacing="1" cellPadding="1"
        width="100%" border="0">
            <TR>
                <TD>
                    <asp:Label id="Label1" runat="server">
                    Department ID:</asp:Label></TD>
                <TD>
                    <asp:TextBox id="txtDepartmentID"
                    runat="server"
                    Width="106px"></asp:TextBox></TD>
            </TR>
            <TR>
                <TD>
                    <asp:RequiredFieldValidator
                    id="RequiredFieldValidator1" runat="server"
                    ErrorMessage=
                    "You must enter a department name.
                    ControlToValidate="txtDepartmentName">*
                    </asp:RequiredFieldValidator>Department 
                    Name:</TD>
                <TD>
                    <asp:TextBox id="txtDepartmentName"
                    runat="server"
                    Width="343px"></asp:TextBox></TD>
            </TR>
            <TR>
                <TD>
                    <asp:RequiredFieldValidator
                    id="RequiredFieldValidator2" runat="server"
                    ErrorMessage="You must enter a department
                    description."
                    ControlToValidate="txtDepartmentDescription">*
                    </asp:RequiredFieldValidator>Description:</TD>
                <TD>
                    <asp:TextBox id="txtDepartmentDescription"
```

```
                                    runat="server" Width="342px" Rows="10"
                                    Height="213px" TextMode="MultiLine">
                                    </asp:TextBox></TD>
                            </TR>
                            <TR>
                                <TD>
                                    <asp:RequiredFieldValidator
                                     id="RequiredFieldValidator3" runat="server"
                                     ErrorMessage="You must select an image file."
                                     ControlToValidate="txtDepartmentImage">*
                                    </asp:RequiredFieldValidator>Image
                                     file:</TD>
                                <TD>
                                    <asp:TextBox id="txtDepartmentImage"
                                     runat="server" Width="342px"></asp:TextBox>
                                    <asp:Image id="imgDepartment" runat="server">
                                    </asp:Image></TD>
                            </TR>
                        </TABLE>
                    </P>
                    <P>
                        <asp:Button id="btnUpdate" runat="server"
                         Text="Update Department"></asp:Button>
                </form>
                </P>
            </body>
        </HTML>
```

The Page_Load procedure for this page, shown in Listing 10.60, uses the DepartmentID stored in the session variables collection to retrieve information on the department. It also sets the NavigateUrl property for the Hyperlink control that lets the user preview the department in the live store.

Listing 10.60   **ManageDept.aspx.vb Page_Load Procedure**

```
Private Sub Page_Load(ByVal sender As System.Object, _
 ByVal e As System.EventArgs) Handles MyBase.Load
    Dim dr As SqlClient.SqlDataReader
    ' Populate the UI with current information.
    ' First, set the hyperlink jump into the store
    hlPreview.NavigateUrl = "../CDStore/Products.aspx?idDept=" & _
     Session("DepartmentID")
    ' Get the department info from the database
    With cmdManagerRetrieveDepartment
        .Parameters("@DepartmentID").Value = _
         Session("DepartmentID")
        cnn.Open()
        dr = .ExecuteReader()
    End With
```

```
        dr.Read()
        txtDepartmentID.Enabled = True
        txtDepartmentID.Text = dr.GetInt32(0)
        ' Lock the Product ID so they can't change it
        txtDepartmentID.Enabled = False
        txtDepartmentName.Text = dr.GetString(1)
        txtDepartmentDescription.Text = dr.GetString(2)
        txtDepartmentImage.Text = dr.GetString(3)
        imgDepartment.ImageUrl = "../CDStore/Images/" & _
          dr.GetString(3)
        dr.Close()
    End Sub
```

This code uses the procManagerRetrieveDepartment stored procedure to get data from the database. Listing 10.61 shows this stored procedure.

Listing 10.61   procManagerRetrieveDepartment Stored Procedure

```
/*  Retrieve all info on a department

From .NET E-Commerce Programming
by Mike Gunderloy and Noel Jerke
Copyright 2002, Sybex Inc. All Rights Reserved. */
CREATE PROCEDURE procManagerRetrieveDepartment
  @DepartmentID int
AS
  SELECT * FROM Department
  WHERE DepartmentID = @DepartmentID
```

If the user makes changes and clicks the Update Department button, the code shown in Listing 10.62 runs in order to save the changes to the database. Once again, the validation controls check all the data before this procedure is allowed to run.

Listing 10.62   ManageDept.aspx.vb btnUpdate_Click Procedure

```
Private Sub btnUpdate_Click(ByVal sender As System.Object, _
  ByVal e As System.EventArgs) Handles btnUpdate.Click
      ' Save the info from the form to the database
      With cmdManagerUpdateDepartment
          .Parameters("@DepartmentID").Value = _
          Session("DepartmentID")
          .Parameters("@DepartmentName").Value = _
          txtDepartmentName.Text
          .Parameters("@DepartmentDescription").Value = _
          txtDepartmentDescription.Text
          .Parameters("@DepartmentImage").Value = _
          txtDepartmentImage.Text
          cnn.Open()
```

```
        .ExecuteNonQuery()
        cnn.Close()
    End With
End Sub
```

The actual update is performed by the procManagerUpdateDepartment stored procedure. Listing 10.63 shows this stored procedure.

Listing 10.63   procManagerUpdateDepartment Stored Procedure

```
/*  Update a department

From .NET E-Commerce Programming
by Mike Gunderloy and Noel Jerke
Copyright 2002, Sybex Inc. All Rights Reserved. */
CREATE PROCEDURE procManagerUpdateDepartment
  @DepartmentID int,
  @DepartmentName varchar(255),
  @DepartmentDescription text,
  @DepartmentImage varchar(255)
AS
  UPDATE Department
    SET DepartmentName = @DepartmentName,
    DepartmentDescription = @DepartmentDescription,
    DepartmentImage = @DepartmentImage
    WHERE DepartmentID = @DepartmentID
```

When the user clicks the LinkButton to delete a department, the control's Click event is fired. This runs the code shown in Listing 10.64. After deleting the department, this code redirects the user to the list of the remaining departments.

Listing 10.64   ManageDept.aspx.vb lbDelete_Click Procedure

```
Private Sub lbDelete_Click(ByVal sender As System.Object, _
  ByVal e As System.EventArgs) Handles lbDelete.Click
    ' Delete the current department
    With cmdManagerDeleteDepartment
        .Parameters("@DepartmentID").Value = _
         Session("DepartmentID")
        cnn.Open()
        .ExecuteNonQuery()
        cnn.Close()
    End With
    ' And go back to the department listing
    Server.Transfer("ListDepts.aspx")
End Sub
```

Of course, the actual deletion operation is performed by a stored procedure—procManagerDeleteDepartment in this case. Listing 10.65 shows this stored procedure. When we drop a department, we also drop all related rows from the DepartmentProduct table.

Listing 10.65   **procManagerDeleteDepartment Stored Procedure**

```
/*  Delete a department

From .NET E-Commerce Programming
by Mike Gunderloy and Noel Jerke
Copyright 2002, Sybex Inc. All Rights Reserved. */
CREATE PROCEDURE procManagerDeleteDepartment
  @DepartmentID int
AS
  /* Delete the product associations */
  DELETE FROM DepartmentProduct
    WHERE DepartmentID = @DepartmentID
  /* Delete the department record */
  DELETE FROM Department
    WHERE DepartmentID = @DepartmentID
```

Obviously, after writing all this code, it's important to test the functions that it implements. To begin demonstrating our new department management functions, Figure 10.17 shows the listing of departments in the store. Note the options to edit existing departments and to add a new one.

FIGURE 10.17:

Department listing

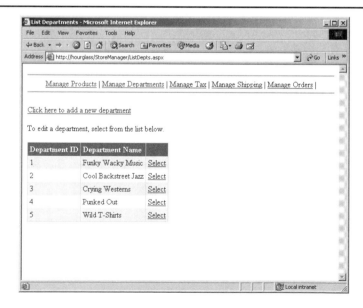

Click the "new department" link in the department listing and, on the new page that appears, fill in the data appropriately. Figure 10.18 shows an example. Click Add Department to submit the form.

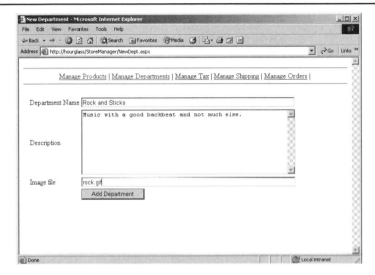

Once you've added the new department to the database, you're ready to edit it. Select the new department from the listing, and you will be taken to the edit page. Figure 10.19 shows the department data ready for editing.

You now have the option to update the department data, remove the department, or preview it. Figure 10.20 shows the department in preview mode. Note that because we haven't yet uploaded a new image for the department, a broken graphic is appearing here.

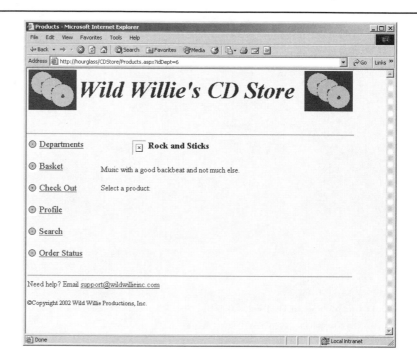

TIP   In our product and department management, we didn't build in user validation. For example, when the user clicks the option to delete a product or department, we might want to have them verify the request before performing the actual deletion.

Summary

In this chapter, we covered the key functions of managing product and department data. This includes editing, adding, and deleting both products and departments, as well as altering the relationships between products and departments. In the next chapter, we'll explore methods for administering the tax and shipping settings in the store.

Managing Taxes and Shipping

- Managing Taxes

- Managing Shipping

axes and shipping are two key areas of business rule management for which we need a convenient management interface. In Chapter 8, "Checking Out," we built a Web Service that extracts information from the database to calculate shipping and tax. In this chapter, we are going to build an ASP.NET interface to manage the Tax and Shipping tables in the database.

It's important to note that these ASP.NET pages will manage the data based on the simple set of business rules that we defined for our store: Tax is based exclusively on the customer's state, and the shipping charge depends only on the quantity of items ordered. If your store requires support for one-day and two-day shipping, tax calculations at various local levels, or other more complex calculations, you'll need to modify these ASP.NET pages, the database, and the Web Service to work together with the new information.

Managing Taxes

Our first task is to work on the management of the tax data. Wild Willie's CD Store calculates tax at the state level. That is, the amount of sales tax charged on an order depends on the state where the shipping address for the order is located. We'll need to be able to update the tax rate for each state. In Chapter 8, we entered tax rates for Virginia and Texas only.

Of course, we'll use an ASP.NET Web Form to handle the updating of tax rates. The design of this form, ManageTax.aspx, is different from the other Web Forms you've seen so far in this book. Because it will be used only by our own staff, we can develop a somewhat more sophisticated user interface. In this case, we'll display all of the current tax rates in a DataGrid on the form and allow the user to edit the rates directly in the DataGrid. Although data will still move between the browser and the server for every edit, it will seem to the user that they are editing data directly in the browser.

Because we're introducing the concepts underlying this form, we'll build it step by step instead of just showing you the completed code. Begin by following these steps to set up a new form with the standard include files for this application:

1. Add a new Web Form to the project. Name it **ManageTax.aspx**.

2. Change the pageLayout property of the form to **FlowLayout**.

3. Change the title property of the form to **Manage Tax**.

4. Switch to HTML view and add a comment to identify the page as well as the special comments for the include files. Listing 11.1 shows the HTML for this page after completing this step.

Listing 11.1   **Skeleton for ManageTax.aspx**

```
<%@ Page Language="vb" AutoEventWireup="false"
 Codebehind="ManageTax.aspx.vb"
 Inherits="StoreManager.ManageTax"%>
<!DOCTYPE HTML PUBLIC "-//W3C//DTD HTML 4.0 Transitional//EN">
<HTML>
    <HEAD>
        <title>Manage Tax</title>
        <meta name="GENERATOR" content="Microsoft Visual Studio.NET 7.0">
        <meta name="CODE_LANGUAGE" content="Visual Basic 7.0">
        <meta name="vs_defaultClientScript" content="JavaScript">
        <meta name="vs_targetSchema"
         content="http://schemas.microsoft.com/intellisense/ie5">
        <!-- ManageTax.aspx - Manage the tax table for the store -->
    </HEAD>
    <body>
        <!-- #Include File="ValidateCheck.inc" -->
        <!-- #Include File="Navbar.inc" -->
        <form id="Form1" method="post" runat="server">
        </form>
    </body>
</HTML>
```

Next, we'll add a DataGrid control to the page and bind it to the Tax table in the database. To do this, follow these steps:

1. Switch the page back to design view.

2. Drag a DataGrid control from the Web Forms tab in the Toolbox and drop it on the page.

3. Click the Auto Format hyperlink beneath the Properties window.

4. Select the Classic 2 format and click OK.

5. Click the Property Builder hyperlink beneath the Properties window.

6. Select the Columns section in the DataGrid1 Properties dialog box.

7. Uncheck the Create Columns Automatically at Run Time check box.

8. Expand the Button Column node in the Available Columns listbox. Select the Edit, Update, Cancel button and add it to the Selected Columns list.

9. Add a Bound Column to the Selected Columns list by choosing Bound Column from the Available Columns list. Set the Header Text property of this column to **Tax ID**. Set the Data Field property of this column to **TaxID**. Uncheck the Visible check box for this column.

10. Add a second Bound Column to the Selected Columns list. Set the Header Text property of this column to **State**. Set the Data Field property of this column to **TaxState**. Check the Read Only check box for this column.

11. Add a third Bound Column to the Selected Columns list. Set the Header Text property of this column to **Rate**. Set the Data Field property of this column to **TaxRate**.

12. Click OK to dismiss the dialog box and save your changes.

13. Change the (ID) property of the DataGrid control to **dgTaxRates**.

14. Change the DataKeyField property of the DataGrid control to **TaxID**.

The next task is to create the stored procedures that this page will use. There will be one stored procedure to retrieve the tax rates and one to update a given tax rate. Listing 11.2 shows the stored procedure to retrieve the tax rates, and Listing 11.3 shows the stored procedure to update the tax rate for a specified state.

Listing 11.2   procManagerGetTaxRates Stored Procedure

```
/*  Retrieve all tax rates

From .NET E-Commerce Programming
by Mike Gunderloy and Noel Jerke
Copyright 2002, Sybex Inc. All Rights Reserved. */
CREATE PROCEDURE procManagerGetTaxRates
AS
SELECT * FROM Tax
</HTML>
```

Listing 11.3   procManagerUpdateTaxRate Stored Procedure

```
/*  Update a specified tax rate

From .NET E-Commerce Programming
by Mike Gunderloy and Noel Jerke
Copyright 2002, Sybex Inc. All Rights Reserved. */
CREATE PROCEDURE procManagerUpdateTaxRate
  @TaxID int,
  @TaxRate float
AS
  UPDATE Tax
    SET TaxRate = @TaxRate
    WHERE TaxID = @TaxID
```

Next, add these two stored procedures to the Web Form by following these steps:

1. In the Server Explorer window, expand the Data Connections tree until you can see the stored procedures in your database.

2. Drag the procManagerGetTaxRates stored procedure from Server Explorer and drop it on the form. This will create a SqlConnection object and a SqlCommand object.

3. Drag the procManagerUpdateTaxRate stored procedure from Server Explorer and drop it on the form. This will create a second SqlCommand object.

4. Rename the SqlConnection object **cnn** and adjust parameters in its ConnectionString property as necessary to connect to your server.

5. Rename the SqlCommand objects **cmdManagerGetTaxRates** and **cmdManager-UpdateTaxRate**.

With all the objects created, you can now add the code to make everything work together. Open the ManageTax.aspx.vb file and, at the top of the file, enter the code shown in Listing 11.4 to import the necessary namespaces.

Listing 11.4   ManageTax.aspx Declarations

```
Imports System.Data
Imports System.Data.SqlClient
```

Finally, to initialize the page and handle the user's actions, enter the code shown in Listing 11.5.

Listing 11.5   ManageTax.aspx.vb Event Procedures

```
Private Sub Page_Load(ByVal sender As System.Object, _
 ByVal e As System.EventArgs) Handles MyBase.Load
    ' Fill the grid when the page is first loaded
    If Not IsPostBack Then
        BindGrid()
    End If
End Sub

Private Sub dgTaxRates_EditCommand(ByVal source As Object, _
 ByVal e As System.Web.UI.WebControls.DataGridCommandEventArgs) _
 Handles dgTaxRates.EditCommand
    ' Show the selected row for editing
    dgTaxRates.EditItemIndex = CInt(e.Item.ItemIndex)
    BindGrid()
End Sub

Private Sub BindGrid()
```

```
        ' Retrieve tax rates from the database and bind them to the DataGrid
        Dim daTaxRates As New SqlDataAdapter()
        Dim dsTaxRates As New DataSet()
        daTaxRates.SelectCommand = cmdManagerGetTaxRates
        daTaxRates.Fill(dsTaxRates, "Tax")
        dgTaxRates.DataSource = dsTaxRates
        dgTaxRates.DataMember = "Tax"
        DataBind()
    End Sub

    Private Sub dgTaxRates_CancelCommand(ByVal source As Object, _
     ByVal e As System.Web.UI.WebControls.DataGridCommandEventArgs) _
     Handles dgTaxRates.CancelCommand
        ' Take the grid out of edit mode
        dgTaxRates.EditItemIndex = -1
        BindGrid()
    End Sub

    Private Sub dgTaxRates_UpdateCommand(ByVal source As Object, _
     ByVal e As System.Web.UI.WebControls.DataGridCommandEventArgs) _
     Handles dgTaxRates.UpdateCommand
        ' Update the selected row in the database
        With cmdManagerUpdateTaxRate
            .Parameters("@TaxID").Value = _
             dgTaxRates.DataKeys(CInt(e.Item.ItemIndex))
            .Parameters("@TaxRate").Value = _
             CType(e.Item.Cells(3).Controls(0), TextBox).Text
            cnn.Open()
            .ExecuteNonQuery()
            cnn.Close()
            dgTaxRates.EditItemIndex = -1
        End With
        BindGrid()
    End Sub
```

The Page_Load procedure calls the BindGrid procedure when the page is first loaded. The BindGrid procedure contains a code structure that you've seen several times now, for binding a DataSet to a DataGrid control. It's split off into its own procedure here because it's called from several different places in the code.

The new concepts are in the other procedures here. As you might guess, they're called when the user clicks buttons (which are visually presented as hyperlinks) in the DataGrid:

- dgTaxRates_EditCommand is called when the user clicks an Edit button.

- dgTaxRates_CancelCommand is called when the user clicks a Cancel button.

- dgTaxRates_UpdateCommand is called when the user clicks an Update button.

The dgTaxRates_EditCommand procedure shows how you can control which row in a DataGrid is available for editing. The DataGrid has an EditItemIndex property. Set this property to –1 to disable editing, or to the (zero-based) row number to enable editing the specified row. In the procedure we've shown, we use the argument passed in by the event to determine which row should be edited.

The dgTaxRates_CancelCommand procedure simply turns off editing by setting the Edit-ItemIndex property to –1.

Finally, the dgTaxRates_UpdateCommand procedure retrieves the current information from the DataGrid and passes it back to the procManagerUpdateTaxRate stored procedure to update the database.

Now you can test this interface for tax management. Run the StoreManager application, log in, and select Manage Tax. Figure 11.1 shows the Manage Tax page, which contains an entry for each state. Note that the tax rates for Texas and Virginia are already set.

FIGURE 11.1:

Manage Tax page

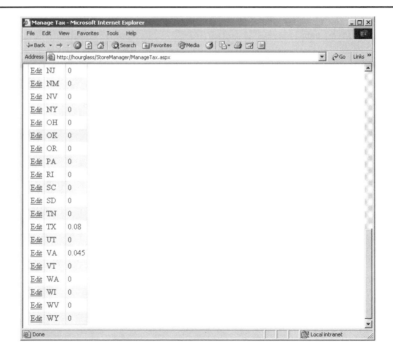

If you click the Edit button for the Pennsylvania entry, you'll get a control where you can enter a new tax rate figure for that state, such as 0.09. Figure 11.2 shows that entry. The code behind the form sets the appropriate row to edit mode, which results in a TextBox control for entering the tax rate. Note that the state abbreviation is still shown as a label because we set the ReadOnly property for that column to True.

Updating
Pennsylvania's
tax rate

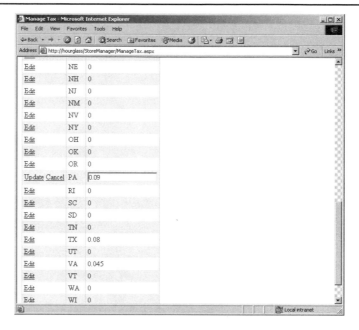

Figure 11.3 shows the result of clicking the Update button to save the change to Pennsylvania's tax rate.

The updated
Pennsylvania
tax rate

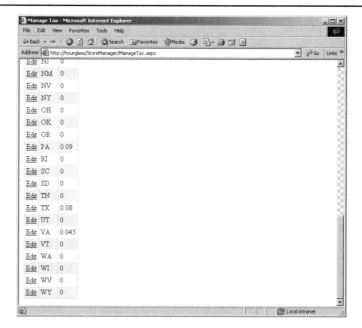

Managing Shipping

Next, let's begin working on the management of the store's shipping calculations. The first page we'll construct is the ManageShipping.aspx page. This page will have the same basic functionality as the ManageTax.aspx page, allowing the user to edit shipping fees directly in a DataGrid control. It will also enable the user to delete fees that are no longer needed and to add new fees.

The page starts like any other page in the StoreManager application, with the headers that are automatically generated by Visual Studio .NET, a descriptive comment, and our two include files. Listing 11.6 shows this section of the HTML.

Listing 11.6   ManageShipping.aspx

```
<%@ Page Language="vb" AutoEventWireup="false"
 Codebehind="ManageShipping.aspx.vb"
 Inherits="StoreManager.ManageShipping"%>
<!DOCTYPE HTML PUBLIC "-//W3C//DTD HTML 4.0 Transitional//EN">
<HTML>
    <HEAD>
        <title>Manage Shipping</title>
        <meta name="GENERATOR" content="Microsoft Visual Studio.NET 7.0">
        <meta name="CODE_LANGUAGE" content="Visual Basic 7.0">
        <meta name="vs_defaultClientScript" content="JavaScript">
        <meta name="vs_targetSchema"
         content="http://schemas.microsoft.com/intellisense/ie5">
        <!-- ManageShipping.aspx -
         Manage the shipping table for the store -->
    </HEAD>
    <body>
        <!-- #Include File="ValidateCheck.inc" -->
        <!-- #Include File="Navbar.inc" -->
```

The next portion of the HTML code, shown in Listing 11.7, defines a DataGrid control to display the shipping information. Of course, you can either edit this HTML or use the Properties dialog boxes to manage the control in design view. Changes in one view are automatically reflected in the other view. Note the additional column in this DataGrid that contains the Delete button.

Listing 11.7   ManageShipping.aspx (continued)

```
<form id="Form1" method="post" runat="server">
    <P>
        <asp:DataGrid id="dgShippingFees" runat="server"
         BorderColor="#DEDFDE" BorderStyle="None" BorderWidth="1px"
         BackColor="White" CellPadding="4" GridLines="Vertical"
         ForeColor="Black" DataKeyField="ShippingID"
         AutoGenerateColumns="False">
            <SelectedItemStyle Font-Bold="True" ForeColor="White"
```

```
        BackColor="#CE5D5A"></SelectedItemStyle>
        <AlternatingItemStyle BackColor="White">
        </AlternatingItemStyle>
        <ItemStyle BackColor="#F7F7DE"></ItemStyle>
        <HeaderStyle Font-Bold="True" ForeColor="White"
         BackColor="#6B696B"></HeaderStyle>
        <FooterStyle BackColor="#CCCC99"></FooterStyle>
        <Columns>
            <asp:EditCommandColumn ButtonType="LinkButton"
             UpdateText="Update" CancelText="Cancel"
             EditText="Edit"></asp:EditCommandColumn>
            <asp:ButtonColumn Text="Delete" CommandName="Delete">
            </asp:ButtonColumn>
            <asp:BoundColumn Visible="False"
             DataField="ShippingID" HeaderText="ShippingID">
            </asp:BoundColumn>
            <asp:BoundColumn DataField="ShippingLowQuantity"
             HeaderText="Low Quantity"></asp:BoundColumn>
            <asp:BoundColumn DataField="ShippingHighQuantity"
             HeaderText="High Quantity"></asp:BoundColumn>
            <asp:BoundColumn DataField="ShippingFee"
             HeaderText="Fee" DataFormatString="{0:c}">
            </asp:BoundColumn>
        </Columns>
        <PagerStyle HorizontalAlign="Right" ForeColor="Black"
         BackColor="#F7F7DE" Mode="NumericPages"></PagerStyle>
    </asp:DataGrid></P>
```

After the DataGrid control, the page contains additional controls to allow the user to enter a new row for the database. Listing 11.8 shows this portion of the HTML for the page.

Listing 11.8   ManageShipping.aspx (continued)

```
<H3>Add a Fee:</H3>
<P>
    <TABLE id="Table1" cellSpacing="1" cellPadding="1"
    width="100%" border="0">
        <TR>
            <TD>
                <asp:Label id="Label1" runat="server">
                 Low Quantity</asp:Label></TD>
            <TD>
                <asp:TextBox id="txtLowQuantity"
                 runat="server">
                </asp:TextBox></TD>
        </TR>
        <TR>
            <TD>
                <asp:Label id="Label2" runat="server">
                 High Quantity</asp:Label></TD>
            <TD>
```

```
                              <asp:TextBox
                               id="txtHighQuantity" runat="server">
                                </asp:TextBox></TD>
                      </TR>
                      <TR>
                          <TD>
                              <asp:Label id="Label3" runat="server">Fee
                                </asp:Label></TD>
                          <TD>
                              <asp:TextBox id="txtFee" runat="server">
                                </asp:TextBox></TD>
                      </TR>
                      <TR>
                          <TD></TD>
                          <TD>
                              <asp:Button id="btnAddFee" runat="server"
                               Text="Add Fee" Width="115px">
                                </asp:Button></TD>
                      </TR>
                  </TABLE>
              </P>
          </form>
      </body>
  </HTML>
```

Figure 11.4 shows this Web Form in design view. As you can see, there are also a number of data objects on this form. You'll see them in use when we review the code-behind file for the page.

FIGURE 11.4:

Designing the
`ManageShipping`
`.aspx` page

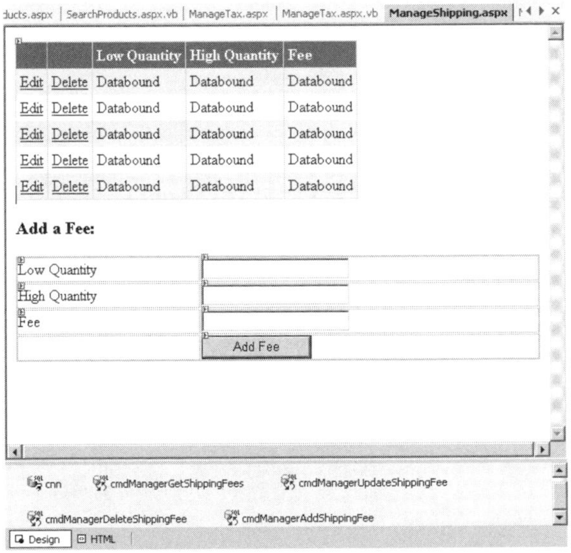

Most of the code behind this page is very similar to the code for `ManageTax.aspx`. Listing 11.9 shows this portion of the code, which includes the non-postback portion of the Page_Load procedure, the BindGrid procedure, and the code to handle the Edit, Update, and Cancel buttons.

Listing 11.9   ManageShipping.aspx.vb Event Procedures

```
Private Sub Page_Load(ByVal sender As System.Object, _
ByVal e As System.EventArgs) Handles MyBase.Load
    If Not IsPostBack Then
        ' Initial form load, so bind the grid
        BindGrid()
    Else
        If txtHighQuantity.Text <> "" Then
            ' Add a new fee to the table
            With cmdManagerAddShippingFee
                .Parameters("@ShippingLowQuantity").Value = _
                 txtLowQuantity.Text
                .Parameters("@ShippingHighQuantity").Value = _
                 txtHighQuantity.Text
                .Parameters("@ShippingFee").Value = _
                 txtFee.Text
                cnn.Open()
                .ExecuteNonQuery()
                cnn.Close()
                dgShippingFees.EditItemIndex = -1
                txtHighQuantity.Text = ""
                txtLowQuantity.Text = ""
                txtFee.Text = ""
            End With
            BindGrid()
        End If
    End If
End Sub

Private Sub BindGrid()
    ' Retrieve shipping fees from the database and
    ' bind them to the DataGrid
    Dim daShippingFees As New SqlDataAdapter()
    Dim dsShippingFees As New DataSet()
    daShippingFees.SelectCommand = cmdManagerGetShippingFees
    daShippingFees.Fill(dsShippingFees, "Tax")
    dgShippingFees.DataSource = dsShippingFees
    dgShippingFees.DataMember = "Tax"
    DataBind()
End Sub

Private Sub dgShippingFees_CancelCommand(ByVal source As Object, _
ByVal e As System.Web.UI.WebControls.DataGridCommandEventArgs) _
Handles dgShippingFees.CancelCommand
    ' Take the grid out of edit mode
```

```
      dgShippingFees.EditItemIndex = -1
      BindGrid()
End Sub

Private Sub dgShippingFees_EditCommand(ByVal source As Object, _
 ByVal e As System.Web.UI.WebControls.DataGridCommandEventArgs) _
 Handles dgShippingFees.EditCommand
    ' Show the selected row for editing
    dgShippingFees.EditItemIndex = CInt(e.Item.ItemIndex)
    BindGrid()
End Sub

Private Sub dgShippingFees_UpdateCommand(ByVal source As Object, _
 ByVal e As System.Web.UI.WebControls.DataGridCommandEventArgs) _
 Handles dgShippingFees.UpdateCommand
    ' Update the selected row in the database
    With cmdManagerUpdateShippingFee
        .Parameters("@ShippingID").Value = _
         dgShippingFees.DataKeys(CInt(e.Item.ItemIndex))
        .Parameters("@ShippingLowQuantity").Value = _
        CType(e.Item.Cells(3).Controls(0), TextBox).Text
        .Parameters("@ShippingHighQuantity").Value = _
        CType(e.Item.Cells(4).Controls(0), TextBox).Text
        .Parameters("@ShippingFee").Value = _
        CType(CType(e.Item.Cells(5).Controls(0), TextBox).Text, _
        Double)
        cnn.Open()
        .ExecuteNonQuery()
        cnn.Close()
        dgShippingFees.EditItemIndex = -1
    End With
    BindGrid()
End Sub
```

There is additional code to handle the new functionality of this form: deleting rows and adding new rows. Listing 11.10 shows the event procedure that's called when the user clicks the Delete button. It's quite similar to the code used to update a row.

Listing 11.10   **ManageShipping.aspx.vb Delete Event Procedure**

```
Private Sub dgShippingFees_DeleteCommand(ByVal source As Object, _
 ByVal e As System.Web.UI.WebControls.DataGridCommandEventArgs) _
 Handles dgShippingFees.DeleteCommand
    ' Delete the selected row from the database
    With cmdManagerDeleteShippingFee
        .Parameters("@ShippingID").Value = _
         dgShippingFees.DataKeys(CInt(e.Item.ItemIndex))
        cnn.Open()
        .ExecuteNonQuery()
        cnn.Close()
        dgShippingFees.EditItemIndex = -1
```

```
      End With
      BindGrid()
   End Sub
```

Finally, Listing 11.11 shows the code that's used to add a new row to the table. As with much of the other code you've seen in this project, it is just a wrapper around a stored procedure. This code is located in the Page_Load procedure, where it will be called when the user clicks the Add button and the form is posted back to the server. The code makes a simple check to make sure that there is data before trying to add a row to the table.

Listing 11.11   **ManageShipping.aspx.vb Page_Load Event Procedure**

```
Private Sub Page_Load(ByVal sender As System.Object, _
  ByVal e As System.EventArgs) Handles MyBase.Load
    If Not IsPostBack Then
        ' Initial form load, so bind the grid
        BindGrid()
    Else
        If txtHighQuantity.Text <> "" Then
            ' Add a new fee to the table
            With cmdManagerAddShippingFee
                .Parameters("@ShippingLowQuantity").Value = _
                 txtLowQuantity.Text
                .Parameters("@ShippingHighQuantity").Value = _
                 txtHighQuantity.Text
                .Parameters("@ShippingFee").Value = _
                 txtFee.Text
                cnn.Open()
                .ExecuteNonQuery()
                cnn.Close()
                dgShippingFees.EditItemIndex = -1
                txtHighQuantity.Text = ""
                txtLowQuantity.Text = ""
                txtFee.Text = ""
            End With
            BindGrid()
        End If
    End If
End Sub
```

The code for ManageShipping.aspx calls four stored procedures on the SQL Server. The first of these, the procManagerGetShippingFees stored procedure, provides the original data to be bound to the DataGrid control. It's shown in Listing 11.12.

Listing 11.12   **procManagerGetShippingFees Stored Procedure**

```
/*  Retrieve all shipping fees
```

```
From .NET E-Commerce Programming
by Mike Gunderloy and Noel Jerke
Copyright 2002, Sybex Inc. All Rights Reserved. */
CREATE PROCEDURE procManagerGetShippingFees
AS
SELECT * FROM Shipping
  ORDER BY ShippingLowQuantity
```

Listing 11.13 shows the procManagerUpdateShippingFee stored procedure, which is used to update an existing row in the table.

Listing 11.13   procManagerUpdateShippingFee Stored Procedure

```
/*  Update a specified shipping fee

From .NET E-Commerce Programming
by Mike Gunderloy and Noel Jerke
Copyright 2002, Sybex Inc. All Rights Reserved. */
CREATE PROCEDURE procManagerUpdateShippingFee
  @ShippingID int,
  @ShippingLowQuantity int,
  @ShippingHighQuantity int,
  @ShippingFee money
AS
  UPDATE Shipping
    SET ShippingLowQuantity = @ShippingLowQuantity,
      ShippingHighQuantity = @ShippingHighQuantity,
      ShippingFee = @ShippingFee
    WHERE ShippingID = @ShippingID
```

The procManagerDeleteShippingFee stored procedure handles deleting a row from the table. Listing 11.14 shows this stored procedure.

Listing 11.14   procManagerDeleteShippingFee Stored Procedure

```
/*  Delete a shipping fee

From .NET E-Commerce Programming
by Mike Gunderloy and Noel Jerke
Copyright 2002, Sybex Inc. All Rights Reserved. */
CREATE PROCEDURE procManagerDeleteShippingFee
  @ShippingID int
AS
  DELETE FROM Shipping
    WHERE ShippingID = @ShippingID
```

Finally, Listing 11.15 shows the procManagerAddShippingFee stored procedure, which is called to add a new row to the Shipping table.

Listing 11.15   **procManagerAddShippingFee Stored Procedure**

```
/*  Add a new shipping fee

From .NET E-Commerce Programming
by Mike Gunderloy and Noel Jerke
Copyright 2002, Sybex Inc. All Rights Reserved. */
CREATE PROCEDURE procManagerAddShippingFee
  @ShippingLowQuantity int,
  @ShippingHighQuantity int,
  @ShippingFee money
AS
  INSERT INTO Shipping (ShippingLowQuantity, ShippingHighQuantity,
    ShippingFee)
  VALUES (@ShippingLowQuantity, @ShippingHighQuantity, @ShippingFee)
```

Now we're ready to test the interface for managing shipping rates. Figure 11.5 shows the Manage Shipping page with the current settings in the database. Note the options to change the existing values and to delete any range. At the bottom of the page is the form to add a new shipping range and its associated fee.

FIGURE 11.5:

Manage Shipping page

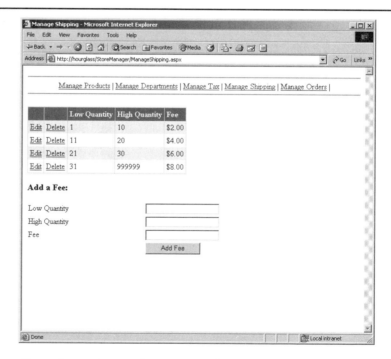

To start the test, we'll use the option to edit a current shipping range. Figure 11.6 shows the process of editing the last range.

FIGURE 11.6:

Editing a
shipping range

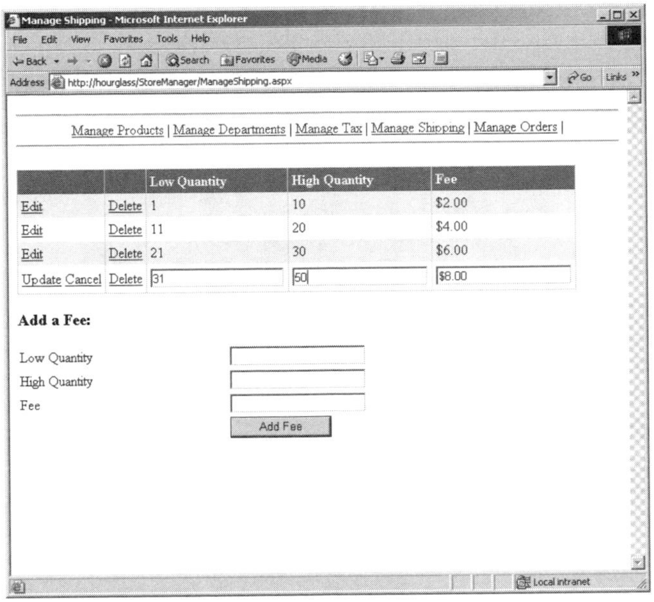

Next, we'll test the option of adding a shipping range and fee. Figure 11.7 shows a shipping range that's about to be added to the list. Note that no checking is being done to ensure that the ranges don't overlap and that the new range doesn't already exist. The presumption is that the user will be smart enough to ensure that each range is valid and that there are no gaps or overlaps.

FIGURE 11.7:

Adding a shipping
range and fee

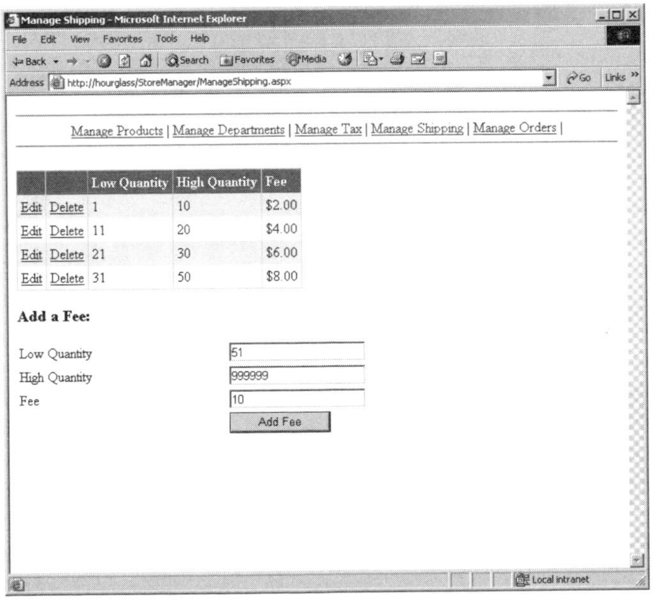

Figure 11.8 shows the updated shipping ranges after the new values are added.

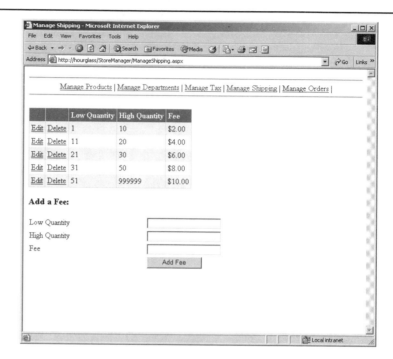

Summary

In this chapter, we designed Web Forms to update the tax and shipping data of our online store. If the business rules for how we calculate the sales tax or the shipping charge change, these pages will also have to change. In Chapter 12, "Managing Orders," we'll finish the job of building the store's management interface with some tools for order management.

CHAPTER 12

Managing Orders

- Searching for Orders

- Editing Item Information

- Deleting an Item

- Saving Changes to Order Information

The last management features that we will build are for order management. It's important that the business managers of the store be able to easily and quickly sift through orders for purposes such as processing, customer service, technical support, and updating the shipping status.

We'll start with a search interface for quickly finding orders in the system that match a specified set of criteria. The management application will respond with a list of matching orders. From there, we'll be able to manage order status and the details of an order.

Searching for Orders

Hopefully, our new online store will sell products left and right. That means that we'll need some sort of interface for managing those orders. We'll start with a page that provides a series of search options for different data fields of the order. This will give us a fast and easy way to retrieve orders that meet certain criteria. This page will also contain a Repeater control to show the results of the search. When the page is initially loaded, the user won't see the Repeater control because the page won't contain any data. After the search criteria are posted back to the page, the Repeater will become visible with the results, and the user will be able to modify their search criteria if necessary to find the exact records that they want.

The page starts with the same header information as the other pages in the StoreManager application. It then contains the code to define the Repeater control. Listing 12.1 shows this portion of the HTML for ManageOrders.aspx.

Listing 12.1   **ManageOrders.aspx**

```
<%@ Page Language="vb" AutoEventWireup="false"
 Codebehind="ManageOrders.aspx.vb" Inherits="StoreManager.ManageOrders"%>
<!DOCTYPE HTML PUBLIC "-//W3C//DTD HTML 4.0 Transitional//EN">
<HTML>
    <HEAD>
        <title>Manage Orders</title>
        <meta content="Microsoft Visual Studio.NET 7.0" name="GENERATOR">
<meta content="Visual Basic 7.0" name="CODE_LANGUAGE">
        <meta content="JavaScript" name="vs_defaultClientScript">
        <meta content="http://schemas.microsoft.com/intellisense/ie5"
         name="vs_targetSchema">
        <!-- ManageOrders.aspx - Manage orders for the store -->
    </HEAD>
    <body>
        <!-- #Include File="ValidateCheck.inc" -->
        <!-- #Include File="Navbar.inc" -->
        <form id="Form1" method="post" runat="server">
            <P><asp:repeater id="rptOrders" runat="server">
                <ItemTemplate>
                    <tr>
```

```
                <td><a href='OrderDetail.aspx?OrderID=
                <%# DataBinder.Eval(Container.DataItem,
                "OrderID") %>&ShopperID=
                <%# DataBinder.Eval(Container.DataItem,
                "ShopperID") %>'>
                <%# DataBinder.Eval(Container.DataItem,
                "OrderID") %></a>
                </td>
                <td><%# DataBinder.Eval(Container.DataItem,
                "OrderDateOrdered") %></td>
                <td><%# DataBinder.Eval(Container.DataItem,
                "BasketTotal", "{0:c}") %></td>
                <td><%# DataBinder.Eval(Container.DataItem,
                "OrderShipLastName") %></td>
                <td><a href='mailto:
                <%# DataBinder.Eval(Container.DataItem,
                "OrderShipEmail") %>'>
                <%# DataBinder.Eval(Container.DataItem,
                "OrderShipEmail") %></a>
                </td>
                <td><%# DataBinder.Eval(Container.DataItem,
                "OrderBillLastName") %></td>
                <td><a href='mailto:
                <%# DataBinder.Eval(Container.DataItem,
                "OrderBillEmail") %>'>
                <%# DataBinder.Eval(Container.DataItem,
                "OrderBillEmail") %></a>
                </td>
                <td><%# DataBinder.Eval(Container.DataItem,
                "Status") %></td>
                <td>
                    <asp:LinkButton id="LinkButton1"
                    runat="server">Delete
                    </asp:LinkButton></td>
            </tr>
    </ItemTemplate>
    <HeaderTemplate>
        <table border="1" cellpadding="3" cellspacing="3">
            <tr>
                <th>
                    Order ID</th>
                <th>
                    Date Ordered</th>
                <th>
                    Order Total</th>
                <th>
                    Ship to<BR>
                    Last Name</th>
                <th>
                    Ship to<BR>
                    Email Address</th>
```

```
                                <th>
                                    Bill to<BR>
                                    Last Name</th>
                                <th>
                                    Bill to<BR>
                                    Email Address</th>
                                <th>
                                    Order Status</th>
                                <th>
                                    Delete</th>
                            </tr>
                        </HeaderTemplate>
                        <FooterTemplate>
                            </table>
                        </FooterTemplate>
                    </asp:repeater></P>
```

Note that the Repeater control makes things easy for the employee who's working with orders. The OrderID column for each order is linked to a detail page for that order (which you'll see later in this chapter), and the shipping and billing e-mail addresses are also set up as hyperlinks. This means that the user can send updates or information to the shopper with a single mouse click. Finally, the Repeater displays a Delete link for each row, so that unwanted orders can be deleted quickly.

The page continues with a set of text boxes that enable the user to input search criteria. Listing 12.2 shows this section of the HTML.

Listing 12.2   **ManageOrders.aspx (continued)**

```
        <P><FONT size="5"> Enter your search criteria:</FONT></P>
        <P>
            <TABLE id="Table1" cellSpacing="1" cellPadding="1"
            width="100%" border="0">
                <TR>
                    <TD>Shopper Name (first or last)</TD>
                    <TD><asp:textbox id="txtName" runat="server">
                    </asp:textbox></TD>
                </TR>
                <TR>
                    <TD>Shopper Email</TD>
                    <TD><asp:textbox id="txtEmail" runat="server">
                    </asp:textbox></TD>
                </TR>
                <TR>
                    <TD>Order Date</TD>
                    <TD><asp:textbox id="txtOrderDate1"
                        runat="server"></asp:textbox> to
                        <asp:textbox id="txtOrderDate2"
                        runat="server"></asp:textbox></TD>
```

```
                    </TR>
                    <TR>
                        <TD>Order Total</TD>
                        <TD><asp:textbox id="txtOrderTotal1"
                            runat="server"></asp:textbox> to
                            <asp:textbox id="txtOrderTotal2"
                            runat="server"></asp:textbox></TD>
                    </TR>
                    <TR>
                        <TD>Product Name</TD>
                        <TD><asp:textbox id="txtProductName"
                         runat="server"></asp:textbox></TD>
                    </TR>
                </TABLE>
            </P>
            <asp:button id="btnSearch" runat="server" Text="Search Now">
            </asp:button>
        </form>
    </body>
</HTML>
```

No code at all runs when this page is first displayed in the browser. As shown in Figure 12.1, it initially shows only a set of data entry controls to the user.

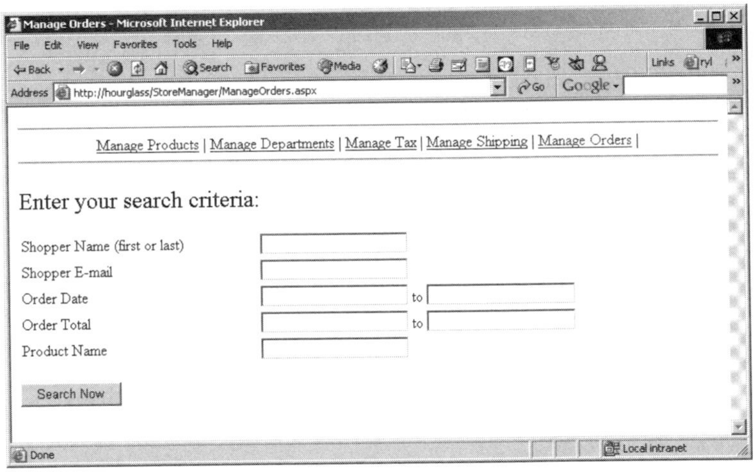

FIGURE 12.1:

The
ManageOrders.aspx
page's initial display

When the user enters some search criteria (or no criteria at all) and then clicks the Search Now button, the Page_Load procedure is called. Listing 12.3 shows this event procedure.

Listing 12.3   **ManageOrders.aspx.vb Page_Load Procedure**

```vb
Dim mstrSQL As String

Private Sub Page_Load(ByVal sender As System.Object, _
   ByVal e As System.EventArgs) Handles MyBase.Load
      ' Process queries when they're posted back
      If IsPostBack Then
         ' Build a SQL statement to retrieve the desired rows.
         ' First, the SELECT statement specifies the columns to return
         mstrSQL = "SELECT DISTINCT [Order].OrderID, " & _
            "OrderDateOrdered, [Order].ShopperID, " & _
            "OrderShipLastName, OrderShipEmail, OrderBillLastName, " & _
            "OrderBillEmail, Status = CASE OrderStatusStage " & _
            "WHEN 0 THEN 'Order Received' " & _
            "WHEN 1 THEN 'Order Fulfilled' " & _
            "WHEN 2 THEN 'Order Shipped' " & _
            "WHEN 3 THEN 'Call Customer Service' " & _
            "END, BasketTotal " & _
            "FROM ((([Order] INNER JOIN OrderStatus " & _
            "ON [Order].OrderID = OrderStatus.OrderID) " & _
            "INNER JOIN Basket " & _
            "ON [Order].BasketID = Basket.BasketID) " & _
            "INNER JOIN BasketItem " & _
            "ON Basket.BasketID = BasketItem.BasketID "

         ' Now create the WHERE clause
         Dim strWhere As String
         ' Search for name data in all of the name columns.
         ' Have to double any quotes in this string data
         If txtName.Text <> "" Then
            Dim strName As String = "'%" & _
             Replace(txtName.Text, "'", "''") & "%'"
            strWhere &= "(OrderShipFirstName LIKE " & strName & _
             " OR OrderShipLastName LIKE " & strName & _
             " OR OrderBillFirstName LIKE " & strName & _
             " OR OrderBillLastName LIKE " & strName & ") "
         End If

         ' Search for e-mail in both e-mail columns
         If txtEmail.Text <> "" Then
            If strWhere <> "" Then
               strWhere &= "AND "
            End If
            Dim strEmail As String = "'%" & _
             Replace(txtEmail.Text, "'", "''") & "%'"
            strWhere &= "(OrderShipEmail LIKE " & strEmail & _
             " OR OrderBillEmail LIKE " & strEmail & ") "
         End If
```

```
' Build clauses to search for orders before or
' after specified dates
If txtOrderDate1.Text <> "" Then
    If strWhere <> "" Then
        strWhere &= "AND "
    End If
    strWhere &= "OrderDateOrdered >= '" & _
     txtOrderDate1.Text & "' "
End If
If txtOrderDate2.Text <> "" Then
    If strWhere <> "" Then
        strWhere &= "AND "
    End If
    strWhere &= "OrderDateOrdered <= '" & _
     txtOrderDate2.Text & "' "
End If

' Search for order totals in any specified range
If txtOrderTotal1.Text <> "" Then
    If strWhere <> "" Then
        strWhere &= "AND "
    End If
    strWhere &= "BasketTotal >= " & _
     txtOrderTotal1.Text & " "
End If
If txtOrderTotal2.Text <> "" Then
    If strWhere <> "" Then
        strWhere &= "AND "
    End If
    strWhere &= "BasketTotal <= " & _
     txtOrderTotal2.Text & " "
End If

' Search for all orders containing a specific product
If txtProductName.Text <> "" Then
    If strWhere <> "" Then
        strWhere &= "AND "
    End If
    strWhere &= "BasketItemProductName LIKE '%" & _
     Replace(txtProductName.Text, "'", "''") & _
     "%'"
End If

' If the WHERE clause isn't empty, tack it onto the
' SELECT clause
If strWhere <> "" Then
    mstrSQL &= " WHERE " & strWhere
End If

' Add the ORDER BY clause in any case
mstrSQL &= " ORDER BY [Order].OrderID DESC"
```

```
              ' And display the data on the user interface
              BindOrders()
        End If
End Sub
```

This procedure works by building a SQL string based on the data entered by the user and storing the string in a module-level variable, *mstrSQL*. We've taken this approach rather than our usual method of passing parameters to a stored procedure because of the free-form nature of the user's input. The user may enter values for all of the search parameters, for any subset of the search parameters, or for no search parameters at all. It's simpler to use the data that the user enters to build an appropriate SQL statement dynamically than to handle these various conditions in a stored procedure.

Note that the varchar fields holding name and e-mail information are searched with clauses containing the LIKE predicate. That way, a user, for example, can search for an address such as "@sybex.com" that will return all orders where the shopper's e-mail address contains that text, without having to enter the entire e-mail address.

After the code builds the SQL statement, it calls the BindOrders procedure to display the results on the form's user interface. Listing 12.4 shows this procedure.

Listing 12.4   ManageOrders.aspx.vb BindOrders Procedure

```
Private Sub BindOrders()
    ' Use the module-level SQL string to show the desired
    ' orders on the user interface

    ' Create a Command object based on the SQL string
    Dim cmdOrders As New SqlCommand()
    cmdOrders.Connection = cnn
    cmdOrders.CommandText = mstrSQL
    cmdOrders.CommandType = CommandType.Text

    ' Use a DataSet and DataAdapter to grab the data
    Dim dsOrders As New DataSet()
    Dim daOrders As New SqlDataAdapter()
    daOrders.SelectCommand = cmdOrders
    daOrders.Fill(dsOrders, "Items")

    ' And bind the items to the user interface
    rptOrders.DataSource = dsOrders
    rptOrders.DataMember = dsOrders.Tables(0).TableName
    DataBind()
End Sub
```

The other code behind this particular Web Form handles clicks on the Delete links. This code passes the OrderID of the specified order to a stored procedure that performs the actual deletion. It then calls the BindOrders procedure to update the data displayed on the form so that the deleted order will no longer be displayed. Listing 12.5 shows this code.

Listing 12.5   ManageOrders.aspx.vb rptOrders_ItemCommand Procedure

```
Private Sub rptOrders_ItemCommand(ByVal source As System.Object, _
  ByVal e As System.Web.UI.WebControls.RepeaterCommandEventArgs) _
  Handles rptOrders.ItemCommand
    ' Delete the specified order
    cmdManagerDeleteOrder.Parameters("@OrderID").Value = _
      rptOrders.DataSource.Tables(0).Rows(e.Item.ItemIndex)(0)
    cnn.Open()
    cmdManagerDeleteOrder.ExecuteNonQuery()
    cnn.Close()
    BindOrders()
End Sub
```

Listing 12.6 shows the procManagerDeleteOrder stored procedure, which performs the actual deletion.

Listing 12.6   procManagerDeleteOrder Stored Procedure

```
/*  Delete an order from the database

From .NET E-Commerce Programming
by Mike Gunderloy and Noel Jerke
Copyright 2002, Sybex Inc. All Rights Reserved. */
CREATE PROCEDURE procManagerDeleteOrder
  @OrderID int
AS
  DECLARE @BasketID int
  /* Find the basket ID for this order */
  SELECT @BasketID = BasketID
    FROM [Order]
    WHERE OrderID = @OrderID
  /* Delete any payments */
  DELETE FROM Payment
    WHERE OrderID = @OrderID
  /* Delete the order status */
  DELETE FROM OrderStatus
    WHERE OrderID = @OrderID
  /* Delete the order */
  DELETE FROM [Order]
    WHERE OrderID = @OrderID
  /* Delete basket items */
  DELETE FROM BasketItem
```

```
      WHERE BasketID = @BasketID
   /* Delete the matching basket */
   DELETE FROM Basket
      WHERE BasketID = @BasketID
```

As you can see, the stored procedure is fairly complex. That's because it has to do more than just delete a row from the Order table. To completely clean up an order, rows need to be deleted from five tables:

- Payment
- OrderStatus
- Order
- BasketItem
- Basket

In addition, foreign key constraints require some of these deletions to be performed in a particular sequence. For example, you can't delete a row from the Basket table if there are still corresponding rows in the BasketItem table. The stored procedure takes care of the details of performing the various deletions in an acceptable order.

The other thing that a user can do on the ManageOrders.aspx page is click the ID of a particular order to see the details of that order. The link loads the OrderDetail.aspx page, passing the OrderID and ShopperID values as the QueryString for the web page. We'll discuss the OrderDetail.aspx page in the next section of this chapter.

But first, let's test the search interface. Our initial test is to simply search for all orders in the system by clicking the Search Now button without entering any search criteria. Figure 12.2 shows the listing of all orders returned. Note all the data that's returned for each order.

Next, we'll perform a very specific search by entering an order date range and order total range (making sure that at least one order meets both requirements). Figure 12.3 shows the search form filled in with our sample data.

FIGURE 12.2:

All orders returned by the search

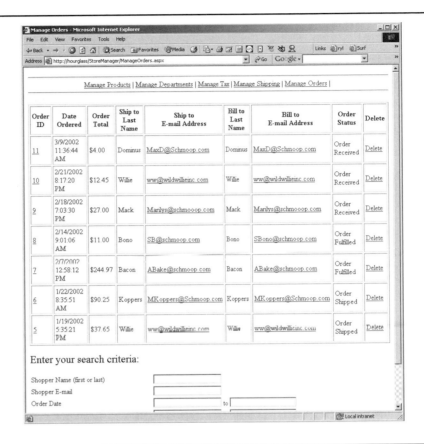

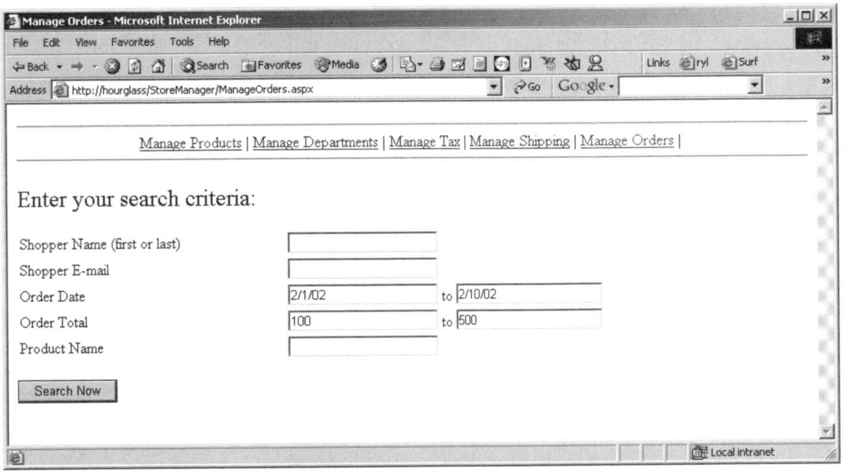

FIGURE 12.3:

Searching by date range and total range

Figure 12.4 shows the search results. Note that the date and total of the order that was returned fall within the ranges that we specified.

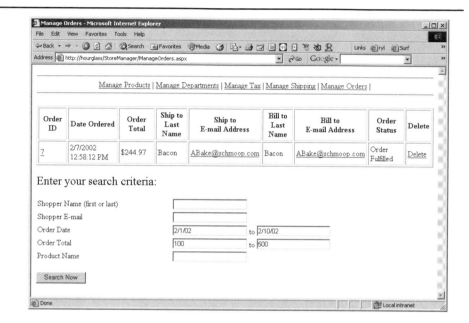

Reviewing and Updating an Order

The OrderDetail.aspx page is the most complex page in the StoreManager application. It displays a wide variety of data from multiple tables and allows the user of the application to make changes if necessary. This is the page that our customer service representatives will use if any adjustments need to be made to a shopper's order.

Despite the page's complexity, it doesn't introduce any new concepts. As you can see in Figure 12.5, the page uses a variety of TextBox controls plus a DataGrid control to display information, and it depends on a large number of stored procedures to do its work.

The page starts with the standard header information and then contains a complex set of tables to display all the information about a particular order. The first part of the HTML, shown in Listing 12.7, displays the order ID, order date, and order status. The status is shown in a DropDownList control that automatically translates the numerical status values into messages.

FIGURE 12.5:
OrderDetail.aspx
in design view

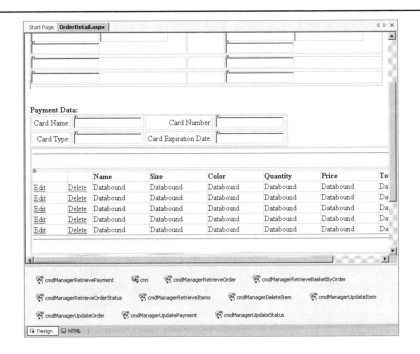

Listing 12.7   **OrderDetail.aspx**

```
<%@ Page Language="vb" AutoEventWireup="false"
 Codebehind="OrderDetail.aspx.vb" Inherits="StoreManager.OrderDetail"%>
<!DOCTYPE HTML PUBLIC "-//W3C//DTD HTML 4.0 Transitional//EN">
<HTML>
    <HEAD>
        <title>Order Detail</title>
        <META http-equiv="Content-Type"
         content="text/html; charset=windows-1252">
        <meta name="GENERATOR" content="Microsoft Visual Studio.NET 7.0">
        <meta name="CODE_LANGUAGE" content="Visual Basic 7.0">
        <meta name="vs_defaultClientScript" content="JavaScript">
        <meta name="vs_targetSchema"
         content="http://schemas.microsoft.com/intellisense/ie5">
        <!-- OrderDetail.aspx - Manage a single order -->
    </HEAD>
    <body>
        <!-- #Include File="ValidateCheck.inc" -->
        <!-- #Include File="Navbar.inc" -->
        <form id="Form1" method="post" runat="server">
            <table>
                <!-- Row to display the order id and the date ordered
                 -->
                <tr>
```

```
            <td><b>
                <asp:Label id="lblOrderNumber"
                  runat="server">Order #</asp:Label></b>
            </td>
            <td width="75"></td>
            <td><b><asp:Label id="lblOrderDate" runat="server">
             Order Date:</asp:Label></b></td>
        <tr>
        <!-- Blank column -->
        <tr>
            <td colspan="3">
                <asp:DropDownList id="ddlOrderStatus"
                  runat="server" Width="369px">
                    <asp:ListItem Value="0">
                     Order Received</asp:ListItem>
                    <asp:ListItem Value="1">
                     Order Fulfilled</asp:ListItem>
                    <asp:ListItem Value="2">
                     Order Shipped</asp:ListItem>
                    <asp:ListItem Value="3">
                     Call Customer Service</asp:ListItem>
                </asp:DropDownList></td>
        </tr>
```

This section sets the pattern for much of the rest of the page. The information will be displayed in Web Form controls whose Text properties can be set when the page is loaded. Note that data that should not be edited, such as the order ID, will be displayed in Label controls. Listing 12.8 shows the section of the page that will display the billing and shipping information for the order.

Listing 12.8   OrderDetail.aspx (continued)

```
<!-- Bill to and Ship to header -->
<tr>
    <td><b>Bill To:</b></td>
    <td width="75"></td>
    <td><b>Ship To:</b></td>
<tr>
<!-- Shipping and Billing information -->
<tr>
    <td>
        <asp:TextBox id="txtBillFirstName" runat="server">
        </asp:TextBox>
        <asp:TextBox id="txtBillLastName" runat="server">
        </asp:TextBox>
    </td>
    <td width="75"></td>
    <td>
        <asp:TextBox id="txtShipFirstName" runat="server">
```

```
                    </asp:TextBox>
                    <asp:TextBox id="txtShipLastName" runat="server">
                    </asp:TextBox>
             </td>
       <tr>
       <!-- Billing and shipping address  -->
       <tr>
             <td>
                    <asp:TextBox id="txtBillAddress" runat="server"></asp:TextBox>
             </td>
             <td width="75"></td>
             <td>
                    <asp:TextBox id="txtShipAddress" runat="server"></asp:TextBox>
             </td>
       <tr>
       <!-- Billing and shipping city, state, zip  -->
       <tr>
             <td>
                    <asp:TextBox id="txtBillCity" runat="server"></asp:TextBox>
                    <asp:TextBox id="txtBillState" runat="server"></asp:TextBox>
                    <asp:TextBox id="txtBillZipCode" runat="server"></asp:TextBox>
             </td>
             <td width="75"></td>
             <td>
                    <asp:TextBox id="txtShipCity" runat="server"></asp:TextBox>
                    <asp:TextBox id="txtShipState" runat="server"></asp:TextBox>
                    <asp:TextBox id="txtShipZipCode" runat="server"></asp:TextBox>
             </td>
       <tr>
       <!-- Billing and shipping phone  -->
       <tr>
             <td>
                    <asp:TextBox id="txtBillPhone" runat="server"></asp:TextBox>
             </td>
             <td width="75"></td>
             <td>
                    <asp:TextBox id="txtShipPhone" runat="server"></asp:TextBox>
             </td>
       <tr>
       <!-- Billing and shipping e-mail -->
       <tr>
             <td>
                    <asp:TextBox id="txtBillEmail" runat="server"></asp:TextBox>
             </td>
             <td width="75"></td>
             <td>
                    <asp:TextBox id="txtShipEmail" runat="server"></asp:TextBox>
             </td>
       <tr>
       </tr>
</table>
```

After the address details, the Web Form displays the payment data for the order in a separate table. This section of the page is shown in Listing 12.9.

Listing 12.9   **OrderDetail.aspx (continued)**

```
<!-- Display the payment data  -->
<BR>
<BR>
<b>Payment Data:</b>
<BR>
<!-- A table is created to display the payment data  -->
<table cellpadding="3" cellspacing="3">
    <tr>
        <!-- Display the card name -->
        <td align="right">Card Name:</td>
        <td>
            <asp:TextBox id="txtCardName" runat="server"></asp:TextBox>
        </td>
        <!-- Display the card number  -->
        <td align="right">Card Number:</td>
        <td>
            <asp:TextBox id="txtCardNumber" runat="server"></asp:TextBox>
        </td>
    </tr>
    <tr>
        <!-- Display the card type  -->
        <td align="right">Card Type:</td>
        <td>
            <asp:TextBox id="txtCardType" runat="server"></asp:TextBox>
        </td>
        <!-- Display the card expiration date  -->
        <td align="right">Card Expiration Date:</td>
        <td>
            <asp:TextBox id="txtCardExpirationDate" runat="server">
            </asp:TextBox>
        </td>
    </tr>
</table>
```

After the payment data, the form will display the individual items in the order. We'll use a DataGrid control to hold this information. The DataGrid is embedded in a table to make sure that it's properly aligned with other elements on the page. Listing 12.10 shows this section of the HTML.

Listing 12.10   **OrderDetail.aspx (continued)**

```
<table border="0" cellpadding="3" cellspacing="2" width="840">
    <TBODY>
```

```
<tr>
    <td colspan="7"><HR>
    </td>
</tr>
<tr>
    <td colspan="7">
        <asp:DataGrid id="dgItems" runat="server"
         AutoGenerateColumns="False" Width="840px"
         DataKeyField="BasketItemID">
            <HeaderStyle Font-Bold="True"></HeaderStyle>
            <Columns>
                <asp:EditCommandColumn ButtonType="LinkButton"
                 UpdateText="Update" CancelText="Cancel"
                 EditText="Edit">
                    <HeaderStyle Width="70px"></HeaderStyle>
                </asp:EditCommandColumn>
                <asp:ButtonColumn Text="Delete"
                 CommandName="Delete">
                    <HeaderStyle Width="50px"></HeaderStyle>
                </asp:ButtonColumn>
                <asp:BoundColumn DataField="BasketItemProductName"
                 HeaderText="Name">
                    <HeaderStyle Width="120px"></HeaderStyle>
                </asp:BoundColumn>
                <asp:BoundColumn DataField="BasketItemSize"
                 HeaderText="Size">
                    <HeaderStyle Width="120px"></HeaderStyle>
                </asp:BoundColumn>
                <asp:BoundColumn DataField="BasketItemColor"
                 HeaderText="Color">
                    <HeaderStyle Width="120px"></HeaderStyle>
                </asp:BoundColumn>
                <asp:BoundColumn DataField="BasketItemQuantity"
                 HeaderText="Quantity">
                    <HeaderStyle Width="120px"></HeaderStyle>
                </asp:BoundColumn>
                <asp:BoundColumn DataField="BasketItemPrice"
                 HeaderText="Price" DataFormatString="{0:c}">
                    <HeaderStyle Width="120px"></HeaderStyle>
                </asp:BoundColumn>
                <asp:BoundColumn DataField="BasketItemTotal"
                 ReadOnly="True" HeaderText="Total"
                 DataFormatString="{0:c}">
                    <HeaderStyle Width="120px"></HeaderStyle>
                </asp:BoundColumn>
                <asp:BoundColumn Visible="False"
                 DataField="BasketItemID"></asp:BoundColumn>
            </Columns>
        </asp:DataGrid><HR>
    </td>
</tr>
```

WARNING The width of the individual columns in the DataGrid is set by assigning a HeaderStyle tag to each column. If you turn off the display of the DataGrid's header, you can't set column widths.

After the item information, the page concludes by showing the billing information for the order and a Submit button, and by closing out all the open tags. Listing 12.11 shows this part of the HTML.

Listing 12.11 **OrderDetail.aspx (continued)**

```
<!-- Show the subtotal of the basket -->
<tr>
    <td colspan="6" align="right"><b>Subtotal:</b>
    </td>
    <td align="right"><asp:Label id="lblSubTotal"
     runat="server">$0.00</asp:Label></td>
</tr>
<!-- Show the shipping total of the basket -->
<tr>
    <td colspan="6" align="right"><b>Shipping:</b>
    </td>
    <td align="right"><asp:Label id="lblShipping"
     runat="server">$0.00</asp:Label></td>
</tr>
<!-- Show the tax total of the basket -->
<tr>
    <td colspan="6" align="right"><b>Tax:</b></td>
    <td align="right"><asp:Label id="lblTax"
     runat="server">$0.00</asp:Label></td>
</tr>
<!-- Show the total of the basket -->
<tr>
    <td colspan="6" align="right"><b>Total:</b></td>
    <td align="right"><asp:Label id="lblTotal"
     runat="server">$0.00</asp:Label></td>
</tr>
<!-- Submit button to process the updates  -->
<tr>
    <td colspan="7">
        <asp:Button id="btnSubmit" runat="server"
         Text="Submit"></asp:Button>
    </td>
    <tr>
    </tr>
</TBODY>
</table>
</form>
</body>
</HTML>
```

The code-behind file for the page starts with a deceptively simple Page_Load procedure. This procedure, shown in Listing 12.12, starts by saving the OrderID and ShopperID that were passed into the page in a pair of session variables. It then calls two other procedures to display the data.

Listing 12.12   OrderDetail.aspx.vb Page_Load Procedure

```
Private Sub Page_Load(ByVal sender As System.Object, _
 ByVal e As System.EventArgs) Handles MyBase.Load
    If Not IsPostBack Then
        ' Save the incoming OrderID and ShopperID
        Session("OrderID") = Request.QueryString("OrderID")
        Session("ShopperID") = Request.QueryString("ShopperID")
        BindMain()
        BindItemGrid()
    End If
End Sub
```

The BindMain procedure, shown in Listing 12.13, uses a combination of SqlCommand objects and a DataReader object to transfer information about a particular order from the database to the Web Form.

Listing 12.13   OrderDetail.aspx.vb BindMain Procedure

```
Private Sub BindMain()
    Dim dr As SqlDataReader
    ' Get the order info
    With cmdManagerRetrieveOrder
        .Parameters("@OrderID").Value = _
         Session("OrderID")
        cnn.Open()
        dr = .ExecuteReader
        With dr
            .Read()
            lblOrderNumber.Text = "Order #" & _
             CType(.GetInt32(0), String)
            If Not dr.IsDBNull(3) Then
                txtShipFirstName.Text = .GetString(3)
            End If
            If Not dr.IsDBNull(4) Then
                txtShipLastName.Text = .GetString(4)
            End If
            If Not dr.IsDBNull(5) Then
                txtShipAddress.Text = .GetString(5)
            End If
            If Not dr.IsDBNull(6) Then
                txtShipCity.Text = .GetString(6)
            End If
```

```
            If Not dr.IsDBNull(7) Then
                txtShipState.Text = .GetString(7)
            End If
            If Not dr.IsDBNull(10) Then
                txtShipZipCode.Text = .GetString(10)
            End If
            If Not dr.IsDBNull(11) Then
                txtShipPhone.Text = .GetString(11)
            End If
            If Not dr.IsDBNull(13) Then
                txtShipEmail.Text = .GetString(13)
            End If
            If Not dr.IsDBNull(14) Then
                txtBillFirstName.Text = .GetString(14)
            End If
            If Not dr.IsDBNull(15) Then
                txtBillLastName.Text = .GetString(15)
            End If
            If Not dr.IsDBNull(16) Then
                txtBillAddress.Text = .GetString(16)
            End If
            If Not dr.IsDBNull(17) Then
                txtBillCity.Text = .GetString(17)
            End If
            If Not dr.IsDBNull(18) Then
                txtBillState.Text = .GetString(18)
            End If
            If Not dr.IsDBNull(21) Then
                txtBillZipCode.Text = .GetString(21)
            End If
            If Not dr.IsDBNull(22) Then
                txtBillPhone.Text = .GetString(22)
            End If
            If Not dr.IsDBNull(24) Then
                txtBillEmail.Text = .GetString(24)
            End If
            If Not dr.IsDBNull(25) Then
                lblOrderDate.Text = "Order Date: " & _
                CType(.GetDateTime(25), String)
            End If
            .Close()
        End With
    End With

    ' Get the payment info
    With cmdManagerRetrievePayment
        .Parameters("@OrderID").Value = _
        Session("OrderID")
        dr = .ExecuteReader
        With dr
            .Read()
```

```
                    If Not dr.IsDBNull(2) Then
                        txtCardType.Text = .GetString(2)
                    End If
                    If Not dr.IsDBNull(3) Then
                        txtCardNumber.Text = .GetString(3)
                    End If
                    If Not dr.IsDBNull(4) Then
                        txtCardExpirationDate.Text = .GetString(4)
                    End If
                    If Not dr.IsDBNull(5) Then
                        txtCardName.Text = .GetString(5)
                    End If
                    .Close()
                End With
            End With

            ' Get order status
            With cmdManagerRetrieveOrderStatus
                .Parameters("@OrderID").Value = _
                 Session("OrderID")
                ddlOrderStatus.SelectedItem.Value = .ExecuteScalar
            End With

            cnn.Close()

    End Sub
```

The BindMain procedure uses several stored procedures to retrieve information from the database. Each of these takes the OrderID as a parameter and uses it to find the desired data. The first of these stored procedures, procManagerRetrieveOrder, gets the row for the order from the Order table, as shown in Listing 12.14.

Listing 12.14   procManagerRetrieveOrder Stored Procedure

```
/*  Retrieve all info on an order

From .NET E-Commerce Programming
by Mike Gunderloy and Noel Jerke
Copyright 2002, Sybex Inc. All Rights Reserved. */
CREATE PROCEDURE procManagerRetrieveOrder
  @OrderID int
AS
  SELECT * FROM [Order]
  WHERE OrderID = @OrderID
```

The procManagerRetrievePayment stored procedure, shown in Listing 12.15, gets the payment information for the order.

⟶ **Listing 12.15**   **procManagerRetrievePayment Stored Procedure**

```
/*  Retrieve payment info on an order

From .NET E-Commerce Programming
by Mike Gunderloy and Noel Jerke
Copyright 2002, Sybex Inc. All Rights Reserved. */
CREATE PROCEDURE procManagerRetrievePayment
  @OrderID int
AS
  SELECT * FROM Payment
  WHERE OrderID = @OrderID
```

The last stored procedure called by the BindMain procedure is procManagerRetrieve-
OrderStatus, which gets the current status for the order. Listing 12.16 shows this stored
procedure.

⟶ **Listing 12.16**   **procManagerRetrieveOrderStatus Stored Procedure**

```
/*  Retrieve totals for an order

From .NET E-Commerce Programming
by Mike Gunderloy and Noel Jerke
Copyright 2002, Sybex Inc. All Rights Reserved. */
CREATE PROCEDURE procManagerRetrieveOrderStatus
  @OrderID int
AS
  SELECT OrderStatusStage FROM OrderStatus
  WHERE OrderID = @OrderID
```

The Page_Load procedure on this page also calls the BindItemGrid procedure. This procedure, shown in Listing 12.17, performs two tasks:

- Retrieve the item information for the order and bind it to the DataGrid control.

- Retrieve the totals for the order and show them in the appropriate label controls.

⟶ **Listing 12.17**   **OrderDetail.aspx.vb BindItemGrid Procedure**

```
Private Sub BindItemGrid()
    Dim dr As SqlDataReader

    ' Get items
    cmdManagerRetrieveItems.Parameters("@OrderID").Value = _
     Session("OrderID")
    Dim daItems As SqlDataAdapter = New SqlDataAdapter()
    Dim dsItems As DataSet = New DataSet()
```

```
daItems.SelectCommand = cmdManagerRetrieveItems
daItems.Fill(dsItems, "Items")
dgItems.DataSource = dsItems
dgItems.DataMember = "Items"
dgItems.DataBind()

' Get the totals info
With cmdManagerRetrieveBasketByOrder
    .Parameters("@OrderID").Value = _
    Session("OrderID")
    cnn.Open()
    dr = .ExecuteReader
    With dr
        .Read()
        If Not dr.IsDBNull(0) Then
            lblSubTotal.Text = Format( _
            dr.GetSqlMoney(0).ToSqlString.Value, "currency")
        End If
        If Not dr.IsDBNull(1) Then
            lblTotal.Text = Format( _
            dr.GetSqlMoney(1).ToSqlString.Value, "currency")
        End If
        If Not dr.IsDBNull(2) Then
            lblShipping.Text = Format( _
            dr.GetSqlMoney(2).ToSqlString.Value, "currency")
        End If
        If Not dr.IsDBNull(3) Then
            lblTax.Text = Format( _
            dr.GetSqlMoney(3).ToSqlString.Value, "currency")
        End If
        .Close()
    End With
    cnn.Close()
End With

End Sub
```

The BindItemGrid procedure calls two stored procedures to get its information. The first of these, procManagerRetrieveItems, is shown in Listing 12.18.

Listing 12.18   procManagerRetrieveItems Stored Procedure

```
/* Retrieve the item information for an order

From .NET E-Commerce Programming
by Mike Gunderloy and Noel Jerke
Copyright 2002, Sybex Inc. All Rights Reserved. */
CREATE PROCEDURE procManagerRetrieveItems
   @OrderID int
AS
```

```
SELECT BasketItem.*, BasketItemTotal =
  BasketItemQuantity * BasketItemPrice
FROM (BasketItem INNER JOIN Basket
  ON BasketItem.BasketID = Basket.BasketID)
INNER JOIN [Order]
  ON [Order].BasketID = Basket.BasketID
  WHERE [Order].OrderID = @OrderID
```

The procManagerRetrieveBasketByOrder stored procedure, shown in Listing 12.19, gets the information on the total charges for the order from the Basket table.

Listing 12.19   **procManagerRetrieveBasketByOrder Stored Procedure**

```
/*  Retrieve totals for an order

From .NET E-Commerce Programming
by Mike Gunderloy and Noel Jerke
Copyright 2002, Sybex Inc. All Rights Reserved. */
CREATE PROCEDURE procManagerRetrieveBasketByOrder
  @OrderID int
AS
  SELECT BasketSubtotal, BasketTotal,
    BasketShipping, BasketTax
    FROM Basket INNER JOIN [Order]
    ON [Order].BasketID = Basket.BasketID
  WHERE OrderID = @OrderID
```

After both BindMain and BindItemGrid have finished executing, the page will be displayed with all of the order information available. At this point, the user can perform several tasks:

- Edit item information in the DataGrid control
- Delete an item from the DataGrid control
- Edit other information on the Web Form and click the Submit button

We'll look at each of these tasks in turn.

Editing Item Information

Editing item information follows the same pattern that you already saw for editing tax and shipping information in Chapter 11, "Managing Taxes and Shipping." The DataGrid control contains a link labeled Edit, which puts the selected row into edit mode. When the row is in edit mode, there are links to update the database or to cancel the update. Listing 12.20 shows the code that's called by the Edit link. This code works by setting the EditItemIndex property for the grid to the number of the row that's passed into the procedure.

Listing 12.20   OrderDetails.aspx.vb dgItems_EditCommand Procedure

```vb
Private Sub dgItems_EditCommand(ByVal source As Object, _
 ByVal e As System.Web.UI.WebControls.DataGridCommandEventArgs) _
 Handles dgItems.EditCommand
    ' Show the selected row for editing
    dgItems.EditItemIndex = CInt(e.Item.ItemIndex)
    BindItemGrid()
End Sub
```

To cancel an edit, the code simply returns the EditItemIndex to its default value of –1 and calls the BindItemGrid method to redisplay the original data. Listing 12.21 shows the code for this procedure.

Listing 12.21   OrderDetails.aspx,vb dgItems_CancelCommand Procedure

```vb
Private Sub dgItems_CancelCommand(ByVal source As Object, _
 ByVal e As System.Web.UI.WebControls.DataGridCommandEventArgs) _
 Handles dgItems.CancelCommand
    ' Take the grid out of edit mode
    dgItems.EditItemIndex = -1
    BindItemGrid()
End Sub
```

Finally, if the user clicks the Update link, the code calls the UpdateCommand procedure. This procedure, shown in Listing 12.22, uses a stored procedure to write any changes back to the database.

Listing 12.22   OrderDetails.aspx.vb dgItems_UpdateCommand Procedure

```vb
Private Sub dgItems_UpdateCommand(ByVal source As Object, _
 ByVal e As System.Web.UI.WebControls.DataGridCommandEventArgs) _
 Handles dgItems.UpdateCommand
    ' Update the selected row in the database
    With cmdManagerUpdateItem
        .Parameters("@BasketItemID").Value = _
        dgItems.DataKeys(CInt(e.Item.ItemIndex))
        .Parameters("@ProductName").Value = _
        CType(e.Item.Cells(2).Controls(0), TextBox).Text
        .Parameters("@Size").Value = _
        CType(e.Item.Cells(3).Controls(0), TextBox).Text
        .Parameters("@Color").Value = _
        CType(e.Item.Cells(4).Controls(0), TextBox).Text
        .Parameters("@Quantity").Value = _
        CType(CType(e.Item.Cells(5).Controls(0), TextBox).Text, _
        Integer)
```

```
      .Parameters("@Price").Value = _
      CType(CType(e.Item.Cells(6).Controls(0), TextBox).Text, _
      Integer)
      cnn.Open()
      .ExecuteNonQuery()
      cnn.Close()
      dgItems.EditItemIndex = -1
    End With
    BindItemGrid()
End Sub
```

The procManagerUpdateItem stored procedure, shown in Listing 12.23, needs to do more than just update the appropriate row in the BasketItem table. That's because changing the quantity or price of an item will affect the charge for the entire order, which must be recalculated. All the calculations are embedded in the stored procedure.

Listing 12.23   **procManagerUpdateItem Stored Procedure**

```
/* Update a specified basket item

From .NET E-Commerce Programming
by Mike Gunderloy and Noel Jerke
Copyright 2002, Sybex Inc. All Rights Reserved. */
CREATE PROCEDURE procManagerUpdateItem
  @BasketItemID int,
  @ProductName varchar(255),
  @Size varchar(50),
  @Color varchar(50),
  @Quantity int,
  @Price money
AS
  DECLARE @BasketID int
  DECLARE @Subtotal money
  DECLARE @BasketQuantity money
  /* Save the basket ID */
  SELECT @BasketID = BasketID
    FROM BasketItem
    WHERE BasketItemID = @BasketItemID
  /* Update the item */
  UPDATE BasketItem
    SET BasketItemProductName = @ProductName,
    BasketItemSize = @Size,
    BasketItemColor = @Color,
    BasketItemQuantity = @Quantity,
    BasketItemPrice = @Price
    WHERE BasketItemID = @BasketItemID
  /* Update the Basket table */
  SELECT @BasketQuantity = SUM(BasketItemQuantity)
    FROM BasketItem
```

```
    WHERE BasketID = @BasketID
SELECT @Subtotal = SUM(BasketItemQuantity *
    BasketItemPrice)
    FROM BasketItem
    WHERE BasketID = @BasketID
UPDATE Basket
    SET BasketQuantity = @BasketQuantity,
    BasketSubtotal = @Subtotal
    WHERE BasketID = @BasketID
UPDATE Basket
    SET BasketTotal = BasketSubtotal + BasketTax
    + BasketShipping
    WHERE BasketID = @BasketID
```

Deleting an Item

To delete an item from the current order, the user clicks the Delete link in the DataGrid.
This calls the DeleteCommand procedure, shown in Listing 12.24.

Listing 12.24   OrderDetails.aspx.vb dgItems_DeleteCommand Procedure

```
Private Sub dgItems_DeleteCommand(ByVal source As Object,
 ByVal e As System.Web.UI.WebControls.DataGridCommandEventArgs) _
 Handles dgItems.DeleteCommand
    ' Delete the selected row from the database
    With cmdManagerDeleteItem
        .Parameters("@BasketItemID").Value = _
        dgItems.DataKeys(CInt(e.Item.ItemIndex))
        cnn.Open()
        .ExecuteNonQuery()
        cnn.Close()
        dgItems.EditItemIndex = -1
    End With
    BindItemGrid()
End Sub
```

This procedure uses the procManagerDeleteItem stored procedure to do its work. Because
deleting an item will always change the total for an order, this stored procedure (shown in
Listing 12.25) must also recalculate the charges for the basket.

Listing 12.25   procManagerDeleteItem Stored Procedure

```
/* Delete a specified basket item

From .NET E-Commerce Programming
by Mike Gunderloy and Noel Jerke
Copyright 2002, Sybex Inc. All Rights Reserved. */
```

```
CREATE PROCEDURE procManagerDeleteItem
  @BasketItemID int
AS
  DECLARE @BasketID int
  DECLARE @Subtotal money
  DECLARE @Quantity money
  /* Save the basket ID */
  SELECT @BasketID = BasketID
    FROM BasketItem
    WHERE BasketItemID = @BasketItemID
  /* Delete the item */
  DELETE FROM BasketItem
    WHERE BasketItemID = @BasketItemID
  /* Update the Basket table */
  SELECT @Quantity = SUM(BasketItemQuantity)
    FROM BasketItem
    WHERE BasketID = @BasketID
  SELECT @Subtotal = SUM(BasketItemQuantity *
    BasketItemPrice)
    FROM BasketItem
    WHERE BasketID = @BasketID
  UPDATE Basket
    SET BasketQuantity = @Quantity,
    BasketSubtotal = @Subtotal
    WHERE BasketID = @BasketID
  UPDATE Basket
    SET BasketTotal = BasketSubtotal + BasketTax
    + BasketShipping
    WHERE BasketID = @BasketID
```

NOTE   For simplicity's sake, we're ignoring any tax and shipping changes that can be caused by editing or deleting an item. To incorporate such changes, you could call the Web Service that we developed to calculate taxes and shipping fees. See Chapter 8, "Checking Out," for the details on this Web Service.

Saving Changes to Order Information

When the user clicks the Submit button at the bottom of the OrderDetail.aspx Web Form, the code takes the entire contents of the form (except for item information) and writes it all back to the appropriate database tables. Listing 12.26 shows the Visual Basic .NET code that manages this activity.

Listing 12.26   **OrderDetails.aspx.vb btnSubmit_Click Procedure**

```
Private Sub btnSubmit_Click(ByVal sender As System.Object, _
  ByVal e As System.EventArgs) Handles btnSubmit.Click
    cnn.Open()
```

```
' Update order
With cmdManagerUpdateOrder
    .Parameters("@OrderID").Value = _
    Session("OrderID")
    .Parameters("@OrderShipFirstName").Value = _
    txtShipFirstName.Text
    .Parameters("@OrderShipLastName").Value = _
    txtShipLastName.Text
    .Parameters("@OrderShipAddress").Value = _
    txtShipAddress.Text
    .Parameters("@OrderShipCity").Value = _
    txtShipCity.Text
    .Parameters("@OrderShipState").Value = _
    txtShipState.Text
    .Parameters("@OrderShipZipCode").Value = _
    txtShipZipCode.Text
    .Parameters("@OrderShipPhone").Value = _
    txtShipPhone.Text
    .Parameters("@OrderShipEmail").Value = _
    txtShipEmail.Text
    .Parameters("@OrderBillFirstName").Value = _
    txtBillFirstName.Text
    .Parameters("@OrderBillLastName").Value = _
    txtBillLastName.Text
    .Parameters("@OrderBillAddress").Value - _
    txtBillAddress.Text
    .Parameters("@OrderBillCity").Value = _
    txtBillCity.Text
    .Parameters("@OrderBillState").Value = _
    txtBillState.Text
    .Parameters("@OrderBillZipCode").Value = _
    txtBillZipCode.Text
    .Parameters("@OrderBillPhone").Value = _
    txtBillPhone.Text
    .Parameters("@OrderBillEmail").Value = _
    txtBillEmail.Text
    .ExecuteNonQuery()
End With

' Update payment info
With cmdManagerUpdatePayment
    .Parameters("@OrderID").Value = _
    Session("OrderID")
    .Parameters("@PaymentCardType").Value = _
    txtCardType.Text
    .Parameters("@PaymentCardNumber").Value = _
    txtCardNumber.Text
    .Parameters("@PaymentExpDate").Value = _
    txtCardExpirationDate.Text
    .Parameters("@PaymentCardName").Value = _
    txtCardName.Text
```

```
        .ExecuteNonQuery()
    End With

    ' Update status
    With cmdManagerUpdateStatus
        .Parameters("@OrderID").Value = _
        Session("OrderID")
        .Parameters("@OrderStatusStage").Value = _
        ddlOrderStatus.SelectedItem.Value
        .Parameters("@DateUpdate").Value = Now
        .ExecuteNonQuery()
    End With

    cnn.Close()
    BindMain()
End Sub
```

As you can see, the code doesn't make any attempt to determine which (if any) pieces of data were changed. It simply writes the entire contents of the form back to the database. This is much easier than trying to keep track of which controls on the form contain changed data; and with the small amount of information displayed on the form, this strategy doesn't impose any significant performance penalty.

The code calls three stored procedures to save the data. The first of these, procManagerUpdateOrder, is shown in Listing 12.27. It handles the task of making changes to the Order table.

Listing 12.27   **procManagerUpdateOrder Stored Procedure**

```
/* Update a specified order

From .NET E-Commerce Programming
by Mike Gunderloy and Noel Jerke
Copyright 2002, Sybex Inc. All Rights Reserved. */
CREATE PROCEDURE procManagerUpdateOrder
  @OrderID int,
  @OrderShipFirstName varchar(50),
  @OrderShipLastName varchar(50),
  @OrderShipAddress varchar(150),
  @OrderShipCity varchar(150),
  @OrderShipState varchar(50),
  @OrderShipZipCode varchar(15),
  @OrderShipPhone varchar(25),
  @OrderShipEmail varchar(100),
  @OrderBillFirstName varchar(50),
  @OrderBillLastName varchar(50),
  @OrderBillAddress varchar(150),
  @OrderBillCity varchar(150),
```

```
    @OrderBillState varchar(50),
    @OrderBillZipCode varchar(15),
    @OrderBillPhone varchar(25),
    @OrderBillEmail varchar(100)
AS
    UPDATE [Order]
    SET OrderShipFirstName = @OrderShipFirstName,
    OrderShipLastName = @OrderShipLastName,
    OrderShipAddress = @OrderShipAddress,
    OrderShipCity = @OrderShipCity,
    OrderShipState = @OrderShipState,
    OrderShipZipCode = @OrderShipZipCode,
    OrderShipPhone = @OrderShipPhone,
    OrderShipEmail = @OrderShipEmail,
    OrderBillFirstName = @OrderBillFirstName,
    OrderBillLastName = @OrderBillLastName,
    OrderBillAddress = @OrderBillAddress,
    OrderBillCity = @OrderBillCity,
    OrderBillState = @OrderBillState,
    OrderBillZipCode = @OrderBillZipCode,
    OrderBillPhone = @OrderBillPhone,
    OrderBillEmail = @OrderBillEmail
    WHERE OrderID = @OrderID
```

NOTE   This page allows the user to enter any data that they like. Unlike the pages in the CDStore application, where we validate all data to ensure that it's reasonable, in this application we're assuming that the user knows what they're doing. The user can type in anything for product name, price, or any other field. Depending on the sophistication of our workforce, we might need to add validation to this page.

The second stored procedure, procManagerUpdatePayment, writes data back to the Payment table. Listing 12.28 shows this stored procedure.

Listing 12.28   procManagerUpdatePayment Stored Procedure

```
/* Update a specified payment

From .NET E-Commerce Programming
by Mike Gunderloy and Noel Jerke
Copyright 2002, Sybex Inc. All Rights Reserved. */
CREATE PROCEDURE procManagerUpdatePayment
    @OrderID int,
    @PaymentCardType varchar(50),
    @PaymentCardNumber varchar(30),
    @PaymentExpDate varchar(25),
    @PaymentCardName varchar(150)
AS
```

```
UPDATE Payment
SET PaymentCardType = @PaymentCardType,
PaymentCardNumber = @PaymentCardNumber,
PaymentExpDate = @PaymentExpDate,
PaymentCardName = @PaymentCardName
WHERE OrderID = @OrderID
```

The last stored procedure called from this piece of code is procManagerUpdateStatus. This stored procedure, shown in Listing 12.29, updates the OrderStatus table. It contains internal logic to update multiple columns if necessary. For example, when the status is changed to indicate that the order has been shipped, the stored procedure automatically updates the column that holds the shipping date.

Listing 12.29   **procManagerUpdateStatus Stored Procedure**

```
/* Update a specified order status

From .NET E-Commerce Programming
by Mike Gunderloy and Noel Jerke
Copyright 2002, Sybex Inc. All Rights Reserved. */
CREATE PROCEDURE procManagerUpdateStatus
  @OrderID int,
  @OrderStatusStage int,
  @DateUpdate datetime
AS
  IF @OrderStatusStage = 0
    UPDATE OrderStatus
    SET OrderStatusStage = 0
    WHERE OrderID = @OrderID
  ELSE
    IF @OrderStatusStage = 1
      UPDATE OrderStatus
      SET OrderStatusStage = 1,
      OrderStatusDateFulfilled = @DateUpdate
      WHERE OrderID = @OrderID
    ELSE
      IF @OrderStatusStage = 2
        UPDATE OrderStatus
        SET OrderStatusStage = 2,
        OrderStatusDateShipped = @DateUpdate
        WHERE OrderID = @OrderID
      ELSE
        IF @OrderStatusStage = 3
          UPDATE OrderStatus
          SET OrderStatusStage = 3
          WHERE OrderID = @OrderID
```

That's all the code that we need to update orders. Figure 12.6 shows a full, displayed order detail. Note that all the key fields are set up for editing.

FIGURE 12.6:

Order detail

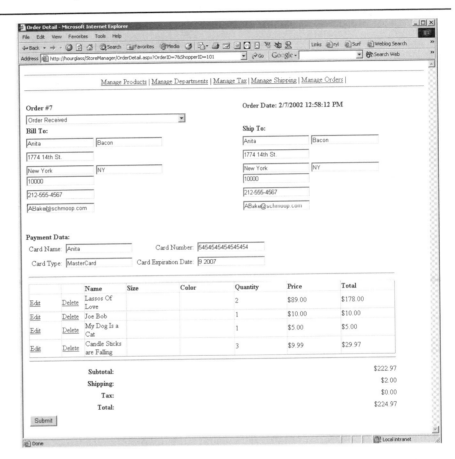

To test our edit capability, let's change the order quantity for the "Joe Bob" CD, as shown in Figure 12.7. This will have a trickle-down effect and force an update of the subtotal and total for the order.

FIGURE 12.7:

Changing an order
quantity

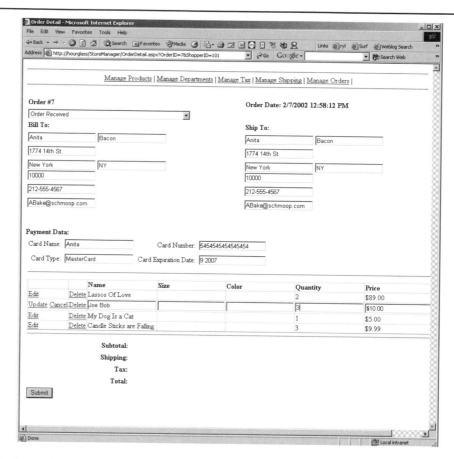

Figure 12.8 shows the updated order detail that you'll see after clicking the Update link. Note that all the calculated columns have been updated appropriately.

FIGURE 12.8:

Updated order

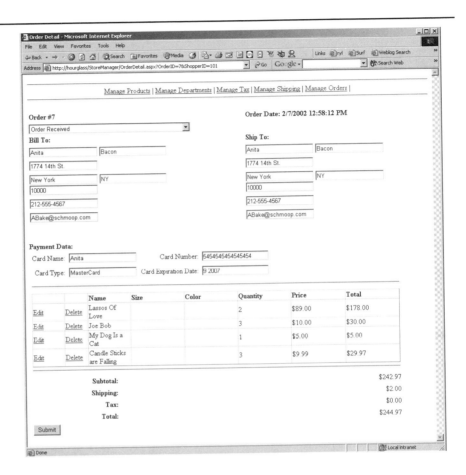

Summary

That's the last of the code in our StoreManager application. Of course, we could add many more features to this application to provide complete store management. In a real business, we would probably need to build links between this application and other applications that handle accounting, inventory, and shipping tasks.

In Part IV, "Promotions," we're going to develop code that will provide different promotional tools on the website. Our goal will be to entice shoppers to spend additional money by offering them attractive prices or suggestions.

Part IV

Promotions

CHAPTER 13

Up-Sell and Cross-Sell

- Designing the Related Products

- Building the Relationships

- Managing Related Products

Now that we have our basic store and management functions in place, we are ready to work on some new promotional functions for the store. In this chapter, we'll build *up-sell* and *cross-sell* functions. Up-selling is giving the shopper the option of purchasing a more expensive product than the one they initially chose, and cross-selling is giving the shopper the option of purchasing related products. By offering these options, we'll make it easy for our shoppers to spend more money in our store!

We need to provide ways for shoppers to find similar or upgraded products. In this chapter, we'll build these features in the user interface and set up the product relationships through an expanded management interface.

Designing the Related Products

Two types of relationships occur in our database. The first type, the cross-sell, relates complementary products. Examples would be a promotional T-shirt that goes with a particular CD, or a second CD in the genre that the shopper has already chosen.

The second type of relationship is an up-sell to a better or more full-featured product (and, of course, a more expensive one) that would replace the product that the shopper originally planned to purchase. For example, we could suggest that the shopper buy a premium T-shirt or an autographed CD rather than the basic models.

To test these functions, we'll first insert several relationships so that we can see the results of our changes to the user interface. Listing 13.1 shows three SQL INSERT statements.

As you'll recall from Chapter 3, "E-Commerce Database Design," the RelatedProduct table consists of three columns:

ProductAID The ProductID of the product that the shopper has already decided to purchase.

ProductBID The ProductID of the product that we want to suggest to the shopper.

RelationType An integer that defines the type of relationship. A RelationType value of 1 indicates a cross-sell product, while a RelationType value of 2 indicates an up-sell product.

We might also offer both cross-sells and up-sells for the same product, or more than one cross-sell or up-sell for a single product. We can accomplish these goals by adding more rows to the RelatedProduct table.

Listing 13.1 **SQL INSERT Code for Related Products**

```
/* T-shirts are cross-sells for each other */
INSERT INTO RelatedProduct
```

```
      (ProductAID, ProductBID, RelationType)
      VALUES (9, 10, 1)
INSERT INTO RelatedProduct
      (ProductAID, ProductBID, RelationType)
      VALUES (10, 9, 1)
/* Up-sell from Circle Sax to Alley Jazz */
INSERT INTO RelatedProduct
      (ProductAID, ProductBID, RelationType)
      VALUES (4, 3, 2)
```

NOTE   These SQL statements are available in the file `RelatedProducts.sql` on this book's companion CD.

Building the Relationships

We are going to build the interface for the relationships in two places. The first will be on the product page. We'll list cross-sell products on that page so that shoppers see related products as they're browsing through the store. This will provide more navigation options so that the shopper can more easily find products that they're interested in.

The second relationship will appear in the shopping basket. When the shopper puts a product into their basket, and the product has an up-sell associated with it, the basket page will suggest that the shopper try the more expensive product. The basket will show a link to the up-sell product. When the shopper clicks that link, we'll display the details of the product. If the shopper then decides to order the up-sell product, it will be inserted into the basket in place of the original product. By default, we'll add the same quantity of the new product as the quantity that the shopper had selected for the original product.

We'll look at the code for these two options separately, starting with the cross-sell functionality.

NOTE   Because this section of the book involves further modification of pages that we developed in earlier chapters, we've provided new versions of the sample projects. You'll find the files that we discuss in this chapter in the CDStore2 and StoreManager2 applications.

Related Cross-Sell Products

To show related cross-sell products, we've added additional code to the Product.aspx page. This code uses a new stored procedure, procRetrieveCrossSellProducts, to get the related products (if any) for the product being displayed. If there are any related products, we'll show a DataList control on the page and populate it with the related products.

NOTE   The code listings in this chapter show only the new sections of the pages that we've modified. You can refer to the earlier chapters, or to the sample files, to see the complete files.

Listing 13.2 shows the changes to the Product.aspx Web Form. The additional controls are added at the bottom of the form on this page. Note that both controls have their Visible attribute set to False, so that by default they won't be displayed. In fact, Web Form controls with their Visible attribute set to False won't even be sent to the client browser.

Listing 13.2   Changes to Product.aspx

```
<P>
    <asp:Label id="lblRelatedProducts" runat="server" Visible="False"
      Font-Size="Medium">Related Products</asp:Label>
</P>
<P>
    <asp:DataList id="dlRelated" runat="server" Visible="False">
        <ItemTemplate>
            <a href='Product.aspx?idProduct=
             <%# DataBinder.Eval(Container.DataItem, "ProductID") %>'>
             <%# DataBinder.Eval(Container.DataItem, "ProductName") %>
            </a>
            <br>
        </ItemTemplate>
    </asp:DataList>
</P>
```

Of course, there's additional code to handle populating these controls. This code, shown in Listing 13.3, is in the Page_Load procedure for the page.

Listing 13.3   Changes to Product.aspx.vb Page_Load Procedure

```
' Set up the cross-sell products (if any)
cmdRetrieveCrossSellProducts.Parameters("@ProductID").Value = _
  Request("idProduct")
Dim dsCrossSell As New DataSet()
Dim daCrossSell As New SqlDataAdapter()
daCrossSell.SelectCommand = cmdRetrieveCrossSellProducts
daCrossSell.Fill(dsCrossSell, "CrossSell")
' Only show the cross-sell section if there
' are cross-sell products
If dsCrossSell.Tables("CrossSell").Rows.Count > 0 Then
    lblRelatedProducts.Visible = True
    dlRelated.Visible = True
    dlRelated.DataSource = dsCrossSell
    dlRelated.DataMember = "CrossSell"
End If
```

Most of that code should be very familiar by now, because it follows the same pattern we've used many times already to retrieve data from the database:

1. Set up a SqlCommand object to represent a stored procedure.

2. Use parameters of the stored procedure to tell the database precisely what data we want to retrieve.

3. Create a SqlDataAdapter object and set its SelectCommand property to the SqlCommand object.

4. Fill a DataSet from the SqlDataAdapter object.

5. Bind the DataSet to a control on the user interface.

The one new twist in this procedure is the check of the number of rows of data that the stored procedure returned. Many products in our database won't have any cross-sell options at all. In that case, we won't even bother to show the Label and DataList controls that hold cross-sell products.

Listing 13.4 shows the stored procedure, procRetrieveCrossSellProducts, that's used in this section of code.

Listing 13.4   procRetrieveCrossSellProducts Stored Procedure

```
/*  Retrieve cross-sell products for a
    specified product

From .NET E-Commerce Programming
by Mike Gunderloy and Noel Jerke
Copyright 2002, Sybex Inc. All Rights Reserved. */
CREATE PROCEDURE procRetrieveCrossSellProducts
  @ProductID int
AS
/* Note that a RelationType of 1 corresponds
   to a cross-sell */
SELECT Product.ProductID, Product.ProductName
  FROM Product INNER JOIN RelatedProduct
  ON Product.ProductID = RelatedProduct.ProductBID
  WHERE RelatedProduct.ProductAID = @ProductID
    AND RelationType = 1
```

If you look again at Listing 13.2, you'll see that the DataList provides links to the Product.aspx page. When the shopper chooses to follow one of these links, the situation is just the same as if the shopper had gotten to that page any other way. We don't need to write any other code to handle cross-sell products beyond simply making them available.

Related Up-Sell Products

Next, we'll work on the up-sell process. The first part of this is to display up-sell products in the shopper's basket. You'll recall that the Basket.aspx page uses a Repeater control to display the items in the basket. Rather than abandon this interface, we'll add rows to the Repeater to display any related up-sell products. This will require a substantially more complicated stored procedure in the SQL Server database; we'll actually build some HTML code in the result of the stored procedure. This will allow us to use the simplest possible code in the page itself.

Listing 13.5 shows the additional HTML code in the Basket.aspx file. We've included a few tags that didn't change in the listing so that you can see how this piece fits into the Repeater control.

NOTE   Ellipses in the listing show where we've omitted additional code.

Listing 13.5   **Changes to Basket.aspx**

```
<asp:repeater id="rptBasket" runat="server">
...
    <ItemTemplate>
        <tr>
...
        </tr>
        <tr>
        <td colspan="7"
         height='<%# DataBinder.Eval(Container.DataItem, "Height") %>'>
         <%# DataBinder.Eval(Container.DataItem, "Message") %></td>
        </tr>
</ItemTemplate>
...
</asp:repeater>
```

The HTML adds a new row to the basket for every item, whether there is an up-sell for that product or not. But note that we've actually used a databound value for the height property of the <td> tag that defines the row. In the stored procedure, we'll set this value to zero for rows where there is no up-sell product. This will have the effect of hiding the extra row when it's not needed. When the row is displayed, the stored procedure will also supply an HTML string in its Message column. It's this value that will link the basket to a page displaying the up-sell product.

TIP   You might also want to add a column to the RelatedProduct table to hold customized supporting text that promotes the particular up-sell. As you'll see shortly, we chose to use a generic message that's the same in all cases.

The only change to the code-behind file for this page is the inclusion of a new stored procedure for filling the Repeater control. The original version of this page used a SqlCommand object named cmdRetrieveBasket. Listing 13.6 shows the portion of the code where that object has been replaced by a new version.

Listing 13.6   Changes to Basket.aspx.vb UpdatePage Procedure

```
' Get the current basket contents
cmdRetrieveBasketWithUpsell.Parameters("@BasketID").Value = _
  Session("idBasket")
Dim dsBasket As New DataSet()
Dim daBasket As New SqlDataAdapter()
daBasket.SelectCommand = cmdRetrieveBasketWithUpsell
daBasket.Fill(dsBasket, "BasketItems")
rptBasket.DataSource = dsBasket
rptBasket.DataMember = "BasketItems"
' And bind it all to the user interface
DataBind()
```

It's the stored procedure underlying this code, procRetrieveBasketWithUpsell, that does the additional work of finding up-sell products and building appropriate links. Listing 13.7 shows this stored procedure.

Listing 13.7   procRetrieveBasketWithUpsell Stored Procedure

```
/* Retrieve the contents of a specified basket by BasketID.
   Also fetch any up-sell products for products in the basket

From .NET E-Commerce Programming
by Mike Gunderloy and Noel Jerke
Copyright 2002, Sybex Inc. All Rights Reserved. */
CREATE PROCEDURE procRetrieveBasketWithUpsell
  @BasketID int
AS
  SELECT BasketItem.ProductID, BasketItemProductName,
    BasketItemColor, BasketItemSize,
    BasketItemPrice, BasketItemQuantity, BasketItemID,
    BasketItemPrice * BasketItemQuantity AS BasketItemTotal,
    'Why not try buying ' +
    '<a href="UpgradeProduct.aspx?Quantity=' +
    CAST(BasketItemQuantity AS varchar(5)) + '&BasketItemID=' +
    CAST(BasketItemID AS varchar(5)) + '&ProductID=' +
    CAST(Product.ProductID AS varchar(5)) + '">' +
    ProductName + '</a> instead?' AS Message,
    ISNULL(RelationType*12, 0) AS Height
  FROM BasketItem LEFT OUTER JOIN
    (RelatedProduct INNER JOIN Product
    ON RelatedProduct.ProductBID = Product.ProductID)
```

```
    ON BasketItem.ProductID = RelatedProduct.ProductAID
    WHERE BasketID = @BasketID
      AND (RelationType = 2 OR RelationType IS NULL)
```

Let's look at the code in this stored procedure one piece at a time. The first piece passes in the BasketID of the shopper's basket and then selects a number of columns to be displayed:

```
CREATE PROCEDURE procRetrieveBasketWithUpsell
  @BasketID int
AS
  SELECT BasketItem.ProductID, BasketItemProductName,
    BasketItemColor, BasketItemSize,
    BasketItemPrice, BasketItemQuantity, BasketItemID,
    BasketItemPrice * BasketItemQuantity AS BasketItemTotal,
```

The next portion of the stored procedure builds up a calculated column named Message:

```
'Why not try buying ' +
'<a href="UpgradeProduct.aspx?Quantity=' +
CAST(BasketItemQuantity AS varchar(5)) + '&BasketItemID=' +
CAST(BasketItemID AS varchar(5)) + '&ProductID=' +
CAST(Product.ProductID AS varchar(5)) + '">' +
ProductName + '</a> instead?' AS Message,
```

The Message column contains the HTML code for a hyperlink to the UpgradeProduct .aspx web page, together with query parameters to hold the current quantity and BasketItemID, and the ProductID of the related product. This is the HTML that will be displayed in the shopper's basket when an up-sell product is available.

The next portion of the stored procedure creates a calculated column named Height:

```
ISNULL(RelationType*12, 0) AS Height
```

The SQL Server ISNULL function takes two arguments. If the first argument is not Null, the value of the function is the value of the first argument. If the first argument is Null, the value of the function is the value of the second argument. In the particular case at hand, the RelationType will be either 2 (if there is an up-sell product) or Null (if there is no such product). If you trace through the logic, you'll see that Height will be set to either 24 (a reasonable height for a row of data on the web page) or 0, depending on whether there is an up-sell product.

The FROM clause of the stored procedure defines the tables that store the data to be retrieved:

```
FROM BasketItem LEFT OUTER JOIN
  (RelatedProduct INNER JOIN Product
   ON RelatedProduct.ProductBID = Product.ProductID)
  ON BasketItem.ProductID = RelatedProduct.ProductAID
```

Note the use of the LEFT OUTER JOIN between the BasketItem table and the other tables. This ensures that the results of the stored procedure will include one row for every row in the BasketItem table, whether there is matching data on related products or not. Finally, the stored procedure closes by limiting the results to items in the current basket, and related items that are up-sells (instead of cross-sells):

```
WHERE BasketID = @BasketID
  AND (RelationType = 2 OR RelationType IS NULL)
```

When the shopper clicks an up-sell link, they are transferred to the UpgradeProduct.aspx page. Although this page is very similar to the regular Product.aspx page, it uses the Add-UpgradeItem.aspx page instead of the AddItem.aspx page to handle orders. It also defaults to displaying the quantity that the shopper has already selected for the original product instead of always displaying 1, as the Product.aspx page does.

Listing 13.8 shows the HTML code for the UpgradeProduct.aspx page.

Listing 13.8   **UpgradeProduct.aspx**

```
<%@ Page Language="vb" AutoEventWireup="false"
 Codebehind="UpgradeProduct.aspx.vb"
 Inherits="CDStore2.UpgradeProduct" %>
<!DOCTYPE HTML PUBLIC "-//W3C//DTD HTML 4.0 Transitional//EN">
<HTML>
    <HEAD>
        <TITLE>Product Detail</TITLE>
    </HEAD>
    <!-- UpgradeProduct.aspx -
     Details and order form for an up-sell product -->
    <meta name="GENERATOR" content="Microsoft Visual Studio.NET 7.0">
    <meta name="CODE_LANGUAGE" content="Visual Basic 7.0">
    <meta name="vs_defaultClientScript" content="JavaScript">
    <meta name="vs_targetSchema"
     content="http://schemas.microsoft.com/intellisense/ie5">
    <!-- #Include File="Header.inc" -->
    <form id="Form1" method="post" runat="server">
        <P>
            <asp:datalist id="dlProduct" runat="server"
             BorderColor="Tan" ForeColor="Black"
             BackColor="LightGoldenrodYellow" CellPadding="2"
             BorderWidth="1px">
                <SelectedItemStyle ForeColor="GhostWhite"
                 BackColor="DarkSlateBlue"></SelectedItemStyle>
                <AlternatingItemStyle BackColor="PaleGoldenrod">
                </AlternatingItemStyle>
                <ItemTemplate>
                    <table>
                        <tr>
                            <td><img src='images/products/
                            <%# DataBinder.Eval(Container.DataItem,
```

```
                    "ProductImage") %>'></td>
                <td valign="top">
                    <center><b><font size="5">
                    <%# DataBinder.Eval(Container.DataItem,
                     "ProductName") %></font></b></center>
                    <br>
                    <br>
                    <%# DataBinder.Eval(Container.DataItem,
                     "ProductDescription") %>
                    <br>
                    <br>
                </td>
            </tr>
            <tr>
                <td align="center"><b>Price:
                        <%# DataBinder.Eval(
                        Container.DataItem, "ProductPrice",
                        "{0:c}") %>
                    </b>
                </td>
                <td align="center">
                    <b>Quantity: <input type="text"
                    value='<%# DataBinder.Eval(
                    Container.DataItem, "Quantity") %>'
                    name="quantity" size="2"></b>
                    <input type="hidden" value='
                    <%# DataBinder.Eval(Container.DataItem,
                     "ProductID") %>' name="ProductID">
                    <input type="hidden" value='
                    <%# DataBinder.Eval(Container.DataItem,
                     "ProductName") %>' name="ProductName">
                    <input type="hidden" value='
                    <%# DataBinder.Eval(Container.DataItem,
                     "ProductPrice") %>' name="ProductPrice">
                </td>
            </tr>
        </table>
    </ItemTemplate>
    <FooterStyle BackColor="Tan"></FooterStyle>
    <HeaderStyle Font-Bold="True" BackColor="Tan">
    </HeaderStyle>
</asp:datalist></P>
<P>
    <asp:Label id="lblColor" runat="server">Color:
    </asp:Label>
    <asp:DropDownList id="ddlColor" runat="server">
    </asp:DropDownList>
    <asp:Label id="lblSize" runat="server">Size:
    </asp:Label>
    <asp:DropDownList id="ddlSize" runat="server">
    </asp:DropDownList></P>
```

```
<P></P>
<P></P>
<P>
    <INPUT type="submit" value="Order" name="Submit">
</P>
<P>
    <asp:Label id="lblRelatedProducts" runat="server"
    Visible="False" Font-Size="Medium">Related Products
    </asp:Label></P>
<P>
    <asp:DataList id="dlRelated" runat="server" Visible="False">
        <ItemTemplate>
            <a href='Product.aspx?idProduct=
             <%# DataBinder.Eval(Container.DataItem,
              "ProductID") %>'>
                <%# DataBinder.Eval(Container.DataItem,
                 "ProductName") %>
            </a>
            <br>
        </ItemTemplate>
    </asp:DataList></P>
</form>
<!-- #Include File="Footer.inc" -->
</HTML>
```

Because this form is so similar to the Product.aspx page, the code behind is very similar as well. Listing 13.9 shows the Page_Load procedure for this page.

Listing 13.9   AddUpgradeItem.aspx.vb Page_Load Procedure

```
Private Sub Page_Load(ByVal sender As System.Object, _
  ByVal e As System.EventArgs) Handles MyBase.Load
    Dim strError As String
    If Not IsPostBack Then
        SessionCheck(Session, Request.Cookies("WWCD"), strError)
        ' Set up the Product data
        cmdRetrieveProduct.Parameters("@idProduct").Value = _
         Request("ProductID")
        Dim dsProduct As New DataSet()
        Dim daProduct As New SqlDataAdapter()
        daProduct.SelectCommand = cmdRetrieveProduct
        daProduct.Fill(dsProduct, "Product")
        dsProduct.Tables("Product").Columns.Add("Quantity", _
         System.Type.GetType("System.Decimal"))
        dsProduct.Tables("Product").Rows(0)("Quantity") _
         = Request("Quantity")
        dlProduct.DataSource = dsProduct
        dlProduct.DataMember = "Product"
        ' Set up the color data
        cmdColor.Parameters("@idProduct").Value = _
```

```
      Request("ProductID")
Dim dsColor As New DataSet()
Dim daColor As New SqlDataAdapter()
daColor.SelectCommand = cmdColor
daColor.Fill(dsColor, "Color")
' Set up the size data
cmdSize.Parameters("@idProduct").Value = _
   Request("ProductID")
Dim dsSize As New DataSet()
Dim daSize As New SqlDataAdapter()
daSize.SelectCommand = cmdSize
daSize.Fill(dsSize, "Size")
' Adjust control properties
If dsColor.Tables("Color").Rows.Count = 0 Then
    ddlColor.Visible = False
    lblColor.Visible = False
Else
    ddlColor.DataSource = dsColor
    ddlColor.DataMember = "Color"
    ddlColor.DataTextField = "AttributeName"
    ddlColor.DataValueField = "AttributeName"
End If
If dsSize.Tables("Size").Rows.Count = 0 Then
    ddlSize.Visible = False
    lblSize.Visible = False
Else
    ddlSize.DataSource = dsSize
    ddlSize.DataMember = "Size"
    ddlSize.DataTextField = "AttributeName"
    ddlSize.DataValueField = "AttributeName"
End If
' Set up the cross-sell products (if any)
cmdRetrieveCrossSellProducts.Parameters("@ProductID").Value = _
   Request("ProductID")
Dim dsCrossSell As New DataSet()
Dim daCrossSell As New SqlDataAdapter()
daCrossSell.SelectCommand = cmdRetrieveCrossSellProducts
daCrossSell.Fill(dsCrossSell, "CrossSell")
' Only show the cross-sell section if there
' are cross-sell products
If dsCrossSell.Tables("CrossSell").Rows.Count > 0 Then
    lblRelatedProducts.Visible = True
    dlRelated.Visible = True
    dlRelated.DataSource = dsCrossSell
    dlRelated.DataMember = "CrossSell"
End If
' Save the information we need to handle the up-sell
Session("BasketItemID") = Request("BasketItemID")
Session("Quantity") = Request("Quantity")
' Bind the data to the user interface
DataBind()
Else
    ' This code is called in response to the user
    ' clicking the Order button. Place some info in
```

```
        ' Session variables and transfer to the AddUpgradeItem page
        Session("Quantity") = Request.Form("Quantity")
        Session("ProductName") = Request.Form("ProductName")
        Session("ProductPrice") = Request.Form("ProductPrice")
        Session("ProductID") = Request("ProductID")
        If Not ddlSize.SelectedItem Is Nothing Then
            Session("Size") = ddlSize.SelectedItem.Value
        End If
        If Not ddlColor.SelectedItem Is Nothing Then
            Session("Color") = ddlColor.SelectedItem.Value
        End If
        Server.Transfer("AddUpgradeItem.aspx")
    End If
End Sub
```

The interesting new section of this procedure adds a Quantity column to the data that's bound to the page for display:

```
dsProduct.Tables("Product").Columns.Add("Quantity", _
  System.Type.GetType("System.Decimal"))
dsProduct.Tables("Product").Rows(0)("Quantity") _
  = Request("Quantity")
```

When this code is executed, the DataSet has already been filled with the Product table. Despite this, we can still add another column without affecting any of the existing data. We also know that there's only one row of data, because this page displays only a single product. So, after adding the new column, we can set the quantity of the first row of the DataSet to the quantity that was passed in as part of the request for the page, and this will be available to the form for display.

The procedure also saves the other parameters (the BasketItemID and the Quantity) that are passed in from the Basket.aspx page to session variables so that they'll be available to the next page in the sequence.

If the shopper clicks the Order button for the up-sell product, the code uses the Server.Transfer method to load the AddUpgradeItem.aspx page. Listing 13.10 shows the HTML code for this page, which has no user interface. As you'll see in Listing 13.11, this page updates the database and then loads another web page immediately.

Listing 13.10   **AddUpgradeItem.aspx**

```
<%@ Page Language="vb" AutoEventWireup="false"
 Codebehind="AddUpgradeItem.aspx.vb" Inherits="CDStore2.AddUpgradeItem"%>
<!DOCTYPE HTML PUBLIC "-//W3C//DTD HTML 4.0 Transitional//EN">
<HTML>
    <HEAD>
        <title>AddUpgradeItem</title>
        <meta name="GENERATOR" content="Microsoft Visual Studio.NET 7.0">
        <meta name="CODE_LANGUAGE" content="Visual Basic 7.0">
        <meta name="vs_defaultClientScript" content="JavaScript">
```

```
        <meta name="vs_targetSchema"
        content="http://schemas.microsoft.com/intellisense/ie5">
    </HEAD>
    <body>
        <form id="Form1" method="post" runat="server">
        </form>
    </body>
</HTML>
```

The Visual Basic .NET code for this page uses a pair of stored procedures to update the items in the basket, as shown in Listing 13.11.

Listing 13.11   AddUpgradeItem.aspx.vb Page_Load Procedure

```
Private Sub Page_Load(ByVal sender As System.Object, _
  ByVal e As System.EventArgs) Handles MyBase.Load
    ' Check for a valid session ID
    Dim strError As String
    SessionCheck(Session, Request.Cookies("WWCD"), strError)

    ' Check to make sure the user supplied a quantity
    If Session("Quantity") = 0 Then
        ' No quantity? Go back where we came from
        Server.Transfer("UpgradeProduct.aspx?ProductID=" & _
        Session("ProductID") & "&BasketItemID=" & _
        Session("BasketID") & "&Quantity=" & _
        Session("Quantity"))
    Else
        ' Insert or update the basket item
        cmdInsertBasketItem.Parameters("@BasketID").Value = _
        Session("idBasket")
        cmdInsertBasketItem.Parameters("@Quantity").Value = _
        Session("Quantity")
        cmdInsertBasketItem.Parameters("@Price").Value = _
        Session("ProductPrice")
        cmdInsertBasketItem.Parameters("@ProductName").Value = _
        Session("ProductName")
        cmdInsertBasketItem.Parameters("@ProductID").Value = _
        Session("ProductID")
        cmdInsertBasketItem.Parameters("@Size").Value = _
        Session("Size")
        cmdInsertBasketItem.Parameters("@Color").Value = _
        Session("Color")
        cnn.Open()
        cmdInsertBasketItem.ExecuteNonQuery()
        cnn.Close()
        ' Remove the item that they're replacing
        cmdRemoveBasketItem.Parameters("@BasketID").Value = _
        Session("idBasket")
        cmdRemoveBasketItem.Parameters("@BasketItemID").Value = _
```

```
        Session("BasketItemID")
        cnn.Open()
        cmdRemoveBasketItem.ExecuteNonQuery()
        cnn.Close()
        ' And take the user to their basket
        Server.Transfer("Basket.aspx")
    End If
End Sub
```

We could have written a single stored procedure to remove the old item and insert the new one, but the database already contains stored procedures to perform the two halves of that process. By reusing the existing procInsertBasketItem and procRemoveBasketItem stored procedures, we can cut down on the number of stored procedures that we need to maintain.

TIP   You'll find the definitions of those two procedures in Chapter 7, "Making a Basket Case."

That's it for the changes that the shopper will see directly. Now let's take a look at the interface in action. Figure 13.1 shows the product page for our excellent "T-Shirt Rip." Because this product has a cross-sell product available, a link appears at the bottom of the page, enticing the shopper to explore further.

FIGURE 13.1:

Product with a cross-sell

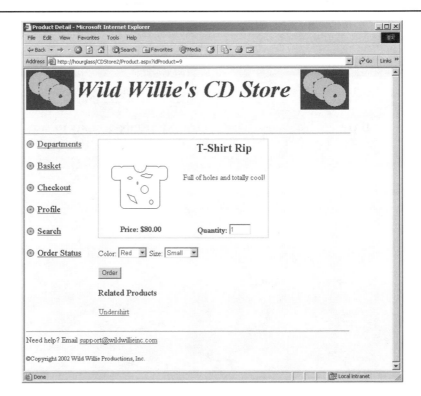

Figure 13.2 shows the shopping basket with an up-sell message. To get this message, add the "Circle Sax" product to the basket.

FIGURE 13.2:

Basket with an up-sell

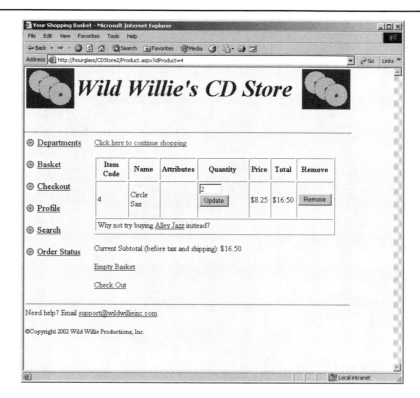

If you click the up-sell link, you'll get the opportunity to buy "Alley Jazz" instead of "Circle Sax." Figure 13.3 shows the result of agreeing to the up-sell.

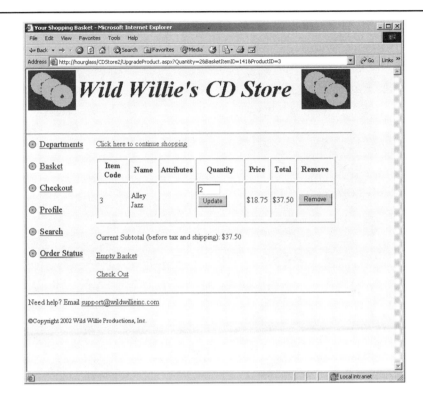

Updated basket

Managing Related Products

Now that we have an interface to display related products to the shopper, we need a way to manage the relationships. There are a couple of different approaches that we could take to accomplish this.

We could provide a separate page in the StoreManager application to manage related products. That page would allow selecting two products and setting the relationship type between them. This approach would allow us to manage all the relationships in the database in one place.

We could also provide relationship management at the product level and allow many different assignments per product. This is the approach we'll take in the StoreManager2 application. Of course, we could also offer both approaches in a single application.

To implement this management tool, we'll need to modify the `ManageProduct.aspx` page. We'll add one more section at the bottom of the page to handle adding, updating, and deleting relationships between products. We'll insert the code for dealing with these operations into the existing page.

Listing 13.12 shows the additional HTML code that we've added to the `ManageProduct` `.aspx` page to handle related products.

Listing 13.12   Changes to ManageProduct.aspx

```
<H3>Relationships for this product:</H3>
<P><asp:datagrid id="dgRelatedProducts" runat="server" ForeColor="Black"
 GridLines="Vertical" CellPadding="4" BackColor="White"
   BorderWidth="1px" BorderStyle="None" BorderColor="#DEDFDE"
     AutoGenerateColumns="False">
        <SelectedItemStyle Font-Bold="True" ForeColor="White"
         BackColor="#CE5D5A"></SelectedItemStyle>
        <AlternatingItemStyle BackColor="White"></AlternatingItemStyle>
        <ItemStyle BackColor="#F7F7DE"></ItemStyle>
        <HeaderStyle Font-Bold="True" ForeColor="White"
         BackColor="#6B696B"></HeaderStyle>
        <FooterStyle BackColor="#CCCC99"></FooterStyle>
        <Columns>
            <asp:BoundColumn Visible="False" DataField="ProductID"
             HeaderText="ProductID"></asp:BoundColumn>
            <asp:BoundColumn DataField="ProductName"
             HeaderText="Product"></asp:BoundColumn>
            <asp:BoundColumn DataField="RelType"
             HeaderText="Type"></asp:BoundColumn>
            <asp:ButtonColumn Text="Delete"
             CommandName="Delete"></asp:ButtonColumn>
        </Columns>
        <PagerStyle HorizontalAlign="Right" ForeColor="Black"
         BackColor="#F7F7DE" Mode="NumericPages"></PagerStyle>
    </asp:datagrid></P>
<P>Select a Related Product to add:</P>
<P>
    <asp:RadioButtonList id="rblRelationType" runat="server"
     RepeatColumns="2">
        <asp:ListItem Value="1" Selected="True">Cross-sell</asp:ListItem>
        <asp:ListItem Value="2">Up-Sell</asp:ListItem>
    </asp:RadioButtonList></P>
<P><asp:dropdownlist id="ddlAddRelatedProduct" runat="server"
 AutoPostBack="True"></asp:dropdownlist></P>
```

We've also made several changes in the code for this Web Form. First, in the Page_Load procedure, we need to retrieve and display the related products. Listing 13.13 shows the code for this task.

Listing 13.13   **Changes to ManageProduct.aspx.vb**

```
' Get the list of related products for this product
cmdManagerRetrieveRelatedProducts.Parameters("@ProductID").Value = _
  Session("ProductID")
dr = cmdManagerRetrieveRelatedProducts.ExecuteReader
dgRelatedProducts.DataSource = dr
dgRelatedProducts.DataBind()
dr.Close()
```

This code uses the procManagerRetrieveRelatedProducts stored procedure, shown in Listing 13.14, to retrieve all existing relationships for the product that the user is working with.

Listing 13.14   **procManagerRetrieveRelatedProducts Stored Procedure**

```
/*  Retrieve all related products for a
    specified product

From .NET E-Commerce Programming
by Mike Gunderloy and Noel Jerke
Copyright 2002, Sybex Inc. All Rights Reserved. */
CREATE PROCEDURE procManagerRetrieveRelatedProducts
  @ProductID int
AS
SELECT Product.ProductID, Product.ProductName,
  CASE RelationType
    WHEN 1 THEN 'Cross-sell'
    WHEN 2 THEN 'Up-sell'
  END AS RelType
  FROM Product INNER JOIN RelatedProduct
  ON Product.ProductID = RelatedProduct.ProductBID
  WHERE RelatedProduct.ProductAID = @ProductID
```

The first time the page is loaded, it also has to initialize the DropDownList control that lists all the products in the database. This is the control that allows the user to choose additional products when creating new relations. Listing 13.15 shows this code.

Listing 13.15   **Changes to ManageProduct.aspx.vb (continued)**

```
' Stock the Related Products dropdownlist
Dim dsRelatedProducts As New DataSet()
Dim daRelatedProducts As New SqlDataAdapter()
daRelatedProducts.SelectCommand = cmdManagerRetrieveAllProducts
daRelatedProducts.Fill(dsRelatedProducts, "RelatedProducts")
ddlAddRelatedProduct.DataSource = dsRelatedProducts
ddlAddRelatedProduct.DataMember = "RelatedProducts"
```

```
ddlAddRelatedProduct.DataTextField = "ProductName"
ddlAddRelatedProduct.DataValueField = "ProductID"
ddlAddRelatedProduct.DataBind()
```

The procManagerRetrieveAllProducts stored procedure, shown in Listing 13.16, pulls the ProductName and ProductID columns from the Product table.

Listing 13.16   procManagerRetrieveAllProducts Stored Procedure

```
/*  Retrieve all product names and IDs

From .NET E-Commerce Programming
by Mike Gunderloy and Noel Jerke
Copyright 2002, Sybex Inc. All Rights Reserved. */
CREATE PROCEDURE procManagerRetrieveAllProducts
AS
   SELECT ProductID, ProductName
   FROM Product
   ORDER BY ProductName
```

Deleting a relationship between products is handled by the ItemCommand event of the DataGrid control that displays the relationship. This code is shown in Listing 13.17.

Listing 13.17   ManageProduct.aspx.vb dgRelatedProducts_ItemCommand Procedure

```
Private Sub dgRelatedProducts_ItemCommand(ByVal source As Object, _
  ByVal e As System.Web.UI.WebControls.DataGridCommandEventArgs) _
  Handles dgRelatedProducts.ItemCommand
      ' Called when the Delete link is clicked for a related product
      ' e.Item is the row of the table where the button was
      ' clicked
      Dim dr As SqlDataReader
      With cmdManagerRemoveRelatedProduct
          .Parameters("@ProductID").Value = _
          Session("ProductID")
          .Parameters("@RelatedProductID").Value = _
          e.Item.Cells(0).Text
          If e.Item.Cells(2).Text = "Cross-sell" Then
              .Parameters("@RelationType").Value = 1
          Else
              .Parameters("@RelationType").Value = 2
          End If
          cnn.Open()
          .ExecuteNonQuery()
      End With
      ' Refresh the list of related products for this product
      cmdManagerRetrieveRelatedProducts.Parameters("@ProductID").Value = _
      Session("ProductID")
```

```
dr = cmdManagerRetrieveRelatedProducts.ExecuteReader
dgRelatedProducts.DataSource = dr
dgRelatedProducts.DataBind()
dr.Close()
cnn.Close()
End Sub
```

When the user chooses to remove a relationship, this procedure calls the procManager-RemoveRelatedProduct stored procedure to do the actual work. Listing 13.18 shows this stored procedure. Once the deletion is done, the user is sent back to the ManageProduct.aspx page to continue editing the product.

Listing 13.18   procManagerRemoveRelatedProduct Stored Procedure

```
/*  Remove a relation between products

From .NET E-Commerce Programming
by Mike Gunderloy and Noel Jerke
Copyright 2002, Sybex Inc. All Rights Reserved. */
CREATE PROCEDURE procManagerRemoveRelatedProduct
  @ProductID int,
  @RelatedProductID int,
  @RelationType int
AS
  DELETE FROM RelatedProduct
  WHERE ProductAID = @ProductID
  AND ProductBID = @RelatedProductID
  AND RelationType = @RelationType
```

Finally, when the user selects a new product in the DropDownList control, it calls code to add a new relationship to the database, as shown in Listing 13.19.

Listing 13.19   ManageProduct.aspx.vb ddlAddRelatedProduct_SelectedItemIndexChanged Procedure

```
Private Sub ddlAddRelatedProduct_SelectedIndexChanged( _
  ByVal sender As Object, ByVal e As System.EventArgs) _
  Handles ddlAddRelatedProduct.SelectedIndexChanged
    Dim dr As SqlDataReader
    ' Add a new related product for this product
    Try
        If ddlAddRelatedProduct.SelectedItem.Value <> 0 Then
            With cmdManagerAddRelatedProduct
                .Parameters("@ProductID").Value = _
                Session("ProductID")
                .Parameters("@RelatedProductID").Value = _
                ddlAddRelatedProduct.SelectedItem.Value
```

```
                    .Parameters("@RelationType").Value = _
                     rblRelationType.SelectedItem.Value
                    cnn.Open()
                    .ExecuteNonQuery()
                End With
                ' Refresh the list of related products for this product
                cmdManagerRetrieveRelatedProducts. _
                 Parameters("@ProductID").Value = _
                 Session("ProductID")
                dr = cmdManagerRetrieveRelatedProducts.ExecuteReader
                dgRelatedProducts.DataSource = dr
                dgRelatedProducts.DataBind()
                dr.Close()
            End If
        Catch ex As Exception
            ' Code will end up here on attempt to add a
            ' duplicate relation. OK to just fall through
            ' in that case
        Finally
            cnn.Close()
        End Try
    End Sub
```

The actual work of adding the product is done by the procManagerAddRelatedProduct stored procedure. This stored procedure, shown in Listing 13.20, completes the programming for this portion of the application.

Listing 13.20   **procManagerAddRelatedProduct Stored Procedure**

```
/*  Add a new relation for a product

From .NET E-Commerce Programming
by Mike Gunderloy and Noel Jerke
Copyright 2002, Sybex Inc. All Rights Reserved. */
CREATE PROCEDURE procManagerAddRelatedProduct
  @ProductID int,
  @RelatedProductID int,
  @RelationType int
AS
  INSERT INTO RelatedProduct(ProductAID,
    ProductBID, RelationType)
    VALUES(@ProductID, @RelatedProductID, @RelationType)
```

Now let's test our management interface. Figure 13.4 shows the related product listing for the "Circle Sax" product. Note the existing relationship with "Alley Jazz."

If you then select the Up-sell radio button and choose a new product in the DropDown-List control, the page will add a new relationship to the database, as shown in Figure 13.5.

FIGURE 13.4:

Related product listing

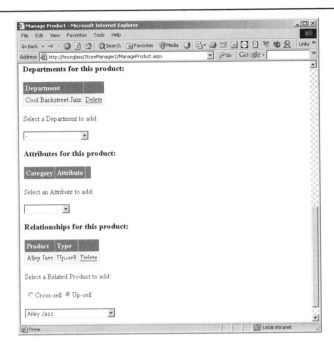

FIGURE 13.5:

Adding a new
relationship

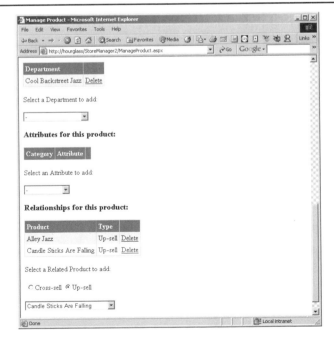

And, of course, you can use the Delete link to remove an existing relationship. Figure 13.6 shows the page after removing the original relationship.

FIGURE 13.6:

Deleting a relationship

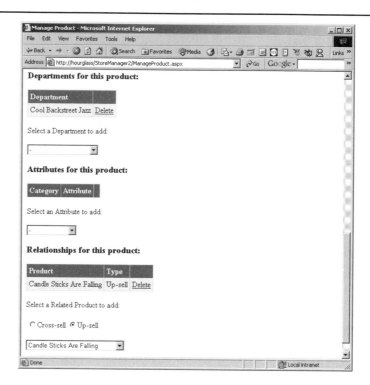

Summary

That completes the programming necessary to handle both cross-sells and up-sells. With these tools in place, we can expect the average shopper to consider purchasing additional or more expensive products. The result should be an improvement to the bottom line.

In the next chapter, we are going to explore how to display "featured products" in our store. The goal will be to showcase products that we especially want to sell, so as to tempt the shopper to buy them.

CHAPTER 14

Featured Products

- Building and Designing the Featured Products

- Programming the User Interface

- Managing Featured Products

n the last chapter, we looked at ways to promote products by relating them to other products. In this chapter, we'll explore different ways to feature products as promotions. If you walk into your local supermarket, you'll see that the products that they most want to sell you are placed at the front of the store, at the end of aisles, and in other prominent spots. We'll develop ways to carry out the virtual equivalent of these product placements.

Building and Designing the Featured Products

In our store, we are going to promote featured products in three spots. The first will be the default page that the shopper sees upon first entering the store. Right now, that page is a bit bland, with just a welcome message and navigation.

We're also going to promote products on the shopping basket page. In that case, we don't want to promote products that are already in the shopping basket, so we'll need to add some logic to list only featured products that haven't been purchased.

Finally, we'll add a notification area to each of the pages in our application. This area will give us the opportunity to display featured products at any time, as well as to include other messages on the user interface of our website.

To manage featured products, we'll use three of the columns in the Product table that we've been ignoring so far. Table 14.1 shows these three columns along with a description of each.

TABLE 14.1: Featured Product Table Columns

Column	Description
ProductFeatured	Set to 1 if the product is featured, or to zero (the default) if the product is not featured.
ProductFeaturedStart	Indicates the first date that the product is featured.
ProductFeaturedEnd	Indicates the last date that the product is featured.

Listing 14.1 shows several sample insert statements that set up a couple of featured products. Two products are updated so that they will be featured beginning on the day that the SQL statements are executed. The features are set to end a month after they start.

Listing 14.1   SQL Insert Code to Create Featured Products

```
UPDATE Product
   SET ProductFeatured = 1,
      ProductFeaturedStart = GETDATE(),
      ProductFeaturedEnd = DATEADD(Month, 1, GETDATE())
```

```
WHERE ProductID = 1

UPDATE Product
  SET ProductFeatured = 1,
    ProductFeaturedStart = GETDATE(),
    ProductFeaturedEnd = DATEADD(Month, 1, GETDATE())
  WHERE ProductID = 2
```

TIP   You'll find these SQL statements in the file `FeaturedProducts.sql` on this book's companion CD.

Programming the User Interface

First, we'll work on the default page. We're going to show the featured products right below the opening introductory text on the `Default.aspx` page.

Once again, we're going to show only the code changes in this chapter; you'll find the complete files in the CDStore2 project on the companion CD. Listing 14.2 shows the new code for the default page. If you compare it with the listings in Chapter 6, "Building the User Interface," you'll see that this section is very similar to the `Products.aspx` page.

Listing 14.2   **Changes to Default.aspx**

```
<P><B>
       <asp:Label id="lblFeaturedProducts" runat="server">
        Or choose from our featured products of the day:
       </asp:Label></B></P>
<P>
    <asp:datalist id="dlFeaturedProducts" runat="server" Width="100%"
     BorderColor="Tan" ForeColor="Black" BackColor="LightGoldenrodYellow"
     CellPadding="2" BorderWidth="1px">
       <SelectedItemStyle ForeColor="GhostWhite"
        BackColor="DarkSlateBlue"></SelectedItemStyle>
       <AlternatingItemStyle BackColor="PaleGoldenrod">
       </AlternatingItemStyle>
       <ItemTemplate>
          <a href='Product.aspx?idProduct=
          <%# DataBinder.Eval(Container.DataItem, "ProductID") %>'>
             <img src='images/products/sm_
             <%# DataBinder.Eval(Container.DataItem,
              "ProductImage") %>'
       align="middle" border="0">
             <%# DataBinder.Eval(Container.DataItem, "ProductName") %>
          </a>
          <BR>
```

```
        <BR>
    </ItemTemplate>
    <FooterStyle BackColor="Tan"></FooterStyle>
    <HeaderStyle Font-Bold="True" BackColor="Tan"></HeaderStyle>
    <AlternatingItemTemplate>
        <a href='Product.aspx?idProduct=<%#
          DataBinder.Eval(Container.DataItem, "ProductID") %>'>
            <%# DataBinder.Eval(Container.DataItem,
              "ProductName") %>
            <img src='images/products/sm_
              <%# DataBinder.Eval(Container.DataItem,
                "ProductImage") %>'
    align="middle" border="0"></a><BR>
        <BR>
    </AlternatingItemTemplate>
</asp:datalist>
```

Notice that we used a server-side label control, rather than simple text on the HTML page, for the caption of the featured products list. That's because we can control the visibility of a server-side control from code. Listing 14.3 shows the code that we added to the Page_Load procedure of the page to manage featured products.

Listing 14.3   **Default.aspx.vb Page_Load Procedure Additions**

```
' Show the featured products
Dim dsFeaturedProducts As New DataSet()
Dim daFeaturedProducts As New SqlDataAdapter()
daFeaturedProducts.SelectCommand = cmdRetrieveFeaturedProducts
daFeaturedProducts.Fill(dsFeaturedProducts, "Products")
' Only show the controls if there are featured products
If dsFeaturedProducts.Tables("Products").Rows.Count > 0 Then
    lblFeaturedProducts.Visible = True
    dlFeaturedProducts.Visible = True
    dlFeaturedProducts.DataSource = dsFeaturedProducts
    dlFeaturedProducts.DataMember = "Products"
    ' And bind it all to the user interface
    DataBind()
Else
    lblFeaturedProducts.Visible = False
    dlFeaturedProducts.Visible = False
End If
```

This code uses the procRetrieveFeaturedProducts stored procedure to retrieve all the featured products that are currently active (see Listing 14.4). The stored procedure checks the FeaturedProduct flag and also compares the range of dates for each product with the current date, to determine which products should be included.

Listing 14.4   **procRetrieveFeaturedProducts**

```
/*  Retrieve the current featured products

From .NET E-Commerce Programming
by Mike Gunderloy and Noel Jerke
Copyright 2002, Sybex Inc. All Rights Reserved. */
CREATE PROCEDURE procRetrieveFeaturedProducts
AS
  SELECT Product.ProductID, ProductName, ProductImage
   FROM Product
   WHERE ProductFeatured = 1
    AND ProductFeaturedStart <= GETDATE()
    AND ProductFeaturedEnd >= GETDATE()
```

That does it for changes to the default page. Next, we'll take a look at the Basket.aspx page. Listing 14.5 shows the HTML changes for this page.

Listing 14.5   **Changes to Basket.aspx**

```
<P>
    <asp:Label id="lblFeaturedProducts" runat="server" Font-Bold="True">
    Or choose from our featured products of the day:</asp:Label></P>
<P>
    <asp:datalist id="dlFeaturedProducts" runat="server"
     BorderWidth="1px" CellPadding="2" BackColor="LightGoldenrodYellow"
     ForeColor="Black" BorderColor="Tan" Width="100%">
        <SelectedItemStyle ForeColor="GhostWhite"
         BackColor="DarkSlateBlue"></SelectedItemStyle>
        <AlternatingItemStyle BackColor="PaleGoldenrod">
        </AlternatingItemStyle>
        <ItemTemplate>
            <a href='Product.aspx?idProduct=<%#
            DataBinder.Eval(Container.DataItem, "ProductID") %>'>
                <%# DataBinder.Eval(Container.DataItem, "ProductName") %>
            </a>
            <BR>
            <BR>
        </ItemTemplate>
        <FooterStyle BackColor="Tan"></FooterStyle>
        <HeaderStyle Font-Bold="True" BackColor="Tan"></HeaderStyle>
        <AlternatingItemTemplate>
            <a href='Product.aspx?idProduct=<%#
            DataBinder.Eval(Container.DataItem, "ProductID") %>'>
                <%# DataBinder.Eval(Container.DataItem, "ProductName") %>
            </a>
            <BR>
            <BR>
        </AlternatingItemTemplate>
    </asp:datalist></P>
```

Once again, the changes consist of adding a label control and a DataList control to the page. This time, though, the DataList doesn't contain any images. If the shopper has been interacting with the store for a while, the basket page might already be pretty cluttered. Listing the products is enough.

Of course, there's some extra Visual Basic .NET code to handle filling the new DataList. Listing 14.6 shows this code.

Listing 14.6   Changes to Basket.aspx.vb UpdatePage Procedure

```
' Show the featured products
Dim dsFeaturedProducts As New DataSet()
Dim daFeaturedProducts As New SqlDataAdapter()
cmdRetrieveNonPurchasedFeaturedProducts.Parameters( _
  "@BasketID").Value = Session("idBasket")
daFeaturedProducts.SelectCommand = _
  cmdRetrieveNonPurchasedFeaturedProducts
daFeaturedProducts.Fill(dsFeaturedProducts, "Products")
' Only show the controls if there are featured products
If dsFeaturedProducts.Tables("Products").Rows.Count > 0 Then
    lblFeaturedProducts.Visible = True
    dlFeaturedProducts.Visible = True
    dlFeaturedProducts.DataSource = dsFeaturedProducts
    dlFeaturedProducts.DataMember = "Products"
    ' And bind it all to the user interface
    DataBind()
Else
    lblFeaturedProducts.Visible = False
    dlFeaturedProducts.Visible = False
End If
```

Once again, this code is very similar to the code for the Products.aspx page and the Default.aspx page. The difference lies in the stored procedure that the code uses to select the featured products to display. In this case, it needs to return all featured products that are not in the list of basket items for the current basket.

The code passes the appropriate BasketID into the stored procedure. The WHERE clause of the stored procedure performs a SELECT statement to return the items that are currently in the basket. It then uses the NOT IN operator to return featured products that are not in the basket item list.

Of course, the stored procedure also has to check the date range in the Product table against the current date. Listing 14.7 shows the code for this stored procedure, proc-RetrieveNonPurchasedFeatureProducts.

Listing 14.7   **procRetrieveNonPurchasedFeatureProducts Stored Procedure**

```
/*  Retrieve the current featured products
    that are not in the specified basket

From .NET E-Commerce Programming
by Mike Gunderloy and Noel Jerke
Copyright 2002, Sybex Inc. All Rights Reserved. */
CREATE PROCEDURE procRetrieveNonPurchasedFeaturedProducts
  @BasketID int
AS
  SELECT Product.ProductID, ProductName, ProductImage
  FROM Product
  WHERE ProductFeatured = 1
    AND ProductFeaturedStart <= GETDATE()
    AND ProductFeaturedEnd >= GETDATE()
    AND ProductID NOT IN
      (SELECT ProductID
       FROM BasketItem
       WHERE BasketID = @BasketID)
```

The last feature that we'll add for this chapter is a special notification area at the top of each page. We'll use this area to show a list of featured products below the navigation links.

The notification area simply consists of a Web Forms label control with the name lblNotification. This control can have any text at design time, because we're going to set its text programmatically at runtime. We've added this control to the top of each page in the CDStore2 site. Figure 14.1 shows the notification area selected in design view on the Default.aspx page.

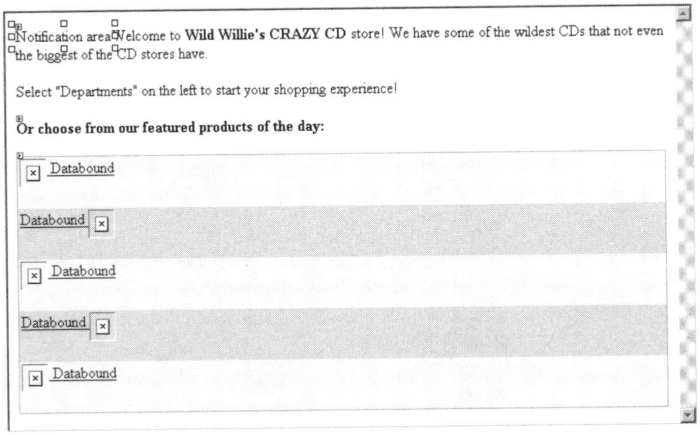

FIGURE 14.1:

The notification area

There's a new line in the Page_Load procedure of each page that features the notification area. This line of code calls a function in the GlobalProcedures.vb file to display text in the notification area:

```
GetNotifications(lblNotification, Request)
```

The first parameter to the GetNotifications procedure is the label that will contain the returned text. The second parameter is the HttpRequest class that was passed to the page by ASP.NET. Having the HttpRequest available makes it easy for the GetNotifications procedure to determine which page it's being called from. Listing 14.8 shows the code for the GetNotifications procedure.

NOTE   As you can see, the GetNotifications procedure is declared with the Friend keyword. Procedures declared with the Friend keyword are available to any code in the same assembly that contains the declaration. Because ASP.NET applications are implemented as a single assembly when they're compiled on the server, this makes the GetNotifications procedure available to all the web pages within the CDStore application.

Listing 14.8   **The GetNotifications Procedure from GlobalProcedures.vb**

```vb
Friend Sub GetNotifications( _
 ByVal lbl As System.Web.UI.WebControls.Label, _
 ByVal r As HttpRequest)
    ' Show any notifications in the supplied label control
    Try
        ' Clear the design-time text
        lbl.Text = ""
        ' On pages other than default and basket,
        ' show the featured products
        If ((InStr(r.Path, "Default.aspx") = 0) And _
        (InStr(r.Path, "Basket.aspx") = 0)) Then
            lbl.Text = "<p>Featured products: "
            Dim cnn As SqlConnection = _
             New SqlClient.SqlConnection("Data Source=(local);" & _
             "Initial Catalog=Store;Integrated Security=SSPI")
            Dim cmd As New SqlCommand()
            With cmd
                .Connection = cnn
                .CommandText = "procRetrieveFeaturedProducts"
                .CommandType = CommandType.StoredProcedure
            End With
            cnn.Open()
            Dim dr As SqlDataReader = cmd.ExecuteReader
            Do While dr.Read
                lbl.Text &= "<a href=""Product.aspx?idProduct=" & _
                dr.GetInt32(0) & """>" & dr.GetString(1) & "</a> "
            Loop
```

```
                dr.Close()
                cnn.Close()
                ' Are there any products?
                If lbl.Text <> "<p>Featured products: " Then
                    ' If so, close the <p> tag
                    lbl.Text &= "</p>"
                Else
                    ' If not, clear the entire label
                    lbl.Text = ""
                End If
            End If
        Catch ex As Exception
            ' If any error, just forget about it and exit
        Finally
        End Try
    End Sub
```

The GetNotifications procedure starts by clearing out any design-time text from the supplied Label control. It then checks to see whether it's being called from the Default.aspx page or Basket.aspx page. If it is, it just returns without setting any text into the control. That's because we're already displaying the featured products on those pages and don't want to display them a second time.

If the GetNotifications procedure is called from any other page, it uses the procRetrieve-FeaturedProducts stored procedure (which you already saw in Listing 14.4) to get the featured products for the day. It then uses a loop to build up a text string containing HTML code to display links to the featured products. This string is returned as the text for the supplied label, which causes the page to render the HTML.

With these changes in place, you can take a look at these features in action. Figure 14.2 shows the new home page with our two featured products. Note that there's no text in the notification area because this is the default page.

Figure 14.3 shows the departments page. Note the list of featured products in the notification area. This list will show up on any page except the default and basket pages.

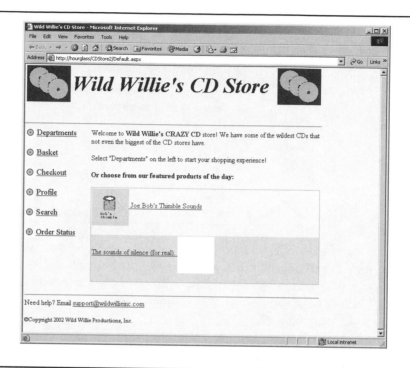

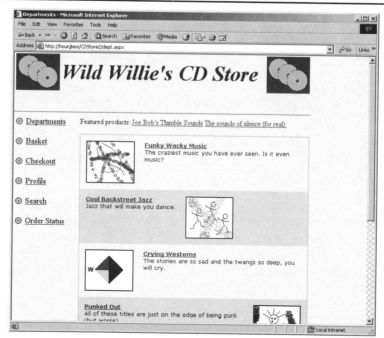

Next, add a product other than one of the featured products to the shopping basket.
Figure 14.4 shows the basket with both featured products shown at the bottom of the page.
Notice that they also show up in the notification area at the top of the page.

FIGURE 14.4:

Basket page with both
featured products
displayed

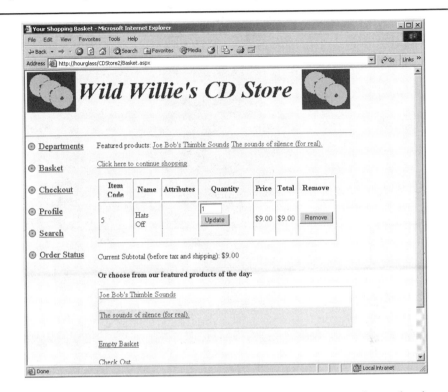

Now add one of the featured products to the shopping basket. Figure 14.5 shows the shopping basket with "Joe Bob's Thimble Sounds" added to the basket. Now only the featured
product "The Sounds of Silence (for Real)" is shown after the shopping basket. Both featured
products still appear in the notification area.

In the rest of the chapter, we'll build an interface to manage the featured products list in
the store manager.

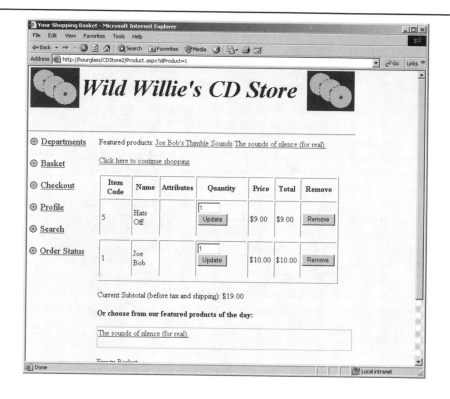

Managing Featured Products

We'll add controls for managing featured products on the ManageProduct.aspx page, where we're already handling the rest of the settings for each product. This requires adding controls for setting the featured product flag, the start date, and the end date.

Listing 14.9 shows the additional HTML for these controls (a check box and two text boxes) on the ManageProduct.aspx page. These controls appear at the end of the table that shows the basic product information.

Listing 14.9   **Changes to ManageProduct.aspx**

```
<TR>
    <TD></TD>
    <TD><asp:checkbox id="chkFeatured" runat="server"
     Text="Check if product is featured."></asp:checkbox></TD>
</TR>
<TR>
```

```
        <TD>Feature Start Date:</TD>
        <TD>
            <asp:TextBox id="txtFeaturedStartDate" runat="server">
            </asp:TextBox></TD>
    </TR>
    <TR>
        <TD>Feature End Date:</TD>
        <TD>
            <asp:TextBox id="txtFeaturedEndDate" runat="server">
            </asp:TextBox></TD>
    </TR>
```

NOTE   ASP.NET also includes a Calendar control for Web Forms. The advantage of this control is that it ensures that any data entered will be properly formatted as a date. We've chosen not to use this control because the page is already quite large, and it takes up a lot of space. We'll depend on our users to enter dates in the Textbox controls instead.

Of course, we also need to add code to the page to initialize these controls, and to use their values in update operations. Listing 14.10 shows the portion of the Page_Load procedure for the ManageProduct.aspx page that handles setting the initial values in the controls.

Listing 14.10   ManageProduct.aspx.vb Page_Load Procedure

```
' Populate the UI with current information
' First, set the hyperlink jump into the store
hlPreview.NavigateUrl = "../CDStore/Product.aspx?idProduct=" & _
 Session("ProductID")
' Get the product info from the database
With cmdManagerRetrieveProduct
    .Parameters("@ProductID").Value = _
     Session("ProductID")
    dr = .ExecuteReader()
End With
dr.Read()
txtProductID.Enabled = True
txtProductID.Text = dr.GetInt32(0)
' Lock the Product ID so they can't change it
txtProductID.Enabled = False
txtProductName.Text = dr.GetString(1)
txtProductDescription.Text = dr.GetString(2)
txtProductImage.Text = dr.GetString(3)
imgProduct.ImageUrl = "../CDStore/Images/Products/sm_" & _
 dr.GetString(3)
txtProductPrice.Text = Format( _
 dr.GetSqlMoney(4).ToSqlString.Value, "currency")
If dr.GetBoolean(7) Then
    chkActive.Checked = True
```

```
Else
    chkActive.Checked = False
End If
If dr.GetBoolean(8) Then
    chkFeatured.Checked = True
Else
    chkFeatured.Checked = False
End If
If Not dr.IsDBNull(9) Then
    txtFeaturedStartDate.Text = dr.GetDateTime(9).ToShortDateString
Else
    txtFeaturedStartDate.Text = ""
End If
If Not dr.IsDBNull(10) Then
    txtFeaturedEndDate.Text = dr.GetDateTime(10).ToShortDateString
Else
    txtFeaturedEndDate.Text = ""
End If

dr.Close()
```

We didn't need to modify the stored procedure that retrieves the data for this page because it already performs a SELECT * operation to retrieve all the columns from the Product table. We just added additional code to retrieve the values in columns 8, 9, and 10 of the results. Note the use of the ToShortDateString method to format the dates for display.

Listing 14.11 shows the procedure that handles updating the database when the user clicks the Update button.

Listing 14.11   ManageProduct.aspx.vb btnUpdate_Click Procedure

```
Private Sub btnUpdate_Click(ByVal sender As System.Object, _
  ByVal e As System.EventArgs) Handles btnUpdate.Click
    ' Save the information from this page back
    ' to the database

    With cmdManagerUpdateProduct2
        .Parameters("@ProductID").Value = _
        Session("ProductID")
        .Parameters("@ProductName").Value = _
        txtProductName.Text
        .Parameters("@ProductDescription").Value = _
        txtProductDescription.Text
        .Parameters("@ProductImage").Value = _
        txtProductImage.Text
        .Parameters("@ProductPrice").Value = _
        CType(txtProductPrice.Text, Decimal)
        If chkActive.Checked Then
            .Parameters("@ProductActive").Value = 1
```

```
        Else
            .Parameters("@ProductActive").Value = 0
        End If
        If chkFeatured.Checked Then
            .Parameters("@ProductFeatured").Value = 1
        Else
            .Parameters("@ProductFeatured").Value = 0
        End If
        If txtFeaturedStartDate.Text = "" Then
            .Parameters("@ProductFeaturedStart").Value = _
            DBNull.Value
        Else
            .Parameters("@ProductFeaturedStart").Value = _
            CDate(txtFeaturedStartDate.Text)
        End If
        If txtFeaturedEndDate.Text = "" Then
            .Parameters("@ProductFeaturedEnd").Value = _
            DBNull.Value
        Else
            .Parameters("@ProductFeaturedEnd").Value = _
            CDate(txtFeaturedEndDate.Text)
        End If

        cnn.Open()
        .ExecuteNonQuery()
        cnn.Close()
    End With
End Sub
```

Rather than modify the existing stored procedure for updating products, we chose to create a new stored procedure named procManagerUpdateProduct2. This stored procedure is identical to procManagerUpdateProduct except for the addition of parameters to handle the new columns. Listing 14.12 shows the new stored procedure.

Listing 14.12   procManagerUpdateProduct2 Stored Procedure

```
/*  Update information on a product

From .NET E-Commerce Programming
by Mike Gunderloy and Noel Jerke
Copyright 2002, Sybex Inc. All Rights Reserved. */
CREATE PROCEDURE procManagerUpdateProduct2
  @ProductID int,
  @ProductName varchar(255),
  @ProductDescription text,
  @ProductImage varchar(255),
  @ProductPrice money,
  @ProductActive bit,
  @ProductFeatured bit,
```

```
      @ProductFeaturedStart datetime,
      @ProductFeaturedEnd datetime
   AS
      UPDATE Product
        SET ProductName = @ProductName,
          ProductDescription = @ProductDescription,
          ProductImage = @ProductImage,
          ProductPrice = @ProductPrice,
          ProductActive = @ProductActive,
          ProductFeatured = @ProductFeatured,
          ProductFeaturedStart = @ProductFeaturedStart,
          ProductFeaturedEnd = @ProductFeaturedEnd
        WHERE ProductID = @ProductID
```

Now we can test the featured product management operations in the StoreManager application. Figure 14.6 shows the product management page with the additional fields that are used for featured products.

FIGURE 14.6:

Product manager page

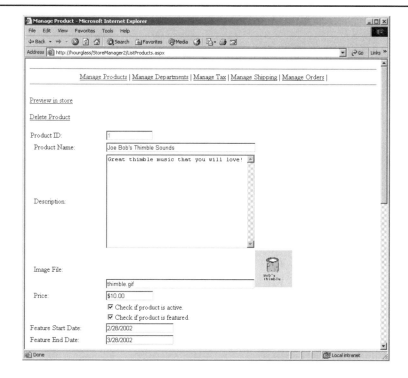

Let's take "Joe Bob's Thimble Sounds" off as a featured product. Uncheck the check box, clear the date fields, and then click the Update button. Figure 14.7 shows the updated product page.

FIGURE 14.7:

Updated product

Figure 14.8 shows the default page for the store after making this change. Note that only one product is now featured.

FIGURE 14.8:

New home page with featured product listing

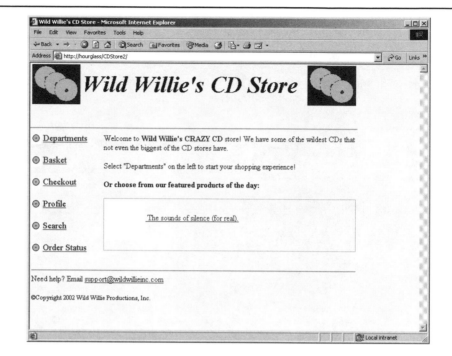

Summary

That's it for handling featured products in the store. Through the tools outlined in this chapter, the StoreManager application can easily highlight new products in the store, fast-selling products, products that are overstocked, or any other products that the store wants to promote. This is a key tool that the StoreManager can exploit to engage with the shopper.

In the next chapter, we'll tackle another important promotional device: sale products. Our approach to sales will be similar to the way we handled featured products, but it will be targeted at reducing prices or lowering the overall cost of the purchase.

CHAPTER 15

On Sale

- Designing the Sale Features

- Building the Shopping Sale Features

- Building the Sale Management Features

I t's a sale! In this chapter, we'll explore how to store sale prices for our products and how to promote those sale products. But sales are not limited to reduced prices. They can also include promotional offers like free shipping, which is another option we will explore.

Designing the Sale Features

We already have columns in our Product table that will support setting sale prices and their effective date ranges:

ProductSalePrice   Stores the sale price for the product.

ProductSaleStart   Stores the starting date of the sale.

ProductSaleEnd   Stores the ending date of the sale.

Listing 15.1 shows SQL code for setting up three initial products to be on sale in our store. When you execute these statements, the three products are placed on sale for one month, starting on the current date. Executing these statements allows us to easily test that our sale functions work properly.

TIP   These SQL statements are available on this book's companion CD in the file `SaleProducts.sql`.

Listing 15.1   **Setting Sale Prices**

```
UPDATE Product
  SET ProductSalePrice = 4.00,
  ProductSaleStart = GETDATE(),
  ProductSaleEnd = DATEADD(Month, 1, GETDATE())
  WHERE ProductID = 1

UPDATE Product
  SET ProductSalePrice = 5.00,
  ProductSaleStart = GETDATE(),
  ProductSaleEnd = DATEADD(Month, 1, GETDATE())
  WHERE ProductID = 2

UPDATE Product
  SET ProductSalePrice = 6.00,
  ProductSaleStart = GETDATE(),
  ProductSaleEnd = DATEADD(Month, 1, GETDATE())
  WHERE ProductID = 3
```

To support our free-shipping promotions, we'll add information to the FreeShip table. This table contains columns to hold the starting date and ending date of each free-shipping promotion. Listing 15.2 shows the SQL statement that adds a one-month free-shipping promotion to the database.

TIP   This SQL statement is available on the companion CD in the file FreeShip.sql.

Listing 15.2   Setting Free Shipping

```
INSERT INTO FreeShip (FreeShipStartDate, FreeShipEndDate)
   VALUES(GETDATE(), DATEADD(Month, 1, GETDATE()))
```

Now we're ready to begin modifying the user interface of our store to include sale prices and free shipping.

Building the Shopping Sale Features

We'll need to make two sets of changes to our code for the store. The first set of changes will support displaying sale items throughout the shopping process. The second set will modify the checkout process to support free shipping.

Implementing Sale Items

To get started, we'll want to show a sale item along with the featured products in the notification area of the store. Remember, we created the notification area in the preceding chapter to show featured products. We have to be careful, though. We may have multiple sale products, and to show all of them on any single page could be overwhelming.

We'll take the approach of selecting a sale product randomly and displaying it directly after the featured products (if any) on the page. Listing 15.3 shows the modified GetNotifications procedure from the GlobalProcedures.vb file.

Listing 15.3   GlobalProcedures.vb GetNotifications Procedure

```
Friend Sub GetNotifications( _
 ByVal lbl As System.Web.UI.WebControls.Label, _
 ByVal r As HttpRequest)
    ' Show any notifications in the supplied label control
   Dim cnn As SqlConnection = _
    New SqlClient.SqlConnection("Data Source=(local);" & _
    "Initial Catalog=Store;Integrated Security=SSPI")
   cnn.Open()
   Try
       ' Clear the design-time text
       lbl.Text = ""
```

```
' On pages other than default and basket,
' show the featured products
If ((InStr(r.Path, "Default.aspx") = 0) And _
 (InStr(r.Path, "Basket.aspx") = 0)) Then
    lbl.Text = "<p>Featured products: "
    Dim cmd As New SqlCommand()
    With cmd
        .Connection = cnn
        .CommandText = "procRetrieveFeaturedProducts"
        .CommandType = CommandType.StoredProcedure
    End With
    Dim dr As SqlDataReader = cmd.ExecuteReader
    Do While dr.Read
        lbl.Text &= "<a href=""Product.aspx?idProduct=" & _
        dr.GetInt32(0) & """>" & dr.GetString(1) & "</a> "
    Loop
    dr.Close()
    ' Are there any products?
    If lbl.Text <> "<p>Featured products: " Then
        ' If so, close the <p> tag
        lbl.Text &= "</p>"
    Else
        ' If not, clear the entire label
        lbl.Text = ""
    End If
End If
' Pick a random sale product and show it on every page.
' First, get the count of sale products and the
' list of sale product IDs
Dim cmdSale As New SqlCommand()
With cmdSale
    .Connection = cnn
    .CommandText = "procRetrieveSaleProductList"
    .CommandType = CommandType.StoredProcedure
End With
Dim daSale As New SqlDataAdapter()
Dim dsSale As New DataSet()
daSale.SelectCommand = cmdSale
daSale.Fill(dsSale, "Sale")
' Check to see whether there ARE any sale products
If dsSale.Tables("Sale").Rows.Count > 0 Then
    ' Pick a random row
    Dim rnd As New Random()
    Dim intRow = rnd.Next(0, dsSale.Tables("Sale").Rows(0)(0))
    ' And get its data
    Dim cmdSaleProduct As New SqlCommand()
    With cmdSaleProduct
        .Connection = cnn
        .CommandText = "procRetrieveSaleProduct"
        .CommandType = CommandType.StoredProcedure
        .Parameters.Add("@ProductID", _
```

```
            dsSale.Tables("Sale").Rows(intRow)(1))
        End With
        Dim drSaleProduct As SqlDataReader = _
         cmdSaleProduct.ExecuteReader
        drSaleProduct.Read()
        ' Format the results for display
        lbl.Text &= "<p><b>On Sale Today: </b>" & _
         "<a href=""Product.aspx?idProduct=" & _
         drSaleProduct.GetInt32(0) & """>" & _
         drSaleProduct.GetString(1) & "</a> " & _
         "<font color='red'>" & _
         Format(drSaleProduct.GetSqlMoney(2). _
         ToString, "Currency") & _
         "</font></p>"
        drSaleProduct.Close()
      End If

    Catch ex As Exception
        ' If any error, just forget about it and exit
    Finally
        cnn.Close()
    End Try
End Sub
```

The new code begins by connecting to the database and retrieving a DataSet that includes the number of currently active sale products in the store and the Product ID for each of those products. It then checks to make sure that the count is greater than zero. If it is (that is, if there are any products currently on sale), the code runs a second stored procedure to retrieve details on one randomly selected product. It then formats a link to that particular product, along with the sale price, and adds that link to the label that's being used as a notification area.

Random Numbers in the .NET Framework

To generate random numbers, the code uses an instance of the Random class, which is a member of the System namespace. Previous versions of Visual Basic provided a set of functions to manage random numbers. The .NET Framework is much more flexible in this regard. Because Random is now a class, you can declare as many independent random-number generators as you need. A random-number generator is simply an instance of the Random class:

```
Dim rnd As New Random()
```

Continued on next page

Random-number generators of the type used in the .NET Framework are deterministic. They work by returning numbers from a long, nonrepeating sequence. The sequence is always exactly the same. By default, the .NET Framework "seeds" a new random-number generator with a value based on the system time, so that the starting point in the sequence is unpredictable. If you want to start at a particular point (for instance, if you're debugging and you want to generate the same sequence of random numbers each time you run the application), you can specify your own seed value in the constructor:

```
Dim rnd As New Random(12345)
```

The Random class implements three methods to return random numbers. The NextDouble method is similar to the Rand() function in Visual Basic 6; it returns a random double-precision number between zero and one:

```
Dim dblRandom = rnd.NextDouble()
```

The code in our store uses the more flexible Next method. Next is overloaded and has three versions. First, you can use it simply to return a positive integer between zero and the maximum number that an Int32 variable can hold (2,147,483,647):

```
Dim intRandom = rnd.Next()
```

Second, you can supply a maximum number that the random value should not exceed. For instance, the following call will return a random number between zero and 47:

```
Dim intRandom = rnd.Next(47)
```

Finally, you can supply both a minimum and a maximum number. This call will return random numbers between 5 and 10:

```
Dim intRandom = rnd.Next(5, 10)
```

The last method of returning random numbers from the Random class is NextBytes. The NextBytes method fills an array of bytes with random positive integers. This is useful when you need to generate many random numbers in one call:

```
Dim abytRandom(10) As Byte
rnd.NextBytes(abytRandom)
```

Listing 15.4 shows the procRetrieveSaleProductList stored procedure, which is used to retrieve the count of sale products and their Product IDs.

Listing 15.4   **procRetrieveSaleProductList Stored Procedure**

```
/*  Retrieve the number of products currently
    on sale together with their Product IDs
```

```
From .NET E-Commerce Programming
by Mike Gunderloy and Noel Jerke
Copyright 2002, Sybex Inc. All Rights Reserved. */
CREATE PROCEDURE procRetrieveSaleProductList
AS
  DECLARE @cnt int

  SELECT @cnt = COUNT(*)
  FROM Product
  WHERE GETDATE() >= ProductSaleStart and GETDATE() <= ProductSaleEnd

  SELECT @cnt AS SaleCount, ProductID
  FROM product
  WHERE GETDATE() >= ProductSaleStart and GETDATE() <= ProductSaleEnd
```

Note that this stored procedure first uses a SELECT COUNT(*) statement to retrieve a constant value that is the number of products currently on sale, and then returns that constant value as a column in the result set for the stored procedure. The results of the stored procedure will look something like this:

```
SaleCount    ProductID
---------    ---------
3            1
3            2
3            3
```

The other stored procedure used by the GetNotifications procedure is procRetrieveSaleProduct. This stored procedure, shown in Listing 15.5, takes a Product ID as an input parameter and returns enough details about that product to allow the code to build a link on the user interface.

Listing 15.5   **procRetrieveSaleProduct Stored Procedure**

```
/*  Retrieve details on a sale product

From .NET E-Commerce Programming
by Mike Gunderloy and Noel Jerke
Copyright 2002, Sybex Inc. All Rights Reserved. */
CREATE PROCEDURE procRetrieveSaleProduct
  @ProductID int
AS
  SELECT ProductID, ProductName, ProductSalePrice
  FROM Product
  WHERE ProductID = @ProductID
```

Now that we've got the sale products displaying in the notification area, we're ready to move to the product page. On the product page we need to show the sale price instead of the regular price so that the shopper will know that they're getting a bargain. We also need to modify the logic so the sale price is used when the product is added to the shopping basket.

Within the HTML code for the Product.aspx page, we need to make two changes. First, we'll add a hidden-form field to the page to hold the sale price, as shown in Listing 15.6

Listing 15.6   **Product.aspx Changes**

```
<input type="hidden" value='<%# DataBinder.Eval(Container.DataItem,
  "ProductSalePrice") %>' name="ProductSalePrice">
```

We also need to add a Label control to display the sale price to the shopper, if the item is on sale. The code for this is shown in Listing 15.7.

Listing 15.7   **Product.aspx Changes (continued)**

```
<asp:Label id="lblSale" runat="server" ForeColor="Red" Font-Size="Large"
  Visible="False" Font-Bold="True">Sale</asp:Label></P>
```

Note that by default the lblSale control has its Visible property set to False. You'll see the code to actually display this control a bit later in the chapter. For now, we're assuming that most products are not on sale.

We also need to modify the stored procedure, procRetrieveProduct, that we use to load product information. That's because we originally designed this stored procedure (in Chapter 6, "Building the User Interface") to retrieve only the columns necessary for nonsale products. Now we need to add the columns for sale products. Listing 15.8 shows the SQL statement that can be used to alter the existing stored procedure to include these columns.

Listing 15.8   **Changes to procRetrieveProduct Stored Procedure**

```
ALTER PROCEDURE procRetrieveProduct
  @idProduct int
AS
  SELECT ProductID, ProductName, ProductImage,
  ProductPrice, ProductDescription,
  ProductSalePrice, ProductSaleStart, ProductSaleEnd
  FROM Product
  WHERE ProductID = @idProduct
```

NOTE   You'll find this change script in the procRetrieveProductAlter.sql file on the companion CD.

Adding additional columns to the SQL statement doesn't affect any of the existing coding for the Product.aspx page, because we're still retrieving all the columns that we started with. That's why we didn't create an entirely new stored procedure in this case. However, two changes still need to be made to the code for this page. First, in the Page_Load event, we need to add code to display the lblSale control and to fill it in with the sale price if the product is on sale. This code is shown in Listing 15.9.

Listing 15.9   **Changes to Product.aspx.vb Page_Load Procedure**

```
' Show the sale price if the product is on sale
If (Not (dsProduct.Tables("Product").Rows(0)("ProductSaleStart") _
  Is DBNull.Value)) And _
  (Not (dsProduct.Tables("Product").Rows(0)("ProductSaleEnd") Is _
  DBNull.Value)) Then
    If (dsProduct.Tables("Product").Rows(0)("ProductSaleStart") _
      <= DateTime.Today) And _
      (dsProduct.Tables("Product").Rows(0)("ProductSaleEnd") _
      >= DateTime.Today) Then
        lblSale.Visible = True
        lblSale.Text = "On Sale Today for " & _
         Format( _
          dsProduct.Tables("Product").Rows(0)("ProductSalePrice"), _
          "Currency")
    End If
End If
```

As you can see, the code to determine whether a product is currently on sale is moderately complex. That's because the ProductSaleStart and ProductSaleEnd columns are nullable. If a particular product has never been on sale, these two columns will both contain Nulls. You'll get an error if you try to compare a Null value to a date value (such as that provided by the DateTime.Today method in the code). So the code first has to make sure that neither of these columns contains Null. If both columns have values, the next step is to check to see whether the sale started before the current date and continues until later than the current date. If that's true, the code then makes the lblSale control visible and fills it in with a message that includes the sale price.

Finally, the code that's called on page postback also has to be altered so that it will use the sale price if a product is on sale. Remember, this code is called when the shopper clicks the Order button to purchase an item. Listing 15.10 shows this code.

Listing 15.10   **Changes to Product.aspx.vb Page_Load Procedure (continued)**

```
' If a sale price is displayed, use that as the
' product price
If lblSale.Visible Then
```

```
    Session("ProductPrice") = Request.Form("ProductSalePrice")
Else
    Session("ProductPrice") = Request.Form("ProductPrice")
End If
```

On postback, the code has full access to all the information that was displayed on the form. This means that we don't need to check the database again to determine whether a product is on sale. All the code needs to do is look at the Visible property of the lblSale control. If the sale price is shown on the page, the product must be on sale, and so the code will use the sale price (retrieved from the ProductSalePrice hidden field on the form) as the product price. That price gets passed to the next page, where the order is actually saved.

TIP   You'll find the code for saving an order in Chapter 7, "Making a Basket Case."

TIP   If you have a limited inventory of sale products, you might need to limit purchases of sale products. For example, you might allow a shopper to purchase only four of any given item within a certain time period if the item is on sale. This could be tracked by the shopper profile.

Now we've made all the changes necessary to manage sale products on the store interface. Let's take a look at these changes in action. Figure 15.1 shows the default page of the store with a sale product listed in the notification area.

Figure 15.2 shows the department page. Here, the notification area lists both featured products and a random sale product.

Next, in Figure 15.3, we have a product that is on sale. Note the sale price in boldface, right above the Order button, where it's hard to miss. (If you view the sale price on-screen, you'll see that it's also red.) Click the Order button to add the sale product to the shopping basket.

Figure 15.4 shows the basket with a sale product added. Note that the price is the sale price. If you update the quantity of a sale product, the price will remain the sale price.

FIGURE 15.1:

Default.aspx
showing a sale
product

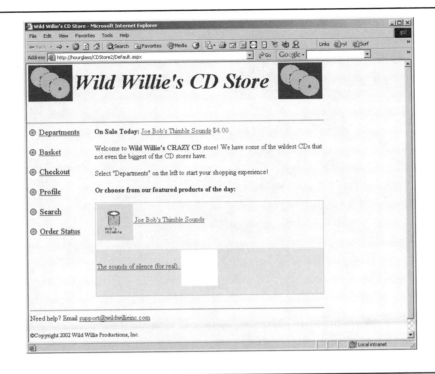

FIGURE 15.2:

Department.aspx
showing a sale
product

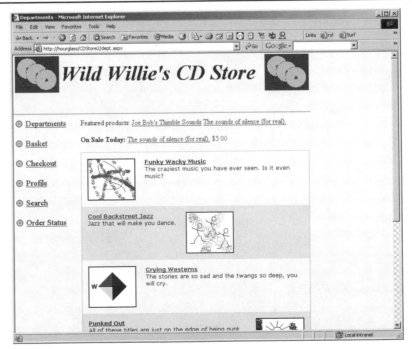

A product on sale

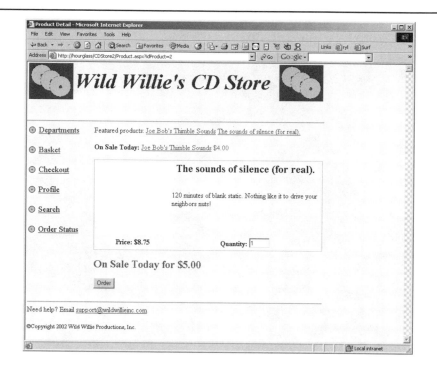

Shopping basket with
a sale price

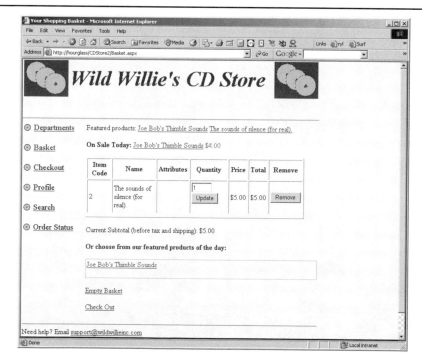

Implementing Free Shipping

Now we can implement free shipping. The idea is to have free shipping on certain days, based on the data in the FreeShip table.

The only page that we need to change is the `Payment.aspx` page, where the shipping costs for an order are calculated. The goal is to intercept the call to the Web Service that would otherwise return a shipping cost, and to set the cost to zero instead.

We'll do this by running a stored procedure that returns zero if today is not a free-shipping day, or a positive number (usually one, but we don't care as long as it isn't zero) if this is a free-shipping day.

If a shipping promotion is currently running, the shipping component isn't called. If a shipping promotion is not on, we call the component as usual. Listing 15.11 shows this set of changes to the Page_Load procedure for `Payment.aspx`.

Listing 15.11   **Payment.aspx.vb Page_Load Changes**

```
' Figure out whether we're in a free-shipping promotion
cnn.Open()
Dim intFreeShip = cmdCheckFreeShip.ExecuteScalar()
cnn.Close()

' Use the Web Services to get the tax and shipping charges
Dim TaxShip As New hourglass.CDStoreServices()
Session("Tax") = TaxShip.GetTaxRate(Session("ShipState")) * _
 Session("Subtotal")
If intFreeShip = 0 Then
    Session("Shipping") = TaxShip.GetShippingFee(Session("Quantity"))
Else
    Session("Shipping") = 0
End If
```

We also need to change the way the shipping total is displayed on the page if we're offering free shipping. We want to display a message to the shopper indicating that free shipping is currently in effect. We'll make this message stand out by setting the properties of the control to red and boldface. Listing 15.12 shows the section of code that handles the display of the message.

Listing 15.12   **Payment.aspx.vb Page_Load Procedure Changes (continued)**

```
If intFreeShip = 0 Then
    lblShipping.Text = Format(Session("Shipping"), "Currency")
Else
    With lblShipping
        .Text = "Free Shipping today"
        .Font.Bold = True
        .ForeColor = System.Drawing.Color.Red
```

```
      End With
   End If
   lblTotal.Text = Format(Session("Total"), "Currency")
```

We use the procCheckFreeShip stored procedure to determine whether free shipping is in effect. This stored procedure checks the start and end dates from the FreeShip table against the current system date using the GETDATE() SQL Server function, as shown in Listing 15.13.

Listing 15.13   **sp_ procCheckFreeShip Stored Procedure**

```
/*  Determine whether free shipping is in effect

From .NET E-Commerce Programming
by Mike Gunderloy and Noel Jerke
Copyright 2002, Sybex Inc. All Rights Reserved. */
CREATE PROCEDURE procCheckFreeShip
AS
SELECT COUNT(*)
FROM FreeShip
WHERE FreeShipStartDate <= GETDATE()
  AND FreeShipEndDate >= GETDATE()
```

That takes care of the display and calculation of the free shipping. Because we're using the same variable to store the shipping cost whether this cost is calculated by the Web Service or set to zero by the code, we don't need to make any other changes. The shipping cost will be stored properly in the database either way.

Shipping Charges

There is more than one way to approach reductions of the shipping charge. We could provide logic that will give free shipping for orders over a certain amount. Or we could provide free shipping on a subset of orders chosen some other way—perhaps based on past buying patterns, or at random. Each of these approaches could be a key feature in providing an incentive for the shopper to make that purchase.

Now let's test our free-shipping logic. To check that free shipping works, be sure to store appropriate values in the FreeShip table by executing the SQL statement from Listing 15.2.

Figure 15.5 shows the payment page for an order, indicating that the user won't be charged for shipping.

Go ahead and place the order. Check the order in the order status or order manager to ensure that the shipping values have been stored properly. Figure 15.6 shows our sample order detail.

FIGURE 15.5:

Free shipping

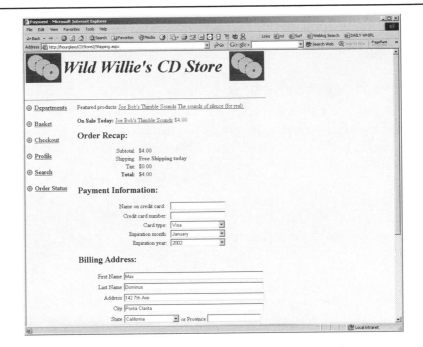

FIGURE 15.6:

Order detail with the sale price and the free-shipping figure

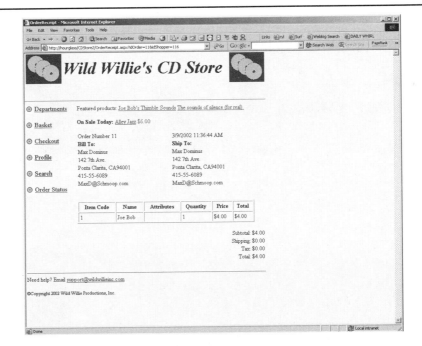

Building the Sale Management Features

Now that everything is working from the shopper's point of view, we're ready to build the management tools necessary to set sale prices and manage the free-shipping settings.

Managing Product Sales

First, we'll add a feature that will enable us to manage sale prices. As with other product-related management features, this will require changing the ManageProduct.aspx page. Listing 15.14 shows the changes to the HTML code for this page, which are quite similar to those required to manage featured products.

Listing 15.14   ManageProduct.aspx Changes

```
<TR>
    <TD>Sale Price:</TD>
    <TD>
        <asp:TextBox id="txtSalePrice" runat="server"></asp:TextBox></TD>
</TR>
<TR>
    <TD>Sale Start Date:</TD>
    <TD>
        <asp:TextBox id="txtSaleStart" runat="server"></asp:TextBox></TD>
</TR>
<TR>
    <TD>Sale End Date:</TD>
    <TD>
        <asp:TextBox id="txtSaleEnd" runat="server"></asp:TextBox></TD>
</TR>
```

The code-behind file for the page needs to be updated as well. Listing 15.15 shows the additional code to show the sale information when the page is first loaded.

Listing 15.15   ManageProduct.aspx.vb Page_Load Procedure Changes

```
If Not dr.IsDBNull(11) Then
    txtSalePrice.Text = Format( _
      dr.GetSqlMoney(11).ToSqlString.Value, "currency")
Else
    txtSalePrice.Text = ""
End If
If Not dr.IsDBNull(5) Then
    txtSaleStart.Text = dr.GetDateTime(5).ToShortDateString
Else
    txtSaleStart.Text = ""
End If
If Not dr.IsDBNull(6) Then
```

```
        txtSaleEnd.Text = dr.GetDateTime(6).ToShortDateString
    Else
        txtSaleEnd.Text = ""
    End If
```

Next, we need to add the additional fields to the code that's called when the user clicks the Update button. Listing 15.16 shows this section of the code.

Listing 15.16   **ManageProduct.aspx.vb btnUpdate_Click Procedure Changes**

```
If txtSaleStart.Text = "" Then
    .Parameters("@ProductSaleStart").Value = _
     DBNull.Value
Else
    .Parameters("@ProductSaleStart").Value = _
     CDate(txtSaleStart.Text)
End If
If txtSaleEnd.Text = "" Then
    .Parameters("@ProductSaleEnd").Value = _
     DBNull.Value
Else
    .Parameters("@ProductSaleEnd").Value = _
     CDate(txtSaleEnd.Text)
End If
```

Because of the need to pass in the additional parameters, we've also modified the stored procedure that updates the product information in the database. Listing 15.17 shows the new version, procManagerUpdateProduct3.

Listing 15.17   **procManagerUpdateProduct3 Stored Procedure**

```
/*  Update information on a product

From .NET E-Commerce Programming
by Mike Gunderloy and Noel Jerke
Copyright 2002, Sybex Inc. All Rights Reserved. */
CREATE PROCEDURE procManagerUpdateProduct3
  @ProductID int,
  @ProductName varchar(255),
  @ProductDescription text,
  @ProductImage varchar(255),
  @ProductPrice money,
  @ProductActive bit,
  @ProductFeatured bit,
  @ProductFeaturedStart datetime,
  @ProductFeaturedEnd datetime,
  @ProductSalePrice money,
  @ProductSaleStart datetime,
```

```
    @ProductSaleEnd datetime
AS
  UPDATE Product
    SET ProductName = @ProductName,
      ProductDescription = @ProductDescription,
      ProductImage = @ProductImage,
      ProductPrice = @ProductPrice,
      ProductActive = @ProductActive,
      ProductFeatured = @ProductFeatured,
      ProductFeaturedStart = @ProductFeaturedStart,
      ProductFeaturedEnd = @ProductFeaturedEnd,
      ProductSalePrice = @ProductSalePrice,
      ProductSaleStart = @ProductSaleStart,
      ProductSaleEnd = @ProductSaleEnd
    WHERE ProductID = @ProductID
```

If you followed the work that we did on the ManageProduct.aspx page in previous chapters, these modifications should strike you as straightforward. Figure 15.7 shows the product manager page with the new sales fields displayed. The user can modify or even delete this information and then click Update Product to save the changes to the database.

FIGURE 15.7:

Managing sale information

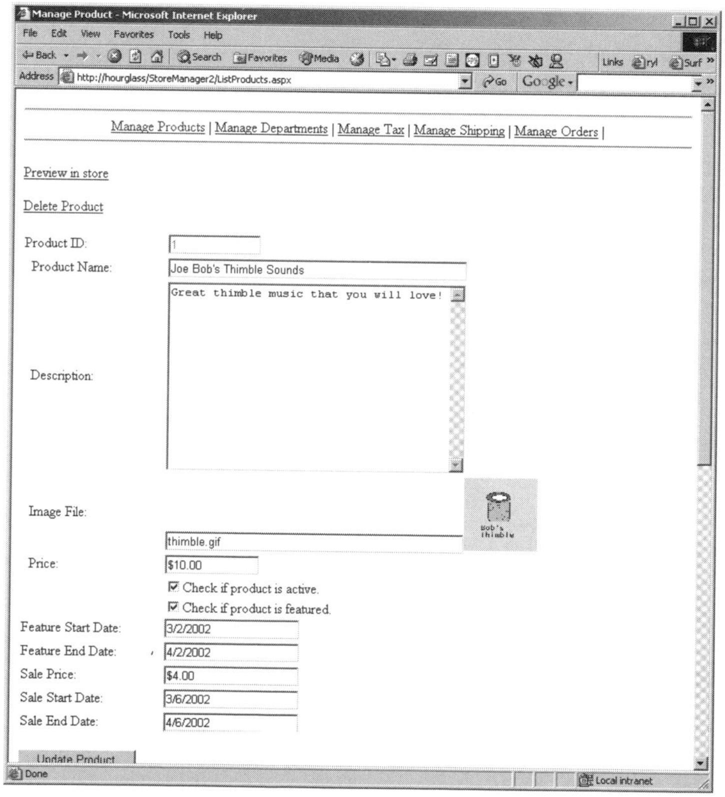

Managing Free Shipping

Currently, we don't have any facility for managing free shipping. To manage free shipping, we'll add one more item to the manager menu and navigation include pages. Listings 15.18 and 15.19 show the updates to the appropriate files for adding free shipping navigation to the StoreManager application.

Listing 15.18   ManagerMenu.aspx Changes

```
<tr>
    <td><a href="ManageFreeShipping.aspx"> Manage Free Shipping</a></td>
</tr>
```

Listing 15.19   NavBar.inc Changes

```
<!--  Link to the management page for free shipping   -->
<a href="ManageFreeShipping.aspx">
Manage Free Shipping</a> |
```

The next step is to add another Web Form to allow editing the FreeShip table. This page will be similar to the one that we developed to handle regular shipping. The basic problem is the same: displaying and updating a single table in the database. Listing 15.20 shows the HTML code for the ManageFreeShipping.aspx page. This page starts with the navigation and security includes, then displays the current contents of the FreeShip table on a DataGrid control. It concludes with a section that allows entering new rows for the table.

Listing 15.20   ManageFreeShipping.aspx

```
<%@ Page Language="vb" AutoEventWireup="false"
 Codebehind="ManageFreeShipping.aspx.vb"
 Inherits="StoreManager.ManageFreeShipping"%>
<!DOCTYPE HTML PUBLIC "-//W3C//DTD HTML 4.0 Transitional//EN">
<HTML>
    <HEAD>
        <title>Manage Shipping</title>
        <meta content="Microsoft Visual Studio.NET 7.0" name="GENERATOR">
        <meta content="Visual Basic 7.0" name="CODE_LANGUAGE">
        <meta content="JavaScript" name="vs_defaultClientScript">
        <meta content="http://schemas.microsoft.com/intellisense/ie5"
         name="vs_targetSchema">
        <!-- ManageFreeShipping.aspx -
         Manage the free shipping table for the store -->
    </HEAD>
    <body>
        <!-- #Include File="ValidateCheck.inc" -->
        <!-- #Include File="Navbar.inc" -->
```

```
<form id="Form1" method="post" runat="server">
    <P><asp:datagrid id="dgFreeShip" runat="server"
    BorderColor="#DEDFDE" BorderStyle="None" BorderWidth="1px"
     BackColor="White" CellPadding="4" GridLines="Vertical"
      ForeColor="Black" DataKeyField="FreeShipID"
       AutoGenerateColumns="False">
            <SelectedItemStyle Font-Bold="True" ForeColor="White"
             BackColor="#CE5D5A"></SelectedItemStyle>
            <AlternatingItemStyle BackColor="White">
            </AlternatingItemStyle>
            <ItemStyle BackColor="#F7F7DE"></ItemStyle>
            <HeaderStyle Font-Bold="True" ForeColor="White"
             BackColor="#6B696B"></HeaderStyle>
            <FooterStyle BackColor="#CCCC99"></FooterStyle>
            <Columns>
                <asp:EditCommandColumn ButtonType="LinkButton"
                 UpdateText="Update" CancelText="Cancel"
                  EditText="Edit"></asp:EditCommandColumn>
                <asp:ButtonColumn Text="Delete"
                 CommandName="Delete"></asp:ButtonColumn>
                <asp:BoundColumn Visible="False"
                 DataField="FreeShipID" HeaderText="FreeShipID">
                  </asp:BoundColumn>
                <asp:BoundColumn DataField="FreeShipStartDate"
                 HeaderText="Starting Date"></asp:BoundColumn>
                <asp:BoundColumn DataField="FreeShipEndDate"
                 HeaderText="Ending Date"></asp:BoundColumn>
            </Columns>
            <PagerStyle HorizontalAlign="Right" ForeColor="Black"
             BackColor="#F7F7DE" Mode="NumericPages">
            </PagerStyle>
    </asp:datagrid></P>
    <H3>Add a Free Shipping Promotion:</H3>
    <P>
        <TABLE id="Table1" cellSpacing="1" cellPadding="1"
        width="100%" border="0">
            <TR>
                <TD><asp:label id="Label1" runat="server">
                Starting Date</asp:label></TD>
                <TD><asp:textbox id="txtStartDate"
                 runat="server"></asp:textbox></TD>
            </TR>
            <TR>
                <TD><asp:label id="Label2" runat="server">
                Ending Date</asp:label></TD>
                <TD><asp:textbox id="txtEndDate"
                 runat="server"></asp:textbox></TD>
            </TR>
            <TR>
```

```
                    <TD></TD>
                    <TD><asp:button id="btnAddPromotion"
                     runat="server" Text="Add Promotion"
                        Width="115px"></asp:button></TD>
                </TR>
            </TABLE>
        </P>
    </form>
  </body>
</HTML>
```

The code behind this page handles the database tasks of retrieving, updating, deleting, and adding data. It starts with the Page_Load procedure shown in Listing 15.21. This procedure displays the initial data when the page is first loaded and updates the database on a postback.

Listing 15.21   ManageFreeShipping.aspx.vb Page_Load Procedure

```
Private Sub Page_Load(ByVal sender As System.Object, _
 ByVal e As System.EventArgs) Handles MyBase.Load
    If Not IsPostBack Then
        ' Initial form load, so bind the grid
        BindGrid()
    Else
        If txtStartDate.Text <> "" Then
            ' Add a new promotion to the table
            With cmdManagerAddFreeShip
                .Parameters("@FreeShipStartDate").Value = _
                CDate(txtStartDate.Text)
                .Parameters("@FreeShipEndDate").Value = _
                CDate(txtEndDate.Text)
                cnn.Open()
                .ExecuteNonQuery()
                cnn.Close()
                dgFreeShip.EditItemIndex = -1
                txtStartDate.Text = ""
                txtEndDate.Text = ""
            End With
            BindGrid()
        End If
    End If
End Sub
```

When the page is first loaded, the Page_Load procedure calls the BindGrid procedure shown in Listing 15.22. We also call this procedure anytime the contents of the table have been edited.

Listing 15.22   **ManageFreeShipping.aspx.vb BindGrid Procedure**

```
Private Sub BindGrid()
    ' Retrieve free shipping promotions from the database
    ' and bind them to the DataGrid
    Dim daFreeShip As New SqlDataAdapter()
    Dim dsFreeShip As New DataSet()
    daFreeShip.SelectCommand = cmdManagerGetFreeShip
    daFreeShip.Fill(dsFreeShip, "FreeShip")
    dgFreeShip.DataSource = dsFreeShip
    dgFreeShip.DataMember = "FreeShip"
    DataBind()
End Sub
```

The BindGrid procedure uses the procManagerGetFreeShip stored procedure, shown in Listing 15.23, to retrieve all of the current data from the FreeShip table.

Listing 15.23   **procManagerGetFreeShip Stored Procedure**

```
/*  Retrieve all free shipping information

From .NET E-Commerce Programming
by Mike Gunderloy and Noel Jerke
Copyright 2002, Sybex Inc. All Rights Reserved. */
CREATE PROCEDURE procManagerGetFreeShip
AS
SELECT * FROM FreeShip
```

When the user adds the information for a new free-shipping promotion and clicks the Add Promotion button, the code calls the procManagerAddFreeShip stored procedure, shown in Listing 15.24.

Listing 15.24   **procManagerAddFreeShip Stored Procedure**

```
/*  Add a new free shipping promotion

From .NET E-Commerce Programming
by Mike Gunderloy and Noel Jerke
Copyright 2002, Sybex Inc. All Rights Reserved. */
CREATE PROCEDURE procManagerAddFreeShip
  @FreeShipStartDate datetime,
  @FreeShipEndDate datetime
AS
  INSERT INTO FreeShip (FreeShipStartDate, FreeShipEndDate)
  VALUES (@FreeShipStartDate, @FreeShipEndDate)
```

The rest of the code behind this page manages operations in the DataGrid control: editing, canceling edits, saving updates, and deleting rows. This code is shown in Listing 15.25.

Listing 15.25   ManageFreeShipping.aspx.vb Event Procedures

```vb
Private Sub dgFreeShip_CancelCommand(ByVal source As System.Object, _
 ByVal e As System.Web.UI.WebControls.DataGridCommandEventArgs) _
 Handles dgFreeShip.CancelCommand
    ' Take the grid out of edit mode
    dgFreeShip.EditItemIndex = -1
    BindGrid()
End Sub

Private Sub dgFreeShip_DeleteCommand(ByVal source As System.Object, _
 ByVal e As System.Web.UI.WebControls.DataGridCommandEventArgs) _
 Handles dgFreeShip.DeleteCommand
    ' Delete the selected row from the database
    With cmdManagerDeleteFreeShip
        .Parameters("@FreeShipID").Value = _
         dgFreeShip.DataKeys(CInt(e.Item.ItemIndex))
        cnn.Open()
        .ExecuteNonQuery()
        cnn.Close()
        dgFreeShip.EditItemIndex = -1
    End With
    BindGrid()
End Sub

Private Sub dgFreeShip_EditCommand(ByVal source As System.Object, _
 ByVal e As System.Web.UI.WebControls.DataGridCommandEventArgs) _
 Handles dgFreeShip.EditCommand
    ' Show the selected row for editing
    dgFreeShip.EditItemIndex = CInt(e.Item.ItemIndex)
    BindGrid()
End Sub

Private Sub dgFreeShip_UpdateCommand(ByVal source As System.Object, _
 ByVal e As System.Web.UI.WebControls.DataGridCommandEventArgs) _
 Handles dgFreeShip.UpdateCommand
    ' Update the selected row in the database
    With cmdManagerUpdateFreeShip
        .Parameters("@FreeShipID").Value = _
         dgFreeShip.DataKeys(CInt(e.Item.ItemIndex))
        .Parameters("@FreeShipStartDate").Value = _
         CDate(CType(e.Item.Cells(3).Controls(0), TextBox).Text)
        .Parameters("@FreeShipEndDate").Value = _
         CDate(CType(e.Item.Cells(4).Controls(0), TextBox).Text)
        cnn.Open()
        .ExecuteNonQuery()
        cnn.Close()
```

```
        dgFreeShip.EditItemIndex = -1
    End With
    BindGrid()
End Sub
```

These event procedures call two stored procedures to do their work. The procManager-UpdateFreeShip stored procedure, shown in Listing 15.26, saves any changes from the grid back to the database.

Listing 15.26   procManagerUpdateFreeShip Stored Procedure

```
/*  Update a free shipping promotion

From .NET E-Commerce Programming
by Mike Gunderloy and Noel Jerke
Copyright 2002, Sybex Inc. All Rights Reserved. */
CREATE PROCEDURE procManagerUpdateFreeShip
  @FreeShipID int,
  @FreeShipStartDate datetime,
  @FreeShipEndDate datetime
AS
  UPDATE FreeShip
    SET FreeShipStartDate = @FreeShipStartDate,
      FreeShipEndDate = @FreeShipEndDate
    WHERE FreeShipID = @FreeShipID
```

Finally, the procManagerDeleteFreeShip stored procedure, shown in Listing 15.27, is called to delete a row from the table.

Listing 15.27   procManagerDeleteFreeShip Stored Procedure

```
/*  Delete a free shipping promotion

From .NET E-Commerce Programming
by Mike Gunderloy and Noel Jerke
Copyright 2002, Sybex Inc. All Rights Reserved. */
CREATE PROCEDURE procManagerDeleteFreeShip
  @FreeShipID int
AS
  DELETE FROM FreeShip
    WHERE FreeShipID = @FreeShipID
```

When it comes to working with orders for which free shipping was in effect when the orders were placed, we have a choice to make. We could add additional code to the Store-Manager application to check whether an order originally had free shipping and to prevent users from adding shipping charges to such an order. However, that wouldn't be consistent with the rest of the order management functionality in the StoreManager application. As the application stands now, we allow users to change anything about an order, rather than limit their actions. This is necessary so that they can deal with whatever shopper problems may arise.

It's easy to come up with reasons why a customer service agent might want to alter the shipping status for an order. For instance, it may sometimes make sense to apply free shipping to an order even though it wasn't placed during a free-shipping promotion, perhaps to placate an irate customer. On the other hand, if a customer wants to add many items to an existing order, the customer may be willing to pay reasonable shipping costs, no matter when the initial order was placed.

In view of these considerations, we've opted not to limit the changes that our users can make to shipping charges through the StoreManager application.

We'll conclude the chapter by taking a look at free-shipping management in action. Figure 15.8 shows the manager menu with the addition of the free-shipping management.

FIGURE 15.8:

Manager menu

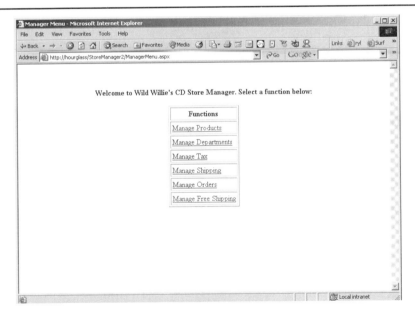

Clicking the Manage Free Shipping link opens the page shown in Figure 15.9.

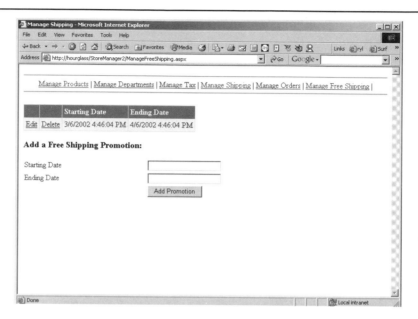

Figure 15.10 shows the same page after adding a second free-shipping promotion to the database. You can experiment with the page to see the edit and delete functionalities as well.

Summary

We've now finished building both our store application and our management application! Of course, we could implement many other promotional ideas. For example, we might want to create a complete sale department, where all items are on sale. Another idea would be to implement quantity discounts for large purchases.

In the next part of the book, we'll explore some advanced topics that you might need to consider as you create your own e-commerce application. These include localizing your user interface into multiple languages, best practices, and scalability considerations for growing businesses.

Part V

Advanced Topics

CHAPTER 16

Localization

- What Is Localization?

- Understanding Cultures

- Localizing ASP.NET Pages

- Working with Resource Files

In the days before the Internet, most software developers never worried about localization. The majority of applications were written in a single human language, and all the users and developers spoke the same language. But when you're doing business on the Internet, things are different. Your next user is as likely to be in Tokyo as in Toledo. Unless you're simply going to refuse to do business with residents of other countries, you need to think about translating your application into multiple languages—a process known as "localization." Fortunately, the .NET Framework provides excellent support for localizing applications. In this chapter, we'll look at the general facilities that the .NET Framework supplies for localization and then see how those facilities can be used to localize part of our e-commerce application.

What Is Localization?

Suppose you're planning to ship an application to customers in the United States, France, and China. There are two basic ways that you could undertake this task:

- Develop the application for the three different customers using three completely different sets of source code.

- Develop the application using a single set of source code, customized as necessary for the three different customers.

In most cases, the first of these alternatives is prohibitively expensive. Developing different sets of source code for different versions of an application requires more developers, more testers, and more managers. Worse, a bug that's fixed in one version might slip through the cracks in another version. Also, if you need to add a fourth language to the mix, you need to go through all the effort of developing the application again.

More commonly, applications are developed from a single code base, which is then customized for individual languages. (As you'll see later in the chapter, customization can also extend far beyond language translation.) This allows you to quickly produce new versions of your application without excess expense.

The Localization Process

The process of preparing an application for shipment in a new language is called *localization*. Microsoft divides the process of preparing a "world-ready application" into three phases:

Globalization   *Globalization* is the process of preparing an application to be localized. This step involves identifying all the localizable resources in an application and separating them from executable code so that they can be modified easily.

Localizability   In the *localizability* phase of the process, you check to ensure that translating the application won't require code changes. If you've planned for localization all along, this phase can be performed as part of your normal quality assurance (QA) process.

Localization   Finally, in the *localization* phase of the process, you customize your application for new locales. This consists primarily of translating the resources identified during the globalization phase into new languages.

TIP   Globalization has taken on increasing importance in recent years as the software market expands worldwide. One way to keep up with developments in this area is to monitor the Microsoft Global Software Development website at www.microsoft.com/globaldev/.

What Should Be Localized?

The most obvious portion of an application that needs to be localized is the text that appears on the user interface of the application. But there are many other features of an application that may need to vary from locale to locale. Here is a list of commonly localized resources:

- Text that appears on the user interface.
- Other text in the application. (For example, menu items, error messages, and message boxes will need to be translated.)
- The display format for dates and times.
- The display format for currency.
- The display format for numbers (for example, whether commas or periods are used as thousands separators in long numbers).
- Data input fields. (For example, zip codes are unique to the United States.)
- Maps and other graphics containing local information.
- Shortcut keys. (Not every character you know appears on every keyboard.)
- Calendars. (Not everyone uses the Gregorian calendar.)
- Alphabetical sorting order.
- Control size. A phrase of 15 characters in English might be 30 or more in German. You need to either resize controls for different locales or make your controls large enough to hold the text in any language.

Of course, not every application will contain all these resources. And even if an application contains a particular resource, you may choose not to localize it. For example, you might decide that showing input fields for address, state, province, postal code, and country is preferable to researching street address formats around the world, no matter what languages you use for the user interface.

Understanding Cultures

The .NET Framework identifies the target audience for localized content by specifying a *culture*. A culture is a more precise concept than a language. For example, U.S. English and U.K. English are two different cultures in the .NET Framework. To completely localize an application, you must depend on cultures rather than languages. This should be obvious if you think about the list of resources that may need to be localized. For example, the formatting of currency and date values differs between the United States and the United Kingdom, even though these countries share (for the most part) a single language.

Culture Codes

The .NET Framework identifies cultures by a set of abbreviations. Each abbreviation consists of a culture code followed by one or more subculture codes. By convention, culture codes are written in lowercase, while subculture codes are written in uppercase. Here are some examples:

- **es** identifies the Spanish culture. This is a *neutral culture*—that is, one that doesn't specify a subculture code. Generally, you won't use neutral cultures in your applications.

- **nl-BE** identifies the Dutch (Belgium) culture. This *specific culture* includes enough information to localize an application for use by Dutch speakers who live in Belgium.

- **sr-SP-Latn** is an example of a specific culture with multiple subculture codes. It identifies Serbian in Serbia written in Latin characters.

The .NET Framework culture codes are a subset of those defined in RFC 1766. RFC stands for "Request for Comments"; the numbered RFCs are a series of documents that define protocols and conventions for the Internet. You can find the text of RFC 1766 at `www.faqs.org/rfcs/rfc1766.html` if you'd like to learn more.

At this point, you may be wondering which cultures the .NET Framework supports. To answer that question, you'll need to know something about the System.Globalization namespace.

The System.Globalization Namespace

The System.Globalization namespace in the .NET Framework contains classes that handle culture-specific information. Table 16.1 lists the classes in this namespace.

TABLE 16.1: Classes in the System.Globalization Namespace

Class	Description
Calendar	An abstract class that represents the general notion of a culture-specific calendar
CompareInfo	A collection of methods for culture-specific string comparisons
CultureInfo	Information about all aspects of a particular culture
DateTimeFormatInfo	Information about formatting dates and times
DaylightTime	Information about daylight savings time
GregorianCalendar	An implementation of the Calendar class that represents the Gregorian (common Western) calendar
HebrewCalendar	An implementation of the Calendar class that represents the Hebrew calendar
HijriCalendar	An implementation of the Calendar class that represents the Hijri (Islamic) calendar
JapaneseCalendar	An implementation of the Calendar class that represents the Japanese calendar
JulianCalendar	An implementation of the Calendar class that represents the Julian (older Western) calendar
KoreanCalendar	An implementation of the Calendar class that represents the Korean calendar
NumberFormatInfo	Information about formatting numbers and currency values
RegionInfo	Information about a particular region or country
SortKey	Information for sorting strings
StringInfo	Provides methods to split a string into elements and iterate over those elements
TaiwanCalendar	An implementation of the Calendar class that represents the Taiwanese calendar
TextElementEnumerator	Used in conjunction with StringInfo to iterate elements in a string
TextInfo	Information about formatting text
ThaiBuddhistCalendar	An implementation of the Calendar class that represents the Thai Buddhist calendar

You can use the CultureInfo class in conjunction with other classes from the System.Globalization namespace to retrieve information on any culture that the .NET Framework supports. Figure 16.1 shows the frmInfo form, which is displaying information about a particular culture. You'll find the frmInfo form in the Cultures sample project on this book's companion CD.

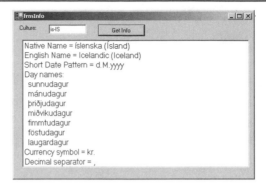

Listing 16.1 shows the code that generated the culture information shown in Figure 16.1.

Listing 16.1   **frmInfo.vb btnGetInfo_Click Procedure**

```vb
Private Sub btnGetInfo_Click(ByVal sender As System.Object, _
ByVal e As System.EventArgs) Handles btnGetInfo.Click
    ' Create a CultureInfo object for the requested culture
    Dim ci As CultureInfo = New CultureInfo(txtCulture.Text)
    With lboInfo.Items
        .Clear()
        ' Get some basic information about the culture
        .Add("Native Name = " & ci.NativeName)
        .Add("English Name = " & ci.EnglishName)
        ' Get some date formatting information
        Dim dtfi As DateTimeFormatInfo = ci.DateTimeFormat
        .Add("Short Date Pattern = " & dtfi.ShortDatePattern)
        Dim strDayNames() As String = dtfi.DayNames
        Dim strDay As String
        .Add("Day names: ")
        For Each strDay In strDayNames
            .Add("   " & strDay)
        Next
        ' Get some numeric formatting information
        Dim nfi As NumberFormatInfo = ci.NumberFormat
        .Add("Currency symbol = " & nfi.CurrencySymbol)
        .Add("Decimal separator = " & nfi.NumberDecimalSeparator)
    End With
End Sub
```

The CultureInfo Class

The key class in the System.Globalization namespace is the CultureInfo class. Table 16.2
shows some of the methods and properties of this class.

TABLE 16.2: Members of the CultureInfo Class

Member	Type	Description
Calendar	Property	The default Calendar object for the culture
ClearCachedData	Method	Refreshes cached culture-related information (for example, the user's setting for date formats)
CompareInfo	Property	A CompareInfo object for the culture
CurrentCulture	Property	The culture being used by the current thread
CurrentUICulture	Property	The culture being used to look up resources
DateTimeFormat	Property	A DateTimeFormatInfo object for the culture
DisplayName	Property	The name of the culture in the language of the installed version of the .NET Framework
EnglishName	Property	The name of the culture in English
GetCultures	Method	Gets a list of supported cultures
InstalledUICulture	Property	The culture of the current version of the operating system
InvariantCulture	Property	A special culture that isn't localized
Name	Property	The culture and subculture codes for this culture
NativeName	Property	The name of the culture in its own language
NumberFormat	Property	A NumberFormatInfo object for the culture
TextInfo	Property	A TextInfo object for the culture

As you'll see later in the chapter, creating a CultureInfo object and setting its properties are keys to localizing your applications. Two properties in particular are critical to making sure that your application uses the correct resources for the chosen culture: CurrentUI-Culture and CurrentCulture.

The CurrentUICulture Property

You'll actually find the CurrentUICulture property on two different objects. As you've already seen, this is a property of the CultureInfo object; but it's also a property of the Thread object, which you'll find in the System.Threading namespace.

A Thread object represents a thread of execution in a running application. In particular, the Thread.CurrentThread property returns a static Thread object that represents the currently executing thread. The CurrentUICulture property of this object is the culture that will be used by the .NET Framework as the user interface culture for the application. The .NET Framework retrieves this culture and uses it to look up culture-specific resources at runtime.

Although you set this property through the Thread.CurrentThread object, you can retrieve its value from any CultureInfo object. For example, consider this code snippet:

```
Imports System.Threading
Imports System.Globalization
...
Thread.CurrentThread.CurrentUICulture = New CultureInfo("de-DE")
MessageBox.Show (Thread.CurrentThread.CurrentUICulture.Name)
Dim ci As New CultureInfo("en-US")
MessageBox.Show (ci.CurrentUICulture.Name)
```

This code sets the user interface culture to German (Germany) by creating a new Culture-Info object and then assigning it to the Thread.CurrentThread.CurrentUICulture property. As you'd expect, the first MessageBox statement returns de-DE as the name of the Culture-Info retrieved from the thread at that point. The code then goes on to create an independent CultureInfo object representing the English (United States) culture. What you might *not* expect is that the second MessageBox statement also returns de-DE. Although the new Cul-tureInfo object uses the en-US culture, it still knows that the CurrentUICulture value is the one that is set on the executing thread.

The CurrentCulture Property

The CurrentCulture property is very similar to the CurrentUICulture property. It appears on the same two objects, and it can be set and retrieved the same way. For example, you could translate the preceding code snippet to work with the CurrentCulture property instead of the CurrentUICulture property:

```
Imports System.Threading
Imports System.Globalization
...
Thread.CurrentThread.CurrentCulture = New CultureInfo("de-DE")
MessageBox.Show (Thread.CurrentThread.CurrentCulture.Name)
Dim ci As New CultureInfo("en-US")
MessageBox.Show (ci.CurrentCulture.Name)
```

Just as in the previous example, both MessageBox calls will return de-DE as the Current-Culture name.

The difference between CurrentCulture and CurrentUICulture is in their use by the .NET Framework. The CurrentUICulture property is used to retrieve culture-specific resources (most importantly, text for the user interface) from an appropriate file. The Cur-rentCulture property is used to set the format for dates, times, currency, and numbers, as well as other culture-specific functionality, including sorting order, string comparison rules, and casing rules.

Enumerating Cultures

So, now that you've seen the class representation of cultures, how do you get a list of all available cultures? The answer lies in the GetCultures method of the CultureInfo object. This method takes a CultureTypes parameter that specifies a set of cultures to be returned. Table 16.3 shows the available values for the CultureTypes parameter.

TABLE 16.3: Values for the CultureTypes Parameter

Value	Meaning
AllCultures	All cultures understood by the .NET Framework
InstalledWin32Cultures	All cultures installed on the operating system
NeutralCultures	All neutral cultures
SpecificCultures	All specific cultures

The GetCultures method returns an array of CultureInfo objects. So, to see all the cultures that the .NET Framework supports, you can retrieve an array using GetCultures(AllCultures) and iterate through its contents. Listing 16.2 shows the code that accomplishes this task; it's from frmCultures.vb in the Cultures sample project.

Listing 16.2   **frmCultures.vb ShowCultures Procedure**

```
Private Sub ShowCultures()
    Dim ci As CultureInfo
    Dim lvi As New ListViewItem()
    ' Clear any information already in the ListView
    lvwCultures.Items.Clear()
    ' Decide which cultures to get, based on the
    ' user's choice in the combo box
    Select Case cboCultureTypes.Text
        Case "AllCultures"
            For Each ci In CultureInfo.GetCultures( _
              CultureTypes.AllCultures)
                lvi = lvwCultures.Items.Add(ci.Name)
                lvi.SubItems.Add(ci.EnglishName)
            Next
        Case "InstalledWin32Cultures"
            For Each ci In CultureInfo.GetCultures( _
              CultureTypes.InstalledWin32Cultures)
                lvi = lvwCultures.Items.Add(ci.Name)
                lvi.SubItems.Add(ci.EnglishName)
            Next
        Case "NeutralCultures"
            For Each ci In CultureInfo.GetCultures( _
              CultureTypes.NeutralCultures)
```

```
            lvi = lvwCultures.Items.Add(ci.Name)
            lvi.SubItems.Add(ci.EnglishName)
        Next
    Case "SpecificCultures"
        For Each ci In CultureInfo.GetCultures( _
        CultureTypes.SpecificCultures)
            lvi = lvwCultures.Items.Add(ci.Name)
            lvi.SubItems.Add(ci.EnglishName)
        Next
    End Select
End Sub
```

Figure 16.2 shows this code in action.

FIGURE 16.2:

Enumerating .NET
cultures

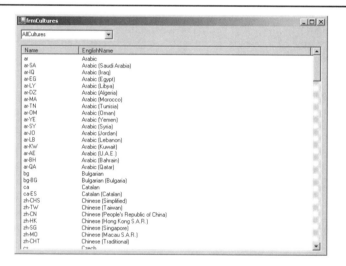

As you can see in the figure, the .NET Framework supports a great variety of cultures, even in its first release. In fact, counting all of the neutral cultures and specific cultures, there are 202 supported cultures in the .NET Framework. Certainly that doesn't cover every culture on the face of the planet, but it's enough for most applications.

The Invariant Culture

If you run the code in Listing 16.2 and inspect the list of all cultures, you'll find a curious one at the end of the list: the invariant culture, which doesn't have an abbreviation. This culture has two purposes:

- Interacting with other software, such as system services, where no user is involved

- Storing data in a culture-independent format that won't be displayed directly to end users

You can create a CultureInfo object for the invariant culture in one of two ways. The following two lines of code produce exactly the same result:

```
Dim ciInv As CultureInfo = New CultureInfo("")
Dim ciInv As CultureInfo = CultureInfo.InvariantCulture
```

Displaying Localized Information

Now that you've seen the CultureInfo class, it's time to see how to use it in code. Figure 16.3 shows the frmInvariant form in the Cultures sample project. This form displays a DateTime value and a Currency value using the invariant culture. You can then select any other culture from the combo box, and the form will use a CultureInfo object to convert the invariant versions of the information to localized versions.

FIGURE 16.3:

Displaying invariant and localized information

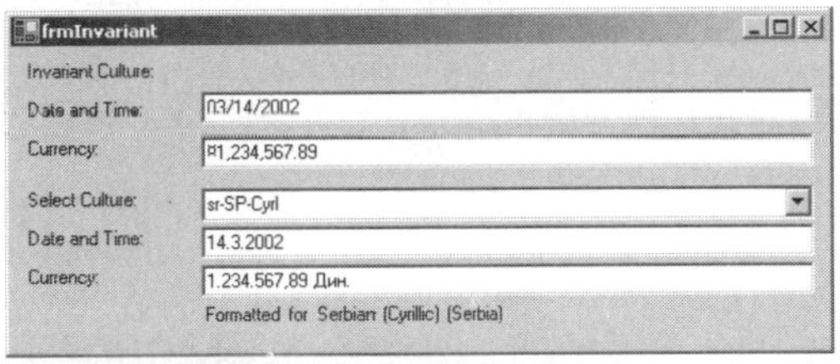

The code from this sample introduces some of the essential techniques for localizing information in code. Listing 16.3 shows the Form_Load procedure, which sets up the user interface when the form is first loaded.

Listing 16.3   frmInvariant Form_Load Procedure

```
Private Sub frmInvariant_Load(ByVal sender As System.Object, _
ByVal e As System.EventArgs) Handles MyBase.Load
    ' Get all specific cultures into the combo box
    Dim ci As CultureInfo
    For Each ci In CultureInfo.GetCultures( _
    CultureTypes.SpecificCultures)
        cboSelectCulture.Items.Add(ci.Name)
    Next
    ' Get a date and a currency value to work with
    Dim dtTest As Date = DateTime.Now
    Dim curTest As Double = 1234567.89
    ' Get the invariant culture
    Dim ciInv As CultureInfo = CultureInfo.InvariantCulture
    ' And use it to format the values
    txtInvariantDateTime.Text = dtTest.ToString("d", ciInv)
    txtInvariantCurrency.Text = curTest.ToString("c", ciInv)
End Sub
```

This block of code creates two variables; one holds a DateTime value, and the other holds a numeric value that the program will interpret as currency. It then creates an instance of the CultureInfo object for the invariant culture. This allows the code to store the two values in a culture-neutral fashion. As you can see, the ToString method of both variables is overloaded to accept both a format string (here, `"d"` for short date, or `"c"` for currency) and a Culture-Info that specifies the target culture for the result.

When the user selects a culture from the combo box, the code in Listing 16.4 is executed by the .NET Framework.

Listing 16.4 **frmInvariant cboSelectCulture_SelectIndexChanged Procedure**

```
Private Sub cboSelectCulture_SelectedIndexChanged( _
 ByVal sender As Object, ByVal e As System.EventArgs) _
 Handles cboSelectCulture.SelectedIndexChanged
    Dim dttest As Date
    Dim curTest As Double
    ' Get the invariant culture
    Dim ciInv As CultureInfo = CultureInfo.InvariantCulture
    ' And use it to parse the invariant values back to variables
    dttest = DateTime.Parse(txtInvariantDateTime.Text, ciInv)
    curTest = Double.Parse(txtInvariantCurrency.Text, _
     NumberStyles.Currency, ciInv)
    ' Get the selected culture
    Dim ci As CultureInfo = New CultureInfo(cboSelectCulture.Text)
    lblCulture.Text = "Formatted for " & ci.EnglishName
    ' And use it to format the values
    txtCultureDateTime.Text = dttest.ToString("d", ci)
    txtCultureCurrency.Text = curTest.ToString("c", ci)
End Sub
```

Here again, the code begins with an invariant culture CultureInfo object. This object is used in conjunction with the Parse methods of the appropriate data types to retrieve the original values from the invariant-formatted versions of the data. Then the code creates a localized CultureInfo object based on the user's selection and uses this new object to format the values for display in that culture.

If you experiment with this form, you'll see that the date and currency formats change as you move from culture to culture. All of this functionality is built directly into the .NET Framework; we don't need to put a single culture-specific formatting string or currency symbol into the code.

Localizing ASP.NET Pages

Now that you've seen the classes provided by the .NET Framework to help with localization, it's time to investigate an actual application. Rather than localize the entire CDStore or StoreManager application, we'll use a single page from the StoreManager application to demonstrate the principles of localizing ASP.NET applications.

The StoreManagerLocalize application contains copies of the `ManageOrders.aspx` and `OrderDetails.aspx` pages from the StoreManager application. It also contains additional code that demonstrates localization of the `OrderDetails.aspx` page.

NOTE   You'll find a copy of the `StoreManagerLocalize` application, together with installation instructions, on the companion CD.

Setting the Culture Properties

In order to display localized information in an ASP.NET application, you need to set the CurrentCulture and CurrentUICulture properties of the executing thread to appropriate values. You can't depend on the values of Thread.CurrentThread.CurrentCulture and Thread.CurrentThread.CurrentUICulture to be correct for the user of the application. That's because those values will be set by default from the language of the server's operating system, not from the language of the client. Remember, ASP.NET code executes exclusively on your web server. What's sent to the client is the pure HTML result of executing that code.

You have two choices for setting these properties: You can set them based on information sent by the user's web browser, or you can provide a user interface to let the user choose a culture.

If you want the application to automatically sense the culture to use, you can retrieve the value of Request.UserLanguages(0) when you're processing a page. The ASP.NET Request object returns an array of strings specifying the language that the user's browser has set. The first member of this array will be the default language of the browser, in RFC 1766 format. You can use this value to create an appropriate CultureInfo object for the current thread. Here's an example:

```
Thread.CurrentThread.CurrentCulture = _
  New CultureInfo(Request.UserLanguages(0))
```

There are several reasons, though, why this strategy is often unworkable in practice:

- Web browsers aren't required to specify a user language when sending an HTTP request for a web page.

- Even if a web browser specifies one or more acceptable languages, there's no guarantee that any of those languages will exactly match a culture that the .NET Framework makes available.

- The user may well be using a web browser whose language doesn't match the user's own preferred language.

For these reasons (and for ease of testing our localization code), we've opted to use the second strategy in the StoreManagerLocalize application. The application starts with a web page, ChooseCultures.aspx, that allows the user to explicitly specify both their preferred culture and their preferred user interface culture. Listing 16.5 shows the HTML code for this page.

Listing 16.5   **ChooseCultures.aspx**

```
<%@ Page Language="vb" AutoEventWireup="false"
 Codebehind="ChooseCultures.aspx.vb"
 Inherits="StoreManagerLocalize.ChooseCultures"%>
<!DOCTYPE HTML PUBLIC "-//W3C//DTD HTML 4.0 Transitional//EN">
<HTML>
    <HEAD>
        <title>Choose Cultures</title>
        <meta name="GENERATOR" content="Microsoft Visual Studio.NET 7.0">
        <meta name="CODE_LANGUAGE" content="Visual Basic 7.0">
        <meta name="vs_defaultClientScript" content="JavaScript">
        <meta name="vs_targetSchema"
         content="http://schemas.microsoft.com/intellisense/ie5">
    </HEAD>
    <body>
        <form id="Form1" method="post" runat="server">
            <P>Culture for detail page:</P>
            <P><asp:RadioButtonList id="rblCurrentCulture"
             runat="server" Height="16px" RepeatColumns="2">
                    <asp:ListItem Value="English" Selected="True">
                    English</asp:ListItem>
                    <asp:ListItem Value="Swedish">Swedish</asp:ListItem>
                </asp:RadioButtonList></P>
            <P>User interface culture for detail page:</P>
            <P><asp:RadioButtonList id="rblCurrentUICulture"
             runat="server" Height="16px" RepeatColumns="2">
                    <asp:ListItem Value="English" Selected="True">
                    English</asp:ListItem>
                    <asp:ListItem Value="Swedish">Swedish</asp:ListItem>
                </asp:RadioButtonList></P>
            <P>
                <asp:Button id="btnSubmit" runat="server" Text="Submit">
                </asp:Button></P>
        </form>
    </body>
</HTML>
```

4

This page contains two sets of radio buttons, which allow the user to choose between English and Swedish for both the CurrentCulture and CurrentUICulture properties. Figure 16.4 shows this page in the web browser.

NOTE   In a real application, you would almost certainly offer only one set of controls for choosing cultures and would set the CurrentCulture and CurrentUICulture properties to the same value. We're using two choices in this application so that you can see the effects of the choices individually.

FIGURE 16.4:

Selecting cultures for an application

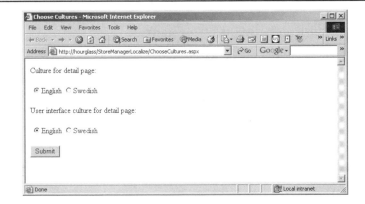

When the user clicks the Submit button on the ChooseCultures.aspx page, the code behind the page stores the user's choices in session variables, as shown in Listing 16.6.

Listing 16.6   **ChooseCultures.aspx.vb Page_Load Procedure**

```
Private Sub Page_Load(ByVal sender As System.Object, _
    ByVal e As System.EventArgs) Handles MyBase.Load
    If IsPostBack Then
        ' Set the CurrentCulture for the application
        If rblCurrentCulture.SelectedItem.Value = "English" Then
            Session("CurrentCulture") = "en-US"
        Else
            Session("CurrentCulture") = "sv-SE"
        End If
        ' Set the CurrentUICulture for the application
        If rblCurrentUICulture.SelectedItem.Value = "English" Then
            Session("CurrentUICulture") = "en-US"
        Else
            Session("CurrentUICulture") = "sv-SE"
```

```
            End If
            Server.Transfer("ManageOrders.aspx")
        End If
    End Sub
```

By placing these choices into session variables, the page makes them available to all other web pages loaded during the session. Note that it wouldn't do any good to use the choices to set the Thread.CurrentThread properties directly. Because each ASP.NET page is generated anew when it's requested, the thread that's processing the ChooseCultures.aspx page won't necessarily be the same thread that delivers any other page.

Handling CurrentCulture Changes

The CurrentCulture property, as you've already seen, handles the formatting of dates, times, currency values, and so on. If you set this property in code, the .NET Framework will handle the details for you. The OrderDetail.aspx.vb web page includes this code in its Page_Load procedure to handle the CurrentCulture property:

```
' Set the CurrentCulture for the page
Thread.CurrentThread.CurrentCulture = _
    New CultureInfo(CStr(Session("CurrentCulture")))
```

By executing that code, the page tells the .NET Framework how to format the information on the page. Figure 16.5 shows the OrderDetail.aspx web page with the CurrentCulture property set to sv-SE, the value for Swedish in Sweden. As you can see, the order date is displayed using Swedish formatting, and currency values are represented in kroner, the currency of Sweden.

> **NOTE**   You'll need to use the search page to get to the detail page, just as in the full version of the StoreManager application.

> **NOTE**   Of course, there isn't any attempt here to convert the actual monetary values from dollars to kroner! Localization deals strictly with the formatting of information, not with changing business rules.

FIGURE 16.5:

Web page with
CurrentCulture
set to sv-SE

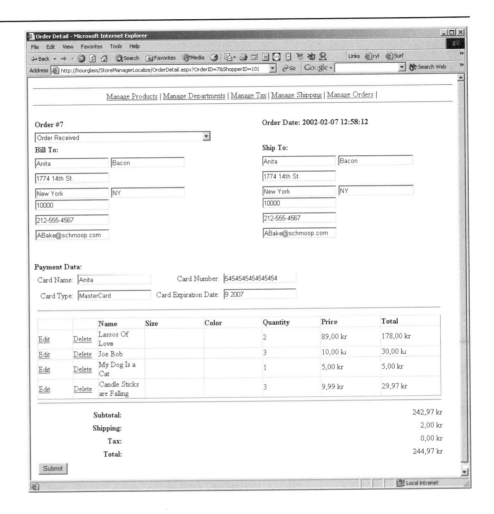

Working with Resource Files

Of course, localizing the display of currency and dates is only part of the job. Localizing the text on the user interface is perhaps even more important. The .NET Framework offers several places to store localized versions of text resources:

External resource files   For each supported culture, you can create a file containing the resources for that culture. Each of these files is created by first building a plain-text file with key and value pairs, and then using the resgen.exe tool to compile a file with the extension .resources. External resource files are useful when you're depending on an outside translator to provide localized text. You can ship the text files to the translator, and the translator won't need any special tools to localize the text.

Satellite assemblies   Satellite assemblies are made by compiling external resource files into a Windows library (DLL) file. You need to create one satellite assembly for each supported culture and store the assemblies in special locations on the hard drive of your web server. At runtime, you can load the appropriate assembly by using methods from the System.Reflection namespace. Satellite assemblies are useful if you need to be able to make changes to localized text without shutting down your web application, because assemblies, like other DLL files, are copied to a shadow folder.

Assembly resource files   Assembly resource files are specially formatted XML files that contain localized text. You need to create one assembly resource file for each supported culture. These assembly resource files can be included directly in your web application, and .NET will choose the correct set of resources at runtime based on the CurrentUI-Culture property of the executing thread.

In our sample application, we've chosen to use assembly resource files to hold the localized text.

Creating Assembly Resource Files

To add an assembly resource file to a web application, follow these steps:

1. Select Project ➤ Add New Item from the Visual Studio .NET menu.

2. Select the Assembly resource file template. Assign a name to the template, keeping the default extension .resx.

3. Click Open to create the file. The blank file will open in the Visual Studio IDE, where you can edit the file in a grid.

4. For each string that you want to localize, assign a name and a value by typing in the grid. Optionally, you can also enter a comment for each string—perhaps to remind you where the string is used on the user interface.

Figure 16.6 shows an assembly resource file that's open in the default editor.

FIGURE 16.6:

Creating an assembly
resource file

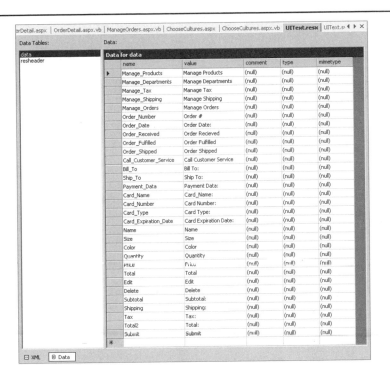

You don't need to worry about the Type and Mimetype columns when you're creating an
assembly resource file of text strings. Use these columns only if you're creating a file with
localized versions of other objects, such as graphics or sounds.

Although Visual Studio .NET does provide this dedicated editor for assembly resource
files, these files are really just XML files. Listing 16.7 shows this particular assembly resource
file as raw XML, which is available by clicking the XML tab at the bottom of the editor.

Listing 16.7   UIText.resx

```xml
<?xml version="1.0" encoding="utf-8" ?>
<root>
    <xsd:schema id="root" xmlns=""
     xmlns:xsd="http://www.w3.org/2001/XMLSchema"
     xmlns:msdata="urn:schemas-microsoft-com:xml-msdata">
        <xsd:element name="root" msdata:IsDataSet="true">
            <xsd:complexType>
                <xsd:choice maxOccurs="unbounded">
                    <xsd:element name="data">
                        <xsd:complexType>
```

```
                            <xsd:sequence>
                                <xsd:element name="value"
                                 type="xsd:string" minOccurs="0"
                                 msdata:Ordinal="1" />
                                <xsd:element name="comment"
                                 type="xsd:string" minOccurs="0"
                                 msdata:Ordinal="2" />
                            </xsd:sequence>
                            <xsd:attribute name="name"
                             type="xsd:string" />
                            <xsd:attribute name="type"
                             type="xsd:string" />
                            <xsd:attribute name="mimetype"
                             type="xsd:string" />
                        </xsd:complexType>
                    </xsd:element>
                    <xsd:element name="resheader">
                        <xsd:complexType>
                            <xsd:sequence>
                                <xsd:element name="value"
                                 type="xsd:string" minOccurs="0"
                                 msdata:Ordinal="1" />
                            </xsd:sequence>
                            <xsd:attribute name="name"
                             type="xsd:string" use="required" />
                        </xsd:complexType>
                    </xsd:element>
                </xsd:choice>
            </xsd:complexType>
        </xsd:element>
</xsd:schema>
<resheader name="ResMimeType">
    <value>text/microsoft-resx</value>
</resheader>
<resheader name="Version">
    <value>1.0.0.0</value>
</resheader>
<resheader name="Reader">
    <value>System.Resources.ResXResourceReader,
     System.Windows.Forms, Version=1.0.3300.0, Culture=neutral,
     PublicKeyToken=b77a5c561934e089</value>
</resheader>
<resheader name="Writer">
    <value>System.Resources.ResXResourceWriter,
     System.Windows.Forms, Version=1.0.3300.0, Culture=neutral,
     PublicKeyToken=b77a5c561934e089</value>
</resheader>
<data name="Manage_Products">
    <value>Manage Products</value>
</data>
<data name="Manage_Departments">
```

```xml
        <value>Manage Departments</value>
</data>
<data name="Manage_Tax">
        <value>Manage Tax</value>
</data>
<data name="Manage_Shipping">
        <value>Manage Shipping</value>
</data>
<data name="Manage_Orders">
        <value>Manage Orders</value>
</data>
<data name="Order_Number">
        <value>Order #</value>
</data>
<data name="Order_Date">
        <value>Order Date:</value>
</data>
<data name="Order_Received">
        <value>Order Received</value>
</data>
<data name="Order_Fulfilled">
        <value>Order Fulfilled</value>
</data>
<data name="Order_Shipped">
        <value>Order Shipped</value>
</data>
<data name="Call_Customer_Service">
        <value>Call Customer Service</value>
</data>
<data name="Bill_To">
        <value>Bill To:</value>
</data>
<data name="Ship_To">
        <value>Ship To:</value>
</data>
<data name="Payment_Data">
        <value>Payment Data:</value>
</data>
<data name="Card_Name">
        <value>Card_Name:</value>
</data>
<data name="Card_Number">
        <value>Card Number:</value>
</data>
<data name="Card_Type">
        <value>Card Type:</value>
</data>
<data name="Card_Expiration_Date">
        <value>Card Expiration Date:</value>
</data>
<data name="Name">
```

```xml
        <value>Name</value>
    </data>
    <data name="Size">
        <value>Size</value>
    </data>
    <data name="Color">
        <value>Color</value>
    </data>
    <data name="Quantity">
        <value>Quantity</value>
    </data>
    <data name="Price">
        <value>Price</value>
    </data>
    <data name="Total">
        <value>Total</value>
    </data>
    <data name="Edit">
        <value>Edit</value>
    </data>
    <data name="Delete">
        <value>Delete</value>
    </data>
    <data name="Subtotal">
        <value>Subtotal:</value>
    </data>
    <data name="Shipping">
        <value>Shipping:</value>
    </data>
    <data name="Tax">
        <value>Tax:</value>
    </data>
    <data name="Total2">
        <value>Total:</value>
    </data>
    <data name="Submit">
        <value>Submit</value>
    </data>
</root>
```

As you can see, there are three sections to this file. First, there is an embedded XML schema file (whose tags are drawn from the xsd namespace) that describes the rest of the contents of the file. Then comes a section of resheader tags, which describe this as being an assembly resource file. You don't need to edit the resheader tags. Finally, the data in the file is presented as data tags with name attributes and nested value tags.

Using Multiple Resource Files

There's not much point in going to all the effort of creating an assembly resource file for an application that supports only one language. We've added a second assembly resource file, UIText.sv-SE.resx, to the StoreManagerLocalize application. This file contains the same data elements as the UIText.resx file, but this time, the values are in Swedish. Figure 16.7 shows this Swedish assembly resource file.

FIGURE 16.7:

Resources for the sv-SE culture

The naming of this file is no accident. When the .NET Framework retrieves resources, it looks in several places, depending on the setting of the CurrentUICulture property of the current thread. For example, if the CurrentUICulture setting is a CultureInfo representing the sv-SE (Swedish in Sweden) culture, the Framework will check for resources in three files, in this order:

1. A specific culture file—in this case, one with a name such as UIText.sv-SE.resx

2. A neutral culture file—in this case, one with a name such as UIText.sv.resx

3. An invariant file—in this case, one with a name such as UIText.resx

In other words, the Framework will fall back on increasingly less-specific files until it gets to the default file included in the application.

Loading Text Resources at Runtime

The part of the .NET Framework that actually handles the loading of the appropriate resources is the ResourceManager class, a part of the System.Resources namespace. Table 16.4 lists the important members of this class.

TABLE 16.4: Members of the ResourceManager Class

Member	Type	Description
BaseName	Property	The root name of the files that the ResourceManager searches. In the case of our sample application, this is UIText.
CreateFileBasedResourceManager	Method	Creates a ResourceManager that uses external resource files.
GetObject	Method	Gets a localized object.
GetString	Method	Gets a localized string.
IgnoreCase	Property	True if key values in the resource files are case insensitive.

Listing 16.8 shows the code in the StoreManagerLocalize application that uses a Resource-Manager object to load localized resources.

Listing 16.8   **Working with Localized Resources in OrderDetail.aspx.vb**

```vb
Private Sub Page_Load(ByVal sender As System.Object, _
ByVal e As System.EventArgs) Handles MyBase.Load
    ' Set the CurrentCulture for the page
    Thread.CurrentThread.CurrentCulture = _
    New CultureInfo(CStr(Session("CurrentCulture")))
    ' Set the CurrentUICulture for the page
    Thread.CurrentThread.CurrentUICulture = _
    New CultureInfo(CStr(Session("CurrentUICulture")))

    ' Initialize user interface text
    InitUIText()

    If Not IsPostBack Then
        ' Save the incoming OrderID and ShopperID
        Session("OrderID") = Request.QueryString("OrderID")
        Session("ShopperID") = Request.QueryString("ShopperID")
        BindMain()
```

```
            BindItemGrid()
        End If
End Sub

Private Sub InitUIText()
    Dim li As New ListItem()
    Dim li2 As New ListItem()
    Dim li3 As New ListItem()
    Dim li4 As New ListItem()
    ' Get a ResourceManager for our strings
    Dim rm As ResourceManager = _
     New ResourceManager("StoreManagerLocalize.UIText", _
     GetType(OrderDetail).Assembly)
    ' Fill in static text
    hlManageProducts.Text = rm.GetString("Manage_Products")
    hlManageDepartments.Text = rm.GetString("Manage_Departments")
    hlManageTax.Text = rm.GetString("Manage_Tax")
    hlManageShipping.Text = rm.GetString("Manage_Shipping")
    hlManageOrders.Text = rm.GetString("Manage_Orders")
    lblOrderNumber.Text = rm.GetString("Order_Number")
    lblOrderDate.Text = rm.GetString("Order_Date")
    ' Add values to the DropDownList control
    li.Text = rm.GetString("Order_Received")
    li.Selected = True
    li.Value = 0
    ddlOrderStatus.Items.Add(li)
    li2.Text = rm.GetString("Order_Fulfilled")
    li2.Selected = False
    li2.Value = 1
    ddlOrderStatus.Items.Add(li2)
    li3.Text = rm.GetString("Order_Shipped")
    li3.Selected = False
    li3.Value = 2
    ddlOrderStatus.Items.Add(li3)
    li4.Text = rm.GetString("Call_Customer_Service")
    li4.Selected = False
    li4.Value = 3
    ddlOrderStatus.Items.Add(li4)
    ' Fill in more of the user interface
    lblBillTo.Text = rm.GetString("Bill_To")
    lblShipTo.Text = rm.GetString("Ship_To")
    lblPaymentData.Text = rm.GetString("Payment_Data")
    lblCardName.Text = rm.GetString("Card_Name")
    lblCardNumber.Text = rm.GetString("Card_Number")
    lblCardType.Text = rm.GetString("Card_Type")
    lblCardExpirationDate.Text = rm.GetString("Card_Expiration_Date")
    ' Fill in text on the DataGrid
    Dim e As EditCommandColumn
    e = dgItems.Columns(0)
    e.EditText = rm.GetString("Edit")
    Dim b As ButtonColumn
```

```
    b = dgItems.Columns(1)
    b.Text = rm.GetString("Delete")
    dgItems.Columns(2).HeaderText = rm.GetString("Name")
    dgItems.Columns(3).HeaderText = rm.GetString("Size")
    dgItems.Columns(4).HeaderText = rm.GetString("Color")
    dgItems.Columns(5).HeaderText = rm.GetString("Quantity")
    dgItems.Columns(6).HeaderText = rm.GetString("Price")
    dgItems.Columns(7).HeaderText = rm.GetString("Total")
    ' Fill in the last bits of text
    lblSubtotalCaption.Text = rm.GetString("Subtotal")
    lblTaxCaption.Text = rm.GetString("Tax")
    lblShippingCaption.Text = rm.GetString("Shipping")
    lblTotalCaption.Text = rm.GetString("Total2")
    btnSubmit.Text = rm.GetString("Submit")
End Sub
```

To make this code work, we made one major change to the Web Form (compared to the version in the non-localized StoreManager application): All the text on the form is now stored in server-side Web Form controls. With server-side controls, we can use code to set the text properties of the controls before they're rendered. That makes it easy to display the correct language at runtime.

As you can see, there are also a few things to do besides just setting text properties of label controls. The items in the DropDownList control need to be set dynamically at runtime, rather than be stored in the control's Items collection at design time. Also, we need to use the object model of the DataGrid control to drill down to the various pieces of text that are displayed within the control.

With this code in place, the work of locating the correct resources is left to the ResourceManager class. The class uses the value of the CurrentUICulture property to decide which resources to load. In Figure 16.8, the OrderDetail.aspx web page is set to use Swedish resources.

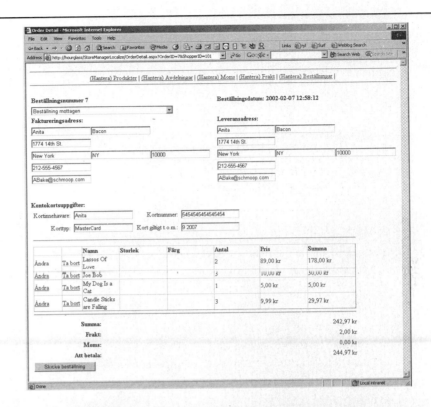

FIGURE 16.8:

Localized text and
other resources

Summary

In this chapter, we've given you a brief introduction to the concepts and code used in localizing ASP.NET applications. Entire books have been written about both localization in general and localization of .NET applications in particular. If you keep in mind the general principles from this chapter, and the code we've demonstrated, you should be able to successfully localize simple applications. As your applications become more complex, you'll need to refer to the documentation for the .NET Framework to learn how to localize objects and to create resource DLLs. At that point, you may also need to enlist the services of a professional translator.

In the final chapter of the book, we'll look at some things you should consider when building an e-commerce website, beyond just writing the code. In particular, we'll discuss some best practices that will help you build more secure and scalable websites.

CHAPTER 17

Best Practices and Scalability

- SQL Server Best Practices

- IIS Best Practices

- Security Best Practices

- Scalability

- Additional Resources

Throughout this book, we've been assuming that you have SQL Server and Internet Information Services available and configured to support your e-commerce applications. But depending on the size of your organization, you may well be the database and server administrator as well as the software developer. So, in this chapter, we're going to take a closer look at the underlying servers. We'll suggest proven ways to get the most from your servers, with the least risk to your business-critical data. Although this chapter won't make you an expert system administrator, it will point out areas where you should make sure your servers are configured properly. We'll break this configuration down into three major areas: best practices, security, and scalability.

SQL Server Best Practices

Most companies employ a dedicated database administrator (DBA) to manage their SQL Server databases. But in smaller organizations, the software developer sometimes does double duty as a DBA. Even if your organization does have a DBA in charge of the SQL Server, it's helpful to understand some of the facets of that person's job. In this section, we'll review some of the areas where a SQL Server DBA's efforts should be concentrated.

Running SQL Server

SQL Server 2000 does a marvelous job of running unattended. The software is designed to dynamically adjust parameters such as the number of locks it makes available and the amount of memory it demands in order to react to changing loads. Nevertheless, you should still monitor your SQL Server to make sure it's performing as desired. In the worst possible case, you need to know whether the server has crashed. Short of that, it's useful to know whether there are any signs of slow performance or other problems.

You should create a checklist of daily tasks to be performed on your SQL Server. Table 17.1 lists suggested items for such a checklist, although you may want to add or delete items to customize the list for your own work environment.

TABLE 17.1: Daily SQL Server Checklist

Task	Comments
Verify that services are up and running.	This applies to the SQL Server, SQL Server Agent, Distributed Transaction, and any other services that your server depends on. You can use the Services MMC snap-in to check the status of services.
Verify connectivity to the server.	Be sure that you can ping the server across the network and that you can successfully log in from a workstation.

Continued on next page

TABLE 17.1 CONTINUED: Daily SQL Server Checklist

Task	Comments
Check the event log.	Use the Event Viewer MMC snap-in on the server to check for warning and error messages.
Check the SQL Server error log.	The SQL Server error log is available from within SQL Server Enterprise Manager.
Check disk space.	If any of your databases are set to automatically allocate size as needed, make sure that you have ample disk space left.
Check SQL Server jobs.	You can use SQL Server Enterprise Manager to make sure that all scheduled jobs completed successfully.
Check for deadlocks and long-running processes.	You can use SQL Server Enterprise Manager to make sure that all processes are completing successfully.
Monitor system utilization.	You can use the System Monitor application to monitor CPU, memory, disk, and network usage for the server.
Update statistics and indexes.	SQL Server 2000 includes an Index Tuning Wizard to help you automate this process.

TIP   If you're new to SQL Server administration, you should pick up a reference such as Mike Gunderloy and Joseph L. Jorden's *Mastering SQL Server 2000* (Sybex, 2000).

You should consider implementing an automated monitoring solution for your SQL Servers. Software in this category includes the following:

- Microsoft Operations Manager (www.microsoft.com/mom/)
- NetIQ SQL Management Suite (www.netiq.com/products/sql/default.asp)
- Quest Software Spotlight (www.quest.com/spotlight_sql/)

These tools are designed to be a part of an enterprise-wide monitoring program for all servers. They can pull together information from a variety of sources to give you an accurate picture of the health of your servers. All these tools can notify you of current problems or dangerous trends in a variety of ways, including via e-mail or pager.

Documenting SQL Server

No matter how you configure your server, it's critical that you document that configuration. Documentation of the server configuration serves two main purposes. First, in the case of absolute disaster, knowing how your server was set up can help you build a replacement server. Second, thorough server documentation can provide a good way for new members of your team to get up to speed on what the server contains and how it fits in with the rest of your e-commerce solution.

Here are some of the things you should consider documenting for your SQL Server installation:

- Maintenance plan configuration
- Service packs and hot fixes that have been installed
- At least one administrative password
- All users and groups in active use
- Location and type of every backup file
- Build scripts for all database objects
- File copies of all DTS packages
- Technical support information about all hardware and software vendors, including logins and passwords for web-based support systems
- Operating system service packs and hot fixes that have been installed
- Physical and logical disk layout
- General hardware information (CPU, RAM, and so on)

Of course, you should keep a copy of this information off site, so that a physical disaster to your production server won't also destroy the documentation.

Availability and Reliability

SQL Server offers a number of features designed to increase the availability and reliability of SQL Server databases. As your database grows, you may need to investigate these features in order to handle the increased volume of data. Table 17.2 summarizes these features.

TABLE 17.2: SQL Server Availability and Reliability Features

Feature	Comments
Log shipping	Log shipping enables you to export transaction logs continuously from your "live" server to a backup server, where they're applied to a copy of your database. In case of a problem with the main server, the backup server can be substituted.

Continued on next page

TABLE 17.2 CONTINUED: SQL Server Availability and Reliability Features

Feature	Comments
Clustering	SQL Server supports the clustering feature of Windows, which allows you to combine two computers with shared disk storage into a single redundant system. If anything goes wrong with the primary computer, applications switch to running on the backup computer with no loss of data.
Linked servers	With linked servers, you can store data on multiple SQL Servers and still query all the data from one database connection. By splitting tables between various servers, you can increase performance when retrieving data from very large tables.
Federated servers	Federated servers allow you to store parts of a single table on multiple SQL Servers. Like linked servers, federated servers can improve query response times for large queries.
Large memory support	SQL Server can support up to 64GB of RAM (with the proper hardware configuration). This allows you to hold the bulk of your database in RAM for very fast querying.

Backups and Maintenance

SQL Server includes excellent support for backing up and maintaining your databases. In particular, SQL Server 2000 includes a Database Maintenance Plan Wizard that can help you set up appropriate maintenance jobs for your server. Here's an overview of the process for using the wizard:

1. Launch SQL Server Enterprise Manager and then connect to your SQL Server.

2. Select Tools ➤ Wizards to launch the Select Wizard dialog box.

3. Expand the Management node, select Database Maintenance Plan Wizard, and click OK.

4. Read the welcome panel of the Database Maintenance Plan Wizard and then click Next.

5. On the Select Databases panel, shown in Figure 17.1, check the databases that you wish to maintain. Click Next.

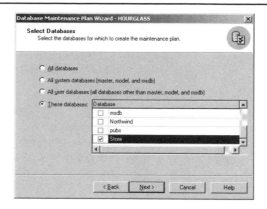

6. On the Update Data Optimization Information panel, you have three choices:

   • Check the Reorganize Data and Index Pages check box to have the wizard rearrange the raw data for faster access. Generally, you won't need to do this unless you frequently delete data or modify primary keys.

   • Check the Update Statistics check box to have the wizard reoptimize views and stored procedures. This is generally a good idea if your database is growing rapidly.

   • Check the Remove Unused Space check box if you wish to have your database compacted to take up less room on the disk. For an e-commerce website that's doing steady business, this option is unlikely to be helpful.

   If you check any of these boxes, you can use the Change button to set a schedule for optimization, or accept the schedule proposed by the wizard. After you've made your choices, click Next.

7. On the Database Integrity Check panel, you can choose whether the wizard should inspect your data and indexes for errors. Although in a perfect world, there would never be data errors in your tables, we recommend that you check this box and schedule the operations. It's cheap insurance for your data. Click Next when you're done.

8. On the Specify the Database Backup Plan panel, shown in Figure 17.2, you should check both the Back Up the Database check box and the Verify check box. Backing up your databases on a regular basis is a critical part of ensuring that you never lose any significant amount of data. If you have a high-speed tape drive, you can back up to tape. Otherwise, you should back up to disk, using a disk drive other than the one where your SQL Server data is stored. Click Next.

FIGURE 17.2:

Selecting backup options

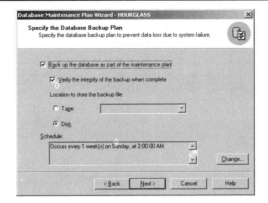

9. If you've chosen to back up your database to disk, the next panel will let you select the location for the backups and the length of time to retain backup files. Click Next.

10. On the Specify Transaction Log Backup Plan panel, you should check the check box to back up the transaction log as part of the maintenance plan. As with the full backup, you can choose where and how often to back up the transaction log. One strategy that's often used is to do a full backup once a week on the weekends and to do a transaction log backup daily. Click Next after scheduling the transaction log backups.

11. If you've chosen to back up your transaction logs to disk, the next panel lets you select the location for the backups and the length of time to retain backup files. Click Next.

12. On the Reports to Generate panel, choose whether you would like a daily report saved to disk or e-mailed to a SQL Server operator. We recommend that you always create a daily report so that you will have a record of any maintenance actions. Click Next.

13. On the Maintenance Plan History panel, choose where to store records of maintenance actions. Click Next.

14. On the final panel of the Database Maintenance Plan Wizard, review your choices and then click Finish. The wizard will then proceed to perform automatic jobs to handle your chosen maintenance tasks.

SQL Server also features an alerting system that can be used to notify you in case of trouble with your database. This system functions by defining *alerts* and then assigning the alerts to *operators*. To get started with the alerting system, follow these steps to create a new SQL Server operator:

1. Launch SQL Server Enterprise Manager and then connect to your SQL Server.

2. Expand the folder in the treeview that corresponds to your server, then the Management folder, and then the SQL Server Agent folder. Figure 17.3 shows this portion of the SQL Server Enterprise Manager tree.

FIGURE 17.3:

Managing operators
and alerts

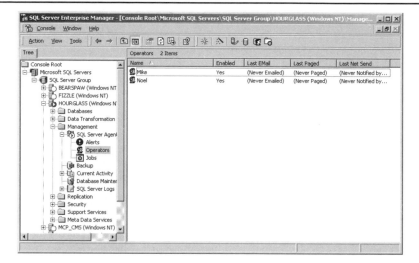

3. SQL Server Agent must be running for operators and alerts to function properly. If the SQL Server Agent node doesn't include a green arrow, right-click it and select Start.

4. Right-click the Operators node and select New Operator.

5. At a minimum, fill in a name and e-mail address for the operator. You can also specify a separate e-mail address for a pager, and a computer address to be used for Net Send messages. You can also specify times and days when the pager address should be used. Click OK to create the operator.

NOTE   To use e-mail or pager notification, you must have configured the SQL Mail service with a valid MAPI profile. See SQL Server Books Online for details on configuring SQL Mail.

Once you've created an operator, you can create an alert by following these steps:

1. Right-click the Alerts node and select New Alert.

2. On the General tab, select an event to trigger the alert. From the Type drop-down list, you can choose either a SQL Server event (error) or a SQL Server performance condition (such as the number of active transactions rising above a fixed limit). You can set error alerts on a particular error number or on a *severity* level that includes a group of related

errors. Figure 17.4 shows the settings for creating an alert that will respond to division-by-zero errors.

FIGURE 17.4:

Creating an alert

3. On the Response tab, select the operators who should be notified when this alert is triggered, and the means by which they should be notified. You can also choose to run a SQL Server job in response to an alert.

4. Click OK to create the alert. In this particular case, you'll get a message warning you that the alert won't be triggered by default because error 8134 is not normally logged. Click Yes to turn on logging for this error.

To test the new alert, launch SQL Query Analyzer and execute this query:

```
SELECT 1/0
```

After a short delay, the specified operator should receive a message warning them of the alert. Figure 17.5 shows the alert in a Net Send message.

FIGURE 17.5:

Alert via a Net Send
message

You'll find much more information on operators, alerts, and jobs in SQL Server Books Online. At a minimum, you should set up alerts to notify operators of all errors of severity 19

or higher. These are the errors that are fatal to the process that was attempting to execute on the server, and whose cause you should try to find immediately.

Database Design and Deployment

You should treat database changes as seriously as code changes in the e-commerce application itself. In particular, don't overlook the necessity of testing all changes to the database before rolling them out to a production environment. Attempting to fix a database problem directly on the same server that's taking orders from your customers is an invitation to disaster. Instead, consider this three-step approach to database development:

1. Each developer should work on their own dedicated SQL Server when designing and implementing new features or fixing bugs in the database. This need not be an excessive expense, because you can almost always use SQL Server Developer Edition running on the developer's individual computer for this purpose.

2. After the developer is satisfied that the change is ready to deploy, it should be tested on an intermediate staging server. The staging server should have a copy of the production database from the "live" store, although this can be a copy with most of the data removed if you're concerned about confidentiality or storage requirements. The developer should create a SQL script and written instructions to make the necessary changes to this server. After the changes are installed, you can test your application on the staging server to make sure that there are no unexpected side effects.

3. After the code has been verified and tested on the staging server, you can use the SQL script and instructions to install it on the production server.

Also, it's prudent to back up both the e-commerce database and the master database just before making any changes. That way, if something does go wrong, you can return to a known good configuration with a minimum of effort.

Consider running SQL Server Profiler on your production server for a few hours. Profiler will capture a trace file of all changes made to the production database and the SQL that was executed to make those changes. You can replay this trace file on your staging server to verify that everything is still performing properly after any changes.

When you're building a change script to apply changes to the staging server (and later, the production server), take the extra time to insert comments in the script. That way, the script can serve as part of the documentation of your system.

When it comes time to deploy changes to your production server, you may face the problem of when to schedule the changes. By their very nature, e-commerce websites are designed to be open 24 hours a day, 7 days a week. If you need to take the server offline to make changes, you may miss sales. If your upgrade can be accomplished quickly, it may be acceptable to do this during off-peak hours. There is another alternative, although it works only if you're using clustered servers. In that case, you can break the cluster and take each copy of the database offline in turn to upgrade it while the other one handles the load of customers. Again, you'll probably want to do this during your store's off-peak hours.

IIS Best Practices

For an e-commerce website, the web server is just as important as the database server. Throughout this book, we've been using Microsoft Internet Information Services (IIS) as the web server for our site. In this section, we'll discuss some of the administrative tasks that need to be performed to keep an IIS server in top condition.

Running IIS

Even before you deploy your web servers, you can begin to develop answers to the most important question of all: How much traffic can the server support? Answering that question is the goal of *capacity analysis*. In performing a capacity analysis, you set up the hardware and software for your IIS server; but instead of connecting the server to the Internet, you use a tool to simulate the load of actual users and to analyze the server's response.

The Microsoft Windows 2000 Server Resource Kit includes two tools for capacity analysis:

- The Web Application Stress Tool simulates requests from multiple clients and reports on key statistics based on the server's response.

- The Web Capacity Analysis Tool uses a client-server configuration to allow higher levels of traffic testing by using multiple computers to make requests.

TIP   You can learn more about the Windows 2000 Server Resource Kit at `www.microsoft` `.com/windows2000/techinfo/reskit/tools/default.asp`.

In addition to examining the maximum load that your application will support, you need to consider the bandwidth between the server and the rest of the Internet. If you're expecting heavy traffic, you may have to install a high-speed link to your own facility. Alternatively, you may choose to collocate your server at your ISP's facility, which presumably already has high-speed Internet connections.

You should monitor critical resources on your web server closely, because web servers tend to be subject to sudden increases in traffic. Of particular interest are the CPU utilization, memory paging (which measures how often applications are swapped to disk), and the number of concurrent client connections. If performance problems develop, you can often gain some time to deal with them by adding memory to the web server.

Two key factors in tuning Internet Information Server are queued requests and threads. IIS tunes the number of threads in its process dynamically. The dynamic values are usually optimal. In extreme cases of very active or underused processors, you might want to adjust the maximum number of threads in the Inetinfo process. If you do change the maximum number of threads, you should continue careful testing to make sure that the change has improved performance. The difference is usually quite subtle.

Tuning the IIS threads has to do with effective computer use. Allowing more threads generally encourages more CPU use. Fewer threads suggest low processor use. For example, if you have a busy website, but the queue length never goes up and the actual processor use is low, you probably have more computer capacity than required. On the other hand, if the queue length goes up and down and the CPU use is still low, the threads should be increased, because you have unused processor capacity.

Configuring the IIS queue is important because busy websites are defined by a high transaction volume. Ideally, each transaction has a very short life cycle. Under a high load, significant slowdowns (blocking) can occur when a component gets called at a greater rate than the number of transactions per second that the component can satisfy. When this occurs, incoming requests are placed in a queue for later first-in/first-out processing. If the blocking occurs for only a few seconds, the queue smoothes out and the request is handled in a timely fashion. However, when the blocking lasts for a longer period, an effect called *queue saturation* may occur. Queue saturation happens when the number of queued services exceeds the maximum number allowed (RequestQueueMax) and IIS returns a Server Too Busy message.

No matter what, there is a limit to what one web server can handle in terms of the number of threads and items in the queue. Carefully monitoring the use of each will have a significant impact on the performance of your site and may allow you to squeeze out better and more performance.

In addition to monitoring resources, you should monitor your web traffic. IIS keeps a log of requests to the server. This log will show you how many visitors you've had, where they came from, what pages they requested while visiting your server, and a wealth of other information. The problem is that the raw log files have too much data for human beings to understand. An active website can quickly accumulate hundreds of megabytes or even gigabytes of logging information. How do you extract useful information from all that data?

The answer is to use a log-file analysis program. Such programs can produce summary reports showing the distribution and trends in the raw log-file data. A wide variety of log-file analysis programs are available, from free packages such as Analog (www.analog.cx) to high-end commercial packages such as WebTrends (www.webtrends.com). Figure 17.6 shows a small portion of an Analog report.

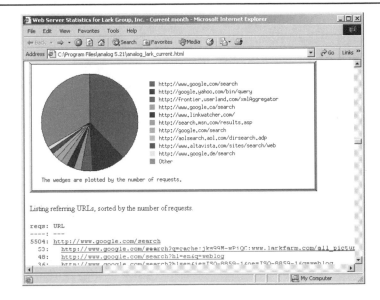

Log-file analysis

Documenting IIS

Here are some of the things you should consider documenting for your IIS Server installation:

- Hot fixes that have been installed
- At least one administrative password
- All users and groups in active use
- Location and type of every backup file
- Configuration information for any external files (such as database connection files)
- Technical support information about hardware and software vendors, including logins and passwords for web-based support systems
- Operating system service packs and hot fixes that have been installed
- Physical and logical disk layout
- General hardware information (CPU, RAM, and so on)
- Site configuration information from Internet Services Manager (the Microsoft Management Console that allows you to administer IIS)
- DNS addresses and service names
- Copies of the `web.config` and `machine.config` files

As with your SQL Server documentation, you should keep a copy of this information off site, so that a physical disaster to your production server won't also destroy the documentation.

Availability and Reliability

IIS offers a number of features designed to increase the availability and reliability of websites. As your e-commerce site attracts additional traffic, you may need to investigate these features to handle the increased volume of data. Table 17.3 summarizes these features.

TABLE 17.3: IIS Availability and Reliability Features

Feature	Comments
Clustering	IIS supports the clustering feature of Windows, which allows you to combine two computers with shared disk storage into a single redundant system. If anything goes wrong with the primary computer, applications switch to running on the backup computer, with no loss of data.
Network Load Balancing	The Network Load Balancing service distributes requests for a single website in round-robin fashion among as many as 32 servers. This allows you to increase the capacity of your site by simply adding more servers.
Isolated applications	IIS allows you to designate an application to run in its own memory space, separate from that of the IIS process itself. This prevents a poorly designed application from crashing the entire web server.
IIS replications	IIS includes a utility, `iissync.exe`, that can replicate configuration information from one computer to another. This is useful when you're adding servers to a cluster.

Security Best Practices

When the Internet was just getting started, people didn't worry much about security. Open protocols and a general spirit of cooperation led to the explosive growth of the Internet. There wasn't much critical data online, and there were very few threats to the data that *was* online.

All of that has changed in the last several years. Viruses, worms, and deliberate attempts to crash or take over servers have become unfortunate facts of the system administrator's life. If you don't pay attention to security before connecting your servers to the Internet, you can assume that they will be quickly taken over and destroyed by malicious users. In this section, we'll cover some of the basics of SQL Server and IIS security configuration.

TIP   The security landscape on the Internet changes very rapidly. If you're responsible for server security, you should monitor some of the many mailing lists and public forums devoted to this subject. The mailing lists maintained by SecurityFocus (`www.security-focus.com`) are an excellent starting point.

Securing servers is always a balancing act. On one hand, you want people to be able to visit your e-commerce store and buy things. On the other hand, you don't want them to be able to walk off with the cash register. As you secure a server, you have to balance the risk against the difficulty and inconvenience of the fix in each case. To secure a server *completely*, you need to turn it off and lock it in a closet. Of course, at that point, the server is no longer of any use.

SQL Server Security

To protect the data you've stored in SQL Server, consider taking these actions:

- Use Windows authentication rather than SQL Server authentication.
- Even if you're using pure Windows authentication, set a strong password for the built-in sa account.
- Be very conservative when adding users to server roles. Many server roles allow users to perform dangerous actions such as reading disk files or manipulating the Registry.
- Be conservative when granting permissions on objects. Deny all permissions and then grant only the necessary permissions to the accounts that need them.
- Grant permissions to groups rather than to users. This makes it easier to manage permissions and also makes it easy to remove a user's access to the database by simply removing the user from the applicable group.
- Remove the guest account from production databases.
- Physically secure sensitive computers. Don't leave them unlocked. Don't leave an account logged in at the computer while it is unattended.
- Stay up-to-date with service packs and hot fixes, for both the operating system and SQL Server itself. You should monitor the Microsoft Security website (`www.microsoft.com/security/`) daily for important news.
- Drop any extended stored procedures that you're not using, because such procedures offer many powerful but dangerous capabilities. For instance, the xp_cmdshell stored procedure gives the user access to an operating system prompt.
- Enable logging of both successful and failed login attempts.

- Use stored procedures and views to access data. Remove user permissions from tables.

- Audit system stored procedures regularly, comparing their code with the code from a fresh installation. This helps ensure than an intruder hasn't introduced any backdoor code into your system.

IIS Security

To protect your web server, consider taking these actions:

- Store all content on NTFS drives. Use Access Control Lists (ACLs) to prevent users from changing the content.

- Protect the IIS log files with ACLs as well. This will prevent malicious users from altering or deleting the log files to cover their tracks.

- Enable logging for all websites.

- Regularly inspect your log files for unusual HTTP requests. Failed requests can offer clues about exploits that have attempted to take over your server.

- If you're not using the remote HTML-based administration tools for IIS, disable the Administration website.

- Don't install any sample ASP or ASP.NET code on production servers.

- Remove any unused application mappings from the IIS server. In Internet Services Manager, open the Properties dialog box for your website. Select the Home Directory tab. Click the Configuration button. This will open the Application Configuration dialog box, shown in Figure 17.7. Use the Remove button to remove all application mappings that you aren't actually using.

FIGURE 17.7:

Removing unused application mappings

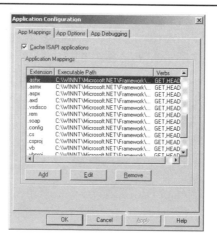

- Don't allow directory browsing. This will prevent people from snooping around to discover vulnerable files.

Scalability

We all hope that our e-commerce efforts will be unqualified successes. But if your store is an overnight success, you're likely to face a sudden problem: Can your servers handle the traffic? The hardware that's adequate for 100 orders a day may be strained by 1,000 orders a day—and may totally collapse when you hit 10,000 orders a day.

The general term for the factors affecting how much load your servers can handle is *scalability*. When you need to increase your servers' capacity, you have two broad choices: *Scaling up* refers to adding additional hardware resources to a single server, while *scaling out* refers to adding additional servers.

TIP   Before you consider either scaling up or scaling out, you should review the efficiency of your application. If the application was created in a hurry, or the code was never properly tested or reviewed, the application may be placing more load than necessary on your servers. In this case, simply improving the code might eliminate the need to invest in additional hardware.

Scaling Up

By adding or changing hardware, you can scale up a single server to handle additional load. Here are some components that are generally considered candidates for scaling up:

CPU   You can add more CPU power to a computer by installing a faster CPU or by adding more CPUs to a computer that has multiple-CPU capabilities.

Memory   Often the first candidate for scaling up is additional memory. A busy server uses gigabytes of memory if it's available, and additional memory is relatively inexpensive.

I/O   You may also be able to scale up by expanding the I/O subsystem (the hard drives and associated controller cards). Additional hard drives can help store more data, and a faster controller can get to the data more quickly. Hardware RAID controllers can help you retrieve data from multiple hard drives more quickly.

Network   Additional network cards or a faster network connection can help a computer deliver more data in a fixed amount of time.

TIP Before investing in additional hardware, you should confirm that there is an actual performance problem that the hardware will fix. The Windows Performance Monitor can help you determine whether CPU, memory, I/O, or network throughput is the bottleneck for your application.

Scaling Out

To fix a problem by scaling out, you add more servers to handle your application, rather than try to do everything on a single computer. We discussed some of the possible architectures for scaling out in Chapter 4, "System Configuration."

Some of the reliability features that we mentioned earlier in this chapter can also contribute to scalability through scaling out:

- Linked SQL Servers
- Federated SQL Servers
- Network Load Balancing service
- IIS replication

In addition to these features, you can scale out an application by *partitioning* it. Partitioning refers to splitting an application so that parts of it run on different servers, as opposed to trying to run the entire application on a single server or a group of identical servers. For example, the design of our e-commerce store includes a Web Service to provide tax and shipping information. There's no reason that this Web Service must be installed on the same IIS server as the main ASP.NET application. You could move the Web Service to another server and call it from the main server. Obviously, you can extend this technique to offload other parts of an application, such as entire static web pages or components that don't need to share session state with the rest of the application.

Additional Resources

We've covered only the bare bones of administration, security, and scalability in this chapter. There are many entire books devoted to such issues, as well as a large amount of online information. Here are a few websites that you might want to visit to get started:

- SQL Server 2000 Operations Guide

  `www.microsoft.com/technet/treeview/default.asp?url=/technet/prodtechnol/`
  `sql/maintain/operate/opsguide/default.asp`

A set of guidelines and procedures for administering a SQL Server.

- SQLSecurity.com

    `www.sqlsecurity.com`

    An independent site devoted to SQL Server security.

- Secure Internet Information Services 5 Checklist

    `www.microsoft.com/technet/treeview/default.asp?url=/technet/security/tools/iis5chk.asp`

    A site from Microsoft devoted to securing IIS.

- Scalability on Microsoft Business

    `www.microsoft.com/business/solutions/scalability.asp`

    Contains links to a number of white papers and technical resources on Windows 2000 Server scalability.

- Microsoft SQL Server 2000 Scalability Project

    `www.microsoft.com/sql/techinfo/administration/2000/BasicCapScalability.asp`

    Shows how to build and tune a SQL Server database to handle one to four terabytes of data.

- SQL Server Case Studies

    `www.microsoft.com/sql/evaluation/casestudies/scalability.asp`

    Real-world examples of how SQL Server is being used to manage large volumes of data in business settings. Useful for understanding the problems and the possible solutions to them.

- Building High-Scalability Server Farms

    `www.microsoft.com/siteserver/ssrk/docs/rk_highscalabilitysite.doc`

    A white paper from the Microsoft Site Server team that discusses the details of both scaling up and scaling out.

Summary

Now that you've finished building an e-commerce website and learned about administrative and security issues, it's time to take the final step: making the site available to real customers. We hope you'll find this a rewarding experience!

APPENDIX A

Database Tables and Stored Procedures

This appendix provides a reference to all of the tables and stored procedures that make up the database for the e-commerce website. We've sorted them alphabetically here so that you can easily find the ones that you're interested in. You'll find a complete build script for the database on the companion CD. Note that in the build script, the objects are sorted in a different order to allow for build dependencies. For example, both the Department and Product tables must exist before the DepartmentProduct table can be created.

Tables

Attribute

```
CREATE TABLE [dbo].[Attribute] (
    [AttributeID] [int] IDENTITY (1, 1) NOT NULL ,
    [AttributeName] [varchar] (255) NOT NULL ,
    [AttributeCategoryID] [int] NOT NULL
)
ALTER TABLE [dbo].[Attribute] WITH NOCHECK ADD
    CONSTRAINT [Attribute_PK] PRIMARY KEY CLUSTERED
    (
        [AttributeID]
    )
ALTER TABLE [dbo].[Attribute] ADD
    CONSTRAINT [AttributeCategory_Attribute_FK1] FOREIGN KEY
    (
        [AttributeCategoryID]
    ) REFERENCES [dbo].[AttributeCategory] (
        [AttributeCategoryID]
    )
```

AttributeCategory

```
CREATE TABLE [dbo].[AttributeCategory] (
    [AttributeCategoryID] [int] IDENTITY (1, 1) NOT NULL ,
    [AttributeCategoryName] [varchar] (255) NOT NULL
)
ALTER TABLE [dbo].[AttributeCategory] WITH NOCHECK ADD
    CONSTRAINT [AttributeCategory_PK] PRIMARY KEY CLUSTERED
    (
        [AttributeCategoryID]
    )
```

Basket

```
CREATE TABLE [dbo].[Basket] (
    [BasketID] [int] IDENTITY (1, 1) NOT NULL ,
```

```
        [ShopperID] [int] NOT NULL ,
        [BasketQuantity] [int] NOT NULL ,
        [BasketDateCreated] [datetime] NOT NULL ,
        [BasketOrderPlaced] [int] NOT NULL ,
        [BasketSubtotal] [money] NOT NULL ,
        [BasketTotal] [money] NOT NULL ,
        [BasketShipping] [money] NOT NULL ,
        [BasketTax] [money] NOT NULL
    )
    ALTER TABLE [dbo].[Basket] WITH NOCHECK ADD
        CONSTRAINT [DF_Basket_BasketQuantity] DEFAULT (0)
         FOR [BasketQuantity],
        CONSTRAINT [DF_Basket_BasketDateCreated] DEFAULT (getdate())
         FOR [BasketDateCreated],
        CONSTRAINT [DF_Basket_BasketOrderPlaced] DEFAULT (0)
         FOR [BasketOrderPlaced],
        CONSTRAINT [DF_Basket_BasketSubtotal] DEFAULT (0)
         FOR [BasketSubtotal],
        CONSTRAINT [DF_Basket_BasketTotal] DEFAULT (0)
         FOR [BasketTotal],
        CONSTRAINT [DF_Basket_BasketShipping] DEFAULT (0)
         FOR [BasketShipping],
        CONSTRAINT [DF_Basket_BasketTax] DEFAULT (0)
         FOR [BasketTax],
        CONSTRAINT [Basket_PK] PRIMARY KEY CLUSTERED
        (
            [BasketID]
        )
    ALTER TABLE [dbo].[Basket] ADD
        CONSTRAINT [Shopper_Basket_FK1] FOREIGN KEY
        (
            [ShopperID]
        ) REFERENCES [dbo].[Shopper] (
            [ShopperID]
        )
```

BasketItem

```
    CREATE TABLE [dbo].[BasketItem] (
        [BasketItemID] [int] IDENTITY (1, 1) NOT NULL ,
        [BasketID] [int] NOT NULL ,
        [ProductID] [int] NOT NULL ,
        [BasketItemPrice] [money] NOT NULL ,
        [BasketItemProductName] [varchar] (255) NOT NULL ,
        [BasketItemQuantity] [int] NOT NULL ,
        [BasketItemSize] [varchar] (50) NULL ,
        [BasketItemColor] [varchar] (50) NULL
```

```
    )
ALTER TABLE [dbo].[BasketItem] WITH NOCHECK ADD
    CONSTRAINT [DF_BasketItem_BasketItemPrice] DEFAULT (0)
    FOR [BasketItemPrice],
    CONSTRAINT [DF_BasketItem_BasketItemQuantity] DEFAULT (0)
    FOR [BasketItemQuantity],
    CONSTRAINT [BasketItem_PK] PRIMARY KEY CLUSTERED
    (
        [BasketItemID]
    )
ALTER TABLE [dbo].[BasketItem] ADD
    CONSTRAINT [Basket_BasketItem_FK1] FOREIGN KEY
    (
        [BasketID]
    ) REFERENCES [dbo].[Basket] (
        [BasketID]
    ),
    CONSTRAINT [Product_BasketItem_FK1] FOREIGN KEY
    (
        [ProductID]
    ) REFERENCES [dbo].[Product] (
        [ProductID]
    )
```

Department

```
CREATE TABLE [dbo].[Department] (
    [DepartmentID] [int] IDENTITY (1, 1) NOT NULL ,
    [DepartmentName] [varchar] (255) NOT NULL ,
    [DepartmentDescription] [text] NULL ,
    [DepartmentImage] [varchar] (255) NULL
) TEXTIMAGE_ON [PRIMARY]
ALTER TABLE [dbo].[Department] WITH NOCHECK ADD
    CONSTRAINT [Department_PK] PRIMARY KEY CLUSTERED
    (
        [DepartmentID]
    )
```

DepartmentProduct

```
CREATE TABLE [dbo].[DepartmentProduct] (
    [DepartmentID] [int] NOT NULL ,
    [ProductID] [int] NOT NULL
)
ALTER TABLE [dbo].[DepartmentProduct] WITH NOCHECK ADD
    CONSTRAINT [Department Product_PK] PRIMARY KEY CLUSTERED
    (
        [DepartmentID],
```

```
        [ProductID]
    )
ALTER TABLE [dbo].[DepartmentProduct] ADD
    CONSTRAINT [Department_Department Product_FK1] FOREIGN KEY
    (
        [DepartmentID]
    ) REFERENCES [dbo].[Department] (
        [DepartmentID]
    ),
    CONSTRAINT [Product_Department Product_FK1] FOREIGN KEY
    (
        [ProductID]
    ) REFERENCES [dbo].[Product] (
        [ProductID]
    )
```

FreeShip

```
CREATE TABLE [dbo].[FreeShip] (
    [FreeShipID] [int] IDENTITY (1, 1) NOT NULL ,
    [FreeShipStartDate] [datetime] NOT NULL ,
    [FreeShipEndDate] [datetime] NOT NULL
)
ALTER TABLE [dbo].[FreeShip] WITH NOCHECK ADD
    CONSTRAINT [FreeShip_PK] PRIMARY KEY CLUSTERED
    (
        [FreeShipID]
    )
```

Order

```
CREATE TABLE [dbo].[Order] (
    [OrderID] [int] IDENTITY (1, 1) NOT NULL ,
    [ShopperID] [int] NOT NULL ,
    [BasketID] [int] NOT NULL ,
    [OrderShipFirstName] [varchar] (50) NULL ,
    [OrderShipLastName] [varchar] (50) NULL ,
    [OrderShipAddress] [varchar] (150) NULL ,
    [OrderShipCity] [varchar] (150) NULL ,
    [OrderShipState] [varchar] (50) NULL ,
    [OrderShipProvince] [varchar] (150) NULL ,
    [OrderShipCountry] [varchar] (100) NULL ,
    [OrderShipZipCode] [varchar] (15) NULL ,
    [OrderShipPhone] [varchar] (25) NULL ,
    [OrderShipFax] [varchar] (25) NULL ,
    [OrderShipEmail] [varchar] (100) NULL ,
    [OrderBillFirstName] [varchar] (50) NULL ,
    [OrderBillLastName] [varchar] (50) NOT NULL ,
```

```
        [OrderBillAddress] [varchar] (150) NULL ,
        [OrderBillCity] [varchar] (150) NULL ,
        [OrderBillState] [varchar] (50) NULL ,
        [OrderBillProvince] [varchar] (150) NULL ,
        [OrderBillCountry] [varchar] (100) NULL ,
        [OrderBillZipCode] [varchar] (15) NULL ,
        [OrderBillPhone] [varchar] (25) NULL ,
        [OrderBillFax] [varchar] (25) NULL ,
        [OrderBillEmail] [varchar] (100) NULL ,
        [OrderDateOrdered] [datetime] NOT NULL
)
ALTER TABLE [dbo].[Order] WITH NOCHECK ADD
    CONSTRAINT [DF_Order_OrderDateOrdered] DEFAULT (getdate())
     FOR [OrderDateOrdered],
    CONSTRAINT [Order_PK] PRIMARY KEY CLUSTERED
    (
        [OrderID]
    ) ,
    CONSTRAINT [Order_AK1_UC1] UNIQUE NONCLUSTERED
    (
        [BasketID]
    )
ALTER TABLE [dbo].[Order] ADD
    CONSTRAINT [Basket_Order_FK1] FOREIGN KEY
    (
        [BasketID]
    ) REFERENCES [dbo].[Basket] (
        [BasketID]
    ),
    CONSTRAINT [Shopper_Order_FK1] FOREIGN KEY
    (
        [ShopperID]
    ) REFERENCES [dbo].[Shopper] (
        [ShopperID]
    )
```

OrderStatus

```
CREATE TABLE [dbo].[OrderStatus] (
    [OrderStatusID] [int] IDENTITY (1, 1) NOT NULL ,
    [OrderStatusStage] [int] NOT NULL ,
    [OrderStatusDateShipped] [datetime] NULL ,
    [OrderStatusDateFulfilled] [datetime] NULL ,
    [OrderStatusDateProcessed] [datetime] NULL ,
    [OrderStatusNotes] [text] NULL ,
    [OrderStatusShippingNumber] [varchar] (30) NULL ,
    [OrderStatusProcessed] [int] NOT NULL ,
```

```
    [OrderID] [int] NOT NULL
) TEXTIMAGE_ON [PRIMARY]
ALTER TABLE [dbo].[OrderStatus] WITH NOCHECK ADD
    CONSTRAINT [DF_OrderStatus_OrderStatusStage] DEFAULT (0)
     FOR [OrderStatusStage],
    CONSTRAINT [OrderStatus_PK] PRIMARY KEY CLUSTERED
    (
        [OrderStatusID]
    )
ALTER TABLE [dbo].[OrderStatus] ADD
    CONSTRAINT [Order_OrderStatus_FK1] FOREIGN KEY
    (
        [OrderID]
    ) REFERENCES [dbo].[Order] (
        [OrderID]
    )
```

Payment

```
CREATE TABLE [dbo].[Payment] (
    [PaymentID] [int] IDENTITY (1, 1) NOT NULL ,
    [OrderID] [int] NOT NULL ,
    [PaymentCardType] [varchar] (50) NOT NULL ,
    [PaymentCardNumber] [varchar] (30) NOT NULL ,
    [PaymentExpDate] [varchar] (25) NOT NULL ,
    [PaymentCardName] [varchar] (150) NOT NULL
)
ALTER TABLE [dbo].[Payment] WITH NOCHECK ADD
    CONSTRAINT [Payment_PK] PRIMARY KEY CLUSTERED
    (
        [PaymentID]
    ) ,
    CONSTRAINT [Payment_AK1_UC1] UNIQUE NONCLUSTERED
    (
        [OrderID]
    )
ALTER TABLE [dbo].[Payment] ADD
    CONSTRAINT [Order_Payment_FK1] FOREIGN KEY
    (
        [OrderID]
    ) REFERENCES [dbo].[Order] (
        [OrderID]
    )
```

Product

```
CREATE TABLE [dbo].[Product] (
    [ProductID] [int] IDENTITY (1, 1) NOT NULL ,
```

```
    [ProductName] [varchar] (255) NOT NULL ,
    [ProductDescription] [text] NULL ,
    [ProductImage] [varchar] (255) NULL ,
    [ProductPrice] [money] NULL ,
    [ProductSaleStart] [datetime] NULL ,
    [ProductSaleEnd] [datetime] NULL ,
    [ProductActive] [bit] NULL ,
    [ProductFeatured] [bit] NULL ,
    [ProductFeaturedStart] [datetime] NULL ,
    [ProductFeaturedEnd] [datetime] NULL ,
    [ProductSalePrice] [money] NULL
) TEXTIMAGE_ON [PRIMARY]
ALTER TABLE [dbo].[Product] WITH NOCHECK ADD
    CONSTRAINT [DF_Product_ProductActive] DEFAULT (1)
     FOR [ProductActive],
    CONSTRAINT [DF_Product_ProductFeatured] DEFAULT (0)
     FOR [ProductFeatured],
    CONSTRAINT [Product_PK] PRIMARY KEY CLUSTERED
    (
        [ProductID]
    )
```

ProductAttribute

```
CREATE TABLE [dbo].[ProductAttribute] (
    [ProductID] [int] NOT NULL ,
    [AttributeID] [int] NOT NULL
)
ALTER TABLE [dbo].[ProductAttribute] WITH NOCHECK ADD
    CONSTRAINT [ProductAttribute_PK] PRIMARY KEY CLUSTERED
    (
        [ProductID],
        [AttributeID]
    )
ALTER TABLE [dbo].[ProductAttribute] ADD
    CONSTRAINT [Attribute_ProductAttribute_FK1] FOREIGN KEY
    (
        [AttributeID]
    ) REFERENCES [dbo].[Attribute] (
        [AttributeID]
    ),
    CONSTRAINT [Product_ProductAttribute_FK1] FOREIGN KEY
    (
        [ProductID]
    ) REFERENCES [dbo].[Product] (
        [ProductID]
    )
```

RelatedProduct

```
CREATE TABLE [dbo].[RelatedProduct] (
    [ProductAID] [int] NOT NULL ,
    [ProductBID] [int] NOT NULL ,
    [RelationType] [int] NOT NULL
)
ALTER TABLE [dbo].[RelatedProduct] WITH NOCHECK ADD
    CONSTRAINT [RelatedProduct_PK] PRIMARY KEY CLUSTERED
    (
        [ProductAID],
        [ProductBID],
        [RelationType]
    )
ALTER TABLE [dbo].[RelatedProduct] ADD
    CONSTRAINT [Product_RelatedProduct_FK1] FOREIGN KEY
    (
        [ProductAID]
    ) REFERENCES [dbo].[Product] (
        [ProductID]
    ),
    CONSTRAINT [Product_RelatedProduct_FK2] FOREIGN KEY
    (
        [ProductBID]
    ) REFERENCES [dbo].[Product] (
        [ProductID]
    )
```

Shipping

```
CREATE TABLE [dbo].[Shipping] (
    [ShippingID] [int] IDENTITY (1, 1) NOT NULL ,
    [ShippingLowQuantity] [int] NOT NULL ,
    [ShippingHighQuantity] [int] NOT NULL ,
    [ShippingFee] [money] NOT NULL
)
ALTER TABLE [dbo].[Shipping] WITH NOCHECK ADD
    CONSTRAINT [Shipping_PK] PRIMARY KEY CLUSTERED
    (
        [ShippingID]
    )
```

Shopper

```
CREATE TABLE [dbo].[Shopper] (
    [ShopperID] [int] IDENTITY (1, 1) NOT NULL ,
    [ShopperFirstName] [varchar] (50) NULL ,
    [ShopperLastName] [varchar] (50) NOT NULL ,
```

```
    [ShopperAddress] [varchar] (150) NULL ,
    [ShopperCity] [varchar] (100) NULL ,
    [ShopperState] [varchar] (2) NULL ,
    [ShopperProvince] [varchar] (150) NULL ,
    [ShopperCountry] [varchar] (100) NULL ,
    [ShopperZipCode] [varchar] (15) NULL ,
    [ShopperPhone] [varchar] (30) NULL ,
    [ShopperFax] [varchar] (30) NULL ,
    [ShopperEmail] [varchar] (150) NULL ,
    [ShopperDateEntered] [datetime] NOT NULL ,
    [ShopperUserName] [varchar] (25) NOT NULL ,
    [ShopperPassword] [varchar] (25) NOT NULL ,
    [ShopperCookie] [tinyint] NOT NULL
)
ALTER TABLE [dbo].[Shopper] WITH NOCHECK ADD
    CONSTRAINT [DF_Shopper_ShopperDateEntered] DEFAULT (getdate())
     FOR [ShopperDateEntered],
    CONSTRAINT [DF_Shopper_ShopperCookie] DEFAULT (0)
     FOR [ShopperCookie],
    CONSTRAINT [Shopper_PK] PRIMARY KEY CLUSTERED
    (
        [ShopperID]
    )
```

Tax

```
CREATE TABLE [dbo].[Tax] (
    [TaxID] [int] IDENTITY (1, 1) NOT NULL ,
    [TaxState] [varchar] (50) NOT NULL ,
    [TaxRate] [float] NOT NULL
)
ALTER TABLE [dbo].[Tax] WITH NOCHECK ADD
    CONSTRAINT [Tax_PK] PRIMARY KEY CLUSTERED
    (
        [TaxID]
    )
```

Stored Procedures

procBasketSubtotal

```
/* Get the subtotal for a basket

From .NET E-Commerce Programming
by Mike Gunderloy and Noel Jerke
Copyright 2002, Sybex Inc. All Rights Reserved. */
```

```
CREATE PROCEDURE procBasketSubtotal
 @BasketID money
AS
 DECLARE @Subtotal money
 SELECT @Subtotal = SUM(BasketItemQuantity * BasketItemPrice)
  FROM BasketItem
  WHERE BasketID = @BasketID
 IF @Subtotal IS NULL
  SELECT 0
 ELSE
  SELECT @Subtotal
```

procCheckFreeShip

```
/* Determine whether free shipping is in effect

From .NET E-Commerce Programming
by Mike Gunderloy and Noel Jerke
Copyright 2002, Sybex Inc. All Rights Reserved. */
CREATE PROCEDURE procCheckFreeShip
AS
SELECT COUNT(*)
FROM FreeShip
WHERE FreeShipStartDate <= GETDATE()
 AND FreeShipEndDate >= GETDATE()
```

procClearBasketItems

```
/* Clear all items from a basket

From .NET E-Commerce Programming
by Mike Gunderloy and Noel Jerke
Copyright 2002, Sybex Inc. All Rights Reserved. */
CREATE PROCEDURE procClearBasketItems
 @BasketID int
AS
 DELETE FROM BasketItem
  WHERE BasketID = @BasketID
```

procCreateBasket

```
/* Creates a new basket and returns the ID

From .NET E-Commerce Programming
by Mike Gunderloy and Noel Jerke
Copyright 2002, Sybex Inc. All Rights Reserved. */
CREATE PROCEDURE procCreateBasket
/* Pass in the ID of the shopper that
```

```
      the basket will belong to, and return
      the ID of the newly created basket
   */
    @ShopperID int,
    @BasketID int OUTPUT
   AS
    INSERT INTO Basket(ShopperID)
     VALUES (@ShopperID)
    SELECT @BasketID = @@IDENTITY
```

procGetShippingFee

```
   /* Retrieve the shipping fee for a particular quantity

   From .NET E-Commerce Programming
   by Mike Gunderloy and Noel Jerke
   Copyright 2002, Sybex Inc. All Rights Reserved. */
   CREATE PROCEDURE procGetShippingFee
    @Quantity int
   AS
    SELECT ShippingFee FROM Shipping
     WHERE ShippingLowQuantity <= @Quantity
     AND ShippingHighQuantity >= @Quantity
```

procGetShopperPassword

```
   /* Given a shopper's e-mail, retrieve their password

   From .NET E-Commerce Programming
   by Mike Gunderloy and Noel Jerke
   Copyright 2002, Sybex Inc. All Rights Reserved. */
   CREATE PROCEDURE procGetShopperPassword
    @Email varchar(150)
   AS
    SELECT ShopperPassword
     FROM Shopper
     WHERE ShopperEmail = @Email
```

procGetTaxRate

```
   /* Return the tax rate for a particular state

   From .NET E-Commerce Programming
   by Mike Gunderloy and Noel Jerke
   Copyright 2002, Sybex Inc. All Rights Reserved. */
   CREATE PROCEDURE procGetTaxRate
    @State varchar(2)
   AS
    SELECT TaxRate FROM Tax
     WHERE TaxState = @State
```

procInitializeOrderStatus

```
/* Initialize the order status table for
   a new order

From .NET E-Commerce Programming
by Mike Gunderloy and Noel Jerke
Copyright 2002, Sybex Inc. All Rights Reserved. */
CREATE PROCEDURE procInitializeOrderStatus
 @OrderID int
AS
 INSERT INTO OrderStatus(OrderID, OrderStatusProcessed)
 VALUES(@OrderID, 0)
```

procInsertBasketItem

```
/* Insert an item into the shopper's basket.
   If they already have this item in their basket,
   increase the quantity for the item instead of
   adding a second instance

From .NET E-Commerce Programming
by Mike Gunderloy and Noel Jerke
Copyright 2002, Sybex Inc. All Rights Reserved. */
CREATE PROCEDURE procInsertBasketItem
/* Pass in the id of the basket, quantity, price,
   product name, ID of the product,
   size of the product, and the color
*/
 @BasketID int,
 @Quantity int,
 @Price money,
 @ProductName varchar(255),
 @ProductID int,
 @Size varchar(50) = NULL,
 @Color varchar(50) = NULL
AS
 DECLARE @Current int
 /* First, see if it's already in the basket */
 SELECT @Current = COUNT(*)
  FROM BasketItem
  WHERE BasketID = @BasketID AND ProductID = @ProductID
 IF @Current = 0
 /* Not already there, so insert it */
  INSERT INTO BasketItem(BasketID, BasketItemQuantity,
   BasketItemPrice, BasketItemProductName, ProductID,
   BasketItemSize, BasketItemColor)
  VALUES(@BasketID, @Quantity, @Price, @ProductName,
```

```
     @ProductID, @Size, @Color)
   ELSE
   /* Already there, update quantity */
    UPDATE BasketItem
     SET BasketItemQuantity = @Quantity + BasketItemQuantity
     WHERE BasketID = @BasketID AND ProductID = @ProductID
```

procInsertOrderData

```
   /* Insert the basic order information
    into the database

   From .NET E-Commerce Programming
   by Mike Gunderloy and Noel Jerke
   Copyright 2002, Sybex Inc. All Rights Reserved. */
   CREATE PROCEDURE procInsertOrderData
     @ShopperID int,
     @ShipFirstName varchar(50),
     @ShipLastName varchar(50),
     @ShipAddress varchar(150),
     @ShipCity varchar(150),
     @ShipState varchar(50),
     @ShipProvince varchar(150),
     @ShipCountry varchar(100),
     @ShipZipCode varchar(15),
     @ShipPhone varchar(25),
     @ShipEmail varchar(100),
     @BillFirstName varchar(50),
     @BillLastName varchar(150),
     @BillAddress varchar(150),
     @BillCity varchar(150),
     @BillState varchar(50),
     @BillProvince varchar(150),
     @BillCountry varchar(100),
     @BillZipCode varchar(15),
     @BillPhone varchar(25),
     @BillEmail varchar(100),
     @BasketID int
   AS
    INSERT INTO [Order](ShopperID, OrderShipFirstName,
     OrderShipLastName, OrderShipAddress,
     OrderShipCity, OrderShipState,
     OrderShipProvince, OrderShipCountry,
     OrderShipZipCode, OrderShipPhone,
     OrderShipEmail, OrderBillFirstName,
     OrderBillLastName, OrderBillAddress,
     OrderBillCity, OrderBillState,
```

```
OrderBillProvince, OrderBillCountry,
OrderBillZipCode, OrderBillPhone,
OrderBillEmail, BasketID)
VALUES(@ShopperID, @ShipFirstName,
@ShipLastName, @ShipAddress,
@ShipCity, @ShipState,
@ShipProvince, @ShipCountry,
@ShipZipCode, @ShipPhone,
@ShipEmail, @BillFirstName,
@BillLastName, @BillAddress,
@BillCity, @BillState,
@BillProvince, @BillCountry,
@BillZipCode, @BillPhone,
@BillEmail, @BasketID)
/* Return the autogenerated ID as the value
   of this stored procedure */
SELECT @@IDENTITY
```

procInsertPaymentData

```
/* Save the payment data for an order

From .NET E-Commerce Programming
by Mike Gunderloy and Noel Jerke
Copyright 2002, Sybex Inc. All Rights Reserved. */
CREATE PROCEDURE procInsertPaymentData
 @OrderID int,
 @CardType varchar(50),
 @CardNumber varchar(30),
 @ExpDate varchar(25),
 @CardName varchar(150)
AS
 INSERT INTO Payment (OrderID, PaymentCardType,
  PaymentCardNumber, PaymentExpDate,
  PaymentCardName)
 VALUES (@OrderID, @CardType,
  @CardNumber, @ExpDate,
  @CardName)
```

procInsertProduct

```
/* Add a new product to the store

From .NET E-Commerce Programming
by Mike Gunderloy and Noel Jerke
Copyright 2002, Sybex Inc. All Rights Reserved. */
CREATE PROCEDURE procInsertProduct
 @ProductName varchar(255),
```

```
@ProductDescription text,
@ProductImage varchar(255),
@ProductPrice money,
@ProductActive bit
AS
 INSERT INTO Products(ProductName, ProductDescription,
  ProductImage, ProductPrice, ProductActive)
 VALUES(@ProductName, @ProductDescription,
  @ProductImage, @ProductPrice, @ProductActive)
 /* Return the ID of the new product */
 SELECT @@IDENTITY
```

procInsertShopper

```
/* Insert a new shopper into the database,
   setting the required fields to empty strings

From .NET E-Commerce Programming
by Mike Gunderloy and Noel Jerke
Copyright 2002, Sybex Inc. All Rights Reserved. */
CREATE PROC procInsertShopper
AS
 INSERT INTO Shopper(ShopperLastName, ShopperUserName, ShopperPassword)
 VALUES('', '', '')
 SELECT @@IDENTITY
```

procManagerAddFreeShip

```
/* Add a new free shipping promotion

From .NET E-Commerce Programming
by Mike Gunderloy and Noel Jerke
Copyright 2002, Sybex Inc. All Rights Reserved. */
CREATE PROCEDURE procManagerAddFreeShip
 @FreeShipStartDate datetime,
 @FreeShipEndDate datetime
AS
 INSERT INTO FreeShip (FreeShipStartDate, FreeShipEndDate)
 VALUES (@FreeShipStartDate, @FreeShipEndDate)
```

procManagerAddProductAttribute

```
/* Add a new attribute for a product

From .NET E-Commerce Programming
by Mike Gunderloy and Noel Jerke
Copyright 2002, Sybex Inc. All Rights Reserved. */
CREATE PROCEDURE procManagerAddProductAttribute
```

```
 @ProductID int,
 @AttributeID int
AS
 INSERT INTO ProductAttribute(ProductID, AttributeID)
  VALUES(@ProductID, @AttributeID)
```

procManagerAddProductDept

```
/* Add a new department for a product

From .NET E-Commerce Programming
by Mike Gunderloy and Noel Jerke
Copyright 2002, Sybex Inc. All Rights Reserved. */
CREATE PROCEDURE procManagerAddProductDept
 @ProductID int,
 @DepartmentID int
AS
 INSERT INTO DepartmentProduct(ProductID, DepartmentID)
  VALUES(@ProductID, @DepartmentID)
```

procManagerAddRelatedProduct

```
/* Add a new relation for a product

From .NET E-Commerce Programming
by Mike Gunderloy and Noel Jerke
Copyright 2002, Sybex Inc. All Rights Reserved. */
CREATE PROCEDURE procManagerAddRelatedProduct
 @ProductID int,
 @RelatedProductID int,
 @RelationType int
AS
 INSERT INTO RelatedProduct(ProductAID,
  ProductBID, RelationType)
   VALUES(@ProductID, @RelatedProductID, @RelationType)
```

procManagerAddShippingFee

```
/* Add a new shipping fee

From .NET E-Commerce Programming
by Mike Gunderloy and Noel Jerke
Copyright 2002, Sybex Inc. All Rights Reserved. */
CREATE PROCEDURE procManagerAddShippingFee
 @ShippingLowQuantity int,
 @ShippingHighQuantity int,
 @ShippingFee money
AS
```

```
INSERT INTO Shipping (ShippingLowQuantity, ShippingHighQuantity,
  ShippingFee)
VALUES (@ShippingLowQuantity, @ShippingHighQuantity, @ShippingFee)
```

procManagerDeleteDepartment

```
/* Delete a department

From .NET E-Commerce Programming
by Mike Gunderloy and Noel Jerke
Copyright 2002, Sybex Inc. All Rights Reserved. */
CREATE PROCEDURE procManagerDeleteDepartment
 @DepartmentID int
AS
 /* Delete the product associations */
 DELETE FROM DepartmentProduct
  WHERE DepartmentID = @DepartmentID
 /* Delete the department record */
 DELETE FROM Department
  WHERE DepartmentID = @DepartmentID
```

procManagerDeleteFreeShip

```
/* Delete a free shipping promotion

From .NET E-Commerce Programming
by Mike Gunderloy and Noel Jerke
Copyright 2002, Sybex Inc. All Rights Reserved. */
CREATE PROCEDURE procManagerDeleteFreeShip
 @FreeShipID int
AS
 DELETE FROM FreeShip
  WHERE FreeShipID = @FreeShipID
```

procManagerDeleteItem

```
/* Delete a specified basket item

From .NET E-Commerce Programming
by Mike Gunderloy and Noel Jerke
Copyright 2002, Sybex Inc. All Rights Reserved. */
CREATE PROCEDURE procManagerDeleteItem
 @BasketItemID int
AS
 DECLARE @BasketID int
 DECLARE @Subtotal money
 DECLARE @Quantity money
 /* Save the basket ID */
```

```
SELECT @BasketID = BasketID
 FROM BasketItem
 WHERE BasketItemID = @BasketItemID
/* Delete the item */
DELETE FROM BasketItem
 WHERE BasketItemID = @BasketItemID
/* Update the Basket table */
SELECT @Quantity = SUM(BasketItemQuantity)
 FROM BasketItem
 WHERE BasketID = @BasketID
SELECT @Subtotal = SUM(BasketItemQuantity *
 BasketItemPrice)
 FROM BasketItem
 WHERE BasketID = @BasketID
UPDATE Basket
 SET BasketQuantity = @Quantity,
 BasketSubtotal = @Subtotal
 WHERE BasketID = @BasketID
UPDATE Basket
 SET BasketTotal = BasketSubtotal + BasketTax
 + BasketShipping
 WHERE BasketID = @BasketID
```

procManagerDeleteOrder

```
/* Delete an order from the database

From .NET E-Commerce Programming
by Mike Gunderloy and Noel Jerke
Copyright 2002, Sybex Inc. All Rights Reserved. */
CREATE PROCEDURE procManagerDeleteOrder
 @OrderID int
AS
 DECLARE @BasketID int
 /* Find the basket ID for this order */
 SELECT @BasketID = BasketID
  FROM [Order]
  WHERE OrderID = @OrderID
 /* Delete any payments */
 DELETE FROM Payment
  WHERE OrderID = @OrderID
 /* Delete the order status */
 DELETE FROM OrderStatus
  WHERE OrderID = @OrderID
 /* Delete the order */
 DELETE FROM [Order]
  WHERE OrderID = @OrderID
```

```
/* Delete basket items */
DELETE FROM BasketItem
 WHERE BasketID = @BasketID
/* Delete the matching basket */
 DELETE FROM Basket
 WHERE BasketID = @BasketID
```

procManagerDeleteProduct

```
/* Delete a product from the database

From .NET E-Commerce Programming
by Mike Gunderloy and Noel Jerke
Copyright 2002, Sybex Inc. All Rights Reserved. */
CREATE PROCEDURE procManagerDeleteProduct
 @ProductID int
AS
 /* Delete department associations */
 DELETE FROM DepartmentProduct
  WHERE ProductID = @ProductID
 /* Delete attribute associations */
 DELETE FROM ProductAttribute
  WHERE ProductID = @ProductID
 /* Delete the product itself */
 DELETE FROM Product
  WHERE ProductID = @ProductID
```

procManagerDeleteShippingFee

```
/* Delete a shipping fee

From .NET E-Commerce Programming
by Mike Gunderloy and Noel Jerke
Copyright 2002, Sybex Inc. All Rights Reserved. */
CREATE PROCEDURE procManagerDeleteShippingFee
 @ShippingID int
AS
 DELETE FROM Shipping
  WHERE ShippingID = @ShippingID
```

procManagerGetFreeShipping

```
/* Retrieve all free shipping information

From .NET E-Commerce Programming
by Mike Gunderloy and Noel Jerke
Copyright 2002, Sybex Inc. All Rights Reserved. */
CREATE PROCEDURE procManagerGetFreeShipping
AS
SELECT * FROM FreeShipping
```

procManagerGetShippingCharges

```
/* Retrieve all shipping charges

From .NET E-Commerce Programming
by Mike Gunderloy and Noel Jerke
Copyright 2002, Sybex Inc. All Rights Reserved. */
CREATE PROCEDURE procManagerGetShippingCharges
AS
SELECT * FROM Shipping
 ORDER BY ShippingLowQuantity
```

procManagerGetShippingFees

```
/* Retrieve all shipping fees

From .NET E-Commerce Programming
by Mike Gunderloy and Noel Jerke
Copyright 2002, Sybex Inc. All Rights Reserved. */
CREATE PROCEDURE procManagerGetShippingFees
AS
SELECT * FROM Shipping
 ORDER BY ShippingLowQuantity
```

procManagerGetTaxRates

```
/* Retrieve all tax rates

From .NET E-Commerce Programming
by Mike Gunderloy and Noel Jerke
Copyright 2002, Sybex Inc. All Rights Reserved. */
CREATE PROCEDURE procManagerGetTaxRates
AS
SELECT * FROM Tax
 ORDER BY TaxState
```

procManagerInsertDepartment

```
/* Add a new department to the store

From .NET E-Commerce Programming
by Mike Gunderloy and Noel Jerke
Copyright 2002, Sybex Inc. All Rights Reserved. */
CREATE PROCEDURE procManagerInsertDepartment
 @DepartmentName varchar(255),
 @DepartmentDescription text,
 @DepartmentImage varchar(255)
AS
 INSERT INTO Department(DepartmentName,
```

```
DepartmentDescription, DepartmentImage)
VALUES(@DepartmentName,
 @DepartmentDescription, @DepartmentImage)
/* Return the ID of the new department */
SELECT @@IDENTITY
```

procManagerInsertProduct

```
/* Add a new product to the store

From .NET E-Commerce Programming
by Mike Gunderloy and Noel Jerke
Copyright 2002, Sybex Inc. All Rights Reserved. */
CREATE PROCEDURE procManagerInsertProduct
 @ProductName varchar(255),
 @ProductDescription text,
 @ProductImage varchar(255),
 @ProductPrice money,
 @ProductActive bit
AS
 INSERT INTO Product(ProductName, ProductDescription,
  ProductImage, ProductPrice, ProductActive)
 VALUES(@ProductName, @ProductDescription,
  @ProductImage, @ProductPrice, @ProductActive)
 /* Return the ID of the new product */
 SELECT @@IDENTITY
```

procManagerMaxProductID

```
/* Get the highest product ID

From .NET E-Commerce Programming
by Mike Gunderloy and Noel Jerke
Copyright 2002, Sybex Inc. All Rights Reserved. */
CREATE PROCEDURE procManagerMaxProductID
AS
SELECT Max(ProductID) FROM Product
```

procManagerMaxSearchProductID

```
/* Get the highest product ID for a product search

From .NET E-Commerce Programming
by Mike Gunderloy and Noel Jerke
Copyright 2002, Sybex Inc. All Rights Reserved. */
CREATE PROCEDURE procManagerMaxSearchProductID
  @SearchText varchar(255)
AS
 SELECT Max(ProductID) FROM Product
  WHERE ProductName LIKE '%' + @SearchText + '%'
```

procManagerRemoveProductAttribute

```
/* Remove an attribute for a product

From .NET E-Commerce Programming
by Mike Gunderloy and Noel Jerke
Copyright 2002, Sybex Inc. All Rights Reserved. */
CREATE PROCEDURE procManagerRemoveProductAttribute
 @ProductID int,
 @AttributeID int
AS
 DELETE FROM ProductAttribute
   WHERE ProductID = @ProductID AND AttributeID = @AttributeID
```

procManagerRemoveProductDept

```
/* Delete a department for a product

From .NET E-Commerce Programming
by Mike Gunderloy and Noel Jerke
Copyright 2002, Sybex Inc. All Rights Reserved. */
CREATE PROCEDURE procManagerRemoveProductDept
 @ProductID int,
 @DepartmentID int
AS
 DELETE FROM DepartmentProduct
   WHERE ProductID = @ProductID AND DepartmentID = @DepartmentID
```

procManagerRemoveRelatedProduct

```
/* Remove a relation between products

From .NET E-Commerce Programming
by Mike Gunderloy and Noel Jerke
Copyright 2002, Sybex Inc. All Rights Reserved. */
CREATE PROCEDURE procManagerRemoveRelatedProduct
 @ProductID int,
 @RelatedProductID int,
 @RelationType int
AS
 DELETE FROM RelatedProduct
 WHERE ProductAID = @ProductID
 AND ProductBID = @RelatedProductID
 AND RelationType = @RelationType
```

procManagerRetrieveAllProducts

```
/* Retrieve all product names and IDs

From .NET E-Commerce Programming
```

```
by Mike Gunderloy and Noel Jerke
Copyright 2002, Sybex Inc. All Rights Reserved. */
CREATE PROCEDURE procManagerRetrieveAllProducts
AS
 SELECT ProductID, ProductName
 FROM Product
 ORDER BY ProductName
```

procManagerRetrieveAttributeByProd

```
/* Retrieve all attributes for a product

From .NET E-Commerce Programming
by Mike Gunderloy and Noel Jerke
Copyright 2002, Sybex Inc. All Rights Reserved. */
CREATE PROCEDURE procManagerRetrieveAttributeByProd
 @ProductID int
AS
 SELECT AttributeCategoryName, Attribute.AttributeID, AttributeName
  FROM (Attribute INNER JOIN AttributeCategory
  ON Attribute.AttributeCategoryID =
    AttributeCategory.AttributeCategoryID)
  INNER JOIN ProductAttribute
  ON Attribute.AttributeID = ProductAttribute.AttributeID
  WHERE ProductID = @ProductID
```

procManagerRetrieveAttributes

```
/* Retrieve all attributes in the database

From .NET E-Commerce Programming
by Mike Gunderloy and Noel Jerke
Copyright 2002, Sybex Inc. All Rights Reserved. */
CREATE PROCEDURE procManagerRetrieveAttributes
AS
 SELECT '-' AS Attr, 0 AS AttributeID
  UNION
 SELECT AttributeCategoryName + ': ' +
  AttributeName AS Attr, Attribute.AttributeID
  FROM Attribute INNER JOIN AttributeCategory
  ON Attribute.AttributeCategoryID =
    AttributeCategory.AttributeCategoryID
```

procManagerRetrieveBasketByOrder

```
/* Retrieve totals for an order

From .NET E-Commerce Programming
```

```
by Mike Gunderloy and Noel Jerke
Copyright 2002, Sybex Inc. All Rights Reserved. */
CREATE PROCEDURE procManagerRetrieveBasketByOrder
 @OrderID int
AS
 SELECT BasketSubtotal, BasketTotal,
  BasketShipping, BasketTax
  FROM Basket INNER JOIN [Order]
  ON [Order].BasketID = Basket.BasketID
 WHERE OrderID = @OrderID
```

procManagerRetrieveDepartment

```
/* Retrieve all info on a department

From .NET E-Commerce Programming
by Mike Gunderloy and Noel Jerke
Copyright 2002, Sybex Inc. All Rights Reserved. */
CREATE PROCEDURE procManagerRetrieveDepartment
 @DepartmentID int
AS
 SELECT * FROM Department
 WHERE DepartmentID = @DepartmentID
```

procManagerRetrieveDeptByProd

```
/* Retrieve all departments for a product

From .NET E-Commerce Programming
by Mike Gunderloy and Noel Jerke
Copyright 2002, Sybex Inc. All Rights Reserved. */
CREATE PROCEDURE procManagerRetrieveDeptByProd
 @ProductID int
AS
 SELECT Department.DepartmentID, DepartmentName
  FROM Department INNER JOIN DepartmentProduct
  ON Department.DepartmentID = DepartmentProduct.DepartmentID
 WHERE ProductID = @ProductID
```

procManagerRetrieveDeptListing

```
/* Retrieve all departments in the store

From .NET E-Commerce Programming
by Mike Gunderloy and Noel Jerke
Copyright 2002, Sybex Inc. All Rights Reserved. */
CREATE PROCEDURE procManagerRetrieveDeptListing
AS
 SELECT DepartmentID, DepartmentName
  FROM Department
```

procManagerRetrieveDepts

```
/* Retrieve all departments in the store

From .NET E-Commerce Programming
by Mike Gunderloy and Noel Jerke
Copyright 2002, Sybex Inc. All Rights Reserved. */
CREATE PROCEDURE procManagerRetrieveDepts
AS
 SELECT 0 AS DepartmentID, '-' AS DepartmentName
  UNION
 SELECT DepartmentID, DepartmentName
  FROM Department
```

procManagerRetrieveItems

```
/* Retrieve the item information for an order

From .NET E-Commerce Programming
by Mike Gunderloy and Noel Jerke
Copyright 2002, Sybex Inc. All Rights Reserved. */
CREATE PROCEDURE procManagerRetrieveItems
 @OrderID int
AS
 SELECT BasketItem.*, BasketItemTotal =
  BasketItemQuantity * BasketItemPrice
 FROM (BasketItem INNER JOIN Basket
  ON BasketItem.BasketID = Basket.BasketID)
 INNER JOIN [Order]
  ON [Order].BasketID = Basket.BasketID
  WHERE [Order].OrderID = @OrderID
```

procManagerRetrieveNextProducts

```
/* Retrieve basic product information

From .NET E-Commerce Programming
by Mike Gunderloy and Noel Jerke
Copyright 2002, Sybex Inc. All Rights Reserved. */
CREATE PROCEDURE procManagerRetrieveNextProducts
 @ProductID int,
 @Count int
AS
 EXEC('SELECT TOP ' + @Count + 'ProductID, ProductName, ProductPrice
  FROM Product
  WHERE ProductID > ' + @ProductID +
  ' ORDER BY ProductID')
```

procManagerRetrieveOrder

```
/* Retrieve all info on an order

From .NET E-Commerce Programming
by Mike Gunderloy and Noel Jerke
Copyright 2002, Sybex Inc. All Rights Reserved. */
CREATE PROCEDURE procManagerRetrieveOrder
 @OrderID int
AS
 SELECT * FROM [Order]
 WHERE OrderID = @OrderID
```

procManagerRetrieveOrderStatus

```
/* Retrieve totals for an order

From .NET E-Commerce Programming
by Mike Gunderloy and Noel Jerke
Copyright 2002, Sybex Inc. All Rights Reserved. */
CREATE PROCEDURE procManagerRetrieveOrderStatus
 @OrderID int
AS
 SELECT OrderStatusStage FROM OrderStatus
 WHERE OrderID = @OrderID
```

procManagerRetrievePayment

```
/* Retrieve payment info on an order

From .NET E-Commerce Programming
by Mike Gunderloy and Noel Jerke
Copyright 2002, Sybex Inc. All Rights Reserved. */
CREATE PROCEDURE procManagerRetrievePayment
 @OrderID int
AS
 SELECT * FROM Payment
 WHERE OrderID = @OrderID
```

procManagerRetrievePreviousProducts

```
/* Retrieve basic product information

From .NET E-Commerce Programming
by Mike Gunderloy and Noel Jerke
Copyright 2002, Sybex Inc. All Rights Reserved. */
CREATE PROCEDURE procManagerRetrievePreviousProducts
 @ProductID int,
 @Count int
```

```
AS
 CREATE TABLE #ProductTemp
  (ProductID int, ProductName varchar(255), ProductPrice money)
 INSERT #ProductTemp
  EXEC('SELECT TOP ' + @Count + 'ProductID, ProductName, ProductPrice
   FROM Product
   WHERE ProductID < ' + @ProductID +
   ' ORDER BY ProductID DESC')
 SELECT * FROM #ProductTemp ORDER BY ProductID
```

procManagerRetrieveProduct

```
/* Retrieve all info on a product

From .NET E-Commerce Programming
by Mike Gunderloy and Noel Jerke
Copyright 2002, Sybex Inc. All Rights Reserved. */
CREATE PROCEDURE procManagerRetrieveProduct
 @ProductID int
AS
 SELECT * FROM Product
 WHERE ProductID = @ProductID
```

procManagerRetrieveProducts

```
/* Retrieve basic product information

From .NET E-Commerce Programming
by Mike Gunderloy and Noel Jerke
Copyright 2002, Sybex Inc. All Rights Reserved. */
CREATE PROCEDURE procManagerRetrieveProducts
AS
SELECT ProductID, ProductName, ProductPrice
  FROM Product
  ORDER BY ProductID
```

procManagerRetrieveRelatedProducts

```
/* Retrieve all related products for a
  specified product

From .NET E-Commerce Programming
by Mike Gunderloy and Noel Jerke
Copyright 2002, Sybex Inc. All Rights Reserved. */
CREATE PROCEDURE procManagerRetrieveRelatedProducts
 @ProductID int
AS
SELECT Product.ProductID, Product.ProductName,
```

```
CASE RelationType
 WHEN 1 THEN 'Cross-sell'
 WHEN 2 THEN 'Up-sell'
END AS RelType
FROM Product INNER JOIN RelatedProduct
ON Product.ProductID = RelatedProduct.ProductBID
WHERE RelatedProduct.ProductAID = @ProductID
```

procManagerRetrieveSearchNextProducts

```
/* Retrieve basic product information

From .NET E-Commerce Programming
by Mike Gunderloy and Noel Jerke
Copyright 2002, Sybex Inc. All Rights Reserved. */
CREATE PROCEDURE procManagerRetrieveSearchNextProducts
 @ProductID int,
 @Count int,
 @SearchText varchar(255)
AS
 EXEC('SELECT TOP ' + @Count + 'ProductID, ProductName, ProductPrice
  FROM Product
  WHERE ProductID > ' + @ProductID +
  ' AND ProductName LIKE ''%'' + ''' +
  @SearchText + ''' + ''%'' ORDER BY ProductID')
```

procManagerRetrieveSearchPreviousProducts

```
/* Retrieve basic product information

From .NET E-Commerce Programming
by Mike Gunderloy and Noel Jerke
Copyright 2002, Sybex Inc. All Rights Reserved. */
CREATE PROCEDURE procManagerRetrieveSearchPreviousProducts
 @ProductID int,
 @Count int,
 @SearchText varchar(255)
AS
 CREATE TABLE #ProductTemp
  (ProductID int, ProductName varchar(255), ProductPrice money)
 INSERT #ProductTemp
  EXEC('SELECT TOP ' + @Count + 'ProductID, ProductName, ProductPrice
   FROM Product
   WHERE ProductID < ' + @ProductID +
   ' AND ProductName LIKE ''%'' + ''' +
  @SearchText + ''' + ''%'' ORDER BY ProductID DESC')
 SELECT * FROM #ProductTemp ORDER BY ProductID
```

procManagerUpdateDepartment

```
/* Update a department

From .NET E-Commerce Programming
by Mike Gunderloy and Noel Jerke
Copyright 2002, Sybex Inc. All Rights Reserved. */
CREATE PROCEDURE procManagerUpdateDepartment
 @DepartmentID int,
 @DepartmentName varchar(255),
 @DepartmentDescription text,
 @DepartmentImage varchar(255)
AS
 UPDATE Department
  SET DepartmentName = @DepartmentName,
  DepartmentDescription = @DepartmentDescription,
  DepartmentImage = @DepartmentImage
  WHERE DepartmentID = @DepartmentID
```

procManagerUpdateFreeShip

```
/* Update a free shipping promotion

From .NET E-Commerce Programming
by Mike Gunderloy and Noel Jerke
Copyright 2002, Sybex Inc. All Rights Reserved. */
CREATE PROCEDURE procManagerUpdateFreeShip
 @FreeShipID int,
 @FreeShipStartDate datetime,
 @FreeShipEndDate datetime
AS
 UPDATE FreeShip
  SET FreeShipStartDate = @FreeShipStartDate,
   FreeShipEndDate = @FreeShipEndDate
  WHERE FreeShipID = @FreeShipID
```

procManagerUpdateItem

```
/* Update a specified basket item

From .NET E-Commerce Programming
by Mike Gunderloy and Noel Jerke
Copyright 2002, Sybex Inc. All Rights Reserved. */
CREATE PROCEDURE procManagerUpdateItem
 @BasketItemID int,
 @ProductName varchar(255),
 @Size varchar(50),
 @Color varchar(50),
```

```
   @Quantity int,
   @Price money
  AS
   DECLARE @BasketID int
   DECLARE @Subtotal money
   DECLARE @BasketQuantity money
   /* Save the basket ID */
   SELECT @BasketID = BasketID
    FROM BasketItem
    WHERE BasketItemID = @BasketItemID
   /* Update the item */
   UPDATE BasketItem
    SET BasketItemProductName = @ProductName,
    BasketItemSize = @Size,
    BasketItemColor = @Color,
    BasketItemQuantity = @Quantity,
    BasketItemPrice = @Price
    WHERE BasketItemID = @BasketItemID
   /* Update the Basket table */
   SELECT @BasketQuantity = SUM(BasketItemQuantity)
    FROM BasketItem
    WHERE BasketID = @BasketID
   SELECT @Subtotal = SUM(BasketItemQuantity *
    BasketItemPrice)
    FROM BasketItem
    WHERE BasketID = @BasketID
   UPDATE Basket
    SET BasketQuantity = @BasketQuantity,
    BasketSubtotal = @Subtotal
    WHERE BasketID = @BasketID
   UPDATE Basket
    SET BasketTotal = BasketSubtotal + BasketTax
    + BasketShipping
    WHERE BasketID = @BasketID
```

procManagerUpdateOrder

```
   /* Update a specified order

   From .NET E-Commerce Programming
   by Mike Gunderloy and Noel Jerke
   Copyright 2002, Sybex Inc. All Rights Reserved. */
   CREATE PROCEDURE procManagerUpdateOrder
    @OrderID int,
    @OrderShipFirstName varchar(50),
    @OrderShipLastName varchar(50),
    @OrderShipAddress varchar(150),
```

```
@OrderShipCity varchar(150),
@OrderShipState varchar(50),
@OrderShipZipCode varchar(15),
@OrderShipPhone varchar(25),
@OrderShipEmail varchar(100),
@OrderBillFirstName varchar(50),
@OrderBillLastName varchar(50),
@OrderBillAddress varchar(150),
@OrderBillCity varchar(150),
@OrderBillState varchar(50),
@OrderBillZipCode varchar(15),
@OrderBillPhone varchar(25),
@OrderBillEmail varchar(100)
AS
UPDATE [Order]
SET OrderShipFirstName = @OrderShipFirstName,
OrderShipLastName = @OrderShipLastName,
OrderShipAddress = @OrderShipAddress,
OrderShipCity = @OrderShipCity,
OrderShipState = @OrderShipState,
OrderShipZipCode = @OrderShipZipCode,
OrderShipPhone = @OrderShipPhone,
OrderShipEmail = @OrderShipEmail,
OrderBillFirstName = @OrderBillFirstName,
OrderBillLastName = @OrderBillLastName,
OrderBillAddress = @OrderBillAddress,
OrderBillCity = @OrderBillCity,
OrderBillState = @OrderBillState,
OrderBillZipCode = @OrderBillZipCode,
OrderBillPhone = @OrderBillPhone,
OrderBillEmail = @OrderBillEmail
WHERE OrderID = @OrderID
```

procManagerUpdatePayment

```
/* Update a specified payment

From .NET E-Commerce Programming
by Mike Gunderloy and Noel Jerke
Copyright 2002, Sybex Inc. All Rights Reserved. */
CREATE PROCEDURE procManagerUpdatePayment
@OrderID int,
@PaymentCardType varchar(50),
@PaymentCardNumber varchar(30),
@PaymentExpDate varchar(25),
@PaymentCardName varchar(150)
AS
```

```
UPDATE Payment
SET PaymentCardType = @PaymentCardType,
PaymentCardNumber = @PaymentCardNumber,
PaymentExpDate = @PaymentExpDate,
PaymentCardName = @PaymentCardName
WHERE OrderID = @OrderID
```

procManagerUpdateProduct

```
/* Update information on a product

From .NET E-Commerce Programming
by Mike Gunderloy and Noel Jerke
Copyright 2002, Sybex Inc. All Rights Reserved. */
CREATE PROCEDURE procManagerUpdateProduct
 @ProductID int,
 @ProductName varchar(255),
 @ProductDescription text,
 @ProductImage varchar(255),
 @ProductPrice money,
 @ProductActive bit
AS
 UPDATE Product
  SET ProductName = @ProductName,
   ProductDescription = @ProductDescription,
   ProductImage = @ProductImage,
   ProductPrice = @ProductPrice,
   ProductActive = @ProductActive
  WHERE ProductID = @ProductID
```

procManagerUpdateProduct2

```
/* Update information on a product

From .NET E-Commerce Programming
by Mike Gunderloy and Noel Jerke
Copyright 2002, Sybex Inc. All Rights Reserved. */
CREATE PROCEDURE procManagerUpdateProduct2
 @ProductID int,
 @ProductName varchar(255),
 @ProductDescription text,
 @ProductImage varchar(255),
 @ProductPrice money,
 @ProductActive bit,
 @ProductFeatured bit,
 @ProductFeaturedStart datetime,
 @ProductFeaturedEnd datetime
AS
```

```
UPDATE Product
 SET ProductName = @ProductName,
  ProductDescription = @ProductDescription,
  ProductImage = @ProductImage,
  ProductPrice = @ProductPrice,
  ProductActive = @ProductActive,
  ProductFeatured = @ProductFeatured,
  ProductFeaturedStart = @ProductFeaturedStart,
  ProductFeaturedEnd = @ProductFeaturedEnd
 WHERE ProductID = @ProductID
```

procManagerUpdateProduct3

```
/* Update information on a product

From .NET E-Commerce Programming
by Mike Gunderloy and Noel Jerke
Copyright 2002, Sybex Inc. All Rights Reserved. */
CREATE PROCEDURE procManagerUpdateProduct3
 @ProductID int,
 @ProductName varchar(255),
 @ProductDescription text,
 @ProductImage varchar(255),
 @ProductPrice money,
 @ProductActive bit,
 @ProductFeatured bit,
 @ProductFeaturedStart datetime,
 @ProductFeaturedEnd datetime,
 @ProductSalePrice money,
 @ProductSaleStart datetime,
 @ProductSaleEnd datetime
AS
 UPDATE Product
  SET ProductName = @ProductName,
   ProductDescription = @ProductDescription,
   ProductImage = @ProductImage,
   ProductPrice = @ProductPrice,
   ProductActive = @ProductActive,
   ProductFeatured = @ProductFeatured,
   ProductFeaturedStart = @ProductFeaturedStart,
   ProductFeaturedEnd = @ProductFeaturedEnd,
   ProductSalePrice = @ProductSalePrice,
   ProductSaleStart = @ProductSaleStart,
   ProductSaleEnd = @ProductSaleEnd
  WHERE ProductID = @ProductID
```

procManagerUpdateShippingFee

```
/* Update a specified shipping fee

From .NET E-Commerce Programming
by Mike Gunderloy and Noel Jerke
Copyright 2002, Sybex Inc. All Rights Reserved. */
CREATE PROCEDURE procManagerUpdateShippingFee
 @ShippingID int,
 @ShippingLowQuantity int,
 @ShippingHighQuantity int,
 @ShippingFee money
AS
 UPDATE Shipping
  SET ShippingLowQuantity = @ShippingLowQuantity,
   ShippingHighQuantity = @ShippingHighQuantity,
   ShippingFee = @ShippingFee
  WHERE ShippingID = @ShippingID
```

procManagerUpdateStatus

```
/* Update a specified order status

From .NET E-Commerce Programming
by Mike Gunderloy and Noel Jerke
Copyright 2002, Sybex Inc. All Rights Reserved. */
CREATE PROCEDURE procManagerUpdateStatus
 @OrderID int,
 @OrderStatusStage int,
 @DateUpdate datetime
AS
 IF @OrderStatusStage = 0
  UPDATE OrderStatus
  SET OrderStatusStage = 0
  WHERE OrderID = @OrderID
 ELSE
  IF @OrderStatusStage = 1
   UPDATE OrderStatus
   SET OrderStatusStage = 1,
   OrderStatusDateFulfilled = @DateUpdate
   WHERE OrderID = @OrderID
  ELSE
   IF @OrderStatusStage = 2
    UPDATE OrderStatus
    SET OrderStatusStage = 2,
    OrderStatusDateShipped = @DateUpdate
    WHERE OrderID = @OrderID
   ELSE
```

```
    IF @OrderStatusStage = 3
    UPDATE OrderStatus
    SET OrderStatusStage = 3
    WHERE OrderID = @OrderID
```

procManagerUpdateTaxRate

```
/* Update a specified tax rate

From .NET E-Commerce Programming
by Mike Gunderloy and Noel Jerke
Copyright 2002, Sybex Inc. All Rights Reserved. */
CREATE PROCEDURE procManagerUpdateTaxRate
 @TaxID int,
 @TaxRate float
AS
 UPDATE Tax
   SET TaxRate = @TaxRate
   WHERE TaxID = @TaxID
```

procProductAttributes

```
/* Returns the attributes of a specified type
   for a specified product

From .NET E-Commerce Programming
by Mike Gunderloy and Noel Jerke
Copyright 2002, Sybex Inc. All Rights Reserved. */
CREATE PROCEDURE procProductAttributes
 @idProduct int, @AttributeCategoryName varchar(255)
AS
 SELECT Attribute.AttributeName
   FROM ((Product INNER JOIN ProductAttribute
   ON Product.ProductID = ProductAttribute.ProductID)
   INNER JOIN Attribute
   ON ProductAttribute.AttributeID = Attribute.AttributeID)
   INNER JOIN AttributeCategory
   ON Attribute.AttributeCategoryID =
     AttributeCategory.AttributeCategoryID
   WHERE Product.ProductID = @idProduct
   AND AttributeCategory.AttributeCategoryName = @AttributeCategoryName
```

procRemoveBasketItem

```
/* Remove a particular item from the basket

From .NET E-Commerce Programming
by Mike Gunderloy and Noel Jerke
```

```
Copyright 2002, Sybex Inc. All Rights Reserved. */
CREATE PROCEDURE procRemoveBasketItem
 @BasketID int,
 @BasketItemID int
AS
 DELETE BasketItem
 WHERE BasketID = @BasketID AND BasketItemID = @BasketItemID
```

procRetrieveBasket

```
/* Retrieve the contents of a specified basket by BasketID

From .NET E-Commerce Programming
by Mike Gunderloy and Noel Jerke
Copyright 2002, Sybex Inc. All Rights Reserved. */
CREATE PROCEDURE procRetrieveBasket
 @BasketID int
AS
 SELECT ProductID, BasketItemProductName, BasketItemColor,
  BasketItemSize,
  BasketItemPrice, BasketItemQuantity, BasketItemID,
  BasketItemPrice * BasketItemQuantity AS BasketItemTotal
  FROM BasketItem
  WHERE BasketID = @BasketID
```

procRetrieveBasketWithUpsell

```
/* Retrieve the contents of a specified basket by BasketID.
  Also fetch any up-sell products for products in the basket

From .NET E-Commerce Programming
by Mike Gunderloy and Noel Jerke
Copyright 2002, Sybex Inc. All Rights Reserved. */
CREATE PROCEDURE procRetrieveBasketWithUpsell
 @BasketID int
AS
 SELECT BasketItem.ProductID, BasketItemProductName,
  BasketItemColor, BasketItemSize,
  BasketItemPrice, BasketItemQuantity, BasketItemID,
  BasketItemPrice * BasketItemQuantity AS BasketItemTotal,
  'Why not try buying ' +
  '<a href="UpgradeProduct.aspx?Quantity=' +
  CAST(BasketItemQuantity AS varchar(5)) + '&BasketItemID=' +
  CAST(BasketItemID AS varchar(5)) + '&ProductID=' +
  CAST(Product.ProductID AS varchar(5)) + '">' +
  ProductName + '</a> instead?' AS Message,
  ISNULL(RelationType*12, 0) AS Height
  FROM BasketItem LEFT OUTER JOIN
```

```
    (RelatedProduct INNER JOIN Product
      ON RelatedProduct.ProductBID = Product.ProductID)
    ON BasketItem.ProductID = RelatedProduct.ProductAID
    WHERE BasketID = @BasketID
      AND (RelationType = 2 OR RelationType IS NULL)
```

procRetrieveCrossSellProducts

```
    /* Retrieve cross-sell products for a specified product

    From .NET E-Commerce Programming
    by Mike Gunderloy and Noel Jerke
    Copyright 2002, Sybex Inc. All Rights Reserved. */
    CREATE PROCEDURE procRetrieveCrossSellProducts
     @ProductID int
    AS
    /* Note that a RelationType of 1 corresponds
      to a cross-sell */
    SELECT Product.ProductID, Product.ProductName
     FROM Product INNER JOIN RelatedProduct
     ON Product.ProductID = RelatedProduct.ProductBID
     WHERE RelatedProduct.ProductAID = @ProductID
      AND RelationType = 1
```

procRetrieveDept

```
    /* Retrieve the information about a specified department

    From .NET E-Commerce Programming
    by Mike Gunderloy and Noel Jerke
    Copyright 2002, Sybex Inc. All Rights Reserved. */
    CREATE PROCEDURE procRetrieveDept
     @idDepartment int
    AS
     SELECT * FROM Department
      WHERE DepartmentID = @idDepartment
```

procRetrieveDeptProducts

```
    /* Retrieve the products for a specified department

    From .NET E-Commerce Programming
    by Mike Gunderloy and Noel Jerke
    Copyright 2002, Sybex Inc. All Rights Reserved. */
    CREATE PROCEDURE procRetrieveDeptProducts
     @idDept int
    AS
     SELECT Product.ProductID, ProductName, ProductImage
```

```
FROM Product INNER JOIN DepartmentProduct
ON Product.ProductID = DepartmentProduct.ProductID
WHERE DepartmentProduct.DepartmentID = @idDept
```

procRetrieveDepts

```
/* Retrieve departments from the store

From .NET E-Commerce Programming
by Mike Gunderloy and Noel Jerke
Copyright 2002, Sybex Inc. All Rights Reserved. */
CREATE PROCEDURE procRetrieveDepts
AS
 SELECT * FROM Department
```

procRetrieveFeaturedProducts

```
/* Retrieve the current featured products

From .NET E-Commerce Programming
by Mike Gunderloy and Noel Jerke
Copyright 2002, Sybex Inc. All Rights Reserved. */
CREATE PROCEDURE procRetrieveFeaturedProducts
AS
 SELECT Product.ProductID, ProductName, ProductImage
  FROM Product
  WHERE ProductFeatured = 1
  AND ProductFeaturedStart <= GETDATE()
  AND ProductFeaturedEnd >= GETDATE()
```

procRetrieveLastBasket

```
/* Retrieve the last basket ID for the shopper,
  or 0 if there is no saved basket

From .NET E-Commerce Programming
by Mike Gunderloy and Noel Jerke
Copyright 2002, Sybex Inc. All Rights Reserved. */
CREATE PROCEDURE procRetrieveLastBasket
  @ShopperID int
AS
 DECLARE @BasketID int
 SET @BasketID = (SELECT TOP 1 BasketID FROM Basket
 WHERE ShopperID = @ShopperID AND BasketOrderPlaced =0
 AND BasketTotal = 0
 ORDER BY BasketDateCreated DESC)
 IF @BasketID IS NULL
 SELECT 0
 ELSE
 SELECT @BasketID
```

procRetrieveNonPurchasedFeaturedProducts

```
/* Retrieve the current featured products
  that are not in the specified basket

From .NET E-Commerce Programming
by Mike Gunderloy and Noel Jerke
Copyright 2002, Sybex Inc. All Rights Reserved. */
CREATE PROCEDURE procRetrieveNonPurchasedFeaturedProducts
 @BasketID int
AS
 SELECT Product.ProductID, ProductName, ProductImage
  FROM Product
  WHERE ProductFeatured = 1
  AND ProductFeaturedStart <= GETDATE()
  AND ProductFeaturedEnd >= GETDATE()
  AND ProductID NOT IN
   (SELECT ProductID
    FROM BasketItem
    WHERE BasketID = @BasketID)
```

procRetrieveOrders

```
/* Retrieve basic order information for a shopper

From .NET E-Commerce Programming
by Mike Gunderloy and Noel Jerke
Copyright 2002, Sybex Inc. All Rights Reserved. */
CREATE PROCEDURE procRetrieveOrders
 @ShopperID int
AS
 SELECT
  OrderStatus = CASE OrderStatus.OrderStatusStage
   WHEN 0 THEN 'Order received and to be processed'
   WHEN 1 THEN 'Order ready to ship'
   WHEN 2 THEN 'Order Shipped, Confirmation #' +
    OrderStatus.OrderStatusShippingNumber
   WHEN 3 THEN 'Please call customer service'
  END,
  [Order].OrderID, [Order].ShopperID,
  [Order].OrderDateOrdered, Basket.BasketTotal
  FROM ([Order] INNER JOIN OrderStatus
   ON [Order].OrderID = OrderStatus.OrderID)
  INNER JOIN Basket
   ON [Order].BasketID = Basket.BasketID
  WHERE [Order].ShopperID = @ShopperID
  ORDER BY [Order].OrderDateOrdered
```

procRetrieveProduct

```
/* Retrieve the details for a single product

From .NET E-Commerce Programming
by Mike Gunderloy and Noel Jerke
Copyright 2002, Sybex Inc. All Rights Reserved. */
CREATE PROCEDURE procRetrieveProduct
 @idProduct int
AS
 SELECT ProductID, ProductName, ProductImage, ProductPrice,
  ProductDescription,
  ProductSalePrice, ProductSaleStart, ProductSaleEnd
  FROM Product
  WHERE ProductID = @idProduct
```

procRetrieveProfile

```
/* Retrieve a profile based on e-mail and password

From .NET E-Commerce Programming
by Mike Gunderloy and Noel Jerke
Copyright 2002, Sybex Inc. All Rights Reserved. */
CREATE PROCEDURE procRetrieveProfile
 @Email varchar(150),
 @Password varchar(25)
AS
 SELECT * FROM Shopper
  WHERE ShopperEmail = @Email
  AND ShopperPassword = @Password
```

procRetrieveProfileByID

```
/* Retrieve the shopper profile. */
/* Given a shopper's ID, retrieve their other
   information. All information is put into
   output parameters to avoid the overhead of
   building a DataSet to hold one row of data

From .NET E-Commerce Programming
by Mike Gunderloy and Noel Jerke
Copyright 2002, Sybex Inc. All Rights Reserved. */
CREATE PROCEDURE procRetrieveProfileByID
 @ShopperID int,
 @ShopperFirstName varchar(50) OUTPUT,
 @ShopperLastName varchar(50) OUTPUT,
 @ShopperAddress varchar(50) OUTPUT,
 @ShopperCity varchar(100) OUTPUT,
```

```
@ShopperState varchar(2) OUTPUT,
@ShopperProvince varchar(150) OUTPUT,
@ShopperCountry varchar(100) OUTPUT,
@ShopperZipCode varchar(15) OUTPUT,
@ShopperPhone varchar(30) OUTPUT,
@ShopperEmail varchar(150) OUTPUT,
@ShopperPassword varchar(25) OUTPUT,
@ShopperCookie tinyint OUTPUT
AS
 SELECT @ShopperFirstName = ShopperFirstName,
  @ShopperLastName = ShopperLastName,
  @ShopperAddress = ShopperAddress,
  @ShopperCity = ShopperCity,
  @ShopperState = ShopperState,
  @ShopperProvince = ShopperProvince,
  @ShopperCountry = ShopperCountry,
  @ShopperZipCode = ShopperZipCode,
  @ShopperPhone = ShopperPhone,
  @ShopperEmail = ShopperEmail,
  @ShopperPassword = ShopperPassword,
  @ShopperCookie = ShopperCookie
 FROM Shopper
 WHERE ShopperID = @ShopperID
```

procRetrieveReceiptHeader

```
/* Retrieve the header information for a receipt,
  given the Order ID and the Shopper ID

From .NET E-Commerce Programming
by Mike Gunderloy and Noel Jerke
Copyright 2002, Sybex Inc. All Rights Reserved. */
CREATE PROCEDURE procRetrieveReceiptHeader
 @ShopperID int,
 @OrderID int
AS
 SELECT * FROM [ORDER] INNER JOIN Basket
  ON [Order].BasketID = Basket.BasketID
  WHERE [Order].OrderID = @OrderID
   AND [Order].ShopperID = @ShopperID
```

procRetrieveReceiptItems

```
/* Retrieve the item information for a receipt,
  given the Order ID and the Shopper ID

From .NET E-Commerce Programming
by Mike Gunderloy and Noel Jerke
```

```
Copyright 2002, Sybex Inc. All Rights Reserved. */
CREATE PROCEDURE procRetrieveReceiptItems
 @ShopperID int,
 @OrderID int
AS
 SELECT BasketItem.*, BasketItemTotal =
  BasketItemQuantity * BasketItemPrice
 FROM (BasketItem INNER JOIN Basket
  ON BasketItem.BasketID = Basket.BasketID)
 INNER JOIN [Order]
  ON [Order].BasketID = Basket.BasketID
  WHERE [Order].OrderID = @OrderID
   AND [Order].ShopperID = @ShopperID
```

procRetrieveRelatedProducts

```
/* Retrieve all related products for a specified product

From .NET E-Commerce Programming
by Mike Gunderloy and Noel Jerke
Copyright 2002, Sybex Inc. All Rights Reserved. */
CREATE PROCFDURE procRetrieveRelatedProducts
 @ProductID int
AS
SELECT Product.ProductID, Product.ProductName,
 CASE RelationType
  WHEN 1 THEN 'Cross-sell'
  WHEN 2 THEN 'Up-sell'
 END AS RelType
 FROM Product INNER JOIN RelatedProduct
 ON Product.ProductID = RelatedProduct.ProductBID
 WHERE RelatedProduct.ProductAID = @ProductID
```

procRetrieveSaleProduct

```
/* Retrieve details on a sale product

From .NET E-Commerce Programming
by Mike Gunderloy and Noel Jerke
Copyright 2002, Sybex Inc. All Rights Reserved. */
CREATE PROCEDURE procRetrieveSaleProduct
 @ProductID int
AS
 SELECT ProductID, ProductName, ProductSalePrice
 FROM Product
 WHERE ProductID = @ProductID
```

procRetrieveSaleProductList

```
/* Retrieve the number of products currently
   on sale together with their Product IDs

From .NET E-Commerce Programming
by Mike Gunderloy and Noel Jerke
Copyright 2002, Sybex Inc. All Rights Reserved. */
CREATE PROCEDURE procRetrieveSaleProductList
AS
 DECLARE @cnt int
 SELECT @cnt = COUNT(*)
 FROM Product
 WHERE GETDATE() >= ProductSaleStart and GETDATE() <= ProductSaleEnd
 SELECT @cnt AS SaleCount, ProductID
 FROM product
 WHERE GETDATE() >= ProductSaleStart and GETDATE() <= ProductSaleEnd
```

procRetrieveUpSellProducts

```
/* Retrieve up-sell products for a specified product

From .NET E-Commerce Programming
by Mike Gunderloy and Noel Jerke
Copyright 2002, Sybex Inc. All Rights Reserved. */
CREATE PROCEDURE procRetrieveUpSellProducts
 @ProductID int
AS
/* Note that a RelationType of 2 corresponds
   to an up-sell */
SELECT Product.ProductID, Product.ProductName
 FROM Product INNER JOIN RelatedProduct
 ON Product.ProductID = RelatedProduct.ProductBID
 WHERE RelatedProduct.ProductAID = @ProductID
  AND RelationType = 2
```

procSearchProducts

```
/* Stored procedure to search for products
   based on passed-in parameters

From .NET E-Commerce Programming
by Mike Gunderloy and Noel Jerke
Copyright 2002, Sybex Inc. All Rights Reserved. */
CREATE PROCEDURE procSearchProducts
 @SearchText varchar(255),
 @Low int,
 @High int
```

```
AS
 SELECT ProductID, ProductName from Product
  WHERE (ProductName LIKE '%' + @SearchText+ '%' OR
  ProductDescription LIKE '%' + @SearchText + '%') AND
  (ProductPrice >= @low and ProductPrice <= @High)
  ORDER BY ProductName
```

procUpdateBasket

```
/* Update the basket with final order totals

From .NET E-Commerce Programming
by Mike Gunderloy and Noel Jerke
Copyright 2002, Sybex Inc. All Rights Reserved. */
CREATE PROCEDURE procUpdateBasket
 @BasketID int,
 @Quantity int,
 @Subtotal money,
 @Shipping money,
 @Tax money,
 @Total money
AS
 UPDATE Basket
  SET BasketQuantity = @Quantity,
  BasketSubtotal = @Subtotal,
  BasketShipping = @Shipping,
  BasketTax = @Tax,
  BasketTotal = @Total
 WHERE
  BasketID = @BasketID
```

procUpdateBasketItemQuantity

```
/* Update the quantity for a specified item
   in a specified basket

From .NET E-Commerce Programming
by Mike Gunderloy and Noel Jerke
Copyright 2002, Sybex Inc. All Rights Reserved. */
CREATE PROCEDURE procUpdateBasketItemQuantity
 @BasketID int,
 @ProductID int,
 @Quantity int
AS
 UPDATE BasketItem
 SET BasketItemQuantity = @Quantity
 WHERE BasketID = @BasketID AND ProductID = @ProductID
```

procUpdateShopper

```
/* Update the shopper with final billing information

From .NET E-Commerce Programming
by Mike Gunderloy and Noel Jerke
Copyright 2002, Sybex Inc. All Rights Reserved. */
CREATE PROCEDURE procUpdateShopper
 @ShopperID int,
 @FirstName varchar(50),
 @LastName varchar(50),
 @Address varchar(150),
 @City varchar(100),
 @State varchar(2),
 @Province varchar(150),
 @Country varchar(100),
 @ZipCode varchar(15),
 @Phone varchar(30),
 @Email varchar(150),
 @Password varchar(25),
 @Cookie tinyint
AS
 UPDATE Shopper
  SET ShopperFirstName = @FirstName,
  ShopperLastName = @LastName,
  ShopperAddress = @Address,
  ShopperCity = @City,
  ShopperState = @State,
  ShopperProvince = @Province,
  ShopperCountry = @Country,
  ShopperZipCode = @ZipCode,
  ShopperPhone = @Phone,
  ShopperEmail = @Email,
  ShopperPassword = @Password,
  ShopperCookie = @Cookie
  WHERE ShopperID = @ShopperID
```

Index

Note to the Reader: Page numbers in **bold** indicate the principle discussion of a topic or the definition of a term. Page numbers in *italic* indicate illustrations.

D

Q

W

X

The quotation on the bottom of the front cover is taken from the ninth chapter of Lao Tzu's Tao Te Ching, the classic work of Taoist philosophy. This particular verse is from the translation by D. C. Lau (copyright 1963) and communicates the importance of humility as one of the necessary virtues. This verse follows one that says: "Rather than fill it to the brim by keeping it upright/Better to have stopped in time."

It is traditionally held that Lao Tzu lived in the fifth century B.C. in China, during the Chou dynasty, but it is unclear whether he was actually a historical figure. It is said that he was a teacher of Confucius. The concepts embodied in the Tao Te Ching influenced religious thinking in the Far East, including Zen Buddhism in Japan. Many in the West, however, have wrongly understood the Tao Te Ching to be primarily a mystical work; in fact, much of the advice in the book is grounded in a practical moral philosophy governing personal conduct.